D1462186

KARL MARX
FREDERICK ENGELS
COLLECTED WORKS
VOLUME
30

KARL MARX
FREDERICK ENGELS

COLLECTED
WORKS

INTERNATIONAL PUBLISHERS

NEW YORK

KARL MARX
FREDERICK ENGELS

Volume
30

KARL MARX: 1861-63

INTERNATIONAL PUBLISHERS

NEW YORK

This volume has been prepared jointly by Lawrence & Wishart Ltd., London, International Publishers Co. Inc., New York, and Progress Publishers, Moscow, in collaboration with the Institute of Marxism-Leninism, Moscow.

Editorial commissions:
GREAT BRITAIN: Eric Hobsbawm, John Hoffman, Nicholas Jacobs, Monty Johnstone, Martin Milligan, Jeff Skelley, Ernst Wangermann.
USA: Louis Diskin, Philip S. Foner, James E. Jackson, Leonard B. Levenson, Victor Perlo, Betty Smith, Dirk J. Struik.
USSR: for Progress Publishers—A. K. Avelichev, N. P. Karmanova, M. K. Shcheglova; for the Institute of Marxism-Leninism—P. N. Fedoseyev, L. I. Golman, A. I. Malysh, M. P. Mchedlov, V. N. Pospelova, G. L. Smirnov.

Copyright © Progress Publishers, Moscow, 1988

Library of Congress Cataloging in Publication Data

Marx, Karl, 1818-1883.
    Karl Marx, Frederick Engels: collected works.

    1. Socialism—Collected works. 2. Economics—Collected works. I. Engels, Friedrich, 1820-1895. Works. English. 1975. II. Title.
HX 39. 5. A 16 1975 335.4 73-84671
ISBN 0-7178-0530-1 (v. 30).

Printed in the Union of Soviet Socialist Republics

Contents

NOTES AND INDEXES

ILLUSTRATIONS

Translated by

BEN FOWKES: Notebooks I-V
EMILE BURNS: Notebooks VI, VII

Preface

Volumes 30 to 34 of the *Collected Works* of Marx and Engels contain Marx's manuscript, *A Contribution to the Critique of Political Economy*, written between August 1861 and July 1863. Consisting of 23 notebooks with on-going pagination (overall volume: about 1,472 large pages), the manuscript represents an important stage in the development of Marx's economic theory. It investigates the economic laws governing the movement of capitalist production and brings out the content of the converted forms in which this movement is manifested on the surface of bourgeois society. It was through the critique of bourgeois political economy that Marx arrived at his discoveries, and this critique is presented in detail in the central section, *Theories of Surplus Value.*

In view of its great bulk the manuscript is published in five volumes. Volume 30 includes notebooks I to VII, comprising three sections of the chapter on the production process of capital and the beginning of the *Theories of Surplus Value* (pp. 1-210 and 220-99 of the manuscript).

Published in Volume 31 are notebooks VII to XII, which contain the continuation of the *Theories of Surplus Value* (pp. 300-636 of the manuscript).

Volume 32, corresponding to notebooks XII-XV, contains the conclusion of the *Theories of Surplus Value* (pp. 636-944 of the manuscript).

Volume 33 includes notebooks XV to XVIII, V (the closing part), XIX and XX (pp. 944-1157, 211-19, 1159-1251).

Volume 34 contains notebooks XX-XXIII (pp. 1251-1472 of the manuscript) and also the draft of the concluding part of Book I of *Capital* (Chapter Six. The Results of the Direct Process of Production).

The fundamentals of proletarian political economy were formulated in the late 1850s. In his economic manuscript of 1857-58 (see
present edition, vols 28 and 29), which represents the first version
of *Capital*, Marx revealed the inner mechanism of bourgeois
society and showed that the development of capitalism's contradictions was inevitably leading to its replacement by a more highly
organised social system.

This conclusion followed from Marx's theory of surplus value.
By working out his economic doctrine he had turned the
materialist conception of history, first formulated by him and
Engels as early as the 1840s, from a hypothesis into "a
scientifically proven proposition" (V. I. Lenin, *Collected Works*,
Vol. 1, Progress Publishers, Moscow, 1986, p. 142).

In 1859, Marx began to publish the results of his research in a
work entitled *A Contribution to the Critique of Political Economy*. Part
One, which contained an exposition of his theory of value and
theory of money. In this work, as Marx put it, "the *specifically*
social, by no means *absolute*, character of bourgeois production is
analysed straight away in its simplest form, that of the *commodity*"
(present edition, Vol. 40, p. 473).

Marx originally intended to follow this first part with a second
instalment, devoted to the analysis of capital, the dominant
relation of production in bourgeois society. He characterised the
second instalment as being "of crucial importance. It does, in fact,
contain the pith of all the bourgeois stuff" (present edition,
Vol. 40, p. 523).

Initially, the manuscript of 1861-63 was written as the direct
continuation of Part One, under the same overall title, *A Contribution to the Critique of Political Economy*, with the subtitle
"Third Chapter. Capital in General". Since it was, in effect, the
second version of *Capital*, the manuscript of 1861-63 covered
practically all the problems which Marx intended to deal with in
his principal work. About half of it is taken up by the "Theories
of Surplus Value", described by Engels as a detailed critical history
of the pith and marrow of political economy. The manuscript also
works out the theory of productive and unproductive labour, and
of the formal and real subsumption of labour under capital, and
also many questions of the theory of crises which he never
specifically discussed elsewhere. In the final version of *Capital*
Marx confined himself to general conclusions, summing up the
research into these problems which he had conducted in the
present manuscript.

In the manuscript of 1861-63 Marx used the key propositions of his theory of value and surplus value, evolved in the 1850s, to continue his analysis of the relations between labour and capital, investigating a broad range of questions relating to the antagonistic contradictions of the capitalist mode of production, and the condition and struggle of the working class in bourgeois society.

In his study of the genesis of surplus value Marx demonstrated the correspondence between the process of capitalist exploitation—the production and appropriation of surplus value—and the law of value, of the exchange of equivalents. This constitutes one of his major theoretical achievements. "The economists have never been able to reconcile surplus value with the law of equivalence they themselves have postulated. The socialists have always held onto this contradiction and harped on it, instead of understanding the specific nature of this commodity, labour capacity, whose use value is itself the activity which creates exchange value" (Notebook I, p. 47). In the manuscript of 1857-58 Marx began the analysis of the commodity "labour power" (or, in his terminology of the 1850s and early 1860s, "labour capacity"). In the manuscript of 1861-63 he examines this specific commodity in a more detailed, indeed comprehensive manner.

To begin with, he reveals its distinctive feature—the capacity to create surplus value. Bourgeois economists treated the capitalist relations merely as relations of simple commodity owners confronting each other on the market, and regarded surplus value as deriving, in effect, from commercial fraud, from the violation of the principle of equal exchange between seller and buyer. Marx, in contrast, shows that the capitalist relation of production, far from being reducible to simple commodity-money relations, is their more developed form. "...The formation of the capital-relation demonstrates from the outset that it can only enter the picture at a definite historical stage of the economic development of society—of the social relations of production and the productive forces. The capital-relation appears straight away as a historically determined economic relation, a relation that belongs to a definite historical period of economic development, of social production" (I-19). It is only at a definite stage of the economic development of society that the money owner finds on the market the worker deprived of all means of labour and possessing only one commodity for sale—his labour power. It was impossible to find out the source of surplus value without making a distinction between labour capacity and the labour process proper. Marx therefore stresses: the commodity offered by the worker is merely the potential possibility of labour, separated both from labour itself and from the conditions for its realisation.

Like any other commodity, it has use value and value. The use value consists in the fact that the consumption of this commodity, the process of its realisation, constitutes the process of labour itself. But since labour as such is a perennial condition of social life, the vulgar economists, seeking to prove that bourgeois society is an eternal, "natural" institution, treat capitalist production in terms of production in general. "...The apologists of capital confuse or identify it with a moment of the simple labour process as such" (I-33).

However, the process of capitalist production is not merely a process of labour, but simultaneously a process of the self-valorisation of value. And here the value of the commodity "labour power", the way it compares with the value newly created in the labour process, moves to the fore.

In substantiating his theory of surplus value, Marx attached extraordinary importance to determining the value magnitude of the commodity "labour power" (labour capacity) and of its monetary expression, wages. Bourgeois economists, beginning with the Physiocrats, had regarded the value of this commodity (they spoke of the "value of labour") as an immutable magnitude independent of the stage of historical development. They put forward the theory of the "minimum wage", maintaining that the magnitude of wages was determined by the value of a set of means of subsistence—given once and for all—that was necessary for the physical existence of the worker. In the manuscript of 1861-63, Marx for the first time demonstrated that this theory was untenable, and he was thereby enabled to justify the struggle of the working class for higher wages and a shorter working day.

Marx shows that "the extent of the so-called primary requirements for life and the manner of their satisfaction depend to a large degree on the level of civilisation of the society, are themselves the product of history" (I-22). Therefore determining the magnitude of wages, as well as of the value of "labour power", is not simply a matter of determining the ultimate limit of physical necessity, although the capitalists do seek to reduce the value and price of labour power to the minimum. Hence the economic necessity for the working class to pursue an unrelenting struggle for higher wages and shorter working hours.

In the 1861-63 manuscript Marx not only demonstrated the need for such a struggle, but also the *possibility* of waging it. The minimum wage theory was itself a product of historical conditions. At a certain stage of development of bourgeois economic theory, Marx emphasised, it had served a useful purpose, for it made possible the realisation that surplus value was value created by the worker over and above the value of his labour power. It also helped Marx's predecessors to establish that wage increases do not increase the value of commodities, but only reduce the capitalists' rate of profit. The credit for drawing this important conclusion belongs to Ricardo, but it was Marx who provided the definitive proof. Marx also went beyond the inconsistent outlook of classical bourgeois political economy, which did allow that wage rises could cause commodity values to rise, for from Adam Smith on wages had been regarded as a constituent element of the value of commodities (see VI-263, 265). This mistaken premiss led to the mistaken conclusion that the workers' struggle for higher wages was pointless since wage increases inevitably brought higher commodity prices in their wake.

Considerable space in the manuscript is taken up by the analysis of the capitalist mode of production in its historical development. For the first time, Marx examines in detail the essence and stages of the formal and real subsumption of labour under capital, with the production of absolute surplus value playing the dominant part at the first stage and of relative surplus value at the second.

At the first stage capital subjects the actual production process to itself only in form, without changing anything in its technological organisation. The salient feature of this stage is that the labour process and the worker himself are brought under the control, or command, of capital. Compared with the precapitalist modes of production only the nature of coercion changes. Direct, extra-economic coercion is replaced by coercion based on the "free", purely economic, relation between seller and buyer. The real subsumption of labour under capital results from the technological subordination of labour, the worker being unable to function as such outside the production process organised along capitalist lines.

Marx discusses in detail what he calls the *transitional forms*, which develop within the framework of the precapitalist formations and under which capital exploits labour even before it has assumed the form of productive capital, or labour has taken on the form of wage labour. He shows the role played by commercial and usurer's capital in the transition to capitalist production and notes that the transitional forms are constantly reproduced within, and partly reproduced by, the bourgeois mode of production itself (XXI-1314).

Marx traces the *genesis* of the formal subsumption of labour under capital and describes the historical conditions that made possible the rise of capitalist relations, which supplant either slavery and serfdom, or the independent labour of peasants and artisans. While causing no change in the technical characteristics of the mode of production, the transition to capitalist exploitation within the framework of the formal subsumption of labour under capital increases the continuity and, hence, the intensity and productivity of labour. Moreover, it alters the very substance of relations between the exploiters and the exploited. The transformation of the serf or slave into a wage labourer appears here as a rise to a higher social stage. The changed relations make the activity of the free worker more intensive, more continuous, more agile and more skilful than that of the slave, not to mention the fact that they make him capable of entirely different historical action (XXI-1305).

At the same time, Marx points out that the formal subordination of labour, "the assumption of control over it by capital" (I-49), although historically preceding the actual subordination, which presupposes the establishment of the specifically capitalist mode of production, is fully retained at the stage of developed capitalism, as is its result, absolute surplus value. All the social strata which do not directly take part in material production live on the surplus labour of the workers, obtaining the material means of subsistence and the free time they need for carrying on some non-productive activity or just for idleness. The free time enjoyed by others means excessive labour for the workers. "The whole of civilisation and social development so far has been founded on this antagonism," Marx writes in this manuscript (III-105).

Marx deployed a wealth of statistics, drawn above all from the reports of British factory inspectors, to demonstrate capital's tendency to increase surplus labour beyond every limit. He presents an appalling picture of capitalist exploitation. Excessive labour at the early stages of bourgeois society, within the framework of the production of absolute surplus value, reduces the period of the normal functioning of labour power, accelerates the "destruction" of its value, which is a violation of the normal conditions under which the worker sells his labour capacity. Marx describes the historically conditioned task that is being accomplished by the capitalist mode of production and defines the place capitalism holds in preparing the premisses for the society of the future. He writes (the text here is in English): "The capitalistic production is ... most economical of *realised labour*.... It is a greater spendthrift than any other mode of production of man, of living labour, spendthrift not only of flesh and blood and muscles, but of brains and nerves. It is, in fact, only at the greatest waste of individual development that the development of general men is secured in those epochs of history which prelude to a socialist constitution of mankind" (II-92).

Capitalist production has a direct stake in extracting excessive labour from the working class, and only the resistance of organised workers can counteract the realisation of capital's boundless claims. The isolated efforts of individual workers can do nothing to curb this exorbitant lust for surplus labour. What is required is resistance from the working class as a whole. Marx stresses that the workers in themselves—unless they act as a class upon the state, and, through the state, upon capital—are unable to save from the predatory claws of capital even what leisure is needed for their physical survival (XX-1283).

He analyses the working-class struggle which led to the legal limitation of the working day in Britain and a number of other European countries. He notes that, although the relevant laws not infrequently became a dead letter, this process as a whole had an extremely beneficial effect in improving the physical, moral and intellectual condition of the working classes in England, as the statistics demonstrate (V-219).

The formal subsumption of labour under capital, and, corresponding to this, the production of absolute surplus value—while of course constituting the basis of the capitalist relation, of capital's command over labour—sets very narrow limits to the development of the capitalist mode of production. In this connection Marx emphasises that "only in the course of its development does capital not only formally subsume the labour process but transform it, give the very mode of production a new shape and thus first create the mode of production peculiar to it" (I-49). This point highlights the importance of Marx's theory of the formal and real subsumption of labour under capital for further developing and concretising the materialist conception of history: the active role played by the capitalist production relation in changing the mode of production is used here as an example demonstrating the powerful retroactive effect of the production relations on the development of the productive forces.

In his analysis of the real subsumption of labour under capital, Marx stresses the growing dominance of things, of material wealth, over the individual under capitalist conditions. The creation of *great wealth existing in the form of things* appears as the end, to which the labour capacities are merely the means, an end which is only attained by these capacities themselves being turned into *something one-sided and dehumanised* (XXI-1319). At the same time, in describing the formal and real subsumption of labour under capital, the production of absolute and relative surplus value respectively, he notes that it is the tendency of capital to develop surplus value simultaneously in both forms (XX-1283).

But the resistance of the working class sets certain limits to the growth of surplus value obtained through lengthening the working day, in other words to the production of absolute surplus value. Apart from this, there is also a purely physical barrier to this lengthening. The capitalist class seeks to overcome these limits by developing the productive forces, i.e. by raising the productivity of labour, thus ensuring the growth of relative surplus value. The volume of the means of subsistence consumed by the worker may increase in the process, though their value declines. The possible improvement of the worker's living conditions, Marx points out, "in no way alters the *nature* and the *law of relative surplus value*—that a greater part of the working day is appropriated by capital as a result of rises in productivity. Hence the preposterousness of wanting to refute this law by statistical demonstrations that the material condition of the worker has improved here or there, in this or that aspect, as a result of the development of the productive power of labour" (IV-140/141).

In the manuscript of 1861-63 Marx, for the first time ever, analyses in detail three successive stages in the growth of labour productivity within the framework of the capitalist mode of production, stages which he calls "Cooperation", "Division of Labour" and "Machinery. Utilisation of the Forces of Nature and of Science". They represent, simultaneously, three stages in the development of the real subsumption of labour under capital and hence in the intensification of capitalist exploitation.

Cooperation, the joint action of many workers to achieve a common result, while constituting a special historical stage in the development of capitalism, is also "the *general form* on which all social arrangements for increasing the productivity of social labour are based" (IV-143). Cooperation makes labour more efficient. The sphere of its action is expanded, the time required to obtain a certain result is reduced, and such a development of the productive power of labour is achieved as is absolutely beyond the reach of the isolated worker. To the extent that cooperation reduces necessary labour time, it increases the relative surplus value appropriated by the capitalist for nothing. In this sense, "cooperation, which is a productive power of social labour, appears as a productive power of capital, not of labour" (IV-146). A "displacement" of this kind occurs in respect of all the productive forces of bourgeois society; what takes place here is "a process of divestiture of labour, of alienation, whereby its own social forms are presented as alien powers" (V-184).

Under the conditions of capitalist cooperation, when the interconnection of workers is a relation alien to them, there emerges a specific kind of labour, the labour of supervision. The function of directing labour is an objective necessity where there is concentration of workers, but the form which the direction of the labour process is bound to take "in conditions of association", says Marx, has nothing in common with the command of labour under capitalism.

The division of labour in capitalist manufactories is character- ised by Marx as a developed form of cooperation, highly effective in raising productivity and increasing relative surplus value. The manufactory division of labour develops on the basis of the social division of labour, the latter giving rise to commodity exchange, and represents the cooperation of specialised, "partial" kinds of labour to produce a single use value. In the manuscript of 1861-63 Marx investigates in detail the interaction of the two types of division of labour and notes, in this context, that the division of labour "is in a certain respect the category of categories of political economy" (IV-151). The division of labour within society corre- sponds to commodity relations in general, that within production is a specifically capitalist form. The fact that the two principal types of division of labour condition each other—this was discovered by Marx—implied that "the general laws formulated in respect of the commodity ... first come to be realised with the development of capitalist production, i.e. of capital", and "only on the basis of capital, of capitalist production, does the commodity in fact become the general elementary form of wealth" (V-185).

Historically, the division of labour within the process of capitalist production "presupposes *manufacture*, as a specific *mode of production*" (IV-151). Manufacture, which initially consisted in the bringing together of workers producing one and the same commodity and the concentration of the means of labour in one workshop, under the direction of the capitalist, contained all the prerequisites for the development, within it, of the division of labour and hence for the growth of labour productivity. This, precisely, gave capital a decisive advantage over patriarchal guild-based production. Marx demonstrates that, contrary to the assertions of bourgeois economists, capitalist manufacture was characterised not by the distribution of the different kinds of labour among the workers, but, conversely, by the distribution of the workers among the different labour processes, "each of which becomes the exclusive life-process of one of them" (IV-158). The obverse of this distribution is the combination of labour in manufacture. The workers are merely "the building blocks" of this combination and they are entirely dependent on the mechanism as a whole.

In discussing the genesis of manufacture, Marx makes an important methodological remark: Just as in the case of the succession of the different geological formations, so also in that of the rise of the different socio-economic formations, one should not think in terms of periods which suddenly occur, or are sharply divided off from each other (XIX-1199). Marx draws attention to the fact that such important inventions as that of gunpowder, the compass, or printing were made in the craft period of bourgeois society. The *general law*, operating at all stages, is that the material prerequisites for the subsequent form are created within the preceding one—both the technological conditions and the corresponding economic structure of the factory (XIX-1199).

Marx discusses the differentiation and specialisation of the instruments of labour as the technological prerequisites of machine production. He regards the dispute about the distinction between tool and machine as purely scholastic and shows that what is required is such a revolution in the means of labour employed as transforms the mode of production and therefore also the relations of production (XIX-1160). The industrial revolution affects first the working parts of the machine, then its motive force. This second process, the employment of the steam engine as a machine producing motion, is described by Marx as the second revolution (XIX-1162).

Characteristic of large-scale machine production is the massive application by capital of the forces of nature and science. Earlier, in his manuscript of 1857-58, Marx noted the tendency to turn science into a direct productive force. Now he concretises this important proposition by pointing out that capitalist production for the first time turns the material process of production into the application of *science to production*—science introduced into practice (XX-1265). This process is manifested in the creation of social productive forces of labour, above all machinery and automatic factories, which embody the achievements of science, but are appropriated by capital and utilised by it alone. There takes place an *exploitation of science*, of the theoretical progress of mankind (XX-1262). Moreover, capital turns science, as a social productive force, against the workers. Science appears as an *alien* force, *hostile* to labour and *ruling over* it (XX-1262).

The mode of production based on the application of machinery finds its classical expression in the automatic factory. The automatic factory is the perfected mode of production corresponding to machinery, and it is the more perfected the more complete a system of mechanisms it constitutes and the fewer individual processes still need to be mediated by human labour (XIX-1237).

Considerable space in the section on machinery is devoted to the prerequisites for and effects of the capitalist application of machines. As with any advance in the productive forces taking place on the basis of capitalism, the introduction of machinery aims above all at reducing the paid part of the working day and lengthening the unpaid part, i.e. increasing surplus labour time. Therefore, as Marx shows, the introduction of new machines requires, first and foremost, concentration of the conditions of labour and their joint, hence more economical, employment by the associated workers. Only owing to this can they be used in such a way that their higher efficiency in the labour process is accompanied by lower expenses (XIX-1235). Marx discusses the tendency of machine production to combine originally independent branches and turn them into a continuous system of production. His detailed statistical analysis of spinning and weaving, based on factory reports, led him to conclude that combined enterprises are characterised by a higher degree of concentration of production, more intensive use of energy and more economical employment of labour power.

The absolute or relative lengthening of labour time is an objective tendency of machine production. This tendency, the capitalist's striving to speed up the replacement of the fixed capital and ensure its uninterrupted functioning, is manifested in the introduction of night work and the intensification, "condensation", of labour. In the manuscript of 1861-63 Marx brings out the dual impact of the capitalist intensification of labour on the condition of the working class. He points to the link between the legal introduction of the ten-hour working day in Britain and the subsequent technological progress which raised the intensity of labour. The great expansion in industrial production which resulted was *enforced* by the external limit which legislation set to the exploitation of the workers (V-218). This limit did not cause the profits of the British manufacturers to decline. At the same time, Marx shows that at every given stage of the development of production the intensification of labour comes up against objective limits.

One of the most important effects of technological progress is the replacement of manual labour by machinery and the ousting of workers from production proper. Marx draws attention to the tendency of the industrial proletariat to decline in relative terms, although, as he points out, its absolute numbers grow. "Although the number of workers grows absolutely, it declines relatively, not only in proportion to the constant capital which absorbs their labour, but also in proportion to the part of society not directly involved in material production or indeed engaged in no kind of production whatsoever" (V-179). The capitalist employment of machinery thus objectively results in a new stage in the development of the real subsumption of labour under capital. Only when this stage has been reached, does *the formation of a superfluity of workers* become *a pronounced and deliberate tendency operating on a large scale* (XX-1257). The antagonistic contradiction between labour and capital reaches its highest expression here, because capital now appears not only as a means of depreciating living labour capacity but also of rendering it *superfluous* (XX-1259). At the same time Marx points to the opposite tendency of machine production—the constant enlistment of fresh workers, the expansion of the sphere of exploitation.

The manuscript of 1861-63 deals at considerable length with the problem of productive and unproductive labour in capitalist society. Marx notes that to work out a criterion of productive labour means to develop and concretise the basic propositions of the theory of surplus value. "Productive labour is only a concise term for the whole relationship and the form and manner in which labour capacity figures in the capitalist production process. The distinction from *other* kinds of labour is however of the greatest importance since this distinction expresses precisely the specific form of the labour on which the whole capitalist mode of production and capital itself is based" (XXI-1322). "*Productive labour* is therefore—in the system of capitalist production—labour which produces *surplus value* for its employer, or which transforms the objective conditions of labour into capital and their owner into a capitalist" (XXI-1322).

The concept of productive labour is therefore socially conditioned. Marx points out, with reference to bourgeois society, that one and the same kind of labour may be productive if organised along capitalist lines, and unproductive if it merely serves to satisfy the requirements of the working individual. "A singer who sells her singing for her own account is an *unproductive labourer*. But the same singer commissioned by an entrepreneur to sing in order to make money for him is a *productive labourer*; for she produces capital" (XXI-1324).

Defining productive labour as labour producing surplus value implies recognition of the fact that what matters under the capitalist mode of production is not labour productivity as such, but only the relative growth of labour productivity—growth of the rate and volume of surplus value. From the viewpoint of the capitalist, all of the workers' necessary labour is therefore unproductive labour. Speaking of the class of productive workers itself, "the labour which they perform for themselves appears as 'unproductive labour'" (VII-309).

But as well as defining productive labour in terms of capitalist production, Marx also defines it as labour realised in commodities, in material wealth. This definition proceeds from the material content of the process of social production. Marx considered a twofold definition essential because labour in material production must be distinguished from any other kind of labour. "This difference must be kept in mind and the fact that all other kinds of activity influence material production and vice versa in no way affects the necessity for making this distinction" (XVIII-1145).

The theory of productive labour enables Marx to draw a number of important conclusions about the position of the working class in bourgeois society. Above all, he shows that the growth of labour productivity logically leads to a relative decline in the number of those employed in material production. "A country is the richer the smaller its productive population is *relatively* to the total product..." (IX-377). Here we see a further advance in the theory of scientific socialism. In the *Manifesto of the Communist Party* (see present edition, Vol. 6, p. 494) Marx and Engels wrote that as bourgeois production develops "the other classes decay and finally disappear". Now Marx, proceeding from his comprehensive analysis of the capitalist mode of production, in particular from his investigation of the production of relative surplus value, demonstrates that there is an objective basis for the "longevity" of the intermediate strata under capitalism. The relative decrease in the number of industrial workers leads to the growth of the non-productive sphere, the proletarianisation of some sections of the productive classes, an increase in the intermediate strata standing between worker and capitalist. Marx speaks of "the constantly growing number of the middle classes, those who stand between the workman on the one hand and the capitalist and landlord on the other. The middle classes maintain themselves to an ever increasing extent directly out of revenue, they are a burden weighing heavily on the working base and increase the social security and power of the upper ten thousand" (XIII-746).

In analysing productive labour, Marx also draws the important conclusion that the capitalist mode of production artificially divides mental and physical labour. On the other hand, as capitalism develops the material product increasingly becomes the fruit of the efforts of representatives of both kinds of labour. People engaged in either kind now appear as wage labourers in relation to capital (see XXI-1330). Here, therefore, Marx registers an expansion of the scope of wage labour and the sphere of material production. Included among the productive workers are now "all those who contribute in one way or another to the production of the commodity, from the actual operative to the manager or engineer (as distinct from the capitalist)" (VII-303).

In the course of his critical analysis of Ricardo's theory of accumulation in the manuscript of 1861-63, Marx works out his own theory of reproduction and, based on it, his conception of economic crises under capitalism. In contrast to the classical bourgeois political economists, who focussed on the surplus product and failed to give due attention to constant capital, he put the replacement of constant capital in the centre of his theory of reproduction. Marx asserts that there is a portion of the aggregate product which is not reducible to income (Smith and other economists held that all of the product was income) and which can only be consumed productively. In this manuscript Marx put forward, for the first time ever, a proposition of supreme importance for the theory of reproduction: that the product must be replaced in two senses, in line with the two basic aspects of the reproduction process—it must be replaced in value and in its natural form (VI-272). He also considered in detail the division of social production—and, correspondingly, of the social product—into two basic categories according to the natural form of the product: the production of means of production, and the production of objects for consumption (XIV-855/856). His detailed analysis of the theory of reproduction enabled Marx to draw a whole series of important conclusions on the nature of crises under capitalism.

Earlier on, in the economic manuscripts of 1857-58, Marx pointed out that even the simplest economic relation, the act of sale and purchase, contained the abstract possibility of crises. However, the theory of economic crises demonstrating the inevitably cyclical development of capitalism can only be derived, as Marx stressed in the manuscript of 1861-63, "from the real movement of capitalist production, competition and credit" (XIII-715). In considering the problem of capitalist crises one can no longer proceed, e.g., from the assumption that all commodities are sold at their value. A specific analysis of the capitalist economy is required here.

Marx showed that the Ricardians' denial of the possibility of overproduction was to a considerable extent due to a failure to understand "the actual composition of society". In this connection he notes that bourgeois society "by no means consists only of two classes, workers and industrial capitalists", and that "therefore consumers and producers are not identical categories" in it (XIII-704). At the same time, he demonstrates further on that bourgeois political economy seeks to abstract from the contradictions of capitalist production by presenting it as production for the sake of consumption and treating the various moments of capitalist reproduction as forming a unity. It ignores their antagonistic nature and turns a blind eye to the real disproportions of capitalist production. Bourgeois economists identify the capitalist mode of production either with simple commodity production or with the fiction of a harmoniously developing system of production, i.e. they regard capitalism "as *social* production, implying that society, as if according to a plan, distributes its means of production and productive forces in the degree and measure which is required for the fulfilment of the various social needs" (XIII-722). Since they treat capitalism as an eternal, absolute mode of production, bourgeois economists speak of production in general, of consumption in general, of the limitless nature of human needs, etc. In reality, however, it is essential to consider needs backed by money, and their level is artificially kept down. Overproduction "is only concerned with demand that is backed by ability to pay. It is not a question of absolute overproduction" (XIII-712). In the context of capitalist society it is not a matter of overproduction seen in relation to absolute needs, but of relative overproduction—in relation to effective demand. As far as satisfaction of the vital needs of the working people is concerned, "on the basis of capitalist production, there is constant *underproduction* in this sense" (XIII-721).

Without undertaking to give, at this stage, a comprehensive theory or picture of actual crises, Marx does use his preceding analysis to characterise the general conditions under which overproduction precipitates a crisis. He links them to the objective laws of capitalist reproduction. The general form of the movement of capital, $M—C—M'$, is the form in which reproduction takes place under capitalism. Any disturbance in the conditions of reproduction involves an interruption in the normal functioning of capital. Just as in Marx's theory of reproduction, so also in his views on crises does a special place belong to constant capital, which forms the link between different branches of capitalist production. The close interlinking of the reproduction processes of individual capitals forms the specific "connection between the mutual claims and obligations, the sales and purchases, through which the possibility [of a crisis] can develop into actuality" (XIII-715).

The replacement of the capital advanced, both in its natural form and in value, is one of the principal conditions of reproduction. The fluctuations of market prices—whether upward or downward—upset the hitherto existing ratio between the magnitudes of the money expression of value and use value in the reproduction process of capital, and therefore lead to complications in this process and, as a result, to crises.

In the manuscript of 1861-63 considerable attention is given to the specific forms of manifestation of value and surplus value. An analysis of the inner structure of the capitalist mode of production would be incomplete if it failed to give the derivation of the converted forms in which capitalism's intrinsic categories figure on the surface of capitalist society. At the end of 1861, parallel with his investigation into the production of relative surplus value, Marx began writing the section "Capital and Profit", in which the analysis of the capitalist mode of production was to be completed by stating the form in which the general law of capitalist production, the law of surplus value, is manifested. In this section, too, Marx took an important step forward compared with the manuscripts of 1857-58.

Already in that earlier manuscript, the first version of *Capital*, Marx showed, in general terms, that profit as a converted form of surplus value appears as the immediate regulator of capitalist production. In the manuscript of 1861-63 he formulates this more closely, stating that the real embodiment of this regulator is average profit and the average rate of profit. Empirical or average profit, therefore, can only be the distribution of the total profit (and the total surplus value, or total surplus labour, represented by it) among the individual capitals in each individual sphere of production at equal rates or, which is the same thing, according to the difference in the magnitude of the capitals rather than in the proportion in which they directly represent the production of this total profit (XVI-992). Although Marx initially did not propose to consider the actual mechanism of calculating average profit, he wrote, even then, that one agency by which this calculation is brought about is the *competition of capitals* among themselves (XVI-992). The effect of competition, he wrote, was also manifest in the fact that the intrinsic laws of capitalist production appeared on the surface in a distorted form. Hence the vulgar economists' tendency to describe capitalist relations in the form in which they appear in competition. Marx makes the trenchant observation that vulgar political economy explains everything it does not understand by competition. In other words, to express a phenomenon in its most superficial form means the same to it as uncovering its laws (XVI-994).

In this part of the manuscript, Marx develops his views, first formulated in the manuscripts of 1857-58, on the factors behind the law that as capitalist production progresses the rate of profit has a tendency to decline, and the way this law operates (XVI-999). Bourgeois political economy was unable to explain the decline in the rate of profit it predicted. Marx provided the solution by pointing to changes in the organic composition of capital, i.e. in the ratio of constant capital to variable, changes brought about by technological progress and the growth of fixed capital.

The analysis of this law, the tendency of the rate of profit to decline, shows that capitalism is conditioned historically and is historically transient. *The development of the productive forces of social labour is the historical* task and justification of capital. It is precisely by doing this that it unconsciously creates the material conditions for a higher mode of production. On the other hand, it is precisely with the development of the productive forces that profit—the stimulus of capitalist production and also the condition for and urge to accumulation—is endangered by the very law which governs the development of production. Displayed in this in a *purely economic* way, from the standpoint of capitalist production itself, is its limit, its *relativity*, the fact that it is not an *absolute* but merely a historical *mode of production*, one corresponding to a definite limited period in the development of the material conditions of production (XVI-1006).

Originally Marx did not intend to consider the conversion of value into the price of production in detail, but in the course of his polemic against Rodbertus in the *Theories of Surplus Value* on the theoretical basis of the possibility of absolute rent he came to the conclusion that this problem had to be considered already at this stage, along with the problem of rent in general—as an illustration of "the difference between value and price of production" (XVIII-1139). For the very question as to whether absolute rent was at all possible could not be answered without bringing out the general laws of the capitalist mode of production, on the one hand, and demonstrating the untenability of the notions bourgeois political economy held on the matter, on the other.

Marx shows that classical political economy in the persons of Adam Smith and David Ricardo made it appear that the competition among capitals, by evening up the rate of profit, caused commodities to be sold at their value. Proceeding from this Ricardo concluded that absolute rent was impossible. But the differences in the organic composition of capital and other specific factors operating in different spheres of production, on the contrary, ought to have suggested to the bourgeois economists that competition brings about a general rate of profit "by converting the values of the commodities into average prices, in which a part of surplus value is transferred from one commodity to another" (X-451). Marx traces the modification of the law of value into the law of the price of production under the impact of two kinds of competition.

The first kind takes place within a given sphere of production and brings about a uniform market value for the given kind of commodity. "Thus competition, partly among the capitalists themselves, partly between them and the buyers of the commodity and partly among the latter themselves, brings it about here that the value of each individual commodity in a particular sphere of production is determined by the *total mass of social labour time* required by the *total mass of the commodities of this particular sphere of social production* and not by the individual values of the separate commodities or the labour time the individual commodity has cost its *particular* producer and seller" (XI-544).

The second kind of competition takes place between the

different branches of production and leads to the evening up of the different rates of profit in the different branches, resulting in a general or average rate of profit, and to the transformation of the market value into the price of production, according to which the total surplus value is divided. "The capitalists, like hostile brothers, divide among themselves the loot of other people's labour which they have appropriated so that on an average one receives the same amount of unpaid labour as another" (X-451). In this way Marx's critique advances beyond the view held by Smith and Ricardo that value and price of production are identical and shows that they were unable to explain the apparent contradiction between the determination of the value of the commodity by the labour expended, and the reality of capitalism expressed in the fact that equal capitals yield equal profit. Ricardo, says Marx, "did not understand the genesis of the general rate of profit" (XIV-846), hence his erroneous conception. In connection with this analysis Marx emphasises a basic methodological proposition of his theory, the need for introducing the mediating links, which make it possible to resolve the apparent contradiction between the universal and the converted, superficial forms of existence of value and surplus value. In this connection he discusses the difference between surplus value and profit (and, accordingly, the difference between the rate of surplus value and the rate of profit), the determination of the organic composition of capital in different branches of production and, lastly, the mechanism by which the various rates of profit are evened up in the average profit. It was by thus concretising his theoretical investigation that Marx obtained confirmation of the thesis that the price of production "can be comprehended only on the basis of value and its laws, and becomes a meaningless absurdity without that premiss" (XIV-789).

It was, furthermore, this analysis of the conversion of value into the price of production which enabled Marx to discuss more concretely the converted forms of surplus value—rent and interest, and also commercial profit.

His solution of the problem of rent is based on the difference between the organic composition of capital in industry and that in agriculture, and on the monopoly of private property in land as the real relation that sets limits to the freedom of competition. He points out that there existed, in the nineteenth century, a historically evolved difference in the ratio between the component parts of capital in industry and agriculture, so that the surplus value produced in agriculture exceeded the average rate of surplus value obtained in industry. But owing to the monopoly of private property in land, value here is not converted into the price of production. Landed property fixes the excess surplus value in the form of absolute rent. In contrast to certain bourgeois political economists who sought to explain absolute rent exclusively by the sale of agricultural products above their value, Marx demonstrated that absolute rent was possible on the basis of the law of value. Moreover, he was able, in the context of the problem of market value, to give a more detailed theoretical justification for differential rent and to demonstrate the limitations of Ricardo's theory of rent. He points to Ricardo's one-sided understanding of the formation of market value in agriculture and stresses that the law under which "the market *value* cannot be *above* the individual *value* of that product which is produced under the *worst conditions of production* but provides a part of the necessary supply, Ricardo distorts into the assertion that the market value cannot fall *below* the value of that product and must therefore always be determined by it" (XI-580). Thus the theory of rent, as set forth in the manuscript of 1861-63, further substantiates and concretises the theory of average profit and the price of production.

By way of expanding his theory of the average rate of profit and the price of production Marx, in the manuscript of 1861-63, for the first time considers such converted forms of surplus value as commercial profit and interest, giving a detailed analysis of commercial and loan capital. He examines these two special forms of capital from the historical angle, tracing their rise in the course of development of money circulation and discussing the transformation of merchant's capital into commercial capital, and of usurer's capital into loan capital. He shows the part these "antediluvian" forms played in history and demonstrates that, once the capitalist mode of production has developed, commercial and money capital are merely forms of productive capital which operate in the sphere of circulation, and their specific functions should be explained by the form of the commodity's metamorphosis, hence by the movements of the form which are peculiar to circulation as such (XV-960). But the changes of form accompanying the sale and purchase of commodities, though admittedly involving an expenditure of labour time, create no surplus value for the capital employed in the sphere of circulation. Where, then, does the profit of the commercial and money capitalist come from? The predominant view in bourgeois political economy was that commercial profit derived simply from a surcharge on the value of the commodity. In contrast to this view Marx, in the manuscript of 1861-63, for the first time explains commercial profit and interest by the law of value and the law of surplus value. Commercial capital as such creates neither value nor surplus value. But it reduces circulation time and thereby helps productive capital in the creation of surplus value. The merchant's participation, alongside productive capital, in the reproduction of the commodity entitles him to share in the total surplus value and to receive the average rate of profit in the form of commercial profit, even though he is not immediately involved in its production.

In the manuscript of 1861-63 Marx also discusses, likewise for the first time, the difference between wage workers in commerce and workers employed directly in the sphere of material production. He takes as his point of departure the distinction between the sphere of direct production and that of reproduction as a whole: The clerk's relation to the direct *reproduction* of alien wealth is the same as the worker's relation to its direct *production*. His labour, like the worker's, is only a means for the reproduction of capital as the power ruling over him, and just as the worker creates surplus value, the clerk helps to realise it, both doing so not for themselves but for capital (XVII-1033).

In his further analysis of the movement of capital, Marx traces the process by which interest becomes established as a special form of surplus value. The separation of interest-bearing capital from industrial capital "is a *necessary* product of the development of industrial capital, of the capitalist mode of production itself" (XV-902). At the same time, the separation of interest is conditioned by the fact that money appears now as a converted form of capital. Money assumes the property of being directly representative of capital and in this form becomes the specific source of interest as the money capitalist's revenue. Parallel with this, wages and rent acquire independent existence as the two other basic forms of revenue. Marx emphasises that this is an objective process. "This assumption of independent forms by the various parts [of surplus value]—and their confrontation as independent forms—is completed as a result of each of these parts being related to a particular element as its measure and its special source..." (XV-912). In this way the connection with the inner processes of capitalist production is completely mystified.

The results of this process—interest, profit, every form of revenue in general—increasingly appear as its conditions, both with respect to the individual capital and capitalist production as a whole. The separation of the specific forms of surplus value turns the antagonism of the worker-capitalist relation into its exact opposite, the "harmony of interests" proclaimed by the vulgar economists. As a result, the agents of capitalist production appear on the surface of bourgeois society, and also in the notions of bourgeois apologists, as mutually indifferent and neutral persons, and therefore, Marx points out, the impression arises that "they do not stand in any hostile connection to one another because they have no inner connection whatsoever" (XV-922).

This phenomenon of bourgeois thinking exists not merely in theory, it reflects actual processes at work in capitalist production when its results—the various forms of surplus value—become ossified and fixed as its premises. In the everyday consciousness of the capitalist and in his practical activity they are such in reality, too, since rent and interest appear to him as portions of the production costs which he has advanced. As Marx points out, to the vulgar economist, to whom the mediating links in the analysis of the production and circulation of capital do not exist and who proceeds from these ossified forms of surplus value, it is quite "obvious" that each part of surplus value derives from a different source based on its own material elements.

Marx concludes his theoretical examination of the capitalist mode of production with a discussion of the process of reproduction in the shape of revenues and their sources, thus taking his analysis up to the forms in which the capitalist relations of production appear on the surface, divorced from the concealed and completely mystified inner connection.

The manuscript of 1861-63 is significant in another way, too: in it, for the first time, Marx provides a comprehensive presentation of the history of bourgeois political economy. Above all, he traces the evolution of views on surplus value, the central concept of economic theory. As he critically analyses the reflection of capitalist production relations in the minds and theories of bourgeois economists, he arrives at a complete conception of bourgeois production.

Two features characterise Marx's research into the history of bourgeois views on capitalist production. First, he shows that they are conditioned by the level of development of the society's productive forces and of class antagonisms, and he lays bare the class nature of the various economic concepts, showing the material interests of the ruling classes of capitalist society that underlie them. Second, he shows the methodological roots of these economic theories and consistently demonstrates how the advantages and disadvantages of the method used by individual bourgeois economists affect their arguments. Marx's conclusions are corroborated by the whole history of bourgeois economic science. He determines the place and role of a given economist in the history of economic thought by the degree of adequacy with which his views reflected the economic realities of his age. From this angle, Marx studies the entire history of bourgeois political economy, from its birth (mercantilism), through its classical period (the Physiocrats, Adam Smith and David Ricardo), and up to its decline (the disintegration of the Ricardian school, and vulgar political economy).

In considering the mercantilists Marx discovers that their views were conditioned by the initial period in the development of the capitalist mode of production, the period of the primitive accumulation of capital. They expressed "the standpoint of emerging capitalist society, to which what matters is exchange value, not use value; wealth, not enjoyment" (IX-400). Not fortuitously, it was in the heyday of merchant's and usurer's capital that mercantilism's principal proposition was put forward: that wealth as such is money. The notion that surplus value derived from circulation was based on a whole series of contemporary economic realities. At the same time, the views of the spokesmen of the nascent bourgeoisie were clearly coloured by their class affiliation. For instance, the polemic waged by some seventeenth-century English economists against interest as an independent form of surplus value "reflects the struggle of the rising industrial bourgeoisie against the old-fashioned usurers, who monopolised the pecuniary resources at that time" (XV-899).

The Physiocrats' view that agricultural labour was the only productive kind of labour stemmed, Marx says, from the preponderance of farming in the French economy. The limitations of their outlook, expressed in their overestimation of agricultural production, led them to proclaim Nature the ultimate source of surplus value.

In contrast to the Physiocrats, Adam Smith's theoretical system reflects the industrial stage in the development of capitalism in Britain, the stage of manufacture proper. The antagonistic contradictions inherent in bourgeois production being as yet undeveloped, he was able to advance, from the position of the revolutionary bourgeoisie, "the view that the capitalist mode of production is the most productive mode (which it absolutely is, in comparison with previous forms)" (VIII-357). On the other hand, it was precisely because the social productive forces were as yet inadequately developed that Adam Smith held the Physiocratic view of agricultural labour as being the most productive. With him political economy for the first time becomes a comprehensive system. Bourgeois production appears in it in a dual shape—in its concealed inner structure and in its superficial aspect, in which the intrinsic connection of the categories is manifested in the phenomena of competition. This feature of Adam Smith's method, Marx notes, makes it possible to vulgarise his theory—fully to divorce one mode of presentation from the other. To a certain extent, this was indeed the case with Adam Smith himself, for his examination of the inner physiology of bourgeois society and his description of the external phenomena of its life "proceed independently of one another" (XI-524).

David Ricardo was the central figure of the classical school of bourgeois political economy. His theory strikingly displays the furthest point a scientist moving within the scope of the bourgeois outlook is capable of attaining in the study of economic reality. The historical limitations of bourgeois science as the ideology of a particular exploiting class are also plain in Ricardo's theory. As a witness of an increasingly accelerated growth of large-scale industry, Ricardo glorifies the development of the productive forces of his age and regards their capitalist form as most fully corresponding to the needs of this development. "Ricardo's conception," Marx wrote, "is, on the whole, in the interests of the *industrial bourgeoisie*, only *because*, and *in so far as*, its interests coincide with those of production or the productive development of human labour. Where the bourgeoisie comes into conflict with this, he is just as *ruthless* towards it as he is at other times towards the proletariat and the aristocracy" (XI-497). Ricardo considers that this development is expressed in the growth of society's wealth, the rise of its value, and he therefore concerns himself, among other things, with the question of how the value that has been created is distributed among the different classes.

Ricardo's merit, Marx says, is that, in discussing distribution, he analyses the inner structure of capitalist production, that he "exposes and describes the economic antagonism of classes—as shown by the intrinsic nexus—and that consequently political economy perceives, discovers the root of the historical struggle and development" (XI-525). However, Ricardo's class narrowness is immediately revealed at this point: he considers the antagonism of labour and capital in bourgeois society a natural relation. To him the capitalist organisation of production is its only true organisation. "Ricardo regards bourgeois, or more precisely,

capitalist production as the *absolute form* of production, whose
specific forms of production relations can therefore never enter
into contradiction with ... the aim of production..." (XIV-775).
Attempts to overcome this narrowness to a certain extent were
made, on the one hand, by Sir George Ramsay, Antoine
Cherbuliez and Richard Jones, Ricardo's bourgeois followers, who
declared "the *capitalist form* of production, and consequently
capital, to be not an absolute, but merely an 'accidental', historical
condition of production" (XVIII-1087), and, on the other hand,
by the Ricardian socialists who concluded from his theory that
"the capitalist as functionary of production has become just as
superfluous to the workers as the landlord appears to the capitalist
with regard to bourgeois production" (XV-919). But both groups
remained the prisoners of bourgeois narrow-mindedness. Marx
demonstrated this specifically when discussing the views of
Ricardo's proletarian opponents, who said, "'We need capital, but
not the capitalists'" (XV-878).

In analysing the history of bourgeois political economy Marx
attached great importance to characterising its method. The
service rendered by classical political economy (above all Adam
Smith and David Ricardo) consisted in that it was able "to reduce
the various fixed and mutually alien forms of wealth to their inner
unity by means of analysis and to strip away the form in which
they exist independently alongside one another. It seeks to grasp
the inner connection in contrast to the multiplicity of outward
forms" (XV-920). Marx notes that on this path, by ultimately
reducing all forms of revenue to unpaid labour, the classical
school came very close to comprehending the essence of surplus
value. But here the limitations of its method were also displayed to
the full: classical political economy, Marx writes, "is not interested
in elaborating how the various forms come into being, but seeks to
reduce them to their unity by means of analysis, because it starts
from them as given premises" (XV-921). Manifest in this are the
lack of an historical approach and the class bias of the bourgeois
economists, who regarded the material conditions of the capitalist
system not only as ready-made, but as the eternal, natural
prerequisites of any production. Marx uses the disintegration of
the Ricardian school as an example of the way in which the
misconceptions of classical political economy increasingly lead it
towards an abandonment of its original starting-point—the
exclusive determination of value by labour time.

Even in Ricardo, Marx repeatedly noted an absence of interest
in the genetic derivation of the more highly developed forms, a

tendency to reduce them one-sidedly and forcibly to simple ones. For all his efforts, Ricardo, for instance, failed to reconcile the equality of profits on equal capitals with the principle of value. In defending his doctrine against Malthus, Ricardo's followers sought to eliminate this and other contradictions in his views. But they retained his method. As Marx points out, "here the contradiction between the general law and further developments in the concrete circumstances is to be resolved not by the discovery of the connecting links but by directly subordinating and immediately adapting the concrete to the abstract. This moreover is to be brought about by a *verbal fiction*" (XIV-793).

While the Ricardian school was disintegrating, vulgar political economy was taking shape as an independent trend within bourgeois political economy. In proportion as the antagonistic inner contradictions of capitalist production developed and the working-class struggle rose to a higher pitch, the vulgar trend became predominant in bourgeois economic science. The Ricardian school, for all its shortcomings, was concerned with the contradictions in Ricardo's doctrine, above all those which reflected the inner contradictions of capitalist production. The vulgar economists were increasingly preoccupied with the superficial forms of capitalist production and with the opinions and motives of individual capitalists. "Vulgar political economy does nothing more than express in doctrinaire fashion this [the individual capitalists'] consciousness, which, in respect of its motives and notions, remains in thrall to the appearance of the capitalist mode of production. And the more it clings to the shallow, superficial appearance, only bringing it into some sort of order, the more it considers that it is acting 'naturally' and avoiding all abstract subtleties" (XV-912).

This incapacity of the bourgeoisie to further develop political economy as a science clearly coincides with that stage of bourgeois society at which the proletariat begins to become conscious of being a class in its own right. Only after this stage had been reached, and the working class had developed its standpoint as the agent of a new type of social progress, did the revolution accomplished in political economy by Marx through applying the method of dialectical materialism to the study of capitalist reality become possible.

Also included in this group of economic volumes in the present edition is the draft of the concluding part of Book I of *Capital*.

Written before the summer of 1864, it is entitled: Chapter Six.
The Results of the Direct Process of Production. It was not
included in the final text of *Capital*.

According to Marx's original intention, the chapter was to
provide an interim summary of the analysis of capitalist production and also, in its closing section, a transition to Book II—the
process of capital circulation (p. 441 of the manuscript).

Among other things, Chapter Six examines the formal and real
subsumption of labour under capital, and also productive labour,
which had been discussed in considerable detail in the manuscript
of 1861-63.

The chapter gives a rather extensive analysis of capitalist
production as the production and reproduction of the specifically
capitalist relation of production. The process of capitalist production reproduces not only the means of production and labour
power, but also the capitalist relation and, hence, the social status
of the agents of production in relation to each other. Marx notes
that the capitalist relation differs only externally from other, more
direct forms of enslavement of labour and property in labour by
the owners of the conditions of production (p. 493). But in
contrast to the previous forms, under which those enslaved could
only be kept in subjection by direct non-economic compulsion,
capitalism formally creates the free worker, and the capitalist
keeps him in subjection by economic compulsion alone. An
analysis of the reproduction of capital shows that within the
framework of the bourgeois system the worker is not in a position
to break out of these fetters.

In Chapter Six Marx comes back to the historical role of
capitalist production. He characterises capitalism as a necessary
stage in creating the unlimited productive forces of social labour
which alone can form the material basis of a free human society
(p. 466).

The reproduction of the capitalist relations of production
involves the creation of new productive forces which in turn
influence the mode of production and thereby bring about a
complete economic revolution (p. 494). This revolution will create
the conditions for a new mode of production which will supersede
the contradictory, capitalist relations. In other words, it will create
the material basis of a newly organised social life-process and
thereby of a new social formation (ibid.).

* * *

The Economic Manuscript of 1861-63, which makes up volumes 30 to 34 of the present edition, is reproduced here in accordance with its new publication in the languages of the original in *Marx-Engels Gesamtausgabe (MEGA)*. Zweite Abteilung. Bd. 3, Teile 1-6. Berlin, 1976-1982. Only the part of the manuscript comprising the *Theories of Surplus Value* was published in English previously. Chapter Six, The Results of the Direct Process of Production, in Volume 34, has been checked against the text in *Marx-Engels Gesamtausgabe (MEGA)*, II/4. 1, Berlin, 1988.

In preparing the present publication, a few minor alterations have been made in the text of the manuscript as compared with *MEGA*. In particular, Marx's excerpts from the manuscripts of 1857-58 have been transferred to the relevant passages in the main body of the text.

Obvious slips of the pen in Marx's text have been corrected by the Editors without comment. The proper and geographical names and other words abbreviated by the author are given in full. Defects in the manuscript are indicated in footnotes, places where the text is damaged or illegible are marked by dots. Where possible, editorial reconstructions are given in square brackets.

Foreign words and phrases are given as used by Marx, with the translation supplied in footnotes where necessary. English phrases, expressions and individual words occurring in the original are set in small caps. Longer passages and quotations in English are given in asterisks. The passages from English economists quoted by Marx in French are given according to the English editions used by the author. In all cases the form of quoting used by Marx is respected. The language in which Marx quotes is indicated unless it is German.

The text of and notes to Volume 30 were prepared by Mikhail Ternovsky (notebooks I-V) and Lyubov Zalunina (notebooks VI-VII). The Preface was written by Mikhail Ternovsky. The volume was edited by Larisa Miskievich (Institute of Marxism-Leninism of the CC CPSU). The name index, the index of quoted and mentioned literature and the index of periodicals were compiled by Vardan Azatian (Institute of Marxism-Leninism of the CC CPSU).

The translation was done by Ben Fowkes (Lawrence and Wishart) and edited by Victor Schnittke and Andrei Skvarsky. The section from the *Theories of Surplus Value* was translated by Emile Burns and edited by Salo Ryazanskaya and Natalia Karmanova

(Progress Publishers). The volume was prepared for the press by Alla Varavitskaya (Progress Publishers).

Scientific editor for this volume was Vitaly Vygodsky (Institute of Marxism-Leninism of the CC CPSU).

KARL MARX

ECONOMIC WORKS

1861-1863

ECONOMIC MANUSCRIPT
OF 1861-63

A CONTRIBUTION TO THE CRITIQUE
OF POLITICAL ECONOMY [1]

THIRD CHAPTER
CAPITAL IN GENERAL

[I-A] *August. 1861. Third Chapter. Capital in General*[2]
    I. *The Production Process of Capital*
        1) *Transformation of Money into Capital*
        a) The Most General Form of Capital. b) Difficulties.
        c) Exchange of Capital with Labour Capacity.
        d) Value of Labour Capacity. e) Labour Process.
        f) Valorisation Process. g) *Capitalist Production*
[II-A] I.1) h) *The Two Components of the Transformation Process*[3]

Cover page of Notebook I of the Economic Manuscript of 1861-63

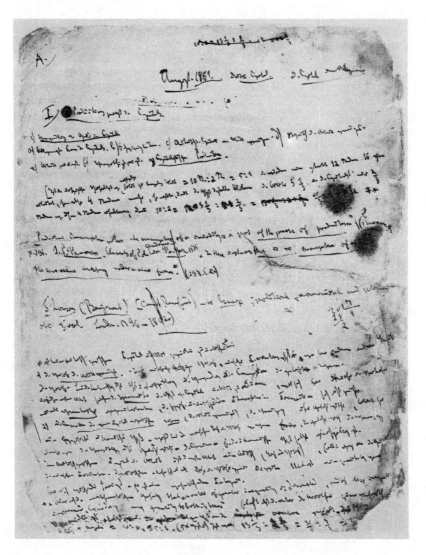

Inside cover page of Notebook I of the Economic Manuscript of 1861-63

9

[I-1] I. THE PRODUCTION PROCESS OF CAPITAL

1) TRANSFORMATION OF MONEY INTO CAPITAL

a) *M—C—M. THE MOST GENERAL FORM OF CAPITAL*

How does money become capital? Or how does the owner of
money (i.e. *the owner of commodities*) become a capitalist?
Let us look first at the form *M—C—M*: the exchange of money
for the commodity, i.e. *buying* in order to exchange the
commodity for money again, i.e. in order to *sell.* We have already
noted [a] that in the form of circulation *C—M—C* the extremes *C*
and *C* are qualitatively distinct, even though they are equal in
magnitude of value, hence in this form a real exchange of
materials takes place (different use values are exchanged for each
other), therefore the result *C—C*—the exchange of commodity
for commodity, in fact the exchange of use values for one
another—has an obvious purpose. In the form *M—C—M* in
contrast (buying in order to sell) the two extremes *M* and *M* are
qualitatively *the same*, namely they are money. Indeed, if I
exchange *M* (money) for *C* (commodity), in order to exchange the
commodity (*C*) in turn for *M* (money), i.e. if I buy in order to
sell, the result will be that I have exchanged money for money. In
actual fact the circulation *M—C—M* (buying in order to sell) falls
into the following acts: first, *M—C*, the exchange of money for
the commodity, purchase; second, *C—M*, the exchange of the
commodity for money, sale; and the unity of the two acts, or the
passage through both stages, *M—C—M*, the exchange of money
for the commodity in order to exchange the commodity for
money, buying in order to sell. The result of the process, however,
is *M—M*, the exchange of money for money. If I buy cotton for

---

[a] K. Marx, *A Contribution to the Critique of Political Economy*. Part One (present
edition, Vol. 29, pp. 324, 332).— *Ed.*

100 thalers and sell the cotton again for a hundred thalers, I have at the end of the process 100 thalers just as I had at the beginning; the whole movement consists in my expending 100 thalers by the purchase and then taking in 100 thalers again by the sale. The result is thus $M—M$: I have in fact exchanged 100 thalers for 100 thalers. Such an operation appears to be without purpose, however, and therefore absurd.* At the end of the process, as at the beginning, I have money, which is qualitatively the same commodity and quantitatively the same magnitude of value. Money is the starting-point and the finishing-point of the process (of the movement). The same person gives out the money as purchaser to receive it back as seller. The point from which the money departs in this movement is the point to which it returns. Because the extremes M, M, are *qualitatively* the same in $M—C—M$, the process of buying in order to sell, this process can only receive a content and a purpose if they differ *quantitatively*. If I buy cotton for 100 thalers and sell the same cotton for 110 thalers, I have in fact exchanged 100 thalers for 110 thalers, i.e. I have bought 110 thalers for 100. Thus the form of circulation [I-2] $M—C—M$, buying in order to sell, receives a content as a result of the fact that the extremes M, M, although qualitatively the same—money—are quantitatively different, since the second M represents a higher magnitude of value, a greater sum of value, than the first. The commodity is bought so as to be sold dearer; in other words, it is bought cheaper than it is sold.

Let us look first at the form $M—C—M$ (buying in order to sell) and compare it with the circulation form $C—M—C$ (selling in order to buy) which we examined earlier.[a] First of all, the circulation $M—C—M$, like the circulation $C—M—C$, splits up into two distinct acts of exchange, of which it is the unity: namely $M—C$, the exchange of money for the commodity, or purchase— in this act of exchange a buyer confronts a seller—and secondly $C—M$, sale, the exchange of the commodity for money—in this act, as in the first, two persons, the buyer and the seller, confront

---

* This is quite correct. Nevertheless the form does occur (and the purpose is irrelevant here). For example, a purchaser may not be in a position to sell the commodity dearer than he bought it. He may be compelled to sell it cheaper than he bought it. In both cases the result of the operation contradicts its purpose. Even so, this does not prevent it from having the form $M—C—M$, in common with the operation which does correspond to its purpose.

---

[a] K. Marx, *A Contribution to the Critique of Political Economy*. Part One (present edition, Vol. 29, pp. 324-34).— *Ed.*

each other. The buyer buys from the one and sells to the other. The buyer, with whom the movement originates, is involved in both acts. First he buys and then he sells. Or his money goes through both stages. It appears as starting-point in the first stage and result in the second. The two persons with whom he exchanges, in contrast, each perform only one act of exchange. The one with whom the buyer makes his first exchange sells the commodity. The other person, with whom he makes the last exchange, buys the commodity. Therefore the commodity sold by the one and the money with which the other buys it do not pass through the two opposed phases of circulation; each rather completes just a single act. Neither of these one-sided acts of sale and purchase performed by these two persons presents us with a new phenomenon. What is new is the whole process which the buyer, who is also its originator, passes through. Let us therefore look instead at the whole movement passed through by the buyer who sells again, or by the money with which he started the operation.

M—C—M. The starting-point is money, the converted form of the commodity, in which it is always exchangeable, in which the labour contained in it has the form of general social labour, i.e. in which it is *exchange value become independent.* The starting-point of this form of circulation, this movement, is therefore itself already a product of the circulation of commodities, i.e. it comes from circulation, for only in and through circulation does the commodity obtain the form of money, only in this way is it changed into money or does it develop its exchange value, the particular independent forms which present themselves as various formal determinations of money. Secondly, the value emerging in this way from circulation and assuming an independent existence in the form of money enters again into circulation, becomes a commodity, but returns again from the commodity form to its monetary form, having at the same time increased its magnitude.

The money which passes through this movement is *capital*, i.e. value become independent in money and passing through this process is the form in which capital initially presents itself or appears.

We can translate the form *M—C—M*: value become independent in money (if we employ the word *value* without defining it more closely, it must always be understood as *exchange value*⁴), hence value emerging from circulation, enters again into circulation, maintains itself in it and returns from it multiplied (returns as a greater magnitude of value). In so far as money constantly describes this circuit afresh, it is value emerging from circulation, entering into it again, perpetuating (maintaining) itself in circulation and multiplied in it.

[I-3] In the first stage of the process money becomes a commodity, in the second stage the commodity again becomes money. The extreme from which the process starts, money—itself already a form of the commodity arisen from circulation, in which it has taken on independence in its determination as exchange value—is at once the point of departure and the point of return. Value is thus preserved in the process it passes through and at the conclusion of the process returns again to its independent form. At the same time, however, the result of the movement, whilst changing nothing in this form (of value), namely its being money, is that the magnitude of the value has grown. The value is thus not only preserved as value, but grows as well, multiplies, increases its magnitude in this movement.

"Capital ... permanent, self-multiplying value" (Sismondi, *Nouveaux principes etc.*, Vol. 1, p. 89).

In $M—C—M$ exchange value appears just as much the prerequisite as the result of circulation.

Value (*money*) resulting from circulation as adequate exchange value (money), taking on an independent form, but entering again into circulation, preserving and multiplying (increasing) itself in and through it, is *capital.*

In $M—C—M$ exchange value becomes the content and the end in itself of circulation. In selling in order to buy the purpose is use value; in buying to sell it is value itself.

Two points must be stressed here. Firstly, $M—C—M$ is *value-in-process*, exchange value as a process that takes its course through various acts of exchange or stages of circulation, and at the same time dominates over them. *Secondly*: In this process value is not only preserved, it increases its magnitude, it is multiplied, increases itself, i.e. it creates in this movement a *surplus value*. It is thus not only self-preserving but self-*valorising* value, *value that posits value.*

Firstly: Let us initially look at $M—C—M$ from the point of view of its form, disregarding the fact that the second M is a value of greater magnitude than the first M. The value exists first as money, then as commodity, then again as money. It is preserved in the alternation of these forms and returns out of them to its original form again. It passes through changes of form in which it is, however, preserved, and it therefore appears as the subject of these changes. The alternation of these forms therefore appears as its own process, or, in other words, value as it presents itself here is value-in-process, the subject of a process. Money and the commodity each appear only as particular forms of existence of the value which is preserved in passing over from one to the other and always returns to itself as money, in the form in which it has become independent. Money and commodity thus appear as the forms of existence of value-in-process or capital. Hence the interpretations of capital. On the one hand, the one above, given by Sismondi. Capital is self-preserving value.

"It is not matter which makes capital, but the value of that matter" (J. B. Say, *Traité d'économie politique etc.*, 3rd ed., Vol. 2, Paris, 1817, p. 429).[a]

On the other hand, when it is conceived not as the whole movement but in each of its forms of existence—the forms in which it exists each time—: capital is money, capital is commodity.

"CAPITAL IS COMMODITIES" (J. Mill, *Elements of Political Economy*, London, 1821, [p.] 74).

"*CURRENCY* EMPLOYED TO PRODUCTIVE PURPOSES IS *CAPITAL*" (McLeod, *The Theory and Practice of Banking etc.*, Vol. I, London, 1855, Ch. 1).[5]

In the form of circulation *C—M—C* the commodity passes through two metamorphoses, the result of which is that it remains behind as a use value. It is the commodity—as unity of use value and exchange value, or as use value, with the exchange value of the commodity figuring as a mere form, an evanescent form— which passes through this process. But in *M—C—M* money and the commodity appear only as different forms of existence of exchange value, which is seen on the one occasion in its general form as money, and on the other in its particular form as the commodity, at the same time figuring as the dominant and self-asserting element in both forms. [I-4] Money is in itself the form of existence of exchange value become independent, but the commodity too appears here only as the repository of exchange value's material embodiment.

[I-16][6] It can easily be understood that if there exist classes which do not take part in the production of commodities, and yet possess commodities or money, which is only a form of the commodity, they have a share in the commodities without exchange, through a title gained either by law or force, not to be discussed any further at this point. The commodity owner or producer—for the moment we can only understand the commodity owner as a commodity producer—must give up to those classes

---

[a] Marx quotes in French.— *Ed.*

4*

a portion of his commodities or of the money he receives for their sale. By virtue of this money, for which they have given no equivalent, they would then be consumers, buyers, without ever having been sellers. These buyers, however, can only be explained as participants in the commodities of the seller (co-owners), a position they have reached through a process inexplicable here.[a] If therefore they buy commodities, they merely give back to the commodity owners and producers a portion of those commodities in exchange for other commodities, commodities they received from the latter without exchange.

It is entirely explicable that if all the producers of commodities sell them at more than their value they will receive from these buyers more than they gave them, but they will only get back more of a sum of value which belonged to the commodity producers in the first place. If someone steals 100 thalers from me and I sell him a commodity worth only 90 thalers for 100 thalers, I make a profit of 10 thalers from him. This is a method of taking away from this buyer, who is a consumer without being a producer, by way of trade a part of the sum of value of 100 thalers that originally belonged to me. If he takes 100 thalers a year from me and I sell him commodities valued at 90 thalers similarly for 100 every year, I admittedly gain 10 thalers a year from him, but only because I lose 100 thalers a year to him. If his taking away of 100 thalers is an institution, the trading that follows is a means of cancelling out this institution in part, here to the extent of $1/10$. However, no surplus value arises in this way and the extent to which this buyer can be defrauded by me, i.e. the number of transactions in which I can sell him 90 thalers' worth of commodities for 100, depends precisely on the number of times he takes 100 thalers from me without giving any equivalent whatever. It is therefore not a transaction through which capital, value preserving and increasing itself in circulation, can be explained, still less the surplus value of capital. Not only Torrens, but *Malthus* himself makes leaps of this kind, and is reproached for it with moral indignation by the Ricardians.[7] Thus Malthus thinks—and correctly under the given conditions—that the income of the mere CONSUMERS, mere buyers, must be increased so that the producers can make a profit from them, so as to encourage production.

* "The zeal for 'encouraging consumption', as supposed necessary for trade in general, springs from the real usefulness of it with regard to the venders of a

---

[a] See this volume, pp. 190-91.— *Ed.*

particular trade" * ([p.] 60). * " 'What we want are people who buy our goods'... But they have nothing in the world to give you for your goods, but what you gave them first. No property can originate in their hands; it must have come from yours. Landlords, placemen, stockholders, servants, be they what they may, their whole means of buying your goods was once your means, and you gave it up to them" * ([pp. 61-]62. * "The object of selling your goods is to make a certain amount of money; it never can answer to part with that amount of money for nothing, to another person, that he may bring it back to you, and buy your goods with it: you might as well have just burnt your goods at once, and you would have been in the same situation" * ([p.] 63) (*An Inquiry into those Principles, Respecting the Nature of Demand and the Necessity of Consumption, Lately* [I-17] *Advocated by Mr. Malthus etc.,* London, 1821).

* "Mr. Malthus sometimes talks as if there were two distinct funds, capital and revenue, supply and demand, production and consumption, which must take care to keep pace with each other, and neither outrun the other. As if, besides the whole mass of commodities produced, there was required another mass, fallen from Heaven, I suppose, to purchase them with.... The fund for consumption, such as he requires, can only be had at the expense of production" * (l.c., [pp.] 49, 50). * "When a man is in want of *demand,* does Mr. Malthus recommend him to pay some other person to take off his goods?" * ([p.] 55).

[I-4] In the form of circulation *C—M—C,* viewed as the total metamorphosis of the commodity, the value admittedly exists as well, first as the price of the commodity, then in money as the realised price, and finally in the price of the commodity again (or, in general, in its exchange value); but it only puts in a transitory appearance here. The commodity exchanged by means of the money becomes a use value; the exchange value disappears, as the irrelevant form of the commodity, and it drops out of circulation altogether.

In simple commodity circulation—*C—M—C*—money always appears in all its forms as merely the result of circulation.[a] In *M—C—M* it appears, to an equal extent, as starting-point and as result of circulation, so that exchange value is not, as in the first form of circulation, the merely transitory form of commodity circulation—the form of the commodity itself taking shape within the exchange of commodities and in turn vanishing—but on the contrary the purpose, the content and the propulsive heart of circulation.

The starting-point of this circulation is money, exchange value become independent. Historically the formation of capital also proceeds everywhere from monetary wealth, and the first conception of capital is that it is money, but money that passes through certain processes.

---

[a] K. Marx, *A Contribution to the Critique of Political Economy.* Part One (present edition, Vol. 29, p. 372).— *Ed.*

The form of circulation $M—C—M$, or money-in-process, self-valorising value, takes as its starting-point money, the product of the simple circulation $C—M—C$. It therefore presupposes not just the circulation of commodities but a circulation of commodities which has already developed all the forms of money. The formation of capital is therefore only possible where the circulation of commodities—the exchange of products as commodities and the establishment of exchange value's independence in money and the latter's various forms—has already developed. In order to pass through the process in which it appears as starting-point and result, exchange value must have already attained its independent, abstract shape in money.

The first act of the form $M—C—M$, namely $M—C$, or purchase, is the last act of the form $C—M—C$, namely $M—C$ once again. In the last act, however, the commodity is bought, money is converted into a commodity, so that the latter may be consumed as a use value. The money is *expended.* By contrast, in $M—C$ as the first stage of $M—C—M$, the money is converted into a commodity, exchanged for a commodity, only so that the commodity may be converted back into money, so that the money may be recovered, retrieved from circulation again by means of the commodity. The money therefore appears only to have been given out so that it may return, only thrown into circulation so that it may be withdrawn again through the commodity. Hence it is only *advanced.*

* "When a thing is bought, in order to be sold again, the sum employed is called money *advanced*; when it is bought not to be sold, it may be said to be *expended*" * (James Steuart, *Works etc.*, ed. by General Sir James Steuart, his son etc., Vol. I, London, 1805,[8] [p.] 274).[a]

If we look at the form $C—M—C$, in its first act, $C—M$, the commodity appears as a mere materialisation of exchange value (hence a mere means of exchange) for the seller. Its use value is not as such use value for himself—the seller—but for a third factor, the buyer. He therefore sells it, converts it into money, in order with that money to buy a commodity which is a use value for himself. The price of the commodity he buys has value for him only in so far as it determines the quantity—the quantity of use values—he obtains for his money. *In purchase* therefore the exchange value of the commodity appears here only as a transitory form of the commodity, and similarly the independence of this

---

[a] J. Steuart, *An Inquiry into the Principles of Political Oeconomy.* In: J. Steuart, *The Works, Political, Metaphysical, and Chronological.— Ed.*

exchange value in money only puts in a transitory appearance. In $M—C—M$, on the other hand, [I-5] where the purchase forms not the second but rather the first act of circulation or the processes of exchange, the commodity into which the money is converted is equally no more than a materialisation of exchange value for the buyer, just a disguised form of money, so to speak. Here both M and C appear merely as specific forms, modes of existence of exchange value, between which it alternates; money as the general, the commodity as a particular form of exchange value. The exchange value is not lost in the transition from one mode of existence to the other; it merely changes its form and hence always returns to itself in its general form. It appears as dominating over its two modes of existence, money and the commodity, and precisely for that reason it appears as the subject of the process, in which it presents itself now as the one and now as the other, hence either as *money-in-process* or as *value-in-process.*

Secondly. As we have already noted, $M—C—M$ would, however, be a movement without content if the extremes M, M, which are qualitatively the same, were not quantitatively different. The process would be without content if a certain sum of value were cast into circulation as money, so that the same sum of value could be withdrawn again from circulation in the form of money, thus leaving everything as it was before, at the starting-point of the movement, as a result of two acts of exchange in opposite directions. The characteristic feature of the process is rather that the extremes M, M, although qualitatively the same, are quantitatively different, quantitative distinction being altogether the only thing exchange value as such—and in money it exists as such—is capable of by its nature. As a result of the two acts of buying and selling, the conversion of money into a commodity and the reconversion of the commodity into money, at the end of the movement more money, a larger sum of money, hence an enhanced value, emerges from circulation: more money than the amount cast into circulation at the beginning.

If, for example, the money was originally, at the start of the movement, 100 thalers, it is 110 at the end. The value has therefore not only maintained itself but has in the course of circulation posited a new value, or *surplus value,* as we shall call it. Value has produced value. Or value appears to us here for the first time as *self-valorising.* Hence value as it appears in the movement $M—C—M$ is value coming out of circulation, entering it, maintaining itself in it, and *valorising itself,* positing surplus value. As such it is *capital.*

In hoarding, which one might recall here, value does not valorise itself.[a] The commodity is converted into money, sold, and in this shape withdrawn from circulation, laid aside. The same magnitude of value as existed previously in the form of the commodity now exists in the form of money. The commodity has not increased its magnitude of value; it has simply taken on the general form of exchange value, the money form. This was a purely qualitative change, not a quantitative one.

In the present case, however, the commodity is already presupposed in the form of money as the starting-point of the process. It gives up this form temporarily in order to reassume it at the end as an increased magnitude of value. Money as hoard, in contrast, remains fixed in its form as exchange value become independent, and, far from being *valorised*, is withdrawn from circulation. Its power of acting as exchange value is retained *in petto*[b] for the future, but suspended for the present. Not only does the magnitude of its value remain unaltered, it loses its function, its quality, of exchange value—as long as it remains a hoard— since it does not function as money, whether means of purchase or means of payment. Apart from this it has no direct use value as money, and has therefore also lost the use value it possessed as a commodity. It can only win this use value back [I-6] by acting again as money, being thrown into circulation and thereby giving up its character as the presence of exchange value. The only thing that takes place in hoarding is that the commodity is given the form of money, the adequate form of exchange value, by the sale of the commodity at its price. In place of valorisation—i.e. an increase of the original value—there occurs no utilisation at all of the money fixed as a hoard; it possesses only a potential value, in actuality it is valueless. Thus this relation of self-valorising value or capital has nothing in common with hoarding, except that both of them are concerned with exchange value, with the hoarder, however, employing an illusory method of increasing it.

In C—M—C, selling in order to buy, in which use value and therefore the satisfaction of needs is the ultimate purpose, there is nothing in the form itself that directly requires its repetition once the process has taken place. The commodity is exchanged by means of money for another commodity, which now drops out of circulation as a use value. With this the movement has come to an

[a] K. Marx, *A Contribution to the Critique of Political Economy.* Part One (present edition, Vol. 29, pp. 359-70).— *Ed.*

[b] Literally: "in the breast". In a figurative sense: "in a secret place", "in a concealed form", "in reserve".— *Ed.*

end. In $M-C-M$, by contrast, the very form of the movement implies that no end is at hand: the end of the movement already contains the principle and the driving force of its resumption. For since money, abstract wealth, exchange value is the starting-point of the movement and its multiplication is the purpose; since the result and the starting-point are qualitatively the same, being a sum of money or value, whose quantitative limit appears at the end as much as at the beginning of the process as a barrier to its general concept—for the more the quantity of exchange value or money is increased the more it corresponds to its concept—(money as such can be exchanged for all wealth, all commodities, but the degree to which it is exchangeable depends on its own mass or magnitude of value)—self-valorisation remains as much a necessary activity for the money which emerges from the process as for the money which started it off—consequently the principle of the movement's resumption is already given with the movement's end. Moreover, it emerges at the end as what it was at the beginning, namely the prerequisite of the same movement in the same form. This is what this movement has in common with hoarding: the absolute drive for enrichment, the drive to gain possession of wealth in its general form.

//At this point it will be necessary to go in detail into Aristotle's discussion, *Republic* I, 1, ch. 9.[9]//

It is the money owner (or commodity owner, for money is after all only the converted shape of the commodity) who makes his money, or the value he possesses in the form of money, pass through the process $M-C-M$. This movement is the content of his activity and he therefore appears only as the personification of capital defined in this way, as the *capitalist*. His person (or rather his pocket) is the starting-point of M, and it is the point of return. He is the conscious vehicle of this process. Just as the result of the process is the preservation and increase of value, the self-valorisation of value, what forms the content of the movement appears in him as a conscious purpose. *To increase the amount of value he possesses* appears thus as his sole purpose. His purpose is the ever-growing appropriation of wealth in its general form, *exchange value*, and only in so far as it appears as his sole driving motive is he a capitalist or a conscious subject of the movement $M-C-M$. Never use value, only exchange value must therefore be regarded as his direct purpose. The need he satisfies is for enrichment as such. It goes without saying, incidentally, that he continuously increases his control over real wealth, over the world of use values. For whatever the productivity of labour, at a given stage of production a higher exchange value is always represented by a larger mass of use values than a smaller.[10] [I-6]

[I-14][11] In order to develop the concept of capital we must begin to not with labour but with *value*, or, more precisely, with the exchange value already developed in the movement of circulation. It is just as impossible to pass directly from labour to capital from the different races of men directly to the banker, or from nature to the steam-engine.[12]

As soon as money is posited as exchange value which not merely makes itself independent of circulation (as in hoarding) but maintains itself inside it, it is no longer money, for money as such does not extend beyond the negative determination; it is *capital*. Hence money is also the first form in which exchange value proceeds to the character of capital, and historically it is the first *form* in which capital *appears*, being as a result historically confused with capital itself. For capital, circulation appears not only, as with money, as a movement in which exchange value vanishes, but also as a movement in which it is preserved and is itself the alternation of the two determinations of money and commodity. In simple circulation, in contrast, exchange value is not realised as such. It is always realised only in the moment of its disappearance. If the commodity becomes money and the money again becomes commodity, the exchange value determination of the commodity disappears, for it only served to obtain a quantity of the second commodity corresponding to the first commodity, the second commodity to the corresponding amount, whereupon the latter commodity as a use value is swallowed up in consumption. The commodity becomes indifferent towards this form and ceases to be more than the direct object of need. If the commodity is exchanged for money, the form of exchange value, money, persists only as long as it stays *outside* exchange, puts itself in a negative relation to circulation. The imperishability money strove for by taking up a negative stance towards circulation is achieved by capital, in that the latter preserves itself precisely by self-abandonment to circulation. [I-14]

[I-7] b) *DIFFICULTIES ARISING FROM THE NATURE OF VALUE, ETC.*

We first examined the form of capital in which it is directly presented or appears for observation. It can, however, be easily shown that the form $M—C—M$, value re-entering circulation, preserving and valorising itself within it, seems utterly incompatible with the nature of money, the commodity, value and circulation itself.

Circulation, in which the commodity is now represented as commodity, now as money, involves a change of form for the commodity; the manner in which its exchange value is represented changes but the exchange value itself remains unaltered. The magnitude of its value does not change, it is not affected by this change of form. If we take a commodity, a ton of iron for example, its exchange value, the labour time contained in it, is expressed (represented) in its price, say £3. If it is now sold, it is converted into £3, into the quantity of money indicated by its price, money which contains an identical amount of labour time. Now it exists no longer as a commodity but as money, as independent exchange value. The magnitude of value remains unaltered, being the same in the one form as in the other. Only the form in which the same exchange value exists has altered. The change in the form of the commodity which constitutes circulation, buying and selling, has in itself nothing to do with the magnitude of the commodity's value: this magnitude is rather pre-posited to circulation as a given factor. The money form is merely another form of the commodity itself, in which no change takes place in its exchange value except that it now appears in its independent form.

But in the circulation $C—M—C$ (selling in order to buy) there is a simple confrontation of commodity owners, one of whom possesses the commodity in its original shape, the other in its converted shape as money. Like the circulation $C—M—C$, the circulation $M—C—M$ contains the two acts of sale and purchase and no more. The one starts with a sale and ends with a purchase; the other starts with a purchase and ends with a sale. Each of the acts of exchange needs only to be considered for itself in order to see that the sequence of these acts cannot change their nature in any way. In the first act, $M—C$, what we have called capital exists only as money; in the second act, $C—M$, it exists only as a commodity. In both acts, therefore, it can only have the effect of money and commodity. In the first it confronts the other commodity owner as the buyer, the money owner, in the second as seller, commodity owner. If we assume that through some inexplicable circumstance the buyers have the opportunity of buying cheaper, i.e. buying the commodity at less than its value and selling it at its value or at more than its value, our man is admittedly a buyer in the first act $(M—C)$ and would therefore buy the commodity at less than its value, but in the second act $(C—M)$ he is a seller and another commodity owner confronts him as buyer; the latter would in turn have the privilege of purchasing the commodity from him at less than its value. What he gained with one hand would be lost with the other. If, on the other hand, one assumes that he sells the commodity at more than its value, this being a privilege enjoyed by the seller, then in the first act, before he himself acquired the commodity in order to sell it later, someone else confronted him as the seller and sold him his commodity too dear. If they all sell their commodities e.g. 10% too dear, i.e. at 10% over their value—and we have here only commodity owners confronting each other, whether they possess their commodities in the commodity or the money form; in fact they will possess them alternately in one form and then the other—then it will be exactly the same as if they sold them to each other at their real value. Similarly if they all buy the commodities at, for example, 10% under their value.

It is clear, in so far as one considers the simple use value of the commodities, that both parties can gain by the exchange. [I-8] In this sense it can be said that "exchange is a transaction in which both sides only gain" (Destutt de Tracy, *Élémens d'idéologie. Traité de la volonté et de ses effets* (forms part IV and V), Paris, 1826, p. 68. It says there:

"Exchange is an admirable transaction in which the two contracting parties *always gain*, both of them" [a]).

To the extent that the whole circulation is only a mediating movement to exchange one commodity for another, each person alienates the commodity he does not need as a use value and appropriates the commodity he does need as a use value. They both gain from this process, therefore, and they only enter into it because they both gain. Yet another point: A, who sells iron and buys grain, possibly produces more iron over a given labour time than the grain farmer B could produce in the same time, and B for his part produces more grain in the same labour time than A could produce. By means of the exchange, therefore, whether mediated through money or not, A receives more grain for the same exchange value, and B more iron, than they would if the exchange had not taken place. In so far as it is a matter of the use values iron and grain, then, both sides gain by the exchange. Similarly, if we regard each of the two acts of circulation, buying

---

[a] Marx quotes in French.— *Ed.*

and selling, in isolation, and limit our consideration to use value, both parties gain. The seller, who converts his commodity into money, gains because he now has it for the first time in a generally exchangeable form, and only thus does it become general means of exchange for him. The buyer, who converts his money back into a commodity, gains because he has taken it out of this form which is required for circulation, but is otherwise useless, and turned it into a use value for himself. There is not the slightest difficulty in understanding, therefore, that both sides gain by the exchange, in so far as it is a question of use value.

It is entirely different with exchange value. Here the reverse is the case: "Where there is equality there is no gain"

(Galiani, *Della moneta*, Custodi. *Autore etc.*, *Parte Moderna*, Vol. IV, [p.] 244... "Dove è eguaglità, non è lucro").

It is clear that if A and B exchange equivalents, quantities of exchange value or objectified labour time of equal magnitude, whether in the form of money or of commodities, they both bring back from the exchange the same exchange value as they threw into it. If A sells his commodity at its value, he now possesses in the form of money the same quantity of objectified labour time (or a draft on the same quantity, which is for him in practice the same) as he previously possessed in the form of the commodity, i.e. the same exchange value. The same thing holds good, but inversely, for B, who has bought the commodity with his money. He now possesses in the form of the commodity the same exchange value as he previously possessed in the form of money. The sum of the two exchange values remains the same, as also the exchange value possessed by each of them. It is impossible that A should buy the commodity from B under its value and thus receive back in the commodity a higher exchange value than he gave B in money, while B simultaneously sells the commodity above its [value] and thus receives from A in the money form more exchange value than he gave him in the commodity form.

(* "A cannot obtain from B more corn for the same quantity of cloth, at the same time that B obtains from A more cloth for the same quantity of corn" *) (*A Critical Dissertation on the Nature, Measures, and Causes of Value etc.*, London, 1825, [p. 65]).

(The anonymous author is Bailey.) *

* That commodities are exchanged *in accordance with their value*, or, with regard to the particular form of exchange which occurs in the circulation process, are sold and bought, means nothing more than that *equivalents*, equal magnitudes of value, are exchanged, replace each other, i.e. commodities are exchanged in proportion as their use values contain equal magnitudes of worked-up labour time, are *quanta* of labour of equal size.

It is of course possible that one person may lose what the other gains, with the result that the two exchangers are exchanging *non-equivalents*. Hence one person will draw from the exchange a higher exchange value than he threw in, and indeed precisely in the proportion in which the other person draws a lower exchange value from the exchange than he threw into it. Let us suppose that the value of 100 lbs of cotton is 100 shillings. If A now sells 150 pounds of cotton at 100 shillings to B, B has won 50 shillings, but only because A has lost 50 shillings.

[I-9] If 150 lbs of cotton with a price of 150s. (the price is here only its value expressed, measured, in money) are sold at 100s., the sum of the two values is 250s. after the sale as well as before. Hence the total sum of value present in circulation has not increased, has *not valorised* itself, has posited no surplus value. It has, rather, remained unaltered. All that has taken place within the exchange or by means of the sale is a change in the distribution of the value *pre-posited* to it, which existed before it and independently of it. 50s. have passed from one side to the other. It is therefore clear that the fraud which has occurred on one side or the other, whether committed by the buyer or by the seller, does not increase the sum of exchange values present in circulation (whether they exist in the commodity or the money form) but only alters (changes) their distribution among the various commodity owners. Let us assume in the above example that A sells 150 lbs of cotton with a value of 150s. to B for 100s., and B sells it at 150s. to C. In this way B gains 50s., or it appears that his value of 100s. has posited a value of 150. But in fact the same amount is present after the transaction as before it: 100s. in A's possession, 150s. in B's, commodities to the value of 150s. in C's. *Summa summarum*[a]: 400s. Originally there were present: commodities to the value of 150s. in A's possession, 100s. in B's, 150s. in C's. *Summa summarum*: 400s. No further change has taken place except the change in the distribution of the 400s. between A, B and C. 50s. have travelled from A's pocket to B's, and A has become poorer precisely to the extent that B has been enriched. What applies to one sale and one purchase applies equally to the sum total of all sales and purchases, in short to the whole of the circulation of commodities taking place between the whole of the owners of commodities within any period of time. If one commodity owner, or a number of them, take advantage of the rest and thereby draw a surplus value from circulation, its quantity

---

[a] Grand total.— *Ed.*

can be exactly measured by the reduction in the value drawn from circulation by the other commodity owners. Some of them extract more value from circulation than they threw in because, and to the extent that, the others extract less value, suffer a deduction from, a lessening in, the value they originally laid out. The sum total of existing values is not thereby altered, only their distribution.

"The exchange of two equal values neither increases nor diminishes the amount of the values available in society. Nor does the exchange of two unequal values ... change anything in the sum of social values, although it adds to the wealth of one person what it removes from the wealth of another" (J. B. Say, *Traité d'économie politique*, 3rd ed., Vol. 2, Paris, 1817, pp. 443-44).[a]

If we take all the capitalists of a country and the sum total of purchases and sales between them in the course of a year, for example, one capitalist may admittedly defraud the other and hence draw from circulation more value than he threw in, but this operation would not increase by one iota the sum total of the circulating value of the capital. In other words: the class of capitalists taken as a whole cannot enrich itself as a class, it cannot increase its total capital, or produce a surplus value, by one capitalist's gaining what another loses. The class as a whole cannot defraud itself. The sum total of capital in circulation cannot be increased by changes in the distribution of its individual components between its owners. Operations of this kind, therefore, however large a number of them one may imagine, will not produce any increase in the sum total of value, any new or surplus value, or any gain on top of the total capital in circulation.

To say that *equivalents* are exchanged is in fact to say nothing more than that commodities are exchanged at their exchange value, that they are bought and sold and bought at their exchange value.

"In fact the exchange value of one commodity expressed in the use value of another commodity represents equivalence" (I-15).[b]

Where exchange has developed into the form of circulation, however, the exchange value of the commodity is expressed, by means of the price, in money (the material of the commodity which serves as the measure of values and hence as money). Its price is its exchange value expressed in money. Therefore, the fact that it is sold in return for an equivalent in money means nothing

---

[a] Marx quotes in French.— *Ed.*

[b] K. Marx, *A Contribution to the Critique of Political Economy.* Part One (present edition, Vol. 29, pp. 279-80).— *Ed.*

more than that it is sold at its price, i.e. its value. Similarly, in the case of a purchase, the money buys the commodity at its price, i.e. here the identical sum of money. [I-10] The *prerequisite* that commodities are exchanged for their *equivalents* is the same as that they are exchanged at their value, bought and sold at their value.

Two things follow from this.

Firstly. If the commodities are bought and sold *at their value, equivalents* are exchanged. The value cast by each hand into circulation returns back from circulation into the same hand. It is therefore not increased, it is not affected at all by the act of exchange. Capital, i.e. value which valorises itself in and through circulation, i.e. increasing value, value which posits a surplus value, would thereby be impossible if the commodities were bought and sold at their value.

Secondly. If, however, the commodities are not sold or bought at their value, this is only possible—and, altogether, non-equivalents .can only be exchanged—if one side takes advantage of the other, i.e. if one person receives through the exchange exactly as much more than the value he laid out as the other receives less than the value he laid out. But the sum total of the values exchanged is not thereby altered and no new value has therefore arisen through the exchange. A possesses 100 lbs of cotton to the value of 100s. B buys it for 50s. B has gained 50s., because A has lost 50s. The total sum of values before the exchange was 150s. It is the same after the exchange. But B owned $^1/_3$ of this sum before the exchange, and afterwards he owns $^2/_3$. A in contrast owned $^2/_3$ before the exchange and only owns $^1/_3$ afterwards. All that has happened, therefore, is a change in the distribution of the sum of values, 150s. The sum itself has remained unchanged.

According to this, capital, self-valorising value, would once again be impossible as a general form of wealth, as in the first case, since an increase of value on the one side would imply a corresponding reduction of value on the other, hence the value as such would not rise. In circulation, one value would only increase because the other value declined, hence was not even maintained.

It is therefore clear that exchange as such, whether in the form of direct barter or in the form of circulation, leaves the values cast into it unchanged, adds no value.

* "Exchange confers no value at all upon products" * (F. Wayland, *The Elements of Political Economy*, Boston, 1843, [p.] 169).

Even so, one still meets with the nonsensical assertion, even from renowned modern economists, that surplus value as such derives from things being sold dearer than their purchase price. Thus, e.g., Mr. Torrens:

* "Effectual demand consists in the power and inclination, on the part of the consumers, to give for commodities, either by immediate or circuitous barter, some greater portion of all the ingredients of capital than their production costs" * (Torrens, *An Essay on the Production of Wealth etc.*, London, 1821, p. 349).

Here we merely have seller and buyer before us. The question whether the commodity owner (the seller) has produced the commodity by himself, and whether the other, the buyer (whose money, however, must also have originated from the sale of commodities, is only their converted form) wants to buy the commodity for consumption, to buy it as a consumer, does not alter the relation in any way. The seller always represents use value. The [economists'] phrase, reduced to its essential content, and with its incidental accoutrement stripped off, means nothing more than this, that all buyers buy their commodities at more than their value, hence the seller in general sells his commodity at more than its value, and the buyer always buys at less than the value of his money. To bring in the producer and the consumer does not alter things in the least; for they do not confront each other in the act of exchange as consumer and producer but as seller and buyer. Yet where the individuals exchange solely as commodity owners each of them must be both producer and consumer, and each can only be the one in so far as he is the other. Each would lose as buyer what he gains as seller.

On the one hand, then, if a *surplus value*, as we still can call every form of gain here, is to emerge from the exchange, it must already have been present before the exchange, as a result of some act which is, however, invisible, not perceptible, in the formula $M—C—M$.

* "*Profit* * (this is a special form of surplus value),* in the usual condition of the market, *is not made by exchanging*. Had it not existed before, neither could it after that transaction" * (G. Ramsay, *An Essay on the Distribution of Wealth*, Edinburgh, [London,] 1836, p. 184).

Ramsay says in the same place:

* "The idea of profits being paid by the consumers, is, assuredly, very absurd. Who are the consumers?" * etc. (p. 183).

There are only commodity owners facing each other, each of whom is just as much a CONSUMER as a PRODUCER; and each of them can only be the one to the extent that he is the other. But if one thinks, anticipating, of classes which consume without [I-11] producing, even so their wealth can only consist of a share of the commodities of the producers, and one cannot explain the increase in value by saying that classes which are given values for nothing are defrauded when an exchange is made in return for those values. (See *Malthus.*[13]) The surplus value or the self-valorisation of value cannot arise from exchange, from circulation. On the other hand, value which as such creates value can only be a product of exchange, of circulation, for only in exchange can it function as exchange value. In itself, isolated, it would be a hoard and as such it no more valorises itself than it serves as a use value. Or if, e.g., one were to say: the money owner buys the commodity, but he works on it, applies it productively, and in that way adds value to it, and then in turn sells it, the surplus value would have arisen entirely and exclusively from his labour. Value as such would not have functioned, would not have valorised itself. He does not obtain more value because he has *value*: the increase of value comes instead from the addition of labour.

In any case, if capital is a specific form of wealth, a potentiality of value, it must be developed on the basis that equivalents are exchanged, i.e. that the commodities are sold at their value, i.e. in proportion to the labour time contained in them. This seems impossible, however. If equivalents are exchanged for each other in $M—C—M$, both in the act $M—C$ and in the act $C—M$, how can more money emerge from the process than went into it?

The investigation of the origins of surplus value has therefore formed the most important problem of political economy from the Physiocrats to the present day. It is in fact the question of how money (or the commodity, as money is only the converted form of the commodity), a sum of values in general, becomes transformed into capital, how capital originates.

The apparent contradictions which lie in the problem—in the conditions of the task—led Franklin to the following utterance:

* "There are only 3 ways of increasing the riches of a state: the first is by war: that is robbery; the second is by commerce: this is cheating; and the third is by agriculture: this is the only honest way" * ([*The*] *Works of B. Franklin,* Vol. II, ed. Sparks, [p. 373,] "Positions to be examined concerning National Wealth").[14]

Here one can already see why two forms of capital[a] that correspond most closely to the ordinary conception of capital and are, in fact, historically the oldest forms of existence of capital—capital in two functions, for its appearance as a particular sort of capital depends on whether it functions in one form or the other—do not come into consideration here at all, for we are

---

[a] Merchant's capital and usurer's capital.— *Ed.*

dealing with capital as such, but must rather be developed later as derived, secondary forms of capital.[15]

The movement $M—C—M$ is shown most clearly in merchant's capital proper. It was therefore realised at an early stage that its purpose is to increase the value or the money cast into circulation, and that the form in which this is achieved is through buying in order to sell again.

"All the orders of merchants have in common that they *buy in order to re-sell*" (*Réflexions sur la formation et la distribution des richesses*, (appeared in 1766) in *Oeuvres de Turgot*, ed. by Eugène Daire, Vol. 1, Paris, 1844, p. 43).[a]

On the other hand, surplus value appears here to originate purely in circulation, in that the merchant sells dearer than he buys, whether by buying cheaper than he sells (buying the commodity at less than its value and selling it at or above its value) or by buying the commodity at its value but selling it above its value. He buys the commodity from one person, sells it to another, representing money to the one and the commodity to the other; and when he begins the movement all over again, he sells also in order to buy, but the commodity as such is never his goal, the latter movement serving him only as [I-12] a mediation for the first. He alternately represents the different sides (phases) of circulation towards the buyer and the seller, and the whole of his movement falls within circulation, or rather, he appears as its vehicle, as the representative of money, just as in simple commodity circulation the' whole movement seems to proceed from the medium of circulation, from money as medium of circulation.[b] He appears only as the intermediary of the different phases the commodity has to pass through in circulation and he therefore mediates only between available extremes, available sellers and buyers, who represent available commodities and available money. Since no other process is added here to the circulation process, the surplus value (profit) the merchant makes by alternately selling and buying—for all his operations can be reduced to sales and purchases—the increase in the money or value brought by him into circulation seems to be explained purely by his taking advantage of the parties with whom he is alternately concerned; the explanation appears to lie in the exchange of non-equivalents, whereby he always draws out of circulation a greater value than he puts into it. His gain—the surplus value

---

a Marx quotes in French.— *Ed.*

b K. Marx, *A Contribution to the Critique of Political Economy*. Part One (present edition, Vol. 29, p. 337).— *Ed.*

created for him by the value he has brought into the exchange—
thus appears to stem exclusively from circulation and hence only
to be made up of the losses of the people trading with him.

Merchant wealth can in fact originate purely in this manner,
and the wealth of the trading peoples which conduct a carrying
trade between industrially less developed nations originated to a
large extent in this manner. Merchant's capital can act between
nations standing at very diverse stages of production and of the
economic structure of society in general. It can therefore act
between nations where the capitalist mode of production does not
occur, hence long before capital is developed in its main forms.
But if the gain made by the merchant, or the self-valorisation of
the merchant's wealth, is not merely to be explained by his taking
advantage of the commodity owners; if, therefore, it is to be more
than just a different distribution of previously existing sums of
value, it must evidently be derived only from prerequisites which
do not appear in its movement, in its specific function, and its
gain, its self-valorisation, appears as a purely derivative, secondary
form, the origin of which must be sought elsewhere. Indeed, if its
specific form is viewed independently, for itself, commerce must
appear, in Franklin's words, as mere cheating, and if equivalents
are exchanged, or commodities are sold and bought at their
exchange value, it must appear altogether impossible.

* "Under the rule of invariable equivalents commerce would be impossible" *
(G. Opdyke, *A Treatise on Political Economy*, New York, 1851, [p.] 67).

(Hence Engels, in his *Outlines of a Critique of Political Economy*—
see *Deutsch-Französische Jahrbücher*, Paris, 1844—sought in similar
fashion to explain the difference between exchange value and
price by saying that commerce was impossible as long as
commodities were exchanged at their value.[a])

Another form of capital, similarly age-old, is money lent out at
interest, interest-bearing money capital, from which popular
opinion has taken its concept of capital. Here we do not see the
movement $M-C-M$, the exchange of money for the commodity
followed by the exchange of the commodity for more money. All
we see is the result of the movement $M-M$: money is exchanged
for more money. It returns to its starting-point, but augmented. If
it was originally 100 thalers, it is now 110. The money, the value
represented by the 100 thalers, has preserved and valorised itself,
i.e. it has posited a surplus value of 10 thalers. We find

---

[a] See present edition, Vol. 3, p. 427.— *Ed.*

interest-bearing money, money that posits money, formally therefore *capital*, in almost all countries and epochs of history, however
primitive the mode of production of the society and however
undeveloped its economic structure. One side of capital comes still
closer here to the [popular] conception than was the case with
merchant's wealth. [I-13] (The κεφάλαιον of the Greeks is our
capital in its etymological formation as well.[16]) Namely the fact that
value as such valorises itself, posits surplus value, because it (enters
into circulation) already exists previously as value, independent
value (money), and that, in general, value is only posited, and the
[original] value is only preserved and multiplied, because value—
value as value—was pre-posited, because it functions as self-
valorising. It is sufficient to remark here (*we shall return to this on
another occasion*[17]):
Firstly: If money is lent out as capital in the modern sense of the
word, it is already assumed that money—a sum of value—is in
itself capital; i.e. that the person to whom the money is lent can or
will apply it as productive capital, as self-valorising value, and will
have to pay a portion of the surplus value thereby created to the
person who has lent him the money as capital. Here, then,
interest-bearing money capital is manifestly not only a derived
form of capital, capital in a particular function, but capital is
assumed to be already fully developed, so that now a sum of
value—whether in the money or the commodity form—can be
lent as capital, not as money and commodity, i.e. *capital* itself can
be thrown into circulation as a *commodity* sui generis.[a] Here capital
is already presupposed in finished form as a power of money or
the commodity, of value in general, so that it can be thrown into
circulation as this potentiated value. Interest-bearing money capital
in this sense therefore already assumes the development of capital.
The capital-relation must already be complete before it can appear
in this specific form. The self-valorising nature of value is here
already presupposed as rooted in it, so that a sum of value could
be sold as self-valorising value, disposed of to a third person on
certain conditions. Similarly, interest appears then merely as a
particular form and branch of surplus value, just as the latter
divides altogether later on into different forms, which constitute
different kinds of revenue, such as profit, rent, interest. All
questions about the magnitude of the interest, etc., therefore
appear as questions of the distribution of the available surplus

---

[a] Of a special kind.— *Ed.*

value between different sorts of capitalist. The existence of surplus value as such is *presupposed* here.

In order that money or commodities, a sum of value in general, may be lent as *capital,* capital is already so far presupposed as a specific potentiated form of value that, just as money and commodities are presupposed as material elements over against capital in general, the capital form of value is here presupposed as the identical inherent quality of money and commodities, so that money or commodities can be made over as capital to a third person, since commodities or money are not developed as capital during circulation but can instead be cast into circulation as finished capital, as *capital in itself,* as a *particular commodity,* which also has its own particular form of alienation.

On the basis of capitalist production itself, therefore, interest-bearing capital appears as a derived, secondary form.

Secondly. Interest-bearing money appears as the first form of interest-bearing capital, just as money in general appears as the starting-point of capital formation, since value first becomes independent in money, hence the increase of money initially appears as an increase in value in itself, and in money the standard is available for the measurement of, first, the value of all commodities, but then the self-valorisation of value. Money can now be lent out to productive purposes, hence formally as *capital,* although capital has not yet taken control of production, there is no capitalist production yet, hence no capital exists yet in the strict sense of the word, whether because production takes place on the basis of slavery, or the surplus product belongs to the LANDLORD (as in Asia and in feudal times), or craft industry or peasant economy and the like is the rule. This form of capital is therefore just as independent of the development of the stages of production as merchant's wealth (the only presupposition being that the circulation of commodities has proceeded far enough to create money), and hence appears historically before the development of capitalist production, on the basis of which it is only a secondary form. Like merchant's wealth it only needs to be *formally* capital, capital in a function in which it can exist before it has taken control of production; the latter capital alone is the basis of an historical mode of social production of its own.[18]

[I-14] *Thirdly.* Money can be borrowed (just like commodities) for *buying,* not for productive employment, but for consumption, to expend it. In this case no surplus value is formed, there is merely a change in distribution, a displacement of the available values.

Fourthly. Money can be borrowed for *payment.* Money can be borrowed as a means of payment. If this is done to cover debts arising out of consumption, it is the same case as 3, the only difference being that there money is borrowed to buy use values, here to pay for use values which have been consumed. But the payment may be required as an act of the circulation process of capital. *Discount.* The examination of this case belongs in the doctrine of credit.[19]

After this digression back to the subject.

In developing capital it is important to keep in mind that the sole prerequisite—the sole material we start out from—is commodity circulation and money circulation, commodities and money, and that individuals only confront each other as commodity owners.[20] The second prerequisite is that the change of form the commodity undergoes in circulation is only formal, i.e. that in all forms the value remains unchanged, that although the commodity exists at one time as a use value and next time as money, there is no alteration in the magnitude of its value, that the commodities are therefore bought and sold at their *value,* in proportion to the labour time contained in them: in other words, that equivalents alone are exchanged.

Of course, if one looks at the form *C—M—C*, one finds that here too the value is preserved. It exists first in the form of the commodity, then in that of money, then in that of the commodity again. E.g. if a ton of iron is sold at a price of £3, the same £3 then exist as money, and after that as wheat at a price of £3. The magnitude of the value, £3, has therefore been preserved in this process, but the grain, as a use value, now drops out of circulation into consumption and with this the value is annihilated. Even though the value is preserved in this case as long as the commodity stays in circulation, this appears a purely formal matter.[a]

[I-15] γ) *EXCHANGE WITH LABOUR. LABOUR PROCESS. VALORISATION PROCESS*

In the process *M—C—M* the value (a given sum of value) should be maintained and increased while it enters into circulation, i.e. alternately takes on the forms of commodity and money. Circulation should not be a mere change of form but should raise

---

[a] K. Marx, *A Contribution to the Critique of Political Economy.* Part One (present edition, Vol. 29, p. 324). See also this volume, p. 20.— *Ed.*

the magnitude of value, should add to the value already present a new value, or surplus value. As capital the value should be, as it were, raised to the second power, potentiated.

The exchange value of the commodity is the quantity of equal social labour objectified in its use value, or the quantity of labour which has been embodied, worked up in it. The magnitude of this quantity is measured by time: the labour time that is required to produce the use value, and is therefore objectified in it.

Money is distinguished from the commodity solely by the form in which this objectified labour is expressed. In money, the objectified labour is expressed as social labour (in general), which is therefore directly exchangeable with all other commodities in proportion as they contain the same amount of labour. In the commodity, the exchange value it contains, or the labour objectified in it, is only expressed in its *price*, i.e. in an equation with money; it is only expressed notionally in gold (the material of money and the measure of values). Both forms, however, are forms of the same magnitude of value and, viewed in terms of their substance, forms of the same quantity of objectified labour, thus they are objectified labour in general. (As we have seen,[a] money can be replaced in internal circulation both as means of purchase and of payment by tokens of value, tokens of itself. This in no way alters the essence of the matter, as the token represents the same value, the same labour time, as is contained in the money.)

In the movement $M—C—M$, and in the concept of capital in general, money is the starting-point. This means nothing more than that the starting-point is the independent form assumed by the value contained in the commodity, or by the labour contained in it: the form in which labour time is present as labour time in general, regardless of the use value in which it was originally embodied. Value, both in the form of money and of the commodity, is an *objectified* quantity of labour. If money is converted into a commodity, or a commodity into money, the value changes only its form, not its substance, which consists in its being objectified labour, nor its magnitude, whereby it is a definite quantity of objectified labour. All commodities therefore differ only formally from money; money is only a particular form of existence taken on by commodities in and for circulation. As objectified labour they are the same thing, value. The change of

---

[a] K. Marx, *A Contribution to the Critique of Political Economy*. Part One (present edition, Vol. 29, pp. 348-51).— *Ed.*

form, the fact that this value is present now as money, now as commodity, ought on our assumption to be irrelevant to capital, or it is a prerequisite—assuming that capital in each of these forms is self-maintaining value—without which money, and value in general, does not become capital at all. In general, it should only be a matter of the same content changing its form. The sole antithesis to objectified labour is non-objectified, *living labour*. The one is present in space, the other in time, the one is in the past, the other in the present, the one is already embodied in a use value, the other, as human activity-in-process, is currently engaged in the process of self-objectification, the one is value, the other is value-creating. If a given value is exchanged for the value-creating activity, if objectified labour is exchanged for living labour, in short if money is exchanged for labour, the possibility seems to be available that by means of this process of exchange the existing value can be preserved or increased. Let us therefore assume that the money-owner buys labour, hence the seller sells not a commodity but labour. This relation cannot be explained on the basis of the relation of the circulation of commodities, considered previously, where the only parties confronting each other are [I-16] the owners of commodities.[20] For the moment we shall not inquire here into the conditions for this relation, and simply assume it as a fact.[21] Our money-owner's sole aim in buying labour is to increase the value he possesses. The particular kind of labour he purchases is therefore a matter of indifference to him. All that is necessary is that it should be useful labour, producing a particular use value, hence a specific kind of labour, e.g. the labour of a linen-weaver. We do not as yet know anything about the value of this labour; nor do we know how the value of labour in general is determined.

[I-17] It is therefore clear that the magnitude of the value of a given quantity of labour cannot be changed, let alone *increased*, by the mere fact of its existing first in the form of money, the commodity in which the value of all other commodities is measured, and then in any other use value; in other words, by its existing first in the form of money and then in the form of the commodity. It is impossible to conceive how a given sum of value, a definite quantity of objectified labour, should even be *preserved* as such via a metamorphosis of this kind. When it is in the form of money, the value of the commodity—or the commodity itself, in so far as it is exchange value, a definite quantity of objectified labour,—exists in its immutable form. The money form is precisely the form in which the value of the commodity is maintained, conserved as value or as a definite quantity of objectified labour. If I transform money into a commodity, I transform value from a form in which it is preserved into a form in which it is not preserved; and in the movement of buying in order to sell, value would first be transformed from its immutable form into a form in which it does not preserve itself, so that it could then be retransformed into money again, the immutable form. This transformation may or may not be successful in circulation. But the result would be that I possessed the sum of value, the objectified labour in its immutable form, as a definite sum of money, both before and after the process. This is an entirely useless operation, indeed it runs counter to my purpose. If, however, I keep hold of the money as such, it is a hoard, it has a use value again, and it is preserved as an exchange value only because it does not act as such. It is preserved, as it were, as petrified exchange value, by staying out of circulation, relating to it negatively. On the other hand, in the commodity form the value perishes with the use value in which it is contained, since use value is a transitory thing and as such would be dissolved simply by the metabolic process of nature. And if it is really utilised as a use value, i.e. consumed, the exchange value contained in the use value perishes along with it.

An increase in value means nothing other than an increase in objectified labour; but it is only through living labour that objectified labour can be preserved or increased.

[I-18] Value, the *objectified* labour which exists in the form of money, could grow only by exchange with a commodity whose *use value* itself consisted in the ability to increase exchange value, whose consumption would be equivalent to the creation of value or the objectification of labour. (*No* commodity has any direct use value at all for the value which is to be valorised, except in so far as its use itself constitutes the creation of value; in so far as it is useful for increasing value.) But such use value is only possessed by *living labour capacity*. Value, money, can therefore only be transformed into capital through exchange with living labour capacity. Its transformation into capital requires that it be exchanged, on the one hand, for labour capacity and, on the other, for the material conditions prerequisite to the objectification of labour capacity.

Here the basis is the circulation of commodities, in which absolutely no dependency relations between the participants in exchange are presupposed apart from those given by the process of circulation itself; the exchangers are distinguished solely as buyers and sellers.[20] Accordingly, money can only buy *labour capacity* to the extent that the latter is itself offered for sale as a commodity, sold by its owner, the living possessor of labour capacity. The condition for this is first of all that the possessor of labour capacity should have the disposition of his own labour capacity, that he should be able to dispose of it as a commodity. For this to be possible, he must be its proprietor. Otherwise he could not *sell* it as a commodity. But a second condition, already contained in the first, is that he *himself* must bring his labour capacity as a commodity to the market, and sell it, because he no longer has labour to sell in the form of another commodity, another use value composed of *objectified* labour (labour existing outside his subjectivity). Instead, the sole commodity he has to offer, to sell, is precisely his living labour capacity, present in his own living corporeity.[21] (*Capacity* is here absolutely not to be conceived as *fortuna*, FORTUNE, but as potency, δύναμις.[a])

Instead of selling a commodity in which his labour is objectified, he must be compelled to sell his own labour capacity, that commodity which is specifically distinct from all other commodities, whether they exist in the commodity form or the money form. A prerequisite for this is the absence of the objective conditions for the realisation of his labour capacity, the conditions for the objectification of his labour; these must have been lost to him, becoming instead subject to an alien will, as a world of wealth, of objective wealth confronting him in circulation as the property of the commodity owners, as alien property. Later on we shall be able to be more precise about the kind of conditions required for the realisation of his labour capacity, i.e. the objective conditions for labour, labour *in processu*, conceived as activity realising itself in a use value.[b]

If then the condition for the transformation of money into capital is its exchange with living labour capacity, or the purchase of living labour capacity from its proprietor, money can, in general, be transformed into capital, or the money owner turn into a capitalist, only to the extent that the free worker is *available* on the commodity market, within circulation; free, that is, in so far as he, on the one hand, has at his disposal his own labour capacity as a commodity, and, on the other hand, has no other commodity at his disposal, is free, completely rid of, all the objective conditions for the realisation of his labour capacity; and therefore,

---

[a] Ability.— *Ed.*
[b] See this volume, pp. 55-66.— *Ed.*

as a mere subject, a mere personification of his own labour capacity, is a *worker* in the same sense as the money owner is a *capitalist*, as subject and repository of objectified labour, of value sticking fast to itself.

This free worker, however, is evidently himself the product, the result, of a prior historical development, the summation of many economic transformations; and his existence presupposes the fall of other social relations of production and a definite development of the productive forces of social labour. The same is therefore also true of the exchange between the money owner and the owner of labour capacity, between capital and labour, between capitalist and worker. The definite historical conditions [I-19] associated with the relation presupposed here will emerge of themselves from the later analysis of that relation.[22] In any case, capitalist production proceeds from the *presupposition* that free workers, i.e. sellers who have nothing but their own labour capacity to sell, will be *found available* within the sphere of circulation, on the market. Thus the formation of the capital-relation demonstrates from the outset that it can only enter the picture at a definite historical stage of the economic development of society—of the social relations of production and the productive forces. The capital-relation appears straight away as a historically determined economic relation, a relation that belongs to a definite historical period of economic development, of social production.[21]

We started out from the way the commodity appears on the surface of bourgeois society, as the simplest economic relation, the element of bourgeois wealth. The analysis of the commodity showed that definite historical conditions were wrapped up in its existence, too.[a] For example, if the products are only produced by the producers as use values, the use value does not become a commodity. This presupposes that the relations among the members of society are historically determined. If we had pursued the question further, asking under what circumstances the products are generally produced as commodities, or under what conditions the product in its existence as commodity appears as the universal and necessary form of all products, it would have turned out that this only takes place on the basis of one particular historical mode of production, the capitalist one. But this way of looking at things would not have been relevant to the analysis of

---

[a] K. Marx, *A Contribution to the Critique of Political Economy.* Part One (present edition, Vol. 29, pp. 282-83, 292).— *Ed.*

the commodity as such, for in that analysis we were only concerned with the products, the use values, to the extent that they appeared in the commodity form, and not with the question of the socio-economic basis for the appearance of every product as a commodity. We were proceeding instead from the fact that the commodity is found to be present in bourgeois production as such a universal elementary form of wealth.[20] The production and therefore the circulation of commodities can, however, take place between different communities or between different organs of the same community, even though the major part of what is produced may be produced as use values, for the producers' own direct personal requirements, and therefore may never take on the commodity form. The circulation of money, for its part, and hence the development of the different elementary functions and forms of money, presupposes nothing more than commodity circulation itself, and crudely developed commodity circulation at that.[23] Of course, this is also a historical prerequisite, but owing to the nature of the commodity it may be fulfilled at very different stages of the social production process. A closer analysis of the individual forms of money, e.g. the development of money as a hoard and of money as means of payment, pointed to very different historical stages of the social production process. These are historical differences, arising out of the sheer form of these different functions of money[24]; but the mere existence of money in the form of a hoard or of means of payment was shown to be in equal degree a feature of every halfway developed stage of commodity circulation. Money is therefore not restricted to a particular period of production, being as characteristic of pre-bourgeois stages of the production process as of bourgeois production. Capital, however, steps forth from the outset as a relation which can only be the result of a definite historical process and the basis of a definite epoch in the social mode of production.

Let us now look at labour capacity itself in its antithesis to the commodity, which confronts it in the form of money, or in its antithesis to objectified labour, to value, which is personified in the money owner or capitalist and in this person has become a will in its own right, being-for-itself,[25] a conscious end in itself.

Labour capacity appears on the one hand as *absolute poverty*, in that the whole world of material wealth as well as its general form, exchange value, confronts it as alien commodity and alien money, whereas it is itself merely the possibility of labour, available and confined within the living body of the worker,[a] a possibility which

---

[a] In the manuscript, "subject" is written above "worker".— *Ed.*

is, however, utterly separated from all the objective conditions of its realisation, hence from its own reality, denuded of them, and existing independently over against them. To the extent that all the objective conditions for labour to come to life, for its actual process, for really setting it in motion—all the conditions for its objectification—mediate between the capacity for labour and actual labour, they can all be described as *means of labour.* In order that labour capacity may as an independent factor come to meet the [I-20] objectified labour represented by the owners of money and commodities, that it may confront the value personified by the capitalist, it must be denuded of its own means of labour and step forth in its independent shape as the worker who is obliged to offer his labour capacity as such for sale as a commodity. Since *actual* labour is the appropriation of nature for the satisfaction of human needs,[26] the activity through which the metabolism between man and nature is mediated, to denude labour capacity of the means of labour, the objective conditions for the appropriation of nature through labour, is to denude it, also, of the *means of life,* for as we saw earlier,[a] the use value of commodities can quite generally be characterised as the *means of life.* Labour capacity denuded of the means of labour and the means of life is therefore absolute poverty as such, and the worker, as the mere personification of the labour capacity, has his needs in actuality, whereas the activity of satisfying them is only possessed by him as a non-objective capacity (a possibility) confined within his own subjectivity. As such, conceptually speaking, he is a PAUPER, he is the personification and repository of this capacity which exists for itself, in isolation from its objectivity.

On the other hand, since material wealth, the world of use values, exclusively consists of natural materials modified by labour, hence appropriated solely through labour, and the social form of this wealth, exchange value, is nothing but a particular social form of the objectified labour contained in the use values; and since the use value, the real use of labour capacity is labour itself, i.e. the activity which mediates use values and creates exchange value, it follows that labour capacity is, just as much, the general possibility of material wealth and the sole source of wealth in the particular social form wealth has as exchange value. Value as objectified labour is after all only the objectified activity of labour capacity. Hence, if in dealing with the capital-relation one starts from the

---

[a] K. Marx, *A Contribution to the Critique of Political Economy.* Part One (present edition, Vol. 29, pp. 269-70).— *Ed.*

presupposition that objectified labour is preserved and increased, that value is preserved and increased, by the fact that the owners of money or commodities continuously find available in circulation a section of the population who are mere personifications of labour capacity, mere workers, and therefore sell their labour capacity as a commodity, continuously offering it on the market, then the paradox which seems to be the starting-point of modern political economy stems from the nature of the case.[27] While on the one hand political economy proclaims labour to be the source of wealth, in both its material substance and its social form, as regards both use values and exchange values, on the other hand it proclaims, just as much, the necessity for the worker to be in absolute poverty, a poverty which means nothing else than that his labour capacity is the sole remaining commodity he can sell, that he confronts objective, real wealth as mere labour capacity. This contradiction is present in the fact that, whether value appears in the form of the commodity or of money, it confronts labour capacity as such as a special kind of commodity.

A further antithesis is this: in contrast to money (or value in general) as *objectified labour*, labour capacity appears as a capacity of the living subject; the former is past labour, labour already performed, the latter is future labour, whose existence can only be the living activity, the currently present activity of the living subject itself.[28]

Just as on the side of the capitalist there stands value as such, which has its social, universally valid, general existence as objectified labour in money, and for which every particular form of existence, existence in the use value of every particular commodity, only means a particular and in itself indifferent embodiment, value as such being wealth in the abstract, so he is confronted, in the shape of the worker as the mere personification of labour capacity, by labour as such, the general possibility of wealth, value-creating activity (as a capacity) in general. Whatever the particular kind of actual labour the capitalist may wish to buy, this particular kind of labour capacity only retains its validity to the extent that its use value is the objectification of labour in general, hence value-creating activity in general. The capitalist, who represents value as such, is confronted by the worker, as labour capacity pure and simple, as worker in general, so that the antithesis between [I-21] self-valorising value, self-valorising objectified labour, and living value-creating labour capacity forms the point and the actual content of the relation. They confront each other as capital and labour, as capitalist and worker. This abstract opposition can be found for example in industry under the guild system, where the relation between master and journeyman is of an entirely different nature.[29] // This point, and probably the whole of this passage, should be put in first in the section "Capital and Wage Labour".[30] //

VALUE OF LABOUR CAPACITY.
MINIMUM SALARY OR AVERAGE WAGE OF LABOUR

Labour capacity is specifically distinguished as *use value* from the use values of all other commodities. Firstly, because it exists as a mere ability in the living body of the seller, the worker; and secondly (this is something that imprints on it an entirely characteristic difference from all other use values) because its use value—its actual realisation as a use value, i.e. its consumption—is labour itself, hence the substance of exchange value; because it is the creative substance of exchange value itself. Its actual using-up, its consumption, posits exchange value. Its specific use value is that it creates exchange value.

As a commodity, however, labour capacity itself possesses an *exchange value*. The question is, how to determine this value? In so far as a commodity is considered from the point of view of exchange value, it is always viewed as a result of the productive activity that is required for the creation of its use value. Its exchange value is equal to the quantity of labour used in working on it, objectified in it, and the measure of this is labour time itself. As exchange value, commodities are distinguished from each other only quantitatively, but from the point of view of its substance each commodity is a certain quantity of average social labour, of necessary labour time, which is required to produce, and therefore also to reproduce, this particular use value under the given general conditions of production. Hence the value of labour capacity, like that of every other use value, is equal to the quantity of labour worked up in it, the labour time required to produce labour capacity (under the given general conditions of production). Labour capacity exists only as an ability of the living body of the worker. Once labour capacity is presupposed as given, its production comes down to reproduction, preservation, as does the production of every living thing. The value of labour capacity can therefore be resolved at the outset into the value of the means of subsistence needed to maintain it, i.e. to maintain the worker's life as a worker, so that having worked today he will be able to repeat the same process under the same conditions the next day.

Secondly: Before the worker has developed his labour capacity, before he is able to work, he must live. Thus if capital is continuously to find sellers of their own labour capacity available on the market, within circulation—and this is a prerequisite for money to develop into capital, for the capital-relation to occur —it is necessary, the worker being mortal, that he should receive, apart from his own means of subsistence, enough of the means of subsistence to perpetuate the race of workers, to increase their number, or at the very least to maintain it at its given level, so that the labour capacities withdrawn from the market through unsuitability or death are replaced by fresh ones. In other words, he must receive adequate means of subsistence to nourish children until they themselves can live as workers. In order to develop a particular labour capacity, in order to modify his general nature in such a way that he is capable of performing a particular kind of labour, the worker requires practice or training: an education which must itself be paid for, and is more or less expensive according to the particular kind of productive labour he is learning to do. This therefore also forms a part of the cost of production of labour capacity. Important as the latter consideration becomes when it is a matter [I-22] of analysing the differing values of individual branches of labour, here it is irrelevant, for we are only concerned with the general relationship between capital and labour, and therefore have in view ordinary, average labour, seeing all labour as only a multiple of this average labour, the training costs of which are infinitesimally small. In any case, the training costs—the outgoings required to develop the nature of the worker so that he has expertise and dexterity in a particular branch of labour—are always included in the means of subsistence the worker requires to convert his children, his replacements, in turn into labour capacities. These costs form part of the means of subsistence required for the worker to reproduce himself as a worker.

The value of labour capacity can therefore be resolved into the values of the means of subsistence required for the worker to maintain himself as a worker, to live as a worker, and to procreate. These values for their part can be resolved into the particular amount of labour time needed, the quantity of labour expended, in order to create means of subsistence or the use values necessary for the maintenance and propagation of labour capacity.

The means of subsistence needed for the maintenance or reproduction of labour capacity can all be reduced to commodities, which possess more or less value as the productive power of labour varies, i.e. according to whether they require a shorter or longer labour time for their production, so that the same use values contain more or less objectified labour time. The value of the means of subsistence required for the maintenance of labour capacity therefore varies, but it is always precisely measured by the quantity of labour necessary to produce the means of subsistence needed for the maintenance and reproduction of labour capacity, or to maintain or reproduce labour capacity itself. The magnitude of the labour time required for this purpose is subject to variation, but a definite portion of labour time—larger or smaller—is always available, and must be devoted to the reproduction of labour capacity. The living existence of this capacity itself is to be regarded as the objectification of that labour time.

Naturally, the means of subsistence needed by the worker to live as a worker differ from one country to another and from one level of civilisation to another. Natural needs themselves, e.g. the need for nourishment, clothing, housing, heating, are greater or smaller according to climatic differences. Similarly, since the extent of the so-called primary requirements for life and the manner of their satisfaction depend to a large degree on the level of civilisation of the society, are themselves the product of history, the necessary means of subsistence in one country or epoch include things not included in another. The range of these necessary means of subsistence is, however, given in a particular country and a particular period.

Even the level of the *value* of labour rises or falls when one compares different epochs of the bourgeois period in the same country. Finally, the market price of labour capacity at one time rises above and at another falls below the level of its *value*. This applies to labour capacity as to all other commodities, and is a matter of indifference here, where we are proceeding from the presupposition that commodities are exchanged as equivalents or realise their value in circulation. (This value of commodities in general, just like the value of labour capacity, is represented in reality as their average price, arrived at by the mutual compensation of the alternately falling and rising market prices, with the result that the value of the commodities is realised, made manifest, in these fluctuations of the market price itself.[31]) The problem of these movements in the level of the workers' needs, as also that of the rise and fall of the market price of labour capacity above or below this level, do not belong here, where the general capital-relation is to be developed, but in the doctrine of the wages of labour.[32] It will be seen in the further course of this investigation that whether one assumes the level of workers' needs to be higher or lower is completely irrelevant to the end result.[33] The only thing of importance is that it should be viewed as given, determinate. All questions relating to it as not a given but a variable magnitude belong to the investigation of [I-23] wage labour in particular and do not touch its general relationship to capital. Incidentally, every capitalist who for example sets up a factory and establishes his business necessarily regards wages as given in the place where and the time when he sets himself up in business.

// "Diminish the cost of subsistence of men, by diminishing the natural price of the food and clothing, BY WHICH LIFE IS SUSTAINED, AND WAGES WILL ULTIMATELY FALL, NOTWITHSTANDING THAT THE DEMAND FOR LABOURERS MAY VERY GREATLY INCREASE" (Ricardo, *On the Principles of Political Economy*, 3rd ed., London, 1821, p. 460). //

// "The *natural price of labour* is that price which is necessary to enable the labourers, ONE WITH ANOTHER, to subsist and to perpetuate their race, without either increase or diminution. The power of the labourer to support himself and his family does not depend on the quantity of money which he may receive for wages, but on the quantity of FOOD, NECESSARIES, and CONVENIENCES which that money can purchase. The natural price of labour, therefore, depends on the PRICE OF the FOOD, NECESSARIES, and CONVENIENCES.... With a rise in the price of FOOD and NECESSARIES, the natural price of labour will rise; with a fall in their price, it will fall" (Ricardo, l.c., p. 86). //

// The English PECK (a measure of corn) = $^{1}/_{4}$ BUSHEL. There are 8 BUSHELS to 1 quarter. The STANDARD BUSHEL contains 2,218 AND $^{1}/_{5}$ cubic INCHES, AND MEASURES $19^{1}/_{2}$ INCHES IN DIAMETER, AND $8^{1}/_{4}$ INCHES DEEP. Malthus says:

"From a comparative review of corn prices and wages from the reign of Edward III onwards we may draw the inference that during the course of 500 years, the EARNINGS OF A DAY'S LABOUR IN THIS COUNTRY have been more frequently below than above a PECK of wheat; that 1 PECK of wheat may be considered as something like a MIDDLE POINT, or a point RATHER ABOVE THE MIDDLE, ABOUT WHICH THE CORN WAGES OF LABOUR, VARYING ACCORDING TO THE DEMAND AND SUPPLY, HAVE OSCILLATED" (Malthus, *Principles of Political Economy etc.*, 2nd ed., London, 1836, [pp. 240,] 254). //

If a lower-grade commodity is put in the place of a higher and more valuable one, which formed the worker's main means of subsistence, e.g. if corn, wheat, replaces meat, or potatoes are put in the place of wheat and rye, the level of the *value* of labour capacity naturally falls, because the level of its needs has been pushed down. In our investigation, however, we shall everywhere assume that the amount and quality of the means of subsistence, and therefore also the extent of needs, at a given level of civilisation, is never pushed down, because this investigation of the rise and fall of the level itself (particularly its artificial lowering)

6*

does not alter anything in the consideration of the general relationship.

Among the Scots, for example, there are many families that live for whole months on OAT MEAL and barley meal, mixed with only water and salt, instead of on wheat and rye, "AND THAT VERY COMFORTABLY", says Eden in his *The State of the Poor etc.*, Vol. I, London, 1797, b. II, Ch. II.

That curious philanthropist and ennobled Yankee, Count Rumford, exerted his limited brainpower at the end of the last century in the artificial creation of a low AVERAGE. His *Essays*[a] are a fine cookery book with recipes of all kinds of the cheapest possible grub for replacing the present expensive normal food with surrogates for the workers. The cheapest meal which can be prepared, according to this "philosopher", is a soup of barley, Indian corn, pepper, salt, vinegar, sweet herbs and 4 herrings in 8 gallons of water. In the work cited above Eden heartily recommends this pretty pig-swill to workhouse overseers. 5 lbs of barley, 5 lbs of Indian corn, 3d. worth of herring, 1d. salt, 1d. vinegar, 2d. pepper and herbs, in all $20^3/_4$d., provide a soup for 64 people, and given the average price of corn it should be possible to reduce the cost per portion to $^1/_4$d.

// "The mere workman, who has only his arms and his industry, has nothing unless he succeeds in selling his labour to others.... In every kind of work it cannot fail to happen, and as a matter of fact it does happen, that the wages of the workman are limited to what is necessary to procure him his subsistence" (Turgot, *Réflexions sur la formation et la distribution des richesses,* (appeared first in 1766) in *Oeuvres de Turgot,*[34] ed. by Eugène Daire, Vol. 1, Paris, 1844, [p.] 10).[b] //

[I-26] //[35] It is possible, on the one hand, to bring down the level of the value of labour capacity by reducing the value of the means of subsistence or the way needs are satisfied, through replacing better by cheaper and inferior provisions, or in general through reducing the scope, the volume of provisions. But in view of the fact that the nourishment of women and children enters into the determination of the level, the average level, it is also possible, on the other hand, to push down this level by forcing them to work. Children are already made use of for work during the time when they should be developing. But we are leaving this case out of consideration, like all other cases affecting the level of the value of labour.[36] We are therefore giving capital a FAIR CHANCE by assuming precisely its greatest abominations to be non-

---

[a] B. [Thompson,] Count of Rumford, *Essays, Political, Economical and Philosophical*, Vol. I, London, 1796, p. 294.— *Ed.*

[b] Marx quotes in French.— *Ed.*

existent. // //The level can equally be lowered by reducing the period of apprenticeship or its cost as near to zero as possible through simplification of work. //

//The following passage from the Whig sycophant Macaulay can be adduced here, in reference to the early exploitation of children as workers.[a] It is characteristic of the kind of history-writing, and the kind of attitude in the economic sphere too, which, while not being *laudator temporis acti*,[b] limits its audacity to the retrospective, transferring it into the passive. Concerning child labour in factories, similar things in the 17th century. But the passage dealing with the historical process or the machine, etc., is better [suited for it].[37] See Factory Reports, 1856.// [I-26]

[I-24] It was naturally of the highest importance for grasping the capital-relation to determine the *value of labour capacity*, since the capital-relation rests on the sale of that capacity. What had above all to be established was the way in which the value of this commodity is determined, for the essential feature of the relation is that labour capacity is offered as a commodity; but as a commodity the determination of its exchange value is the decisive factor. Since the exchange value of labour capacity is determined by the values or the prices of the means of subsistence, the use values necessary for labour capacity's preservation and reproduction, the Physiocrats were able to form on the whole a correct conception of its value however little they grasped the nature of value in general. Hence this wage of labour, which is determined by the average necessities of life, plays an important role with these people, who established the first rational conceptions of capital in general.[c]

// In his anonymously published work *A Critical Dissertation on the Nature, Measures, and Causes of Value etc.*, London, 1825, directed against Ricardo's theory of value altogether, Bailey remarks as follows on the former's determination of the *value* of labour capacity:

* "Mr. Ricardo, ingeniously enough, avoids a difficulty, which, on a first view, threatens to encumber his doctrine, that value depends on the quantity of labour employed in production. If this principle is rigidly adhered to, it follows *that the value of labour* depends on the quantity of labour *employed in producing it*—which is evidently absurd. By a dexterous turn, therefore, Mr. Ricardo makes the value of labour depend on the quantity of labour required to produce wages; or, to give

---

[a] The passage in question—Marx does not quote it here—occurs in Th. B. Macaulay's *The History of England from the Accession of James the Second*, Vol. I, London, 1854.— *Ed.*

[b] A laudator of times gone by (Horace, *Ars poetica*).— *Ed.*

[c] See this volume, pp. 353-54.— *Ed.*

him the benefit of his own language, he maintains *that the value of labour is to be estimated* by the quantity of labour required to produce wages; by which he means the quantity of labour required to produce the money or commodities given to the labourer. This is similar to saying, that the value of cloth is to be estimated, not by the quantity of labour bestowed upon its production, but by the quantity of labour bestowed on the production of the silver for which the cloth is exchanged" * ([pp.] 50-51).[38]

The only thing right about this polemic is that Ricardo has the capitalist use his money to buy *labour* directly, instead of disposition over labour capacity. Labour as such is not directly a commodity, for this is necessarily objectified labour, worked up in a use value. Ricardo does not distinguish between labour capacity as the commodity the worker sells, use value, which has a definite exchange value, and labour, which is merely the use of this capacity *in actu.* He is therefore incapable, leaving aside the contradiction picked out by Bailey—that living labour cannot be estimated by the quantity of labour EMPLOYED IN ITS PRODUCTION—of demonstrating how surplus value can emerge, namely the inequality between the quantity of labour the capitalist gives to the worker as a wage and the quantity of living labour the capitalist buys for this amount of objectified labour. For the rest Bailey's remark is SILLY. The price of CLOTH does indeed consist also of the price of the cotton yarn consumed in it, just as the price of labour capacity consists of the means of subsistence that enter into it through the metabolic process. Incidentally, the reproduction of living, organic things does not depend on the labour directly applied to them, the labour worked up in them, but on the means of subsistence they consume—and this is the way of reproducing them. Bailey could also have seen this in the determination of animals' value; even in the case of machines, in so far as coal, oil and other *matières instrumentales*[a] consumed by them enter into their cost. To the extent that labour is not restricted merely to the maintaining of life, the need being rather for a special kind of labour which directly modifies labour capacity itself, develops it in such a way that it can practise a particular skill, this too enters into the value of labour—as is the case with more complex labour—and here it is directly incorporated in the worker, is labour expended to produce him. Otherwise Bailey's joke only has the upshot that the labour applied to the reproduction of the organic body is applied to its means of subsistence, not directly to the body itself, since the appropriation of these means of subsistence through consumption is not work but rather enjoyment. //

---

[a] Instrumental materials.— *Ed.*

[I-25] The necessities of life are renewed daily. If we take for example the mass of necessities of life that are required during a year for the worker to be able to live as a worker and maintain himself as a labour capacity, and the exchange value of this sum—i.e. the quantity of labour time that is worked up, objectified, contained in these means of subsistence—the total quantity of the means of subsistence the worker requires on the average in a day, taking one day with another, and the value of the same needed to live the whole year through, represent the value of his labour capacity on each day, or the quantity of the means of subsistence required on one day so that this labour capacity may continue to exist, be reproduced, as living labour capacity.

Some of the means of subsistence are consumed more quickly, others more slowly. For example, the use values that serve daily as sustenance are also consumed daily, and the same is true of the use values that serve for heating, soap (cleanliness) and lighting. Other necessary means of subsistence, in contrast, such as clothes or housing, are worn out more slowly, although they are used and needed every day. Some means of subsistence must be bought afresh every day, renewed (*replaced*) every day, others, like for example clothes, need replacing or renewing only at longer intervals although they have to be used every day. This is because they continue to serve as use values for longer periods of time and only become worn out, unserviceable, at the end of these periods.

If the total amount of the means of subsistence the worker must consume every day in order to live as a worker=A, in 365 days it=365A. In contrast to this, if the total amount of all the other means of subsistence he needs, which only need replacing, i.e. buying anew, three times a year,=B, he would only need 3B in the whole year. Taking them together, therefore, he would need 365A+3B in a year; and every day $\frac{365A+3B}{365}$. This would be the average amount of the means of subsistence he needed every day, and the value of this amount would be the daily value of his labour capacity, i.e. the value required day by day, counting one day as equivalent to another, to buy the means of subsistence necessary for the maintenance of his labour capacity.

(If one counts the year as 365 days it will contain 52 Sundays, leaving 313 working days; one can therefore take an average of 310 working days.) If now the value of $\frac{365A+3B}{365}$ =1 thaler, the daily value of his labour capacity would=1 thaler. He must earn this amount every day in order to be able to live through the year day by day, and nothing in this is altered by the fact that the use value of certain commodities is not renewed every day. The annual total of his necessities of life is therefore given; then we take their value or price; then we take the daily average, i.e. we divide the total by 365, and we thus obtain the value of the worker's average necessities of life or the average daily value of his labour capacity. (The price of $365A+3B=365$ thalers, hence the price of his daily necessities of life $= \dfrac{365A+3B}{365} = \dfrac{365}{365} = 1$ thaler.)

EXCHANGE OF MONEY WITH LABOUR CAPACITY

Labour capacity has a specific character and is therefore a specific commodity—just as money was both a commodity in general and a specific commodity, though with money its specific character was produced by the way all commodities related to any commodity which happened to be chosen as the exclusive commodity,[a] whereas here it is produced by the nature of the commodity's use value—but despite this it is like every other commodity 1) a *use value*, a particular object whose use satisfies particular needs, and 2) it has an *exchange value*, i.e. a definite quantity of labour has been used up, objectified, in it as object, as use value. As objectification of labour time in general it is value. The magnitude of its value is determined by the quantity of labour used up in it. This value, expressed in money, is the price of labour capacity. As we are proceeding here from the presupposition [I-26] that all commodities are sold according to their value,[b] price is in general distinguished from value only by the fact that it is the value estimated or measured or expressed in the material of money. The commodity is therefore sold at its value when it is sold at its price. Similarly, one should understand under the price of labour capacity nothing but its value expressed in money. The value of labour capacity for a day or a week is therefore paid when the price of the means of subsistence required for the maintenance of labour capacity during a day or a week is paid. This price or value, however, is not just determined by the means of subsistence entirely consumed by labour capacity each day, but equally by the means of subsistence it makes use of

---

[a] K. Marx, *A Contribution to the Critique of Political Economy*. Part One (present edition, Vol. 29, pp. 287-89).— *Ed.*

[b] See this volume, p. 33.— *Ed.*

each day, such as clothes, for example, but does not entirely use up each day thereby necessitating their constant renewal; they therefore need to be renewed or replaced only over a certain period of time. Even if all objects relating to clothing were only used up once within one year (vessels for eating and drinking, e.g., do not need to be replaced so quickly as clothing, because they do not wear out so rapidly, and this applies still more to furniture, beds, tables, chairs, etc.), the value of these articles of clothing would still be consumed during the whole year for the maintenance of labour capacity, and the worker would have to be able to replace them after the end of the year. He would therefore have to receive every day on an average an amount such that after deduction of the daily expenditure for daily consumption enough was left over to replace worn-out clothing by new after the year had run its course; hence a daily requirement of, if not the such and such portion of a coat, at least one day's aliquot part of the value of a coat. The maintenance of labour capacity, if it is to be continuous, which is a prerequisite with the capital-relation, is not determined only by the price of the means of subsistence consumed in a day and therefore to be renewed, replaced on the next day: there must also be added the daily average of the price of the means of subsistence which need replacing over a longer period of time but must be used every day. It amounts to a difference in payment. A use value like a coat, for example, must be bought as a whole and used up as a whole. It is paid for by holding in reserve every day $1/x$ of the price of labour.

Since labour capacity is available only as an ability, an aptitude, a power enclosed in the living body of the worker, its maintenance means nothing other than the maintenance of the worker himself at the level of strength, health, vitality in general, which is needed for the exercise of his labour capacity.

[I-27] We must therefore state the following:

The commodity the worker offers for sale on the market in the sphere of circulation, the commodity he has to sell, is his *own labour capacity*, which, like every other commodity, has an objective existence so far as it is a use value, even if it is here only an ability, a power in the living body of the individual himself (it is hardly necessary to mention here that the head belongs to the body as well as the hand). Its functioning as a use value, however, the consumption of this commodity, its use as a use value, consists in labour itself, just like wheat, which only really functions as a use value when it is used up in the nutrition process, when it takes effect as an alimentary substance.

The use value of this commodity, like that of every other commodity, is only realised in the process of its consumption, hence only after it has passed from the hand of the seller into that of the buyer, but it has nothing to do with the process of sale itself except that it is a motive for the buyer. This use value, which exists as labour capacity before it is consumed, has in addition an *exchange value*, which, as in the case of every other commodity, is equal to the quantity of labour contained in it and therefore required for its reproduction; and as we have seen it is exactly measured by the labour time required to create the means of subsistence necessary for the maintenance of the worker. Time is the measure for life itself, just as e.g. weight is the measure for metals; hence the labour time required on an average to keep the worker alive for one day would be the daily value of his labour capacity, by virtue of which it is reproduced from one day to the next, or, what is the same thing here, preserved under the same conditions. As we have already said,[a] the range of these conditions is not prescribed by simple natural need but by natural need historically modified at a certain level of civilisation.

This *value* of labour capacity expressed in money is its *price*, and we presuppose that it is paid, since we in general assume that equivalents are exchanged or that commodities are sold at their value. This price of labour is called the *wage*. The wage which corresponds to the value of labour capacity is its average price, as we have explained it[b]; it is the *average wage*, which is also called the *minimum wage or salary*, whereby we understand by minimum not the extreme limit of physical necessity but the average daily wage over e.g. one year, in which are balanced out the prices of labour capacity during that time, which now stand above their value, and now fall below it.

It lies in the nature of this particular commodity, labour capacity, that its real use value only really passes from one hand to the other, from the hand of the seller to that of the buyer, after it has been consumed. The real use of labour capacity is labour. But it is sold as a capacity, a mere possibility before the labour has been performed, as a mere power, whose real manifestation only takes place after its alienation to the buyer. Since here the formal alienation [by sale] of the use value and its actual handing over are not simultaneous occurrences, the money of the buyer in this exchange mostly functions as *means of payment*. Labour capacity is

---

a See this volume, p. 44.— *Ed.*
b Ibid., pp. 44-45.— *Ed.*

paid for daily, weekly, etc., but not at the moment when it is bought, rather after it has really been consumed in a day, a week, etc. In all countries where the capital-relation is developed the worker's labour capacity is only paid for after it has functioned as such. In this connection it can be said that everywhere the worker gives credit to the capitalist, by the day or by the week; this is due to the special nature of the commodity he is selling. The worker hands over to him the use of the commodity he sells, and only receives its exchange value or price after it has been consumed. // In times of crisis, and even with isolated bankruptcies, it is then revealed that this credit given by the workers is no mere phrase, since they do not get paid. // Nevertheless this does not initially alter the exchange process. The price is laid down by contract, hence the value of labour capacity is estimated in money, although it is only realised, paid, later. The determination of price is therefore related to the value of labour capacity, not the value of the product which accrues to the buyer of labour capacity as a result of its consumption, its actual utilisation. Nor is it related to the value of labour, which is not a commodity as such.

[I-28] We now know in fact what is paid to the worker by the owner of money who wants to transform his money into capital, and therefore buys labour capacity: he in fact pays him e.g. the daily *value* of his labour capacity, a price or daily wage corresponding to its daily value, in that he pays him a sum of money=the value of the means of subsistence necessary to the daily maintenance of labour capacity; a sum of money which represents exactly as much labour time as is required for the production of these means of subsistence, i.e. for the daily reproduction of labour capacity.

We do not yet know what the buyer receives for his part. It is bound up with the specific nature of this commodity, labour capacity, and with the specific purpose of its purchase by the buyer—namely that he may prove himself as representative of self-valorising value—that the operations occurring after the sale are of a specific nature and must therefore be considered separately. In addition—and this is the essential point—the specific use value of the commodity and its realisation as use value concern the economic relationship, the determinate economic form itself, and are therefore relevant to our analysis. It can be pointed out here in passing that use value originally appears as a matter of indifference, as any material prerequisite one cares to choose. In the analysis of the commodity the real use value of the individual commodities is completely irrelevant,[39] and the same therefore holds for the specific character of the commodities altogether. What is alone important here is the general distinction between use value and exchange value, out of which money develops, etc. (See above.[40]) // What the worker has in fact sold to the money owner is the disposition over his labour capacity, and the latter has to employ it in accordance with its nature, its specific character. Within what limits, will be seen later.[a] // [I-28].

THE LABOUR PROCESS

[I-A][41] In considering the exchange between capital and labour we have to distinguish two things:

1) *The sale of labour capacity.* This is a simple sale and purchase, a simple relation of circulation, like any other sale and purchase. In investigating this relation the employment or consumption of the commodity purchased is irrelevant.

The *harmonisers* seek to reduce the relation of capital and labour to this first act, because here buyer and seller meet each other only as *commodity owners,* and the specific and distinctive character of the transaction is not apparent.[42]

2) *The consumption of the commodity obtained in this exchange by capital* (of labour capacity), the using up of its use value, forms here a specific economic relation; whereas with the simple sale and purchase of commodities the use value of the commodity, just like the realisation of this use value, consumption, is irrelevant to the economic relation itself.

In the exchange between capital and labour the first act is an exchange (purchase or sale), comes entirely within the sphere of simple circulation. The exchangers only confront each other as buyer and seller. The second act is a process qualitatively distinct from the exchange. It is an essentially different category. [I-A]

[I-28] After the owner of money has bought labour capacity—made the exchange for labour capacity (the purchase is complete once the two sides have reached an agreement, even if payment takes place later)—he applies it as use value, consumes it. But the realisation, the actual use, of labour capacity, is living labour itself. The *consumption process* of this specific commodity sold by the worker therefore coincides with, or rather is, the *labour process* itself. Since labour is the activity of the worker himself, the realisation of his own labour capacity, he enters into this process as a labouring person, a worker, and for the buyer he has in this

---

[a] See this volume, pp. 182-85.— *Ed.*

process no other existence than that of labour capacity in action. It is therefore not a person, but active labour capacity personified in the worker, that is working. It is characteristic that in England the name for workers, HANDS, is derived from the main organ with which their labour capacity performs its function, namely their own hands.

Real labour is purposeful activity aimed at the creation of a use value, at the appropriation of natural material in a manner which corresponds to particular needs.[43] Whether the muscles or the nerves suffer greater wear through this activity is in this connection irrelevant, as is the degree of idealisation the materials of nature have already undergone.[44]

All real labour is *particular* labour, the exercise of a particular branch of labour distinct from the others. Just as one commodity is distinguished from another by its specific use value, so a specific kind of activity, of labour, is embodied in it. Since the conversion of money into capital or the formation of capital presupposes a developed circulation of commodities, it presupposes a developed division of labour, a division of labour understood here in the manner in which it is manifest (appears) in the multiplicity of commodities in circulation, hence as a division of the totality, of the whole of social labour, into manifold modes of labour, hence a totality of specific modes of labour.[45] The labour performed by the worker will therefore belong exclusively to a specific branch of labour, just as his labour capacity is itself specific. The particular content or purpose, and therefore the particular mode of labour, concern us here just as little as the particular material or use value of the commodity concerns us when we analyse the commodity.[39] Which specific branch of labour the worker works in is irrelevant, although of course the purchaser can only buy labour of a specific kind. The sole point to be kept in view here is the specificity of labour where it appears as a real process. It will be seen below that this indifference towards the specific content of labour is not only an abstraction made by us; it is also made by capital, and it belongs to its essential [1-29] character.[16] // Just as the investigation of the *use values* of commodities as such belongs in *commercial knowledge*, so the investigation of the labour process in its reality belongs in *technology*.[47] //

In looking at the labour process we are only interested in the entirely general moments into which it falls and which belong to it as labour process. These general moments must emerge from the nature of labour itself. Before the worker had sold the disposition over his labour capacity, he could not set the latter in motion as labour, could not realise it, because it was separated from the *objective conditions* of its activity. This separation is overcome in the actual labour process. Labour capacity now functions, because in accordance with its nature it appropriates its objective conditions. It comes into action because it enters into contact, into process, into association with the objective factors without which it cannot realise itself. These factors can be described in entirely general terms as *means of labour.* But the means of labour themselves fall necessarily into an object which is worked on, and which we want to call the *material of labour,* and the actual *means of labour,* an object which human labour, activity, interposes as a means between itself and the material of labour, and which serves in this way as a conductor of human activity. (This object does not need to be an instrument, it can be e.g. a chemical process.) [48]

A precise analysis will always reveal that all labour involves the employment of a material of labour and a means of labour. It is possible that the material of labour, the object to be appropriated by means of labour for a specific need, is available in nature without the assistance of human labour: the fish caught in water for example, or the wood felled in the primeval forest, or the ore brought up out of the pit. In such a case only the means of labour itself is a product of previous human labour. This characterises everything that can be called extractive industry; it only applies to agriculture to the extent that, say, virgin soil is being cultivated. Here, however, the seed is both means and material of labour, just as everything organic is both at once, the animal in stock-breeding for example. In contrast to this, it can only occur at the most primitive stages of economic development, hence only in conditions where the formation of the capital-relation does not come into question, that the instrument of labour is available in nature without further mediation. It is apparent of itself, and follows from the nature of the case, that the development of human labour capacity is displayed in particular in the development of the *means of labour* or *instrument of production.* It displays, namely, the degree to which man has heightened the impact of his direct labour on the natural world through the interposition for his working purposes of a nature already ordered, regulated and subjected to his will as a conductor.

The *means of labour,* in contrast to the material of labour, comprise not only the *instruments of production,* from the simplest tool or container up to the most highly developed system of machinery, but also the *objective conditions* without which the labour process cannot occur at all, e.g. the house in which the work is done or the field on which sowing takes place, etc. These do not enter directly into the labour process, but they are conditions without which it cannot occur, and therefore necessary means of labour. They appear as conditions for the occurrence of the whole process, not as factors enclosed within the process. The *means of labour* equally include substances consumed in order to make use of the means of labour as such, like oil, coal, etc., or chemical substances used to call forth a certain modification in the material of labour, as e.g. chlorine for bleaching, etc. There is no point in going into details here.

With the exception of the production of raw materials the material of labour will always have itself already passed through a previous labour process. What appears as material of labour and hence raw material in one branch of labour appears as result in another. The great majority even of things regarded as products of nature, e.g. plants and animals, are the result, in the form in which they are now utilised by human beings and produced anew, of a previous transformation effected by means of human labour over many generations under human control, during which their form and substance have changed. As we have already noted, the means of labour in one labour process is the result of labour in another.

[I-30] Hence in order to consume labour capacity it is not sufficient for the money owner to buy labour capacity // temporary disposition over it //; he must also buy the means of labour, a bigger or smaller quantity of them: the material of labour and the means of labour. We shall come back to this afterwards.[a] Here we only need to remark that for the money owner who has bought labour capacity to be able to proceed to its consumption, i.e. to the actual *labour process,* he must, with another part of his money, have bought the objective conditions of labour, which roll round within circulation as commodities. Only in combination with them can labour capacity make the transition to the actual labour process.

The money owner also buys commodities, but commodities whose use values are to be consumed by living labour, consumed as factors in the labour process: in part as use values which are to constitute the material of labour, and hence the element of a higher use value; and in part as means of labour, which serve as a conductor for the operation of labour on the material of labour. To consume commodities—here initially the use values of commodities—in this way in the labour process is *to consume them*

---

[a] See this volume, pp. 66-67.— *Ed.*

productively, namely to consume them only as the means or object through and in which labour creates a higher use value. It is the industrial consumption of commodities (use values).[49] So much for the money owner, who transforms his money into capital by making the exchange with labour capacity.

Within the actual labour process itself commodities are only available as use values, not exchange values; for they confront real living labour only as its conditions, as means for its realisation, as factors determined by the nature of labour itself, which it requires for its realisation in a particular use value. The linen weaver, for example, is related in the act of weaving to the material of his labour, the linen yarn, only as material of this particular activity, weaving, only as an element in the fabrication of the product, linen. He is not related to it in so far as it has an exchange value, is the result of previous labour, but as a thing in front of him, whose properties he utilises for its rearrangement. In the same way, the fact that the loom is a commodity, the repository of exchange value, is of no concern at all here, it only matters as the means of the weaver's labour. Only as such is it used and consumed in the labour process. The material of labour and the means of labour, although they are themselves commodities and therefore use values which possess an exchange value, confront actual labour only as moments, as factors of its process. This being so, it is obvious that in this process they do not confront labour as capital either. Actual labour appropriates the instrument as its means and the material as the material of its activity. It is the process of appropriation of these objects as of the animated body, the organs of labour itself. Here the material appears as the inorganic nature of labour, and the means of labour as the organ of the appropriating activity itself.[50]

When we speak here of "higher" use values, this should not be understood in a moral sense; we do not even mean that the new use value necessarily occupies a higher rank in the system of needs. Grain distilled into schnapps is a lower use value than schnapps. Every use value that is preposited as an element in the formation of a new one is a lower use value vis-à-vis this new one, because it forms its elementary prerequisite, and the more labour processes have been undergone by the elements out of which a use value has been freshly formed, i.e. the more mediate its existence, the higher that use value is.[51]

The labour process is therefore a process in which the worker performs a particular purposive activity, a movement which is both the exertion of his labour capacity, his mental and physical

powers, and their expenditure and using-up. Through it he gives
the material of labour a new shape, in which the movement is
materialised. This applies whether the change of form is chemical
or mechanical, whether it proceeds of itself, through the control of
physiological processes, or merely consists in the removal of the
object to a distance (alteration of its spatial location), or only
involves separating it from the body of the earth. Whilst labour
materialises itself in this manner in the object of labour, it forms it
and uses up, consumes the means of labour as its organ.[52] The
labour goes over from the form of activity to the form of being,
the form of the object. As alteration of the object it alters its own
shape. The form-giving activity consumes the object and itself; it
forms the object and materialises itself; it consumes itself in its
subjective form as activity and consumes the objective character of
the object, i.e. it abolishes the object's indifference towards the
purpose of the labour. Finally, the labour consumes the means of
labour, which likewise made the transition during the process
from mere possibility to actuality, by becoming the real conductor
of labour, but thereby also got used up, in the form [I-31] in
which it had been at rest, through the mechanical or chemical
process it had entered.

All 3 moments of the process, whose subject is labour and whose
factors are the material on which and the means of labour with
which it operates, come together in a neutral result—the *product*.
In the product labour has combined with the material of labour
through the agency of the means of labour. The product, the
neutral result in which the labour process ends, is a new *use value*.
A use value in general appears as a product of the labour process.
This use value may now either have attained the final form in
which it can serve as means of subsistence for individual
consumption, or, even in this form, it can again become a factor in
a new labour process, as e.g. corn may be consumed not by human
beings but by horses, may serve for the production of horses; or it
can serve as an element for a higher, more complex use value; or
the use value is a finished means of labour which is to serve as
such in a fresh labour process; or, finally, the use value is an
unfinished, a semi-manufactured product, which has to enter
again as material of labour into a longer or shorter series of
further labour processes, distinct from the labour process from
which it has emerged as product, and also pass through a series of
material changes. But with respect to the labour process from
which it has emerged as product, it appears as a finished,
conclusive result, as a new use value whose fabrication formed the

content of the labour process and the immanent purpose of labour's activity; formed the expenditure of the labour capacity, its consumption.

Therefore in the labour process the products of previous labour processes are employed, consumed by labour, in order to manufacture new products of higher, i.e. more mediated, use value. Within the limits of the particular labour process itself, in which the objective factors of labour only appear as the objective conditions of their realisation, this determination of use values, that they are themselves already products, is entirely irrelevant. It does however demonstrate the mutual material dependence of the different social modes of labour and the way they supplement each other to form a totality of social modes of labour.

To the extent that past labour is considered in its material aspect, i.e. to the extent that in looking at a use value which serves as means or material of labour in a labour process the circumstance is kept in mind that this use value is itself already a combination of natural material and labour, the past concrete labour objectified in use values serves as a means to the realisation of fresh labour, or, and this is the same thing, the formation of fresh use values. But one should certainly keep in mind the sense in which this is the case in the actual labour process. For example, *loom and cotton yarn serve in weaving only in the qualities they possess for this process as material and means of weaving, only through the physical qualities they possess for this particular labour process.* Cotton, wood and iron have taken on the forms in which they perform these services in the labour process, the one as yarn, the others as the loom. The fact that they have acquired this particular employment of their use value through the agency of previous labour, that they themselves already represent a combination of labour and natural material, is, as such, a circumstance which— just like the circumstance that wheat performs the particular services, finds the particular employment of its use value we see in the nourishment process—is irrelevant for *this* particular labour process as such, since they serve in a particular manner as use values, acquire a specific useful application. The process could not however, take place if cotton, iron and wood had not acquired the shape and therefore the specifically applicable qualities they possess as yarn and loom as a result of an earlier, past labour process.

Looked at purely materially, from the point of view of the actual labour process itself, a definite past labour process therefore appears as a preliminary stage and a condition for the entry into action of the new labour process. But then this labour process itself becomes merely a condition for the manufacture of a particular use value, even viewed from the standpoint of use value. In the consumption of a use value in general the labour contained in it is irrelevant and the use value only functions as use value, in other words it satisfies certain needs according to its qualities in the process of consumption, hence only the qualities it possesses as this object and the services it renders as this object are of interest; equally, in the labour process, which is itself only a definite, specific process of the consumption of use values, a particular, specific manner of using them up, what matters is only the qualities the products of earlier labour have for this process, not their existence as the materialisation of past labour. The qualities acquired by any natural material through earlier labour are now its own physical qualities, with which it functions or serves. The fact that these qualities are mediated by earlier labour, this mediation itself, is cancelled out, extinguished, in the product.

[I-32] What was the specific mode, the driving purpose, the activity of labour, now appears in its result, in the alteration in the object brought about by labour in the product, as an object with particular new qualities which it has for use, for the satisfaction of needs. If we are reminded in the labour process itself that the material and means of labour are the product of earlier labour, this only happens in so far as they fail to develop the necessary qualities, e.g. a saw that does not saw, a knife that does not cut, etc. This recalls to us the imperfection of the labour which has provided a factor for the labour process currently under way. Where products of earlier labour processes enter into a new labour process as factors, as material or means, it is only the quality of the past labour that interests us. We want to know whether its product really possesses the useful qualities it claims to have, whether the work was *good* or *bad*. It is labour in its material effect and reality that interests us here. For the rest, where the means and the material of labour serve as such use values in the actual labour process and possess the appropriate qualities — though whether they possess these qualities as use values at a higher or lower level, whether they serve their purpose more or less perfectly, depends on the past labour whose products they are — it is entirely irrelevant that they are the products of previous labour. If they fell ready-made from the sky they would perform the same service. If they interest us as products, i.e. as the results of past labour, it is only as the results of *specific* labour. We are interested in the quality of this specific labour, on which depends

7*

the quality of the results as use values, the degree to which they really serve [as] use values for this specific consumption process. Similarly, in a given labour process the labour is only of interest to the extent that it functions as this particular purposive activity; but the particular material content, and the degree to which the product is good or bad, to which it really possesses, acquires, the use value it ought to acquire in the labour process, depends on the higher or lower quality of the labour, on its thoroughness and suitability to the purpose.[53]

On the other hand, products which are destined to enter as use values into a fresh labour process, hence are either means of labour or unfinished products, i.e. products which need further treatment in order to become real use values, to serve for individual or productive consumption; products which are there-fore either means or materials of labour for a further labour process, are realised as such only by entering into contact with living labour, which overcomes their dead objectivity, consumes them, transforms them from use values which only exist potential-ly into real and effective use values by consuming and utilising them as the objective factors of its own living movement. A machine that does not serve in the labour process is useless, dead wood and iron. Apart from this it falls victim to consumption by elemental forces, to the universal metabolism [of nature]. Iron rusts, wood rots. Yarn that is not woven or knitted, etc., is only wasted cotton, cotton unfitted for the other useful applications it possessed in its state as cotton, as raw material.

Since every use value can be made use of in various ways, every thing having various qualities in which it can serve to satisfy needs, it loses these qualities by acquiring use value in a particular direction through an earlier labour process, acquiring qualities with which it can only be useful in a particular subsequent labour process; hence products which can only serve as means and material of labour not only lose their quality as products which they acquired through the earlier labour, their quality as these particular use values, but also the raw material of which they consist is spoiled, pointlessly squandered, and along with the useful form it acquired as a result of labour previously carried out it falls victim to the dissolving action of natural forces. In the labour process the products of an earlier labour process, the material and means of labour, are as it were awakened from the dead. They only become *real* use values by entering as factors into the labour process, only in that process do they act as use values and only through it are they withdrawn from the dissolving action of the universal metabolic process so as to re-appear in the product as a new formation.

The labour process also destroys the machine, but as a machine. It lives and acts as a machine, for it to be consumed is the same thing as to be effective, and in the changed form of the material its movement is realised, fixed, as the quality of a new object. Similarly, it is only in the labour process itself that the material of labour develops the useful qualities it possesses as such. The process of its consumption is a process of refashioning, alteration, from which it emerges as a use value of a higher order.[51]

[I-33] Hence if existing products, the results of earlier labour, mediate the realisation of living labour as its objective conditions, living labour, for its part, mediates the realisation of these products as use values, as products, and preserves them, withdraws them from the universal metabolism of nature, by breathing life into them as the elements of a "new formation".

In so far as actual labour creates use values, is appropriation of the natural world for human needs, whether these needs are needs of production or individual consumption, it is the universal condition for the metabolic interaction between nature and man, and as such a natural condition of human life it is independent of, equally common to, all particular social forms of human life.[43] The same is true of the labour process in its general forms; it is after all nothing but living labour, split up into its specific elements, whose unity is the labour process itself, the impact of labour on the material of labour working through the means of labour. The labour process itself appears in its general form, hence still in *no* specific *economic determinateness*. This form does not express any particular historical (social) *relation of production* entered into by human beings in the production of their social life; it is rather the general form, and the general elements, into which labour must be uniformly divided in all social modes of production in order to function as labour.

The form of the labour process which has been examined here is only its abstract form, a form divorced from all particular historical characteristics and fitting equally well with every kind of labour process, irrespective of the social relations human beings may enter into with each other in its course. Just as little as one can tell from the taste of wheat whether it has been produced by a Russian serf or a French peasant, equally little can one tell from the labour process in its general forms, the general forms of this labour process, whether it is happening under the whip of the slave-driver or the eye of the industrial capitalist, or indeed whether the process is that of a savage dispatching wild beasts with his bow.[54]

With his money, the money owner has in part bought disposition over labour capacity, in part material and means of labour, so that he can use up, consume, this labour capacity as such, i.e. have it operate as actual labour, in short, so that he can have the worker really work. The universal determinants of this labour, which it has in common with every other manner of working, are not altered by the fact that it is done here for the money owner or appears here as the process of his consumption of labour capacity. He has subsumed the labour process under his dominion, appropriated it, but thereby left its general nature unchanged. To what extent the character of the labour process is itself changed by its subsumption under capital is a question which has nothing to do with the general form of the labour process and will be discussed later on.[55]

The wheat I eat, whether I have bought it or produced it myself, functions in either case in the nourishment process according to its own natural characteristics. Similarly, it does not change anything in the labour process in its general form, i.e. it changes nothing in the conceptual moments of work in general, whether I work for myself with my own material and instrument of labour, or I work for the money owner, to whom I have temporarily sold my labour capacity. The consumption of this labour capacity, i.e. its actual operation as labour power, actual labour, *which in itself is a process wherein an activity enters into certain relations with objects, remains the same as before* and moves within the same general forms. The labour process or actual work implies precisely that the separation in which the worker found himself before the sale of his labour capacity from the objective conditions which alone permit him to activate his labour capacity, to work—that this separation has been overcome, that he now enters into the natural relation as worker to the objective conditions of his labour, that he enters into the labour process. Hence in considering the general moments of this process I am only considering the general moments of actual labour in general.

(The practical application of this is namely that the apologists of capital confuse or identify it with a moment of the simple labour process as such, maintaining that a product intended for the production of another product is capital, that raw material is capital or that the tool of labour, the instrument of production is capital, that therefore capital is—whatever the relations of distribution and forms of social production—a factor of the labour process as such, a factor of production. It will be better to deal with this point when once the valorisation process has been treated.[56] For money to be transformed into capital (productive capital), it must be transformed into material of labour, instrument of labour and labour capacity, all of them products of past labour, use values provided through the agency of labour and employed for new production. Viewed from its material side capital thus appears now—in so far as it exists as use value—[I-34] as existing, present in the form of products which serve for new production, raw material, tools (but also as labour). The converse, however, by no means follows: these things are not as such capital. They only become capital given certain social pre-conditions. Otherwise it could just as well be said that labour is in and for itself capital, hence the usefulness of labour could be used to demonstrate to the worker the usefulness of capital, since in the labour process the labour belongs to the capitalist just as much as the tool does.)

The moments of the labour process, considered in relation to labour itself, have been specified as material of labour, means of labour and labour itself. If these moments are considered with regard to the purpose of the whole process, the product to be manufactured, they can be described as material of production, means of production and productive labour (perhaps not this last expression).[57]

The product is the result of the labour process. But products appear just as much as its prerequisite, with which it does not end but from whose existence it starts out as a condition. Not only is the labour capacity itself a product; the means of subsistence the worker receives as money from the money owner for the sale of his labour capacity are already finished products for individual consumption. Likewise, his material and means of labour, one or the other, or both, are already products. Products are therefore presupposed to production; products both for individual and for productive consumption. Nature itself is originally the store-house in which the human being, equally presupposed as a natural product, finds available for consumption finished natural products, as well as finding available in part, in the very organs of his own body, the first instruments of production for the appropriation of these products. The means of labour, the means of production, appears as the first product produced by the human being; and the first forms of this product, stones, etc., are also found present in nature by him.[58]

As we have said, the labour process as such has nothing to do with the act of purchasing the labour capacity on the part of the capitalist.[a] He has bought the labour capacity. Now he must employ it as use value. The use value of labour is work itself, the labour process. We therefore ask what this process consists in, in its general moments, i.e. independently of the future capitalist, in the same way as if we were to say: he buys wheat and now wants to use it as a means of nourishment.[b] In what does the process of nourishment by cereals consist, or rather, what are the general moments of the nourishment process as such?

THE VALORISATION PROCESS

In so far as the result of the labour process is still viewed in relation to the process itself, as the crystallised labour process, whose different factors have come together in a static object, a combination of subjective activity and its material content, this result is the *product*. But this product viewed for itself, in the independence in which it appears as a result of the labour process, is a particular *use value*. The material of labour has acquired the form, the particular qualities, whose manufacture was the purpose of the entire labour process and which as the driving objective determined the specific way the labour itself was carried on. This product is a *use value* in so far as it is now present as the result, with the labour process lying behind it as past, as the history of its origin. What money has acquired by its exchange with the labour capacity, or what the money owner has acquired by the consumption of the labour capacity he has bought—this consumption being however by the nature of the labour capacity an industrial, productive consumption or a labour process—is a *use value*. This use value belongs to him; he has bought it by giving an equivalent for it, namely he has bought the material of labour and the means of labour. But the *labour itself* likewise belonged to him, for owing to his purchase of the labour capacity—hence *before* any actual work was done—the use value of this commodity belongs to him, and this is labour itself. The product belongs to him just as much as if he had consumed his own labour capacity, i.e. himself worked on the raw material. The whole labour process only takes place after he has provided himself with all its elements on the basis of commodity exchange and in accordance with its laws, namely by purchasing these elements at their price, which is their value expressed, estimated, in money. To the extent that his

---

[a] See this volume, pp. 54-55.— *Ed.*
[b] Ibid., p. 52.— *Ed.*

money has been converted into the elements of the labour process and the whole labour process itself appears merely as the consumption of the labour capacity bought by the money, the labour process itself appears as a transformation that money passes through by being exchanged not for an available use value but for a process which is its own process. The labour process is as it were incorporated in it, subsumed under it.

Yet, the purpose of the exchange of money for the labour capacity was by no means use value; it was the transformation of money into capital. Value, become independent in money, was to maintain, increase itself in this exchange, assume a self-sufficient character, and the money owner was to become a capitalist precisely by representing value dominant over circulation and asserting itself [I-35] as subject within it. What was at stake here was exchange value, not use value. Value asserts itself as exchange value only if the use value created in the labour process, the product of actual labour, is itself a repository of exchange value, i.e. a *commodity*. For the money that was being turned into capital, therefore, it was a matter of the production of a commodity, not a mere use value. The use value was important only in so far as it was a necessary condition, a material substratum of exchange value. What was involved, in fact, was the *production* of exchange value, its preservation and its increase. It will now be necessary, therefore, to calculate the exchange value obtained in the product, in the new use value. (It is a matter of the valorisation of value. Hence not only a labour process but a valorisation process.)

Just one more preliminary remark before we proceed to this calculation. All the prerequisites of the labour process, all the things that went into it, were not just use values but commodities, use values with a price expressing their exchange value. Commodities were present in advance as elements of this process, and must emerge from it again. Nothing of this is shown when we look at the simple labour process as material production. The labour process therefore constitutes only one side, the material side of the production process. As the commodity is itself from one aspect use value, from another exchange value, so naturally must the commodity *in actu*,[a] in the process of its origin, be a two-sided process: [on the one hand] its production as use value, as product of useful labour, on the other hand its production as exchange value, and these two processes must only appear as two different

---

[a] In process.— *Ed.*

forms of the same process, exactly as the commodity is a unity of use value and exchange value. The commodity, from which we proceeded as something already given,[a] is viewed here in the process of its becoming. The production process is not the process of the production of use value, but of the commodity, hence of the unity of use value and exchange value. Even so, this would not yet make the mode of production into a capitalist one. All that is required so far is that the product, the use value, be destined not for personal consumption but for alienation, for sale. Capitalist production, however, requires not only that the commodities thrown into the labour process should be valorised, should acquire a new value by the addition of labour—industrial consumption is nothing but the addition of new labour—but also that the values thrown into industrial consumption—for the use values thrown into it all had value to the extent that they were commodities—should valorise themselves as values, should produce new value owing to the fact that they were values. If it was just a matter of the first requirement we should not have passed beyond the simple commodity.

We assume that the elements of the labour process are not use values to be found in the possession of the money owner himself, but were originally acquired as commodities by purchase and that this forms the prerequisite of the entire labour process. We have seen that it is not necessary for every kind of industry that in addition to the means of labour the material of labour as well should be a commodity, i.e. a product already mediated by labour, that it should be exchange value—a commodity—as objectified labour.[b] Here, however, we proceed from the presupposition that all elements of the process are bought, as is the case in manufacturing. We take the phenomenon in the form in which it appears most completely. This does not detract from the correctness of the analysis, since one only has to set one factor=0 for other cases. Thus in fishing the material of labour is not itself a product, hence does not circulate beforehand like a commodity, and so one factor of the labour process, namely the material of labour, if considered as exchange value, as a commodity, can be set=0.

It is however an *essential* presupposition that the money owner should buy more than just the labour capacity. In other words, not

---

[a] K. Marx, *A Contribution to the Critique of Political Economy.* Part One (present edition, Vol. 29, p. 269).— *Ed.*

[b] See this volume, p. 56.— *Ed.*

only must money be exchanged for the labour capacity, but equally for the other objective conditions of the labour process, material of labour and means of labour; and under these headings there may lie a great multiplicity of things, of commodities, depending on whether the labour process is of a simpler or a more complex nature. To begin with, this presupposition is methodologically necessary at the stage of development presently being considered. We have to see how money is transformed into capital. But every money owner who wants to transform his money into industrial capital goes through this process every day. He must buy the material and the means of labour in order to be able to consume alien labour.—Necessary for real insight into the nature of the capital-relation. The latter proceeds from the circulation of commodities as its basis.[20] It implies the supersession of the mode of production in which personal consumption is the main purpose of production, and in which only the surplus is sold as a commodity. It is the more completely developed the more the elements that concern it are themselves commodities, hence can only be appropriated through purchase. The more production itself acquires its elements from circulation—i.e. as commodities—so that they enter into it as exchange values already, the more is this production capitalist production. If we here theoretically presuppose the existence of circulation before the formation of capital, and therefore proceed from money, this is also the course followed by history.[59] [I-36] Capital develops out of monetary wealth, and the formation of capital presupposes that commercial relations, formed at a stage of production that precedes it, are already highly developed. Money and the commodity are the presuppositions from which we must proceed in considering the bourgeois economy. Further consideration of capital will demonstrate that it is in fact capitalist production alone whose surface presents the commodity as the elementary form of wealth.[60]

One therefore sees the absurdity of the custom introduced by J. B. Say with his French schematism, but not followed by any of the classical economists. Because he was on the whole merely a vulgariser of Adam Smith, all he could do was provide a pretty or uniform arrangement for material he had by no means assimilated. He examines first production, then exchange, then distribution, and finally consumption, also sometimes distributing these four rubrics somewhat differently.[61] The specific mode of production we are to consider presupposes from the outset as one of its forms a particular mode of exchange, and produces a particular mode of distribution and a particular mode of consumption, in so far as consideration of the latter falls within the sphere of political economy at all. (This must be returned to later.)[62]

So, now *ad rem*.[a]

The exchange value of the product (of the use value) that emerged from the labour process consists of the total amount of labour time materialised in it, of the total quantity of labour worked up, objectified, in it.* It therefore consists firstly of the value of the raw material contained in the product, or the labour time required to produce this, the material of labour. Let us assume it to be 100 working days. This value is however already expressed in the price at which the material of labour was bought, say, e.g. a price of 100 thalers. The value of this part of the product enters into it already determined as price. Secondly, as regards the means of labour, tools, etc., the tool will not necessarily be completely worn out; it can continue to function as a means of labour in fresh labour processes. Hence only that part of the tool can enter into the calculation that has been used up, since it alone has entered into the product. Later on the method of calculating the wear and tear on the means of labour will be shown more precisely,[63] but at this point we shall assume that the whole of it is worn out in the one labour process. This assumption makes the less difference to the case in that actually the tool only enters the calculation in so far as it is consumed in the labour process, hence is transferred to the product; hence only the worn out means of labour enters the calculation. This is equally purchased. Hence the labour time contained in it, say of 16 working days, is expressed in its price of 16 thalers.

Before we now go further we ought to discuss here how the value of the material and means of labour is preserved in the labour process, so that it re-appears as a finished, *presupposed* constituent of the value of the product, or, what is the same thing, how the material and means of labour are consumed, altered in the labour process, either altered or completely destroyed (as with the means of labour), but their value is not destroyed, re-appearing instead in the product as a constituent, a *presupposed* constituent of its value.

// Capital has been regarded from its material side as a simple production process, a labour process. But, from the side of its

---

* Quesnay, etc., base their proof of the unproductiveness of all labour SAVE AGRICULTURAL LABOUR on this *addition*.[64]

---

[a] To the matter in hand.— *Ed.*

formal determination, this process is a *process of self-valorisation.* Self-valorisation includes preservation of the preposited value as well as its multiplication. Labour is purposeful activity and from the material side it is therefore presupposed that the labour has employed its means to the appropriate purpose in the production process so as to give the material of labour the intended new use value.//

// Since the labour process is a process of the consumption of labour capacity by the capitalist—for the labour belongs to the capitalist—he has, in the labour process, consumed his material and means of labour by labour, and has consumed the labour itself by his material, etc.//[65]

[I-37] For the labour process as such, or in the labour process as such, effective labour capacity, the real worker, is concerned with the material and means of labour only as the objective prerequisites of the creative unrest that is labour itself, in fact only as the objective means to the realisation of labour. They are this through their objective qualities alone, through the qualities they possess as material and means of this particular labour. Where they are themselves products of earlier labour, this fact is extinguished in their capacity as things. The table that serves me for writing upon has its own form and its own characteristics; these appeared previously in the form-giving quality or specificity of the joiner's labour. In using the table as a means for further labour I have to do with it to the extent that it serves as a use value, has a particular useful application as a table. The fact that the material out of which it consists has acquired this form through earlier labour, the labour of the joiner, has disappeared, is extinguished in its existence as an object. It serves as a table in the labour process, quite regardless of the labour that turned it into a table.

In exchange value, in contrast, what matters is the quantity of labour materialised in this particular use value, or the quantity of labour time required to produce it. In this labour its own quality, the quality of being, for example, a joiner's labour, is extinguished, for it is reduced to a definite quantity of equal, general, undifferentiated, social, abstract labour.[66] The material specificity of the labour, hence of the use value in which it has been fixed, is thereby extinguished, vanished, irrelevant. It is presupposed that it was useful labour, that is, labour which resulted in a use value. The nature of this use value, hence the particular nature of the labour's usefulness, is extinguished in the existence of the commodity as exchange value, for as exchange value it is an equivalent, expressible in every other use value, hence in every other form of useful labour which constitutes a quantity of social labour of the same magnitude. In respect of value therefore—i.e. considered as quantities of objectified labour time—the material of labour and the worn out means of labour can always be regarded as if they were moments of the same labour process, so that what is required to manufacture the product, the new use value, is 1) the labour time objectified in the material of labour, and 2) the labour time materialised in the means of labour. The material of labour is admittedly different in its original form, although it also re-appears in substance in the new use value. The means of labour has disappeared entirely, although it re-appears in the form of the new use value as effect, result. The particular material specificity, usefulness, of the acts of labour that were present in the material and means of labour, is just as extinguished as the use values in which they resulted have themselves vanished or changed. But as exchange values, and even before they entered this new labour process, they were merely a materialisation of labour in general, they were nothing but a quantity of labour time as such, absorbed in an object. For this labour time the particular character of the actual work being done, as well as the particular nature of the use value in which it was realised, was a matter of indifference.

After the new labour process the relationship is exactly the same as it was before. The quantity of labour time necessary e.g. to produce the cotton and the spindle is a quantity of labour time necessary to manufacture the yarn, in so far as cotton and spindle are used up in the yarn. That this quantity of labour time now appears as yarn is entirely irrelevant, since it continues to appear in a use value for whose manufacture it is necessary. If I for example exchange cotton and spindle to the value of 100 thalers for a quantity of yarn which is equally worth 100 thalers, in this case too the labour time contained in the cotton and spindle exists as labour time contained in the yarn. The fact that in their actual material transformation into yarn the cotton and the spindle also undergo changes in their material, with the one acquiring another form and the other entirely perishing in its material form, makes no difference, *because* this concerns them only as use values, hence in a shape towards which they are, as exchange values, essentially indifferent. Since as exchange values they are only a particular quantity of materialised social labour time, hence equal magnitudes, equivalents, for every other use value which represents a quantity of materialised social labour time of the same magnitude, it makes no difference to them that they appear now as the factors of a new use value. The sole conditions are these, that they should 1) appear as labour time necessary for the creation of the new use value, and 2) really result in another use value—hence in use value [I-38] in general.

They are labour time necessary for the creation of the new use value because the use values in which they were originally crystallised were factors necessary for the new labour process. Secondly, however, according to our condition, the use values, as they existed before the labour process—as cotton and spindle— have in fact resulted through the new labour process in a new use value, the product, the yarn.

(That only such quantities of the material and means of labour should enter into the new product as are necessary for its creation, hence that no more labour time should be used than is necessary in these definite quantities; in other words that neither material nor means of production should be squandered, is a condition which has to do not with the material and means of labour as such but with the suitability and productivity of the new labour which uses them up in the labour process as its material and means; it is therefore a point that has to be considered in dealing with this labour itself. Here, however, the assumption is that the means and the material of labour only enter into the new process in quantities in which they are really required as such for the realisation of the new labour, are really objective conditions of the new labour process.)

Two results therefore.

Firstly: The labour time required for the manufacture of the material and means of labour used up in the product is labour time required for the manufacture of the product. In so far as exchange value is considered, the labour time materialised in the material and means of labour can be regarded as if the latter were moments of the same labour process. All the labour time contained in the product belongs to the past; hence it is materialised labour. The labour time which perished in the material and means of labour passed away earlier; it belongs to an earlier period than the labour time functioning directly in the last labour process. But this changes nothing. They merely constitute earlier periods during which [part of] the labour time contained in the product was worked up, as against the part which represents the labour entering into it directly. *The values of the material and means of labour therefore appear again in the product as constituents of its value.* This value is *presupposed,* since the labour time contained in the material and means of labour was expressed in their prices in its general form, as social labour; these are the prices at which the money owner bought them as commodities before he began the labour process. The use values in which they consisted have perished but they themselves have remained unaltered and remain unaltered in the new use value. The only change that has taken place is that they appear as mere constituents, factors of his value, as factors of a new value. To the extent that the commodity is exchange value at all, the particular use value, the particular material determinateness in which it exists is after all only a particular mode of its manifestation; it is in fact a universal equivalent and can therefore exchange this incarnation for any other. Through circulation and first of all through being transformed into money it is indeed capable of giving itself the substance of every other use value.

Secondly: The values of the means of labour and the material of labour are therefore preserved in the value of the product, enter as factors into the value of the product. *But they only re-appear in it* because the real alteration the use values have received in them did not affect their substance at all, but only the forms of use value in which they existed before, as after, the process; and the particular form of use value in which the value of the product exists, or indeed the specific usefulness of the labour, which is reduced in that value to abstract labour, does not, in the nature of things, affect the essential character of value at all.

However, it is a *conditio sine qua non*[a] for the re-appearance of the value of the material and means of labour in the product that the labour process really proceed to its end, to the product, that it really result in the product. If, therefore, it is a matter of use values whose production extends over a long period, one sees what an essential moment *the continuity* of the labour process is for the valorisation process in general, even so far as merely the preservation of existing use values is concerned. // This however implies, according to our presupposition, that the labour process proceeds on the basis of the appropriation of labour capacity by purchase on the part of money, by the continuous transformation of money into capital. The assumption is therefore that the *working class* is constantly in existence. This constancy is itself first created by capital. At earlier stages of production too an earlier working class may be present sporadically, not however as [I-39] a *universal* prerequisite of production. The case of *colonies* (see

---

[a] Necessary condition.— *Ed.*

Wakefield,[67] come back to this later) shows how this relation is itself a product of capitalist production.//

As far as the preservation of the values of the material and means of labour is concerned—assuming therefore that the labour process eventuates in a product—this is simply attained by the fact that these use values are consumed as such by living labour in the labour process, that they figure as actual moments of the labour process, but only by their contact with, and incorporation into, living labour as the conditions of its purposeful activity. *Living labour only adds value in the labour process to the value preposited in the material and means of labour* to the extent that it is itself a new quantity of labour as such; it does not do so as actual, useful labour, not as viewed from the angle of its material determinateness. The yarn only has greater value than the sum of the values of the cotton and the spindle consumed in it because a new quantity of labour has been added in the labour process, in order to convert those use values into the new use value, yarn; the reason, therefore, is that the yarn now contains an extra, newly added quantity of labour over and above the quantity contained in the cotton and the spindle. But the exchange values of the cotton and the spindle are *preserved* simply by the fact that the actual labour, spinning, converts them into the new use value, yarn, hence consumes them to the purpose, makes them *vital factors of its own process.* The values entering the labour process are therefore preserved simply by the *quality* of the living labour, the nature of its expression. Those dead objects, in which the preposited values are present as their use values, are now really seized upon as use values by this new useful labour, spinning, and made into moments of new labour. *They are preserved as values by entering as use values into the labour process,* i.e. by playing their conceptually determined roles of material and means of labour towards actual useful labour.

Let us stay with our example. Cotton and spindle are used up as use values because they enter as material and means into the particular labour of spinning; because they are placed in the actual spinning process, one as the object, the other as the organ of this living purposeful activity. They are therefore preserved as values by being preserved as use values for labour. *In general, they are preserved as exchange values because they are consumed as use values by labour.* But the labour which consumes them in this way as use values is actual labour, labour considered in its material determinateness, this particular useful labour which is related exclusively to these specific use values as material and means of labour, related to them as such in its living manifestation. It is this particular useful labour, spinning, which preserves the use values cotton and spindle as exchange values, and therefore lets them re-appear as an exchange-value component in the product, in the use value yarn, because in the actual process it relates to them as its material and its means, as the organs of its realisation, because it breathes life into them as its own organs and makes them function as such. And thus the values of all commodities which in line with the nature of their use values do not enter into direct individual consumption, but are destined for new production, are only preserved in this way, that as material and means of labour, which they are only potentially, they become really the material and means of labour, and are utilised as such by the particular labour they are as such able to serve. They are only preserved as exchange values by being consumed as use values by living labour in accordance with their conceptual determination. *They are, however, only use values of this kind — material and means of labour — for actual, definite and specific labour.* I can only use up cotton and spindle as use values in the act of spinning, not in the acts of milling or boot-making.— In general, all commodities are only use values potentially. They only become real use values by being actually used, consumed, and their consumption in this case is the specifically determined labour itself, the specific labour process.

[I-40] The material and means of labour are therefore only preserved as exchange values by being consumed in the labour process as use values, i.e. when living labour relates to them *actu*[a] as to its use values, lets them play the role of its material and means, in its living unrest both posits and supersedes them as means and material. But in so far as it does that, labour is *actual* labour, a specific purposeful activity, labour as it appears in the labour process, materially determined, as a specific kind of useful labour. It is, however, not labour in this specific determinateness which adds — or it is not in this specific determinateness that labour adds — *new* exchange value to the product, or to the objects — use values — which enter into the labour process.

Spinning, for example. Spinning preserves in yarn the values of the cotton and spindle consumed in it, because this process really uses up cotton and spindle in spinning, consumes them as material and means for the production of a new use value, the yarn, or lets cotton and spindle really function in the spinning process as

---

[a] In action.— *Ed.*

material and means of this specific living labour, spinning. If, however, the spinning raises the value of the product, yarn, or adds new value to the values already present beforehand in the yarn, which simply re-appear, the values of the spindle and the cotton, this only occurs to the extent that *new labour time is added to the labour time contained in the cotton and the spindle* by spinning.

Firstly, in accordance with its substance, spinning creates value, not as this concrete, specific, materially determined labour of spinning, but as labour in general, abstract, equal, social labour. Therefore, it does not create value to the extent that it is objectified as spun yarn, but to the extent that it is a materialisation of social labour in general, i.e. is objectified in a universal equivalent.

Secondly, the magnitude of the value added depends exclusively on the quantity of labour added, on the labour time that is added. If, as a result of some invention, the spinner were able to convert into yarn a particular quantity of cotton, using a given number of spindles, in half a day's labour instead of a whole day, only *half the value would have been added* to the yarn compared with the first case. But the *entire value* of the cotton and the spindles would have been preserved in the product, yarn, in one case as much as the other, whether a day or half a day or an hour of labour time is required to convert the cotton into yarn. These values are preserved by the very fact that cotton is converted into yarn, that cotton and spindles have become the material and means of spinning, have entered into the spinning process. The labour time required by this process is here entirely irrelevant.

Let us assume that the spinner adds to the cotton only as much labour time as is necessary to produce his own wages, hence as much labour time as the capitalist expended in the price of the spinner's labour. In this case the value of the product would be exactly equal to the value of the capital advanced; namely equal to the price of the material+the price of the means of labour+the price of labour. No more labour time would be contained in the product than was present in the sum of money before it was transformed into the elements of the production process. No new value would have been added, but after as before the value of the cotton and spindle would be contained in the yarn. Spinning adds value to cotton in so far as it is reduced to equal social labour in general, reduced to this abstract form of labour, and the amount of value it adds depends not on its content as spinning but on its duration. *The spinner therefore does not need two periods of labour, one to preserve the value of cotton and spindle, the other to add new value to them.* It is rather that while he spins the cotton, makes it into an objectification of new labour time, adds new value to it, he is at the same time preserving the value cotton and the worn out spindle had before they entered the labour process. *Merely by adding new value, new labour time, he preserves the old values, the labour time that was already contained in the material and means of labour.* It is as spinning, however, that spinning preserves them; not as labour in general and not as labour time, but in its material determinateness, through its quality as this specific, living, actual labour, which in the labour process, as living activity with a definite purpose, snatches the use values cotton and spindle out of their indifferent objectivity, not abandoning them as indifferent objects to nature's metabolism, but making them into real moments of the labour process.

But whatever the specific character of particular, actual labour may be, what every variety of this labour has in common with every other is that by its process—through the contact, the living interaction it enters into with its objective conditions—it makes them play the roles of means and material of labour appropriate to their nature and purpose, transforms them into conceptually determined moments of the labour process itself and thus *preserves* them as *exchange values by using them up as real use values.* [I-41] It is therefore through its quality as living labour, which converts the products available in the labour process into the material and means of its own activity, its own realisation, that it preserves the exchange values of these products and use values in the new product and use values. It preserves their value because it consumes them as use values. But it only consumes them as use values because, as this specific labour, it awakens them from the dead and makes them into its material and means of labour. In so far as it creates exchange value labour is only a definite social form of labour, actual labour reduced to a definite social formula, and in this form labour time is the sole measure of the magnitude of value.

Because the preservation of the values of the material and means of labour is so to speak the natural gift of living, actual labour, and hence the old values are preserved in the same process as increases value—*since new value cannot be added without the preservation of the old values,* because this effect stems from the essential nature of labour as use value, as useful activity, originates from the use value of labour itself—so the preservation of these values costs nothing either to the worker or to the capitalist. The latter therefore receives the preservation of the preposited values in the new product gratis.

Although his purpose is not the preservation but the increase of the preposited value, this free gift by labour shows its decisive importance e.g. in industrial crises, during which the actual labour process is interrupted. The machine becomes rusty, the material spoils. They lose their exchange values: these are not preserved, because they are not entering as use values into the labour process, they are not coming into contact with living labour; their values are not being preserved because they are not being increased. They can only be increased, new labour time can only be added to the old, to the extent that a start is made again with the actual labour process.

Hence values are preserved in the labour process by labour as actual living labour, whereas new value is added to the values by labour only as abstract social labour, labour time.

The actual labour process appears as *productive consumption*. The latter can now be defined more closely in the sense that the preposited values of the products are preserved in the labour process by these products being used up, consumed, as use values—material and means of labour—and converted into real use values for the formation of a new use value.

//But the values of the material and means of labour only re-appear in the product of the labour process to the extent that they were preposited to the latter as values, i.e. were values before they entered into the process. Their value is equal to the social labour time materialised in them; it is equal to the labour time necessary to produce them under given general social conditions of production. If later on more or less labour time were to be required to manufacture these particular use values, owing to some alteration in the productivity of the labour of which they are the products, their value would have risen in the first case and fallen in the second; for the labour time contained in their value only determines it to the extent that it is general, social, and necessary labour time. Hence although they entered the labour process with a definite value, they may come out of it with a value that is larger or smaller, because the labour time society needs for their production has undergone a general change, a revolution has occurred in their production costs, i.e. in the magnitude of the labour time necessary for their manufacture. In this case more or less labour time than previously would be required to reproduce them, to manufacture a new sample of the same kind. But this change in the value of the material and means of labour involves absolutely no alteration in the circumstance that in the labour process into which they enter as material and means they are always preposited as given values, values of a given magnitude. For in this process itself they only emerge as values in so far as they entered as values. A change in their value never results from this labour process itself but rather from the conditions of the labour process of which they are or were the products and to which they therefore are not preposited as products. If their general conditions of production have changed, this reacts back upon them. They are an objectification of more or less labour time, of more or less value than they were originally; but only because a greater or smaller amount of labour time is now required than originally for their production. The reaction is due to the fact that as values they are a materialisation of social labour time but the labour time contained in them only counts to the extent that it is reduced to general [I-42] social labour time, raised to the power of equal social labour time. These changes in their value, however, always arise from changes in the productivity of the labour of which they are the products, and have nothing to do with the labour processes into which they enter as finished products with a given value. If this value changes before the new product of which they are the elements is finished they nevertheless relate to it as independent, given values preposited to it. Their change of value stems from alterations in their own conditions of production, which occur outside and independently of the labour process into which they enter as material and means; not as a result of an operation occurring within the labour process. For it they are always values of a given, preposited magnitude, even though owing to external agencies, acting outside the labour process, they are now preposited as of greater or smaller magnitude than was originally the case.//

We saw that just as the product is the result of the labour process so are its products prerequisites for the same process[a]; but now it must equally be said that if the commodity, i.e. a unity of use value and exchange value, is the result of the labour process, commodities are just as much its prerequisites. The products only emerge from the valorisation process as commodities because they have entered it as commodities, products with a definite exchange value. The difference is this: the products are changed as use values so that a new use value can be formed. Their exchange values are not affected by this change in the material, and they

---

[a] See this volume, p. 65.— *Ed.*

therefore re-appear unchanged in the new product. If use value is the product of the labour process, exchange value must be regarded as the product of the valorisation process, and thus the commodity, the unity of exchange value and use value, must be regarded as the product of both processes, which are merely two forms of the same process. If one wished to disregard the fact that commodities are preposited to production as its elements, the only matter of concern in the production process would be the use of products for the formation of new products; and this can, indeed, occur in states of society in which the product has not developed into the commodity, still less the commodity into capital.[68]

We now know two components of the value of the product: 1) the value of the material consumed in it; 2) the value of the means of production consumed in it. If these are equal respectively to A and B, the value of the product will initially consist of the sum of the values of A and B, or P (the product). $P = A + B + x$. With x we denote the as yet undetermined portion of value that has been added to the material A by labour in the labour process. Therefore, we now come to consider this third component.

We know what price or value the money owner has paid for disposition over labour capacity or the temporary purchase of labour capacity, but we do not yet know what equivalent he receives in return for this.—We proceed, furthermore, from the assumption that the labour performed by the worker is ordinary average labour, labour of the quality or rather the qualitylessness in which it forms the substance of exchange value.[69] We shall see in the course of our investigation that the power of the labour, the question whether it is more or less potentiated simple labour, is a matter of complete indifference for the relation to be developed here.[a] We proceed therefore from the assumption that whatever the particular material determinateness of the labour, whatever specific branch of labour it belongs to, whatever particular use value it produces, it is only the expression, the activity of average labour capacity, so that whether this manifests itself in spinning or weaving, etc., or farming, concerns only its use value, the manner of its application. It does not concern what it cost to produce the labour capacity itself, hence not its own exchange value. It will also be seen that differences in the wage paid for different working days, higher or lower, the unequal *distribution of wages* between the

---

[a] See this volume, pp. 90 and 225-26.— *Ed.*

different branches of labour, do not affect the general relation between capital and wage labour.[32]—

What the money owner gets back from the purchase of labour capacity can only become manifest in the actual labour process. The value added by labour in the labour process to the already existing value of the material is exactly equal to its duration. It is naturally presupposed that over a definite period of time, e.g. one day, precisely as much labour is employed on the product of this day as is necessary to produce it at the given general productive level of labour (under the given general conditions of production).[70] That is, it is presupposed that the labour time employed for the manufacture of the product is *necessary labour time*, the labour time required to give a certain quantity of material the form of the new use value. If, under the general conditions of production we have presupposed, 6 lbs of COTTON can be converted into twist in the course of 1 day of 12 hours, only a day in which 6 lbs of COTTON is converted into twist is regarded as a working day of 12 hours. On the one hand, therefore, *necessary* labour time is presupposed; on the other hand, it is presupposed that the particular labour performed in the labour process is ordinary *average labour*, whatever specific form it may have as spinning, weaving, digging, etc. (and the same is true of the labour employed in the production of the precious metals[71]). It follows, accordingly, that the quantity of value or the quantity of objectified general [I-43] labour time which this labour adds to the existing value is exactly equal to its own duration. This, under the given assumptions, simply means that precisely as much labour is objectified as the time taken for the process during which the labour is objectifying itself.

Let us say that 6 lbs of cotton can be spun into twist, say 5 lbs of twist, in a day of 12 hours. During the labour process the labour is continuously passing from the form of unrest and motion into the objective form. (5 lbs=80 ounces.) (Over 12 hours this would make exactly $6^2/_3$ ounces an hour.) The spinning constantly results in yarn. If one hour is required to turn 8 ounces of cotton into yarn, say $6^2/_3$ ounces of yarn, 12 hours would be required to turn 6 lbs of cotton into 5 lbs of yarn. What interests us here, however, is not that one hour of spinning turns 8 ounces of COTTON into yarn and 12 hours 6 lbs, but that in the first case 1 hour of labour is added to the value of the COTTON, and in the second 12 hours. In other words, we are only interested in the product from this point of view to the extent that it is the materialisation of new labour time and this naturally depends on the labour time itself. We are interested only in the quantity of labour absorbed in the product. Here we do not look at spinning as spinning, we do not look at it in so far as it gives the COTTON a definite form, a new use value, but only in so far as it is labour in general, labour time and its materialisation, which is present in the yarn, the materialisation of general labour time as such. It is entirely irrelevant whether the same labour time is employed in the form of any other particular labour or to produce any other particular exchange value.

Originally, it is true, we were able to measure *labour capacity* with money, because it was itself already objectified labour, and the capitalist could therefore buy it; but were unable to measure *labour itself* directly, for as bare activity it escaped our standard of measurement. Now, however, in the measure to which, in the labour process, labour capacity proceeds to its real manifestation, to labour, the latter is realised, appears itself in the product as objectified labour time. The possibility is now available for comparing what the capitalist gives in wages with what he gets back in exchange for wages through the consumption of labour capacity. At the end of a certain measure of labour time, e.g. hours, a certain quantity of labour time has been objectified in a use value, say twist, and now exists as the latter's exchange value.

Let us assume that the labour time realised in the spinner's labour capacity amounts to 10 hours. We are speaking here only of the labour time realised *daily* in his labour capacity. In the price the money owner has paid the labour time required to produce or reproduce the labour capacity of the spinner every day is already expressed *in average labour*. We assume on the other hand that his own labour is *the same* quality of labour, i.e. *the same average labour,* as forms the substance of value, and in which his own labour capacity is evaluated.

Let us therefore assume initially that the spinner works 10 hours for the money owner or gives him, has sold him, 10 hours' disposition over his labour capacity. This 10-hour disposition over the spinner's labour capacity is consumed by the money owner in the labour process. This means, in other words, simply that he has the spinner spin for 10 hours, has him work in general, since here the particular form in which he has him do this is irrelevant. The spinner has therefore added to the value of the cotton through the agency of the means of labour 10 hours of labour in the shape of the spun thread, the yarn. If, therefore, the value of the product, the spun thread, the yarn, *disregarding* the newly added labour, was equal to A+B, it now=A+B+10 hours of labour. The capitalist pays for these 10 hours of labour with 10d. Let us call these 10d. C. The product of the yarn now=A+B+C, i.e. it equals the labour time contained in the cotton, in the spindles (to the extent that they have been consumed) and finally in the newly added labour time.

Let the sum of A+B+C be=D. D is then equal to the sum of money the money owner laid out in material of labour, means of labour, and labour capacity before he began the labour process. That is to say, the value of the product—the yarn—is equal to the value of the elements of which the yarn consists, i.e.=the value of the material of labour and the means of labour (which is entirely consumed in the product on our assumption)+the value of the newly added labour, which has combined with the other two in the labour process to form yarn. Therefore 100 thalers of cotton, 16 thalers of instrument, and 16 thalers of labour capacity=132 thalers. In this case the values advanced would admittedly have been preserved, but not increased. The only alteration that would have taken place before the money was transformed into capital [I-44] would have been a purely formal one. This value was originally=132 thalers, a definite quantity of objectified labour time. The same unity re-appears in the product, as 132 thalers. The magnitude of value is the same, but this is now the sum of the value components 100, 16 and 16, i.e. the values of the factors into which the money originally advanced is divided in the labour process, and each of which has been purchased separately by that money.

In itself this result is not in the least absurd. If I buy yarn for 132 thalers, merely by converting money into yarn—i.e. by way of simple circulation—I pay for the material, means and labour contained in the yarn in order to acquire this particular use value and consume it in one way or the other. If the money owner has a house built in order to live in it, he pays an equivalent for the house. In short, when he goes through the circulation C—M—C, he in fact does nothing other than this. The money with which he buys is equal to the value of the commodity originally in his possession. The new commodity he buys is equal to the money in which the value of the commodity originally possessed by him has acquired an independent shape as exchange value.

Yet the purpose of the capitalist in transforming money into the commodity is not the commodity's use value but the *increase* of the money or value laid out in the commodity—*the self-valorisation of value.* He does not buy for his own consumption but in order to draw out of circulation a higher exchange value than he originally threw into it.

If he were to re-sell the yarn, which is worth A+B+C, at, say, A+B+C+x, we should come back to the same contradiction. He would not sell his commodity as an equivalent, but above its equivalent. In circulation, however, no surplus value, no value over and above the equivalent, can arise unless one of the parties to the exchange receives a value *below* its equivalent.[a]

The transformation of money into the elements of the labour process—or the actual consumption of the labour capacity that has been purchased, which is the same thing—would therefore be completely purposeless under the assumption that the money owner sets the worker to work for the same period of labour time as that he has paid him as an equivalent for his labour capacity. Whether he buys yarn for 132 thalers, so as to re-sell the yarn at 132 thalers, or converts the 132 thalers into 100 thalers of cotton, 16 thalers of spindles, etc., and 16 thalers of objectified labour, i.e. the consumption of labour capacity for the period of labour time contained in 16 thalers, so as to sell the 132 thalers' worth of yarn thus produced at 132 thalers once again, the process is entirely the same from the point of view of its result, except that the tautological outcome of the process would have been arrived at by a more roundabout route in one case than in the other.

A *surplus value*, i.e. a value which forms an excess over the values that originally entered the labour process, can evidently only originate in that process if the money owner has bought disposition over the employment of labour capacity during a longer period than the amount of labour time required by the labour capacity for its own reproduction, i.e. than the labour time which is incorporated in the labour capacity itself, forms its own value and as such is expressed in its price. Let us apply this to the case mentioned above. If the cotton and the spindle belonged to the spinner himself, he would have to add 10 hours of labour to them in order to live, i.e. in order to reproduce himself as a spinner for the next day. If he were now to set a worker to work for 11 hours instead of 10, a surplus value of 1 hour would be produced, because the labour objectified in the labour process would contain an hour more of labour time than is necessary to reproduce the labour capacity itself, i.e. to keep alive the worker as worker, the spinner day in day out as spinner. Every portion of time worked by the spinner in the labour process over and above the 10 hours, [I-45] all *surplus labour* in excess of the quantity of labour incorporated in his own labour capacity, would form a

---

[a] See this volume, pp. 23-29.—*Ed.*

surplus value, because it would be surplus labour, hence more spun thread, more labour objectified as yarn.

If the worker must work for 10 hours in order to live for the whole day, which consists of 24 hours (in which are naturally included the hours during which he must as an organism rest from labour, sleep, etc., is unable to work), he can work over the whole day for 12, 14 hours, although he only needs 10 out of these 12, 14 hours for the reproduction of himself as a worker, as living labour capacity.

If we now assume that this process corresponds to the general law of commodity exchange, that equal quantities of labour time are alone being exchanged, i.e. that the exchange value of the commodity is equal to the quantity of any other use value that expresses the same exchange value, i.e. the same quantity of objectified labour, the general form of capital— M — C — M —will have lost its absurdity and acquired content. Since the commodity, here the yarn, for whose elements the money owner exchanged his money before the labour process, would have received an addition to the original quantity of objectified labour, in the shape of the *product* of the labour process, the new use value, the yarn, the product would possess a greater value than the sum of the values preposited in its elements. If it was originally=132 thalers, it would now be=143, if instead of 16 thalers (1 thaler=1 day of labour) x more days of labour were contained in it. The value would now be=100+16+16+11, and if the capitalist re-sold the product of the labour process, the yarn, at its value, he would gain 11 thalers from the 132 thalers. The original value would have been not only preserved but increased.

One must ask whether this process does not contradict the law originally presupposed, that commodities are exchanged as equivalents, i.e. at their exchange values; the law, therefore, that governs the exchange of commodities?[a]

It does not, for two reasons. Firstly, because money finds this specific object, living labour capacity, on the market, in circulation, as a commodity. Secondly, owing to the specific nature of this commodity. Its peculiar character consists namely in the fact that, whereas its exchange value, like that of all other commodities=the labour time incorporated in its own actual existence, in its existence as labour capacity, i.e.=the labour time necessary to keep alive this living labour capacity as such, or, what is the same thing,

---

[a] See this volume, p. 33.— *Ed.*

to keep the worker alive as a worker,—its *use value* is labour itself, i.e. precisely the substance which posits exchange value, the particular fluid activity which fixes itself as exchange value and creates it.[72] With commodities, however, only their exchange value is paid for.

One does not pay for oil's quality of being oil on top of paying for the labour contained in it, any more than one pays for the drinking of wine in addition to the labour contained in it, or for the enjoyment when paying for the drinking. Similarly therefore with labour capacity: what is paid for is its own exchange value, the labour time contained in it itself. But since its use value is in turn labour itself, the substance that creates exchange value, it in no way contradicts the law of the exchange of commodities that the actual consumption of labour capacity, its actual use as a use value, posits more labour, manifests itself in more objectified labour, than is present within it itself as exchange value.

The sole condition required for this relationship to come into existence is that [I-46] labour capacity itself should step forth as a commodity to meet money, or value in general. But this confrontation is conditioned by a definite historical process which narrows down the worker to pure labour capacity; this is the same as saying that this process confronts labour capacity with the conditions of its realisation, hence confronts actual labour with its objective elements, as alien powers, separated from it, as commodities in the possession of other keepers of commodities.[21] Under this *historical* presupposition labour capacity is a *commodity,* and under the presupposition that it is a commodity it by no means contradicts the law of the exchange of commodities, it much rather corresponds to it, that the labour time objectified in labour capacity or its exchange value does not determine its *use value.* The latter, however, is in turn itself labour. Hence in the actual consumption of this use value, i.e. in and through the labour process, the money owner can receive back more objectified labour time than he paid out for the exchange value of the labour capacity. *So that although he has paid an equivalent for this specific commodity* he receives back as a consequence of its specific nature—that its use value itself posits exchange value, is the creative substance of exchange value—a greater value by its use than he had advanced by its purchase, in which he paid for its exchange value alone, in line with the law of the exchange of commodities.

Therefore, presupposing a relationship in which labour capacity exists as mere labour capacity, hence as a commodity, and in which it is accordingly confronted by money as the form of all objective wealth, the money owner, being only concerned with value as such, will only purchase labour capacity on condition that he acquires disposition over it for a longer period, or that the worker binds himself to work for him during the labour process for a longer period, than the labour time the worker would have to put in in order to keep himself alive as a worker, as living labour capacity, if he himself owned the material and means of labour. This difference between the labour time which measures the exchange value of labour capacity itself and the labour time during which it is used as use value, is the labour time worked by labour capacity beyond the labour time contained in its own exchange value, hence beyond the value it cost originally. As such it is surplus labour— *surplus value.*

If the money owner makes this exchange of money with living labour capacity and with the objective conditions for the consumption of this labour capacity—i.e. with the material and means of labour corresponding to its particular material determinateness— he thereby transforms money into capital, i.e. into self-preserving and self-augmenting, self-valorising value. At no time does he contravene the law of simple circulation, of the exchange of commodities, whereby equivalents are exchanged or the commodities—on the average—are sold at their exchange values, i.e. exchange values of equal magnitude, whatever use values they may exist in, replace each other as equal magnitudes. At the same time he fulfils the formula $M-C-M$, i.e. the exchange of money for the commodity so as to exchange the commodity for more money, and accordingly does not contravene the law of equivalence, acting instead entirely in line with it.

Firstly: Say, a normal working day=1 thaler, is expressed in the quantity of silver denominated by a thaler. The money owner expends 100 thalers for raw material; 16 thalers for instrument; and 16 thalers for the 16 labour capacities which he employs and whose exchange value=16 thalers. Thus he advances 132 thalers, which *re-appear* in the product (result) of the labour process, [I-47] i.e. in the consumption of the labour capacity he has bought, the labour process, productive consumption. But the commodity he has bought at its exchange value of 15 days of labour provides as a use value, say, 30 days of labour, a day of 6 hours provides 12 hours, objectifies itself in 12 hours of labour; i.e. it posits as a use value twice as great a value as it possesses as exchange value. But the use value of a commodity is independent of its exchange value and has nothing to do with the price at which it is sold—this is determined by the amount of labour time objectified in it. The product therefore $= A+B+C+15$ hours of labour time. It is thus greater by 15 hours of labour time than the value preposited to the labour process. If A was $=100$, $B=16$, $C=16$, the product $=143$, i.e. 11 thalers' more value than the capital advanced. If he re-sells this commodity at its value, he gains 11 thalers, although the law of the exchange of commodities was not infringed at any moment of the whole operation, the commodities having on the contrary been exchanged at every moment at their exchange values and therefore as equivalents.

Simple as this process is, it has so far been very little understood. The economists have never been able to reconcile surplus value with the law of equivalence they themselves have postulated. The socialists have always held onto this contradiction and harped on it, instead of understanding the specific nature of this commodity, labour capacity, whose use value is itself the activity which creates exchange value.[73]

Through this process, therefore, the exchange of money with labour capacity and the subsequent consumption of the latter, money is transformed into *capital*. The economists call this *the transformation of money into productive capital*, on the one hand in reference to other forms of capital, in which this basic process admittedly exists as a prerequisite but is extinguished in the form; and on the other hand in reference to the fact that money, in so far as it is confronted with labour capacity as a commodity, is *the possibility* of this transformation into capital, therefore is *in itself* capital, even if it is only through this process itself that it is transformed into actual capital. It has however the possibility of being transformed into *capital*.

It is clear that if surplus labour is to be realised, more of the material of labour is needed; more of the instrument of labour only in exceptional cases. If in 10 hours 10a pounds of cotton can be converted into twist, $10a+2a$ will be converted in 12 hours. In this case, therefore, more cotton is needed or it must be assumed from the outset that the capitalist buys an adequate quantity of cotton to *absorb* the surplus labour. But it is also possible, for example, that the same material can only be worked up into a half-finished state in half a day and completely finished in a whole day. Even so, in this case too, more labour has been consumed in the material and if the process is to continue from day to day, to be a continuous production process, more of the material of labour would still be required than if the worker only replaced by his work in the labour process the labour time objectified in his own wages. Whether more of the means of labour is required and to what extent—and the means of labour is not limited to what are actually tools—depends on the technological nature of the particular labour, hence on the nature of the means consumed by it.

In every case more new labour must have been *absorbed* into the material of labour at the end of the labour process, and therefore objectified, than the amount of labour time objectified in the worker's wage. Let us simply stick to the example of the manufacturer. This *surplus absorption* of labour manifests itself as the working up of more material or the working up of the same material to a higher level than could be attained with less labour time.

[I-48] If we compare the valorisation process with the labour process, the distinction is strikingly apparent between actual labour, which produces use value, and the form of this labour which appears as the element of exchange value, as the activity that creates exchange value.

It is apparent that the particular kind of labour being performed, its material determinateness, does not affect its relation to capital, which is the only issue here. But we started out from the assumption that the labour of the worker was common average labour. Yet the *casus* is not altered if it is assumed that his labour has a higher specific gravity, is potentiated average labour.[69] Simple labour or average labour, the labour of the spinner, the miller, the tiller or the engineer, what the capitalist acquires objectified in the labour process, appropriates for himself through it, is the particular labour of the worker, spinning, milling, tilling the fields, building machines. The surplus value he produces always consists in the surplus quantity of labour, of labour time, during which the worker spins, mills, tills the fields, builds machines for longer than is necessary to produce his own wage. It therefore always consists in a surplus quantity of his own labour, which the capitalist receives for nothing, whatever the character of that labour may be, whether simple or potentiated. The relation, for example, in which potentiated labour stands to average social labour alters nothing in the relation of this potentiated labour to itself, it does not change the fact that an hour of it creates only half as much value as two hours, or that it is realised in proportion to its duration. Hence so far as the relation between labour and surplus labour—or labour which creates surplus value—comes into consideration, it is always a matter of the same kind of labour, and here the following is

correct, although it would not be correct in reference to exchange
value positing labour as such:

* "When reference is made to labour as a measure of value, it necessarily
implies *labour of one particular kind and a given duration*; the proportion which the
other kinds bear to it being easily ascertained by the respective remuneration given
to each" * ([J. Cazenove,] *Outlines of Political Economy,* London, 1832, [pp.] 22-23).

The product obtained by the capitalist in this way is a particular
use value, whose value is equal to the value of the material, the
means of labour, and the quantity of labour added (=the quantity
of labour contained in the wage+the surplus labour, which is not
paid for)=A+B+S+S″. Hence, if he sells the commodity at its
value, he gains exactly as much as the amount of surplus labour.
He does not gain through selling the new commodity at *over* its
value but because he sells it *at* its value, converts the whole of its
value into money. He thereby receives payment of a part of the
value, a part of the labour contained in the product, which he has
not bought and which has cost him nothing. The part of the value
of his product which he has not paid for and sells constitutes his gain.
In circulation, therefore, he merely realises the surplus value he has
received in the labour process. This does not arise from circulation
itself, it does not spring from his selling his commodity *at more than
its value.*[a]

// The value of the material and means of labour consumed in
the labour process—the labour time objectified in them—re-
appears in the product, the new use value. It is preserved, but it
cannot be said in the proper sense of the word that it is
reproduced; for it is not affected by the change of form that has
taken place in the use value, the fact that it now exists in a
different use value from previously. If a day's labour is objectified
in a use value, this objectification, the quantity of labour fixed in
the use value, is not altered by the fact that e.g. the 12th hour of
labour only enters into its composition 11 hours after the first
hour of labour. Thus the labour time contained in the material
and means of labour can be regarded as if it had only entered into
the product at an earlier stage of the production process necessary
for the manufacture of the whole product, hence of all its
elements.

As against this, the situation is otherwise with labour capacity, in
so far as it enters the valorisation process. It replaces the value
contained in itself and therefore paid for itself or the objectified
labour time paid for in its price, in the wage, by adding an equal

---

[a] See this volume, p. 21 et seq.— *Ed.*

quantity of new living labour to the material of labour. It therefore reproduces the value present in itself in advance of the labour process, quite apart from the fact that it also adds a surplus, surplus labour, over and above this quantity. The value of the material and means of labour only re-appears in the product because the material and means of labour possess this value *before* the labour process and independently [I-49] of it. But the value, and more than the value, of the labour capacity re-appears in the product[a] because it is replaced, hence reproduced, by a greater quantity of new living labour in the labour process (even so, in *this* distinction the surplus quantity is at first irrelevant). //

UNITY OF THE LABOUR PROCESS AND THE VALORISATION PROCESS.
(THE CAPITALIST PRODUCTION PROCESS)

The actual production process, which occurs as soon as money has been transformed into capital by being exchanged for living labour capacity and ditto for the objective conditions for the realisation of this capacity—the material and means of labour—this production process is a unity of the labour process and the valorisation process, just as its result, the commodity, is a unity of use value and exchange value.

The production process of capital, looked at from its material side, the production of use values, is, first of all, a *labour process* in general, and as such it displays the general factors which pertain to this process as such under the most varied forms of social production. These factors are determined, namely, by the nature of labour as labour. Historically, in fact, at the start of its formation, we see capital take under its control (subsume under itself) not only the labour process in general but the specific actual labour processes as it finds them available in the existing technology, and in the form in which they have developed on the basis of non-capitalist relations of production. It finds in existence the actual production process—the particular mode of production—and at the beginning it only subsumes it *formally*, without making any changes in its specific technological character. Only in the course of its development does capital not only formally subsume the labour process but transform it, give the very mode of production a new shape and thus first create the mode of production peculiar to it.[55] But whatever its changed shape may

---

[a] Above the word "product" Marx wrote: "(partial product)".— *Ed.*

be, as a labour process in general, i.e. as a labour process viewed in abstraction from its historical determinateness, it always contains the general moments of the labour process as such.

This *formal* subsumption of the labour process, the assumption of control over it by capital, consists in the worker's subjection as worker to the supervision and therefore to the command of capital or the capitalist. Capital becomes command over labour, not in the sense of Adam Smith's statement that wealth is absolutely command over labour,[a] but in the sense that the worker as worker comes under the command of the capitalist. For as soon as he has sold his labour capacity for a definite period of time to the capitalist in return for a wage he must enter into the labour process as a worker, as one of the factors with which capital works.

If the actual labour process is the productive consumption of the use values that enter into it through labour, hence through the activity of the worker himself, it is also just as much the consumption of labour capacity by capital or the capitalist.[74] He employs the worker's labour capacity by having him work. All the factors of the labour process, the material of labour, the means of labour and living labour itself, as the activity, the consumption, of the labour capacity he has bought, belong to him; so the whole labour process belongs to him just as much as if he himself were working with his own material and his own means of labour. But since labour is at the same time the expression of the worker's own life, the manifestation of his own personal skill and capacity—a manifestation which depends on his will and is simultaneously an expression of his will—the capitalist supervises the worker, controls the functioning of labour capacity as an action belonging to him. He will make sure that the material of labour is used for the right purpose: consumed as material of labour. If any material is wasted, it does not enter into the labour process, is not consumed as material of labour. The same is true of the means of labour, when, e.g. the worker wears out their material substance in a manner other than that prescribed by the labour process itself. Lastly, the capitalist will make sure that the worker really works, works the whole time required, and expends *necessary labour time only*, i.e. does the normal quantity of work over a given time. In all these aspects, the labour process and thereby labour and the worker himself come under the control of capital, under its command. I call this the *formal subsumption* of the labour process under capital.[75]

---

a See this volume, p. 383.—*Ed.*

In the whole of the following investigation the labour the capitalist himself may perhaps perform is never reckoned among the components of the product's value. If it consists of simple labour, it has nothing to do with the relation as such, and the capitalist [I-50] is not operating as capitalist, as mere personification, capital incarnate. If, however, it is a form of labour that arises from the peculiar functions of capital as such, hence from the capitalist mode of production as such, we shall subject it later on to a more specific and precise examination as "LABOUR OF SUPERINTENDENCE".[76]

This formal subsumption of the labour process under capital, or the command of the capitalist over the worker, has nothing in common with, e.g., the relation that prevailed in the guild industry of the Middle Ages between the master and the journeymen and apprentices.[29] It emerges instead, purely and simply, from the fact that productive consumption, or the production process, is at the same time a process of the consumption of labour capacity by capital, that the content and determining purpose of this consumption is nothing but the preservation and increase of the value of capital, and that this preservation and increase can only be attained by the most effective, most exact organisation of the actual labour process, which depends on the will, the hard work, etc., of the worker, and which is therefore taken under the control and supervision of the capitalist will.

// One more remark with reference to the production process: Money, *in order to be transformed into capital, must be transformed into the factors of the labour process—i.e. into commodities which can figure as use values in the labour process*; hence it must be transformed into *means of consumption for labour capacity—i.e. the worker's means of subsistence—or into the material and means of labour.* All commodities, therefore, or all products, which cannot be employed in this manner or are not destined to be thus employed, belong to the consumption fund of society, but not to capital (here we understand under capital the objects wherein capital exists). Nevertheless, as long as these products remain *commodities*, they are themselves a mode of existence of capital. If capitalist production is presupposed, capital produces all products without exception, and it is entirely irrelevant whether these products are destined for productive consumption or are unable to enter into it, unable therefore to become the body of capital again. But they then remain capital as long as they remain commodities, i.e. are present in circulation. As soon as they are definitively sold, they cease to be capital in this sense. To the extent that capital is not at the stage of the labour process, it must absolutely be on hand in the form of commodity or money (if only perhaps a mere claim on money, etc.). But they cannot enter into the labour process or the production process as use values. //

In the same measure as the worker is active as a worker, i.e. *externalises* his labour capacity, he *alienates* it, since it has already been *alienated by sale* as a self-externalising capacity to the money owner before the labour process begins. As labour realises itself—on the one hand, as the form of raw material (as use value and product) and, on the other hand, as exchange value, *objectified* social labour in general—it is transformed into *capital.*

In general, to say that capital is a product, employed as a means for new production, is, as already remarked above, to misconstrue the capital-relation as covering the *objective conditions* of every labour process.[56] On the other hand, the same confusion may arise—and is even to be found in part in Ricardo himself[77]—when capital is described as ACCUMULATED LABOUR[a] employed for the production of more ACCUMULATED LABOUR. The expression is ambiguous, since one needs to understand no more by accumulated labour than products which are employed for the production of new use values. But the expression can also be understood in the sense that the product (as exchange value) is, in general, nothing but a definite quantity of *objectified* labour, expended in order to make this quantity grow—hence the *process of self-valorisation.* Although the second process presupposes the first, the first process, in contrast, does not necessarily imply the second.

To the extent that the *objective conditions* of labour, the material and means of labour, serve directly in the labour process, they are employed by the worker. But IT IS NOT LABOUR WHICH EMPLOYS CAPITAL, IT IS CAPITAL WHICH EMPLOYS LABOUR.[78] It is this specific position taken up by value in general towards labour capacity, by objectified, past labour towards living, present labour, by the conditions of labour towards labour itself, which forms the specific nature of capital. We shall go into this in somewhat more detail at the end of this section I. 1) (Transformation of Money into Capital).[b] Here it suffices to say, for the moment, that in the production process—in so far as this is a valorisation process and hence a process of the self-valorisation of the preposited value or money—value (i.e. objectified general social labour), past labour, [I-51] preserves and increases itself, posits surplus value, through exchange, through

---

a Marx gives the English term in brackets after its German equivalent.— *Ed.*
b See this volume, pp. 105-115.— *Ed.*

the relative appropriation of living labour, an exchange mediated by the purchase of labour capacity. It thus appears as value-in-process, and preserving and maintaining itself in the process. It thus appears as a *self*—the incarnation of this self is the capitalist— *the selfhood of value.* Labour (living) appears only as the means, the AGENCY through which capital (value) reproduces and increases itself.

* "Labour is the agency by which capital is made productive of wages, profit, or revenue" * (John Wade, *History of the Middle and Working Classes etc.*, 3rd ed., London, 1835, p. 161).

(In the abstract economic section of his book Wade has some original points for his time, e.g. on commercial crises, etc. The whole of the historical part is, in contrast, a striking example of the shameless plagiarism that predominates among the English economists. It is in fact copied almost word for word from Sir F. Morton Eden, *The State of the Poor etc.*, 3 vols, London, 1797.) [79]

Value, objectified labour, acquires this relation to living labour only to the extent that it is confronted by labour *capacity* as such, i.e. to the extent that, conversely, the *objective conditions* of labour—and hence the conditions for the realisation of labour capacity—confront labour capacity itself in separation and independence, under the control of an alien will. Hence although the means and material of labour are not as such capital, they themselves appear as *capital* because their independence, their existence as entities in their own right vis-à-vis the worker and therefore labour itself, is rooted in their being. Just as gold and silver appear as money, and are, notionally, directly connected with the social relation of production of which they are the vehicles. [80]

Within capitalist production, the relationship between the labour process and the valorisation process is that the latter appears as the purpose, the former only as the means. The former is therefore STOPPED when the latter is no longer possible or not yet possible. On the other hand, it is revealed in times of so-called speculative fashions, of crises of speculation (shares and so forth), that the labour process (actual material production) is only a burdensome requirement, and the capitalist nations are seized by a universal mania for attaining the goal (the valorisation process) without using the means (the labour process). The labour process as such could only provide its own purpose if the capitalist were concerned with the use value of the product. He is, however, *only* concerned with alienating it by sale as a commodity, converting it back into money, and, since it was money originally, with the increase of this sum of money. In this sense it can be said:

"The value makes the product" (Say, *Cours complet*, p. 510).[a][81]

(This is in fact true for all production of *commodities*. On the other hand, it is also correct that only capitalist production is *commodity production* to the broadest extent, i.e. production for the individual's own use entirely disappears and the elements of production, even in agriculture, are to a greater and greater degree already *commodities* when they enter the production process.[60])

Here, in dealing with the transformation of money into capital, we only need to point generally to the form in which money appears (since we shall be returning to this in dealing with circulation[82]). In any case this has already been done for the most part, in I. 1) a) (*The Most General Form of Capital*).

A further remark needs to be made with regard to the valorisation process: It is not merely value, but a sum of value, that is preposited to it. A value of a definite magnitude, a point which will be developed still further later on.[b] It must (even as capitalist *in nuce*[c]) at least be capable of buying 1 worker and the material and instrument needed for him. In short, the sum of value is here determined from the outset by the exchange values of the commodities which enter directly into the labour process.

We therefore call the whole thing the capitalist production process on the basis of capital. It is not a question of producing a product but a commodity—a product destined to be sold. And it is not a question of simply producing commodities in order by selling them to gain possession in this way of the use values available in circulation, but of producing commodities in order to preserve and increase the preposited value.

[I-52] // If the labour process is viewed entirely abstractly, it can be said that originally only two factors come into play—man and nature. (Labour and the natural material of labour.) His first tools are his own limbs, and even these he must first appropriate for himself. Only with the first product that is employed for new production—even if it is just a stone thrown at an animal to kill it—does the labour process proper begin.[83] One of the first tools appropriated by man is the animal (domesticated animal). (See on this point the passage in Turgot.[84]) To this extent, from the point

---

a Marx quotes in French.— *Ed.*
b See this volume, p. 186 et seq.— *Ed.*
c In embryo.— *Ed.*

of view of labour, Franklin is right to define man as "A TOOL-MAKING ANIMAL" or "ENGINEER".[85] The earth and labour would then be the original factors of production; the products destined for labour, produced material of labour, means of labour, means of subsistence, would only be derivative factors.

"The earth is *necessary*; capital is *useful*. And labour with the earth produces capital" (Colins, *L'économie politique. Source des révolutions et des utopies prétendues socialistes*, Vol. III, Paris, 1857, [p.] 288).[a]

// Colins believes that this achievement of independence by value, see VII-153, 154,[86] which is contained in the concept of capital, was invented by the economists. //

The above-mentioned ambiguity is also present in *James Mill.*

* "All capital" * //here CAPITAL in the merely material sense // * "consists really in commodities.... The first capital must have been the result of pure labour. The first commodities could not be made by any commodities existing before them" * (James Mill, *Elements of Political Economy*, London, 1821, [p.] 72).

However, this separation of production into the factors man, as vehicle of labour, and earth (actually nature) as object of labour, is also totally abstract. For man does not originally confront nature as a worker but as a proprietor, and it is not man as a solitary individual but man as member of a tribe, a clan, a family, etc., as soon as one can at all speak of man leading a human existence.[87]

// In the same Mill:

* "Labour and Capital ... the one, *immediate* labour ... the other, *hoarded labour*, that which has been the result of former labour" * (l.c., [p.] 75). //

If, on the one hand, capital is reduced in the labour process to its merely material mode of existence—if it is separated into its factors— *in order* in general to smuggle it in as a *necessary* element of all production,[56] it is, on the other hand, also conceded that capital is of a purely notional nature, because it is value (*Say, Sismondi*, etc.).[b]

If it is said that capital is *a product as opposed to a commodity* (Proudhon, Wayland, etc.)[c] or that it is the instrument of labour and the material of labour, or that it also consists of the products the worker receives, etc., it is forgotten that in the labour process labour has already been incorporated into capital and belongs to it just as much as the means and material of labour.

* "When the labourers receive wages for their labour ... the capitalist is the *owner*, not of the capital only" * (in this material sense), * "but of *the labour also*. If

---

a Marx quotes in French.— *Ed.*
b See this volume, p. 150.— *Ed.*
c Ibid., p. 154.— *Ed.*

what is paid as wages is included, as it commonly is, in the term capital, it is absurd to talk of labour separately from capital. The word capital, as thus employed, includes labour and capital both"* (James Mill, l.c., [pp.] 70, 71).

Just as it is convenient for the apologists of capital to confuse it with the use value in which it exists, and to call use value as such capital, in order to present capital as an eternal factor of production, as a relation independent of all social forms, immanent in every labour process, hence immanent in the labour process in general, so equally does it happen that it suits Messieurs the economists when reasoning away some of the phenomena which belong peculiarly to the capitalist mode of production to forget the essential feature of capital, namely that it is value positing itself as value, hence not only self-preserving but at the same time self-multiplying value. This is convenient e.g. for proving the impossibility of overproduction.[88] The capitalist is here conceived as someone who is only concerned with the consumption of certain products (their appropriation by means of the sale of his commodity), not with the increase of the preposited value, purchasing power as such, abstract wealth as such.

Through the transformation of money into capital (effected by the exchange of money with labour) the general formula for capital, $M—C—M$, has now acquired a content. Money is the independent existence of exchange value. Viewed from the angle of its quality, it is the material representative of abstract wealth, *the material existence of abstract wealth*. But, the degree [I-53] to which it is this, the extent to which it corresponds to its concept, depends on its own quantity or mass. In the increase of money— corresponds to the increase of value as such—this increase is an end in itself. To make money by means of money is the purpose of the capitalist production process—the increase of wealth in its general form, of the quantity of objectified social labour which is, as this labour, expressed in money. Whether the existing values figure merely as money of account in the ledger, or in whatever other form, as tokens of value, etc., is initially a matter of indifference. Money appears here only as the form of independent value which capital assumes at its starting-point as also at its point of return, but constantly abandons again. A more detailed treatment of this belongs in II) *The Circulation Process of Capital.*[82]

Capital is here money-in-process, for which its forms as money and commodity are themselves merely alternating forms. It is continuously estimated in money of account—and is only valid as this money's material existence, even as long as it exists as a commodity; and no sooner does it assume the form of money than

it must, in order to valorise itself, abandon that form again. To say
the capitalist is concerned with money is to say nothing but that he
is concerned purely with exchange value, with the increase of
exchange value, with abstract enrichment. But this is solely
expressed as such in money.

"THE GREAT OBJECT OF THE MONIED CAPITALIST, IN FACT, IS TO ADD TO THE
NOMINAL AMOUNT OF HIS FORTUNE. IT IS THAT, IF EXPRESSED PECUNIARILY THIS YEAR
BY £20,000 for example, IT SHOULD BE EXPRESSED PECUNIARILY NEXT YEAR BY
£24,000. TO ADVANCE HIS CAPITAL, AS ESTIMATED IN MONEY, IS THE ONLY WAY IN
WHICH HE CAN ADVANCE HIS INTEREST AS A MERCHANT. The IMPORTANCE of this
OBJECT to him is not affected by FLUCTUATIONS IN the CURRENCY or BY A CHANGE IN
THE REAL VALUE OF MONEY. For instance, he may have advanced his fortune, by the
business of one year, from £20,000 to £24,000; and yet, from a decline in the value of
money, he may not HAVE INCREASED HIS COMMAND over the COMFORTS, etc. Still it was as
much his interest [to have engaged in the business], as if money had not fallen; for
else, HIS MONIED FORTUNE WOULD HAVE REMAINED STATIONARY, and his REAL WEALTH
WOULD HAVE DECLINED IN THE PROPORTION OF 24 TO 20.... COMMODITIES are, therefore,
not the TERMINATING OBJECT of the TRADING CAPITALIST, save in the spending of his
REVENUE, and when he purchases for the SAKE OF CONSUMPTION. IN THE OUTLAY OF HIS
CAPITAL, AND WHEN HE PURCHASES FOR THE SAKE OF PRODUCTION, MONEY IS HIS
TERMINATING OBJECT" (Thomas Chalmers, On Political Economy in Connexion with the
Moral State and Moral Prospects of Society, 2nd ed., London, 1832, [pp.] 165-66).

// Another point in relation to the formula **M—C—M.** Value as
capital, self-valorising value, is *value raised to a second power*. Not
only does it have an independent expression, as in money, but it
compares itself with itself (or is compared by the capitalist),
measures itself at one period (the magnitude of value in which it
was preposited to the production process) against itself in another
period, namely after its return from circulation—after the
commodity has been sold and re-converted into money. Value
therefore appears as the same subject in two different periods,
and indeed this is its own movement, the movement that
characterises capital. Only in this movement does value appear as
capital. See in opposition to this "*A Critical Dissertation on the
Nature, Measures, and Causes of Value; Chiefly in Reference to the
Writings of Mr. Ricardo and His Followers.* By the Author of Essays on the Formation and Publication of Opinions."
// S. Bailey, // London, 1825. //

Bailey's main argument against the whole determination of
value by labour time is this: Value is only the *relation* according to
which different commodities are exchanged. Value is only a
RELATION between 2 commodities.

Value is nothing *"intrinsic or absolute"* (l.c., p. 23). *"It is impossible to
designate, or express the value of a commodity, except by a quantity of some other

commodity" * (l.c., [p.] 26). * "Instead of regarding value as a relation between 2 objects, they" * (THE RICARDIANS) (and Ricardo himself) * "consider it as a positive result produced by a definite quantity of labour" * (l.c., [p.] 30). * "Because the values of A and B, according to their doctrine, are to each other as the quantities of producing labour, or ... are determined by the quantities of producing labour, they appear to have concluded, that the value of A alone, without reference to anything else, is as the quantity of its producing labour. There is no meaning certainly in the last proposition" * (pp. 31-32). They speak of * "value as a sort of general and independent property" * (l.c., [p.] 35). * "The value of a commodity must be its value in something" * (l.c.)

As objectification of social labour the commodity is expressed as something relative. For [if the]^a labour contained [in A]^a is equated to all others, this is only as a particular form of existence of social labour. In this, however, the individual is already not viewed in isolation, but if Bailey wishes it, his labour is posited relatively and the commodity is itself posited as the form of existence of this relative thing.

[II-54] The same Bailey says (l.c., p. 72):

* "Value is a relation between *contemporary* commodities, because such only admit of being exchanged for each other; and if we compare the value of a commodity at one time with its value at another, it is only a comparison of the relation in which it stood at these different times to some other commodity." *

He says this as an argument against "COMPARING COMMODITIES AT DIFFERENT PERIODS" as if for example in the turnover of capital the capitalist HAD NOT CONTINUOUSLY TO COMPARE THE VALUE OF ONE PERIOD TO THE VALUE OF ANOTHER PERIOD.[38]

// It could now be asked, what is the relationship in which capital's monetary expression stands to capital itself. Once money exists in the form of money, the constituent elements for which it is exchanged in its transformation into productive capital confront it as commodities. Here, therefore, the laws developed in the metamorphosis of the commodity or in the simple turnover of money are valid.^{b} If tokens of value circulate, whether they serve as means of circulation or means of payment, they merely represent the value of the commodities estimated in money or they directly represent money, which is equal in quantity to the amounts of money expressed in the prices of the commodities. As such they have no value. They are therefore not yet capital in the sense that the latter is objectified labour. They represent instead in full the price of the capital, as they previously represented that

---

a MS damaged.— *Ed.*

b K. Marx, *A Contribution to the Critique of Political Economy.* Part One (present edition, Vol. 29, pp. 324-34).— *Ed.*

of the commodity. If real money circulates, this is itself objectified labour—capital—(because commodity).

If we divide the total sum of money turning over by the number of times it turns over, we get the quantity of money really engaged in the process of turning over, and this is a constituent element of the capital, fixed or circulating according to the view one wishes to take of it. I can buy commodities for 120 thalers with the same 6 thalers if they turn over 20 times in a day: they represent the value of 120 thalers in the course of a day. But the 6 thalers themselves must be added to this. So the whole amount of capital turning over in the course of the day=126 thalers.

If a capital=100 thalers, and it buys commodities with those 100 thalers, then the same 100 thalers now represent a 2nd capital of 100 thalers and so on. If they turn over 6 times in the day, they have successively represented a capital of 600 thalers. How much or how little capital they represent on a given day therefore depends on their velocity of turnover = the speed of the commodity's metamorphosis, which appears here as the metamorphosis of capital, alternately assuming and abandoning its forms of money and commodity. If the money functions as means of payment, 600 thalers of money can pay for any amount of capital, since its negative and positive charges cancel out, leaving a balance of 600 thalers.

Whereas originally, in the simple circulation of commodities, money appears as a point of transition, the metamorphosis of the commodity,[a] the commodity transformed into money appears as the point of departure and conclusion of the movement of capital, and the commodity appears as metamorphosis of capital, as a mere point of transition.

The only distinguishing marks of money in so far as it appears as a form of capital—as real money, not as money of account—are these: 1) It returns to its point of departure, and in increased quantity. Money expended for consumption does not return to its point of departure; capital—money advanced for the purpose of production—returns in increased quantity to its point of departure. 2) Money which has been expended remains in circulation, from which it withdraws the commodity; capital throws back into circulation more commodities than it withdrew and it therefore also constantly withdraws anew from circulation the money it has expended. The more rapid this cyclic movement, i.e. the more

---

[a] K. Marx, *A Contribution to the Critique of Political Economy*. Part One (present edition, Vol. 29, pp. 332).— *Ed.*

rapid the circulation or metamorphosis of capital, the more rapid the turnover of money, and since this movement of capital is many-sided, the more does money serve as means of payment and the more do debts and assets balance each other. //

Capital transformed into money in the way we have described becomes *productive capital* in so far as it has subsumed the production process, functions as buyer and employer of labour. Only where capital has subjected production itself to its control, hence where the capitalist produces, does capital exist as the dominant, specific form of a period of production. Formally speaking, it may already have emerged previously in other functions, and it appears in these functions in its own period too. But then these are only derivative and secondary forms of capital, such as commercial and interest-bearing capital, etc.[15] So when we speak of productive capital, the whole of this relation is to be understood, not as if one of the forms of use value in which it appears in the labour process were in itself productive, with the machine or the material of labour producing value, etc.[89]

From the valorisation process, whose result is the value advanced and a SURPLUS, a surplus value (in the labour process itself capital appears as a real use value; i.e. as real consumption, for only in consumption is [II-55] use value realised as use value; this process of the consumption of capital itself forms an economic relation, has a definite economic form and is not indifferent, falling outside the form, as in the concept of the mere commodity[39]; these use values of which capital consists are conceptually determined by the activity of labour capacity, which consumes them) it follows that the actual specific product of capital, so far as it produces as capital, is *surplus value* itself and *that in production by capital the specific* product of labour, so far as capital incorporates labour, is not this or that product but *capital*. The labour process itself appears only as the means of the valorisation process, just as, in general, use value appears here as only the repository of exchange value.

THE 2 COMPONENTS INTO WHICH THE TRANSFORMATION
OF MONEY INTO CAPITAL IS DIVIDED

[II-A][90] What the worker sells is disposition over his labour capacity—temporally limited disposition over it. The piece-work system of payment does, admittedly, introduce the semblance that the worker obtains a definite *share in the product*. But this is only another form of measuring labour time. Instead of saying: you will work for 12 hours, it is said: you will receive such and such an amount per piece, i.e. we measure the number of hours by the product, as the size of the AVERAGE product of an hour has been established by experience. The worker who cannot supply this minimum is dismissed. (See *Ure*.[91])

In accordance with the general relation of purchase and sale, the *exchange value* of the worker's commodity cannot be determined by the way in which the purchaser *uses* the commodity; it is determined solely by the quantity of objectified labour contained in the commodity itself; here, therefore, by the quantity of labour it costs to produce the worker himself, for the commodity he offers exists only as an ability, a capacity, and has no existence outside his bodily form, his person. The labour time necessary both to maintain him physically and to modify him to develop this *special* capacity is the labour time necessary to produce the worker as such.

In this exchange the worker in fact only receives money as *coin*, i.e. merely a transitory form of the means of subsistence for which he exchanges it. Means of subsistence, not wealth, are for him the purpose of the exchange.

Labour capacity has been called the capital of the worker in so far as it is the fund he does not consume by an isolated exchange, but is able to repeat the exchange again and again for the *duration of his life as a worker*. On this argument everything that formed a fund for repeated processes by the same subject would be capital; e.g. the eye would be the capital of sight. Phrases.[92] The fact that, as long as he is capable of working, labour is always a source of exchange for the worker, and not exchange absolutely but exchange with capital, is inherent in the definition of the concept, according to which he only sells the *temporary disposition* over his labour capacity, hence can always begin the same act of exchange anew once he has half satisfied his hunger and slept half long enough, taken in the appropriate quantity of substances to be able to reproduce afresh the manifestation of his life.

Instead of wondering at this and presenting to the worker the fact that he lives at all, hence is able to repeat certain life processes every day, as a great service rendered by capital, the whitewashing sycophants of bourgeois political economy should rather have fixed their attention on the fact that after constantly repeated labour he always has *only* his living, direct labour itself to exchange. The repetition itself is, IN FACT, merely an apparent one. *What he exchanges for capital* (even if it is represented in relation to him by different, successive capitalists) is *his entire labour capacity*, which he expends over 30 years, SAY. It is paid for in doses, just as he sells it in doses. This changes absolutely nothing in the essence of the matter, and in no way justifies the conclusion that, because the worker must sleep for a certain number of hours before he is capable of repeating his labour and his exchange with capital, labour forms *his capital*. Hence what IN FACT is here conceived as his capital is the limit to his labour, its interruption, the fact that he is not a *perpetuum mobile*. The struggle for the normal working day proves that the capitalist would like nothing better than for the worker to *squander his dosages of vital force, as far as possible, without interruption*. [II-A]

[II-55] The whole movement that money performs to be converted into capital therefore falls into two distinct processes: the first is an act of simple circulation, purchase on one side, sale on the other; the second is the consumption of the purchased article by the buyer, an act which lies outside circulation, takes place behind its back. The consumption of the purchased article, in consequence of the latter's specific nature, here itself constitutes an economic relation.[39] In this consumption process the buyer and the seller enter into a new relation with each other, which is at the same time a *relation of production*.

The two acts may be entirely separate in time; and whether the sale is realised straight away or first concluded nominally and subsequently realised, it must always, at least nominally, as a stipulation made between buyer and seller, precede as a specific act the second act, the process of consumption of the purchased commodities—although their stipulated price is not paid until later.

The first act fully corresponds to the laws of commodity circulation, to which it belongs. Equivalents are exchanged for equivalents. The money owner pays out on the one hand the value of the material and means of labour, on the other hand the *value of the labour capacity*. In this purchase he therefore gives in money exactly as much objectified labour as he withdraws from circulation in the form of commodities—labour capacity, material of labour and means of labour. If this first act did not correspond to the laws of the exchange of commodities, it could not appear at all as the act of a mode of production whose foundation is namely that the most elementary relationship individuals enter with each other is that of commodity owners.[20] A different foundation of production would have to be assumed in order to explain it. But, inversely, it is precisely the mode of production whose product always has the elementary form of the commodity, and not that of use value, which is based on capital, on the exchange of money for labour capacity.

The second act displays a phenomenon which in its result and its conditions is not only entirely alien to the laws of simple circulation but even appears to be at odds with it. In the first place, the social position of the seller and the buyer changes in the production process itself. The buyer takes command of the seller, to the extent that the latter himself enters into the buyer's consumption process with his person as a worker. There comes into being, outside the simple exchange process, a relation of domination and servitude, which is however distinguished from all other historical relations of this kind by the fact that it only follows from the specific nature of the commodity which is being sold by the seller; by the fact, therefore, that this relation only arises here from purchase and sale, from the position of both parties as commodity owners, therefore in itself once again includes political, etc., relationships. The buyer becomes the chief, lord (MASTER), the seller becomes his worker (MAN, HAND). In the same way as the relation of buyer and seller, as soon as it is inverted to become the relation of creditor and debtor, alters the social position of both parties—but there it is only a temporary change. Here it is permanent.[93]

But if one considers the result itself, it completely contradicts the laws of simple circulation, and this becomes even more striking when, as is usually the case, payment is only made after the labour has been delivered, the purchase being therefore in fact realised only at the end of the production process. For now labour capacity no longer confronts the buyer as such. It has become objectified in the commodity, say for example 12 hours of labour time, or 1 day's labour. The buyer therefore receives a value of 12 hours of labour. But he only pays for a value of say 10 hours of labour. Here equivalents would not really be exchanged for each other; but in fact no exchange is taking place at all now. One could only say: even assuming—and this is a favourite phrase—assuming that Act I has not taken place in the manner described but [II-56] instead the buyer pays not for the labour capacity but rather for the labour itself that has been provided. It can only be imagined. The product is now ready, but its value only exists in the form of its price. It must first be realised as money. If, then, the capitalist immediately realises for the worker his part of the product in money, it is in order that the worker should be content with a lesser equivalent in money than he has given up in the commodity. From a general point of view this is absurd. For it adds up to the assertion that the seller must always be satisfied with a lesser equivalent in money than he provides in the commodity. Once the buyer transforms his money into a commodity, buys, the value only continues to exist in the commodity he buys as price; it no longer exists as realised value, as money. *He receives no compensation* for the fact that his commodity has lost the form of exchange value, of money. On the other hand, he has gained by the transaction, in that it now exists in the form of the commodity.

But, it is further argued, if I buy a commodity for my own consumption, that is something different; I am interested in its use value. There, it is only a matter of transforming exchange value into means of subsistence. In contrast to this, if I buy a commodity in order to re-sell it, I evidently suffer an initial loss when I exchange my money for it. For I am only concerned with exchange value and by the act of purchase my money loses the form of money. The exchange value exists now only as price, as an equation with money which has yet to be realised. But the intention with which I buy a commodity has nothing to do with its value. The phenomenon that in buying in order to sell a surplus value emerges would here be derived from the *intention* of the buyer that this surplus value should emerge, which is obviously absurd. When I sell a commodity I am completely indifferent to the use the buyer intends to make of it, as also to the misuse. Let us assume that the commodity owner has insufficient money to buy labour, but enough to buy the material and means of labour. The sellers of the material and means of labour would laugh him to scorn if he were to say: the material and means of labour are incomplete products; one is so in the nature of things, the other, likewise, only forms a constituent element of a later product and has no value except in so far as it enters into that product. Let us say that in fact the material of labour costs 100 thalers, the means of labour 20, and the labour I add to them, measured in money, is equal to 30 thalers. The value of the product would then be 150 thalers, and as soon as I am done with my work I have a commodity of 150 thalers, which, however, must first be sold in order to exist in the form of exchange value, as 150 thalers. I have given 100 thalers to the seller of the material, and 20 thalers to the seller of the means of labour; these form constituent elements of my commodity's value; they form 80% of its price. This 80% of my as yet unsold commodity—which I must first turn back into money—has been realised in money by the sellers of the raw material and the means of labour in that they sold them to me, before the product was finished, and furthermore before it was sold. I am therefore making them an advance by the mere act of buying, and they ought accordingly to sell me their commodities at less than their value. The case is just the. same.

In both cases I have a commodity of 150 thalers in my hands, but it must first be sold, realised in money. In the first case I have myself added the value of the labour, but I have paid in advance the value of the material and means of labour, not only before the product has been sold, but before it is finished. In the second case the worker has added the value and I have paid him before the sale of the commodity. So one would always arrive at the absurd conclusion that the buyer as such has the privilege of buying cheaper, whereby he would lose just as much in his capacity of seller as he would have gained as buyer. At the end of the day for example the worker has added a day's labour to the product and I possess this labour of his in objectified form, as exchange value; I only pay him for this when I give back to him the same exchange value in money. The form of use value in which the value exists changes the magnitude of value just as little as it is changed by existing in the form of the commodity rather than that of money, as realised rather than non-realised value.

What creeps into this conception is the recollection of cash discount. If I have commodities ready, and either have money advanced on them—without selling them (or only making a conditional sale)—or draw out money on a bond of payment for a commodity which is already sold but for which payment first falls due later—for which I therefore have received in payment a bond, a bill of exchange or the like, only to be realised later—in both of these cases I pay discount. I pay for having received money without selling the commodity, or for having received money before the commodity is payable, before the sale is actually realised; in one or the other form I borrow money, and I pay for this. I give up part [II-57] of the price of the commodity, yielding it to the person who advances me money for the commodity as yet unsold or the commodity whose price is not yet payable. Here, therefore, I am paying for the metamorphosis of the commodities.

But if I am the buyer of labour—once it has been objectified in the product—this relation does not fill the bill, to begin with. For whether money is advanced [on unsold commodities] or the payment bond is discounted, in both cases the advancer of the money is not the buyer of the commodity but a third person who interposes himself between buyer and seller. But in our case the capitalist confronts the worker who has provided him with the commodity—a definite amount of labour time objectified in a particular use value—as buyer, and he pays when he has already received the equivalent in the commodity. Secondly, this whole relation between the industrial capitalist and the capitalist advancing money at interest presumes that the capital-relation already exists. It is assumed that money—value in general—possesses as such the quality of valorising itself within a definite period of time, the ability to create a certain surplus value, and payment is made for its use on this assumption. Here, therefore, a derived form of capital is being presupposed in order to explain its original form—a particular form in order to explain its general form.[94]

In any case, the upshot of the whole thing is always this: The worker cannot wait until the product is sold. In other words, he does not have a *commodity* to sell, only his own labour. If he had *commodities* to sell, this would imply that in order to exist as a seller of commodities—since he does not live off the product and the commodity is not a use value for himself—he would always have to have in stock in the form of money as much of the commodities as he needs to live, to buy provisions, until his new commodity is finished and sold. Once again we have the same presupposition as in the first act, namely that the worker is faced, as mere labour capacity, with the objective conditions of labour, which include both his means of subsistence—the means to living while he works—and the conditions for the realisation of his labour itself.[21] Under the pretext of reasoning out of existence the first relation on which everything depends, and which is decisive, it is thus re-established.

Another form is just as idiotic: By receiving his wages, the worker has already received his share of the product or the value of the product, hence he has no further demands to make. Capitalist and worker are *associés*,[a] joint proprietors of the product or its value, but one PARTNER has his share paid to him by the other and thereby loses his right to the value resulting from the sale of the product and the profit realised therein. Arising from this we have to distinguish between two FALLACIES. If the worker had received an equivalent for the labour added by him to the raw material, he would in fact have no further claim. He would have received his share payment at its full value. This would of course show why he has nothing further to do with either the commodity or its value, but it by no means shows why he receives an equivalent in money

---

[a] Partners.— *Ed.*

which is *smaller* than he provided in the *labour objectified* in the product.

Thus in the above example the seller of raw material at 100 thalers and the seller of the means of labour at 20, which were bought from them by the producer of the new commodity, have no claim to the new commodity and its value of 150 thalers. It does not, however, follow from this that the one received only 80 thalers instead of 100 and the other only 10 instead of 20. It only proves that if the worker has received his equivalent before the sale of the commodities—he has, however, sold *his* commodity—he has nothing further to demand. But it does not prove that he has to sell his commodity *at less than the equivalent.* Now of course a second illusion creeps in. The capitalist now sells the commodity at a profit. The worker, who has already obtained his equivalent, has already waived his claim to the profit which arises from this subsequent operation. Here then we once again have the old illusion that profit—surplus value—arises from circulation and therefore that the commodity is sold over its value and the buyer is defrauded. The worker would have no share in this fraud carried out by one capitalist on another; but the profit of the one capitalist would be equal to the loss of the other, and thus no surplus value would exist in and for itself, for capital as a whole.[a]

There are of course particular forms of wage labour in which it *appears* as if the worker sold not his labour capacity but his *labour* itself, already *objectified* in the commodities. In the *piece wage* for example. However, this is [II-58] only another form of measuring labour time and supervising labour (of only paying for *necessary* labour).[b] If I know, for example, that average labour can deliver 24 units of some article in 12 hours, then 2 units would be equivalent to 1 hour of labour. If the worker receives payment for 10 of the 12 hours he works, hence if he works 2 hours of surplus time, this is the same as if in every hour he provided $^1/_6$ of an hour of surplus labour (labour for nothing). (10 minutes, hence 120 minutes over the whole day=2 hours.)

Assuming that 12 hours of labour, evaluated in money,=6s., then 1 hour=$^6/_{12}$s.=$^1/_2$s.=6d. The 24 units therefore=6s., or a single unit=$^1/_4$s.=3d. It is all the same whether the worker adds 2 hours to 10 or 4 units to 20. Each unit of 3d.=$^1/_2$ hour of labour of 3d. The worker, however, receives not 3d. but 2$^1/_2$d. And if he delivers 24 units, he receives 48d.+12d.=60d.=5s., while the

---

a See this volume, pp. 25-26.— *Ed.*

b Ibid., pp. 103-04.— *Ed.*

capitalist sells the commodity at 6s. It is therefore only another way of measuring labour time (and equally of supervising the quality of the labour). These different forms of wage labour have nothing to do with the general relationship. It is in any case obvious that the same question arises with piece wages: where does the surplus value come from? It is clear that the piece is not completely paid for; that more labour is absorbed in the piece than is paid for in money.

Hence the whole phenomenon can only be explained (all other ways of explaining it ultimately return to presupposing its existence) by the fact that the worker does not sell his labour as a commodity—and it is a commodity as soon as it is objectified, in whatever use value, hence always as a result of the labour process, hence mostly before the labour has been *paid for*—but his labour capacity, before it has been set to work and realised itself as labour.

The result—that the preposited value, or the sum of money the buyer cast into circulation, has not only been reproduced but valorised itself, grown in a definite proportion, that a surplus value has been added to the value—this result is only realised in the direct production process, for only here does labour capacity become actual labour, only here is labour objectified in a commodity. The result is that the buyer gets back more objectified labour in the form of the commodity than he advanced in the form of money. This surplus value—this surplus of objectified labour time—arose first during the labour process itself; later the buyer throws it back into circulation by selling the new commodity.

But this second act, in which surplus value really arises and capital in fact becomes productive capital, can only occur as a result of the first act and is only a consequence of the specific use value of the commodity, which is in the first act exchanged for money at *its value*. The first act, however, only takes place under certain historical conditions.[21] The worker must be free, in order to be able to dispose of his labour capacity as his property, he must therefore be neither slave, nor serf, nor bondsman. Equally, he must on the other hand have forfeited the conditions for the realisation of his labour capacity. He must therefore be neither a peasant farming for his own needs nor a craftsman; he must have altogether ceased to be an owner of property. It is assumed that he *works* as *a non-proprietor* and that *the conditions of his labour* confront *him as alien property.* Thus these conditions also imply that the earth confronts him as alien property; that he is excluded from the use of nature and its products. This is the point at which landed property appears as a necessary prerequisite for wage labour and therefore for capital. But in any case this does not have to be borne in mind any further in considering capital as such, since the form of landed property corresponding to the capitalist form of production is itself a historical product of the capitalist mode of production.[95] There therefore lies hidden in the existence of labour capacity offered as a commodity by the worker himself a whole range of historical conditions which alone permit labour to become wage labour, hence money to become capital.

Here, of course, it is a matter of production's resting in general on this basis; wage labour and its employment by capital should not occur as sporadic phenomena on the surface of the society, but should constitute the [II-59] dominant relation.

For labour to be wage labour, for the worker to work as a non-proprietor, for him to sell not commodities but disposition over his own labour capacity—to sell his labour capacity itself in the sole manner in which it can be sold—the conditions for the realisation of his labour must confront him as *alienated conditions,* as *alien powers,* conditions under the sway of an alien will, as alien property. *Objectified labour,* value as such, confronts him as an *entity in its own right,* as *capital,* the vehicle of which is the capitalist—hence it also confronts him as the *capitalist.*

What the worker *buys* is a result, a definite value; the quantity of labour time equal to the quantity contained in his own labour capacity, hence an amount of money necessary to keep him alive *qua* worker. For what he buys is money, hence merely another form for the exchange value he himself already possesses as labour capacity, and in the same quantity.

What the capitalist buys, in contrast, and what the worker sells, is the use value of labour capacity, i.e. labour itself, the power which creates and enhances value. This value-creating and value-enhancing power therefore belongs not to the worker but to capital. By incorporating into itself this power, capital comes alive and begins TO WORK "as if its body were by love possessed".[a] Living labour thus becomes a means whereby objectified labour is preserved and increased. To the extent that the worker creates wealth, living labour becomes a power of capital; similarly, all development of the productive forces of labour is development of the productive forces of capital. What the worker himself sells—and this is always replaced with an equivalent—is labour capacity itself, a definite value, whose magnitude may oscillate

---

[a] Goethe, *Faust,* Der Tragödie erster Teil, "Auerbachs Keller in Leipzig".— *Ed.*

between wider or narrower limits, but which is always reducible conceptually to a definite amount of the means of subsistence required for the maintenance of labour capacity as such, i.e. so that the worker may continue to live as a worker. Objectified, past labour thereby becomes the sovereign of living, present labour. The relation of subject and object is inverted. If already in the presupposition the objective conditions for the realisation of the worker's labour capacity and therefore for actual labour appear to the worker as alien, independent powers, which relate to living labour rather as the conditions of their own preservation and increase—the tool, the material [of labour] and the means of subsistence only giving themselves up to labour in order to absorb more of it—this inversion is still more pronounced in the result. The objective conditions of labour are themselves the products of labour and to the extent that they are viewed from the angle of exchange value they are nothing but labour time in objective form.

In both directions, therefore, the objective conditions of labour are the result of labour itself, they are *its own objectification,* and it is its own objectification, labour itself as its result, that confronts labour as an *alien power,* as an *independent power*; while labour confronts the latter again and again in the same objectlessness, as mere labour capacity.[96]

If the worker needs to work only for half a day in order to live for a whole day, i.e. in order to produce the means of subsistence necessary for his daily maintenance as a worker, the exchange value of his daily labour capacity=half a day's labour. The use value of this capacity, on the other hand, consists not in the labour time needed to preserve and produce, or reproduce, that capacity itself, but in the labour time it can itself work. Its use value therefore consists for example in a day's labour, whereas its exchange value is only half a day's labour. The capitalist buys it at its exchange value, at the labour time required to preserve it; what he receives, in contrast, is the labour time during which it can itself work; hence in the above case a whole day, if he has paid for a half. The size of his profit depends on the length of the period of time for which the worker places his labour capacity at his disposal. But in all circumstances the relation consists in this, that the worker puts it at his disposal for longer than the amount of labour time necessary for his own reproduction. The capitalist only buys it because it has this use value.

Capital and wage labour only express two factors of the same relation. Money cannot become capital without being exchanged for labour capacity as a commodity sold by the worker himself; therefore without finding this specific commodity available on the market. On the other hand, labour can only appear as wage labour once the specific conditions of its realisation, its *own* objective conditions, confront it as powers in their own right, alien property, value-being-for-itself[25] and holding fast to [II-60] itself, in short as capital. Hence if capital from its material side—or in terms of the use values in which it exists—can only consist of the objective conditions of labour itself, the means of subsistence and means of production (the latter in part material of labour, in part means of labour), from its formal side these objective conditions must confront labour as *alienated*, as *independent* powers, as value—objectified labour—which relates to living labour as the mere means of its own preservation and increase.

Wage labour—or the wage system—(the wage as the price of labour) is therefore a necessary social form of labour for capitalist production, just as capital, potentiated value, is a necessary social form the objective conditions of labour must have for labour to be wage labour. One thus sees what a deep understanding of this social relation of production is possessed by e.g. a Bastiat, who says the form of the wage system is not to blame for the evils the socialists complain of. //More on this subject later.// The fellow thinks that if the workers had enough money to live until the sale of the commodity, they would be able to share with the capitalists on more favourable terms. That is, in other words, if they were not wage labourers, if they could sell the product of their labour instead of their labour capacity. The fact that they cannot do this makes them precisely wage labourers and their buyers capitalists. Thus the essential form of the relation is regarded by Mr. Bastiat as an accidental circumstance.[97]

There are a few more questions attached to this, which will be looked at immediately. First, though, one more remark. We have seen that by adding new labour in the labour process—and this is the only labour he sells to the capitalist—the worker preserves the value of the labour objectified in the material of labour and the means of labour. And indeed he does this for nothing. It happens in virtue of the living quality of labour as labour, not that a fresh quantity of labour would be required for this.

//Where e.g. the instrument of labour has to be improved, etc., requires new labour for its maintenance, it is the same thing as if a new tool or an aliquot part of a new means of labour were to be bought by the capitalist and thrown into the labour process.//

The capitalist receives this for nothing. Just *as the worker advances his labour to him, in that it is only paid for after it is objectified.* (This is a point to be made against those who speak of the price of labour's being advanced.[98] The labour is paid for after it has been provided. The product as such does not concern the worker. The commodity he sells has already passed into the possession of the capitalist before it is paid for.)

But yet a further result comes to pass owing to the whole transaction, and the capitalist also gets this for nothing. After the end of a labour process of, for example, one day the worker has turned the money he receives from the capitalist into means of subsistence and has thereby preserved, reproduced his labour capacity, so that the same exchange between capital and labour capacity can begin again afresh.* But this is a condition for the valorisation of capital, for its further existence in general, which allows it to be a continuous relation of production. This reproduction of labour capacity as such means the reproduction of the sole condition under which commodities can be transformed into capital. The worker's consumption of his wage is productive for the capitalist not only because the latter receives in return labour, and a greater quantity of labour than is represented by the wage, but also because it reproduces for him the condition [for capital's further existence], labour capacity. Hence the result of the capitalist process of production is not just commodities and surplus value; it is the *reproduction of this relation* itself (its reproduction on an ever growing scale, as will be seen later).[100]

In so far as labour is objectified in the production process, it is objectified as *capital*, as not-labour, and in so far as capital yields itself up in the exchange to the worker, it only turns into the means of reproducing his *labour capacity*. At the end of the process, therefore, its original conditions, its original factors and their original [mutual] relation, are again in place. The relation of *capital and wage labour* is therefore reproduced by this mode of production just as much as commodities and surplus value are

---

* [II-61] "The material undergoes changes.... The instruments, or machinery, employed ... undergo changes. The several instruments, in the course of production, are gradually destroyed or consumed.... The various kinds of food, clothing, and shelter, necessary for the existence and comfort of the human being, are also changed. They are consumed, from [II-62] time to time, and their value reappears, in that new vigor imparted to his body and mind, which forms a fresh capital, to be employed again in the work of production" (F. Wayland, *The Elements of Political Economy*, Boston, 1843, [p.] 32). [II-62] [a][99]

---

[a] Marx quotes in English.— *Ed.*

produced. All that emerges at the end of the process is what entered at the start: on the one hand objectified labour as capital, on the other hand objectless labour as mere labour capacity, so that the same exchange is constantly repeated afresh. In colonies, where the domination of capital—or the basis of capitalist production—is not yet sufficiently developed, so that the worker receives more than [II-61] is required for the reproduction of his labour capacity and very soon becomes a peasant farming independently, etc., the original relation is not constantly reproduced; hence great lamentations by the capitalists and attempts to introduce the relation of capital and wage labour artificially (*Wakefield*[67]).

Linked with this reproduction of the total relationship—with the fact that by and large the wage labourer only emerges from the process to find himself in the same position in which he entered it—is the importance for the workers of the nature of the original conditions under which they reproduce their labour capacity and of the average wage or the limits within which they have traditionally to live in order to live as workers. This is more or less obliterated in the course of capitalist production, but it takes a long time. What means of subsistence are needed to maintain the worker—i.e. what kind of means of subsistence and in what quantity in general they are considered necessary—on this see *Thornton*.[a] But this is a striking demonstration that wages are made up of means of subsistence alone, and that the worker continues to result merely as labour capacity. The difference lies only in the more or the less of a thing that counts as the measure of his requirements. He always works only for consumption; the difference is only in whether his consumption costs (=production costs) are larger or smaller.

Wage labour is therefore a necessary condition for the formation of capital and it remains the constant, necessary prerequisite for capitalist production. Therefore although the first act, the exchange of money for labour capacity or the sale of labour capacity, does not enter as such into the direct production process (labour process), it does enter into the production of the whole relation. Without it, money does not become capital, labour does not become wage labour and therefore the whole labour process is not brought under the control of capital, either, not subsumed under it; hence the production of surplus value in the manner defined earlier does not take place either. This question—

---

[a] W. Th. Thornton, *Over-population and its Remedy*, London, 1846, p. 19.—*Ed.*

of whether this first act belongs to the production process of capital—is the actual subject of discussion in the dispute between the economists as to whether the part of capital laid out in wages—or, what is the same thing, the means of subsistence for which the worker exchanges his wage—does constitute a part of capital. (See Rossi, Mill, Ramsay.)[101]

The question: are *wages productive* is in fact the same misunderstanding as the question: is capital productive?

In the latter case capital is understood to mean nothing other than the use values of the commodities in which it exists (the physical objects which comprise capital), not the formal determination, the definite social relation of production of which the commodities are the vehicles. In the former case the emphasis is on the fact that the wage as such does not enter into the direct labour process.

It is not the price of a machine which is productive but the machine itself, to the extent that it functions as a use value in the labour process. When the value of the machine reappears in the value of the product, the price of the machine in the price of the commodity, this only occurs because it has a price. This price produces nothing; it does not preserve, still less does it increase itself. From one aspect wages are a deduction from the productivity of labour; for surplus labour is limited by the labour time the worker requires for his own reproduction, preservation. Hence the surplus value is limited. From another aspect they are productive, in so far as they produce labour capacity itself, which is the source of valorisation altogether and the basis of the whole relation.

The portion of capital expended in wages, i.e. the price of labour capacity, does not enter directly into the labour process, although it does indeed in part, since the worker has to consume means of subsistence several times a day in order to continue with his work. Nevertheless, this consumption process falls outside the actual labour process. (Like coal, oil, etc., in the case of the machine, perhaps?[102]) As *matière instrumentale* of labour capacity? The preposited values only enter into the valorisation process at all to the extent that they are available. With the wage it is different, for this is reproduced; replaced by fresh labour. In any case, if wages themselves—split up into means of subsistence—are regarded merely as the coal and oil needed to keep the machine of labour in motion, they only enter into the labour process as use values to the extent to which they are consumed by the worker as means of subsistence and they are productive to the extent to which they keep him in motion as a working machine. But they do this in so far as they are means of subsistence, not because these means of subsistence [II-62] have a price. The price of these means of subsistence, however, the wage, does not come in here, for the worker must reproduce it. With the consumption of the means of subsistence the value contained in them is annihilated. He replaces this value with a fresh quantity of labour. It is therefore this labour which is productive, not its price.

//We have seen that the value contained in the material and means of labour is simply preserved by their being used up as material and means of labour, hence by their becoming factors of new labour, hence by the addition of new labour to them.[a]

Let us now assume [that this is done] in order to carry on a production process on a particular scale—and this scale is itself determined, for only necessary labour time is to be employed, hence only as much labour time as is necessary at the given social stage of development of the productive forces. This given stage of development is however expressed in a certain quantity of machinery, etc., a certain quantity of products required for fresh production. Hence do not weave with a handloom when the POWERLOOM is predominant, etc. In other words, in order that only necessary labour time be applied, labour must be placed in conditions which correspond to the mode of production. These conditions are themselves expressed as a certain quantity of machinery, etc., in short as means of labour which are prerequisites for ensuring that only as much labour time be employed for the manufacture of the product as is necessary at the given stage of development. Thus to spin yarn at least a minimum size of factory is needed, a steam engine with so and so much horsepower, MULES with so and so many spindles, etc. Hence in order to preserve the value contained in these conditions of production— and spinning with machines in turn implies that a definite quantity of cotton must be consumed every day—it is necessary not only to add fresh labour but to add a *certain quantity* of that labour, so that the quantity of material determined by the stage of production itself should be used up as material, and that the particular time during which the machine must be in motion (must be utilised every day as instrument) should really be available as the machine's period of utilisation.

If I have a machine which is constructed in such a way as to require the spinning of 600 lbs of cotton a day, and if 1 working

---

[a] See this volume, pp. 70-80.— *Ed.*

day is needed to spin 6 lbs, 100 working days must be absorbed by these means of production, so as to preserve the value of the machinery. It is not that the fresh labour is in any way employed in the preservation of this value; all it does is add new value, while the old value re-appears unchanged in the product. But the old value is only preserved by the addition of new value. To re-appear in the product it must proceed as far as the product. Hence if 600 lbs of cotton must be spun so that the machinery is used as machinery, this 600 lbs must be transformed into product, i.e. there must be added to it the quantity of labour time which is necessary to transform it into product. In the product itself the value of the 600 lbs of cotton and the aliquot part of the machine that has been worn out simply reappears; the freshly added labour changes nothing in this, but it increases the value of the product. One part of it replaces the price of the wage (of labour capacity); another creates surplus value. If, however, the whole of this labour had not been added, the value of the raw material and the machinery would not have been preserved either. This part of the labour, in which the worker reproduces only the value of his own labour capacity, hence only adds this afresh, therefore preserves only the part of the value of material and instrument which has absorbed this quantity of labour. The other part of the labour, which creates the surplus value, preserves a further component of the value of the material and the machinery.

Let us assume that the raw material (the 600 lbs) costs 600d.=50s.=£2 10s. The worn out machinery=£1, but the 12 hours of labour add £1 10s. (replacement of wage, and surplus value), so that the total price of the commodity=£5. Assuming the wage amounts to £1, 10s. expresses the surplus labour. Value preserved in the commodity=£2 10s., or half of it [of the £5]. The total product of the working day (one may imagine that this is a working day×100, i.e. a working day of 100 workers, since each one works for 12 hours)=£5. This makes 8 $\frac{1}{3}$s. per hour, or 8s. 4d. In one hour, therefore, 4s. 2d. of raw material and machinery is replaced and 4s. 2d. is added in labour (necessary and surplus labour).

The product of 6 hours of labour is [II-63]=50s.=£2 10s.; preserved in this are raw material and machinery to the value of £1 5s. But in order to use machines so productively, 12 hours must be worked, hence as much raw material must be consumed as 12 hours of labour will absorb. The capitalist can therefore view the matter like this: in the first 6 hours alone the price of the raw material is replaced, amounting to precisely £2 10s. (50s.), the value of the product of 6 hours of labour. 6 hours of labour can only preserve, through the labour thereby added, the value of the material needed for 6 hours of labour. But the capitalist makes his calculations as if the first 6 hours had merely preserved the value of the cotton and machinery, because he must use his machine as a machine, let 12 hours be worked, hence also consume 600 lbs of cotton, in order to extract a definite surplus value. On our assumption, however, the *value of the cotton was £1 10s.=30s.*, $^3/_{10}$ of the whole.[103]

To simplify matters—since the figures are here a matter of indifference—let us assume that £2 worth of cotton (hence 80 lbs, each lb. costing 6d.) is spun in 12 hours of labour; that £2 worth of machinery is used up in 12 hours of labour; and finally that £2 of value is added by fresh labour, of which £1 for wages, £1 for surplus value, surplus labour. £2 (40s.) for 12 hours would come to $3^1/_3$s. per hour (3s. 4d.), expressing the value of an hour of labour in money; similarly $3^1/_3$s. worth of cotton is used up each hour, on our assumption $6^2/_3$ lbs; lastly $3^1/_3$s. worth of machinery is worn out each hour. The value of the commodities finished each hour=10s. But of this 10s. $6^2/_3$s. (6s. 8d.) or $66^2/_3$% is merely preposited value, which only re-appears in the commodity because $3^1/_3$s. of machinery and $6^2/_3$ lbs of cotton are required to absorb 1 hour of labour; because they have entered into the labour process as material and machinery—as material and machinery in these proportions—hence the exchange value contained in this quantity [of material and machinery] has gone over to the new commodity, the twist for example.

The value of the yarn produced in 4 hours=40s. or £2, of which in turn $^1/_3$ (namely $13^1/_3$s.) is newly added labour, and $^2/_3$ or $26^2/_3$s. is merely the preservation of the value contained in the worked up material and the machinery. And indeed this is only preserved because the new value of $13^1/_3$s. is added to the material, i.e. 4 hours of labour are absorbed in it; or this is the quantity of material and machinery needed by the 4 hours of spinning labour for its realisation. In these 4 hours no value has been created apart from the 4 hours of labour which, objectified,=$13^1/_3$s. But the value of the commodity, or of the product of these 4 hours, $^2/_3$ of which is preposited value preserved,=£2 (or 40s.), is exactly equal to the value of the cotton which needs to be spun (consumed) in 12 hours of labour by the spinning process. If, therefore, the manufacturer sells the product of the first 4 hours, he has thereby replaced the value of the cotton which he requires over the 12 hours, or which he requires so as to absorb 12 hours of labour time. But why? Because on our assumption the value of the cotton that enters into the product of 12 hours=$^1/_3$ of the value of the total product. In $^1/_3$ of the labour time he consumes only $^1/_3$ of the cotton and therefore only preserves the value of this one third. If he adds another $^2/_3$ of labour, he thereby consumes $^2/_3$ more cotton and in 12 hours he has preserved in the product the total value of the cotton, because all 80 lbs of cotton have really entered into the product, into the labour process. Now, if he were to sell the product of 4 hours of labour, whose value=$^1/_3$ of the total product, which is also the part of the value of the total product formed by the cotton, he might imagine that he had reproduced the value of the cotton in these first 4 hours, that it had been reproduced in 4 hours of labour. In actual fact, however, only $^1/_3$ of the cotton enters these 4 hours, hence only $^1/_3$ of its value. He assumes that the cotton consumed in the 12 hours was reproduced in the 4 hours. But the calculation only works because he included in the cotton $^1/_3$ for the instrument and $^1/_3$ for labour (objectified), which together form $^2/_3$ of the price of the product of the 4 hours. They=26$^2/_3$s., and in price therefore=53$^1/_3$ lbs of cotton. If he were only to work for 4 hours, he would only have in his commodity $^1/_3$ of the value of the total product of 12 hours. Since the cotton forms $^1/_3$ of the value of the total product, he can reckon that in the product of 4 hours he brings forth the value of the cotton needed for 12 hours of labour.

[II-64] If he works for a further 4 hours, this again=$^1/_3$ of the value of the total product, and since the machinery=$^1/_3$ of the latter, he can imagine that in the 2nd third of the labour time he has replaced the value of the machinery needed for 12 hours. Indeed, if he sells the product of this 2nd third, or of these other 4 hours, the value of the machinery used up in 12 hours has been replaced. On this calculation the product of the last 4 hours contains neither raw material nor machinery, whose value it would include, but simply labour. Newly created value, therefore, so that 2 hours=the reproduced wage (£1) and 2 hours are surplus value, surplus labour (also £1). In reality, the labour added in the last 4 hours only adds 4 hours of value, hence 13$^1/_3$s. But it is presupposed that the value of the raw material and means [of labour], which enter to 66$^2/_3$% into the product of these 4 hours, merely replaces the labour added. The value added by labour in the 12 hours is thus conceived as if it were added by labour in 4 hours. The whole calculation comes out because it is presupposed that $^1/_3$ of the labour time not only creates itself but also the value of the $^2/_3$ of the preposited values contained in the labour's product.[a]

If it is assumed in this way that the product of a whole third part of the labour time is merely the value added by labour—although this value is only $^1/_3$—the result is naturally the same as if over 3×4 hours the real third part were calculated on labour and the $^2/_3$ on the preposited values. This calculation may be quite practical for the capitalist, but it entirely distorts the real relationship and leads to the greatest absurdity, if it is supposed to have theoretical validity. The *preposited* value of raw material and machinery alone forms $66^2/_3\%$ of the new commodity, whilst the added labour only forms $33^1/_3\%$. The $66^2/_3\%$ represents 24 hours of objectified labour time; how ridiculous therefore the requirement that the 12 hours of new labour should objectify not only itself but in addition a further 24 hours, hence 36 hours altogether.

The point, then, is this:

The price of the product of 4 hours of labour, i.e. of a third of the total working day of 12 hours, $=^1/_3$ of the price of the total product. According to our assumption, the price of the cotton forms $^1/_3$ of the price of the total product. Hence the price of the product of 4 hours of labour, of $^1/_3$ of the total working day, $=$ the price of the cotton that enters into the total product, or is spun in 12 hours of labour. The manufacturer therefore says that the first 4 hours of labour replace only the price of the cotton that is consumed during the 12 hours of labour. But in fact the price of the product of the first 4 hours of labour $=^1/_3$ of the value added in the labour process, i.e. $13^1/_3$s. labour (in our example), $13^1/_3$s. cotton, and $13^1/_3$s. machinery, the last two components only re-appearing in the price of the product because they have been consumed by the four hours' labour in their shape as use values, hence re-appear in a new use value, and have therefore preserved their old exchange value.

What is added in the 4 hours to the $26^2/_3$s. of cotton and machinery (which possessed this value before they entered into the labour process, and only re-appear in the value of the new product because they have entered into the new product through the agency of the four-hour spinning process) is nothing other than $13^1/_3$s., i.e. the newly added labour. (The quantity of newly added labour time.) If we therefore deduct the 4 hours from the

---

[a] This should read: "...but also the value of the preposited values, contained in the labour's product to the amount of $^2/_3$ of that product".— *Ed.*

price of the product, the $26\,^2/_3$s. advanced from the 40s., only $13\,^1/_3$s. remains as value really created in the process, the four hours of labour expressed in money. If now $^2/_3$ of the price of the product, namely the one third or $13\,^1/_3$s. which represents the machinery, and the other third or $13\,^1/_3$s. which represents the labour, is evaluated in cotton, there emerges the price of the cotton that is consumed in the 12 hours.

In other words: In 4 hours of labour time only 4 hours of labour time is in fact added to the values previously present. But these values appear again—the values of the quantities of cotton and machinery—because they have absorbed this 4 hours of labour time or because as factors in the spinning they have become constituents of the yarn. The price of the cotton which re-appears in the value of the product of 4 hours of labour therefore=only the value of the quantity of cotton which has really entered as material into this 4-hour labour process, has been consumed; hence it=$13\,^1/_3$s., according to the [original] assumption. But the *price* of the total product of 4 hours of labour=the *price* of the cotton consumed in 12 hours, because the product of 4 hours of labour time=$^1/_3$ of the total product of 12 hours, and the price of the cotton constitutes $^1/_3$ of the price of the total product of 12 hours.

[II-65] What is true of 12 hours of labour is true of one hour. The proportion between 4 hours and 12 hours is the same as between $^1/_3$ hour and 1 hour. Hence in order to simplify the whole example even more let us reduce it to 1 hour. On the given assumption the value of the product of 1 hour=10s., of which $3\,^1/_3$s. is cotton ($6\,^2/_3$ lbs of cotton), $3\,^1/_3$ machinery, and $3\,^1/_3$ labour time. If an hour of labour time is added, the value of the whole product=10s. or 3 hours of labour time, because the values of the material consumed and the machinery consumed, which re-appear in the new product, the yarn,=$6\,^2/_3$s., which=2 hours of labour on our assumption. The manner in which the values of the cotton and the spindle re-appear in the value of the yarn and the manner in which the freshly added labour enters into it are now to be distinguished.

Firstly: The value of the whole product=3 hours of labour time, or 10s. Of this, 2 hours were labour time contained in the cotton and spindle and *in existence prior to* the labour process, i. e. they were values of cotton and spindle before these entered into the labour process. They therefore simply re-appear, are merely preserved, in the value of the total product, of which they form $^2/_3$. The excess of the value of the new product over the values of its material constituents is only=$^1/_3$,=3$^1/_3$s. This is the sole new value created in this labour process. The old values, which existed independently of it, have merely been preserved.

But, *secondly*: How have they been preserved? Through being applied by living labour as material and means, through being consumed by it as factors in the formation of a new use value, that of yarn. The labour has only preserved their exchange value because it related to them as use values, i. e. consumed them as the elements in the formation of a new use value, of yarn. The exchange values of the cotton and the spindle therefore re-appear in the exchange value of the yarn, not because labour in general, abstract labour, pure labour time—labour as it forms the element of exchange value—has been added to them, but this particular, real labour, spinning, useful labour which is realised in a particular use value, in yarn, and which as this specific purposeful activity consumes cotton and spindle as its use values, ulilises them as its factors, making them, through its own purposeful activity, into the formative elements of yarn.

If the spinner—therefore the labour of spinning—were able to convert 6$^2/_3$ lbs of cotton into yarn in half an hour instead of 1 hour with a more ingenious machine, which nevertheless had the same value relation, the value of the product would=3$^1/_3$s. (for cotton)+3$^1/_3$s. (for machine)+1$^2/_3$s. of labour, since half an hour of labour time would be expressed in 1$^2/_3$s. on our assumption. The value of the product would therefore=8$^1/_3$s., in which the value of the cotton and the machinery would re-appear entirely, as in the first case, although the labour time added to them would amount to 50% less than in the first case. They would re-appear entirely, because no more than half an hour of spinning was required to convert them into yarn. Hence they re-appear entirely because they entered entirely into the product of half an hour's spinning, into the new use value, yarn. The labour, so far as it preserves them as exchange values, does so only to the extent that it is real labour, a specific purposeful activity aimed at producing a particular use value. It does this as spinning, not as abstract social labour time which is indifferent to its content. Only as *spinning* does the labour preserve here the values of cotton and spindle in the product, the yarn.

On the other hand, in this process in which it preserves the exchange values of cotton and spindle the labour, spinning, relates to them not as exchange values, but as use values, elements of this particular labour, spinning. If by using certain machinery the spinner can convert 6$^1/_3$ lbs of cotton into yarn, it is for this process quite irrelevant whether the lb. of cotton costs 6d. or 6s., for he consumes it in the spinning process as cotton, as the material of spinning. There must be as much of this material as is required to absorb 1 hour of spinning labour. The price of the material has nothing to do with this. The same applies to the machinery. If the same machinery cost only half the price and performed the same service, this would not affect the spinning process in any way. The sole condition for the spinner is that he should possess material (cotton) and spindle (machinery) to the extent, in such *quanta*, as are required for spinning over the course of an hour.[a] The values or prices of cotton and spindle do not concern the spinning process as such. They are the result of the labour time objectified in themselves. They therefore only re-appear in the product to the extent that they were preposited to it as given values, and they re-appear only because the commodities cotton and spindle are required as use values, in their material determinateness, for the spinning of yarn, because they enter as factors into the spinning process.

On the other hand, however, spinning adds to the value of cotton and spindle a new value not to the extent that it is this particular labour of spinning but only because it is labour in general, and the labour time of the spinner is general labour time, for which it is a matter of indifference whatever [II-66] use value it is objectified in and whatever specific useful character, specific purpose it has, or whatever the specific kind or mode of existence of the labour as whose time (measure) it is present. An hour of spinning labour is here equated with an hour of labour time as such (whether this=one hour or several has no bearing on the matter). This hour of objectified labour time adds to the combination of cotton and spindle $3\,^1/_3$s., for example, because this sum objectifies the same labour time in money.

If the 5 lbs of yarn (6 lbs of spun COTTON) [104] could be produced in half an hour instead of a whole hour, the same use value would be preserved at the end of half an hour as in the other case at the end of the whole hour. The same quantity of use value of the same quality, 5 lbs of yarn of a given quality. The labour, to the extent that it is concrete labour, spinning, activity directed at producing a use value, would have achieved in the half hour as much as previously in the whole hour, it would have created the same use value. As spinning it achieves the same in both cases, although the duration of the spinning is twice as long in one case

---

[a] Above the words "an hour" Marx wrote: "a definite time".— *Ed.*

as in the other. To the extent that labour itself is use value, i.e. purposeful activity directed at producing a use value, the necessary time required, the time labour must last, to produce this use value is completely irrelevant; whether labour needs 1 hour or $^1/_2$ hour to spin 5 lbs of yarn. On the contrary. The less time it needs to produce the same use value, the more productive and useful it is. But the value it adds, the value it creates, is measured purely by the labour's duration. In 1 hour, the labour of spinning adds twice as great a value as in $^1/_2$, and in 2 hours twice as great a value as in one, etc. The value it adds is measured by the labour's own duration and, as value, the product is nothing but the materialisation of a definite amount of labour time in general. It is not the product of this specific labour of spinning, or spinning only comes into consideration to the extent that it is labour in general and its duration is labour time in general. The values of cotton and spindle are preserved because the labour of spinning converts them into yarn, hence because they are employed as the material and means of this specific mode of labour; the value of the 6 lbs of cotton is only increased because it has absorbed 1 hour of labour time; in the product, yarn, 1 hour more of labour time is objectified than was contained in the value elements cotton and spindle.

However, labour time can only be added to existing products or, in general, to existing material of labour to the extent that it is the time of a specific labour, which relates to the material and means of labour as to *its own* material and means; hence 1 hour of labour time can only be added to the cotton and the spindle in that an hour of spinning labour is added to them. The fact that their values are preserved derives merely from the specific character of the labour, from its material determinateness, from its being spinning, precisely the particular labour for which cotton and spindle serve as the means for the production of yarn; and further, from its being living labour in general, purposeful activity. The fact that value is added to them derives merely from spinning labour's being labour in general, abstract social labour in general, and from the hour of spinning labour being equivalent to an hour of social labour in general, an hour of social labour time. Hence the values of the material and means of labour are preserved and re-appear as value components in the total value of the product merely through the process of valorisation—which is in fact merely an abstract expression for actual labour—through the process of adding new labour time—since this must be added in a particular useful and purposeful form. But the work is not done twice, once to add value, the next time to preserve the existing values; instead, since the *labour time can only be added in the form of useful labour, specific labour, like spinning, it automatically preserves the values of material and means* [of labour] *by adding new value to them, i.e. by adding labour time.*

It is now clear, furthermore, that the quantity of existing values preserved by the new labour stands in a definite relation to the quantity of value the new labour adds to them, or that the quantity of already objectified labour that is preserved stands in a definite relation to the quantity of new labour time that is added, is objectified for the first time; that, in a word, a definite relation occurs between the direct labour process and the valorisation process.

If the labour time *necessary* to spin 6 lbs of cotton, using up x amount of machinery, is 1 hour under given general conditions of production, only 6 lbs of cotton can be converted into yarn in the one hour and only x amount of machinery can be used up, hence only 5 lbs of yarn can be produced; so that for every hour of labour by which the value of the yarn is higher than the value of the cotton and x spindles there would be 2 hours of labour (of objectified labour time), 6 lbs of cotton and x spindles ($3\,^1/_3$s.) preserved in the yarn. Cotton can only be valorised (i.e. obtain a surplus value) by 1 hour of labour, $3\,^1/_3$s., in so far as 6 lbs of cotton and x amount of machinery is used up; on the other hand, these can only be used up, and therefore their values can only re-appear in the yarn, if 1 hour of labour time is added. Thus if the value of 72 lbs[104] of cotton is to re-appear in the product [II-67] as a value component of the yarn, 12 hours of labour must be added. A definite quantity of material only absorbs a definite quantity of labour time. Its value is only preserved in proportion as it absorbs the latter (with a given productivity of labour). Therefore the value of the 72 lbs of cotton cannot be preserved unless it is all spun into yarn. But this requires a labour time of 12 hours, on our assumption.

If the productivity of labour—i.e. the quantity of use value it can provide in a definite time—is given, the quantity of given values it preserves depends purely on its *own duration*; or the amount of value of material [and] means [of labour] that is preserved depends purely on the labour time that is added, hence on the measure in which new value is created. The preservation of values falls and rises in direct proportion to the fall or rise in the addition of value. If on the other hand the material and means of labour are given, their preservation as values depends purely on the productivity of the labour added, on whether this labour needs more or less time to convert them into a new use value. Here, therefore, the preservation of the given values stands in an inverse relation to the addition of value,[a] i.e. if the labour is more productive, they require less labour time to be preserved; and vice versa.

// But now a peculiar circumstance comes into the picture, through the division of labour, and still more through machinery.

Labour time as the element, substance, of value is *necessary labour time*; hence labour time required under given general social conditions of production. If for example 1 hour is the labour time necessary for the conversion of 6 lbs of COTTON into yarn, it is the duration of a labour of spinning which needs certain conditions for its realisation: e.g. a MULE with so and so many spindles, a steam engine with such and such horse-power, etc. The whole of this apparatus would be necessary to convert 6 lbs of COTTON into yarn over a period of 1 hour. But this CASE belongs to a later discussion.[b]//

Now back to our example. 6 lbs of cotton spun in one hour. Value of the cotton=3$\frac{1}{3}$s., value of the spindle, etc., used up=3$\frac{1}{3}$s., value of the labour added=3$\frac{1}{3}$s. Therefore value of the product=10s. The given values=2 hours of labour, as the cotton and the spindle are each equal to 1 hour of labour. The price of the total product at the end of the hour=the sum of prices;=10s.; or 3 hours of objectified labour time, of which 2 hours, the hours accounted for by the cotton and the spindle, merely re-appear in the product, and 1 hour alone represents the creation of new value or added labour. The price of each of the factors forms $\frac{1}{3}$ of the total price of the product of 1 hour of labour. Hence the price of the product of $\frac{1}{3}$ of an hour of labour=the price of $\frac{1}{3}$ of the total product, hence=the price of the labour, or cotton, or machinery, contained in the total product, as each of these 3 elements of the total product constitutes $\frac{1}{3}$ of its price. Therefore, if $\frac{1}{3}$ of an hour's work is done, the product=2 lbs of yarn of a value of 3$\frac{1}{3}$s., with which I could buy cotton to the amount of 6 lbs. Or the price of the product of $\frac{1}{3}$ of an hour=the price of the cotton consumed in a whole hour of labour. The price of the 2nd third=the price of the machinery used up. The price of the product, e.g. $\frac{1}{3}$ of an hour=the price of the whole of the labour added (both the part

[a] Above "the addition of value" Marx wrote "labour productivity".— Ed.
[b] See this volume, pp. 318-43.— Ed.

which constitutes an equivalent for the wage and the part which constitutes surplus value or profit).

The manufacturer can therefore calculate as follows: I work $1/3$ of an hour to pay the price of the cotton, $1/3$ of an hour to replace the price of the machinery worn out, and $1/3$ of an hour of which $1/6$ replaces wages, $1/6$ forms the surplus value. Correct as this calculation is in practice, it is completely absurd if it is meant to explain the real formation of value (valorisation process) and therefore the relation between necessary and surplus labour. In particular the preposterous notion creeps in here that $1/3$ of an hour of labour creates or replaces the value of the cotton that has been used, $1/3$ replaces the value of the worn out machinery, while $1/3$ forms the newly added labour or the newly created value, which is the common fund for wages and profit. It is in fact only a trivial method of expressing the relation in which the given values of cotton and means of labour re-appear in ,the product of the whole of the labour time (the hour's labour), or the relation in which given values, objectified labour, are preserved in the labour process by the addition of an hour of labour time.

If I say: the price of the product of $1/3$ of an hour of labour=the price of the cotton spun in a whole hour of labour, let us say=the price of 6 lbs of cotton, 3 $1/3$s., I know that the product of 1 hour of labour=3 times the product of $1/3$ of an hour of labour. If, then, the price of the product of $1/3$ of an hour of labour=the price of the cotton which is spun in $3/3$, or 1 hour of labour, this only means that the price of the cotton=$1/3$ of the price of the total product, that 6 lbs of cotton enter into the total product, hence its value re-appears and this value forms $1/3$ of the value of the total product. Ditto with the value of the machinery. Ditto with the labour.

If I therefore say that the price of the product of $2/3$ of the time that labour is [II-68] in general carried on, i. e. for example the price of the product of $2/3$ of the hour of labour=the price of the material and the price of the machinery which is worked up in $3/3$ or 1 hour of labour, this is only another way of expressing the fact that the prices of the material and means of labour enter to an extent of $2/3$ into the price of the total product of the hour, hence the hour of labour added is only $1/3$ of the whole value objectified in the product. The fact that the *price of the product* of a part of the hour, $1/3$, or $2/3$, etc., is equal to the price of the raw material, the machinery, etc., definitely does not mean, therefore, that the price of the raw material, the machinery, is produced or even *reproduced* in the proper sense of the word in the course of $1/3$ or

$^2/_3$, etc., of an hour; it means rather that the price of these partial products, or these products of aliquot parts of labour time=the price of the raw material, etc., which re-appears, is preserved, in the total product.

The absurdness of the other conception is best seen if one looks at the final third, which represents the price of the labour added, the quantity of value added, or the quantity of new objectified labour. The *price of the product* of this last third is on our assumption equal to $1\,^1/_9$s. of cotton,$=^1/_3$ of an hour of labour;$+1\,^1/_9$s. of machinery$=^1/_3$ of an hour of labour;$+^1/_3$ of an hour of labour, which is, however, newly added. The sum total therefore$=^3/_3$ of an hour of labour, or 1 hour of labour. This price is therefore, in fact, the monetary expression of the whole of the labour time added to the raw material. But according to the confused notion mentioned earlier $^1/_3$ of an hour of labour would be represented by $3\,^1/_3$s., i.e. by the product of $^3/_3$ of an hour of labour. Similarly in the first third, where the *price of the product* of $^1/_3$ of an hour of labour=the price of the cotton. This price consists of the price of 2 lbs of cotton at $1\,^1/_9$s. ($^1/_3$ of an hour of labour), the price of the machinery at $1\,^1/_9$s. ($^1/_3$ of an hour of labour) and $^1/_3$ of what really is newly added labour, the labour time, indeed, that was required to convert 2 lbs of cotton into yarn. The sum total therefore=1 hour of labour,$=3\,^1/_3$s. But this is also the price of the cotton that is required in $^3/_3$ of an hour of labour. In fact, therefore, the value of $^2/_3$ of an hour of labour ($=2\,^2/_9$s.) is only preserved in this first third, as in every subsequent third, of an hour of labour because x amount of cotton has been spun, and hence the value of the cotton and the machinery used up re-appears. Only the $^1/_3$ of newly objectified labour has been added to this as new value.

But in this way it does look as if the manufacturer is right in saying that the first 4 hours of labour (or $^1/_3$ of an hour of labour) only replace the price of the cotton he needs in 12 hours of labour, the second 4 hours of labour only replace the price of the machinery he uses up in 12 hours of labour, and the last 4 hours of labour alone form the new value, one part of which replaces the wages and the other constitutes the surplus value he gets as the result of the whole production process. He thereby forgets, however, that he is assuming that the product of the last 4 hours objectifies only newly added labour time, hence 12 hours of labour, namely the 4 hours of labour in the material, the 4 hours of labour in the machinery used up, and finally the 4 hours of labour that have really been newly added; and he obtains the result that the price of the total product consists of 36 hours of labour, 24 of which merely represent the value the cotton and the machinery had before they were worked up into yarn, while 12 hours of labour, $1/3$ of the total price, represent the newly added labour, the new value, which is exactly equal to the newly added labour. //

// The fact that the worker, placed face to face with money, offers his labour capacity for sale as a commodity implies [21]:

1) That the conditions of labour, the objective conditions of labour, confront him as *alien powers*, alienated conditions. Alien property. This also implies, among other things, the earth as landed property, it implies that the earth confronts him as alien property. *Mere labour capacity.*

2) That he is related as a person both to the conditions of labour, which have been alienated from him, and to his own labour capacity; that he therefore disposes of the latter as proprietor and does not himself belong among the objective conditions of labour, i. e. is not himself possessed by others as an instrument of labour. *Free worker.*

3) That the objective conditions of his labour themselves confront him as merely *objectified labour*, i. e. as value, as money and commodities; as objectified labour which only exchanges with living labour to preserve and increase itself, to valorise itself, to turn into more money, and for which the worker exchanges his labour capacity in order to gain possession of a part of it, to the extent that it consists of his own means of subsistence. Hence in this relation the objective conditions of labour appear only as *value*, which has become *more independent*, holds onto itself and aims only at increasing itself.

The whole content of the relation, and the mode of appearance of the conditions of the worker's labour alienated from labour, are therefore [II-69] present in their pure economic form, without any political, religious or other trimmings. It is a pure money-relation. Capitalist and worker. Objectified labour and living labour capacity. Not master and servant, priest and layman, feudal lord and vassal, master craftsman and journeyman, etc. In all states of society the class that rules (or the classes) is always the one that has possession of the objective conditions of labour, and the re-positories of those conditions, in so far as they do work, do so not as workers but as proprietors, and the serving class is always the one that is either itself, as labour capacity, a possession of the proprietors (slavery), or disposes only over its labour capacity (even if, as e. g. in India, Egypt, etc., it possesses land, the proprietor of which is however the king, or a caste, etc.). But all these forms are distinguished from capital by this relation being veiled in them, by appearing as a relation of masters to servants, of free men to slaves, of demigods to ordinary mortals, etc., and existing in the consciousness of both sides as a relation of this kind. In capital alone are all political, religious and other ideal trimmings stripped from this relation. It is reduced—in the consciousness of both sides—to a relation of mere purchase and sale. The conditions of labour confront labour nakedly as such, and they confront it as *objectified labour, value, money,* which knows itself as mere form of labour and only exchanges with labour in order to preserve and increase itself as *objectified labour.* The relation therefore emerges in its purity as a mere relation of production—a purely economic relation. And where relations of domination develop again on this basis, it is known that they proceed purely from the relation in which the buyer, the representative of the conditions of labour, confronts the seller, the owner of labour capacity.//[93]

Let us therefore now return to the question of the wage system.

We have seen that in the labour process—hence in the production process, to the extent that it is production of a use value, realisation of labour as purposeful activity—the values of the material and means of labour simply do not exist for labour itself.[a] They exist only as objective conditions for the realisation of labour, as objective factors of labour, and as such they are consumed by it. However, the fact that the exchange values of the material and means of labour do not enter into the labour process as such signifies, in other words, simply that they do not enter into it as commodities. The machine serves as a machine, cotton as cotton, and neither of them because they represent a definite quantity of social labour. Rather, as materialisation of this social labour their use value is extinguished in them, they are money. There are in fact labour processes in which the material costs nothing, e. g. fish in the sea, coal in the mine.

But it would be wrong to conclude from this that their character as a commodity has absolutely nothing to do with the production process; for this process produces not only use value, but exchange value, not only product, but commodity; or its product is no mere use value, but a use value with a definite exchange value, and the latter is in part determined by the exchange values which

---

[a] See this volume, p. 117.— *Ed.*

the material and means of labour themselves possess as commodities. They enter into the production process as commodities; otherwise they could not emerge from it as commodities. If one were to say, therefore, that the values of the material and means of labour had nothing to do with the production process, their quality as commodities had nothing to do with it, because they figure in the labour process not as commodities, but simply as use values, this would be the same thing as saying that it was irrelevant for the production process that it is not only a labour process, but at the same time a valorisation process; and this in turn amounts to saying that the production process takes place for personal consumption.[68] Which contradicts the presupposition. But with respect to the pure valorisation process too, their values are not productive for they merely re-appear in the product, are merely preserved.

Now let us consider the wage, or price of labour capacity. The price of labour capacity or the wage *is not productive*, i. e. if it is understood by "productive" that it must enter as an element into the labour process as such. It is the worker himself—the human being bringing his labour capacity into action—who produces use value, purposefully employs the material and means of labour, not the price at which he has sold his labour capacity. Or, when he enters into the labour process, he enters as the activation, the energy of his labour capacity—as labour. Now it can be said [II-70] that the wage comes down to the means of subsistence necessary for the worker to live as a worker, for his self-preservation as living labour capacity, in short, for the maintenance of his life during the work. The means of subsistence which keep the worker in motion as a worker enter into the labour process just as much as the coal and oil, etc., which are consumed by the machine.[102] The worker's costs of maintenance during the work are just as much a moment of the labour process as are the *matières instrumentales* consumed by the machine, etc. Even so, here too—in the case of the machine—the coal, oil, etc., in short the *matières instrumentales*, enter into the labour process as use values alone. Their prices have nothing to do with the matter. Is this also true of the price of the worker's means of subsistence, his wage?

Here the question only has importance in the following way: Are the means of subsistence the worker consumes—and which therefore form his cost of maintenance as a worker—to be viewed as if capital itself consumes them as a moment of its production process (in the way that it consumes the *matières instrumentales*)? This is of course the case in practice. Nevertheless the first act always remains an act of exchange.

The point at issue among the economists is this: Do the means of subsistence the worker consumes, which are represented by the price of his labour, the wage of labour, constitute a part of capital, just as much as the means of labour?[101] (Material and means of labour.) The means of labour are, *d'abord*,[a] also means of subsistence, as it is assumed that the individuals only confront each other as commodity owners, whether in the form of buyers or sellers[20]; hence he who lacks the means of labour has no commodity to exchange (assuming also that production for one's own consumption is OUT OF THE QUESTION; assuming that the product being considered is, in general, a commodity) and therefore no means of subsistence to get in return. On the other hand, the direct means of subsistence are equally means of labour; for in order to work he must live, and in order to live he must consume such and such an amount of the means of subsistence every day.

Labour capacity, which confronts the material conditions of its realisation, its own reality, as mere labour capacity, deprived of the object, therefore stands in the same position towards the means of subsistence or the means of labour, or both of them confront it uniformly as *capital.* Capital is admittedly money, the independent existence of exchange value, objectified general social labour. But this is only its form. Once it has to realise itself as capital—i. e. as self-preserving and self-increasing value—it must transform itself into the conditions of labour; in other words, these conditions form its material existence, they are the real use values within which it exists as exchange value. But the chief condition for the labour process is the worker himself. What is essential, therefore, is the component of capital which buys labour capacity. If there were no means of subsistence on the market, it would be pointless for capital to pay the worker in money. The money is only a promissory note the worker receives on a definite quantity of the means of subsistence available on the market. The capitalist therefore has these δυνάμει[b] and they form a component part of his power. Moreover, even if there were no capitalist production, the costs of maintenance (originally provided by nature free of charge[58]) would continue to be just as necessary conditions of the labour process as the material and means of labour. All the objective moments, however, which labour needs at all for its

---

[a] In the first place.— *Ed.*
[b] Potentially.— *Ed.*

realisation, appear as alienated from it, as standing on the side of capital, the means of subsistence no less than the means of labour.[80]

Rossi,[105] etc., want to say, or say in fact (whether they want to or not) nothing more, actually, than that *wage labour* as such is not a necessary condition of the labour process. They only forget that the same would then be true of *capital*.

// We must go into this further (in the additions[a]) in countering Say's nonsense about the same capital—but here he means value—which is *doubly* consumed, productively for the capitalist, unproductively for the worker. //

// *Property in the instrument of labour* is characteristic of guild industry, or the medieval form of labour.[106] //

The social mode of production in which the production process is subsumed under capital, or which rests on the relation of capital and wage labour, and indeed in such a way that it is the determining, dominant mode of production, we call *capitalist production*.

The worker goes through the form of circulation $C—M—C$. He sells in order to buy. He exchanges his labour capacity for money, in order to swap the money for commodities—to the extent that they are use values, means of subsistence. The purpose is individual consumption. In line with the nature of simple circulation, he can proceed at most to the formation of a hoard, through thrift and extraordinary industry; he cannot create wealth. The capitalist, in contrast, goes through $M—C—M$. He buys in order to sell. The purpose of this [II-71] movement is exchange value, i.e. enrichment.

By wage labour we understand exclusively free labour which is exchanged for capital, is converted into capital and valorises capital. All so-called *services* are excluded from this. Whatever their character otherwise, money is expended for them; it is not advanced. With them, money is always exchange value as evanescent form, a means of getting hold of a use value. There is as little connection between the services the capitalist consumes as a private person—outside the process of the production of commodities—and productive consumption, i.e. productive from the capitalist point of view, as there is between the purchase of commodities in order to consume them (not to consume them through labour) and productive consumption. No matter how

---

[a] See this volume, pp. 137-39.— Ed.

useful, etc., they are. Their content is here completely irrelevant. Of course, the services themselves are differently valued—in so far as they are estimated in economic terms—on the basis of capitalist production from under other relations of production. But an investigation of this only becomes possible once the fundamental factors of capitalist production have themselves been made clear.[107]

With all services, whether they themselves directly create commodities, e.g. the tailor who sews a pair of trousers for me; or not, e.g. the soldier who protects me, similarly the judge, etc., or the musician whose music-making I buy to provide me with aesthetic enjoyment, or the doctor I buy to set a leg back into position, it is always a matter of the material content of the labour, its usefulness, while the circumstance that it is labour is quite irrelevant to me. With wage labour, which creates capital, the content is in fact irrelevant. The particular mode of labour only counts for me in so far as it is social labour as such and therefore the substance of exchange value; money. The above-mentioned workers, performers of services, from prostitute to pope, are therefore never employed in the direct production process. // As for the rest, it would be better to put closer consideration of "productive labour" into the section "Capital and Labour".[108] // With the purchase of one kind of labour I make money, with that of the other I spend money. The one enriches, the other impoverishes. It is possible that the latter may itself be one of the conditions for making money, as policemen, judges, soldiers, executioners. But as such a condition it is always merely an "aggravating circumstance" and has nothing to do with the direct process.

We started out from circulation in order to come to capitalist production. This is also the course of events *historically*, and the development of capitalist production therefore already presupposes in every country the development of trade on another, earlier production basis. // We shall have to speak of this in more detail.[109] //

What we have to consider more closely in the following is the development of *surplus value*. In doing so we shall see that as the production of surplus value becomes the actual purpose of production or as production becomes capitalist production, the originally merely formal subsumption of the labour process under capital, of living labour under objectified, of present labour under past, considerably modifies the manner in which the labour process is itself carried on: hence the capital-relation—where it emerges in a developed form—implies a particular mode of production and development of the productive forces.[55]

// With services too I admittedly consume the labour capacity of the person performing the service; but not because the use value of the labour capacity is labour, rather because his labour has a particular use value. // [107]

ADDITIONS

It says in *An Inquiry into those Principles, Respecting the Nature of Demand and the Necessity of Consumption, Lately Advocated by Mr. Malthus etc.*, London, 1821, in reference to Say's comments in his *letters to Malthus*, Paris-Londres, 1820 (p. 36):

"THESE AFFECTED WAYS OF TALKING CONSTITUTE, IN GREAT PART, WHAT M. Say CALLS HIS *DOCTRINE*.... 'If all these propositions appear paradoxical to you, look at the *things* they express, and I venture to believe that they will then appear very simple and very rational.' DOUBTLESS; AND, AT THE SAME TIME, THEY WILL VERY PROBABLY APPEAR, BY THE SAME PROCESS, NOT AT ALL ORIGINAL OR IMPORTANT. 'Without this analysis I defy you to explain the whole of the *facts*; to explain for example how *the same* [II-72] *capital is consumed twice: productively* by a manufacturer and unproductively by his worker.' IT SEEMS TO BE AGREED 'in most parts of Europe', TO CALL A FANTASTICAL MODE OF EXPRESSION A *FACT*" (l.c., p. 110, Note XI).[a]

The joke is that exchange, in the particular case, purchase, is called by Say *consumption* of money, which is sold.

If the capitalist buys labour for 100 thalers, Say thinks these 100 thalers have been consumed twice, productively by the capitalist, unproductively by the worker. If the capitalist exchanges 100 thalers for labour capacity, he has not consumed the 100 thalers, either productively or unproductively, although he has expended them for a "productive" purpose. He has done nothing but convert them from the money form to the commodity form, and it is this commodity—labour capacity—which he has bought with the money, that he productively consumes. He could also consume it unproductively if he employed the workers to provide him with use values for his own consumption, i.e. if he used them to perform services. The money first becomes capital precisely through this exchange with labour capacity: it is not *consumed as* capital but rather produced, preserved, confirmed.

The worker on the other hand does not consume capital; the money in his hand has just ceased to be capital, and for him it is only means of circulation. (And at the same time, of course, like

---

[a] Marx quotes partly in English and partly in French.— *Ed.*

every means of circulation for which a commodity is exchanged, it is the existence of his commodity in the form of exchange value, which here is and must be, however, only an evanescent form given up in exchange for the means of subsistence.) Labour capacity, in so far as it is consumed, is converted into capital; the capitalist's money, in so far as it is consumed by the worker, is converted into means of subsistence for him and ceases to be capital or a component of capital (δυνάμει[a]) once it is transferred from the hand of the capitalist to that of the worker.

But what actually underlies Say's nonsense is this: He believes that the same value (with him capital is nothing but a *sum of values*[110]) is consumed twice, once by the capitalist, the second time by the worker. He forgets that here two commodities with the same value are being exchanged, not 1 value but 2 values are involved; money on the one hand, the commodity *(labour capacity)* on the other. What the worker consumes unproductively (i.e. without thereby creating wealth for himself) is his own labour capacity (not the money of the capitalist); what the capitalist consumes productively is not his money but the labour capacity of the worker. On both sides the consumption process is mediated through exchange.

In every purchase or sale where the purpose of the buyer is individual consumption of the commodity and the purpose of the seller is production, *the same* value would according to Say be consumed twice, productively by the seller, who converts his commodity into money (exchange value), and unproductively by the buyer, who dissolves his money into transient enjoyments. However, there are 2 commodities and 2 values involved here. Say's phrase would have a meaning only in the sense in which he does not mean it. Namely that the capitalist productively consumes the same value twice: first by his ·productive consumption of labour capacity and second by the unproductive consumption of his money by the worker, the result of which is the reproduction of labour capacity, hence the reproduction of the relation on which the functioning of capital as capital depends. Hence Malthus rightly hits on the last point. // Malthus's point is this: in so far as his consumption is, in general, a condition for his working, hence for his producing for the capitalist. //

* "He" (the workman) "is a *productive consumer to the person who employs him* and to the state but not strictly speaking *to himself*" * (Malthus, *Definitions in Political Economy*, ed. John Cazenove, London, 1853, p. 30).

---

[a] Potentially.—*Ed.*

Ramsay declares that the part of capital which is converted into the wage is not a *necessary* part of capital, but only forms part of it *accidentally* owing to the "DEPLORABLE" poverty of the workers. By FIXED CAPITAL he understands namely the material and means of labour. By CIRCULATING CAPITAL the worker's means of subsistence. He then says:

> * "*Circulating Capital* consists only of subsistence and other necessaries advanced to the workmen, previous to the completion of the produce of their labour" * (George Ramsay, *An Essay on the Distribution of Wealth*, Edinburgh, 1836, [p.] 23).
> * "Fixed capital alone, not circulating, is properly speaking a source of national wealth" * (l.c.).
> * "*Were we to suppose* the labourers not to be paid until the completion of the product, there would be no occasion whatever [II-73] for circulating capital." *

(What does that mean except that an objective condition of labour—the means of subsistence—will not assume the form of capital? This already contains the admission that these objective conditions of production are, as s u c h, not capital, but only become capital as the expression of a particular social relation of production.) (The means of subsistence will not cease to be means of subsistence; just as little would they cease to be a necessary condition of production; but they would cease to be — *capital*.)

> "Production would be just as great. This proves that * *circulating capital*[111] is not an *immediate agent* in production, *not even essential to it at all*, but *merely a convenience rendered necessary by the deplorable poverty of the mass of the people*" * (l.c., [p.] 24).

I.e., in other words: Wage labour is not an absolute, but rather a historical form of labour. It is not necessary for production that the worker's means of subsistence should confront him in an alienated form as *capital*. But the same is true of the other elements of capital and of capital in general. Conversely. If this one part of capital did not assume the form of capital, the other would not either, for the whole relation whereby money becomes capital, or the conditions of labour confront labour as an independent power, would not come into existence. What constitutes the essential form of capital therefore appears to him as "MERELY A CONVENIENCE RENDERED NECESSARY BY THE DEPLORABLE POVERTY OF THE MASS OF THE PEOPLE" [p. 24]. The means of subsistence become capital by being "ADVANCED TO THE WORKMEN" [p. 23]. The wider sense of Ramsay's remarks emerges still more clearly in the proposition:

> * "The fixed capital" * (material and means of labour) * "alone constitutes an *element of cost of production* in a national point of view" * (l. c., [p.] 26).

For the capitalist the wage, i.e. the price he pays for labour capacity, is a cost of production—*money advanced*, advanced to make more money, money that is a mere means to make money. If the worker were not a worker but a working proprietor, the means of subsistence he consumes before the product is finished would not appear to him as *costs of production* in this sense, since the whole production process would appear to him inversely only as a means to create his means of subsistence. Ramsay, on the other hand, thinks that the material and means of labour, products which must be employed, consumed, in order to create new products, are necessary conditions of the production process and must always enter into it, not only from the capitalist's standpoint but from the nation's—i.e., with him, from the point of view of production for society and not for particular classes of society. So here *capital* means nothing to him but the objective conditions of the labour process as such, and, expressing absolutely no social relation, is merely another name for the *objects* that are required in every production process, whatever social form it may have; capital is accordingly only a thing, technological-ly determined. The precise feature that makes it capital is thereby extinguished.[56] Ramsay might just as well have said: it is merely a "CONVENIENCE" that the means of production appear as value in its own right, as independent powers over against labour. If they were the ·social property of the workers, there would be no opportunity there for "fixed capital". And production would remain just the same as before.[112]

// The valorisation process is in reality nothing but the labour process in a particular social form—or a particular social form of the labour process. It is not, as it were, two distinct real processes, but *the same* process, viewed at one time in terms of its content, at the other time according to its form. Despite this, we have already seen that in the valorisation process the relation of the different factors of the labour process takes on new determinations. One further aspect should be brought out here (which will be important later on in dealing with circulation, the determination of fixed capital, etc.). The means of production, e.g. the tool, machinery, factory building, etc., is employed as a whole in the labour process; but, with the exception of the so-called *matières instrumentales*, it is only exceptionally *consumed* (all at once) in the same (single, unique) labour process. It serves in repeated processes of the same kind. But it only enters into the [II-74] valorisation process—or, what is the same thing, it only re-appears as an element in the value of the product—in so far as it is used up in the *labour process*.[113] //

Similar to Ramsay is *Rossi*. First, in *leçon* XXVII, he gives a general definition of capital.[a]

"Capital is that portion of the wealth *produced* which is *destined* for reproduction" (p. 364).

However this only applies to capital in so far as it is use value—applies to its *material* content, not to its form. No wonder, then, that the same Rossi proclaims the component of capital explicable solely from its form—the *approvisionnement*,[b] the part that is exchanged for labour capacity—to be no necessary component of capital, in fact not to be part of capital's *concept* at all. Thus he says, on the one hand, that *capital* is a necessary agent of production, and, on the other hand, that *wage labour* is not a necessary agent of production or relation of production. Actually he understands by capital only "*instrument of production*".[105] According to him one could, it is true, distinguish between *capital-instrument* and *capital-matière*, but actually the political economists are wrong to call raw materials capital; for

"Is it" (the raw material) "really an instrument of production there? Is it not rather an object which is acted upon by the instrument of production?" (*leçons. etc.*, p. 367).

Later on he says:

"*Instrument of production*, that is to say a material which operates on itself, which is at once object and subject, thing acted upon and agent" (l.c., p. 372).

He also calls capital simply "*moyen de production*"[c] on p. 372. In reference to Rossi's polemic against the idea that *approvisionnement* forms a part of capital, we must distinguish two things; or, he confuses two things.

Firstly he views wage labour in general—the capitalist's advancing of the wage—as not a necessary form of production; or wage labour as not a necessary form of labour; thereby forgetting only that *capital* is not a necessary form (i.e. not an absolute, rather merely a particular historical form) of the conditions of labour or production. In other words: the labour process can take place without being subsumed under capital; this particular social form is not a necessary prerequisite for it; the production process as such is not a necessarily capitalist production process. But here he again makes the mistake of viewing the purchase of labour

---

[a] P. Rossi, *Cours d'économie politique. Année 1836-1837*. In: *Cours d'économie politique*, Brussels, 1843. Marx quotes Rossi in French.— *Ed.*

[b] Means of subsistence, provisions.— *Ed.*

[c] Means of production.— *Ed.*

capacity by capital as not *essential* for wage labour but as something accidental. For production the conditions of production are required; but not *capital*, i.e. not the relation which emerges from the appropriation of the conditions of production by a specific class and the existence of labour capacity as a commodity. His stupidity consists in recognising wage labour (or also the independent form of capital) and seeking to argue out of existence the relation of wage labour to capital, which constitutes the former. To say that *capital* is not a necessary form of social production is merely to say that *wage labour* is only a transitory historical form of social labour.

Not only does the rise of capitalist production presuppose a historical process of the separation of the workers from the conditions of labour; capitalist production *reproduces this relation on an ever increasing scale* and gives it a sharper character.[100] This is already evident in considering the general concept of capital, and becomes still clearer later on in the context of competition, which essentially effects this separation (concentration, etc.).[114] In the actual production process the objects of which capital consists do not confront the worker as capital but as the material and means of labour.[a] He is of course conscious that they are alien property, etc., capital. But the same thing is true of his *sold* labour, which belongs not to him but to the capitalist.[b]

[II-75] *Secondly*, however, one further point creeps into the Rossian polemic. (The first point was: exchange of money for labour capacity. Rossi is right in so far as he declares that this operation is not necessary for production as such. He is wrong in so far as he views this relation, without which capitalist production would not exist at all, as an inessential, accidental moment of the latter.)

Namely this: we have seen: First the worker sells his labour capacity, i.e. temporary disposition over it.[c] This includes his bartering it for the means of subsistence that are necessary to preserve him as a worker at all, and more specifically his possession of the means of subsistence "during the work of production" [p. 370]. This is a prerequisite for his entry as a worker into the production process, and for his activation, realisation, of his labour capacity during that process. As we have seen, Rossi understands by capital nothing but the means of

---

[a] See this volume, p. 58.— *Ed.*
[b] Ibid., pp. 66-67.— *Ed.*
[c] Ibid., pp. 51, 81 and 103.— *Ed.*

production (*matière, instrument*) required for the manufacture of a new product. The question is: Do the worker's means of subsistence belong there, like, e.g., the coal, oil, etc., consumed by the machine or the fodder eaten by the cattle? In short the *matières instrumentales*.[102] Do the worker's means of subsistence belong to this category as well? With the slave there is no question but that his means of subsistence are to be counted among the *matières instrumentales*; he is a mere instrument of production, hence what he consumes is a mere *matière instrumentale*. (As we have already remarked, this confirms the point that the price of labour (the wage) does not enter into the labour process proper any more than the prices of the material and means of labour do; although all three, even if in different ways, enter into the valorisation process.[a]) To answer the question it is necessary to subdivide it into two questions:

Firstly: To consider the labour process as such, independently of capital; since the people who raise the question here call the moments of the labour process as such capital.[56] *Secondly*: To ask how far this is modified once the labour process is subsumed under capital.

Firstly, then: If we consider the labour process as such, its objective conditions are the material of labour and the means of labour, they are simply objective conditions of labour itself, as the purposeful activity of a human being directed at producing a use value.[b] The worker relates to them as subject. To be sure, he is presupposed as worker, to allow his labour capacity to function, and the provisions necessary for his subsistence, for the development of labour capacity, are therefore also presupposed. But they do not enter as such into the labour process.

He enters the process as a working proprietor. However, if the different moments of the labour process are viewed with regard to its result, the product, the relation is altered. With regard to the product all 3 moments appear as moments of its mediation, hence as means of production. The material of production, the instrument of production, and productive activity itself, are all means for the manufacture of the product, hence means of production.[c] Here the means of maintaining the machine (oil, coal, etc.), entirely leaving aside their *price*, form part of the means of production, but so equally do the means of maintaining the

---

a See this volume, pp. 117 and 131-32.— *Ed.*
b Ibid., p. 71.— *Ed.*
c Ibid., pp. 55-58.— *Ed.*

worker during the production process itself.[102] For all that, the working proprietor will continue to regard the product as such only as a means of subsistence, not his means of subsistence as prerequisites for the manufacture of the product. However, the way of looking at things does not alter the state of affairs one whit. The proportion of the means of subsistence he must consume as worker, without which his labour capacity cannot function as such at all, is just as indispensable for the production process as the coal and oil consumed by the machine. In that sense the consumption fund of society forms part of its means of production (this disappears again on further consideration, in so far as the whole production process itself appears as simply the reproduction process of society or of the social human being), and the worker's consumption is not economically distinguished within these limits from the consumption of the working horse or the machine.

Thus the part of capital that pays labour capacity or forms the wage enters into the actual production process in so far as the means of subsistence the worker consumes are directly consumed, and have to be consumed, in the production process itself. But the part of the capital given out in this way which does not enter directly into the production process also forms a part of the capital before it is exchanged for labour capacity, and for the formation of the capital-relation this is a necessary prerequisite.

[II-76] The capitalist has paid for labour capacity. The major part of the means of subsistence the workers have thus obtained is expended during the labour process itself, and necessarily so. If the workers were slaves, the capitalist would have to advance this part to them as simple *matières instrumentales*. Here the worker does this for him. For him the worker is a mere agent of production, and the means of subsistence he consumes are the coal and oil necessary to keep this agent of production in motion. This is how the capitalist sees it, and he acts accordingly. If an ox or a machine is a cheaper agent of production, the worker is replaced by one or the other. The opinion is economically incorrect in so far as it is of the essence of wage labour that the 2 processes are distinguished, namely 1) the exchange of money for labour capacity; 2) the consumption process of this labour capacity—the labour process (production process).

Let us now look in some detail at Rossi's criticisms, without coming back to the CASE considered last (under 2).

With regard to this Rossi makes the following statement:

"Those who only regard *economic science from the point of view of the entrepreneur,* and who only consider the net and exchangeable product that each entrepreneur can obtain, such people must in fact see no difference between a man, an ox and a steam-engine: in their eyes there is only one question worthy of serious attention, and that is the question of the cost price, the question of knowing how much it costs the entrepreneur to obtain what he requires from the steam, the ox, the worker" (Rossi, *De la méthode en économie politique etc.,* in *Économie politique. Recueil de monographies etc. Année 1844,* Vol. I, Brussels, 1844, p. 83).[a]

It does appear, then, that the point of view of the entrepreneur, i.e. of the capitalist, is in any case an essential moment in considering capitalist production. But that belongs to the relation of capital and labour.

Our essential concern, however, in considering Mr. Rossi is the way he on the one hand admits that *wage labour,* hence also capitalist production, is not a necessary (absolute) form of labour and production; but then repudiates this admission, being ALTOGETHER miles away from any historical understanding.

Rossi's first objection is this:

"If the worker lives from his income, if he lives from the remuneration of his labour, how can the same thing appear twice in *the phenomenon of production,* in the calculation of *productive forces,* once as the *remuneration of labour* and a second time as capital?" (*leçons,* p. 369).[b]

Here one must remark at the outset: This means, expressed in general terms, that the wage appears twice, once as relation of production, once as relation of distribution. Rossi holds this to be incorrect, and he is right as against the political economists in so far as they view the two different forms in which *the same thing* appears as two mutually independent relations which have nothing to do with each other. We shall return to this subject and demonstrate in general that the relation of production is a relation of distribution and vice versa.[62] But, in addition to this, the wage can enter into the phenomenon of production, i.e. constitute a relation of production, without entering into the *calculation of productive forces,* namely if Mr. Rossi understands by productive force not the development of the productive forces in so far as it is conditioned by the relation of production, but nothing other than the moments that belong to the labour process in general or the production process in general, as such, disregarding all particular social forms.

On the other hand: The means of subsistence form a component of capital as long as they have not yet been *exchanged*

a Marx quotes in French.— *Ed.*
b Marx quotes partly in German and partly in French.— *Ed.*

for labour capacity. This exchange would not, however, take place unless they formed a component of capital *before* it happened. If they are exchanged, they cease to be capital and become income. Indeed it is not the wage but only labour capacity that enters into the direct production process itself. If I have produced grain, it forms a part of my capital until I have sold it. It forms the income of a consumer. (At least it can do so, if it is employed in individual consumption, not in production.) But in fact the means of subsistence [II-77] continue to be a *productive force of capital* even after the worker has received it as income and consumed it as income, for the reproduction of the worker is the reproduction of the principal productive force of capital.

"One says the remuneration of the worker is capital, because the capitalist *advances* it to him. If only there were families of workers who had sufficient to subsist for a year, *wages would not exist.* The worker could say to the capitalist: you advance the capital for the common project, I will bring the labour to it; the product will be shared among us in certain proportions. As soon as the product has been realised, each of us will take his share. Then there would be no *advance* for the workers. Even if work were at a standstill, they would still consume. What they would consume belongs to the consumption fund, not to capital. Therefore: the advances for the workers are not *necessary.* Therefore *wages are not a constituent element of production. They are only of an accidental nature, a form arising from our social condition.* Capital, land, labour, on the other hand, are necessary for production. *Secondly*: The word wages is employed in a double sense. One says that wages are a capital, but what do they represent? Labour. He who says wages says labour and vice versa. Hence, if the wages advanced constituted a part of capital, one would have to speak only of 2 instruments of production: capital and land" (l.c., p[p. 369-]370).[115]

In the same way as Rossi says: if the worker possessed the means of subsistence for a year, the capitalist would not need to advance them to him, he could just as well continue: if the worker possessed the material and means of labour for a year, he would not need the interposition of the capitalist for these conditions of labour. Thus the circumstance that "material of labour and means of labour" appear as capital is "*not a constituent element of production*". "*They are only of an accidental nature, a form arising from our social condition*", which makes them into this. They would still belong to the "production fund", by no means to capital. Capital would not exist at all. If the particular form which makes labour into *wage labour* is a social accident, a particular historico-social form of labour, the same can be said of the form which makes the objective conditions of labour into *capital* or the *conditions of production* into capital. And it is the same social accident that makes labour into *wage labour* and the *conditions of production* into *capital.* Indeed, if the workers had in their possession even this one condition of production—a year's means of subsistence—their labour would not be wage labour, and they would have possession of all the *conditions of production*. They would only need to sell a part of these surplus means of subsistence in order to buy in return the means of production (material and instrument) and produce commodities themselves. What Mr. Rossi is trying to get clear about here, without entirely succeeding, is that a particular social form of production, although it may be a *historical* necessity, is not on that account an *absolute* necessity, and therefore cannot be described as an eternal, unalterable condition of production. The admission we shall accept, but not its incorrect application.

So, in order to produce it is not absolutely necessary for labour to be wage labour and therefore, among other things, for the means of subsistence to have confronted the worker originally as a component of capital. But Rossi continues: "Capital, land, labour by contrast are necessary for production." If he had said: "*Land* (material of labour, working space and in the first instance means of subsistence); *means of labour* (instruments, etc.); and *labour* by contrast are necessary for production", but "rent, capital and wage labour" are not necessarily required, the proposition would have been correct. But his way of speaking strips away from labour and land the particular social form in which they may appear in the bourgeois economy—their forms as wage labour and landed property, and allows the means of labour in contrast to retain their economic character as *capital.* He [II-78] conceives them not only as material conditions of production but in their particular social form of *capital* and therefore arrives at the absurd conclusion that capital is possible without the appropriation of the soil and without wage labour.

Further: If the wage advanced forms part of capital, says Rossi, there are only 2 instruments of production, land and capital, and not 3, as the political economists all assume, land, capital and labour. In reality, here it is a question of the simple moments of the labour process as such, and in this there figure only the material of labour (land), the means of labour (which Rossi incorrectly calls capital) and labour. But definitely not capital. Yet in so far as the whole labour process is subsumed under capital, and the 3 elements which appear in it are appropriated by the capitalist, all 3 elements, material, means, labour, appear as material elements of *capital*; they have been subsumed under a particular social relation, which has absolutely nothing to do with the labour process considered *abstractly*—i.e. in so far as it is equally common to all social forms of the labour process. It remains characteristic of Rossi that he regards the relation between the personified product of labour and living labour capacity, a relation which forms the quintessence of the relation of capital and wage labour, as an *inessential* form, a mere accident of capitalist production itself. (See the wretched *Bastiat*.[97] With Rossi there is at least an inkling that capital and wage labour are not eternal social forms of production.)

We have now already had the argument twice from Rossi that if the wage forms a part of capital (originally), the same thing appears twice. First as a relation of production and second as a relation of distribution. Secondly: that in that case one should not enumerate 3 factors of production (material, means, labour) in the labour process, but only 2, namely material (which he calls here *land*) and means of labour, which he calls here *capital*.

"What occurs between the entrepreneur and the worker? If all products were started in the morning and finished in the evening, and if there were always buyers present on the market, ready to buy the commodities offered, there would be *properly speaking no wage*. It is not so. Months, years are required to realise a product.... The *worker, who possesses only his arms*, cannot wait for the completion (the end) of the project. He says to the entrepreneur, capitalist, farmer, manufacturer what he could say to a third party, a bystander. He could propose to him (the third party) that he buy his claim on the product. He could say to him: I contribute to the production of so-and-so many lengths of cloth, will you buy the remuneration to which I am entitled? Assuming that the third person, the bystander, accepts the proposal and pays the agreed price, can one say that the money expended by the bystander forms a part of the capital of the entrepreneur? That his contract with the worker is one of the phenomena of production? No, he has made a good or bad speculation, which adds nothing to public wealth and takes nothing away from it. *That is wages*. The worker proposes to the manufacturer what he could have proposed to a third party. *The entrepreneur goes along with this arrangement in so far as it may facilitate production. But this is nothing but a second operation, an operation of a quite different nature grafted on to a productive operation. It is not a fact indispensable to production. It could disappear if labour were organised differently.* Even today there are spheres of production in which it has no place. *Wages are therefore a form of the distribution of wealth, not an element of production.* The part of the fund which the entrepreneur devotes to the payment of wages does not constitute a part of capital, any more than the sums of money a manufacturer might employ to discount bills of exchange, or to speculate on the stock-exchange. It is a *distinct operation*, which undoubtedly may promote the course of production but which cannot be called a *direct instrument of production*" (l.c., p. 370).

[II-79] Here the point emerges clearly. A *relation of production* (however the social relation between individuals within production as a whole is viewed) is "*not a direct instrument of production*". The relation of capital and wage labour, whereby the exchange of labour capacity for money is conditioned, is not a "direct instrument of production". Thus the value of the commodity is not a "direct instrument of production", although the essence of the production process changes according to whether it is only a question of the production of products as such or of the production of commodities. The *"value"* of the machine, its existence as fixed capital, etc., is not a "direct instrument of production". A machine would also be productive in a society where there were no commodities at all, no exchange value. The question is by no means whether this "relation of production could disappear in another organisation of labour"; it is rather to investigate the significance of this relation in the capitalist organisation of labour. Rossi concedes that there would be "properly speaking no wage" under such conditions (p. 370). And he will permit me to cease describing as a wage what is "not properly a wage". He only forgets that there would then be no longer any "capital proper" either.

"Since everyone could wait for the products of one's labour, the *present form of the wage could disappear.* There would be partnership between the workers and the capitalists, just as today there is partnership between the capitalists properly so called and the capitalists who are simultaneously workers" (p. 371).[a]

Rossi is not clear about what would become of the present form of production in these circumstances. To be sure, he may treat this as completely irrelevant if he views production as a purely technological process, disregarding the social forms of production, and if, on the other hand, he understands by capital nothing but a product used for the fabrication of new products. He has at least in his favour his pronouncement that the form of the wage is not a "fact indispensable to production".

"To conceive the power of labour, while ignoring the workers' means of subsistence during the work of production, is to conceive *an imagined being.* He who says labour or the power of labour says worker and means of subsistence, worker and wage ... The same element re-appears under the name of capital; as if the same thing could simultaneously form part of two distinct instruments of production" (l.c., pp. 370, 371).[a]

Pure labour capacity is indeed *"a phantom"*. But this phantom exists. Hence when the worker ceases to be able to sell his labour capacity, he starves. And capitalist production is based on the reduction of the labour capacity to such a phantom.

Sismondi is therefore correct to say:

"Labour capacity ... is *nothing* if it is not sold" (Sismondi, *Nouveaux principes etc.*, Vol. 1, p. 114).

What is stupid about Rossi is his attempt to present "wage labour" as "inessential" for capitalist production.

---

[a] Marx quotes in French.— *Ed.*

He could also say of the machine: It is the machine that constitutes part of capital, not its value. The *value* of the machine, he could say, is paid to the machine manufacturer, and perhaps consumed by him as income. The value of the machine, therefore, ought not to figure twice in the production process, the first time as the takings of the machine manufacturer, the other time as capital or a constituent of the capital of the COTTON spinner, etc.

Incidentally, it is characteristic that Rossi says wages, i.e. wage labour, would be superfluous if the workers were rich, while Mr. John Stuart Mill says they would be superfluous if labour were to be had for *nothing*:

"Wages have NO PRODUCTIVE POWER; they are the price of a PRODUCTIVE POWER. WAGES do not contribute, apart from labour, to the production of commodities //should be: to the production of products, use values //, no more than the *price of machines* contributes ALONG WITH THE MACHINES THEMSELVES. *If labour could be had without purchase*, WAGES MIGHT BE DISPENSED WITH" (John Stuart Mill, *Essays on Some Unsettled Questions of Political Economy*, London, 1844, p[p. 90-]91).

[II-80] Where the purely general form of capital as self-preserving and self-valorising value is being considered, it is declared to be something immaterial, and therefore, from the point of view of the political economist, a mere idea; for he knows of nothing but either tangible objects or ideas—relations do not exist for him. As value, capital is indifferent towards its particular material forms of existence, the use values of which it consists. These material elements do not make capital into capital.

"*Capital is always immaterial by nature, since* it is not matter which makes capital, but the *value* of that matter, value which has nothing corporeal about it" (Say, *Traité d'économie politique*, 3rd ed., Vol. 2, Paris, 1817, p. 429).

Or, Sismondi:

"Capital is a commercial *idea*" (Sismondi, LX, *Études etc.*, Vol. 2, p. 273).[a][116]

While all capitals are values, the values as such are still not capital. And so the political economists take flight once again back to the material shape of capital within the labour process. In so far as the labour process itself appears as the production process of capital and is subsumed under capital, and according to whether some specific aspect of the labour process is fixed upon (as we have seen, the labour process as such by no means presupposes capital but is a feature of all modes of production), it can be said that capital becomes a product, or is a means of production, a raw material, an instrument of labour.[56] Thus Ramsay says that raw

[a] Marx quotes Say and Sismondi in French.— *Ed.*

material and means of labour form capital.[a] Rossi says that only the instrument is actually capital.[b] The elements of the labour process are viewed here outside any specific economic determinateness. (It will become evident later that also within the labour process this *extinction of the determinateness of form* is only a semblance.[117]) The labour process (production process of capital), reduced to its simple form, does not appear as production process of capital, but as production process in the absolute sense, and capital appears here *in distinction from labour* solely in its material determinateness of raw material and instrument of labour. (But here too *labour* is in fact capital's own existence, is embodied in it.) The political economists fix on this side, which is not only an arbitrary abstraction, but one which itself vanishes in the process, in order to present capital as a necessary element of all production.[118] Of course, they only do this by arbitrarily fixing on a single aspect.

* "Labour and capital ... the one, *immediate* labour ... the other, *hoarded labour*, that which has been the result of former labour"* (James Mill, *Elements of Political Economy*, London, 1821, [p.] 75).

* "*Accumulated* labour ... immediate labour"* (R. Torrens, *An Essay on the Production of Wealth etc.*, London, 1821, Ch. 1).[119]

Ricardo, *Principles*, p. 89: "*Capital* is that part of the wealth of a country which is employed in production, and consists of FOOD, CLOTHING, TOOLS, RAW MATERIAL, MACHINERY, etc., necessary TO GIVE EFFECT TO LABOUR."

"*Capital*... is but A PARTICULAR SPECIES OF WEALTH, namely that which is destined, not TO THE IMMEDIATE SUPPLYING OF OUR WANTS, BUT TO THE OBTAINING OF OTHER ARTICLES OF UTILITY" (Torrens, l.c., p. 5).

"In the first stone which the savage flings at the wild animal he pursues, in the first stick that he seizes to strike down the fruit which hangs ABOVE HIS REACH, we see the appropriation of one article for the purpose OF AIDING IN THE ACQUISITION OF ANOTHER, and THUS DISCOVER THE ORIGIN OF CAPITAL" (Torrens, l.c., pp. 70-71).

CAPITAL "*ALL ARTICLES POSSESSING EXCHANGEABLE VALUE*", THE ACCUMULATED RESULTS OF PAST LABOUR (H. C. Carey, *Principles of Political Economy*, Part I, Philadelphia, 1837, p. 294).

"When a fund is devoted to material production, it takes the name of *capital*" (H. Storch, *Cours d'économie politique*, ed. Say, Vol. I, Paris, 1823, [p.] 207).[c]

"Wealth is only capital in so far as it serves for production" (l.c., p. 219).[c]

"The elements of the national capital are[d]: 1) improvements of the soil; 2) buildings; 3) tools or instruments of the trade; 4) means of subsistence; 5) materials; 6) completed work" (l.c., pp. 229 sq.).

[II-81] "Every productive force which is neither land nor labour is *capital*. It comprises all the forces, either completely or partially produced, that are applied to reproduction" (Rossi, l.c., p. 271).[c]

---

[a] See this volume, p. 139.— *Ed.*
[b] Ibid., p. 141.— *Ed.*
[c] Marx quotes in French.— *Ed.*
[d] Marx quotes the rest of the paragraph in French.— *Ed.*

"There is no difference between *capital* and any other part of wealth: a thing only becomes *capital* by the *use* that is made of it, that is to say, when it is employed in a productive operation, as raw material, as instrument, or as means of subsistence" (Cherbuliez, *Richesse ou pauvreté*, 1841, p. 18).[a]

But in capitalist production it is by no means just a matter of producing a product or even a commodity; what is aimed at is a greater value than was thrown into production.[b] Hence these definitions:

Capital is the part of WEALTH which is employed in production and GENERALLY FOR THE PURPOSE OF OBTAINING PROFIT (Th. Chalmers, *On Political Economy etc.*, London, 1832, 2nd ed., [p.] 75).

It is above all Malthus who has introduced this element into the definition of capital. (Sismondi's definition is more precise; since profit is already a more developed form of surplus value.[c])

* "*Capital.* That portion of the stock" (i.e. accumulated wealth) "of a country which is kept or employed with a view to profit in the production and distribution of wealth" * (T. R. Malthus, *Definitions in Political Economy*, New Ed. etc. by John Cazenove, London, 1853, [p.] 10).

* "*Antecedent labour* (capital) ... *present labour*" * (E. G. Wakefield's commentary to A. Smith, *Wealth of Nations*, Vol. 1, London, 1835, note to p[p. 230-]31).

Thus we have 1) capital is money; capital is commodity; if the first form in which it emerges is being considered; 2) ACCUMULATED (ANTECEDENT) LABOUR as opposed to IMMEDIATE, PRESENT LABOUR, where it is being considered in contrast to living labour, and value simultaneously as its substance; 3) means of labour, material of labour, in general products used to form new products, where the labour process, the material production process, is being considered. Means of subsistence, where the component of capital which is exchanged for labour capacity is being considered, according to its use value.

In so far as the whole labour process (direct production process) comes together in the product as its result, capital now exists as product. This is, however, simply its presence as use value, except that now the latter is available as the result of the labour process or production process—the process capital has passed through. If this is taken as fixed, and it is forgotten that the labour process is at the same time a process of valorisation, hence its result is not only use value (product) but at the same time exchange value, a unity of use value and exchange value (=the commodity), the absurd notion may arise that capital has been transformed into a

---

[a] Marx quotes in French.— *Ed.*
[b] See this volume, p. 97.— *Ed.*
[c] Ibid., p. 12.— *Ed.*

simple product, and will only become capital again by being sold, by becoming a commodity. The same absurd notion can be put forward from another point of view. In the labour process itself it is irrelevant (the fact disappears) that the material and means of labour are already products, hence commodities (since on our assumption every product is a commodity). Hence the commodity, and the product itself, only counts here to the extent that it is a use value, e.g. raw material. It can therefore be said that what was previously capital has now been converted into raw material; this is a form of expressing the fact that what was the result of one production process is the raw material (the prerequisite) of the other (or the instrument of labour). Proudhon, for example, argues in this manner:

"What causes the sudden transformation of the *notion of product* into that of *capital*? It is *the idea of value.* This means that the product, in order to become capital, must have passed through an authentic valuation, must have been bought or sold, its price discussed and fixed by a kind of legal convention." E.g. "hides, coming from the butcher's shop, are the *product of the butcher.* Have these hides been bought by a tanner? At once he adds either them or their value to his working capital. By the work of the tanner this capital becomes a product again" (*Gratuité du crédit* [pp. 178-80]) (see XVI, 29 etc.).[a] [120]

[II-82] Mr. Proudhon altogether has a penchant for appropriating elementary notions, combining them with an incorrect metaphysical apparatus and reproducing this for the public. Does he perhaps believe that the leather does not figure as a value in the butcher's ledger before leaving the butcher's shop? In reality all he is saying is that the commodity=capital, which is wrong, since though every capital exists as commodity or money, this does not yet make commodity or money as such into capital. What is needed is precisely to develop how the "notion" of capital develops out of the "notion" of money and commodity. He sees the labour process, but not the valorisation process; it is a result of the latter that the product of the overall production process is not only a use value, but a use value with a definite exchange value, i.e. a commodity. Whether this commodity is sold above or below its value, its passage through a legal convention gives it no new determination of form, it does not make the product into a commodity, still less does it make the commodity into capital. The production process of capital is here fixed upon one-sidedly as a labour process, with its result use value. Capital is viewed as a thing; a thing pure and simple.

---

[a] Marx quotes in French.— *Ed.*

Equally stupidly—and this is characteristic of the way in which declamatory socialism regards *society* in relation to economic determinations—Proudhon says:

> "*For society, the difference between capital and product does not exist.* This difference is entirely *subjective,* and related to individuals" [p. 250].[a]

He calls the specific social form subjective and he calls the subjective abstraction society. The product as such is a feature of every mode of labour, whatever its specific social form may be. The product only becomes *capital* to the extent that it expresses a particular, historically determined, social relation of production. Mr. Proudhon's contemplation from the standpoint of society means overlooking, abstracting from, precisely the *differences* which express the particular *social* relation or the determinateness of the economic form. As if someone were to say: Looking from the point of view of society there are no slaves and CITIZENS, both are human beings. They are much rather this *outside* society. To be a slave, to be a CITIZEN, are particular modes of the social existence of human beings *a* and *b.* Human being *a* is as such not a slave. He is a slave in and through the society he belongs to. To be a slave, to be a CITIZEN, are social determinations, relations between human beings *a* and *b.* What Proudhon says here about capital and product means for him that from the point of view of society there is no difference between capitalists and workers; a difference which exists precisely from the social standpoint alone.[121] It is characteristic of him to conceal his inability to proceed from the category (notion) commodity to the category capital beneath a high-sounding phrase.

Incidentally, one finds other political economists talking the same nonsense about the transformation of the product into capital—in fact this is only a special application of the general narrow-minded conception of capital as a thing—but there it is presented less pretentiously.[56] E.g. Francis Wayland, *The Elements of Political Economy,* Tenth Thousand, Boston, 1843, p. 25.

> * "The material which ... we obtain for the purpose of combining it with our own industry, and forming it into a product, is called *capital*; and, after the labour has been exerted, and the value created, it is called a *product.* Thus, the same article may be *product* to one, and *capital* to another. Leather is the product of the currier, and the capital of the shoemaker." *

[II-83] With Mr. J. B. Say nothing would surprise us. He tells us for example:

---

a Marx quotes in French.— *Ed.*

"*Work* on the land, that of animals and machines, is also a *value, because a price is set upon it and it is bought.*"[a][122]

He does so after he has told us that "value" is "what a thing is worth", and "price" is the "value of a thing expressed [in money]".[a] Then he declares the wage to be "*le loyer d'une faculté industrielle*"—the rent of labour capacity—and continues, as a sign that he does not understand his own expression, "*ou plus rigoureusement le prix de l'achat d'un service productif industriel*".[b][123]

Here labour is taken merely as it appears in the labour process: as an activity aimed at producing a *use value*. In this sense *services productifs* are also performed in the labour process by raw material, by the land, using this expression in a general way, and by the means of production (capital). The labour process is precisely the activity of their *use value*. Once all the elements of production have been reduced in this way to mere factors of the use values involved in the labour process, profit and rent then appear as the prices of the *services productifs* of land and products, just as the wage appears as the price of the *services productifs* of labour. The specific forms of exchange value are always explained here by reference to use value, although they are entirely independent of it.

// The whole of the Mercantile System is based on the notion that surplus value arises simply from circulation, i.e. from the altered distribution of already existing values.[c] //

// The extent to which the concept of capital implies not only the preservation and reproduction of value but *its valorisation*, i.e. the multiplication of value, the positing of surplus value, can be seen from, among other examples (as we shall see later, this is most strikingly evident in the case of the Physiocrats[d]), the earlier Italian political economists, who applied the term *reproduction of value* only to this production of surplus value. For example *Verri*:

"The *value reproduced* is that part of the price of an agricultural or industrial product which exceeds the *original value* of the material and the outlay on consumption incurred while it is being produced. In agriculture the seed and the consumption of the peasant must be deducted: equally in manufacture one must deduct the raw material and the worker's consumption; and so every year a *reproduced value* is created, to the amount of the part that remains" (P. Verri,

---

[a] Marx quotes in French.— *Ed.*

[b] "Or, strictly speaking, the purchasing price of a productive labour service." — *Ed.*

[c] See this volume, p. 351.— *Ed.*

[d] Ibid., pp. 352-76.— *Ed.*

Meditazioni sulla economia politica, Custodi, *Parte Moderna,* Vol. XV, [pp.] 26-27).[a][124] //

// The same *P. Verri* (although a Mercantilist) admits that if commodities are sold at their value or their average price (*prezzo comune*) it is unimportant who is the buyer and who the seller; or, in other words, that the surplus value cannot originate from the difference between buyer and seller. He says: We must regard it as irrelevant whether someone is buyer or seller in the act of exchange.

"The average price is that in which the buyer can become seller and the seller buyer without perceptible loss or gain. If for example the average price of silk is a *gigliato* per pound, I say that a person who possesses 100 pounds of silk is just as rich as he who possesses 100 *gigliati,* since the first can easily have 100 *gigliati* by handing over the silk, and similarly the second can have 100 pounds of silk by handing over 100 *gigliati.... The average price is that at which none of the contracting parties becomes poorer"* (l.c., [pp.] 34, 35).[a] //

[II-84] Only that which preserves and increases capital has *use value* for capital as such. *Labour,* therefore, or *labour capacity.* (Labour is after all only a function, realisation, activity of labour capacity.) // The conditions for the realisation of labour are *eo ipso*[b] included, since capital cannot employ, consume labour capacity without them. // Labour is therefore not *a* use value for capital. It is *the* use value of the latter.

* "The immediate market for capital, or field for capital, may be said to be *labour"* * (*An Inquiry into those Principles, Respecting the Nature of Demand and the Necessity of Consumption, Lately Advocated by Mr. Malthus,* London, 1821, [p.] 20).

// *On the exchange of capital with labour capacity*:

"WAGES ARE NOTHING MORE THAN THE MARKET PRICE OF LABOUR, and when the labourer has received them, he has received the full value of the commodity he has disposed of. Beyond this he can have no claim" (John Wade, *History of the Middle and Working Classes,* 3rd ed., London, 1835, p. 177). //

// *Productive consumption.*

* "Productive consumption, where the consumption of a commodity is a part of the *process of production....* In these instances there is *no consumption of value,* the same value existing in a new form" * (S. P. Newman, *Elements of Political Economy,* Andover and New York, 1835, [p.] 296). //

("*Capital* is consumed just as much as the consumption *fund*; but in being consumed it is *reproduced.* A capital is a quantity of wealth destined for *industrial consumption,* that is for *reproduction"* (H. Storch, *Cours d'économie politique,* ed. Say, Vol. I, Paris, 1823, p. 209)).[c]

It is labour *capacity,* not *labour,* which is exchanged for capital in the buying process:

---

[a] Marx quotes in Italian.— *Ed.*

[b] By that very fact.— *Ed.*

[c] Marx quotes in French.— *Ed.*

*"If you call labour a *commodity*, it is not like a commodity which is first produced in order to exchange, and then brought to market where it must exchange with other commodities according to the respective quantities of each which there may be in the market at the time; labour is *created* at the moment it is brought to market; nay it is brought to market *before* it is created"* (*Observations on Certain Verbal Disputes in Political Economy etc.*, London, 1821, [pp.] 75-76).

Viewed as a whole, the production process of capital is divided into 2 sections:

1) exchange of capital for labour capacity, which includes as a corollary the exchange of certain components of capital existing as money (value) for the objective conditions of labour, in so far as they themselves are commodities (hence also products of previous labour). This first act includes the conversion of a part of the existing capital into the worker's means of subsistence, hence simultaneously into the means of the preservation and reproduction of labour capacity. // In that a part of these means of subsistence has been consumed *during* the labour process itself, in order to produce labour, the means of subsistence the worker consumes can be counted (as maintenance costs) among the objective conditions of labour into which capital is divided in the production process just as much as can the raw material and the means of production. Or they can be regarded as a moment in reproductive consumption. Or, finally, they can be regarded just as much as means of production of the product, rather like the coal and oil the machine consumes during the production process.[102] // 2) In the actual labour process *labour* is converted into *capital.* I.e. it becomes *objectified labour* (objective labour)— and indeed objectified labour which confronts living labour capacity *independently*, as the property of the capitalist, the economic existence of the capitalist. *On this conversion of labour into capital*:

"They" (the workers) "exchange their labour for grain" // i.e. means of subsistence in general //. "This becomes income *for them*" // consumption fund // "...while *their labour* has become *capital* for their master" (Sismondi, *Nouveaux principes*, Vol. 1, p. 90).

"He" (the worker) "required the *means of subsistence* to *live*, the boss required *labour* to *make a profit*" (Sismondi, l.c., p. 91).[a]

"The workers who, giving their labour for the exchange, convert it into *capital*" (Sismondi, l.c., p. 105).

"Whatever advantages a rapid growth of wealth may provide for the wage workers, it does not heal the causes of their misery.... They remain deprived of any right to capital, consequently obliged to *sell their labour* and to renounce any pretensions to the products of that labour" (Cherbuliez, *Richesse ou pauvreté*, p. 68).

// "In the social order, wealth has *acquired the characteristic* of reproducing itself

---

[a] Marx quotes this sentence in French.— *Ed.*

by means of *alien labour*, without any assistance from its owner. Wealth, *like labour* and *through labour*, yields an *annual fruit*, which can be destroyed every year without making the rich man poorer thereby. The fruit is the *income* which arises from *capital*" (Sismondi, *Nouveaux principes*, Vol. 1, p. 82). //

[II-85] // The different forms of income (leaving aside wages), such as profit, interest, rent, etc. (taxes too), are only the different elements into which *surplus value* divides, is distributed among different classes. For the moment we shall simply examine them in their general form, surplus value. Of course, whatever subdivision it may subsequently undergo changes nothing, either in its quantity or its quality. Moreover, it is also well known that the industrial capitalist is the person in the middle, who pays interest, rent, etc.

"Labour is the source of wealth; wealth is its product; income, as a part of wealth, must emerge from this common origin; it is customary to derive 3 kinds of income, *rent, profit, wages*, from 3 different sources, land, accumulated capital and labour. These 3 subdivisions of income are only 3 different ways of participating in the fruits of human labour" (Sismondi, *Nouveaux principes*, Vol. 1, p. 85). //

// "The products are appropriated before they are converted into capital; this conversion[a] does not release them from appropriation" (Cherbuliez, [*Richesse ou pauvreté,*] p. 54). //

// "In *selling* his labour for a definite amount of *approvisionnement* the worker completely renounces any right to the other parts of capital. The allocation of these products remains the same as before; it is in no way modified by the above-mentioned contract" (l.c., p. 58). //

In this conversion of labour into capital lies, in fact, the whole secret of the capital-relation.

If one looks at capitalist production as a whole, the conclusion is: We should not regard the *commodity* alone (still less the mere *use value* of the commodity, the *product*) as the actual product of this process; not just the *surplus value* either, although it is a result that is kept in view as the purpose of the whole process, and characterises it. It is not just this single thing that is produced— the commodity, a commodity greater in value than the capital originally advanced—but also capital and wage labour; or, the relation is reproduced and perpetuated. This will in any case be shown in more detail after the production process has been further discussed.[125]

- Both the surplus value and the wage appear here in a form we have not yet met, namely the form of *income*, hence a *distribution form*, on the one hand, and therefore a particular mode of the *consumption fund*, on the other. But since this determination is still superfluous (although it will become necessary once we get to I,4,

---

a Marx quotes the rest of the sentence in French.— *Ed.*

primitive accumulation [126]), we shall only investigate the characteristics of this form when we have examined the production process of capital more closely. Here the wage appears to us as a *production form* because it is as wage system the prerequisite for capitalist production; just as we have included *surplus value* and its creation in the concept of *capital* as a relation of production. Only in the SECOND INSTANCE must it be demonstrated how these relations of production appear simultaneously as relations of distribution [62] (in this context we must also throw more light on the stupidity of considering labour capacity to be the capital of the worker [92]). This is necessitated in part by the need to show what nonsense it is to regard bourgeois relations of production and of distribution as different in kind. Thus J. St. Mill and many other political economists conceive the relations of production as natural, eternal laws, but regard relations of distribution as artificial, of historical origin, and subject to the control, etc., of human society. [61] On the other hand, the description of surplus value e.g. as income (hence the category of income in general) is a formula for simplification, as e.g. in examining the accumulation of capital. [127]

The questions of what labour is productive, whether wages or capital are productive, and the use of the formulation "income" for wages and surplus value, are to be dealt with at the end of the examination of relative surplus value (or also in part in the relation of wage labour and capital?). (Similarly the worker as *C—M—C*, the capitalist as *M—C—M*, saving and HOARDING by the former, etc. [128])

// *Additions from my Notebook.* [129] As *use value*, labour exists *only for capital*, and is *the* use value of capital itself, i.e. the mediating activity through which it *valorises* itself. Therefore labour does not exist as a use value for the worker, it is not a *force productive of* wealth for him, in the sense of a means or activity of enrichment. A *use value* for [II-86] capital, labour is a *mere exchange value* for the worker, an available exchange value. It is posited as such in the act of exchange with capital, through its sale for money. The use value of a thing does not concern the seller as such, only its buyer. The labour (capacity) which the worker sells as a *use value* to capital is for the worker his *exchange value*, which he wishes to realise, but which is already *determined* (like the prices of commodities in general) before this act of exchange, and presupposed to it as a condition. The exchange value of labour capacity, the realisation of which occurs in the process of the exchange with capital, is therefore *presupposed*, determined in advance, and only undergoes formal modification (through conversion into money). It is not determined by the use value of labour. For the worker himself labour only has use value in so far as it *is exchange value*, not in so far as it produces exchange value. For capital it only has exchange value in so far as it is use value. It is a use value, as distinct from its exchange value, not for the worker himself, but only for capital. The worker therefore exchanges labour as a simple, previously determined exchange value, determined by a past process—he exchanges labour as itself *objectified labour*, only in so far as this is a definite quantity of labour; hence only in so far as its equivalent is already measured, given. Capital obtains it through exchange as living labour, as the general productive force of wealth; activity which increases wealth. It is clear, therefore, that the worker cannot *enrich* himself through this exchange, since in exchange for the available value magnitude of his labour capacity he surrenders its *creative power* like Esau his birthright for a mess of pottage.[a] Rather, he has to impoverish himself, because the creative power of his labour becomes established as the power of capital, as an *alien power* confronting him. He *divests* himself of labour as the force productive of wealth; capital appropriates it, as such. The separation of labour from property in the product of labour, of labour from wealth, is thus posited in this very act of exchange. What appears paradoxical as result is already implied by the presupposition itself. Thus the productivity of the worker's labour *comes to confront him as an alien power*; as indeed does his labour in general, in so far as it is *actual* labour, not a *capacity* but motion. Capital, inversely, valorises itself through the *appropriation of alien labour*. At least, the possibility of valorisation is thereby posited, as a result of the exchange between capital and labour. The relation is first *realised* in the act of production itself (where capital really consumes the alien labour). Just as labour capacity, as a *presupposed* exchange value, is exchanged for an equivalent in money, so the latter is again exchanged for an equivalent in commodities, which are consumed. In this process of exchange, labour is not productive; it becomes so only for capital. It can take out of circulation only what it has thrown in, a predetermined quantity of commodities, which are as little its own product as they are its own value. // Thus all advances of civilisation, in other words every increase in the productive forces of society—the productive forces of labour itself—enrich not the worker, but the capitalist. Hence they only magnify the power ruling over labour, only increase the

---

[a] Genesis 25:27-32.— *Ed.*

productive power of capital—the *objective power* over labour. //
The transformation of labour into capital is *in itself* the result of
the act of exchange between capital and labour. *This transformation
is posited* only in the *production process* itself. //

// With *Say* and his associates the instrument, etc., has a claim to
REMUNERATION owing to the *service productif* it performs, and this
remuneration is handed over to the owner of the instrument. The
independence of the instrument of labour, its *social* determination,
i.e. its determination as capital, is presupposed in this way so as to
substantiate the claims of the capitalist. //

//*"Profit is not made by exchanging. Had it not existed before, neither could
it after that transaction"* (Ramsay, l.c., p. 184).//

//"Every space of land is the raw material of agriculture" (P. Verri, l.c.,
[p.] 218).[a]//

[II-87] // Engels gave me this example [130]: 10,000 spindles at 1 lb.
per week=10,000 lbs=£550 of yarn=1 lb. of yarn for $1\,^1/_{10}$s.

Raw material = 10,000 lbs of yarn.
Waste 15%   = 1,500=11,500.
at 7d. a lb. =11,500   £336.   Profit 60.

10,000 spindles at £1 per spindle cost £10,000
Annual wear and tear $12\,^1/_2\% =$ £1,250

Hence per week 24	
Coal, oil, etc. 40	84 ($5^5/_6$ of 490)
Wear and tear on the steam engine 20	

Wages 70; price of lb. of yarn $1^1/_{10}$s.; hence price of the
10,000 lbs £550

                                                    £490
                                                    £ 60

                            490. (Wages are $^1/_7$ of 490.)

Therefore *raw material* $^{490}/_{336}=68^4/_7\%$. *Wages.* $14^2/_7\%$.
Machinery, etc., $17\,^1/_7\%$. Therefore raw material and machi-
nery=$85\,^5/_7$; wages $14\,^2/_7$. Wages $^1/_7$ (70), raw material and machinery $^6/_7$ (420). Hence $^1/_7$ wages, $^6/_7$ machinery and raw material. Out of this $^6/_7$, $^4/_7$ comes under raw material+$^4/_5$ of $^1/_7$. $^1/_7$
and $^1/_5$ of $^1/_7$ come under machinery. Thus *raw material* accounts
for somewhat less than $^5/_7$, *machinery* for somewhat over $^1/_7$, and
workers for $^1/_7$. //

---

a Marx quotes in Italian.— *Ed.*

This comment from *The Manchester Guardian,* September 18, 1861, MONEY ARTICLE [131]:

* "In reference to coarse spinning we have received the following statement from a gentleman of high standing:

Sept. 17, 1860	Per lb.	Margin	Cost of Spinning per lb.
His cotton cost	6 1/4 d.		
His 16's warps		...... 4d. .... 3d.	
sold for	10 1/4 d.		
Profit 1d. per lb.			
Sept. 17, 1861			
His cotton costs	9d.		
For his 16's		...... 2d. .... 3 1/2 d.	
warps to ask	11d.		
Loss 1 1/2 d. per lb." *			

From the *first* example it follows that the value of lb. WARPS is 10¹/₄d. (1860), of which 1d. is profit. His outlay is 9¹/₄d. 1d. on this comes to $10\frac{30}{37}\%$. But if we subtract the raw material (6¹/₄) there remain 4d.; of which 3d. must be deducted for COST OF SPINNING. Even if we assume that wages here amount to one half of this, which is wrong, we arrive at a surplus value of 1d. on 1¹/₂d. Hence 3:2, or $66\frac{2}{3}\%$. $66\frac{2}{3}\%$ is exactly $=\frac{2}{3}$ of the unit. [II-88] Expressing this in hours, the worker works 2 hours for his MASTER for every 3 hours he works for himself. Thus for each hour ...²/₃ of an hour. Hence if he works for 10 hours altogether, 6 hours belong to him, and 4 (¹²/₃) to his MASTER. (3:2=6:4) If he gives 4 hours out of 10 to his MASTER, he gives ⁴/₁₀ of an hour out of 1 hour=24 minutes. In 1 hour he works 36 minutes for himself (36:24=3:2) // for 36×2=72 and 24×3=72 //.

We have seen in the labour process that all its factors can be characterised with reference to the result—the product—as *means of production.* If, in contrast to this, one looks at the *value* of the different factors required for the manufacture of the product—the values *advanced* for its manufacture (values expended)—they are called the *production costs* of the product. The production costs therefore come down to the sum of labour time required for the manufacture of the product (whether this is the labour time contained in the material and means of labour, or the labour time newly added in the labour process)—the total labour time objectified, worked up, in the product. The formula *production costs* is for us a mere name initially; it adds nothing new to the definitions already arrived at. The value of the product=the sum of the values of the material, the means [of labour] and the labour added to the material through the agency of the means of labour.

The proposition is purely analytic. It is in reality only another way of saying that the value of the commodity is determined by the quantity of the labour time objectified in it. Only later on in this investigation shall we find an opportunity to discuss the formula of the production costs. (Namely in dealing with capital and profit; there an antinomy enters because on the one hand the value of the product=the production costs, i.e. the value advanced for the manufacture of the product, while on the other hand (this is of the nature of profit) the value of the product, in that it includes the surplus value, is greater than the value of the production costs. This results from the fact that the production costs for the capitalist are only the sum of the values he has advanced; hence the value of the product=the value of the capital advanced. On the other hand, the real production cost of the product=the sum of the labour time contained in that product. But the sum of the labour time contained in it is greater than the sum of the labour time advanced or paid for by the capitalist. And this surplus value of the product over and above the value *paid for* or *advanced* by the capitalist forms, precisely, the surplus value; in our definition the *absolute magnitude* of which the profit consists.[132])

[II-89][133] *On the Division of Labour.*

Thomas Hodgskin, *Popular Political Economy etc.*, London, 1827.

"INVENTION and KNOWLEDGE necessarily precedes the division of labour. Savages learned TO MAKE BOWS and ARROWS, TO CATCH ANIMALS AND FISH, TO CULTIVATE THE GROUND AND WEAVE CLOTH, BEFORE SOME OF THEM DEDICATED THEMSELVES EXCLUSIVELY TO MAKING THESE INSTRUMENTS, TO HUNTING, FISHING, AGRICULTURE AND WEAVING.... THE ART OF WORKING IN METALS, LEATHER OR WOOD, WAS UNQUESTIONABLY KNOWN TO A CERTAIN EXTENT, BEFORE THERE WERE SMITHS, SHOEMAKERS and CARPENTERS. IN VERY MODERN TIMES, STEAM ENGINES AND SPINNING MULES WERE INVENTED, BEFORE SOME MEN MADE IT THEIR CHIEF OR ONLY BUSINESS TO MANUFACTURE MULES AND STEAM ENGINES" ([pp.] 79-80).

"IMPORTANT INVENTIONS are the RESULT OF THE NECESSITY TO LABOUR AND OF THE NATURAL INCREASE OF POPULATION. If for example the SPONTANEOUS FRUITS are exhausted, man becomes a fisherman, etc." ([p.] 85).

"NECESSITY IS THE MOTHER OF INVENTION; and the CONTINUAL EXISTENCE OF NECESSITY CAN ONLY BE EXPLAINED BY THE CONTINUAL INCREASE OF PEOPLE. E.g. the RISE in the PRICE OF CATTLE is caused by an INCREASE OF PEOPLE AND BY AN INCREASE IN THEIR MANUFACTURING OR OTHER PRODUCE. The RISE in the PRICE OF CATTLE LEADS TO CULTIVATING FOOD FOR THEM, AUGMENTING MANURE AND OCCASIONING THAT INCREASED QUANTITY OF PRODUCE, which in this country amounts to nearly $1/_3$ of the whole" ([pp.] 86-87).

"No one doubts that *RAPID COMMUNICATION* between the different parts of the country CONTRIBUTES BOTH TO THE INCREASE OF KNOWLEDGE AND WEALTH.... *NUM-BERS* OF MINDS ARE INSTANTLY SET TO WORK EVEN BY A HINT; and every DISCOVERY IS INSTANTLY APPRECIATED, and almost as instantaneously improved. The CHANCES OF IMPROVEMENT are great in proportion as the *PERSONS ARE MULTIPLIED* WHOSE ATTENTION IS DEVOTED TO ANY PARTICULAR SUBJECT. An INCREASE IN THE NUMBER OF

PERSONS PRODUCES THE SAME EFFECT AS *COMMUNICATION*; for the latter only operates BY BRINGING NUMBERS TO THINK ON THE SAME SUBJECT" ([pp.] 93-94).

Causes of the division of labour.

"*D'abord*ᵃ division of labour between the sexes in the family. Then differences of age. Then PECULIARITIES OF CONSTITUTION. THE DIFFERENCE OF SEX, OF AGE, OF BODILY AND MENTAL POWER, OR DIFFERENCE OF ORGANIZATION, IS THE CHIEF SOURCE OF DIVISION OF LABOUR, AND IT IS CONTINUALLY EXTENDED IN THE PROGRESS OF SOCIETY BY THE DIFFERENT TASTES, DISPOSITIONS, AND TALENTS OF INDIVIDUALS, AND THEIR DIFFERENT APTITUDES FOR DIFFERENT EMPLOYMENTS" ([pp.] 111 et seq.).

"Apart from the different APTITUDES in those who WORK there are DIFFERENT APTITUDES AND CAPACITIES IN THE NATURAL INSTRUMENTS THEY WORK WITH. DIVERSITIES OF SOIL, CLIMATE, AND SITUATION, AND PECULIARITIES IN THE SPONTANEOUS PRODUCTIONS OF THE EARTH, AND OF THE MINERALS CONTAINED IN ITS BOWELS, ADAPT CERTAIN SPOTS TO CERTAIN ARTS ... *TERRITORIAL DIVISION* OF LABOUR" ([pp.] 127 et seq.).

Limits to the division of labour.

1) "*EXTENT OF MARKET*.... THE COMMODITY PRODUCED BY ONE LABOURER ... CONSTITUTES IN REALITY AND ULTIMATELY THE MARKET FOR THE COMMODITIES PRODUCED BY OTHER LABOURERS; AND THEY AND THEIR PRODUCTIONS ARE MUTUALLY THE MARKET FOR ONE ANOTHER ... THE *EXTENT OF THE MARKET* must mean the NUMBER OF LABOURERS and THEIR PRODUCTIVE POWER; and rather the former than the latter.... AS THE NUMBER OF LABOURERS INCREASES, THE PRODUCTIVE POWER OF SOCIETY AUGMENTS IN THE COMPOUND RATIO OF THAT INCREASE, MULTIPLIED BY THE EFFECTS OF THE DIVISION OF LABOUR AND THE INCREASE OF KNOWLEDGE.... *IMPROVED METHODS OF CONVEYANCE*, like RAIL-ROADS, STEAM-VESSELS, CANALS, ALL MEANS OF FACILITATING INTERCOURSE BETWEEN DISTANT COUNTRIES, have, as far as division of labour is concerned, the same effects as AN *ACTUAL INCREASE IN THE NUMBER OF PEOPLE*; THEY BRING MORE LABOURERS INTO COMMUNICATION with each other, and MORE PRODUCE TO BE EXCHANGED" ([pp.] 115 et seq.).

Second limit. THE NATURE OF DIFFERENT EMPLOYMENTS.

"As science advances, this apparent limit disappears. In particular, machinery moves it farther away. THE APPLICATION OF STEAM ENGINES TO WORKING POWERLOOMS ENABLES ONE MAN TO PERFORM THE OPERATIONS OF SEVERAL; OR TO WEAVE AS MUCH CLOTH AS 3 OR 4 PERSONS CAN WEAVE BY THE HANDLOOM. THIS IS A COMPLICATION OF EMPLOYMENTS ... but then there follows in turn a SUBSEQUENT SIMPLIFICATION ... hence a PERPETUAL RENEWAL OF OCCASIONS FOR THE FARTHER DIVISION OF LABOUR" ([pp.] 127 et seq.).

[II-90] SURPLUS LABOUR.

"Owing to the CUPIDITY of the CAPITALISTS, etc., there is a *CONSTANT TENDENCY* TO EXTEND *THE NUMBER OF WORKING HOURS*, AND THUS BY AUGMENTING THE SUPPLY OF LABOUR, TO LESSEN ITS REMUNERATION.... *THE INCREASE OF FIXED CAPITAL* tends to the same result. FOR WHERE SO GREAT A VALUE IS LODGED IN MACHINERY, BUILDINGS, etc., THE MANUFACTURER IS STRONGLY TEMPTED NOT TO LET SO MUCH STOCK LIE IDLE AND, THEREFORE, WILL EMPLOY NO WORKMEN WHO WILL NOT ENGAGE TO REMAIN FOR MANY HOURS DURING THE DAY. HENCE ALSO THE HORRORS OF NIGHT LABOUR

ᵃ First of all.— *Ed.*

PRACTISED IN SOME ESTABLISHMENTS, ONE SET OF MEN ARRIVING AS OTHERS DEPART"
(G. Ramsay, *An Essay on the Distribution of Wealth*, Edinburgh, [London,] 1836,
[p.] 102).

In the case of *absolute surplus value*, the capital laid out in labour,
the *variable capital*, retains the same magnitude of value while the
value of the total product grows; but it grows on account of the
increase in the portion of the value of the product which
represents the reproduction of the variable capital. In this case
(this relates not to the surplus value as such but to it as profit)
there is, apart from this, a necessary growth in the part of the
constant capital which constitutes raw materials and *matières
instrumentales*. It should not be assumed, except to a very slight
DEGREE, that the outlay (the *real* wastage, even if it is *written off in
advance*) on machinery, buildings, etc., increases thereby.

In the case of *relative surplus value* the portion of the value of
the product in which the variable capital is reproduced remains
the same; but its distribution CHANGES. A LARGER PART REPRESENTS SURPLUS
LABOUR and A SMALLER NECESSARY LABOUR. In this case the given *variable*
capital is diminished by the amount of the reduction in wages.
The constant capital remains the same, except as far as raw
material and *matières instrumentales* are concerned. A part of the
capital, previously laid out in wages, is set free, and can be
converted into machinery, etc. We have investigated the CHANGES in
constant capital elsewhere (in dealing with profit).[134] This can
therefore be left out here, and our consideration confined to the
CHANGES in variable capital. Let the old capital be= c (constant
capital)+£1,000. Let this £1,000 represent the variable capital. Say
the weekly wages of 1,000 men. Now two situations can be
distinguished. The variable capital falls because of falls in the
NECESSARIES produced in other branches of industry (e.g. corn, meat,
boots, etc.). In this case c remains unchanged, and the number of
workers employed, the total amount of labour, remains the same.
No CHANGE has occurred in the *conditions of production*. Let us
assume that owing to falls in the necessaries the variable capital is
reduced (i.e. its value is reduced) by $^1/_{10}$; it therefore falls from
1,000 to 900. Assume the surplus value was £500, hence=half the
variable capital. Then £1,500 would represent the total value of
the labour of 1,000 men (since their working day remains *the same*
on our assumption, its magnitude is not altered) no matter how
these £1,500 may be divided between capital and labour.
In this case the old capital was:

1) $c + 1,000$ $(v) + 500$ (surplus value). Hence surplus labour=$^1/_3$ of the working day.

The new capital would be: 2) $c + 900$ [v]$+600$. Hence surplus labour=$^2/_5$ of the working day. The surplus labour would have risen from $^5/_{15}$ to $^6/_{15}$; the working day=12 hours, thus $^1/_3=4$ hours and $^2/_5=4^4/_5$ hours of labour. Assume that after an INTERVAL the variable capital (wages) again fell by $^1/_{10}$ as a result of the cheapening of means of subsistence which were not produced in this sphere. $^1/_{10}$ of 900=90. The variable capital would fall to 810. We should therefore have:

New capital: 3) $c + 810$ $(v) + 690$ (surplus). Therefore the surplus labour=$^{23}/_{50}$ of the working day, or $^3/_{50}$ more than previously. A capital of 100 is set free in the first case, of 90 in the second; together=£190. This release of capital is also a form of accumulation; it is at once the release of *money capital*, in the form in which we shall find it again when we consider profit.

$c + v + s$ is the product. $v + s$ is a constant magnitude. If now under the given circumstances wages fall, the formula will be $c + (v - x) + (s + x)$.

[II-91] If, in contrast, the relative surplus labour is a result of the cheapening of the article itself, therefore of a CHANGE *in the productive conditions* of the article, e.g. the introduction of machinery, let us assume that $^1/_2$ of the variable capital of 1,000 is converted into machinery. There remains a variable capital of 500, or the labour of 500 men instead of 1,000. The value of their labour=750, since the value of the 1,000 was £1,500. According to this, then, we should have:

Old capital. $c + 1,000$ $(v) + 500$ (s).

New capital. $(c + 500)$, or $c + ^v/_2$, which we shall call c',

$$c' + 500 \ (v) + 250.$$

But since it is presumed that the SURPLUS VALUE grows in consequence of the introduction of machinery, the variable capital declines, by say $^1/_{10}$. We can now either assume that the 500 work up *as much* (raw material) as before or that they are working up more. For the sake of simplification we shall assume that they work up only as much. $^1/_{10}$ of 500=400. Therefore:

Old capital. $c + 1,000$ $(v) + 500$ $(s) = (c + 1,000$ $(v) + ^v/_2)$.

New capital. $(c + 500), = c' + 400$ $(v) + 350$ $(s) = (c'(c + ^1/_2 v) + 400$ $(v) + ^7/_8 v)$.

£100 would be set free thereby. But this would only occur if no addition of at least that proportion were needed to the supply of raw materials and *matières instrumentales*. Only in this case can *money capital* which WAS previously EXPENDED IN THE FORM OF WAGES be released by the introduction of machinery.

In the case of absolute *surplus value* the *matières brutes*[a] and *matières instrumentales* must grow in the same proportion as the absolute amount of labour grows.

Old capital, $c+1{,}000$ $(v)+500$ (s). s here $=^1/_3$ of the working day of 1,000 working days. If the working day$=12$ hours, $s=4$ hours. Assume now that s grows from 500 to 600, hence by $^1/_5$. Since here the value of 12 hours$\times 1{,}000=£1{,}500$, a value of £100 represents 800 hours of labour for the 1,000 men, or $^4/_5$ of an hour of surplus labour for each man. The amount of material, etc., 1 man can work up in $^4/_5$ of an hour depends on how much he can work up in 1 hour, since the working conditions remain the same. We shall denote this by x. Thus:

New capital: $(c+x,$ *or* $c')+1{,}000$ $(v)+500$ $(s)+100$ (s'). Here there is an increase in the capital laid out and a double increase in the product: due to the increase in the capital laid out and due to the increase in the surplus value.

The determination of value itself remains the essential matter— the foundation—hence the basis is that the value is determined, regardless of the level of the productivity of labour, by the necessary labour time [10]; hence it is, for example, always expressed in the same sum of money, if money is assumed to be of constant value.

By the *Urbarium*[b] of Maria Theresia,[135] which abolished serfdom proper in Hungary, the peasants owed the LANDLORDS, in return for the SESSIONS they received //LANDS ON EACH ESTATE, ALLOTTED TO THE MAINTENANCE OF THE SERFS, 35-40 ENGLISH ACRES each//, *unpaid labour* of 104 DAYS per annum, not to mention a series of lesser obligations, [the handing over of] FOWLS, EGGS, etc., [II-92] the spinning of 6 lbs of wool or hemp, provided by the LANDLORD, and besides all this a further $^1/_{10}$ of all their products to be paid to the church, and $^1/_2$ (??) to the LANDLORD.[c] In the year 1771 the LANDLORDS still constituted $^1/_{21}$ of a population of 8 MILLIONS in Hungary, and there were only 30,921 ARTISANS: these are the kind of FACTS which give the doctrine of the Physiocrats its historical backing.[64]

---

a Raw materials.— *Ed.*
b Land survey.— *Ed.*
c Jones has: "...and one-ninth to the lord".— *Ed.*

15 men are KILLED every week in the English coal mines ON AN AVERAGE.[136] In the course of the 10 years CONCLUDING WITH 1861 ABOUT 10,000 PEOPLE were KILLED. MOSTLY BY THE SORDID AVARICE OF THE OWNERS OF THE COAL MINES. This *generally to be remarked. The capitalistic production is—to a certain degree, when we abstract from the whole process of circulation and the immense complications of commercial and monetary transactions resulting from the basis, the value in exchange—most economical of *realised labour*, labour realised in commodities. It is a greater spendthrift than any other mode of production of man, of living labour, spendthrift not only of flesh and blood and muscles, but of brains and nerves. It is, in fact, only at the greatest waste of individual development that the development of general men is secured in those epochs of history which prelude to a socialist constitution of mankind.*

> "Should this torture then torment us
> Since it brings us greater pleasure?
> Were not through the rule of Timur
> Souls devoured without measure?" [a]

* * *

We have to distinguish between more parts in the *value of the product* than in the *value* of the capital advanced. The latter $= c + v$. The former $= c + a$. (The part of the product which expresses the newly added labour.) But $a = v + s$, $=$ the value of the variable capital + the surplus value.

* * *

If *concentration* of the means of production in the hands of relatively few people—AS COMPARED TO THE MASS OF THE LABOURING MULTITUDE—is in general the condition and prerequisite of capitalist production, because, WITHOUT IT, THE MEANS OF PRODUCTION WOULD NOT SEPARATE THEMSELVES FROM THE PRODUCERS, AND THE LATTER WOULD, THEREFORE, NOT BE CONVERTED INTO WAGES LABOURERS—this concentration is also a technological condition for the development of the capitalist mode of production and, with it, of the productive power of society. It is in short a *material* condition for production on a large scale. [II-93] Labour *in common* is developed through concentration—

---

[a] Goethe, "An Suleika", from *Westöstlicher Diwan.—Ed.*

association, division of labour, the employment of machinery, science and the forces of nature. BUT THERE IS STILL ANOTHER POINT CONNECTED WITH IT, which must be considered under the *rate of profit*,[137] but not yet in the analysis of SURPLUS VALUE. The concentration of workers and of the means of labour in a small area, etc., involves ECONOMY OF POWER, the common USE by many people of means such as buildings, etc., heating, etc., the cost of which does not increase in proportion to the numbers they serve; lastly labour too, economy on the overhead costs of production. This is particularly clear in the case of agriculture.

"With the progress of civilisation ALL, AND PERHAPS MORE THAN ALL THE CAPITAL AND LABOUR WHICH ONCE LOOSELY OCCUPIED 500 ACRES, ARE NOW CONCENTRATED FOR THE MORE COMPLETE TILLAGE OF 100" (R. Jones, *An Essay on the Distribution of Wealth etc.*, Part I. *On Rent*, London, 1831, p[p. 190-] 91).

"The COST of getting 24 BUSHELS from 1 ACRE is less than was the cost of getting 24 from 2; the CONCENTRATED SPACE

// this CONCENTRATION *of space* is also important in manufacture. Yet the employment of a shared MOTOR, etc., is still more important here. In agriculture, although SPACE IS CONCENTRATED RELATIVELY TO THE AMOUNT OF CAPITAL AND LABOUR EMPLOYED, IT IS AN ENLARGED SPHERE OF PRODUCTION, AS COMPARED TO THE SPHERE OF PRODUCTION FORMERLY OCCUPIED OR WORKED UPON BY ONE SINGLE, INDEPENDENT AGENT OF PRODUCTION. The sphere is absolutely greater. HENCE THE POSSIBILITY OF EMPLOYING HORSES, etc. //

"in which the OPERATIONS of HUSBANDRY are carried on, MUST GIVE SOME ADVANTAGES AND SAVE SOME EXPENSE; THE FENCING, DRAINING, SEED, HARVEST WORK, etc., LESS WHEN CONFINED TO ONE ACRE, etc." (l.c., [p.] 199).

Ten Hours' BILL and OVERWORKING.

* "Though the *health of a population* is so important a part of the national capital, we are afraid it must be said that the class of employers of labour have not been the most forward to guard and cherish this treasure. 'The men of the West Riding' " * (quotes *The Times* from the Report of the *Registrar General* for October 1861 [a]) * " 'became the clothiers of mankind, and so intent were they on this work, that the health of the workpeople was sacrificed, and the race in a few generations must have degenerated. But a reaction set in. Lord Shaftesbury's Bill limited the hours of children's labour, etc.' The consideration of the health of the operatives' * (adds *The Times*) * "*was forced upon the millowners by society.*" *

In the larger tailoring SHOPS in London a given piece of work, e.g. on trousers, a coat, etc., is called "an hour", "a half hour". (The "hour"=6d.) How much the AVERAGE product of an hour

---

[a] "Every government has its traditions. ...", *The Times*, No. 24082, November 5, 1861.— *Ed.*

comes to is naturally determined by practice. If new fashions or particular improvements and methods of mending emerge, a contest arises between EMPLOYER and WORKMEN over whether a particular piece of work=1 hour, etc., until here too experience has decided the question. Similarly in many London furniture workshops, etc.

(It goes without saying that, apart from certain arrangements for apprenticeship, etc., only those workers are taken on who possess the AVERAGE SKILL and can deliver during the day the AVERAGE amount of product. At times when business is bad, where there is no CONTINUITY OF LABOUR, this latter circumstance is naturally a matter of indifference to the EMPLOYER.)

[III-95a/A] As one of the main advantages of the FACTORY ACTS:

* "A still greater boon is the distinction at last made *clear between the worker's own* time *and his master's.* The worker knows now *when that which he sells is ended,* and *when his own begins*; and, by possessing sure foreknowledge of this, is enabled to pre-arrange his own minutes for his own purposes" * (*Reports of the Inspectors of Factories for the Half Year Ending 31st October 1859.* Report of Mr. Robert Baker, p. 52).[138]

For the worker himself, *labour capacity* only has *use value* in so far as it is *exchange value,* not in so far as it *produces* exchange values.[139] As use value labour exists only *for* capital, and it is *the* use value of capital itself, i.e. it is the mediating activity through which capital is *increased.* Capital is autonomous exchange value as *process,* as *valorisation process.*

The separation of property from labour appears as a necessary law of the exchange between capital and labour. As *not-capital, not-objectified labour* labour capacity appears: 1) *Negatively.* Not-raw material, not-instrument of labour, not-product, not-means of subsistence, not-money: *labour* separated from all the means of labour and life, from the whole of its objectivity, as a mere possibility. This complete denudation, this *possibility of labour* devoid of all objectivity. Labour capacity as *absolute poverty,* i.e. the complete exclusion of objective wealth. The objectivity possessed by labour capacity is only the bodily existence of the worker himself, his own objectivity.

2) *Positively.* Not-*objectified* labour, the unobjective, subjective existence of labour itself. Labour not as object but as activity, as living source of value. In contrast to capital, which is the reality[a] of general wealth, it is the general possibility of the same, asserting itself in action. *As object,* on the one hand, labour is *absolute poverty*; as subject and activity, [on the other,] it is the general possibility of wealth. This is labour, such as it is *presupposed* by capital as antithesis, as the objective existence of capital, and such as for its part it in turn presupposes capital.

What the capitalist pays the worker, as with the buyer of any other commodity, is the *exchange value* of his commodity, which is therefore determined in advance of this exchange process; what the capitalist receives is the *use value* of the labour capacity— labour itself, the enriching activity of which therefore belongs to *him* and *not* to the worker. Hence the worker is not enriched by this process; he rather creates wealth as a power *alien* to him and ruling over him.

---

[a] Here the word "Entelechy" is written in Marx's hand above the line.— *Ed.*

[III-95] 2) ABSOLUTE SURPLUS VALUE

The view presented here is also correct in strictly mathematical terms. Thus in the differential calculus let us take e.g. $y=f(x)+c$, where c is a constant magnitude. THE CHANGE OF x INTO $x+\Delta x$ DOES NOT ALTER THE VALUE OF c. dc would$=0$, because the constant magnitude does not alter. HENCE THE DIFFERENTIAL OF A CONSTANT IS ZERO.[140]

a) *SURPLUS VALUE IS TO BE CONCEIVED AS
A SIMPLE RELATION TO A DEFINITE PORTION
OF CAPITAL, NAMELY THAT LAID OUT IN WAGES*

At the end of the production process capital has a surplus value, which means, expressed in accordance with the general concept of exchange value: The labour time objectified in the product (or the quantity of labour contained in it) is greater than the labour time contained in the original capital, the capital advanced during the production process. This is only possible (assuming that the commodity is sold at its value) because the labour time objectified in the price of labour (the wage of labour) is less than the living labour time by which it is replaced in the production process. What appears as surplus value on the side of capital, appears as *surplus labour*[a] on the side of the worker. Surplus value *is* nothing but the excess labour provided by the worker over and above the quantity of objectified labour he has received in his own wage as the value of his labour capacity.

---

[a] Marx uses two synonymous terms: "*Mehrarbeit* (Surplusarbeit)".— *Ed.*

We have seen that equivalents are exchanged in the exchange between capital and labour capacity.[a] But the result of the transaction, as it appears in the production process and as it forms on the part of the capitalist the whole purpose of the transaction, is this, that the capitalist buys a greater quantity of living labour for a definite quantity of objectified labour, or that the labour time which is objectified in the wage is less than the labour time which the worker works for the capitalist and which is accordingly objectified in the product. The mediatory role of the exchange between capital and labour capacity (or the fact that the labour capacity is sold *at its value*) is a circumstance which is irrelevant in this context, where the question at issue is the analysis of surplus value. What is at stake here is rather the magnitude of the labour time objectified in the wage (the value of labour capacity), on the one hand, and on the other hand the magnitude of the labour time the worker really gives to the capitalist IN RETURN, or *how much* use is made of his labour capacity.

The relation in which objectified labour is exchanged for living labour—hence the difference between the *value of labour capacity* and the *valorisation of that labour capacity* by the capitalist—assumes another form in the production process itself. For there it presents itself as a splitting up of living labour itself into two quantities, both measured by time, and as the ratio between these two quantities. For firstly the worker replaces the value of his labour capacity.

Let us assume the value of his daily means of subsistence to be equal to 10 hours of labour. He reproduces this value by working for 10 hours. Let us call this part of the labour time the *necessary labour time*. Let us assume that the material of labour and the means of labour—the objective conditions of labour—are the property of the worker himself. On our assumption he would have to work 10 hours a day, reproduce a value of 10 hours of labour time a day, in order to be able every following day to appropriate for himself means of subsistence to the amount of 10 hours of labour, to reproduce his own labour capacity, to be able to continue living. The product of his 10 hours of labour would be equal to the labour time contained in the worked up raw material and the tool used up in the process of labour+the 10 hours of new labour he would have added to the raw material. He could only consume the latter portion of the product if he wished to continue producing, i.e. to preserve his conditions of production.

---

[a] See this volume, pp. 50-54.— *Ed.*

For he must deduct the value of the raw material and the means of labour from the value of his product every day in order to be able to replace constantly the raw material and the means of labour; in order to have afresh at his disposal every day as much raw material and means of labour as is required for the realisation (application) of ten hours of labour. If the value of the worker's average daily necessary means of subsistence is equal to 10 hours of labour, he must work a daily average of 10 hours of labour to be able to replace his daily consumption, and provide himself with the conditions needed for his life as a worker. This labour would be *necessary* for him personally, for his [III-96] own self-preservation, quite irrespective of whether he is or is not himself the owner of the conditions of labour—material of labour and means of labour, whether his labour is or is not subsumed under capital. This labour time is necessary for the preservation of the working class itself, and we can call this part of labour time *necessary labour time.*

But we can also call it this from another point of view.

The labour time which is necessary to reproduce the value of labour capacity itself—i.e. the daily production of the worker which is required so that the worker's consumption can be repeated every day—or the labour time with which the worker adds to the product the value he himself receives every day and destroys every day in the form of wages—is also *necessary labour time* from the standpoint of the capitalist in so far as the whole capital-relation presupposes the continuous existence of the working class, its continuing reproduction, and capitalist production has as its necessary prerequisite the continuous availability, preservation and reproduction of a working class.

Further: Let us suppose that the value of the capital advanced for production has to be simply preserved and reproduced, i.e. the capitalist creates no new value in the production process. It is then clear that the value of the product will only be equal to the value of the capital advanced, if the worker adds to the raw material as much labour time as he has received in the form of wages, i.e. if he reproduces the value of his own wage. The labour time which is necessary for the worker to reproduce the value of his own daily means of subsistence is at the same time the labour time necessary for capital simply to preserve and reproduce its value.

We have assumed that a labour time of 10 hours=the labour time contained in the wage; hence the labour time during which the worker only gives back to the capitalist an equivalent for the value of the wage is at the same time the *necessary labour time*, the labour time necessary both for the preservation of the working class itself and for the simple preservation and reproduction of the capital advanced, and, finally, for the possibility of the capital-relation altogether.

On our assumption, then, the first 10 hours the worker works are *necessary labour time* and this is at the same time nothing but an equivalent for the objectified labour time he has received in the form of the wage. Let us call *surplus labour* all the labour time the worker works over and above these 10 hours, this necessary labour time. If he works 11 hours, he has provided 1 hour of surplus labour, if 12, two hours of surplus labour, and so on. In the first case the product possesses a surplus value of one hour in excess of the value of the capital advanced, in the second case a surplus value of 2 hours, and so on. But in all circumstances the surplus value of the product is only the objectification of surplus labour. Surplus value is simply *objectified* surplus labour time, just as value in general is merely objectified labour time. Thus surplus value amounts to labour time the worker works for the capitalist in excess of the necessary labour time.

We have seen that the capitalist pays the worker an equivalent for the daily value of his labour capacity; but he receives in return the right to extract from that labour capacity a value greater than its own value. If 10 hours of labour a day are necessary for the daily reproduction of labour capacity, he sets the worker to work for e.g. 12 hours. In reality, therefore, he exchanges 10 hours of objectified labour time (objectified in the wage) for 12 hours of living labour time. The ratio in which he exchanges objectified labour time (objectified in the capital advanced) for living labour time is the same as the ratio of the worker's necessary labour time to his surplus labour, the labour time he works over and above the necessary labour time. It therefore presents itself as a ratio between two portions of the labour time of the worker himself— necessary labour time and surplus labour. The necessary labour time is the same as the labour time necessary to reproduce the wage. It is therefore a simple equivalent given back to the capitalist by the worker. The latter has received a certain labour time in money; he gives it back in the form of living labour time. The necessary labour time is therefore *paid* labour time. On the other hand, no equivalent has been paid for the surplus labour.* It is rather the valorisation of labour [III-97] capacity by the capitalist in excess of that capacity's own value. It is therefore

---

* Id est, it has not been objectified in an equivalent *for the worker himself.*

unpaid labour time. The ratio in which objectified labour is exchanged for living labour can be resolved into the ratio between the necessary labour time of the worker and his surplus labour, and the latter ratio can be resolved into the ratio of *paid* to *unpaid* labour time. Surplus value is equal to surplus labour is equal to unpaid labour time. Surplus value can therefore be resolved into *unpaid labour time,* and the level of surplus value depends on the ratio in which surplus labour stands to necessary labour, or unpaid to paid labour time.

If we look now at capital, we find that it is originally split up into 3 constituent parts (only two in some industries, such as the extractive industries[a]; but we are taking the most complete form, that of manufacturing industry): raw material, instrument of production, and finally the part of capital which is exchanged for labour capacity in the first instance. Here we are concerned only with the exchange value of capital. As regards the part of the capital's value that is contained in the used up raw material and means of production, we have seen that it simply re-appears in the product.[b] This part of capital never adds more to the value of the product than the value it itself possesses independently of the production process. In reference to the value of the product, we can call this part of the capital its *constant* part. As noted under *heading 1,* its value may rise or fall, but this rising or falling has nothing to do with the production process, in which these values enter as values of the material and the instrument of production.[c]

If 12 hours are worked instead of 10, more raw material is of course necessary so as to absorb the two hours of surplus labour. What we call constant capital will therefore enter the production process in an amount, i.e. an amount of value, a magnitude of value, which varies according to the quantity of labour the raw material has to absorb, in general the quantity of labour to be objectified in the production process. But it is *constant* in so far as its magnitude of value, whatever its ratio towards the total amount of capital advanced, re-appears unchanged in the product. We have seen that it is not itself reproduced in the proper sense of the word.[d] It is rather just preserved because the material and means of labour are (in accordance with their use value), made into factors of the new product by labour, as a result of which the

---

[a] See this volume, p. 56.— *Ed.*

[b] Ibid., pp. 73-75.— *Ed.*

[c] Ibid., pp. 79-80.— *Ed.*

[d] Ibid., pp. 74-78.— *Ed.*

constant capital's value re-appears in this product. And this value is determined simply by the labour time required for its own production. They add to the labour time contained in the product only as much labour time as they themselves contained *before* the production process. It is therefore only the 3rd part of capital, the part exchanged for labour capacity or advanced in wages, which is *variable*. Firstly, it is really reproduced. The value of labour capacity, or the wage of labour, is annihilated (the value and the use value), consumed by the worker. But it is replaced by a new equivalent; an equal quantity of living labour time, added by the worker to the raw material or materialised in the product, steps into the place of the labour time objectified in the wage. And secondly, this part of the value of the capital is not only reproduced, and simply replaced by an equivalent, but also exchanged in the actual production process for a quantity of labour=the labour contained in it+an excess quantity of labour, the surplus labour the worker performs over and above the labour time which is necessary for the reproduction of his own wage, hence is contained in the component of the value of the capital which can be resolved into wages. Therefore, if we call the labour time contained in constant capital c, that contained in variable capital v, and the time the worker has to work over and above the necessary labour time s, the labour time contained in P, or the value of the product, $= c + (v + s)$. The original capital was equal to $c + v$. The excess of its value over its original value therefore $= s$. But the value of c simply re-appears in the product, whereas the value of v is firstly reproduced in v and secondly increased by s. It is therefore only the part of the value of the capital denoted by v which has changed, in that v has reproduced itself as $v + s$. s is therefore only a result of an alteration in v*; and the ratio in which surplus value is created is expressed as $v : s$, the ratio in which the labour time contained in the v component of the value of the total capital has been exchanged for living labour time, [III-98] or, which is the same thing, the ratio of necessary to surplus labour, of $v : s$. The newly created value results from the alteration in v alone, its transformation into $v + s$. It is only this part of capital which increases its value or posits surplus value. The *ratio*, therefore, in which surplus value is posited, is the ratio in which s stands to v, in which the part of the value of capital

---

* If it is assumed that $c = 0$ and that the capitalist has advanced wages alone (variable capital), the magnitude of s remains *the same* although no part of the product replaces c.

expressed in v is not only reproduced but magnified. The best demonstration of this is that if v is simply replaced by an amount of labour time equal to that contained in v itself, no surplus value at all is created; on the contrary, the value of the product is equal to the value of the capital advanced.

If, therefore, surplus value is, in general, nothing but the excess of living labour for which the labour objectified in capital is exchanged, or, which is the same thing, nothing but the unpaid labour time worked by the worker over and above the necessary labour time, the magnitude of the surplus value, the ratio in which it stands to the value it replaces, the ratio in which it grows, is simply determined by the ratio $s:v$, surplus labour to necessary labour, or, and this is the same, the ratio of the labour time advanced by the capitalist in wages to the surplus of labour, etc. Thus if the necessary (wage-reproducing) labour time=10 hours, and the worker works for 12, the surplus value is equal to 2 hours, and the ratio in which the value advanced has increased=$2:10,=^1/_5,=20\%$, whatever may be the amount of labour time contained in c, the constant part of capital, whether it is 50, 60, 100, in short x hours of labour, whatever may be the ratio of the variable to the constant part of capital. As we have seen,[a] the value of this [the constant] part of capital simply re-appears in the product and has absolutely nothing to do with the value-creation that occurs during the production process itself.*

It is very important to keep a strong hold on the idea that surplus value=surplus labour, and that the ratio of surplus value is the ratio of surplus labour to necessary labour. In this connection the customary notion of profit and the rate of profit should initially be entirely forgotten. What kind of relation exists between surplus value and profit will be seen later on.[142]

---

* [I-A] // If the original ratio of necessary labour to surplus labour= 10 hours: 2 hours=5:1, and if now 16 hours are worked instead of 12, hence 4 more hours, the worker would have to receive $3^1/_3$ and the capitalist only $^2/_3$ of an hour from those 4 hours for the ratio to remain the same; for $10:2=3^1/_3:^2/_3=$ $^{10}/_3:^2/_3=10:2$. But under the mathematical law that "A RATIO OF GREATER INEQUALITY IS DIMINISHED, AND OF LESS INEQUALITY INCREASED, BY ADDING ANY QUAN TITY TO BOTH ITS TERMS", the RATIO of wages to surplus value is unchanged if the OVERTIME is divided in accordance with the above ratio. Previously the ratio of [necessary] labour to surplus was 10:2=5:1 (5 times greater). Now it will be $13^1/_3:2^2/_3=^{40}/_3:^8/_3=40[:8=5:1]$. // [141]

---

[a] See this volume, pp. 73-75.— *Ed.*

We shall therefore use a few examples to clarify this conception of surplus value and the rate of surplus value, the ratio in which it grows—the yardstick by which its magnitude is to be measured. These examples are borrowed from statistical sources.[a] Hence labour time always appears here expressed in money. Furthermore, different ITEMS bearing different names appear in the calculations, e.g. side by side with profit there is interest, taxes, rent, etc. These are all different portions of surplus value under different names.[143] How surplus value is distributed among the different classes, i.e. how much of it the industrial capitalist gives up under various headings, and how much he keeps for himself, is completely irrelevant to the conception of surplus value itself. It is, however, entirely clear that all those people—whatever heading they figure under—who do not themselves work, who do not take part in the material process of production themselves as workers, can only participate in the value of the material product in so far as they divide the product's surplus value among themselves, for the value of raw material and machinery, the *constant* part of the value of capital, must be replaced. Similarly with the necessary labour time, for the working class absolutely must first of all work the quantity of labour time necessary to preserve its own life before it can work for others. Only the value x, equal to the workers' surplus labour, hence also the use values that can be purchased with this surplus value, is available for distribution among the non-workers.

It is only the variable part of capital, the quantity of objectified labour which is exchanged in the production process for a greater quantity of living labour time, that undergoes any change at all, that changes its value, posits a surplus value, and the magnitude of this newly created value depends entirely on the ratio between the quantity of living surplus labour obtained in exchange for the variable part of capital and the labour contained in it before the production process.

[III-99] Senior must be cited here as a second example illustrating the political economists' failure to understand surplus labour and surplus value.[144]

Now the following points are still to be examined under surplus value:

// 1) Extent of surplus labour. Drive of capital to spin this out to infinity. 2) Surplus value depends not only on the number of hours the individual worker works over and above the necessary

---

labour time, but also on the number of simultaneous working days, or the number of workers the capitalist employs. 3) The relation of capital as producer of surplus labour: working more than is needed. Civilising character of capital, labour time and free time. Opposition. Surplus labour and surplus product. Hence in the last instance relation of population and capital. 4) Mr. Proudhon's thesis that the worker cannot buy back his own product, or the price of the portion of the product, etc.[145] 5) This form of surplus value is the absolute form. Persists in all modes of production which are founded on the opposition between classes one of which is the possessor of the conditions of production and the other of labour.[a] //

b) RATIO OF SURPLUS LABOUR TO NECESSARY LABOUR. MEASURE OF SURPLUS LABOUR

Capital has in common with hoarding the boundless tendency to self-enrichment.[b] Because surplus value is reducible to surplus labour, capital has a boundless drive to increase surplus labour. Capital endeavours, in return for the objectified labour expended in wages, to obtain the greatest possible quantity of living labour time, i.e. the greatest possible excess of labour time over and above the labour time required for the reproduction of the wage, i.e. the reproduction of the value of the daily means of subsistence of the worker himself. The whole of capital's history is a proof of its unrestrained extravagances in this respect. The tendency is evident everywhere without concealment, and it is only held in check in part by physical conditions, and in part by social obstacles, which we shall not go into in any more detail here (and which that tendency itself is the first to create). All we need do here is note the tendency. In this respect it is interesting for example to compare the modern factory system in England with corvée labour, perhaps in the Danubian Principalities. The two forms, of which one is a developed capitalist form and the other is among the crudest forms of serfdom, display with equal clarity the appropriation of alien excess labour, of surplus labour, as the direct source of enrichment.[c] The special circumstances additionally present in the factory system, in the developed capitalist mode of production, which allow labour time to be

---

[a] See this volume, pp. 252-53.— Ed.
[b] Ibid., p. 18.— Ed.
[c] Ibid., pp. 212-15.— Ed.

lengthened unnaturally, beyond its natural bounds, can only be indicated more closely in the course of this investigation.[a]

In comparing Walachian corvée labour with English wage labour the following point is to be kept in view. If the total daily labour time of a worker consists of 12 or 14 hours, and the necessary labour time in each case amounts to only 10 hours, the worker would provide in the course of 6 days of the week in the first case 6×2 or 12 hours of surplus labour, in the second case 6×4 or 24 hours of surplus labour. In the first case [he] would work one day out of 6 for the capitalist without equivalent, in the second case 2 days. Over the whole year, week in week out, the situation can be resolved into this: he works 1, 2 or x days a week for the capitalist, but the other days of the week he works for himself. This is the form in which the relation appears directly in corvée labour, that of Walachia for example. In essence the general relation is in both cases the same, although the form—the mediation of the relation—is different.

There are, however, natural barriers to the duration of the daily labour time of a particular individual. Leaving aside the time required for the intake of food, the individual needs sleep, relaxation, needs a break during which labour capacity and its organ can enjoy the rest without which they are incapable of continuing the work or starting afresh. The *day* itself can be characterised as the natural measure of labour's duration, and indeed in England the 12 hour day is called the "WORKING DAY". The limits of the working day are however indistinct, and we find it extended from 10 to 17 (18) hours among different nations and in specific branches of industry within the same nation. The periods of work and rest can be displaced, so that for example work can be done during the night, with the daytime for resting, sleeping. Or the working day can be distributed between day and night. In the Russian factories in Moscow, for example, we find that work proceeds for 24 hours, day and night. (This was also the case in large part in the early days of the English cotton industry.) But then two teams (SETS) of workers are employed. The first team works 6 hours during the day and is then replaced by the second team. After that the first team again works for 6 hours during the night and is then again replaced for the following 6 hours by the second team. Or (as in the case of the dressmaker, which is to be cited) (BAKERS too) 30 hours can be worked, one after another, and then a break, etc.[146]

---

[a] See this volume, pp. 331-36.— *Ed.*

[III-100][a] The examples (to be brought in here) on the extraction of labour time are also useful, because they show strikingly how value, i. e. wealth as such, can simply be reduced to labour time.

We have seen that the capitalist pays labour capacity its equivalent, and that the valorisation of labour capacity beyond its value does not stand in contradiction to this operation, which occurs according to the law of the exchange of commodities[b]— namely the law that commodities exchange in proportion to the labour time contained in them, or in proportion to the labour time required to produce them—on the contrary, that it proceeds from the specific nature of the use value of the commodity which is being sold here. Hence the degree to which labour capacity is valorised by the capitalist, or the extent to which the duration of labour time in the actual production process is increased, appears to be a matter of complete indifference, i. e. it does not appear to be given by the nature of the relation itself. That is to say, in other words: The magnitude of the living surplus labour, hence also of the total living labour time obtained by capital in exchange for a particular quantity of objectified labour, determined by the cost of production of labour capacity itself, appears to be subject to just as little restriction by the nature of this economic relation itself as the manner in which a buyer utilises the use value of a commodity is determined by the relation of sale and purchase as such. It is much rather independent of this. The limits that develop here—e. g., later, economically from the relation of supply and demand or from state intervention and the like—do not, by contrast, appear to be included in the general relation itself.

Nevertheless, the following point must be considered: What on capital's side is the valorisation of labour capacity (or, as we previously called it, the consumption of labour capacity[c]—it is of the nature of labour capacity that its consumption is at the same time a process of valorisation, objectification of labour) is on the worker's side work, hence the expenditure of vital force. If labour is prolonged beyond a certain period—or labour capacity is valorised to more than a certain extent—labour capacity will be temporarily or definitively destroyed, instead of being preserved. If the capitalist sets the worker to work for e. g. 20 hours today, tomorrow he will be incapable of working the normal labour time

---

[a] Corrected page number. Marx has [III-160].— *Ed.*

[b] See this volume, pp. 87-88 and 105.— *Ed.*

[c] Ibid., pp. 55-56 and 93-94.— *Ed.*

of 12 hours or perhaps any labour time at all. If the overwork extends over a long period, the worker will perhaps only preserve himself and therefore his labour capacity for 7 years instead of the 20 or 30 years for which he might otherwise have preserved it. It is well known, for example, that before the invention of the COTTON GIN the 2 hours of manufacturing labour (domestic labour) the slaves in the southern states of North America had to perform to separate the cotton wool from its seed, after they had worked in the fields for 12 hours, reduced their average life expectancy to 7 years. This is still at this moment the case in Cuba, where after 12 hours in the fields the Negroes have a further two hours of manufacturing labour to perform in connection with the preparation of sugar or tobacco.

But if the worker sells his labour capacity at its *value*—and we are proceeding from this assumption in our investigation, just as we proceed altogether from the presupposition that commodities are sold at their value[a]—all that is assumed thereby is that he receives an average daily wage which enables him to continue living in his customary manner as a worker, hence that he is in the same normal state of health the day afterwards as the day before (leaving aside the degeneration brought about naturally through age or through the kind of work he does); that his labour capacity is reproduced or preserved, hence can be valorised again in the same way as on the previous day, over a definite normal period of time, e. g. 20 years. Thus if surplus labour is stretched out to an extent of overwork which forcibly shortens, temporarily annihilates, i. e. damages or entirely destroys, the normal duration of labour capacity this condition is breached. The worker places the use of his labour capacity at [the capitalist's] disposal[b]—if he sells it at its value—but only to such an extent as to rule out the destruction of the value of the labour capacity itself, or rather, only to an extent sufficient to ensure that the wage enables him to reproduce his labour capacity, to preserve it throughout a certain normal average time. If the capitalist uses the worker for longer than this normal labour time, he destroys the labour capacity and with that its value. He has, after all, only bought the labour capacity's average daily [III-101] value, hence by no means the value it possesses on the next day as well. In other words, he has not bought in 7 years the value it possesses during 20.

Hence, as, on the one hand, the specific use value of this

---

[a] See this volume, p. 33.— *Ed.*
[b] Ibid., p. 104.— *Ed.*

commodity—labour capacity—implies that its consumption is itself valorisation, the creation of value, so on the other hand, the specific nature of this use value implies that the extent to which it can be consumed, valorised, must be kept within certain limits to prevent the destruction of its own exchange value.

Here, where we are making the overall assumption that the worker sells his labour capacity at its value, we also assume that the total period, the sum of the necessary labour time and the surplus labour time, does not exceed the normal working day, whether this is set at 12, 13 or 14 hours, worked by the worker in order to preserve his labour capacity in its customary state of health and ability to work for a certain normal average period, and to reproduce it every day afresh.

It follows from what has been said, however, that there is an antinomy here in the general relation itself. This antinomy arises in the following way: On the one hand, if we disregard the natural limit which absolutely prohibits the extension of labour time beyond a certain duration, the general relation between capital and labour—the sale of labour capacity—posits no limit to surplus labour. But on the other hand, in so far as surplus labour destroys the value of labour capacity itself, whereas labour capacity's use is only sold to the extent to which it preserves and reproduces itself as labour capacity, implying also the preservation of its value throughout a definite normal period of time, surplus labour which goes beyond a certain indeterminate boundary contradicts the very nature of the relation which is given with the worker's sale of his labour capacity.

We know that in practice it depends on the relative power of the buyer and the seller (which is determined each time economically) whether a commodity is sold at less or more than its value. Similarly here. Whether the worker provides surplus labour of more than the normal amount or not will depend on the power of resistance he is able to oppose to the measureless demands of capital. The history of modern industry teaches us, however, that the measureless demands of capital could never be held in check by the isolated efforts of the worker. The struggle had instead to take on the form of a class struggle, and thereby call forth the intervention of the state power, before the overall daily labour time was confined within certain limits (as yet mostly within certain spheres alone).

One might think that, just as the slaveowner, when he has consumed the Negro in 7 years, is compelled to replace him with a fresh purchase of Negroes, so capital must itself pay for the rapid exhaustion of the workers, since the continuous existence of the working class is capital's fundamental prerequisite. The individual Capitalist A may have enriched himself through this "KILLING NO MURDER",[147] whereas Capitalist B has perhaps to pay the EXPENSES, or Generation B of the capitalists does. Nevertheless, the individual capitalist perpetually rebels against the overall interest of the capitalist class. On the other hand, the history of modern industry has shown that continuous overpopulation is possible, although it consists of a stream of human generations plucked so to speak before they are ripe, quickly wasted and following each other in rapid succession. (See the passage in *Wakefield*.[148])

c) *ADVANTAGE OF OVERWORK*

Let us assume that the average necessary labour time=10 hours, and that the normal surplus labour=2 hours, hence the total daily labour time of the worker=12 hours. Now assume that the capitalist sets the worker to work for 13 hours a day during 6 days of the week, hence 1 hour over the normal or average surplus labour time. These 6 hours amount to $1/2$ working day in the week. Now one has to take into consideration more than this surplus value of 6 hours. In order to appropriate 6 hours of surplus labour, the capitalist would under normal conditions have had to employ 1 worker for 3 days or 3 workers for one day, i. e. he would have had to pay for 30 (3×10) hours of necessary labour time. With this daily extra hour of surplus labour he obtains half a day of surplus labour a week, without having to pay for the 3 days of necessary labour time he would have had to pay for under normal conditions, so as to appropriate the 6 hours of surplus labour. In the first case a surplus value of only 20%; in the second, one of 30%; but the last 10% of surplus value do not cost him any necessary labour time.

[III-102] d) *SIMULTANEOUS WORKING DAYS*

The *amount of surplus value* evidently depends not only on the surplus labour performed by an individual worker above and beyond the necessary labour time; it depends just as much on the number of workers employed simultaneously by capital, or the number of simultaneous working days it makes use of, each of these=necessary labour time+surplus labour time.[149] If the necessary labour time=10 hours, the surplus labour=2, and the total working day of a worker therefore equals 12 hours, the magnitude of the surplus value will depend on its own magnitude×by the number of workers employed by capital, or by the number of simultaneous working days from which the surplus value has resulted. By simultaneous working days we mean the period during which a certain number of workers work on the same day.

If a capitalist employs e.g. 6 workers, each of whom works for 12 hours, the 6 simultaneous working days, or 72 hours, objectified by him in the production process, are transferred to the objective form of value. If the surplus labour of a worker amounts to 2 hours, on top of 10 hours of necessary labour time, the surplus labour of 6 workers$=6\times2=12$ hours. (That is, the surplus labour of the individual worker multiplied by the number of workers simultaneously employed.) With n workers, then, $n\times2$, and it is clear that the magnitude of the product $n\times2$ depends on the magnitude of n, the factor which expresses the number of workers or the number of simultaneous working days. It is equally clear that if the *mass*, the total amount, of surplus value grows with the number of workers and depends on it, the *ratio* of surplus value to necessary labour time, or the ratio in which the capital advanced in the purchase of labour valorises itself, the *proportionate magnitude* of the surplus value, is not thereby altered, hence there is no change in the ratio between the paid and the unpaid labour. $2:10$ is 20%, and so is $2\times6:10\times6$, or $12:60$. ($2:10=12:60$.) (Or, expressed more generally, $2:10=n\times2:n\times10$. For $2\times n\times10=10\times n\times2$.) Assuming that the ratio of surplus value to necessary labour time is given, the amount of surplus value can only grow in proportion to the increase in the number of workers (of simultaneous working days). Assuming that the number of workers is given, the amount, the mass, of surplus value can only grow in the measure to which the surplus value itself grows, i.e. as the duration of the surplus labour increases. $2\times n$ (n being the number of workers) is equal to $4\times{}^n/_2$.

It is therefore clear that if a particular ratio between necessary labour time and surplus labour is given—or if the total time worked by the worker has reached what we shall call the *normal working day*—the amount of the surplus value depends on the number of workers who are simultaneously employed, and it can only grow in so far as this number increases.

We therefore take the normal working day as the *measure* of the consumption and valorisation of labour capacity.

The amount of surplus value therefore depends on the population and other circumstances (size of capital, etc.) which we shall investigate straight away.

This much must be noted before we proceed. For the owner of money or commodities to be able to valorise as capital his money or commodities, in short the value he possesses, and therefore for him to produce as a capitalist, it is necessary in advance that he be capable of employing a certain minimum number of workers simultaneously. From this point of view, too, a certain *minimum magnitude* of value is a prerequisite if it is to be employed as productive capital. The first condition for this magnitude is given from the outset by the fact that, in order to live as a worker, the worker would need merely the amount of raw material (and means of labour) required to absorb the necessary labour time, say 10 hours. The capitalist must be able to buy at least as much more raw material as is required to absorb the surplus labour time (or also as much more of the *matières instrumentales*, etc.). Secondly, however: Suppose the necessary labour time is 10 hours and the surplus labour time is 2 hours. The capitalist, if he does not work himself, would have already to employ 5 workers, so as to take in a value of 10 hours of labour a day in addition to the value of his capital. But what he took in every day in the form of surplus value [III-103] would only enable him to live like one of his workers. And even this only on condition that his purpose was merely the preservation of his life, as with the workers, hence not the increase of his capital, which is the presupposition with capitalist production. If he worked alongside them, so as to earn a wage himself, his mode of life would scarcely differ from that of a worker (it would merely give him the position of a somewhat better paid worker) (and this *boundary* is made hard and fast by the guild regulations). He would in any case still stand very close to the position of a worker, particularly if he were to increase his capital, i.e. capitalise a portion of the surplus value. This is the situation of the guild masters in the Middle Ages, and in part still that of the present master craftsmen. They do not produce as capitalists.

If the necessary labour time is given, and similarly the ratio of surplus labour to it—in a word, the normal *working day*, the overall sum of which=the necessary labour time+the time the surplus labour lasts—the *amount of surplus labour*, hence the *amount of surplus value*, depends on the number of simultaneous working days, or the number of workers who can be set in motion simultaneously by capital. In other words: the amount of surplus value—its total amount—will depend on the number of labour capacities available and present in the market, hence on the magnitude of the working population and the proportion in which this population grows. Hence the natural growth of population, and therefore the increase of the number of labour capacities present in the market, is a *productive power of capital*, since it provides the basis for the growth in the absolute amount of surplus value (i.e. of surplus labour).

It is clear on the other hand that capital must grow in order to employ a greater quantity of workers. Firstly, its *constant* part must grow, i.e. the part the value of which merely re-appears in the product. More raw material is required to absorb more labour. More of the means of labour is also required, though in a more indeterminate proportion. If we assume that manual labour is the main factor, that production is carried on in a handicraft manner (and here, where we are still only considering the absolute form of surplus value, this assumption is valid; for although this form of surplus value remains the fundamental form even of the mode of production transformed by capital, it is still characteristic of capital's mode of production, and it is its sole form as long as capital has only *formally* subsumed the labour process under itself, i.e. actually a previous mode of production, in which human manual labour was the chief factor of production, has merely been brought under capital's control [75]), then the number of instruments and means of labour must grow fairly uniformly with the number of the workers themselves and the quantity of raw material required for labour by the increased number of workers. Thus the value of the whole *constant* part of capital grows proportionately to the growth in the number of workers employed.

Secondly, however, the *variable* part of capital, which is exchanged for labour capacity, must grow (as constant capital grows) in the same proportion as the number of workers or the number of simultaneous working days. This variable part of capital will experience its greatest growth under the conditions of industry of the handicraft type, where the essential factor of production, the manual labour of the individual, only delivers a small amount of product in a given time, hence the material consumed in the production process is small in proportion to the labour employed; likewise the handicraft instruments, which are simple and themselves only represent insignificant values. Since the variable part of capital forms its largest constituent, it will have to grow most of all when capital grows; or since the variable part of capital forms its greatest part, it is precisely this part which will have to grow most significantly when exchanges are made with more labour capacities. If I employ a capital $^2/_5$ of which is constant, and $^3/_5$ of which is laid out in wages, the calculation will be as follows, if the capital is to employ $2 \times n$ workers instead of n

workers: Originally the capital was $= n(^2/_5 + ^3/_5)$. $2n/5 + 3n/5$. Now it will be $4n/5 + 6n/5$. The part of capital laid out in wages, or the variable part, always remains greater than the constant part, in the same proportion as the growth in the number of workers; in the same proportion as it was presupposed to be greater at the outset.

On the one hand, therefore, the population must grow, to allow the amount of surplus value, hence the total capital, to grow under the given conditions; on the other hand, it is presupposed that capital has already grown so that the population may grow. Thus there appears to be a *circulus vitiosus*[a] here // which should be left open as such at this point and not explained. It belongs in Chapter V [150] //.

[III-104] If one assumes that the average wage is sufficient not only for the preservation of the working population but for its constant growth, in whatever proportion, an increasing working population is given in advance for growing capital, while a growth of surplus labour, hence also an increase of capital through the growth in population, is simultaneously given. In analysing capitalist production one must actually proceed from this assumption; for it implies a constant increase in surplus value, i.e. in capital. We do not yet need to investigate how capitalist production itself contributes to the growth of population.[151]

The population numbers working under capital as wage labourers or the number of labour capacities available on the market can grow without any absolute growth in the total population or even in the working population alone. If for example members of working-class families, such as women and children, are pressed into capital's service, and they were not in this position before, the number of wage labourers has increased without any increase in the overall size of the working population. This increase can take place without any increase in the variable part of capital, the part which is exchanged for labour. The family might receive the same wage from which they lived previously. But they would have to provide more labour for the same wage.[152]

On the other hand, the overall working population may grow without any absolute growth in the population as a whole. If sections of the population which were previously in possession of the conditions of labour, and worked with them—such as independent handicraftsmen, allotment-holding peasants, and lastly small capitalists—are robbed of their conditions of labour (of property in them) in consequence of the impact of capitalist

---

[a] Vicious circle.— *Ed.*

production, they may turn into wage labourers and thus increase the absolute number of the working population, without any increase having occurred in the absolute number of the population. There would merely have been an increase in the numerical size of various classes and in their proportional share in the absolute population. But this is known to be one of the effects of the centralisation brought about by capitalist production.[a] In this case the amount of the working population would have risen absolutely. The amount of wealth available and employed in production would not have increased absolutely. But there would have been an increase in the portion of wealth turned into capital and acting as capital.

In both cases there is growth in the number of wage labourers without any absolute increase, in the one case, in the working population, and in the other case, in the total population; without any increase, in the one case, in the amount of capital laid out for wages, and in the other case, in the absolute amount of wealth devoted to reproduction. This would at the same time produce an increase in surplus labour and surplus value and therefore δυνάμει[b] the increase in capital necessary to support the absolute growth of the population. // This will all be considered under Accumulation.[150] //

e) *CHARACTER OF SURPLUS LABOUR*

Once there exists a society in which some people live without working (without participating directly in the production of use values), it is clear that the surplus labour of the workers is the condition of existence of the whole superstructure of the society. They [the non-workers] receive two things from this surplus labour. *Firstly*: the material conditions of life, because they share in, and subsist on and from, the product which the workers provide over and above the product required for the reproduction of their own labour capacity. *Secondly*: The free time they have at their disposal, whether for idleness or for the performance of activities which are not directly productive (as e.g. war, affairs of state) or for the development of human abilities and social potentialities (art, etc., science) which have no directly practical purpose, has as its prerequisite the surplus labour of the mass of workers, i.e. the fact that they have to spend more time in material

---

[a] See this volume, p. 142.— *Ed.*
[b] Potentially.— *Ed.*

production than is required for the production of their own
material life. The *free time* of the non-working parts of society is
based on the *surplus labour* or *overwork,* the *surplus labour time,* of
the working part. The free development of the former is based on
the fact that the workers have to employ the whole of their time,
hence the room for their own development,[153] purely in the
[III-105] production of particular use values; the development of
the human capacities on one side is based on the restriction of
development on the other side. The whole of civilisation and social
development so far has been founded on this antagonism.[154]

On the one hand, therefore, the free time of one section
corresponds to the surplus labour time, the time in thrall to
labour, of the other section—the time of its existence and
functioning as mere labour capacity. *On the other hand*: The
surplus labour is realised not only in a surplus of value but in a
surplus product—an excess of production over and above the
quantity the working class requires and consumes for its own
subsistence.

The value is present in a use value. The surplus value is
therefore present in a surplus product. The surplus labour is
present in surplus production, and this forms the basis for the
existence of all classes not directly absorbed in material production. Society thus develops in contradictory fashion through the
absence of development of the mass of workers, who form its
material basis. The surplus product need not express surplus value
at all. If 2 quarters of wheat are the product of the same amount
of labour time as previously 1 quarter, the 2 QUARTERS will not
express any higher value than the 1 quarter did previously. But if
we presuppose a definite, given development of the productive
forces, surplus value will always be represented by a surplus
product, i.e. the product (use value) created over 2 hours is twice
as large as that created over 1 hour. To put it more definitely: the
surplus labour time worked by the mass of workers over and
above the quantity necessary for the reproduction of their own
labour capacity, their own existence, over and above the *necessary
labour,* this surplus labour time, which presents itself as surplus
value, is simultaneously materialised in extra product, surplus
product, and this surplus product is the material basis for the
existence of all the classes apart from the working classes, of the
whole superstructure of society. It *simultaneously provides free time,*
gives them DISPOSABLE time for the development of their other
capacities. Thus the production of surplus labour time on one side
is at once the production of *free* time on the other. The whole of

human development, so far as it extends beyond the development directly necessary for the natural existence of human beings, consists merely in the employment of this free time and presupposes it as its necessary basis. Thus the free time of society is produced through the production of unfree time, the labour time of workers prolonged beyond that required for their own subsistence. Free time on one side corresponds to subjugated time on the other side.

The form of surplus labour we are examining here—labour prolonged beyond the necessary labour time—is common to capital and all forms of society in which development has taken place beyond the purely natural relation; a development which is therefore antagonistic, making the labour of one section into the natural basis of the social development of another section.[154]

Surplus labour time as considered here—absolute surplus labour time—remains the basis in capitalist production too, although we shall become acquainted with yet another form.

In so far as we have here only the opposition between worker and capitalist, all the classes which do not work must share the product of surplus labour with the capitalist, so that this surplus labour time not only creates the basis of their material existence but also their *free time*, the sphere of their development.

Absolute surplus value, i.e. absolute surplus labour, later too always remains the dominant form.

Just as plants live from the earth, and animals live from the plants or plant-eating animals, so does the part of society which possesses free time, DISPOSABLE time not absorbed in the direct production of subsistence, live from the surplus labour of the workers. Wealth is therefore DISPOSABLE time.[155]

We shall see how the political economists, etc., consider this opposition as natural.[a]

Since surplus value is initially represented in the surplus product, but all other work is DISPOSABLE time in comparison with the labour time employed in the production of the means of nourishment, it is clear why the Physiocrats base surplus value on the surplus product of agriculture; they only make the mistake of regarding it as a simple gift of nature.[126]

[III-106] Here the following can already be remarked:

The branches of labour employed in the production of commodities are distinguished from each other according to their degree of necessity, and this in turn depends on the extent to

---

which the use value they create is necessary for physical existence. This kind of *necessary* labour is related to use value, not exchange value. That is to say, we are concerned here not with the labour time necessary to create a value reducible to the sum of the products necessary to the worker for his existence; rather with the relative necessity of the needs satisfied by the products of different kinds of labour. In this respect the most necessary of all is agricultural labour (understanding by this all work required to procure the immediate means of nourishment). It is agricultural labour which first provides the DISPOSABLE FREE HANDS for industry, as Steuart says.[156] However, we must make a further distinction. While one person employs the whole of his DISPOSABLE time in agriculture, the other can employ it in manufacture. Division of labour. But the surplus labour in all other branches similarly depends on the surplus labour in agriculture, which provides the raw materials for everything else.

* "It is obvious that the relative numbers of persons who can be maintained without agricultural labour, must be measured wholly by the productive powers of cultivation" * (R. Jones, *On the Distribution of Wealth*, London, 1831, pp. 159-60).[157]

ADDITIONS

To b. In the struggle in London between the workers in the building industry and the building masters (capitalists), which is still continuing, the workers make the following objections, among others, to the hour system imposed by the masters (according to which the contract between the two sides is only valid for the hour, the hour being in fact fixed as the normal day):

Firstly: This system, the workers argue, abolishes any normal day (normal working day), hence any boundary to a total day's labour (necessary and surplus labour taken together). But the establishment of a normal day of this kind is the constant goal of the working class, whose members stand at the lowest point of humiliation in every branch where such a normal day, be it in law or in practice, is not in existence, as e.g. among the jobbing labourers of the Thames docks, etc. They stress how a normal day of this kind not only forms the yardstick for the workers' average life expectancy but rules over the whole of their development.

Secondly: They argue that this hour system rules out EXTRA PAY for overwork, i.e. surplus labour performed in excess of its normal and traditional amount. While on the one hand this EXTRA PAY [makes it possible] for the masters to have work done over and above the normal day in extraordinary cases, on the other hand it imposes golden chains on their drive for an indefinite extension of the working day. This was one reason why the workers demanded the EXTRA PAY. The second reason: they demand EXTRA PAY for overwork because the lengthening of the normal day brings with it not only a quantitative but a qualitative difference, and the daily *value* of labour capacity itself must therefore be subjected to an altered valuation. If, for example, a 13-hour working day replaces one of 12 hours, this must be estimated as the average working day of a labour capacity which is used up over, e.g., 15 years, whereas in the other case the average working day is that of a labour capacity which is used up in 20 years.

Thirdly: One group of workers is thereby overworked, a corresponding group becomes unemployed, and the wages of the employed are forced down by the wage at which the unemployed work.

// Taking absolute and relative surplus value together, the following is seen: If the productivity of labour remains the same, and likewise the number of workers, surplus value can only grow to the extent that surplus labour increases, hence the total working day (the yardstick for the use of labour capacity) is extended beyond its given boundary. If the total working day remains the same, and ditto the number of workers, surplus value can only grow if the productivity of labour grows, or, what is the same thing, the part of the working day required for necessary labour is shortened. If the total working day and the productivity of labour remain the same, the rate of surplus value, i.e. its ratio to the necessary labour time, will remain unalterable, but the mass of surplus value can grow in both cases with the increase in the number of simultaneous working days, i.e. with the growth of population. Inversely: The rate of surplus value can fall only if either surplus labour is reduced, hence the total working day is shortened while the productivity of labour remains the same, or if the productivity of labour falls, hence the part of the working day required for necessary labour increases, while the duration of the total working day remains the same. In both cases, the amount of surplus value can fall, while the rate of surplus value remains unchanged, if the number of simultaneous working days falls, that is the population falls (i.e. the working population).

It is presupposed in all these relations that the worker sells his labour capacity at its *value*, i.e. that the *price* of labour, or the wage, corresponds to the *value* of the labour capacity. As we have repeatedly stated, this assumption underlies the whole [III-107] investigation.[a] The question of how far the wage itself can rise above or fall below its value belongs in the chapter on wages, in exactly the same way as does the presentation of the specific forms in which the relative distribution of necessary and surplus labour can appear (daily wage, weekly wage, piece wage, hourly wage, etc.).[35] In the meantime one can make this general remark: If the minimum wage, the cost of production of labour capacity, were itself permanently depressed to a lower level, surplus value would thereby to an equal extent be constantly kept at a higher level, hence surplus labour would increase as if the productivity of labour had increased. It is evidently the same thing, from the point of view of the result, whether out of 12 hours of labour a worker works for himself for only 8 hours instead of 10 hours as previously, because his labour has become more productive and he can produce *the same* means of subsistence in 8 hours as he required 10 hours to produce previously, or whether he receives in future *inferior* means of subsistence, the production of which requires only 8 hours, whereas the previous, superior ones required 10 hours to produce. In both cases the capitalist would gain 2 hours of surplus labour, would exchange the product of 8 hours of labour for that of 12, whereas he previously exchanged the product of 10 hours for that of 12. Further: If no such fall in the value of labour capacity itself were to take place, or no decline, no constant worsening in the worker's mode of life, a temporary reduction of wages below their normal minimum, or, which is the same thing, a fall in the daily price of labour capacity below its daily value, would temporarily coincide—during its time of occurrence— with the above-mentioned case, only that what was there constant would here be temporary. If a capitalist forces wages down below their minimum, in consequence of competition among workers, etc., this means in other words simply that he deducts a portion of that part of the working day that normally forms the necessary labour time, i.e. the part of the labour time allotted to the worker himself. Every reduction in necessary labour time that is not a consequence of an increase in the productivity of labour is in reality not a reduction in necessary labour time but merely an appropriation of necessary labour time by capital, an encroachment by capital beyond its own domain of surplus labour. If the worker receives a lower wage than normal, that is the same thing as receiving the product of less labour time than is necessary for the reproduction of his labour capacity

---

[a] See this volume, p. 33.— *Ed.*

under normal conditions, so that if 10 hours of labour time are required for this, he only receives the product of 8 hours, 2 hours out of his necessary labour time of 10 hours being appropriated by capital. As far as the capitalist's surplus value is concerned, it is naturally all the same for this surplus value, i.e. surplus labour, whether he pays the worker the 10 hours he needs for his normal existence and has him perform 2 hours of surplus labour for capital, or whether he has him work only 10 hours and pays him for 8 hours, whereby he is unable to buy the means of subsistence necessary for his normal existence. A reduction of wages while the productivity of labour remains the same is an increase in surplus labour through the forcible curtailment of necessary labour time as a result of encroachments on its domain. It is clear that for the capitalist it is all one whether he pays less for the same labour time or has the worker work longer for the same wage. //

Addition to e. In so far as in capitalist production capital compels the worker to work over and above his necessary labour time—i.e. over and above the labour time required for the satisfaction of his own vital needs as a worker—capital, as this relation of domination in which past labour stands to living labour, creates, produces *surplus labour* and therewith *surplus value.* Surplus labour is the labour performed by the worker, the individual worker, beyond the limits of his requirements, it is in fact labour for society, although here this surplus labour is initially pocketed, in the name of society, by the capitalist. As we have said, this surplus labour is on the one hand the basis of society's free time, and on the other hand, by virtue of this, the material basis of its whole development and of civilisation in general.[154] In so far as it is capital's compulsion which enforces on the great mass of society this labour over and above its immediate needs, capital creates civilisation; performs a socio-historical function. With this there is created society's industriousness in general, which extends beyond the period necessitated by the immediate physical requirements of the workers themselves.

It is admittedly clear that this same compulsion is exerted, within certain limits, by all ruling classes—within slavery for example, in a much more direct form than in wage labour—and therefore that here too labour is forced beyond the boundaries set for it by purely natural requirements. This is true wherever society rests on class antagonism, so that there are on one side owners of the conditions of production, who rule, and on the other side propertyless people, excluded from ownership of the conditions of production, who must work and maintain themselves and their rulers with their labour. But in all situations where *use value* predominates, the labour time is a matter of less consequence, provided only it is sufficiently extended to provide, apart from the means of subsistence of the workers themselves, a certain mass of use values, a kind of patriarchal wealth, for the rulers.[158] However, in proportion as *exchange value* becomes the determining element of production the lengthening of labour time beyond the measure of natural requirements becomes more and more the decisive feature. Where, for example, slavery and serfdom predominate among peoples which engage in little trade, there can be [III-108] no question of overwork. It is therefore among commercial peoples that slavery and serfdom take on their most hateful form, as e.g. among the Carthaginians; this is even more pronounced among peoples which retain slavery and serfdom as basis of their production in an epoch when they are connected with other peoples in a situation of capitalist production; thus e.g. the southern states of the American Union.

Since in capitalist production exchange value, for the first time ever, dominates over the whole of production and the whole articulation of society, the compulsion capital imposes on labour to go beyond the boundaries of its own requirements is at its greatest. Similarly, since in capitalist production *necessary labour time* (socially necessary labour time) for the first time ever completely determines the magnitude of value of all products, the intensity of labour attains a higher level under that system, since it is only there that the workers are in general compelled in producing an object to employ only the *labour time necessary* under the general social conditions of production. The whip of the slaveowner cannot produce this intensity to the same degree as the compulsion of the capital-relation. In the latter, the free worker, in order to satisfy his essential requirements, must 1) convert his labour time into *necessary labour time*, give it the general, socially determined (by competition) level of intensity; 2) provide surplus labour, in order to be allowed (to be able) to work for the labour time necessary for him himself. The slave, in contrast, has his essential requirements satisfied, like an animal, and it now depends on his natural disposition how far the whip, etc., is cause for him, an adequate motive for him, to provide labour in return for these means of subsistence. The worker works in order to create himself his means of subsistence, to gain his own life. The slave is kept alive by another person in order to be compelled by him to work.

The capital-relation is therefore more productive in this way—for one thing because what is at stake here is labour time as such, exchange value, not the product as such or the use value; and secondly because the free worker can only satisfy the requirements of his existence to the extent that he sells his labour; hence is forced into this by his own interest, not by external compulsion.

A division of labour can only exist at all if every producer of a commodity employs more labour time in the production of that commodity than is required by his own need for the commodity in question. But it does not yet follow from this that his labour time in general will be prolonged beyond the extent of his needs. On the contrary, the extent of his needs—which will of course from the outset expand with advances in the division of labour, of employments—will determine the total amount of his labour time. For example an agriculturalist who produced all his means of subsistence himself would not need to work in the fields for the whole day, but he would have to divide e.g. 12 hours between field labour and various kinds of domestic work. If he now employs the whole of his labour time of 12 hours in agriculture, and exchanges the excess product of these 12 hours for the products of other kinds of work, buys them, this is the same as if he himself had devoted a part of his labour time to agriculture and another part to other branches of business. The 12 hours he works continue to be the labour time required for the satisfaction of his *own needs*, and they are labour time within the limits of his natural or rather social needs. But capital drives beyond these natural or traditional boundaries of labour time, by making the intensity of labour at the same time dependent on the level of social production, and thus withdrawing it from the accustomed routine of the independent producer or the slave who works only under external compulsion.

If all branches of production become subject to capitalist production, it follows simply from the general growth of surplus labour—of general labour time—that there will be an increase in the division of the branches of production, the differentiation of work and the variety of the commodities being exchanged. If 100 men in a branch of business work for as long a time as 110 men did previously—with a smaller amount of surplus labour or shorter duration of labour overall—then 10 men can be thrown into another, new branch of business, and similarly the part of the capital that was previously required to employ those 10 men. The departure—transfer—of labour time beyond its natural or traditional limits will therefore lead in itself to the application of social labour in new branches of production. This due to the fact of *labour time* becoming free, and surplus labour not only creates *free time*, it makes labour capacity which was tied down in one branch of production, labour in general, *free* (this is the point) for new branches of production. But it is a law of the development of human nature that once the satisfaction of a certain sphere of needs [III-109] has been assured *new needs* are set free, created. Therefore when capital pushes labour time beyond the level set for the satisfaction of the worker's natural needs, it impels a greater division of social labour—the labour of society as a whole—a greater diversity of production, an extension of the sphere of social needs and the means for their satisfaction, and therefore also impels the development of human productive capacity and thereby the activation of human dispositions in fresh directions. But just as surplus labour time is a condition for free time, this extension of the sphere of needs and the means for their satisfaction is conditioned by the worker's being chained to the necessary requirements of his life.

Addition to a)

Firstly. Nassau W. Senior says in his pamphlet *Letters on the Factory Act, as It Affects the Cotton Manufacture etc.*, London, 1837 (pp. 12, 13) [144]:

"Under the present law, no mill in which persons under 18 years of age are employed can be worked more than 11 1/2 hours a day, that is, 12 hours during the first 5 days and 9 hours on Saturday. Now, the following analysis will show that in a mill so worked, the whole NET PROFIT IS DERIVED from the *last hour*. A manufacturer invests £100,000: £80,000 in factory buildings and machinery, and £20,000 in raw material and wages. The annual return of that mill, supposing the total capital to be turned once a year, and GROSS PROFITS to be 15%, ought to be goods worth £115,000, reproduced by the constant conversion and reconversion of the £20,000 circulating capital, from money into goods and from goods into money, in periods of rather more than two months. Of this £115,000 each of the 23 half hours of work produces $5/115$ or $1/23$. Of these $23/23$, CONSTITUTING THE WHOLE £115,000, $20/23$, that is to say, £100,000 out of the £115,000, simply replace the capital; $1/23$, or £5,000 out of the £15,000 (gain), makes up for the deterioration of the mill and machinery. The remaining $2/23$, that is, the last two half hours of every day, produce the net profit of 10%. If, therefore (prices remaining the same), the factory could be kept at work 13 hours instead of 11 1/2, by an addition of about £2,600 to the circulating capital, the net profit would be more than doubled. On the other hand, if the hours of working were reduced by one hour per day (prices remaining the same), net profit would be destroyed; if they were reduced by an hour and a half, even gross profit would be destroyed."

Firstly: The correctness or incorrectness of the positive data adduced by Senior is irrelevant to the subject of our investigation. However, it may be remarked in passing that the English Factory

Inspector *Leonard Horner*, a man distinguished as much by his thorough knowledge of the facts as by his incorruptible love of truth, has demonstrated the falsity of these data, presented in 1837 by Mr. Senior, the faithful echo of the Manchester manufacturers. (See Leonard Horner, *A Letter to Mr. Senior etc.*, London, 1837.)

Secondly: the quotation from Senior is characteristic of the hopeless intellectual degeneration the interpreters of science fall victim to as soon as they degrade themselves to be sycophants of a ruling class. Senior wrote the above-quoted pamphlet in the interests of the cotton manufacturers, and before writing it he went to Manchester with the express purpose of receiving the material for the pamphlet from the manufacturers themselves.

In the passage we have quoted, Senior, Professor of Political Economy at Oxford and one of the most renowned living English economists, commits crude errors he would find unforgivable in any of his own students. He makes the assertion that a year's work in a cotton mill, or, what is the same thing, the work of $11\,^1/_2$ [hours], day in day out throughout the year, creates, not only the labour time or value that labour itself adds to the raw material, the cotton, by means of the machinery, [III-110] but also, additionally, the value of the raw material contained in the product and the value of the machinery and factory buildings consumed in the course of production. According to this, the workers in a spinning mill, for example, would simultaneously produce during their $11\,^1/_2$ hours' labour time—apart from the labour of spinning (i.e. the value)—the cotton they work on, ditto the machine with which they work the cotton and the factory building in which this process occurs. Only in this case could Mr. Senior say that the $^{23}/_2$ daily hours of labour during the whole year constitute the £115,000, i.e. the value of the total annual product.

Senior calculates in this way: The workers work so and so many hours during the day to "replace", i.e. to create, the value of the cotton, so and so many hours to "replace" the value of the consumed portion of the machinery and the mill, so and so many hours to produce their own wages, and so and so many hours to produce the profit. This childishly silly notion, according to which the worker, as well as working his own labour time, simultaneously works that contained in the raw material he operates on and in the machinery he uses, that he therefore produces raw material and machinery *at the same time* as they form, as finished products, the conditions of his own labour, can be explained in the following way. Senior, being entirely under the sway of the lessons given him by the manufacturers, introduced a confusion into their practical way of reckoning, which admittedly is itself quite correct theoretically but is for one thing entirely irrelevant to the relation Senior claims to be investigating, namely that of labour time and gain, and for another thing easily gives rise to the absurd notion that the worker produces not only the value he adds to his conditions of labour but also the value of those conditions themselves.

That practical calculation goes like this. Let us assume that the value of the total product of, say, 12 hours of labour time consists, e.g., to $1/3$ of the value of the material of labour, e.g. cotton, to $1/3$ of the value of the means of labour, e.g. machinery, and to $1/3$ of the value of the newly added labour, e.g. spinning. The ratio is not important here. But some particular ratio must always be assumed. Suppose the value of this product is £3 sterling. The manufacturer can calculate like this: The value of the product of $1/3$ of the day's labour time, or 4 hours, is equal to the value of the cotton I need over the 12 hours, or the cotton worked up in the total product. The value of the product of the second $1/3$ of the day's labour time is equal to the value of the machinery I wear out over 12 hours. Finally the value of the product of the third $1/3$ of the day's labour time is equal to wages plus profit. He can therefore say that the first $1/3$ of the day's labour time replaces the value of the cotton, the second $1/3$ replaces the value of the machinery, and finally the third $1/3$ forms the wages and the profit. But in reality this means quite simply that the whole of the day's labour time adds nothing but itself to the value of the cotton and the machinery, which is present independently of it; it adds nothing but the value which forms on the one hand wages, on the other hand profit. That is to say the value of the product of the first third of the day, or the first 4 hours, is equal to $1/3$ of the value of the total product of 12 hours of labour.

The value of the product of these first 4 hours is equal to £1, if the value of the total product of 12 hours=£3. But $2/3$ of the value of this £1, hence $13\,1/3$ shillings, consists of the value of cotton and machinery present in advance (on our assumption). Only $1/3$ of new value has been added, or the value of $6\,2/3$ shillings, of 4 hours of labour. The value of the *product* of the first $1/3$ of the day's labour=£1, because $2/3$ or $13\,1/3$s. in this product consists of the value of the raw material and used-up machinery, which was present beforehand and merely re-appears in the product. In 4 hours the labour has created no more than $6\,2/3$s. of value, hence it creates only 20s. or £1 of value in 12 hours. The value of the *product* of 4 hours of labour is indeed something quite different from the newly created value, the value of the newly *added labour*, the labour of spinning, which on our assumption increases the existing value by only $\frac{1}{3}$. In the first 4 hours the labour of spinning works up the raw material, not of 12 hours, but of 4. If, however, the value of yarn spun in 4 hours is equal to the value of the cotton worked up during 12 hours, this is only due to the fact that on our assumption the value of the cotton forms $\frac{1}{3}$ of the value of the yarn spun in each individual hour, hence also $\frac{1}{3}$ of the value of the yarn produced in 12 hours, i.e. is equal to the value of the yarn produced in 4 hours.

The manufacturer might also calculate that the product of 12 hours of labour replaces the value of cotton for 3 days, without thereby affecting the relation in question in the least. For the manufacturer, the calculation has a practical value. On the level of production at which he works he must work up as much cotton as is required to absorb a definite quantity of labour time. If the cotton forms $\frac{1}{3}$ of the value of the total product of 12 hours, [III-111] the product of $\frac{1}{3}$ of the total working day of 12 hours, i.e. the product of 4 hours, forms the value of the cotton worked up during 12 hours. It can be seen how important it is to keep hold of the fact that in a particular process of production, e.g. spinning, the worker does not create any value apart from that measured by his own labour time (here spinning), one part of this labour time replacing the wage, the other part forming the surplus value which falls to the share of the capitalist.

(In reality the workers do not *produce* or *reproduce* one particle either of the value of the raw material or of that of the machinery, etc. They contribute nothing more than their own labour to the value of the raw material and the value of the machinery consumed in production, and this labour is the newly created value, of which one part is equal to their own wages and the other is equal to the surplus value the capitalist receives. It is therefore not the whole of the product—should production continue—that is divisible between the capitalist and the worker, but only the product less the value of the capital advanced in it. There is not a single hour of labour devoted to the "replacement" of the capital in Senior's sense, such that the labour would produce doubly, would produce its own value and the value of its material, etc. The upshot of Senior's assertion is simply this, that of the $11\frac{1}{2}$ hours the worker works, $10\frac{1}{2}$ form his wages and only $\frac{2}{2}$, or 1 hour, forms his surplus labour time.)

Thirdly: The whole of Mr. Senior's treatment is entirely

unscientific, in the sense that he does not separate out what was essential here, namely the capital laid out in wages, but throws it together with the capital laid out for raw material. Moreover, if the ratio he gives were correct, the workers would, out of the $11\,^1/_2$ hours, or 23 half hours, work 21 half hours for themselves and only provide 2 half hours of surplus labour to the capitalist. According to this, surplus labour would be related to necessary in the proportion $2:21,=1:10\,^1/_2$; hence $9\,^{11}/_{21}\%$, and this is supposed to give a profit of 10% on the whole of the capital! The most peculiar feature, which displays his complete ignorance of the nature of surplus value, is this: He assumes that of the 23 half hours, or $11\,^1/_2$ hours, only 1 hour is surplus labour, hence forms surplus value, and is therefore amazed to find that if the workers were to add to this 1 hour of surplus labour a further $1\,^1/_2$ hours of surplus labour, if they were to work 5 half hours instead of 2 half hours (hence 13 hours altogether), the net gain would increase *more than twofold*. Equally naive is the discovery that, on the assumption that the whole of the surplus labour or surplus value is equal to one hour, the whole net profit would disappear as soon as the labour time were reduced by this one hour, i.e. if no surplus labour were performed at all. On the one hand, we see Senior's astonishment at the discovery that the surplus value, hence the gain too, is reduced to mere surplus labour, and on the other hand simultaneously the failure to grasp this relation, which Mr. Senior, influenced as he is by the manufacturers, notes merely as a curiosity of the cotton industry.

Secondly. The money the worker receives as wages represents the labour time which is present in the commodities required for the satisfaction of his vital needs. Surplus value originates through the fact that the worker gives more labour time in exchange for these commodities than is contained in them, more living labour for a particular quantity of objectified labour. Therefore he buys these commodities, the range of which constitutes his wages, with more labour than is required to produce them.

"Whatever quantity of labour may be requisite to produce any commodity, the labourer must always, in the present state of society, give a great deal more labour to acquire and possess it than is requisite to buy it from nature. Natural Price so increased to the labourer is Social Price" (Th. Hodgskin, *Popular Political Economy*, London, [Edinburgh,] 1827, [p.]220).

"Brotherton, himself a manufacturer, stated in the HOUSE OF COMMONS that the manufacturers would add hundreds of pounds a week to their gain if they could induce their workers" (their MEN, people) "to work but one hour more a day" (Ramsay, l.c.,[a] p. 102).

---

a *An Essay on the Distribution of Wealth.*— Ed.

"Where there is no SURPLUS LABOUR, there can be no SURPLUS PRODUCE, hence no capital" (*The Source and Remedy of the National Difficulties etc.*, London, 1821, [p.] 4).

[III-112] * "The amount of capital which can be invested at a given moment, in a given country, or the world, so as to return not less than *a given rate of profits,* seems principally to depend on *the quantity of labour,* which it is possible, by laying out the capital, to induce the then existing number of human beings to perform" * (*An Inquiry into those Principles, Respecting the Nature of Demand etc., Lately Advocated by Mr. Malthus,* London, 1821, [p.] 20).

For pages 106, 107:

* "If the labourer can be brought to feed on potatoes, instead of bread, it is indisputably true that then more can be exacted from his labour; i.e., if when fed on bread he was obliged to retain for the maintenance of himself and family the labour of Monday and Tuesday, he will, on potatoes, require only half of Monday; and the remaining half of Monday and the whole of Tuesday are available either for the service of the state or the capitalist" * (*The Source and Remedy of the National Difficulties,* London, 1821, [p.] 26).

* "Whatever may be *due* to the capitalist, he *can only receive* the surplus labour of the labourer; for the labourer *must live.* But it is perfectly true, that if capital does not decrease in value as it increases in amount, the capitalist will exact from the labourers the produce of every hour's labour beyond what it is *possible* for the labourer to subsist on: and however horrid or disgusting it may seem, the capitalist may eventually speculate on the food that requires the least labour to produce it, and eventually say to the labourer: 'You sha'n't eat bread, because barley meal is cheaper. You sha'n't eat meat, because it is possible to subsist on beet root and potatoes' " * (l.c., [pp.] 23-24).[159]

Addition to e), p. 107.

* "Wealth is disposable time and nothing more" * (*The Source and Remedy etc.,* p. 6).

In capitalist production the worker's labour is much greater than in the case of the *independent worker,* because the former relation is definitely not determined by the relation between his labour and *his need,* but by capital's unrestricted, boundless need for surplus labour.

"The labour of, for example, the agriculturalist will amount to much more, if only because it is no longer determined by his particular needs" (J. G. Büsch, *Abhandlung von dem Geldumlauf...,* Theil 1, Hamburg and Kiel, 1800, p. 90).[160]

Addition to e, p. 104.

The relation which compels the worker to do surplus labour is the fact that the conditions of his labour exist over against him as capital. He is not subjected to any external compulsion, but in order to live in a world where commodities are determined by their value he is compelled to sell his labour capacity as a commodity, whereas the valorisation of this labour capacity over and above its own value is the prerogative of capital. Thus his surplus labour both increases the variety of production and creates *free time* for others. The political economists like to *conceive* this relation as a *natural relation* or a *divine institution.* As far as industriousness brought about by capital is concerned:

* "Legal constraint" * (to labour) * "is attended with too much trouble, violence and noise; creates ill will etc., whereas *hunger* is not only a peaceable, silent, unremitted pressure, but, as the most natural motive to industry and labour, it calls forth the most powerful exertions" * (*A Dissertation on the Poor Laws.* By a Well-wisher to Mankind (The Rever. Mr. J. Townsend), 1786. Republished, London, 1817, [p.] 15).

Since the capital-relation presupposes that the worker is compelled to sell his labour capacity, hence has essentially only his labour capacity to sell, Townsend says:

* "It seems to be *a law of nature,* that the poor should be to a certain degree improvident, that there always may be some to fulfil the most servile, the most sordid, and the most ignoble affairs in the community. The stock of human happiness is thereby much increased, the more delicate * are relieved from DRUDGERY, and are left at liberty, without interruption, to pursue higher CALLINGS, etc." (l.c., [p.] 39). * "The poor law tends to destroy the harmony and beauty, the symmetry and order of that system, which god and nature [III-113] have established in the world" * (p. 41).

This parson Townsend is admittedly not the actual inventor of the so-called theory of population, but he was the first to give it the form in which Malthus appropriated it and made great literary capital therefrom. It is odd that, with the exception of the Venetian monk Ortes (whose "*Della Economia Nazionale*" *libri sei* of 1774 is much more ingenious than Malthus), it is mainly parsons of the English church who have wrestled with the "URGENT APPETITE" and the, in Townsend's words, "CHECKS WHICH TEND TO BLUNT THE SHAFTS OF CUPID".[161] In opposition to Catholic dogmatism ("SUPERSTITION" says Townsend), they laid claim to the injunction "be fruitful, and multiply"[a] on behalf of the priesthood itself, while preaching celibacy to the working class.

"God ordains that men who carry on trades of primary utility are born in abundance" (Galiani, *Della Moneta,* in Custodi, Vol. III, p. 78).

The progress of the nation's wealth, says *Storch,* "gives birth to this *useful class* of society ... which undertakes the most tedious, sordid and distasteful tasks, which, in a word, by taking upon itself everything that is disagreeable and servile in life procures for the other classes the *time,* the peace of mind and the customary dignity of character they need to embark successfully on work of an elevated kind" (*Cours d'économie politique,* ed. Say, Vol. III, Paris, 1823, p. 223).[b]

"Our zone requires labour for the satisfaction of wants, and *therefore* at least *a portion* of society must *work indefatigably....*" (Sir Morton Eden, *The State of the Poor: or,*

---

[a] Genesis 1:28.— *Ed.*

[b] Marx quotes Storch partly in German and partly in French.— *Ed.*

an History of the Labouring Classes in England, from the Conquest to the Present Period etc.,
Vol. I, London, 1797, Book I, Ch. 1).

Addition to d), p. 102. This law[a] only implies that with a constant
productivity of labour and a given normal day, the amount of
surplus value will grow with the number of workers simultaneously employed. It does not follow from it that in all branches of
production (e.g. agriculture) the productivity of labour remains
the same in the measure to which a greater quantity of labour is
employed. (This is to be put in a note.)

It follows that if other conditions remain the same the wealth of
a country, on the basis of capitalist production, depends on the
size of the proletariat, of the portion of the population dependent
on wage labour.

"The more slaves a master has, the richer he is; it follows, assuming the masses
are equally oppressed, that the more proletarians a country has the richer it is"
(Colins, *L'économie politique. Sources des révolutions et des utopies prétendues socialistes,*
Vol. III, Paris, 1857, [p.] 331).[b]

Addition to a. Illustration of surplus value.

According to Jacob,[c] writing in 1815, the wheat price was 80s.
per quarter and the average product per ACRE was 22 BUSHELS (now
32), giving an average product of £11 per ACRE. He calculates that
the straw pays the expense of harvesting, threshing, and carrying
to the place of sale, reckoning up the ITEMS as follows:

	£	s.		£	s.
Seed (wheat)	1	9	*Tithes, RATES and* TAXES	1	1
Manure	2	10	RENT	1	8
	3	19			
Wages	3	10	*Farmer's profit and* *interest*	1	2
	7	9		3	11

In this table the right hand column, taxes, rates, rent, farmer's
profit and interest, represents only the total surplus value[143] the
farmer (the capitalist) receives, part of which he however gives up
to the state, the LANDLORD, etc., under various names and headings.
The total surplus value therefore = £3 11s. The constant capital
(seed and manure)=£3 19s. The capital advanced for labour=£3
10[s].

---

a See this volume, p. 185.— *Ed.*
b Marx quotes in French.— *Ed.*
c W. Jacob, *A Letter to Samuel Whitbread etc.*, London, 1815, p. 33.— *Ed.*

Page 113 of Notebook III of the Economic Manuscript of 1861-63

It is this [III-114] latter portion of capital, variable capital, which is alone to be considered when we are dealing with surplus value and the ratio of surplus value. In the present case, therefore, the ratio between surplus value and the capital expended on wages, or the rate at which the capital expended on wages increases is given by the ratio £3 11s. to £3 10s. The capital of £3 10[s.] expended on labour is reproduced as a capital of £7 1s. Only £3 10[s.] of this represents the replacement of the wages, whereas £3 11s. represents the surplus value, which therefore amounts to more than 100%. The necessary labour time would accordingly be slightly smaller than the surplus labour, roughly equal to it, so that 6 of the 12 hours of the normal working day would belong to the capitalist (including the various people who share in this surplus value). It may admittedly be the case that e.g., at 80s., the price of the quarter of wheat stands above its value, hence that a part of its price derives from the sale of other commodities in return for wheat at less than their value. But, firstly, it is only a matter of making clear how, in general, surplus value and hence the rate of surplus value are to be understood. On the other hand, if the market price of a bushel of wheat stands, say, 10s. above its value, this can only increase the surplus value received by the farmer provided that he does not pay the agricultural worker, whose labour has risen above its normal value, the amount by which his labour now exceeds the normal value.

Let us take another example from modern English agriculture, namely the following REAL BILL from a HIGH FORMED ESTATE:

Yearly Expenditure in Production Itself		Farmer's Income and Outgoings	
	£		£
Manure	686	Rent	843
Seed	150	Taxes	150
Cattle fodder	100	Tithes	none
Losses, tradesmen's bills, etc.	453	Profit	488
	1,389		1,481
Wages	1,690		
	3,079		

(F. W. Newman, *Lectures on Political Economy*, London, 1851, p. 166 [167]).

In this example, therefore, variable capital, or capital exchanged for living labour, amounts to £1,690. It is reproduced as

£1,690 + 1,481 = £3,171. The surplus value is £1,481, and the ratio of the surplus value to the part of the capital from which it arises = 1,481/1,690, or something over 87%.

// "The inextinguishable passion for gain—the *auri sacri fames*[a]—will always lead capitalists" (McCulloch, *The Principles of Political Economy*, London, 1825, p. 163).//

Addition to e, p. 104.

"It is because one works that the other can rest" (Sismondi, *Nouveaux principes d'économie politique*, Vol. 1, pp. 76-77).[b]

Addition to e, p. 107. Surplus labour and the multiplication of products provides the conditions for the *production of luxuries*, for part of production throwing itself into the production of luxury products, or, what is the same thing, being exchanged for these products (through foreign trade).

"Once there is an overabundance of products, the excess labour must be devoted to luxury objects. The consumption of objects of prime necessity is limited, that of objects of luxury is unlimited" (Sismondi, *Nouveaux principes etc.*, Vol. 1, p. 78). "Luxury is only possible when it is bought with the *labour of others*; assiduous, uninterrupted labour is only possible when it is the sole means of obtaining, not the frivolities, but the necessities of life" (l.c. p. 79).

// The *demand of the workers* for capital is therefore the only thing the capitalist needs, i.e. for him everything turns on the proportion in which living labour offers itself for objectified labour.

* "As to the demand *from* labour, that is, either the giving labour [III-115] in exchange for goods, or, if you choose to consider it in another form, but which comes to the same thing, the giving, in exchange for *complete products*, a future and *accruing addition of value*..., conferred on certain particles of matter entrusted to the labourer. This is the real demand that it is material to the producers to get increased, as far as *any* demand is wanted, extrinsic to that which articles furnish to each other when increased" * (*An Inquiry into those Principles, Respecting the Nature of Demand and the Necessity of Consumption etc.*, London, 1821, [p.] 57). //

When James Mill for example says:

* "To enable a considerable portion of the community to enjoy the advantages of *leisure*, the return to capital must evidently be large" * (James Mill, *Elements of Political Economy*, London, 1821, p. 50),

he means nothing other than this: The wage labourer must slave a good deal so that many people can have leisure, or the free time of one section of society depends on the ratio of the worker's surplus labour time to his necessary labour time.

---

[a] "Passion for accursed gold." The original phrase in Virgil's *Aeneid*, III, 57, is *auri sacra fames* ("accursed passion for gold").— *Ed.*

[b] Here and below Marx quotes Sismondi in French.— *Ed.*

The capitalist's task is to "obtain from the capital expended" (the capital exchanged for living labour) "*the largest possible amount of labour*" (J. G. Courcelle-Seneuil, *Traité théorique et pratique des entreprises industrielles etc.*, 2nd ed., Paris, 1857, p. 62).[a]

That the valorisation of capital, the surplus value it produces over and above its own value, hence its productive power, consists in the surplus labour it appropriates to itself, is stated by *J. St. Mill* for example.

"*Capital*, strictly speaking, has *no productive power*. The only productive power is that of labour; assisted, no doubt, by TOOLS, and ACTING UPON MATERIALS.... The *productive power of capital* can only mean the quantity of real productive power" (labour) "which the capitalist, by means of his capital, can *command*" (J. St. Mill, *Essays on Some Unsettled Questions of Political Economy*, London, 1844, pp. 90, 91).

Addition to a.) It is clear that in the reproduction of capital and its increase the value of the raw material and machinery as such is altogether a matter of indifference for the production process. Take a raw material, e.g. flax. The amount of labour the flax can absorb to be converted into linen for example—if the level of production, a certain degree of technological development, is given—does not depend on its *value* but on its *quantity*, and in the same way the assistance a machine can give to 100 workers depends not on its price but on its use value.

Addition to p. 114.) Or let us take another example. J. C. Symons, *Arts and Artisans at Home and Abroad*, Edinburgh, 1839 [p. 233], gives the following calculation for a Glasgow power-loom factory with 500 LOOMS, CALCULATED TO WEAVE A GOOD FABRIC OF CALICO OR SHIRTING, SUCH AS IS GENERALLY MADE IN Glasgow:

Expense of erecting the factory and machinery	£18,000
Annual produce, 150,000 pieces of 24 yards at 6s.	£45,000
Interest on fixed capital and for DEPRECIATION OF VALUE *of the machinery*, reckoning 900 (5%) for interest	[£] 1,800
Steam-power, oil, tallow, keeping up machinery, etc.	2,000
YARNS AND FLAX	32,000
Wages	7,500
Profit	1,700
	45,000

In this case interest and profit amount to 900+1,700=2,600.

___

a Marx quotes in French.— *Ed.*

The self-reproducing and self-increasing part of capital laid out for labour is £7,500. Surplus value = 2,600; rate of surplus value therefore: nearly 33%.[162]

[III-116] *Addition to b.) p. 99)*

Richard Jones, in his *Essay on the Distribution of Wealth,* London, 1831, rightly regards *corvée* labour, or what he calls LABOUR RENT, as the most primitive form of rent. We have only to consider it here as a particular form of surplus value which falls to the landed proprietor.[163] It is, thus, a form in which the agricultural workers possess a part of the land, and cultivate it to obtain their own subsistence. The labour time they employ for this purpose corresponds to the necessary labour time with which the wage labourer replaces his own wage. However, whereas the modern agricultural day labourer realises the whole of his labour time—both the part that replaces his wages and the part that forms the surplus value—on the same land (which is rented from the farmer)—just as the factory worker employs the same machinery for the realisation of his necessary and his surplus labour—here, in contrast, there takes place not only a division of the time (and much more tangibly than in wage labour) but also a division of the conditions of production (the sphere of production) by means of which this labour time is realised.

For example, the *corvée* labourer cultivates the field assigned to him as his possession on certain days of the week. On other days he works on the seignorial estate, for the landowner. What this form of labour has in common with wage labour is the fact that the worker gives to the owner of the conditions of production not, as in other modes of production, the product, and not money, but *labour itself.* Surplus labour is here more distinctly marked off from necessary labour than in the wage system, because here necessary and surplus labour are performed on two different plots of land. The *corvée* labourer does the labour necessary for the reproduction of his own labour capacity on the field he himself possesses. He performs surplus labour for the landed proprietor on the seignorial estate. This spatial separation makes the division of the total labour time into two parts more clearly apparent, whereas with the wage labourer one may just as well say that he works, e.g., 2 out of 12 hours for the capitalist as that he works for the capitalist for $1/6$ of every hour or of any other aliquot part of the 12 hours.

Firstly, then, the division into necessary labour and surplus labour, labour for the reproduction of one's own labour capacity and labour for the owner of the conditions of production, is more clearly, more distinctly apparent in the form of *corvée* labour than in the form of wage labour. Secondly, however, it follows from its appearing more clearly in the *corvée* form than in wage labour that surplus labour is unpaid labour and that the whole of surplus value can be reduced to surplus labour, i.e. unpaid labour. If the *corvée* labourers work 5 days of the week on their own land, and the 6th day on the landowner's, it is clear that on this 6th day they perform unpaid labour, they work not for themselves but [for] another, and that all the receipts of this other person are the product of their unpaid labour; it is called *corvée* labour precisely for that reason. If factory workers work 2 hours out of 12 every day for the capitalist, it is the same as if they worked 5 days of the week for themselves and 1 for the capitalist, hence in effect the same as if they performed 1 day of *corvée* labour a week for the capitalist.

The form of the wage is absent from the whole *corvée* system, and this makes the relation yet more tangible. The *corvée* labourer receives the conditions of production required for the realisation of his own necessary labour; he is allotted them once and for all. He therefore pays his own wages or directly appropriates the product of his necessary labour. With the wage labourer, in contrast, the whole of his product is first converted into capital, in order to flow back to him subsequently in the form of wages. If the *corvée* labourer, who works 1 day in the week for his lord, had to hand over to him the product of the whole week, so that the lord could convert it into money and pay back $^5/_6$ of this money to the *corvée* labourer, the latter would have been turned into a wage labourer in this respect. Inversely. If the wage labourer, who works 2 hours every day for the capitalist, were himself to pocket the product or the value of the product of 5 days of his labour (deductions from the value for the conditions of production and the material and means of labour take place in both situations, even if in different forms) and work for capital during the 6th day for nothing, he would have turned into a *corvée* labourer. In so far as the nature of necessary labour and surplus labour and their relationship come into consideration, the result is the same.

We find *corvée* labour in larger or smaller quantities combined with all forms of serfdom. But where it appears in its pure form, as the dominant relation of production, which was particularly the case and in part still is the case in the Slav countries and the Danubian provinces occupied by the Romans, we can certainly say [III-117] that it did not arise on the basis of serfdom; instead serfdom arose, inversely, from *corvée* labour. The latter is based on a community, and the surplus labour the members of the commune performed over and above that required for their subsistence, which served partly as a (communal) reserve fund, and partly to cover the costs of their communal, political and religious requirements, gradually became transformed into *corvée* labour performed for the families which had usurped the reserve fund and the political and religious offices as their private property. In the Danubian Principalities, and similarly in Russia, this process of usurpation can be precisely demonstrated. A comparison between the Wallachian boyars and the English manufacturers from the point of view of their thirst for alien labour time is interesting in that the appropriation of alien labour appears in both cases as the direct source of wealth: surplus value as surplus labour.[a]

// * "The employer will be always on the stretch to *economize* time and labour" * (Dugald Stewart, *Lectures on Political Economy*, Vol. I, Edinburgh, 1855, p. 318, in Vol. VIII of the COLLECTED WORKS, ED. BY Sir W. Hamilton). *For p. 107, to the Addition to e.* //

Surplus labour appears in its most primitive "independent", "free" form in *corvée* labour; free in so far as in slavery the whole of the slaves' day, like the cattle's, belongs to the proprietor, and he must naturally feed them.

Even in Moldavia and Wallachia payment in kind still exists alongside the *corvée*.[164] Let us take here the *Règlement organique*, put into effect in 1831.[165] For our present purpose it is irrelevant, and therefore only needs mentioning in passing, that the land, cattle, etc., in fact *belong* to the Wallachian peasants, that the obligations to the proprietors arose through usurpation, and that the Russian *Règlement* raised this usurpation to the level of a law. The payments in kind consist of $^1/_5$ of the hay; $^1/_{20}$ of the wine; and $^1/_{10}$ of all other products (all this in Wallachia). The peasant possesses: 1) 400 *stagenes* (a *stagene* is about 2 square metres) for house and garden on the plain, 300 in the mountains; 2) 3 *pogones* ($1^1/_2$ hectares) of ploughland; 3) 3 *pogones* of grassland (pasture for 5 horned cattle).

Here we must mention incidentally that this code of serfdom was proclaimed a code of freedom by the Russians (under Kiselev) and recognised as such by Europe. Secondly: the boyars in fact

---

[a] See this volume, 180-81.— *Ed.*

edited the *Règlement.* Thirdly: it was much worse, relatively speaking, in Moldavia than in Wallachia.

According to the *Règlement* every peasant owes the proprietor annually: 1) 12 days of general labour; 2) 1 day of field labour; 3) 1 day of wood-carrying. However, these days are measured not by time but by the work to be accomplished. The *Règlement organique* therefore itself lays down that the 12 days of [general] labour are to be the equivalent of 36 days of manual labour, the day of field labour = 3 days, and the day of wood-carrying similarly = 3 days. *Summa summarum*[a] 42 days. But there has to be added to this the so-called *jobbagio* (service, SERVITUDE), i.e. labour for the proprietor's extraordinary production requirements. This extraordinary labour involves the provision by the villages of 4 men for each 100 families, 3 men by villages of 63-75 families, 2 men by villages of 38-50 families, and 1 by villages of 13-25 families. This *jobbagio* is estimated at 14 working days for each Wallachian peasant. Thus the *corvée* prescribed by the *Règlement* itself = 42 + 14 = 56 working days. Owing to the severe climate the agricultural year in Wallachia consists of only 210 days, of which 40 must be deducted for Sundays and holidays, 30 on an average for bad weather; taken together this is 70 days less. There remain 140 days. Subtract from this the 56 *corvée* days. This leaves 84 days: a proportion which is even so no worse than that for the English agricultural workers, if we compare the time they work for their wages with the time they work for the creation of the surplus value which is divided between the farmer, the church, the state, the landowner, etc.

These are the days of *corvée* legally at the disposal of the proprietor, the legally established surplus labour. Yet the *Règlement* made provision for the further extension of the *corvée* without any infringement of the letter of the law. Namely, each day's task was determined in such a way that a certain amount remained over, so that it could only be completed during the next day's labour time. For example, particularly on the maize plantations, "a day's weeding was estimated at twelve perches, thereby imposing a task twice as large as a man could perform in one day".[b] The day's weeding is in fact determined by the *Règlement* in such a way

"that it begins in the month of May and ends in the month of October".[b]
[III-118] "In Moldavia," as one of the grand boyars himself said, "the 12

---

a Grand total.— *Ed.*
b Marx quotes in French.— *Ed.*

working days of the peasant, granted by the *Règlement,* amount in fact to 365 days" [p. 311].[a]

The ingenuity with which the boyars have exploited this law in order to appropriate the peasants' labour time can be explored in further detail in E. Regnault, *Histoire politique et sociale des principautés danubiennes,* Paris, 1855, pp. 305 et seq.

Let us now compare with this the greedy appetite for labour time—surplus labour time—characteristic of capitalist production in England.

It is not my intention here to go into the history of overwork in England since the invention of machinery. The fact is that as a result of these excesses there broke out epidemics whose devastating effects were equally threatening to capitalists and workers; that the state, against tremendous resistance from the capitalists, was compelled to introduce normal [working] days in the factories (later imitated in greater or lesser degree all over the Continent); that, as things are at the moment, this introduction of the normal day has yet to be extended from the factories proper to other branches of labour (bleachworks, printworks, dyeworks); and that this process is still going forward at the present time, the struggle for the normal day continues (e.g. the introduction of the Ten Hours' Bill, the extension of the FACTORY ACTS,[166] e.g., to the LACE MANUFACTURE in Nottingham, etc.). I refer for details on the earlier phases of this process to F. Engels, *Die Lage der arbeitenden Klasse in England,* Leipzig, 1845. Moreover, the practical resistance of the manufacturers was no fiercer than the theoretical resistance offered by their spokesmen and apologists, the professional *economists.* Indeed, Mr. *Newmarch,* the joint editor of Tooke's *History of Prices,* felt himself obliged, as President of the section for economic science, at the last Congress of the BRITISH ASSOCIATION FOR ARTS etc. (the name of the association to be checked), held at Manchester in September 1861, to stress that the understanding of the necessity for legal regulation and compulsory limitation of the normal working day in factories, etc., was one of the very latest achievements of present-day political economy, in virtue of which it was superior to its predecessors[167]!

My purpose here is simply to illustrate the parallel with the greedy appetite of the boyars by adducing certain quotations from the latest Factory Reports; and similarly to bring forward one or two examples in respect of branches of industry where the FACTORY ACTS have not yet been introduced (LACEmaking) or have only just been introduced (PRINTING WORKS). All we need here is a few

---

[a] Marx quotes in French.— *Ed.*

illustrations for a tendency which does not operate any more strongly in Wallachia than in England. *First illustration.* LACE TRADE *in Nottingham. "The Daily Telegraph" of January 17, 1860.*[168]

"It was declared by Mr. Broughton, a county magistrate, who filled the chair at a meeting held in the Nottingham Town Hall on Saturday last (January 14, 1860) that there is an amount of suffering and privation among that portion of the local population connected with the lace trade such as is utterly unknown anywhere else in the civilised world ... children of 9 or 10 years are dragged from their squalid beds at 2, 3, or 4 o'clock in the morning, and compelled to work for a bare subsistance until 10, 11, or 12 at night, their limbs wearing away, their frames dwindling, their faces whitening, and their humanity absolutely sinking into stone—like torpor utterly horrible to contemplate.... We are not surprised that Mr. Mallett or any other manufacturer should stand forward and protest against discussion.... The system, as Rev. Montagu Valpy describes it, is one of unmitigated slavery, socially, physically, morally, and spiritually.... What can be thought of a town which holds a public meeting to petition that the *period of labour for men shall be diminished to 18 hours a day*.... We declaim against the Virginian and Carolinian cottonplanters. Is their black-market, however, their lash, and their barter of human flesh, more detestable than this slow sacrifice of humanity, which takes place in order that veils and collars [III-119] may be fabricated for the benefit of capitalists?" *[a]

[III-119] *Second illustration.* FACTORY REPORTS.

"The fraudulent mill-owner begins work a quarter of an hour (sometimes more, sometimes less), before 6 a.m.; and leaves off a quarter of an hour (sometimes more, sometimes less) after 6 p.m. He takes 5 minutes from the beginning and end of the half hour nominally allowed for breakfast, and 10 minutes at the beginning and end of the hour nominally allowed for dinner. He works for a quarter of an hour (sometimes more, sometimes less) after 2 p.m. on Saturdays.[a]

* [III-120] // *To p. 119.* Since there is in existence that incorrect view that the factory system has become completely *different,* I quote here a note from *General Register Office,* 28 October *1857* ("The Quarterly Return of the Marriages, Births and Deaths", etc. published by authority of the Registrar-General, etc., *No. 35,* p. 6), where it says:

"Mr. Leigh, of the Deans gate subdistrict (Manchester), makes the following judicious remarks, which deserve the careful attention of the people at Manchester: Very sad there is the life of a child.... The total number of deaths, exclusive of coroner's cases, is 224, and of this number 156 were children under 5 years of age.... So large a proportion I have *never before* known. It is evident that whilst the ordinary circumstances affecting adult life have been to a considerable extent in abeyance, those militating against the very young have been in great activity.... 87 of the children died under the age of one year. Neglected diarrhoea, close confinement to ill ventilated rooms during hooping cough, *want of proper nutrition, and free administration of laudanum,* producing marasmus and convulsions, as well as hydrocephalus and congestion of brain, these must explain why ... the mortality (of children) is still so high." //[a] [III-120]

---

[a] Marx quotes in English.— *Ed.*

"THUS HIS *GAIN*" // here directly identified with the surplus labour he has filched // "IS as follows:

* "Before 6 a.m.	15 minutes		
After 6 p.m.	15 ditto		
At breakfast time	10 "		Total for 5 days:
At dinner time	20		300 minutes
	——		
	60		

On Saturdays

Before 6 a.m.	15 m.
At breakfast time	10
After 2 p.m.	15
	——
	40 *

* "*Total weekly gain*: 340 minutes, or 5 hours and 40 minutes weekly, which multiplied by 50 working weeks in the year, allowing two for holidays and occasional stoppages, are equal *to 27 working days*" * (*Suggestions, etc., by Mr. L. Horner*, in "*Factories Regulation Acts*. Ordered by the House of Commons to be printed, *9 August 1859*", pp. 4-5).

* "The profit to be gained by it (overworking over the legal time) appears to be, to many (millowners) a greater temptation than they can resist; they calculate upon the chance of not being found out; and when they see the small amount of penalty and costs, which those who have been convicted have had to pay, they find that if they should de detected there will still be a considerable *balance of gain*" * (*Report of the Inspectors of Factories for the Half Year ending 31st Oct. 1856*, [p.] 34).

* "Five minutes a day's increased work, multiplied by weeks, are equal to $2^{1}/_{2}$ days of production in the year" * (l.c., [p.] 35).

* "In cases where the additional time is gained by *a multiplication of small thefts* in the course of the day, there are insuperable difficulties to the Inspectors making out a case" * (l.c., p. 35).

(Here the OVERTIME appropriated in this way is directly characterised as "*THEFT*" by the official English Factory Inspectors.)

[III-120] These SMALL THEFTS are also described as "*PETTY PILFERINGS OF MINUTES*" (l.c., p. 48), later on AS "*SNATCHING A FEW MINUTES*" (l.c.), "OR AS IT IS TERMED, '*NIBBLING*', OR '*CRIBBLING AT MEAL TIMES*'" (l.c.).

* "'If you allow me,' said a highly respectable master to me, "'to work only 10 minutes in the day over time, you put one thousand a year in my pocket'" * (l.c., p. 48).

According to the Factory Inspectors, the working time is in practice still unrestricted in English PRINTWORKS, and even as late as 1857 children of 8 years and upwards had to work from 6 o'clock in the morning until 9 o'clock in the evening (15 hours).

* "The hours of labour in *printworks* may practically be considered to be unrestricted, notwithstanding the statutory limitation. The only restriction upon labour is contained in 22 of the Printwork act (8 and 9 Victoria C. 29) which enacts

that no child—that is, no child between the ages of 8 and 13 years—shall be employed *during the night*, which is defined to be between 10 p.m. and 6 a.m. of the following morning. *Children, therefore, of the age of 8 years*, may be *lawfully employed* in labour analogous in many respects to factory labour, frequently in rooms in which the temperature is oppressive, *continuously and without any cessation from work for rest or refreshment*, from 6 a.m. to 10 p.m. (16 hours); and a boy, having attained the age of 13, may lawfully be employed day and night for any numbers of hours without any restriction whatever. Children of the age of 8 years and upwards have been employed from 6 a.m. to 9 p.m. during the last half-year in my district" * (*Reports of the Inspectors of Factories, 31st Oct. 1857*, Report of Mr. A. Redgrave, [p.] 39).

* "An *additional hour* a day, gained by small instalments before 6 a.m. and after 6 p.m., and at the beginning and end of the times *nominally* fixed for meals, is nearly equivalent *to making 13 months in the year*" * (*Reports of the Inspectors of Factories. 30th April 1858. Report of Mr. L. Horner*, p. 9 [10]).

So concerned are the Factory Inspectors to make it clear that the GAIN is nothing but labour time, surplus labour time, and the extra GAIN is therefore surplus labour time *over and above* the normal working day.

[III-121] A period of crisis therefore does nothing to change the attempt to have the workers work OVERTIME. If only 3 or 4 days in the week are worked, the profit consists only in the surplus time that is worked during these 3 or 4 days. Hence an EXTRAORDINARY PROFIT is only to be made during the unpaid SURPLUS TIME, which is worked beyond the normal surplus time, and therefore beyond the legally determined normal working day. If I multiply 2 hours of surplus labour by 3 days of the week, the surplus value is of course only half as great as if I multiplied it by 6 days of the week. There is therefore an even greater temptation during crises to have the workers work *overtime*, i.e. more unpaid labour time than would otherwise be worked, on the days *when work actually takes place*. (Other manufacturers do the same thing in practice by reducing wages, i.e. by lessening necessary labour time during the 3 or 4 days on which work is done.) Hence in 1857-58:

* "It may seem inconsistent that there should be any overworking" *

// it is not in the least inconsistent that the manufacturer should try to SNATCH the largest possible portion of *unpaid* labour time during the crisis //

* "at a time when trade is so bad; but that very badness leads to transgressions by unscrupulous men; they get the *extra-profit of it*" * (*Reports etc. 30th April 1858*. Report of Mr. L. Horner, [p. 10]).

// The worse the time and the less business is done, the greater the profit that has to be made on the business done. // Horner therefore remarks, l.c., that at the very time when 122 MILLS in his district had been given up, 143 stood idle, and all the rest were on SHORT-TIME working, OVERWORK OVER THE LEGAL TIME was continuing (l.c.). Similarly another Factory Inspector, T. J. *Howell*, remarks of the same year:

* "I continue, however," * (ALTHOUGH in most of factories only HALF TIME was WORKED owing to the BAD TIME) * "to receive *the usual number of complaints* that half or 3 quarters on an hour in the day are snatched from the workers by encroaching upon the times allowed for rest and refreshment during the working day, and by starting 5 minutes and more before the proper time in the morning and by stopping 5 minutes or more after the proper time in the evening. These petty pilferings, amounting in the whole to from half to three quarters on an hour daily, are very *difficult of detection"* * (*T. J. Howell's Report*, l.c., p. 25).

* "To prove a systematic course of overworking, made up of minutes taken at 6 different times of the day, could manifestly not be done by the observation of an Inspector" * (*Reports*. L. Horner. 31st Oct. 1856 [p. 35]).

* "It is *this general acquiescence in the practice, if not approbation of the principle*, and the general concurrence that the limitation of labour is expedient, etc." * (*Reports etc.* 31st Oct. 1855, p. 77).

The governments on the Continent (France, Prussia, Austria, etc.) were compelled, in proportion with the development there of capitalist production, hence of the factory system, to follow the English example by limiting the working day *d'une manière ou d'une autre*.[a] They have for the most part, with certain modifications, copied, and inevitably so, the English FACTORY LEGISLATION.

[III-122] In France there existed in practice until 1848 no law for the limitation of the working day in factories. The law of March 22, 1841 for the limitation of the work of children in factories (FACTORIES, WORKS and WORKSHOPS EMPLOYING MOVING POWER, OR A CONTINUOUS FIRE, AND ALL ESTABLISHMENTS GIVING EMPLOYMENT TO MORE THAN 20 WORKMEN), the basis of which was 3 and 4 William IV, C. 103, remained *a dead letter* and has up to this day been implemented in practice in the *Département du Nord* alone.[169] In any case, according to this law *children under 13 years old* can be employed even at night (BETWEEN 9 p.m. and 5 a.m.) "UPON THE OCCASION OF URGENT REPAIRS, OR THE STOPPAGE OF A WATERWHEEL". *Children more than 13 years old* can be employed even *during the night* "IF THEIR LABOUR IS INDISPENSABLE".

On March 2, 1848 the Provisional Government promulgated a law limiting the working time to 10 hours in Paris and 11 in the Departments, not only in factories but in all places of manufacture and craft workshops, not only for children but for adult WORKMEN too. The Provisional Government proceeded from the false assumption that the normal working day was 11 hours in Paris and 12 in the Departments. But:

---

[a] In one way or another.— *Ed.*

"In many of the spinning mills the work lasted 14 to 15 hours a day, and even longer, greatly damaging the health and morality of the workers and particularly the children" ([J. A.] Blanqui, *Des classes ouvrières en France, pendant l'année 1848*).

The National Assembly modified this law, by the law of *September 8, 1848*, as follows:

* "The daily labour of the workman in manufactures and works shall not exceed 12 hours. The government has the power to declare exceptions to the above enactment in those cases where the nature of the work or of the apparatus requires it." *

The government put these *exceptions* into effect by the decree of May 17, 1851. Firstly, it listed the various branches of industry to which the law of September 8, 1848 did not apply. In addition, however, the following limitations were made:

* " *The cleaning of machinery at the end of the day*; work rendered necessary by accident to the moving power, the boiler, the machinery, or the building. Labour may be extended in the following cases: For 1 hour at the end of the day for washing and stretching pieces in dye works, bleach works, and cotton print works. For 2 hours in sugar factories, and refineries, and in chemical works. For 2 hours during *120 days* a year, at the choice of the manufacturer, and with the sanction of the Préfet, in dye works, print works, and finishing establishments." *

// FACTORY INSPECTOR A. Redgrave remarks in *Reports etc. 31st October 1855*, p. 80, in regard to the implementation of this law in France:

* "I have been assured by several manufacturers that when they have wished to avail themselves of the permission to extend the working day, the workmen have objected upon the ground that an extension of the working day at one moment would be followed by a curtailment of the ordinary number of hours at another ... and they especially objected to work beyond the 12 hours per day, because the law which fixed those hours is the only good which remains to them of the legislation of the Republic."

* "The *prolongation of the working day* is *optional* with the workmen.... When it is mutually agreed ... the rate per hour (beyond 12) is generally higher than their ordinary pay" * (l.c., p. 80).

A. Redgrave remarks on p. 81 that as a result of overwork and the physical enervation and mental demoralisation bound up with this

* "the labouring population of Rouen and Lille ... have succumbed", become "diminutive in growth", and "many are afflicted with that species of lameness which in England has given to its victims the name of 'factory cripples'".*

* "It must be admitted that a daily labour of 12 hours is a sufficient call upon the human frame, and when the requisite intervals for meals, the time required for going to and returning from work, are added to the hours of labour, the balance at the disposal of the workman is *not excessive*" * (A. Redgrave, l.c., p. 81).

Among the hypocritical pretexts (objections) advanced by the English MANUFACTURERS AGAINST THE *TEN HOURS' BILL* there is the following:

17*

* "One of the many objections made to the Ten Hours' Bill was the danger of throwing upon the hands of the young persons and females *so much leisure time,* which, from their defective education, they would [III-123] either waste or misuse; and it was urged that *until* education progressed, and means were provided for occupying in profitable mental or social employment the leisure Hours which the Ten Hours' Bill proposed to award to the Factory population, it was more advisable, in the interests of morality, that the *whole of the day should be spent in the factory"* (A. Redgrave, l.c., [p.] 87). //

// How much Macaulay distorts the economic FACTS so as to be able to act as Whig apologist for the here-and-now—Cato the Censor[a] towards the past alone, a sycophant towards the present—can be seen from the following passage among others:

* "The practice of setting children prematurely to work, a practice which the state, the legitimate protector of those who cannot protect themselves, has, in our time, wisely and humanely interdicted, prevailed in the 17th century to an extent which, when compared with the extent of the manufacturing system, seems almost incredible. At Norwich, the chief seat of the clothing trade, a little creature of six years old was thought fit for labour. Several writers of that time, and among them some who were considered as eminently benevolent, mention, with exultation, the fact, that in that *single city* boys and girls of tender age, created wealth exceeding what was necessary, for their own subsistence by 12,000 pounds a year. The more carefully we examine the history of the past, the more reason shall we find to dissent from those who imagine that our age has been fruitful of new social evils. The truth is, that the evils are, with scarcely an exception, old. That which is new is the intelligence which discerns and humanity which remedies them"* ([Th. B.] Macaulay, [*The History of*] *England,* Vol. I, p. 417).

This passage proves precisely the opposite, namely that at that time child labour was still an exceptional phenomenon, noted with exultation as particularly praiseworthy by political economists. What modern writer would mention it as something particularly noteworthy that children of tender age were being used up in factories? Anyone who reads writers like Child, Culpeper, etc., with common sense would come to the same conclusion. //

The LEGAL TIME OF WORKING is often EXCEEDED

* "by keeping the children, young persons, and women in the mill to clean the machinery during a part of the meal times, and on Saturdays after 2 o'clock, in place of that work being done within the restricted time"* (*Reports etc. 30th April 1856,* L. Horner, p. 12).

This OVERWORKING also takes place with WORKPEOPLE

* "who are not employed on piece-work, but receive weekly wages"* (*Reports of the Inspectors of Factories. 30th April 1859,* L. Horner, p[p. 8-]9).

(* Mr. Horner, besides being one of the Factory Inquiry Commissioners of 1833, was one of the original Inspectors of Factories, and during the early days of factory supervision had to

---

a I.e. implacable guardian of morality.— *Ed.*

contend with serious difficulties.*) This is what Horner says in his last report, dated *30th April 1859*[170]:

    * "The education of the children, *professedly* provided for, is, in numerous cases, an utter mockery; the protection of the workpeople against bodily injuries and death from unfenced machinery, also *professedly* provided for, has become, practically, a dead letter; the reporting of accidents is, to a great extent, a mere waste of public money.... Overworking to a very considerable extent, still prevails; and, in most instances, with that security against detection and punishment, which the *law itself affords*" * (l.c., pp. 9, 8).

(* Children above 13 years qualified to be employed for the same number of hours as adult men; half-timers children under 13 years.*)

    [III-124] * "The fact is, that prior to the Act of 1833, young persons and children were worked *all night, all day, or both ad libitum*" * (*Reports etc. 30th April 1860*, p[p. 50-]51).

According to the Act of 1833 NIGHT lay BETWEEN 8 $^1/_2$ p.m. and 5 $^1/_2$ a.m. The MILLOWNERS were PERMITTED

    * "to take their legal hours of labour at any period within 5 $^1/_2$ a.m. and 8 $^1/_2$ p.m.".*

* This signification of "day" and "night" continued through all the subsequent Factory acts, though with restricted hours of work until 1850, when, for the first time, the day hours of permitted labour were fixed at from 6 a.m. to 6 p.m., and in winter from 7 a.m. to 7 p.m. if so desired by the mill occupier.* [a]

    * "*The bulk of the accidents happened in the largest mills*.... The perpetual scramble for every minute of time, where work is going on by an unvarying power, which is indicated at perhaps a thousand horses, necessarily *leads to danger. In such mills, moments are the elements of profit*—the attention of everybody's every instant is demanded. It is here, where ... there may be seen a perpetual struggle between life and inorganic forces; where the mental energies must direct, and the animal energies must move and be kept equivalent to the revolutions of the spindles. They must not lag, notwithstanding the strain upon them either by excessive excitement or by heat; nor be suspended for an instant by any counter attention to the various movements around, for in every lagging there is loss" * (*Reports of the Inspectors of Factories. 30th April 1860*, p. 56).

    * "The *Children's Employment Commission*, the reports of which have been published several years, brought to light many enormities, and which still continue,—some of them much greater than any that factories and printworks were ever charged with.... Without an organized system of inspection by paid officers, responsible to Parliament, and kept to their duty by halfyearly reports of their proceedings, the law would soon become inoperative; as was proved by the inefficiency of all the Factory Laws prior to that of 1833, and as is the case at the present day in France: the Factory Law of 1841 containing no provision for systematic inspection" * (*Reports of the Inspectors etc. 31st Oct. 1858*, [p.] 10).

    [a] *Reports of the Inspectors of Factories ... for the Half Year Ending 30th April 1860*, p. 51.— *Ed.*

*The Factory Acts "have put an end to the premature decrepitude of the former long-hour workers; *by making them masters of their own time* they have given them a moral energy which is directing them to the eventual possession of political power"* (*Reports of the Inspectors of Factories. 31st Oct. 1859*, [p.] 47).

* "A still greater boon is, the *distinction* at last made clear *between the worker's own time and his master's. The worker knows now when that which he sells is ended*, and *when his own begins*; and by possessing a sure foreknowledge of this, is enabled to pre-arrange *his own minutes* for his *own purposes!*"* (l.c., p. 52.) a

This is very important with regard to the establishment of a normal working day. Before 1833:

* "The master had no time for anything but money, the servant had no time for anything but labour"* (l.c., p. 48).

* "The cupidity of millowners, whose cruelties in the pursuit of gain have hardly been exceeded by those perpetrated by the Spaniards on the conquest of America, in the pursuit of gold"* (John Wade, *History of the Middle and Working Classes*, 3rd ed., London, 1835, p. 114).

[III-124a] [171] * "Certain classes of workers (such as the adult males, and female weavers) have a direct interest in working overtime, and it may be supposed that they exercise some influence over the more juvenile classes, which latter have, besides, a natural dread of dismissal by giving any evidence or information calculated to implicate their employers ... even when detected (the juvenile workers) in working at illegal times, their evidence to prove the facts before a Bench of Magistrates, can seldom be relied on, as it is given at the risk of losing their employments"* (*Reports of the Inspectors of Factories for the Half Year Ending 31st Oct. 1860*, p. 8).

* "A factory employs 400 people, the half of which work by the 'piece' and have ... a direct interest in working longer hours. The other 200 are paid by the day, work equally long with the others, and get no more money for their overtime. A habit has arisen in some localities of starting systematically 5 minutes before and ceasing 5 minutes after the proper hour. There are 3 starting and 3 leaving off times each day; and thus 5 minutes at 6 different times, equal to half an hour is gained daily, not by one person only, but by 200 who work and are paid by the day. The work of these 200 people for half an hour a day is equal to one person's work for 50 hours, or $5/6$ of one person's labour in a week, and is *a positive gain to the employer*"* (l.c., p. 9).

If piece-wages are paid, the worker has indeed a share in his OVERTIME, and he himself appropriates a portion of the SURPLUS TIME during which he works. But the capitalist, quite apart from the more rapid valorisation of his fixed capital, enjoys a SURPLUS PROFIT even if he pays an hour of OVERTIME at the same rate as, or even higher than, the hours of the normal working day: 1) Because he does not need to increase the number of machines on which the work is done (e.g. spindles, looms). The same worker works at the same POWER LOOM whether he works for 12 or 15 hours. Thus a part of the capital outlay is subtracted with this production of SURPLUS TIME. 2) If the normal working day is 12 hours, of which 2 hours

---

a See this volume, p. 170.— *Ed.*

are surplus labour, 10 hours must be paid for 2 hours of surplus time.

Here of the 30 minutes ($^1/_2$ hour) $^1/_6$ is gained, =5 minutes, and the worker is paid 25 minutes. The surplus time is otherwise dependent on the worker's having first worked 10 hours for himself. Here it is already assumed in advance that he has earned his necessary wages. He can therefore be fobbed off with 1 aliquot part of the OVERTIME.

If the OVERTIME is *gratis*, capital acquires it without paying necessary labour time; 100 hours of OVERTIME, if 10 hours a day are being worked, =the labour time of 10 workers, whose wages are *completely saved*.

[III-124b] The BLEACHING AND DYEING ACTS WERE TO COME INTO OPERATION ON AUGUST 1, 1861.

The *main* provisions of the FACTORY ACTS *proper* are:

* "All persons under 16 years of age must be examined by the certifying surgeon. Children cannot be employed under the age of 8 years. Children between 8 and 13 years of age can only be employed for half-time, and must attend school daily. Females and young persons under the age of 18 years cannot be employed before 6 o'clock in the morning nor after 6 o'clock in the evening, nor after 2 o'clock in the afternoon of Saturdays. Females and young persons cannot be employed during a meal time, nor be allowed to remain in any room in a factory while any manufacturing process is carried on. Children under 13 years of age cannot be employed both before noon and after 1 o'clock on the same day" * ([*Reports*...,] l.c., pp. 22-23).

* "The hours of work are governed by a public clock; generally the clock of the nearest railway station.... It is sometimes advanced by way of excuse, when persons are found in a factory either during a meal hour or at some other illegal time, that they will not leave the mill at the appointed hour, and that compulsion is necessary to force them to cease work, especially on Saturday afternoons. But, if the hands remain in a factory after the machinery has ceased to revolve, and occupy themselves in cleaning their machines and in other like work, they would not have been so employed if sufficient time had been set apart specially for cleaning, etc., either before 6 p.m. or before 2 p.m. on Saturday afternoons" * (l.c., p. 23).

A further provision of the FACTORY ACTS in regard to MEALTIMES:

* "One hour and a half must be given to all young persons and females, at the same time between 7.30 a.m. and 6 p.m.; of this one hour must be given before 3 p.m., and no person can be employed for more than 5 hours before 1 p.m. without an interval of 30 minutes. The usual mealhours of mechanics throughout the country are, half an hour for breakfast and an hour for dinner" * (l.c., [p.] 24).

A further provision of the FACTORY ACTS:

* "The parent is required to cause his child to attend school for 3 hours daily for 5 days in the week. The occupier is restricted from employing children unless he shall have procured on each Monday morning a schoolmaster's certificate that each child has attended school for 3 hours daily for 5 days in the preceding week" * (p. 26).

In earlier centuries too, in the period preceding capitalist production, we likewise find forcible regulation, i.e. regulation by laws, on the part of governments. But the aim then was to force the workers to work for a *definite* period of time, whereas the present regulations all have the opposite objective, to force the capitalist to have them work for *no more than a definite period of time.* In the face of developed capital it is only government compulsion that can limit labour time. At the stage at which capital is only entering on its development, [III-124c] government compulsion steps in to transform the worker forcibly into a wage labourer.

*"When population is scanty, and land abundant, the free labourer is idle and saucy. Artificial regulation has often been found, not only useful, but absolutely necessary to compel him to work. At this day, according to Mr. Carlyle, the emancipated negroes in our West India Islands, having hot sun for nothing, and plenty of pumpkin for next to nothing, will not work. He seems to think legal regulations compelling work absolutely necessary, even for their own sakes. For they are rapidly relapsing into their original barbarism. So in England 500 years ago, it was found, by experience, that the poor need not, and would not work. A great plague in the 14th century having thinned the population, the difficulty of getting men to work *on reasonable terms* grew to such a height as to be quite intolerable, and to threaten the industry of the kingdom. Accordingly, in the year 1349, the Statute 23rd, Edward III, was passed, compelling the poor to work, and interfering with the wages of labour. It was followed with the same view through several centuries by a long series of statutable enactments. The wages of artisans, as well as of agricultural labourers; the prices of piece-work, as well as of day-work; the periods during which the poor were obliged to work, nay, *the very intervals for meals* (as in the Factory acts of the present day) were defined by law. Acts of Parliament regulating wages, but *against* the labourer, and in favour of the master, lasted for the long period of 464 years. Population grew. These laws were then found, and really became, unnecessary and burdensome. In the year 1813, they were all repealed"* ([J. B. Byles,] *Sophisms of Free-Trade etc.,* 7th ed., London, 1850, pp. 205-06).

"It appears from the Statute of 1496 that the diet was considered equivalent to $1/3$ of the income of an artificer and $1/2$ the income of a LABOURER, which indicates a greater degree of independence among the working classes than prevails at present; for the board, both of LABOURERS and ARTIFICERS, is now reckoned at a higher proportion of their WAGES. *The hours for MEALS and RELAXATION were more liberal than at this day.* They amounted to e.g. 1 hour for breakfast from March to September, $1^1/_2$ hours for dinner, and $1/_2$ hour for 'NOON-MEATE'." (Thus 3 hours altogether.) "In winter they worked from 5 o'clock in the morning until it went dark. In the COTTON factories of the present time, in contrast, $1/_2$ hour is allowed for [III-124d] breakfast, 1 hour for DINNER", hence only $1^1/_2$ hours, *exactly half as much as in the 15th century* (John Wade, *History of the Middle and Working Classes,* 3rd ed., London, 1835, pp. 24-25 and 577-78).

The *Bleaching and Dyeing Works Act.* Passed in 1860.
There are different provisions in the *Print Work Act, Bleaching and Dyeing Works Act* and the *Factory Act.*

* "The Bleaching etc Works Act limits the hours of work of all females and young persons between *6 a.m. and 8 p.m.*, but does not permit children to work *after 6 p.m.* The Print Works Act limits the hours of females, young persons and children between 6 a.m. and 10 p.m., provided the children have attended some school for 5 hours in any day but Saturday before 6 o'clock p.m." * (*Reports of the Inspectors of Factories for the Half Year Ending 31st Oct. 1861*, pp. 20-21).

* "The Factory Acts require 1 1/2 hours to be allowed during the day, and that they shall be taken between 7.30 a.m. and 6 p.m. and one hour thereof shall be given before 3 o'clock in the afternoon; and that no child, young person, or female shall be employed more than 5 hours before 1 o'clock in the afternoon of any day without an interval for meal time of at least 30 minutes.... In the Print Works Act there is *no* requisition ... *for any meal time at all*. Accordingly, young persons and females may work from 6 o'clock in the morning till 10 o'clock at night without stopping for meals" * (l.c., p. 21).

* "In Print Works a child may work between 6 o'clock in the morning and 10 o'clock at night.... By the Bleach Works Act a child may only work as under the Factories Act, whilst the labour *of the young persons and females,* with whom it has been previously working during the day, may be continued till 8 o'clock in the evening" * (l.c., [p.] 22).

* " *To take the silk manufacture* for example, since *1850,* it has been lawful to employ children above 11 years of age" * (from 11 to 13 years, therefore) * "in the winding and throwing of raw silk for 10 1/2 hours a day. From 1844 to 1850 their daily work, less Saturday, was limited to 10 hours; and before that period to 9 hours. These alterations took place on the ground that labour in silk mills was lighter than in mills for other fabrics, and less likely, in other respects also, to be prejudicial to health" * (l.c., p. 26).

* "The allegation put forth in 1850 about the manufacture of silk being a healthier occupation than that of other textile fabrics, not only entirely [III-124e] fails of proof, but the proof is quite the other way; for the average death rate is exceedingly high in the silk districts, and amongst the female part of the population is higher even than it is in the cotton districts of Lancashire, where, although it is true that the children only work half time, yet from the conditional causes which render cotton manufacture unhealthy, a high rate of pulmonary mortality might be supposed to be inevitable" * (l.c., p. 27).

Lord Ashley said in his speech on the Ten Hours' Bill (MARCH 15, 1844) that hours of labour in Austrian factories at that time were

* "15, not unfrequently 17 hours a day" * (*Ten Hours' Factory Bill,* London, 1844, p. 5).

* In Switzerland the regulations are very strict * :

* "In the canton of Argovia, no children are allowed to work, under 14 years, more than 12 hours and 1/2; and education is compulsory on the millowners." *

* In the canton of Zurich "the hours of labour are limited to 12; and children under 10 years of age are not allowed to be employed.... In Prussia, by the law of 1839, no child who has not completed his or her 16th year, is to be employed more than 10 hours a day; none under 9 years of age to be employed at all" * (p[p. 5-]6).

[V-196] [172] *Subinspector Baker reports (*Factory Reports,* 1843), as to "having seen several females, who, he was sure, could only just have completed their 18th year, who had been obliged to work from 6 a.m. to 10 p.m., with only 1 1/2 hours for meals. In other cases, he shows, females are obliged to work all night, in a temperature from 70 to 80 degrees.... I found (says Mr. Horner, *Factory Reports,* 1843) many young women, just 18 years of age, at work from half past 5 in the morning until 8 o'clock at night, with no cessation except a quarter of an hour for breakfast, and 3 quarters of an hour for dinner. They may be fairly said to labour for 15 hours and a half[a] out of 24. There are (says Mr. Saunders, *Factory Reports,* 1843) among them females who have been employed for some weeks, with an interval only of a few days, from 6 o'clock in the morning until 12 o'clock at night, less than 2 hours for meals, thus giving them for 5 nights in the week, 6 hours out of its 24 to go to and from their homes, and to obtain rest in bed"* (l.c., [pp.] 20-21).

The earlier wearing out of labour capacity, in other words premature ageing, in consequence of the forcible lengthening of labour time:

"In the year 1833, a letter was addressed to me by Mr. Ashworth, a very considerable millowner in Lancashire, which contains the following curious passage: 'You will next naturally inquire about the old men, who are said to die, or become unfit for work, when they attain 40 years of age, or soon after.' Mark the phrase 'old men' at 40 years of age!" (l.c., p. 12).

* The government commissioner M'Intosh (one of those commissioners, sent expressly to collect evidence against that taken by the committee of 1832), says in his report of 1833: "Although prepared by seeing childhood occupied in such a manner, it is very difficult to *believe the ages* of men advanced in years, as given by themselves, so complete is their premature old age"* (l.c., p. 13).

[III-124e] In 1816 Sir R. Peel PROCURED A COMMITTEE OF THE HOUSE OF COMMONS TO EXAMINE INTO THE APPRENTICE ACT OF 1802 (among other things). According to the EVIDENCE OF John Moss, OVERSEER OF a MILL near Preston,[b] the APPRENTICE ACT WAS CONSTANTLY SET AT NOUGHT. THE WITNESS DID NOT EVEN KNOW OF IT. The CHILDREN in the MILL were almost all APPRENTICES of London PARISHES; they WERE WORKED from 5 o'clock in the morning until 8 at night, all the year round, with 1 hour for the 2 MEALS; THEY INVARIABLY WORKED from 6 on the Sunday morning till 12, IN CLEANING THE MACHINERY FOR THE WEEK (15 hours).

Average working day among the London bakers 17 hours. Regularly 17 hours in the earliest stages of the cotton industry. Shortly after this introduction of night work.

---

[a] Here Marx reproduces an inaccuracy contained in the *Reports.* It should be "13 hours and a half".— *Ed.*

[b] J. Fielden, *The Curse of the Factory System; or, a Short Account of the Origin of Factory Cruelties,* London, [1836,] p. 15.— *Ed.*

RATE OF SURPLUS VALUE

If the worker does 10 hours of NECESSARY LABOUR and 2 hours of SURPLUS LABOUR, the rate=$^2/_{10}$=$^1/_5$=20%. It would result in an incorrect calculation, i.e. the rate of exploitation would be wrongly stated, if one were to consider the whole of the working day of 12 hours, and say, for instance, that the worker receives $^5/_6$ and the capitalist $^1/_6$ of it. The rate would then amount to $^1/_6$ ($^{12}/_6$=2 hours),=16$^2/_3$%. The same error would occur if the product were calculated, and indeed not the ratio of the SURPLUS PRODUCT to the part of the PRODUCT WHICH is equivalent to the wage, but to the SURPLUS PRODUCT AS ALIQUOT PART OF THE AGGREGATE PRODUCT. This point is not only very important for the determination of surplus value but it is later of decisive importance for the correct determination of the rate of profit.[173]

[III-124f] "He" (one of the entrepreneurs in the FIRST period of the development of the COTTON INDUSTRY) "communicated an admirable idea to me, I don't know whether it is his own invention, but it is truly worthy of him: it is the *organisation of night work.* The workers will be divided into two gangs, in such a way that each of them on alternate nights will be awake until the morning: the business will no longer come to a halt. The work, when confined to 17 hours, allowed an enormous capital—the value of the machines, the rent of the buildings, etc.—to lie dormant for 7 whole hours. These 7 whole hours of interest a day will no longer be lost. He explained to me a plan thanks to which he will recover, and more than recover, the expenses of lighting, simply by his way of remunerating night work" (St. Germain Leduc, *Sir Richard Arkwright etc. (1760 à 1792),* Paris, 1842, [pp.] 145-46).[a]

This is now the norm in the COTTON factories of Moscow. Much more frightful at this moment the system followed in the mirror factories of Manchester, with children being used as well. There are two gangs, which relieve each other every 6 hours, day and night, during the whole of the 24 hours. We read in Babbage (*On the Economy of Machinery etc.,* London, 1832):

"The first machines for manufacturing tulle were very expensive when first purchased, at between £1,000 and £1,200 or £1,300 sterling. Every manufacturer who possessed one of these machines soon found that he was manufacturing more, but because its work was limited to 8 hours a day he could not, in view of its price, compete with the old method of manufacture. This disadvantage stemmed from the considerable sum of money devoted to the initial establishment of the machine. Soon, however, the manufacturers noticed that with the same expenditure of initial capital and a small addition to their circulating capital they could set the same machine to work for 24 hours. The advantages thereby realised induced other people to direct their attention to the means of perfecting the machine; so that its purchase price underwent a considerable reduction simultaneously with increases in the speed and quantity of tulle manufacture" (Ch. XXII).[174]

---

[a] Marx quotes Leduc and, below, Macnab in French.— *Ed.*

Dale, Owen's predecessor in the COTTON mill at New Lanark, and himself a philanthropist, still employed children for 13 hours a day, even those under 10 years old.

"To cover the expense of these so well combined arrangements, and for the general upkeep of the premises, it was absolutely necessary to employ these children in the cotton mills from 6 o'clock in the morning until 7 o'clock in the evening, summer and winter alike.... The directors of the workhouses, through misplaced motives of economy, did not want to send the children entrusted to their care, unless the owner of establishment took charge of them from the ages of 6, 7 or 8 years" (Henry Grey Macnab, *Examen impartial des nouvelles vues de M. Robert Owen, et de ses établissements à New-Lanark en Écosse.* Traduit par *Laffon de Ladébat,* Paris, 1821, [p.] 64).

"Thus the arrangements of Mr. Dale and his tender solicitude for the well-being of these children were in the last resort almost entirely useless and unsuccessful. He had taken these children into his service, and without their labour he could not feed them" (l.c., [p.] 65).

"The source of this evil was that the children [III-124g] sent by the workhouses were much too young for the work, and ought to have been kept for four more years, and to have received primary schooling.... If this is the true and not exaggerated picture of the situation of our apprentices emerging from the workhouses, *in our present manufacturing system,* even under the best and most humane regulations, how deplorable must the situation of these children be under a bad management?" (l.c., [p.] 66).

As soon as Owen took over the management:

"The system of accepting apprentices drawn from the workhouses was abolished.... They gave up the practice of employing children of six to eight years of age in the factories" ([p.] 74).

"Working hours, which were 16 out of the 24, have been reduced to 10 and a half per day" ([p.] 98).

This was naturally regarded as subversive of society. A great noise was made by the *économistes* and Benthamite "philosophers".

* * *

"But it is still easier to obtain bread in the eastern islands of the Asian archipelago, where sago grows wild in the forests. When the inhabitants have convinced themselves, by boring a hole in the trunk, that the pith is ripe, the tree is cut down and divided into several pieces, the pith is extracted, mixed with water and filtered: it is then quite fit for use as sago meal. One tree commonly yields 300 pounds, and it may yield 500-600. There, then, one goes into the forest and cuts one's own bread, just as with us one cuts firewood" (J. F. Schouw, *Die Erde, die Pflanzen und der Mensch,* 2nd ed., Leipzig, 1854, [p.] 148).

Suppose that 1 day (of 12 hours) a week is required for this bread-cutter to satisfy all his needs. If capitalist production were introduced, he would have to work 6 days a week in order to appropriate for himself the product of that one day.

Surplus labour naturally consists of the same kind of labour as NECESSARY labour. If the worker is a spinner, his surplus labour consists of spinning, and his SURPLUS PRODUCT of spun yarn. If he is a miner, similarly, etc. It can therefore be seen that the kind of labour it is, its particular quality, the particular branch it belongs to, is entirely irrelevant to the ratio of SURPLUS LABOUR to NECESSARY LABOUR. Equally irrelevant, therefore, is the ratio between the values of different days of labour, or, which is the same thing, the ratio in which A DAY OF MORE OR LESS SKILLED LABOUR IS EQUATED WITH A DAY OF UNSKILLED AVERAGE LABOUR. This equation has no effect at all on the ratio under investigation here. In order to simplify (the presentation) we can therefore always argue as if the labour of all the workers employed by the capitalist=AVERAGE UNSKILLED LABOUR, simple labour.[69] In any case, in the capitalist's own calculations (in the monetary expression of labour), every kind of labour is reduced, in practice and in fact, *to this expression.*

[III-124h] The qualitative differences between the different kinds of *AVERAGE LABOUR,* whereby one requires more dexterity, the other more strength, etc., cancel each other out in practice. But as regards the *individual differences* between workers who perform *the same* labour, the following must be pointed out: These differences are greatest in handicraft production (and in the higher spheres of so-called unproductive labour). They vanish progressively as time goes on, and in developed capitalist production, where division of labour and machinery prevail, their role is limited to a sphere almost too small for calculation. (If we set aside the short period during which APPRENTICES learn their trade.) The AVERAGE wage must be high enough to preserve the AVERAGE worker's life as a worker; and an AVERAGE performance is here the prerequisite the worker must fulfil to be allowed into the workshop at all. He who stands above or below this AVERAGE is an exception, and, viewing the workshop as a whole, its entire personnel provides the AVERAGE product in the AVERAGE time of the branch in question under the AVERAGE conditions of production. In the daily or weekly wage, etc., no regard is in fact taken of these individual DIFFERENCES. They *are* taken into account in the piece-wage system, though. But this does not change the relation between capitalist and worker at all. If the labour time of *A* is higher than that of *B*, his wages are higher too, but also the SURPLUS VALUE he produces. If his performance falls below the AVERAGE, his wages fall, but also the SURPLUS VALUE. The workshop as a whole, however, must provide the AVERAGE. What is above and below the AVERAGE is mutually complementary, and the AVERAGE, which the GREAT BULK OF LABOURERS perform in any case, remains what it was. These matters are to be considered under the wages of labour.[33] For the relation being considered here they are irrelevant. For the rest, the piece-wage was introduced very early on into the English factories. Once it was established how much could be performed ON AN AVERAGE in a given period of labour, the wage was determined accordingly (the number of hours in the working day being simultaneously given). And IN FACT the wage (the AGGREGATE) was then lower if 17 hours a day were worked than if 10 were worked. Only with *extraordinary* OVERTIME WORKING would the workers benefit from the distinction, so that they could APPROPRIATE TO THEMSELVES a PART of this EXTRAORDINARY SURPLUS LABOUR. Which, incidentally, is also the case where there is EXTRAORDINARY SURPLUS LABOUR under the daily wage system, etc.

We have seen that the basis of *value* is the fact that human beings relate to each other's labour as equal, and general, and in this form social, labour. This is an abstraction, like all human thought, and social relations only exist among human beings to the extent that they think, and possess this power of abstraction from sensuous individuality and contingency. The kind of political economist who attacks the determination of value by labour time on the ground that the work performed by 2 individuals during the same time is not *absolutely equal* (although in the same trade), doesn't yet even know what distinguishes human social relations from relations between animals. He is a BEAST. As BEASTS, the same fellows then also have no difficulty in overlooking the fact that no 2 use values are absolutely identical (no 2 leaves, *Leibniz*[175]) and even less difficulty in judging use values, which have no common measure whatever, as exchange values *according to their degree of utility.*

If the MONETARY EXPRESSION (money TO BE SUPPOSED TO KEEP ITS VALUE, AS IT REALLY DOES FOR LONGER PERIODS) of an AVERAGE working day of 12 hours were=10s., it would be clear that the worker who works for 12 hours can never add more than 10s. to the object of labour. If the total amount of the means of subsistence he needs every day is 5s., the capitalist will have to pay 5s. and receive 5s. of SURPLUS VALUE. If it comes to 6 he will only receive 4, if 7 only 3, if 3 in contrast then 7, etc. With a given labour time—length of the working day—it must be firmly grasped that the sum total of the NECESSARY and the SURPLUS LABOUR is represented in a product of constant value and of EQUAL MONETARY EXPRESSION OF THAT VALUE, AS LONG AS THE VALUE OF MONEY REMAINS CONSTANT.

[III-125] 3) RELATIVE SURPLUS VALUE

We call the form of surplus value considered so far *abso-lute surplus value* because its very existence, its rate of growth, and its every increase is at the same time an absolute increase of *created* value (of produced value). It arises, as we have seen,[a] from an extension of the necessary working day beyond its limits, and its absolute magnitude is equal to the magnitude of this extension, whereas its relative magnitude—the proportional surplus value, or the rate of surplus value—is given by the ratio of this extension, this fluxion, to its fluent,[176] necessary labour time. If the necessary labour time is 10 hours, the working day will be extended by 2, 3, 4, 5 hours. As a result, a value of 12-15 hours of labour will be created instead of one of 10. The extension of the *normal working day*, i.e. the total of necessary labour time+surplus labour time, is here the process by which surplus value grows, is increased.

Let us assume that the overall working day has reached its normal limits. Now there emerges, in the manner peculiar to and characteristic of it, capital's tendency to posit surplus value, i.e. surplus labour time. Let the normal working day consist of 12 hours, of which 10 are necessary labour time, and 2 surplus labour time. Let an extension beyond this duration, hence a growth in absolute surplus value, be out of the question. It is of course clear that such a barrier—however one may fix it—is bound to assert itself, to be reached. (One may also assume, in order to have the problem present in its purest form, that the *sum total* of absolute surplus value cannot be raised any further, since the working population is given.) In this case, therefore, where the surplus

---

[a] See this volume, pp. 175-76.— *Ed.*

value cannot be raised any further by lengthening the overall working day, how can it be raised any further at all? By *shortening the necessary labour time.* Given an overall working day of 12 hours (10 hours necessary labour time, 2 hours surplus labour time) the surplus value or the surplus labour time may e.g. grow by 50%, may grow from 2 hours to 3—without any extension of the overall working day—if the necessary labour time is shortened from 10 hours to 9 hours, by $1/10$. The quantum of surplus labour time, consequently surplus value, may grow not only through a direct increase of surplus labour time achieved by a simultaneous lengthening of the overall working day, but also through the shortening of the necessary labour time, hence the *conversion* of labour time from necessary to surplus labour time. The normal working day would not be lengthened, but necessary labour time would be reduced and there would have been a change in the ratio governing the division of the overall working day into labour which replaces wages and labour which creates surplus value.

As we have seen,[a] necessary labour time (as paid labour time) is nothing but the labour time which replaces the labour time contained in the wage, in the purchasing price of labour capacity (which is in reality the labour time required for the production of the wage). It could be reduced by reducing the wage. If the value of the wage is forcibly cut down, so also is the labour time contained in the wage, hence the labour time paid for the reproduction, the replacement, of the wage. As the value fell, so would the equivalent for the value: the equivalent value corresponding to, or rather equal to, this value. This is exactly what happens in practice, of course. The price of labour capacity, like that of every other commodity, does in practice rise and fall above and below its value. But this is of no concern to us, as we proceed from the assumption that the price of the commodity corresponds to its value, or we consider the phenomena *on this assumption.* The reduction of necessary labour time which is under discussion here has therefore to be analysed under the presupposition that labour capacity is sold at its value, that the worker receives the normal wage, and therefore that no reduction occurs in the amount of the means of subsistence which are required for the normal and traditional reproduction of his labour capacity.

[III-126] // An increase in surplus value achieved by reducing wages below their average level (without increasing the productivity of labour) is an increase in profit achieved by forcing the

---

a See this volume, pp. 173-76.— *Ed.*

worker below the level of his normal conditions of life. On the other hand, an increase in wages over their normal average level is, on the part of the worker, a sharing in, an appropriation of, a part of his own surplus labour (similarly assuming the productive power of labour remains constant). In the first case * the capitalist encroaches upon the vital conditions of the workman, and upon the times of labour necessary for its own sustainance.* In the second case * the workman expropriates part of his own surplus labour. In both cases the one loses what the other gains, but the workman loses in life, what the capitalist gains in money, and in the other case the workman gains in enjoyment of life, what the capitalist loses in the rate of appropriating other people's labour.*//

Any reduction in necessary labour time which takes place on the assumption that the price of labour capacity is equal to its value, hence that wages are not forced down below normal wages, is possible only through *an increase in the productivity of labour*, or through a higher *development of the productive forces of labour*, which is the same thing.

We saw when we were considering the commodity [10] that if the productive power of labour increases, the same use value will be produced in a shorter labour time, or a greater quantity of the same use values will be produced in the same labour time (or a shorter time, but this is included in case 2). The use value of the commodity remains the same although its exchange value has fallen, i.e. a smaller quantity of labour time is objectified in it, less labour is required to produce it. The amount of the means of subsistence required for the normal reproduction of labour capacity is not determined by their exchange value but by their use value—qualitatively and quantitatively. It is therefore not determined by the labour time required to produce them, objectified in them, but by the result of this labour time, by the real labour, to the extent that it is present in the product. Hence if the same amount of the means of subsistence can be produced in a shorter working period owing to an increase in the productivity of real labour, the value of labour capacity will fall, and along with that the labour time required for its reproduction, for the production of its equivalent value, the necessary labour time, although labour capacity will continue to be sold at its value. Just as any other commodity continues to be sold at its value if it costs $1/100$ less today than before, because $1/100$ less labour time is contained in it, although it continues to possess the same use value as before. Here the value of labour capacity falls, and therefore the necessary labour time too, not because the price of labour capacity has fallen below its value but because its value has itself fallen, i.e. because less labour time is objectified in the labour capacity, and therefore less labour time is required for its reproduction. In this case surplus labour time grows because necessary labour time has diminished. A part of the overall working day which was previously reserved for necessary labour is now set free, is annexed to the surplus labour time. A part of the necessary labour time is converted into surplus labour time; hence a portion of the overall value of the product, which previously entered the wage, now enters the surplus value (the capitalist's gain). I call this form of surplus value *relative surplus value.*

It is clear from the outset that an increase in the productive power of labour can only lessen the value of its labour capacity or its necessary labour time to the extent that the products of this labour either directly enter into the worker's consumption, such as means of nourishment and heating, housing, clothing, etc., or go into the constant capital (raw material and instrument of labour) which is required for the manufacture of those products. The value of the constant capital entering into the product re-appears in the value of the product, and therefore the value of the product clearly falls, not only when there is a fall in the labour time required for its own manufacture but also, and just as much, when there is a fall in the labour time required for the manufacture of its conditions of production; that is to say the value of the raw material and instrument of labour required for the manufacture of the products which enter into the consumption of the worker, in short the value of the constant capital (*see Ramsay*[177]).

// The distinction between the re-appearance or simple preservation of the value in the product and the reproduction of that value is as follows: In the latter case a new equivalent replaces the exchange value lost through the consumption of the use value in which it was contained. In the first case no new equivalent is put in the place of the original value. For example, the value of the wood which re-appears in the table is not replaced by a newly created equivalent. The value of the wood only re-appears in the table because the wood previously possessed value and the production of its value is a prerequisite for the production of the table's value. //

But, secondly: Take the worker in the branch of labour in which he himself works. If, owing to a rise in the productive power of labour, a worker in a weaving-mill produces 20 yards of calico in one hour, whereas he previously produced only 1 yard, the 20 yards, after deduction of the increased amount of constant capital contained in them, therefore in so far as they are, in general, value created by the worker himself, [III-127] possess no more value than the 1 yard, did previously. If the productive power of labour remains the same in all the other branches as it was before this transformation in the weaving trade, the worker would be unable to buy more of the means of subsistence than before with his 1 hour, despite the heightened productive power of his labour—i.e. he could only buy commodities in which 1 hour of labour is objectified, just as before. The growth of productive power in his own branch of labour, the increased productivity of his own labour, would therefore only cheapen the reproduction of his own labour capacity and hence only diminish his necessary labour time, in so far as and to the extent to which calico enters into his own consumption as, say, an element in his clothing. Only in this proportion. But this is true of every specific branch of production, hence of every individual capital, taken for itself, in the sphere of its own industrial functioning.

If we take the total capital of society, hence the whole capitalist class vis-à-vis the working class, it is clear that the capitalist class can only increase surplus value without extending the overall working day and without lessening the normal wage in so far as a greater productivity of labour, a higher development of the productive power of labour, makes it possible to maintain the working class as a whole with less labour, to produce the total amount of its means of subsistence more cheaply, and therefore to reduce the amount of labour time in total that the working class requires for the reproduction of its own wages. But this total amount consists simply of the total amount of individual means of subsistence and the total amount of the specific branches of labour; hence of the total amount of the individual branches of labour which produce these means of subsistence; hence of the total amount of the reductions in labour time on account of the increased productive power of labour in each of these individual branches. For the purpose of generalising the presentation, however, we are justified in viewing the process as if the worker lived from the use values he produces himself—and we can only view the process by picturing a particular individual capital with particular workers in a particular sphere. (It is not assumed here that the worker's need for necessary labour time declines in the same measure as the amount of product he provides in the same period increases, but that his own product, which has now become cheaper, enters into his own consumption in proportion as his necessary labour time declines. This is valid for the whole of society, hence for the sum total of all the individuals, since the social sum of relative surplus labour is nothing but the sum of all the surplus labours of the individual workers in the individual branches of labour. It is only that compensations and adjustments come into the picture, the consideration of which does not belong here, although they hide the true relation.

A *reduction in necessary labour time* is therefore an *increase in surplus labour time.* The one grows smaller in proportion as the other grows larger, and inversely. This rise and fall does not, however, affect the overall working day and its magnitude.) The worker himself can in fact only create relative surplus value to the extent that he creates it in the sphere of his own activity, i.e. produces products entering into his own consumption in less time than previously. The political economists therefore always take flight to this assumption, in so far as they go into the nature of relative value at all (see *Mill*[178]).

In fact, one looks at the usual course of events. If the working day was = 12 hours, surplus labour time = 2 hours, and the capitalist, in consequence of increased productivity of labour, produces e.g. twice as much. Then surplus value can grow—his gain can emerge—only from two sources. Either the product of labour enters in a certain proportion into the reproduction of labour capacity, and labour capacity is cheapened in this proportion, so that the wage, i.e. the value of labour capacity falls in this ratio, hence there is also a fall in the part of the total working day required until then for the reproduction of this part of the value of labour capacity. Or the manufacturer sells the commodity above its value, i.e. as if the productivity of labour had remained the same. Only in the proportion to which he sells it above its value, hence buys all other commodities below their value, cheaper than the ratio between the amount of labour time contained in them and that contained in his commodity would require, does he posit a new surplus value. The worker, however, only receives the same normal wage as before. He therefore obtains a smaller part of the total value of the product, or a smaller part of that value is *expended in the purchase of labour capacity than before the increase* in the productivity of labour. A smaller *part of his whole day is therefore expended in reproducing his wages, a larger part for the capitalist.* It is the same thing, in practice, *as if his cost of upkeep were lessened as a result of the increased productivity of his labour, or as if he* could buy all other means of subsistence cheaper as a result of *the greater productivity* of his labour in the same proportion as the capitalist receives new value.

[III-128] In any case, we do not need to repeat here that the general presupposition of a sale of commodities above their value negates itself, and competition in fact compensates for sale above the value by sale below the value. What is involved here is the case where an increase in the productivity of labour has not yet become universal in the same branch of business, where the capitalist therefore sells (in a certain proportion at least, for he will always sell cheaper than the other) as if more labour time had been needed for the manufacture of his product than was really necessary. He sells e.g. the product of $^3/_4$ of an hour as the product of 1 hour, because the majority of his competitors still need 1 hour to manufacture this product. If the total working day was 12 hours, he sells, in the given case, as if it had been 15 hours. ($^{12}/_4=3$, $12+3=15$.) He has not lengthened the working day. If necessary labour time was = 10, and surplus labour time was = 2, it is still = 2. Actually, however, he sells as if necessary labour time were only 7 hours and surplus labour 5 hours ($7+5=12$). In fact, the labour of his own workers relates to that of average workers in such a way that they buy with the value of 7 hours as much as the latter buy with the value of 10 (since value has not fallen in proportion to productivity). With the original ratio, he had to give the workers 10 hours out of the 12, i.e. $\frac{5}{6}\left(\frac{12}{6}=2;\quad \frac{5\times12}{6}=10\right)$.

Now, in consequence of the rise in the productivity of labour, he sells 12 at 15. If an hour of labour were paid for as an hour that stands $^1/_4$ above average labour, the workers, instead of 10 hours, would only have to work $10-^{10}/_4$. If the necessary working day until then was 10 hours, and 2 hours of surplus labour, the workers would now only need to work $10\times^3/_4$ hours instead of $10\times^4/_4$ hours (since their labour would count for $^1/_4$ more than the average hour of labour), hence they would need to work $7^1/_2$ hours instead of 10, and the surplus value, just as before, would come to $^1/_5$ of the necessary labour time ($^{10}/_5=2$). It would now be $^1/_5$ of $7^1/_2$ hours, or $^{15}/_2$ hours. $^1/_5$ of $^{15}/_2=^{15}/_{10}=1\,^5/_{10}=1\,^1/_2$, or $^3/_2$, or $^6/_4$. In fact if $^3/_4$ of an hour of this labour = 1, or $^4/_4$ of an hour of average labour, $^6/_4$ of the same labour = $^8/_4$, or 2 hours of labour. The working day would thereby be reduced to $7^1/_2+^3/_2=9$ hours. The capitalist has the workers work 12 hours, as before, pays for the necessary labour time with $7^1/_2$, and therefore pockets $4^1/_2$ hours.

His gain derives from the fact that the necessary labour time of 10 hours has fallen to $7\,^1/_2$, or the worker can buy all his necessary means of subsistence with the product of $7^1/_2$ hours. It is exactly the same as if he were to produce the whole of his means of subsistence himself and were to be able to produce as much in $^3/_4$ of an hour as previously in 1 hour, owing to the higher productivity of his labour, hence producing in $7^1/_2$ hours as much as he previously produced in 10. If with the increased productivity of labour the proportion had remained the same, the overall working day would have become shorter, because necessary labour would have been lessened while the proportion between necessary labour and surplus labour would have remained the same. In practice it comes to exactly the same thing: Whether the value of labour capacity and therefore the necessary labour time is *lessened*, because the worker's product enters into his own consumption in a certain proportion and therefore the necessary labour time declines and the surplus labour time, hence also surplus value, increases in this proportion; or whether as a result of the increased productivity of labour this particular branch of labour rises above the level of the socially average worker in the same branch, therefore the value e.g. of the hour of labour rises relative to all other commodities, the capitalist pays this labour as average labour—according to the previous standard—but sells it as labour of a higher than average level. In both cases a smaller number of hours is sufficient to pay the wage, i.e. the [III-129] necessary labour time has been reduced and in both cases the relative surplus value, i.e. surplus value not attained through an absolute prolongation of the working day, results from the decline in the amount of labour time required for the reproduction of the wage consequent on the increased productivity of labour; relative surplus value results in the one case directly, because the worker produces the same quantity of use values in a lesser labour time, although the product continues to be sold at its value. In the other case it results because a smaller quantity of labour time is equated with a greater quantity of average labour time as a result of the rise in productivity, and the worker therefore receives the same quantity of use values with labour time which is smaller but sold at a higher price. In both cases the relative surplus value results from a reduction in the *necessary labour time.*

The following is in any case clear in itself: If the productivity of labour grows, and the ratio remains the same, the worker would either have to work less labour time to reproduce his wages, say $7^1/_2$ instead of 10 hours, thereby shortening the working day as a whole; or he would have to receive a greater quantity of means of subsistence, his wages would rise above the [average] level. If neither the one thing nor the other takes place, it is clear that the result of the increased productivity of labour has only been to increase the amount of labour he performs for the capitalist, and to reduce the amount of labour he performs for himself.

The whole difficulty arises from this, that when the individual capitalist raises the productivity of labour, he is not thinking directly of a diminution of necessary labour time, but of its sale above its value—of *raising it above average labour time.* Of this raised labour time, however, a smaller proportion is needed for the replacement of wages; i.e. the surplus labour time grows, although this growth presents itself in a roundabout way, through sale above value.

The working day as a whole does not grow along with the growth in relative surplus value, hence relative labour time. It therefore follows that there is only a fall in the *proportion* in which the worker participates in his own working day. There is a fall in relative wages, or the weight of capital rises in relation to labour.

Further: As a result of the growth in the productivity of labour the quantity of products is increased. The same value is present in their total amount (e.g. the total for one working day) as was present previously in a smaller total. The individual product or the individual commodity therefore falls in value, but it is multiplied by a larger factor, which is indicated by the number of products. 6×4 is not more than 12×2. Here, then, we have a growth in the real wealth of use values, without any growth in their exchange value or the labour time contained in them, whereas in the first case—absolute surplus value—the amount of products also grows, but simultaneously with their exchange value, i.e. in proportion to the labour time contained in them.

This is to be understood as follows. If 10 [lbs] of cotton are converted into twist in the same time as previously 1 lb, the 10 lbs have not absorbed more spinning labour than the previous 1 lb. The value added to the 10 lbs is no greater than the value of the 1 lb. Every 1 lb of twist contains ten times less spinning labour in the first case than in the second. And since they both contain the same amount of cotton, every 1 lb of twist, *caeteris paribus,*[a] is $^1/_{10}$ cheaper if the spinning labour amounts to $^1/_{10}$ of the value. [III-130] If the added day of spinning labour=10, and the value of 1 lb of cotton=20 (for the sake of simplicity the instrument is set=0 in both cases), in the first case 1 lb of twist=10+20=30; in the second case 10 lbs of twist=100+10=110, making 1 lb of

---

[a] Other things being equal.— *Ed.*

twist=11, and 10 lbs=110, whereas in the first case 10 lbs=300.

Relative surplus value is therefore distinguished from absolute as follows. In both, surplus value=surplus labour, or, the ratio of surplus value is equal to the ratio of surplus labour time to necessary labour time. In the first case the working day is extended beyond its limits and the surplus value grows (or the surplus labour time grows) in proportion as the working day is *extended* beyond its limit. In the second case the working day is given. Here, the surplus value, or the surplus labour time, is increased owing to the *reduction* of the portion of the working day that was required, or was necessary, for the reproduction of the wage. In the first case a given level of the productivity of labour is presupposed. In the second case the productivity of labour is raised. In the first case the value of an aliquot part of the total product or a part of the product of the working day remains unchanged; in the second the value of the part of the product changes, but its quantity (number of articles) grows in the same proportion as its value diminishes. The value of the total amount thus remains unchanged, whilst the total amount of products or use values has increased. Further the matter is to be presented simply as follows:

As we saw in our analysis of the commodity,[10] the productivity of labour does not increase the *value* of the product or the commodity in which the labour manifests itself. If we presuppose that the labour time contained in the commodities is, under the given conditions, *necessary* labour time, socially necessary labour time[70]—and this is always the presupposition we start from once the value of a commodity is reduced to the labour time contained in it—what takes place is rather the following: *The value of the product of labour is in an inverse ratio to the productivity of labour.* This is in fact an identical proposition. It means nothing more than this: If labour becomes more productive, it can represent a greater quantity of the same use values in the same period, it can embody itself in a greater amount of use values of the same kind. Accordingly, an aliquot part of these use values, e.g. a yard of linen, contains less labour time than previously, has therefore *less exchange value* and indeed the exchange value of the yard of linen has fallen in the same proportion as the productivity of the labour of weaving has grown. Inversely, if more labour time than previously were required to produce a yard of linen (let us say, because more labour time was required to produce a pound of flax), the yard of linen would now contain more labour time, hence would have a higher exchange value. Its exchange value would have increased in the same proportion as the labour required to produce it had become less productive.

If we therefore take the whole working day—the average normal working day—the value of the sum total of its products remains unchanged, whether the labour becomes more or less productive. For the sum total of use values produced comes to one working day, just as before, it continues to represent the same quantity of socially necessary labour time. If, on the other hand, we take an aliquot part of the daily overall production, or a part of the product, its value rises and falls in *inverse* ratio to the productivity of the labour contained in it. For example, if 1 quarter or 8 BUSHELS are the product of a month's labour, let agriculture double its productivity in one case, and halve its productivity in another case. We should then have 3 cases: 8 BUSHELS the product of a month's labour; 16 BUSHELS the product of the same labour time; 4 BUSHELS the product of the same labour time. The value of the total amount produced during the month, 8, 16 or 4 BUSHELS, would continue to contain respectively the same quantity of necessary labour time. The value of this total amount would therefore have remained unchanged, although in one case the productivity of labour would have doubled, in the other case declined to half its original level. But in the first case 1 BUSHEL would contain $^1/_8$ of a month=$^2/_{16}$, in the second case $^1/_4$ or $^2/_8$=$^4/_{16}$, and in the third case only $^1/_{16}$. With the productivity of agriculture doubled, the value of the BUSHELS fell by a half; with productivity declining to half its original level, the value doubled. The *value* of a commodity can therefore never increase as a result of [increases in] the productivity of labour. This would involve a contradiction. Growth in the productivity of labour means that it brings forth the same product (use value) in less time. Growth in the exchange value of the product means that it contains more labour time than previously.

If, therefore, the *value* of the individual commodity stands in an *inverse* ratio to the productivity of labour, whilst the value of the total amount of products in which a *given* labour time is embodied remains untouched, unchanged, by any variation in the productivity of labour, the *surplus value* in contrast depends on the productivity of labour: if, on the one hand, the commodity is sold at its value, and on the other hand the length of the normal working day is given, the *surplus value* can only increase as a result of a rise in the productivity of labour. The surplus value is not related to the commodity; it expresses rather a relation between two parts of the overall working day—a relation namely between the part during which the worker works to replace his wage (the value of his labour capacity) and the part during which he works for the capitalist over and above this replacement. Since these two parts together make up the whole of the working day, since they are parts of the same whole, their magnitudes clearly stand in *inverse* ratio to each other, and the surplus value, i.e. the surplus labour time, rises or falls according to whether the necessary labour time falls or rises. The growth or diminution of the latter, however, stands in *inverse ratio* to the productivity of labour.

[III-131] But if there were to be a general doubling of the productivity of labour, i.e. in all branches of industry providing directly or indirectly the commodities (use values) required for the reproduction of labour capacity, providing products which enter into the consumption of the workers, the value of labour capacity would fall in proportion as this general productivity of labour uniformly increased, hence the labour time necessary for the replacement of this value would fall, and the part of the day which forms surplus time, which is worked for the capitalist, would increase in the same proportion as the former would decline. However, the development of the productive forces in these different branches of labour is neither uniform nor simultaneous, being subject to uneven, diverse and often mutually opposed motions. If the productivity of labour increases in a branch of industry which enters directly or indirectly into the worker's consumption, e.g. the industry supplying fabrics for clothes, we cannot say that the value of labour capacity falls in the same proportion as the productivity of this particular industry grows. It is only this means of subsistence that is produced more cheaply. The cheapening only affects an aliquot part of the worker's vital requirements. The increased productivity of labour in this one branch does not lessen the necessary labour time (i.e. the labour time required for the production of the means of subsistence needed by the workers) in proportion to the growth in productivity, but only in proportion as the product of this labour enters, on the average, into the worker's consumption. No definite calculation of this can be made for each individual branch of industry (excepting perhaps the products of agriculture).

This does not change the general law in any way. It remains correct, just as before, that relative surplus value can only arise and increase in the proportion to which use values (means of subsistence) directly or indirectly entering into the worker's consumption are cheapened, i.e. not in the proportion to which the productivity of a specific branch of industry has grown, but rather in the proportion to which this increase in its productivity lessens necessary labour time, i.e. produces more cheaply a product which enters into the worker's consumption. In considering relative surplus value therefore, we not only can but we must always proceed from the presupposition that the development of productive power or the development of the productivity of labour in every particular branch in which capital investment takes place *directly* reduces the necessary labour time in a definite proportion, i.e. that the product produced by the worker forms a part of his means of subsistence and its cheapening therefore reduces the labour time required for the reproduction of his life in a definite proportion. Since relative surplus value arises only on this condition, we can and must always assume the presence of this condition in considering relative surplus value.

It is clear, further, that the presence and the growth of relative surplus value by no means require as a condition that the worker's *life situation* should remain *unchanged*, i.e. that his average wage should always provide the same quantitatively and qualitatively determined amount of means of subsistence and no more. This is not the case, although relative *surplus value* can neither arise nor grow without a corresponding *fall* in the *value of labour capacity* or the *value of wages* (average wages). Indeed, relative surplus value might well rise continuously, and the *value of labour capacity*, hence the value of average wages, fall continuously, yet despite this the range of the worker's means of subsistence and therefore the pleasures of his life could expand continuously. For this is conditioned by the quality and quantity of the *use values* (commodities) he can appropriate, not by their *exchange value.*

Let us assume a doubling of productivity which is universal, covering all branches of production.[179] Assume that before this doubling the normal day was 12 hours, 10 of them necessary labour time, 2 surplus labour time. The total amount of the worker's daily means of subsistence, which previously cost [10] hours of labour, could now be produced in 5 hours. Instead of needing 10 hours of labour to replace the value (price) of his labour capacity every day, i.e. to provide an equivalent for his daily wages, the worker would now need only [5] hours. The *value* of his labour capacity would have fallen by a half, for the means of subsistence required for its reproduction would now be the product of 5 hours; instead of 10 as before. If the worker now—after this revolution in the productivity of labour—received a daily wage equivalent to 6 hours, that is to say, if he had in future to work 6 hours [IV-138][180] a day, his material living situation would have improved in the same proportion as if, under the previous conditions of production, he had worked the whole day of 12 hours for himself (i.e. for the reproduction of his wages) and a labour time of 0 for the capitalist; as if the whole of the working day necessary labour time had been worked, and no surplus labour time at all. For $5:6=10:12$. $(5\times12=6\times10$.) Nevertheless, surplus labour time would have increased in this case from 2 hours to 6 hours, and a relative surplus value of 4 hours would have been added to the absolute surplus value of 2 hours. Instead of working as before 10 hours for himself and 2 for the capitalist, hence $^{10}/_{12}$ $(=^5/_6)$, therefore $^5/_6$ of the day, for himself and $^2/_{12}=^1/_6$ of the day for the capitalist, the worker now works only $^6/_{12}$ or $^3/_6$ of the day for himself and, instead of $^1/_6$, he also works $^3/_6$, half the day, for the capitalist. Necessary labour time would have fallen from 10 to 6, hence the value of the day's labour capacity, instead of being 10 hours, would only be 6 hours: 4 hours less, i.e. it would have fallen by 40% $(10:4=100:40)$. Surplus value would have increased to 300%, from 2 to 6. // Instead of $^1/_6$ of the day $^3/_6$. $^2/_6$ added to $^1/_6$ gives $^3/_6$, therefore a 200% *increase*. This for the *surplus value*. On the other hand, from $^5/_6$ down to $^3/_6$ is a reduction of $^2/_6$, i.e. the increase on the surplus labour [time] side or the side of the capitalist is exactly as much, viewed absolutely, as the reduction on the necessary labour time side or the value of labour capacity side. It amounts to $^2/_6$ of a day, or 4 hours of labour. $(^2/_6=^4/_{12}$.) But if we look at the increase on one side in proportion to the original surplus labour time, and the decrease on the other side in proportion to the original necessary labour time (or the value of labour capacity), the increase on one side and the decrease on the other are expressed in *different proportions,* although the *absolute magnitude* of the time subtracted from one side and added to the other is *the same identical magnitude.*

Thus in the above case: $^{10}/_{12}$ or $^5/_6$ are related to $^6/_{12}$ or $^3/_6$ or $\dfrac{5-2}{6}$ as 5:3, as 60% (should be 40%, *see the other page*[181]), for $5:3=100:60$ $(5\times60=300$ and 3×100 similarly$=300)$, while $^2/_{12}$ or $^1/_6$ is related to $^6/_{12}$ or to $\dfrac{1+2}{6}$ $(^3/_6)$ as 1:3, i.e. 100:300, hence as 300%. Therefore, although the absolute increase in surplus labour [time]=the absolute decrease in necessary labour time, which has occurred as a result of the raised productivity of labour, the proportion in which the value of labour capacity declines or the necessary labour time falls is not identical with the proportion in which the surplus labour time or the surplus value rises, but depends rather on the *original proportion* in which surplus labour time and necessary labour time *shared* in the normal overall working day, participated in it. //

// It follows from this that in the proportion in which total surplus labour time (both the part of it which arose from the reduction of necessary labour time consequent on the increase in the productivity of labour, and the part which arose from the lengthening of the working day up to its normal limits) already forms a greater part (a more significant portion) of the overall working day, any increase in the productive power of labour and resultant reduction in necessary labour time (or increase in relative surplus value) can only increase *the proportional surplus value* in a smaller ratio. Or that a reduction of necessary labour time causes an increase in surplus labour time in a proportion which is smaller, the greater the already achieved total magnitude of surplus labour time, and greater, the smaller the achieved total magnitude of the surplus labour time. Therefore (and this must be dealt with in more detail under *profit*[182]) the more advanced the industry, the smaller the proportional growth of surplus value, if productive power continues to increase *in the same degree.* Productive power in general, or productive power altogether, to the extent that it influences the reproduction of labour capacity. In other words, the *proportion* in which an increase in the [IV-139] productive power of labour reduces necessary labour time (hence the *value* of labour capacity) and raises surplus labour time, hence surplus value, stands in an *inverse relation* to the *proportion* in which necessary labour time and surplus labour time *originally,* i.e. each time before the coming of the new increase in productive power, shared in, or participated in, the overall working day.

Assume that the working day = 12 hours, 10 hours of necessary labour, and 2 hours of surplus labour. Let there be a general doubling of productive power. Now 5 hours would suffice for necessary labour time, surplus labour time would be increased by 5 hours, by the same amount as the decrease in necessary labour time (hence in the *value* of labour capacity)—i.e. 5 hours. Necessary labour time would have declined from 10 to 5, i.e. by half = 50%. // (If the necessary labour time were to decline from 10 to 6, this would be a reduction of 4 hours. 10:4=100:40, therefore by 40%. I said 60% before.[181] This is wrong, because I calculated 10:6=100:60, whereas in fact what we are concerned with is the ratio of 10 to the remainder of the 10 when 6 is taken away from it, hence the ratio of 10 to 4. After all, the labour time has not been reduced by 6 hours, i.e. not by 60%.) On the other hand surplus labour time has risen from 2 to 7 hours (with the addition of 5 hours of surplus labour time), and 2:7=100:350 (2×350=700 and 7×100 also=700); hence a rise to 350%. It would have increased to three and a half times its original magnitude.

Let us now assume that once this proportion has become established, with the overall working day falling into 5 hours of necessary labour, 7 hours of surplus labour, the general productive power of labour is redoubled, i.e. necessary labour time diminishes by $2\frac{1}{2}$ hours, surplus labour time therefore rising by the same $2\frac{1}{2}$ hours; hence from 7 to $9\frac{1}{2}$ hours. Here the necessary labour time has again fallen by 50%, and surplus labour time risen in the ratio $\frac{14}{2}$ (7) to $\frac{19}{2}$ ($9\frac{1}{2}$), thus 14:19. 14:19=100:x; $x=\frac{1900}{14}$,=$135\frac{5}{7}$%. (19×100=1,900 and 14×$135\frac{5}{7}$ (or $135\frac{10}{14}$) also=1,900). Therefore, although in both cases the productive power of labour has doubled and the necessary labour time has therefore fallen by a half, by 50%, surplus labour time or surplus value would have risen to 350% in one case and only to $135\frac{5}{7}$% in the other. (The proportion in which the productive power *generally increases would always be the same,= the proportion in which the necessary labour time fell as compared with itself, i.e. with its extent before this increase in productive power.*) But in the first case the surplus labour time amounted to only $\frac{1}{6}$ of the whole working day, 2 hours,=$\frac{2}{12}$, before the doubling of the productive power took effect, while in the second case it amounted to 7 hours or $\frac{7}{12}$. (The same peculiarity holds for the increase of money, as has been demonstrated by Jacob, for example. It grew more in the 18th century than in the 17th. But the proportional increase was smaller.[a])

[IV-140] If we now take an actual CASE, in which productive power is e.g. doubled in one branch, but not in the other branches at the same time, perhaps remaining unaltered in the branches of production which provide constant capital for this one branch, so that the expenditure on raw materials remains the same, i.e. grows along with the increase in productive power, and the expenditure on machinery increases, even if not in the same ratio, it is clear that the *profit*, i.e. the ratio of the surplus value to the total value of the capital expended, does not increase in the same proportion as the necessary labour falls through the increase in productive

---

[a] W. Jacob, *An Historical Inquiry into the Production and Consumption of the Precious Metals*, Vol. II, London, 1831, pp. 132, 215.— *Ed.*

power. There are two reasons why this does not happen. Firstly because with the more developed productive power of labour, surplus value does not grow in the same proportion as necessary labour diminishes. Secondly because this surplus value, which has grown in a smaller proportion, is calculated on capital which has increased its value approximately in proportion to the heightening of productive power. //

// One can calculate the diminution in necessary labour time in two ways: 1) in proportion to its own magnitude before the increase in the productive power of labour; 2) in proportion to the whole of the working day. It is clear in the first calculation that—presupposing an overall heightening of productive power— necessary labour time (and therefore the value of labour capacity) declines in the same measure as productive power increases; but the proportional growth of surplus labour time or surplus value depends on the proportion in which the overall working day was originally divided between necessary labour time and surplus labour time. Thus if the working day was 12 hours originally, divided into 10 of necessary and 2 of surplus labour, and if the productive power of labour doubled, necessary labour time would fall from 10 to 5, i.e. by 50%, while productive power doubled. (This proportion is expressed in the case of productive power by a 100% growth, in the case of necessary labour time by a 50% fall. That necessary labour time falls from 10 to 5, i.e. by 50%, means that in 1 hour I can produce as much as I did previously in 2, i.e. twice as much, i.e. the productive power of labour has increased by 100%.) Surplus labour, on the other hand, has grown from 2 to 7, i.e. to 350% (a threefold increase, 2×3, or [6] hours, and a rise by a half, $= ^2/_2 = 1$, thus the whole has gone up from 2 to 7), because it originally only amounted to 2 hours out of 12. If it had originally already amounted to 3 hours, and necessary labour only 9 hours, the latter would have fallen by $4^1/_2$ hours, again by 50%, while surplus labour would have risen from 3 to $7^1/_2$; i.e. to 250% (for $3:7^1/_2$, or $^6/_2:^{15}/_2$, or $6:15,=100:250$. $15 \times 100 = 1500$ and $6 \times 250 = 1500$). If we now consider the whole of the working day, the ratio is *not* altered. [Necessary] labour time originally amounted to 10 hours or $^{10}/_{12}$ of the working day; now it only amounts to $^5/_{12}$ in the first case. (In the second it was originally $^9/_{12}$ of the working day, and afterwards came to no more than $\dfrac{4^1/_2}{12}$.)

It is all the same whether I compare necessary labour time with itself or with the working day as a whole. All that is added is the divisor 12. This FIX has therefore been dealt with. //

Now back to page 138 *before* the bracket.[a] The worker's life situation would have improved despite the fall in the *value* of his labour capacity, the reduction by 4 hours in his necessary labour time and the increase of 4 hours in his surplus labour time for the capitalist, because he himself would have received a share of 1 hour in the time now set free. I.e., the labour time he worked for himself, i.e. for the reproduction of his wages, would *not* have been reduced to the *full extent* of the shortening of this necessary labour time resulting from the [increased] product of the labour. He would receive more use values of less value—i.e. containing less labour time than previously. But the degree in which new surplus labour would have been formed in general, in which relative surplus value would have arisen, would correspond completely to the degree in which a part of his necessary labour time had been converted into surplus labour time for the capitalist, or in which the *value* of his *labour capacity* had declined. This is enough here. Later on the proportional elements in the matter must in general be put together [183] (see also above[b]). Thus this in no way alters the *nature* and the *law of relative surplus value*—that a greater part of the working day is appropriated by capital as a result of rises in productivity. Hence the preposterousness of wanting to refute this law by statistical demonstrations that the material condition of the worker has improved here or there, in this or that aspect, [IV-141] as a result of the development of the productive power of labour.

// *Standard.* October 26, 1861. We read here of proceedings taken by the firm of John Bright and Co. against its workers, before the Rochdale MAGISTRATES,

*to prosecute for intimidation the agents of the *Carpets' Weavers' Trades Unions.* Bright's partners had introduced new machinery which would turn out 240 yards of carpet in the time and with the labour previously required to produce 160 yards. The workmen had no claim whatever to share in the profits made by the investment of their employers' capital in mechanical improvement. Accordingly, Messrs. Bright proposed to lower the rate of pay from $1^1/_2$d. per yard to 1d., leaving the earnings of the men exactly the same as before for the same labour. But there was a nominal reduction, of which the operatives, it is asserted, had not had fair warning beforehand.* [184] // [IV-141]

* * *

---

a See this volume, p. 246, the bracket before "Instead".— *Ed.*
b Ibid.— *Ed.*

[IV-138a] [185] 1) The surplus value capital receives through the development of the productive forces does not flow from an increase in the amount of products or use values created by the same amount of labour, but from a *reduction* in *necessary* labour and an *increase* of the same proportion in surplus labour. The surplus value capital receives through the production process consists in nothing more than the excess of surplus labour over necessary labour.

Surplus value exactly equals surplus labour; an increase in surplus labour is exactly measured by a reduction in necessary labour. With *absolute surplus value* the reduction in necessary labour is *relative*, i.e. necessary labour falls relatively because overtime is increased *directly*. If the necessary labour=10 hours, and the surplus labour=2 hours, and if the latter is now increased by 2 hours, i.e. the total working day is lengthened from 12 hours to 14, the necessary labour remains 10 hours, as it was before. But previously its ratio to the surplus labour was 10:2, i.e. 5:1, and now it is 10:4,=5:2, or, in other words, previously it was equal to $^5/_6$ of the working day, now it is only $^5/_7$. Here, therefore, necessary labour time is reduced *relatively*, because total labour time, and therefore surplus labour time, has grown *absolutely*. In contrast to this, if the normal working day is given, and the increase in *relative* surplus value occurs through an increase in productive forces, the *necessary labour time is lessened* a b s o l u t e l y and the surplus value is thereby increased both absolutely and relatively without any increase in the *value* of the product. In the case of absolute surplus value, therefore, there is a *relative fall in the value* of wages as compared with the absolute growth in surplus value; whereas in the case of relative surplus value there is an *absolute fall in the value* of wages. Nevertheless, the first case is always worse for the worker. In the first case the *price* of labour falls absolutely. In the second case the *price of labour* may rise.

2) The surplus value of the capital is increased not by the multiplier of the productive power but by the fraction of the working day which originally represented the necessary labour time, divided by the multiplier of the productive power.

3) The greater the surplus value *prior to* the new *increase in productive power*, i.e. the greater the part of the day worked for no return already is, and the smaller therefore the paid part of the day, the fraction of the day which forms the worker's equivalent, the less the growth in surplus value which capital obtains from the new increase in productive power. Its surplus value rises, but in an ever smaller proportion to the development of the productive

forces. The barrier remains the ratio between the fraction of the day which expresses *necessary labour* and the whole of the working day. Movement can only take place within these limits. The smaller the fraction allotted to necessary labour, and the greater therefore the surplus labour, the smaller the *ratio* in which an increase in productive power lessens necessary labour time, since the denominator of the fraction is that much larger. The *rate* of capital's self-valorisation therefore grows more slowly in the measure to which it is already valorised. This does not, however, happen because the wage or the worker's share in the product has risen but because the fraction of the working day which represents necessary labour has already fallen very low in proportion to the working day as a whole. [IV-138a]

[IV-141] A certain development of the productivity of labour is in general presupposed, even for the existence of absolute surplus value, i.e. surplus labour in general, and therefore for the existence of capitalist production, as for all earlier modes of production in which one part of society works not only for itself but also for the other part of society.

* "The very existence of the former (the master-capitalists) as a distinct class is dependent on the productiveness of industry" * (Ramsay, *An Essay on the Distribution of Wealth etc.*, Edinburgh, [London,] 1836, [p.] 206).

* "If each man's labour were but enough to produce[a] his own food, there could be no property" * (this word is used here for CAPITAL) (Piercy Ravenstone, *Thoughts on the Funding System, and its Effects*, London, 1824, p. 14).

In any case, the capital-relation develops at a historical stage of the economic formation of society which is already the result of a long series of previous developments. The level of the productivity of labour from which it proceeds is not of natural origin but is something created historically; by that time labour has long emerged from its first raw beginnings. It is clear that if a country possesses soil that is naturally fertile, waters teeming with fish, rich coal deposits (combustible materials in general), metal mines, etc., in comparison with other countries, where these natural conditions for the productivity of labour are present to a lesser degree, less time is required in the first country to produce the necessary means of subsistence, hence a greater quantity of excess labour for others over and above labour for oneself is possible from the outset; and therefore absolute surplus labour time, thus absolute

------

[a] Ravenstone has: "procure".— *Ed.*

surplus value, is greater here from the outset. Capital (or any other relation of production whereby *surplus labour* is enforced) is therefore more productive here than under less favourable natural conditions. The ancients were already aware that natural cheapness of labour capacity, i.e. of its cost of production and reproduction, was a great factor in industrial production. For example, it says in Diodorus' *Historical Library*, b. 1, ch. 80,[a] in relation to the Egyptians:

"It is altogether incredible how little trouble and expense the bringing up of their children causes them. They cook for them the first simple food that comes to hand; they also give them the lower part of the papyrus stem to eat, if it can be roasted in the fire, and the roots and stalks of marsh plants, some raw, some boiled, and some roasted. Most of the children go without shoes and unclothed, since the air is so mild. Hence a child, until he is grown up, costs his parents no more than twenty drachmas altogether. *This is the main reason why the population of Egypt* is so numerous, and, therefore, why it has been possible to undertake so many great works."

// Once the ratio of surplus value is given, its amount depends on the size of the population; if the size of the population is given, it depends on the ratio of surplus to necessary labour. //

All that follows from this is that, in places where the capital-relation predominates (or a similar relation of production which *enforces* absolute surplus labour, for this natural fertility only facilitates the prolongation of surplus labour time and its existence; it does not create relative surplus value in our sense), the productivity of capital is at its greatest—i.e. the most surplus labour is available and therefore the most surplus value, or the value of labour capacity is naturally at its lowest, which is the same thing—where the natural conditions of labour, [IV-142] hence in particular the soil, are at their most fruitful. This by no means implies that the most fertile countries are the most well suited to the development, thus also the fruitfulness, of the capital-relation itself. When Ricardo speaks of the fertility of the soil as one of the main conditions for the productivity of labour, he assumes capitalist production, and the proposition is only uttered on this assumption. He is naturally inclined everywhere to presuppose *bourgeois relations of production* as given. This does not interfere with the development of his argument as he deals exclusively with production in this particular form. The following passage is important, both for the concept of surplus labour in general and

---

[a] Diodor von Sicilien, *Historische Bibliothek*. Übers. von Julius Friedrich Wurm (Abth. 1), Bändchen 1, Stuttgart, 1827, p. 126.— *Ed.*

for the misunderstanding about the point we have just touched on.

  "'In different stages of society, the *accumulation of capital*, or of the *means of employing labour*** is more or less rapid, and must in *all cases depend on the productive powers of labour*. The productive powers of labour are generally greatest, where there is an *abundance of fertile land*² (Ricardo).ᵃ

  "If, in the first sentence, *the productive powers of labour mean the smallness of that aliquot part of any produce that goes to those whose manual labour produced it*, the sentence is nearly identical, because the *remaining aliquot part is the fund whence capital can*, if the owner pleases, *be accumulated*. But then this does not generally happen where there is most fertile land. It does in North America, but that is an artificial state of things. It does not in Mexico. It does not in New Holland.ᵇ The productive powers of labour are, indeed, in *another* sense, greatest where there is much fertile land, viz. the *power of man*, if he chooses it, to raise *much raw produce in proportion to the whole labour he performs*. It is, indeed, a *gift of nature*, that men can *raise more food* than the *lowest quantity* that *they could maintain* and *keep up the existing population on*; but '*surplus produce*' (the term used by Mr. Ricardo p. 93) generally means the *excess of the whole price of a thing above that part of it which goes to the labourers who made it*; a part, which is settled by human arrangement, and not fixed" (*Observations on Certain Verbal Disputes in Political Economy, Particularly Relating to Value, and to Demand and Supply*, London, 1821, pp. 74-75).ᶜ

  This man does not see that in fact "THE SMALLNESS" OR BIGNESS "OF THAT ALIQUOT PART THAT GOES" TO THE LABOURER depends on the PROPORTIONAL QUANTITY OF RAW PRODUCE WHICH "*THE WHOLE LABOUR*" OF A MAN CAN PERFORM DAILY. He is only right against Ricardo to the extent that he says: Natural fertility brings it about that with one day's labour I could produce, IF I CHOSE, much more than what is absolutely necessary for existence (THE LOWEST QUANTITY TO KEEP THE EXISTING POPULATION UPON). It does not mean that I work a lot, hence produce a lot; still less that the work I do over and above what is necessary forms the *fond* of capital. This "IS SETTLED BY HUMAN ARRANGEMENT". For Ricardo the capital-relation is itself a naturally given relation and is therefore presupposed everywhere.

  If capitalist production is presupposed, necessary labour time, i.e. the time required for the reproduction of the worker, will differ in different countries according to how favourable the

---

  * It is only in such passages as this that the nature of capital breaks through in Ricardo. So CAPITAL is not the MEANS OF LABOUR FOR PRODUCING A CERTAIN RESULT, BUT IT IS "THE MEANS FOR *EMPLOYING* LABOUR", AND THIS INVOLVES THAT THE POSSESSOR OF THE MEANS, OR THOSE MEANS THEMSELVES, EMPLOYS LABOUR, THE MEANS ARE THE POWER OVER LABOUR.[186]

  ᵃ D. Ricardo, *On the Principles of Political Economy etc.*, 3rd ed., London, 1821, p. 92.— *Ed.*
  ᵇ Old name of Australia.— *Ed.*
  ᶜ Marx reproduces the above two paragraphs in English.— *Ed.*

natural conditions of labour are, and therefore according to its natural level of productivity, and it will stand in inverse relation to the productivity of labour, hence it will be possible for surplus labour time or surplus value to be greater in one country than in the other, in direct relation, even if the same number of hours is worked.

All this concerns*the very existence of absolute surplus labour, and its relative quantity in different countries according to their respective natural facilities for production*. We do not have to deal with this here.

[IV-143] Since it is assumed that the normal working day is already divided into necessary labour and absolute surplus labour, the existence, and indeed a definite level, of the latter is presupposed, hence a definite natural basis for it is also presupposed. The question here is rather *the productive power of labour*—hence the shortening of necessary labour time, the prolongation of surplus labour time—in so far as it is itself the product of capitalist (in general, of social) production.

The chief forms are: *Cooperation, Division of Labour,* and *Machinery* or the application of SCIENTIFIC POWER, etc.

a) COOPERATION

This is the *basic form.* Division of labour presupposes cooperation or is only a specific form of cooperation. The same is true of a workshop based on the use of machinery, etc. Cooperation is the *general form* on which all social arrangements for increasing the productivity of social labour are based, and it merely receives further specification in each of these. But cooperation is itself at the same time a *specific* form, existing alongside its more highly developed and closely specified forms (just as it is a form which transcends its hitherto developments).

As a form which is distinct from its own further developments or specifications, and which *exists* in distinction, separately from them, *cooperation* is the most rooted in nature, the crudest and the most abstract of its own varieties; but in any case it continues in its simplicity, in its simple form, to be the basis and prerequisite of all its more highly developed forms.

Cooperation is therefore first of all the direct *collective labour*— unmediated by *exchange*—of many workers in order to produce the same result, the same product and the same use value (or utility). In production under slavery. (Cf. Cairnes.) [187]

It is firstly the *collective labour of many workers.* Hence its initial prerequisite is the existence of an *agglomeration*, a *heaping up of many workers* in *the same area* (in one place), all working *at the same time*; or this already constitutes the material existence of cooperation. This prerequisite underlies all its more highly developed forms.

The *simplest*, as yet not further specified mode of cooperation is evidently the performing, not of different operations, but of the *same* one by people working simultaneously and in association in the same area; but their activity must be simultaneous in order to bring about a definite result or to achieve this within a definite time. This side of cooperation, too, persists in its more highly developed forms. Many people do the same thing at the same time under the division of labour as well. Even more so in the automatic workshop.

Hunting presents one of the oldest forms of this kind of cooperation. The same can be said of war, which is only a man-hunt, a more highly developed hunt.[188] The effect produced by, for example, the charge of a cavalry regiment could not be produced by the individual members of the regiment, taking each one in isolation, even though during the charge each individual only acts as an individual, in so far as he acts at all. The gigantic structures erected by the Asiatics are another example of this kind of cooperation, indeed the importance of this simple form of cooperation emerges very strikingly in building. An individual may build a hut, but the construction of a house requires that many people should do the same thing at the same time. An individual may row a small boat; a large skiff requires a definite number of oarsmen. In the division of labour this side of cooperation emerges in the principle of the proportion of MULTIPLES,[a] which are to be apportioned to each particular branch. In the automatic workshop the main effect stems not from the division of labour but from the *sameness* of the work performed by many people at once. For example, the SPINNING MULES set in motion simultaneously by the same motor are watched over simultaneously by so and so many spinners.

The merit of *Wakefield*'s new system of colonisation is not that he discovered or [IV-144] promoted the art of colonisation, nor that he made any fresh discoveries whatsoever in the field of political economy, but that he naively laid bare the narrow-mindedness of political economy without being clear himself as to

---

the importance of these discoveries or being to the slightest degree free from that narrow-mindedness.

The point is that in the colonies, particularly in their earliest stages of development, bourgeois relations are not yet fully formed; not yet presupposed, as they are in old established countries. They are in the process of becoming. The conditions of their origin therefore emerge more clearly. It appears that these *economic relations* are neither present by nature, nor are they *things*, which is the way the political economists are rather inclined to view capital, etc. We shall see later how Mr. Wakefield solves this mystery in the colonies, to his own astonishment.[67] Here we shall confine ourselves, for the time being, to citing a passage which bears on this simple form of cooperation:

* "There are numerous operations of so simple a kind *as not to admit a division into parts*, which cannot be performed *without the cooperation of many pairs of hands*. For instance the lifting of a large tree on a wain, keeping down weeds in a large field of growing crops, shearing a large flock of sheep at the same time, gathering a harvest of corn at a time when it is ripe enough and not too ripe, moving any great weight; everything in short, which cannot be done unless a good many pairs of hands help each other in *the same undivided employment*, and at the same time" * (E. G. Wakefield, *A View of the Art of Colonization etc.*, London, 1849, p. 168).

Catching fish for example. Result when many act at once—as in hunting. Building railways. Digging canals, etc. This kind of cooperation in the public works of the Egyptians and Asiatics. The Romans employed their armies like this in PUBLIC WORKS. (See the passage in *Jones.*[a])

We have already seen, in considering absolute surplus value,[b] that once the rate is given the amount of surplus value depends on the number of workers simultaneously employed; SO FAR, therefore, on their cooperation. However, it is precisely here that the difference between absolute and relative surplus value—in so far as the latter presupposes an increase in and therefore a development of the productive power of labour—emerges in striking fashion. If, in place of 10 workers, each of whom works 2 hours of surplus labour, 20 workers are employed, the result will be 40 surplus hours instead of 20, as in the first case. 1:2=20:40. The ratio is the same for the 20 as for the one. Here we only have the addition or multiplication of the hours worked by the individuals. *Cooperation as such* makes absolutely no difference to the ratio here. Now, in contrast, we are considering cooperation as a natural force of social labour, in so far as the labour of the

---

a See this volume, p. 259.— *Ed.*
b Ibid., 185-90.— *Ed.*

individual attains a productivity by means of cooperation which it
would not have attained as the labour of the isolated individual.
E.g. if 100 people mow simultaneously, each of them only works
as an individual and does the same work. But the result achieved,
that in this definite period of time, before the hay has rotted, etc.,
the mowing has been done—this use value has been produced—is
alone the result of the fact that 100 people have *simultaneously*
borne a hand in this work. In other cases an actual increase of
strength occurs. E.g. in lifting etc. Loading a heavy burden. A
power is created here which is not possessed by the individual in
isolation, but only when he works together with others *at the same
time*. In the first case he could not extend his sphere of action as
far afield as would be necessary for the achievement of the result.
In the second case he could not develop the necessary power at
all, or only with infinite loss of time. The time taken by 10 people
to load a tree into a cart is less than one-tenth of the time one
individual would take to achieve the same result (if he could do it
at all). The result is that through cooperation things can be
produced in a shorter time than would be possible for the same
individuals when working in the same numbers but scattered
about in isolation, or use values can be produced which would
otherwise be impossible to produce at all. An individual cannot do
in 100 days, indeed often 100 individuals cannot do in 100 days,
what 100 can do in one day through cooperation. Here, therefore,
the productive power of the individual is increased by the social
[IV-145] form of labour. Since this makes it possible to produce
more in less time, the necessary means of subsistence or the
conditions required for their production can be produced in less
time. Necessary labour time diminishes. Relative surplus time is
thereby made possible. The latter can be extended, the former
reduced.

"The strength of each man is very small, but the union of a number of very
small forces produces a collective force which is greater than *the sum of these partial
forces,* so that merely by being joined together these forces can reduce the time
required, and extend their field of action" (G. R. Carli, note 1, p. 196, to Pietro
Verri, *Meditazioni sulla economia politica etc.,* Custodi, *Parte Moderna,* Vol. XV).[a]

// It may perhaps be recalled here that in many branches of
industry this simple form of cooperation permits the communal
use of the conditions of labour, e.g. fuel, buildings, etc. But this
does not concern us here. It should rather be considered under
Profit.[189] Here we only need to look at how far the ratio of

---

[a] Marx quotes in Italian.— *Ed.*

necessary to surplus labour is directly affected, not the ratio of surplus labour to the total amount of capital laid out. This must also be kept in mind in the sections that follow. // // It is not absolutely necessary for the workers to be united together in the same location. If 10 astronomers make the same observations from the observatories of different countries, etc., that is not a *division of labour* but the performance of the same labour in different places, a form of cooperation. // But also, at the same time, *concentration of the means of labour.*

Extension of the sphere of action; curtailment of the time during which a particular result is attained; and finally, the creation of forces of production the isolated worker is completely incapable of developing: all these are characteristic both of simple cooperation and of its more differentiated forms.

In simple cooperation it is only the amount of human force which produces the effect. The place of the one individual with two eyes, etc., is taken by a many-eyed, many-armed, etc., monster. Hence the gigantic works of the Roman armies. The great public works of Asia and Egypt. Here, where the state spends the revenue of the whole country, it has the power to set in motion great masses of people.

* "It has happened in times past that these Oriental States, after supplying the expenses of their civil and military establishments, have found themselves in possession of a surplus which they could apply to works of magnificence or utility, and in the construction of these *their command over the hands and arms of almost the entire non-agricultural population* [...], and this food, belonging to the monarch and the priesthood, afforded the means of creating the mighty monuments which filled the land ... in moving the colossal statues and vast masses, of which the transport creates wonder, human labour almost alone was prodigally used ... topes and reservoirs of Ceylon, the Wall of China, the numerous works of which the ruins cover the plains of Assyria and Mesopotamia" * (Richard Jones, *Text-book of Lectures on the Political Economy of Nations,* Hertford, 1852, p. 77).

* *"The number of the labourers, and the concentration of their efforts suffticed."* *

// *The number and concentration of workers* is the basis of simple cooperation. //

* "We see mighty coral reefs rising from the depths of the ocean into islands and firm land, yet each individual depositor is puny, weak and contemptible. The non-agricultural labourers of an Asiatic monarchy have little but their individual bodily exertions to bring [IV-146] to the task; but *their number is their strength,* and the *power of directing these masses* gave rise to the palaces and temples etc. It is *that confinement of the revenues which feed them, to one or a few hands, which makes such undertakings possible"* * (l.c., [p.] 78).

// *Continuity* of labour is, in general, peculiar to capitalist production; but it only develops fully with the development of fixed capital, which we shall discuss later.[190] //

This power of the Egyptian and Asiatic kings and priests or the Etruscan theocrats in the ancient world has in bourgeois society passed to capital and therewith to the capitalists.

Simple cooperation, as also its more developed forms, and altogether any means of heightening the productive power of labour, fall under the labour process, not the process of valorisation. They heighten the EFFICIENCY of LABOUR. The *value* of the product of LABOUR, on the other hand, depends on the necessary labour time required for its manufacture. EFFICIENCY of LABOUR can therefore only reduce the value of a particular product, it cannot raise it. But all the methods which are employed to heighten the EFFICIENCY of the labour process reduce necessary labour time (TO A CERTAIN DEGREE), and thus increase surplus value, the part of the value which accrues to the capitalist, although the value of the total product remains determined as before by the total quantity of labour time employed.

"The mathematical principle that the whole is equal to the sum of its parts becomes false when applied to our subject. REGARDING LABOUR, THE GREAT PILLAR OF HUMAN EXISTENCE, IT MAY BE SAID, that the entire product of combined exertion infinitely EXCEEDS all which individual and DISCONNECTED EFFORTS could possibly accomplish" (Michael Thomas Sadler, *The Law of Population*, Vol. 1, p. 84).

Cooperation—i.e. its application by the capitalist, i.e. the owner of money or commodities—naturally requires concentration in his hand of means of labour, and likewise of means of subsistence (the part of capital exchanged for labour). The employment of one man for 360 days during the year requires a capital 360 times smaller than the employment of 360 men on one and the same day.

The social productive power which arises from cooperation is a *free gift.* The individual workers or rather labour capacities are paid, and paid as separate ones. Their cooperation, and the productive power which arises therefrom, is not paid for. The capitalist pays 360 workers; he does not pay for the cooperation of the 360 workers: for the exchange between capital and labour capacity takes place between capital and the individual labour capacity. It is determined by the exchange value of the latter, which is just as independent of the productive power this labour capacity attains under certain social combinations as it is of the fact that the time for which the worker works and can work is longer than the labour time required for his own reproduction.

Cooperation, which is a productive power of social labour, appears as a productive power of capital, not of labour. And this transposition takes place within capitalist production in respect of all the productive powers of social labour. This refers to real labour. Just as the general, abstractly social character [IV-147] of labour—i.e. the exchange value of the commodity—presents itself as *money*, and all the qualities the product possesses as the representation of this general labour present themselves as qualities of money, in the same way does the concrete social character of labour present itself as the character and quality of capital.

In fact: Once the worker enters into the actual labour process he is already incorporated *qua* labour capacity into capital, he no longer belongs to himself but to capital, and therefore the conditions under which he works are rather the conditions under which capital works. However, before he steps into the labour process he enters into contact with the capitalist as the individual owner or seller of a commodity; this commodity is his own labour capacity. He sells it as an isolated commodity. It becomes social once it has entered into the labour process. The metamorphosis his labour capacity undergoes thereby is something external to it, in which it does not participate; it is rather something which is done to it. The capitalist buys not one but many individual labour capacities at the same time, but he buys them all as isolated commodities, belonging to isolated, mutually independent commodity owners. Once they enter into the labour process, they are already incorporated into capital, and their own cooperation is therefore not a relation into which they put themselves; it is the capitalist who puts them into it. Nor is it a relation which belongs to them; instead, they now belong to it, and the relation itself appears as a relation of capital to them. It is not their reciprocal association, but rather a unity which rules over them, and of which the vehicle and director is capital itself. Their own association in labour—cooperation—is in fact a power alien to them; it is the power of capital which confronts the isolated workers. In so far as they have a relation to the capitalist as independent persons, as sellers, it is the relation of isolated, mutually independent workers, who stand in a relation to the capitalist but not to each other. Where they do stand in a relation to each other as functioning labour capacities, they are incorporated into capital, and this relation therefore confronts them as a relation of capital, not as their own relation. They find that they are agglomerated. The cooperation which arises from this agglomeration is for them just as much an effect of capital as the agglomeration itself. Their *interconnection and their unity* lies not in themselves but in capital, or, the social productive power of their labour arising therefrom is a productive power of capital. Just as the power of individual labour capacity not only to replace but to increase itself—surplus labour—appears as a capacity of capital, so does the social character of labour and the productive power which arises from that character.

This is the first stage at which the subsumption of labour under capital no longer appears as a merely formal subsumption but changes the mode of production itself, so that the *capitalist* mode of production is a specific mode of production.[55] The subsumption is formal, in so far as the individual worker, instead of working as an independent commodity owner, now works as a labour capacity belonging to the capitalist, [IV-148] and therefore under his command and supervision; also works no longer for himself but for the capitalist; the means of labour, moreover, no longer appear as means to the realisation of his labour: his labour appears instead as the means of valorisation—i.e. absorption of labour—for the means of labour. This distinction is formal in so far as it can exist without causing the slightest alteration of any kind in the mode of production or the social relations within which production takes place.[75] With cooperation a specific distinction already enters the picture. The work takes place under conditions in which the independent labour of the individual cannot be carried on—and indeed these conditions appear as a relation dominating the individual, as a band with which capital fetters the individual workers.

The collaboration of many people, whose association itself is a relation alien to them, whose unity lies outside them, gives rise to the necessity for command, for overall supervision, as itself a condition of production, as a new kind of labour, LABOUR OF SUPERINTENDENCE, made necessary and conditioned by the cooperation of the workers, just as in any army there is a need for people with the power of command, a need for command, if it is to function as a unified body, even when all its members belong to the same arm of the service.[76] This command is an attribute of capital, although the individual capitalist can in his turn hand over its implementation to specialised workers, who nevertheless represent capital and the capitalist over against the army of workers. (*Slavery, Cairnes.*[187])

In so far as specialised work of this kind arises out of functions created by capitalist production itself, it is of course absurd to use capital's performance of these functions to prove the necessity of its existence. It is a tautology. It is as if one were to wish to justify slavery to the Negroes by saying that as slaves they needed the overseer with his whip, who was as necessary to their production as they themselves. But he is necessary only because and in so far as they are slaves—on the basis of slavery. In contrast to this, in so far as cooperation requires a director, as in an orchestra for example, the form this takes under the conditions of capital and the form it might take otherwise, e.g. in the case of association, are completely different things. In the latter case it is a specialised function of labour alongside others, but not as the power that brings about the workers' own unity as something alien to them, and the exploitation of their labour as an act committed upon them by an alien power.

Cooperation may be continuous; it may also be merely temporary, as in agriculture with the harvest, etc.

The essence of simple cooperation remains *simultaneity* of action, a simultaneity whose results can never be attained by the temporal succession of the activities of the individual workers.

What remains most important is: This first transposition of the social character of labour as social character of capital, of the productive power of social labour as productive power of capital; and finally the first transformation of the formal subsumption under capital into a real alteration of the mode of production itself.

[IV-138a][191] *Destutt de Tracy* distinguishes as means for increasing the productivity of labour:

1) *Concours de forces.* (SIMPLE COOPERATION.)[a] "Is it a matter of defending oneself? Ten men can easily resist an enemy who would have destroyed all of them by attacking them one after another. Is a heavy object to be moved? The burden heavy enough to oppose an invincible resistance to the efforts of a single individual yields straight away to several people acting together. *Is it a question of undertaking a complex piece of labour?* Many things must be done simultaneously. One person does one thing, while another does something else, and they all contribute to an effect that a single man would be unable to produce. One rows while the other holds the rudder, and a third casts the net or harpoons the fish; in this way fishing enjoys a success that would be impossible without this cooperation" (l.c., p. 78).[b]

In this second form of cooperation there is already a division of labour taking place, because many things must be done *simultaneously,* but this is not a division of labour in the true sense. The 3 people can alternately row, steer and fish, although in the act of cooperation each of them only does the one thing. The real division of labour, in contrast, consists in this, that

---

a Destutt de Tracy, *Traité de la volonté et de ses effets*, Paris, 1826, p. 80.— Ed.
b Here and below Marx quotes in French.— Ed.

"when a number of men work for each other, each of them can devote himself *exclusively* to the occupation for which he is most suited, etc." (l.c., p. 79). [IV-138a]

[IV-149] b) *DIVISION OF LABOUR*[192]

The division of labour is a particular, differentiated, further developed form of cooperation, a powerful means of heightening the productive power of labour, performing the same work in less labour time, hence reducing the labour time necessary for the reproduction of labour capacity and extending surplus labour time.

Simple cooperation involves many people working together to perform the *same* work. In the division of labour many workers cooperate under the command of capital to produce *different* parts of *the same commodities*, each particular part requiring a specific kind of labour, a specific operation, and each worker or definite multiple quantity of workers performing one specific operation only, with the others performing others and so forth; the totality of these operations, however, producing *a single commodity*, a particular specific commodity; the latter therefore representing the totality of these specific forms of labour.

We say *commodity* from a twofold point of view. Firstly, a commodity produced under the division of labour can itself be a semi-manufacture, a raw material, a material of labour for another sphere of production. A product of this kind therefore by no means needs to be a use value which has taken on its final form, the form in which it ultimately enters consumption.

If different production processes are required for the manufacture of a use value, e.g. printed calico—spinning, weaving, printing—the printed calico is the result of these different production processes and of the totality of the specific modes of labour, spinning, weaving, printing. No division of labour in the sense we are now considering has yet taken place on that account. If the spun yarn is a *commodity*, the *woven cloth a commodity*, and the printed calico a specific commodity alongside the other two commodities—those use values which are the product of processes which must precede the printing of calico—no division of labour in the sense we are now considering takes place, although there is a social division of labour, because the yarn is the product of spinners, the cloth is the product of weavers and the calico is the product of printers. The labour necessary for the production of printed calico is divided into spinning, weaving and printing and each of these branches forms the occupation of a particular section of workers, each of whom performs only the one particular operation of spinning or weaving or printing. Here, then, what is needed is firstly a totality of particular kinds of labour, in order to produce the printed calico; and secondly the subsumption of different workers under each of these particular labour operations. But it cannot be said that they cooperate in producing *the same commodity*. They rather produce commodities independent of each other. The yarn is on our assumption as much a commodity as the printed calico. The existence of a use value as a commodity does not depend on the nature of that use value, hence it does not depend, either, on its distance from or nearness to the shape in which it finally enters consumption, whether as means of labour or means of subsistence. It depends solely on this, that a definite quantity of labour time is represented in the product and that it forms the material for the satisfaction of certain needs, whether these are the needs of a further production process or those of the consumption process. On the other hand, if the printed calico first came onto the market as a *commodity* after having passed through the processes of spinning, weaving and printing, it would have been produced by *division* of labour.

We have seen that the product only becomes a commodity at all, and the exchange of commodities as a condition of production only takes place at all, given a social division of labour, [IV-150] or a division of social labour.[a] The specific commodities are the repositories of specific modes of labour, and the producer or owner of the individual commodity only takes possession of his aliquot part of social production, i.e. of the products of all the other branches of labour, through exchange, namely the sale of his product, through the conversion of his commodity into money. That he produces a commodity at all implies that his labour is one-sided and does not *directly* produce his means of subsistence, that these are rather obtained only by the exchange of his labour for the products of other branches of labour. This social division of labour, which is presupposed in the existence of the product as a commodity and of the exchange of commodities, differs essentially from the division of labour we are investigating here. The latter presupposes the former as its point of departure and basis.

A division of labour occurs in the former case in so far as every

---

a K. Marx, *A Contribution to the Critique of Political Economy.* Part One (present edition, Vol. 29, p. 292).— *Ed.*

commodity represents the other commodity, hence every commodity owner or producer represents a specific branch of labour vis-à-vis the other one; and the totality of these specific branches of labour, their existence as the whole gamut of social labour, is mediated through the *exchange of commodities,* or, more closely defined, the *circulation of commodities,* which as we have seen includes the circulation of money.[a] A considerable division of labour in this sense may take place without there being any division of labour in the other sense. But the second type cannot occur without the first under conditions of commodity production, although it can occur where products are not produced as commodities at all, where production does not, in general, take place on the basis of the exchange of commodities. The first division of labour shows itself in the fact that the product of a specific branch of labour confronts as a specific commodity the producers of all other branches of labour as independent commodities differing from it. The second division of labour, in contrast, takes place when a specific use value is produced before it comes onto the market, enters into circulation, as a specific, independent commodity. In the first case the different kinds of labour complement each other through the exchange of commodities. In the second there is direct, cooperative action by the different kinds of labour, not mediated through the exchange of commodities, with the aim of manufacturing the same use value under the command of capital. In the first division of labour the producers meet as independent commodity owners and representatives of specific branches of labour. In the second they appear rather as dependent, since they only produce a complete commodity, indeed only produce a commodity at all, through their cooperation, and each of them represents not a specific piece of work, but rather the individual operations which are combined, which meet, in a specific piece of work, while the commodity owner, the producer of the complete commodity, confronts the dependent workers as capitalist.

Adam Smith constantly confuses these very different senses of the division of labour, which admittedly complement each other, but are also in certain respects mutually opposed. In order to avoid confusion, more recent English writers call the first type DIVISION OF LABOUR and the second SUBDIVISION OF LABOUR, although this fails to bring out the conceptual distinction.[193]

---

[a] K. Marx, *A Contribution to the Critique of Political Economy.* Part One (present edition, Vol. 29, Chapter Two, "Money or Simple Circulation").— *Ed.*

Pins and twist are two specific commodities; each of them represent a specific branch of labour and their producers confront each other as commodity owners. They represent a division of social labour, each section of which confronts the other as a specific sphere of production. In contrast to this, the different operations required for the production of a pin constitute a division of labour in the second sense if they represent just as many modes of labour under which particular workers are subsumed—it being presupposed, namely, that the particular parts of the pin do not emerge as specific commodities. Characteristic of this kind of division of labour is the differentiation of the operations within the sphere of production which belongs to a particular *commodity*, and the distribution of each of these operations among particular workers, whose cooperation creates the whole product, the *commodity*, but whose representative is not the worker but the capitalist. [IV-151] Even this form of the division of labour, which we are considering here, by no means exhausts the subject of the division of labour, which is in a certain respect the category of categories of political economy. But here we have only to consider it as a particular productive power of capital.

It is clear, 1) that this division of labour presupposes the social division of labour. First the exchange of commodities develops the differentiation of social labour, and then the branches of labour become so widely separated that each specific branch is traced back to a specialised kind of labour, and the division of labour, its analysis, can take place within this specialised labour. It is equally clear, 2) that the second division of labour must, in its turn, extend the first—reacting back upon it. *Firstly* in so far as it, like all other productive forces, reduces the amount of labour required for a particular use value, therefore sets labour free to take part in a new branch of social labour. Secondly, and this is specific to it, in so far as it is able in its analysis to split up a speciality in such a way that the different *components of the same use value* are now produced as different commodities, independent of each other, or also that the *different varieties of the same use value*, which previously all fell to the share of the same sphere of production, are now allotted to different spheres of production through the analysis of the individual varieties.

The one is division of social labour into different branches of labour, the other is division of labour in the manufacture of a commodity, hence not division of labour in society but social division of labour within one and the same workshop. Division of labour in the latter sense presupposes *manufacture*, as a specific *mode of production*.

Adam Smith does not distinguish these two SENSES of the division of labour. The second division of labour therefore does not appear with him as something specific to capitalist production.

The chapter on the division of labour with which he opens his work (book I, chapter I) (On the Division of Labour) begins like this:

"The effects of the *division of labour*, in the general industry of society, will be more easily understood by considering in what manner these effects operate in some particular manufactures" [Garnier, p. 11] [Vol. I, p. 15].[194]

The division of labour within the *atelier* (which really means workshop, FACTORY, mine, or farm here, the only assumption being that the individuals employed in the production of a particular *commodity cooperate* under the command of capital), the *capitalist* division of labour, is only of interest to him, and he only discusses it in particular, as being a more easily comprehensible, more tangible and clearer example of the effects of the division of labour within society in general and upon the "general industry of society". The following passage proves this:

"It is commonly supposed that this *division* is carried furthest in some manufactures which produce articles of little value; not perhaps that it really is carried further in them than in others of more importance: but in those trifling manufactures which are destined to supply the small wants of but a small number of people, the whole number of workmen must necessarily be small; *and those employed in every different branch of the work can often be collected into the same workhouse*, and placed at once under the view of the spectator. In those great manufactures, on the contrary, which are destined to supply the wants of the great body of the people, *every different branch of the work employs so great a number of workmen that it is impossible to collect them all* [IV-152] *into the same workhouse.* We can seldom see more, at one time, than those employed in one single branch of the work. Though in such manufactures, therefore, the work may really be divided into a much greater number of parts than in those of the first kind, the division is not near so obvious, and has accordingly been much less observed" [l.c., pp. 11-12].

Firstly, this passage demonstrates the small scale on which industrial enterprises still operated in Adam Smith's time.

Secondly, the division of labour in a workshop and the division of a branch of labour within society into distinct, mutually independent branches, are only *subjectively* different matters for him, not *objectively*. In the first case one sees the division at a glance, in the second case one does not. The change is not in the real situation but only in the way the observer sees it. For example, if one looks at the whole of the iron-producing industry, starting from the production of pig iron and going through all the different types of product into which the industry is divided, each of which forms an independent branch of production, an *independent* commodity, whose connection with its preceding or subsequent stages is mediated by the exchange of commodities, the social division of this branch of industry probably involves more subdivisions than we meet with inside a pin factory.

Hence Adam Smith does not grasp the division of labour as a particular, specifically distinct form characteristic of the *capitalist* mode of production.

The division of labour, as we regard it here, presupposes firstly that the social division of labour has already attained a considerable level of development, that the various spheres of production are separated from each other, and that within each sphere there are further divisions into independent subspecies; indeed, capital can only develop on the basis of a circulation of commodities which is already relatively extensive, and is identical with a relatively extensive development of the division (autonomisation) of branches of business within society as a whole. Once this is presupposed, hence e.g. once the production of cotton yarn exists as an independent, autonomous branch of business (hence is no longer e.g. a subsidiary occupation of the countryside), the second prerequisite for the division of labour, which precedes this one and exists before it, is that many workers in this branch should be associated in a workshop under the command of capital. This association, the agglomeration of workers under the command of capital, which is the condition for *capitalist* cooperation, comes about for two reasons. Firstly, surplus value does not depend only on its rate; its absolute amount, magnitude, depends at the same time on the number of workers who are simultaneously being exploited by the same capital. Capital functions as capital in proportion to the number of workers it simultaneously employs. The independence of the workers in their production is thereby at an end. They work under the supervision and command of capital. In so far as they work together and are interconnected, this interconnection exists in capital, or, this interconnection itself is for them merely external, a mode of capital's existence. Their labour becomes *compulsory labour* because once they enter into the labour process it belongs not to them but already to capital, is already incorporated in capital. The workers are subjected to the *discipline* of capital and placed in completely changed conditions of life. The first manufactories in Holland, and in all countries where they developed independently and were not imported ready-made from abroad, were little more than conglomerations of workers who produced the same commodity, with the means of labour being concentrated in the same workshop under the command of the same capital. A developed division of labour was not a feature of those places, the development rather took place first within them as its natural basis. In the medieval guilds the master [IV-153] was prevented from becoming a capitalist by the guild regulations, which restricted to a very low maximum the number of workers he was permitted to employ at any one time.

Secondly, the economic advantages which arose from the common utilisation of the buildings, of furnaces, etc., and soon gave these manufactories such an advantage in productivity over the patriarchal or guild-based enterprises—apart from any effect of the division of labour—do not belong to our subject here, as we have only to consider, not the *economy* made on the *conditions of labour*,[189] but the more productive application of variable capital; the extent to which these means *directly* raise the productivity of the labour employed in a particular sphere of production.

Even where a particular branch of business—see e.g. *Blanqui*[a]— is very subdivided, but patriarchal, so that the product of each part exists as a specific commodity independently of the others, or is only mediated by the exchange of commodities, association in a single workshop is by no means merely formal. In these circumstances the work almost always takes the form of domestic-rural subsidiary labour, there thus being no absolute subsumption of the worker under an entirely one-sided and simple operation. It is not his exclusive task. But then the main feature is lacking. These workers work with their own means of labour. The mode of production itself is in fact not capitalist, instead, the capitalist merely steps between these independent workers and the definitive purchaser of their commodities as *middleman,* as *merchant.* This form, in which capital has not yet taken control of production itself, still predominates over much of the Continent; it always constitutes the transition from the subsidiary industries of the countryside to the capitalist mode of production proper. Here the worker himself appears as commodity owner, producer and seller, and the capitalist still confronts him as *buyer of commodities,* not of *labour.* The basis of capitalist production is therefore still absent.

Where, as in Blanqui's example, the division of labour exists in the form of independent branches of production, a multiplicity of time-consuming and unproductive intermediate processes takes place, conditioned by the existence of the different stages of the

---

a See this volume, pp. 285-86.— *Ed*

commodity as commodities in their own right, and by the fact that their interconnection in the overall production of the commodity has first to be mediated through the exchange of commodities, through sale and purchase. Working for each other in the different branches is subject to all kinds of accidents, irregularities and so on, for it is the compulsion of the workshop which first introduces simultaneity, regularity and proportionality into the mechanism of these different operations, in fact first combines them together into a uniformly operating mechanism.

If the division of labour—once it proceeds, now on the basis of the existing workshops, to a further subdivision of the operations and subsumption under them of definite multiple numbers of workers—if the division of labour *carries itself further*, it is also its opposite. For in so far as the *disjecta membra poetae*[a] were previously autonomous, existing side by side as an equal number of independent commodities, and hence as the products of an equal number of independent commodity owners, the division of labour is also their *combination* in one mechanism; an aspect entirely overlooked by Adam.

Later on[b] we shall investigate in more detail why the division of labour within society, a division which through the exchange of commodities emerges as the totality of production and only has an impact on its individual representatives through competition, the law of supply and demand, develops further at the same pace as, goes hand in hand with, the division of labour within the workshop, the division of labour characteristic of capitalist production, in which the independence of the workers is completely annihilated and they become parts of a social mechanism standing under the command of capital.[55]

[IV-154] This much is clear. Adam Smith did not grasp the *division of labour* as something peculiar to the capitalist mode of production; something whereby, in addition to machinery and simple cooperation, labour is transformed not only formally, but in its reality—through subsumption under capital. He conceives it in the same way as Petty and others of his predecessors after Petty. (See the *East Indian pamphlet*.[c])

Like his predecessors, Smith in fact still views the division of labour from the standpoint of *antiquity,* in so far as they lump it

---

[a] "Scattered limbs of the poet" (Horace, *Satirarum*, I, 4).— *Ed.*
[b] See this volume, pp. 312-16.— *Ed.*
[c] W. Petty, *An Essay Concerning the Multiplication of Mankind*; [H. Martyn,] *The Advantages of the East-India Trade to England* (see this volume, pp. 286-87.— *Ed.*

together with the division of labour within society. They only differ from the conception held by the classical world in their view of the result and purpose of the division of labour. They conceive it as from the outset a productive force of capital, in so far as they stress and almost exclusively discuss the fact that the division of labour *cheapens commodities*, reduces the amount of necessary labour time required to produce a particular commodity, or increases the quantity of commodities that can be produced in the same necessary labour time, thereby lessening the *exchange value* of the individual commodities. They lay all their emphasis on this aspect— *exchange value*—and the *modernity* of their point of view consists in this. And this is of course the decisive point if the division of labour is conceived as a productive force of capital, for it is such a force only in so far as it cheapens the means of subsistence required for the reproduction of labour capacity, reduces the amount of labour time needed for their reproduction. The ancients, on the other hand, had their eyes fixed exclusively on *use value*, in so far as they made any attempt at all to reflect upon and understand the division of labour. The consequence of the division of labour for them was that the products of the individual branches of production attained a *better quality*, whereas the *quantitative* point of view predominates among the moderns. The ancients, therefore, consider the division of labour not in relation to the *commodity* but in relation to the *product* as such. What interests the commodity owners who have become capitalists is the influence of the division of labour on the *commodity*; its influence on the *product* as such only has a bearing on the commodity in so far as it is a matter of the satisfaction of human needs in general, a matter of use value as such. The historical background of the Greeks' views is always *Egypt*, which they regarded as the model of an industrial country, in just the same way as Holland and later England were regarded by the moderns. The division of labour therefore occurs with them, as we shall see later, in relation to the hereditary division of labour and the caste system deriving from it, as it existed in Egypt.

Adam Smith confuses the two forms of the division of labour later on too. Thus he says further in the same book I, chapter I:

"The division of labour, so far as it can be introduced, occasions, in every art, a proportionable increase of the productive powers of labour. *The separation of different trades and employments from one another seems to have taken place in consequence of this advantage.* This separation, too, is generally carried furthest in those countries which enjoy the highest degree of industry and improvement; what is the work of one man in a rude state of society being generally that of several in an improved one" [Garnier, p. 15] [Vol. I, p. 18].

Adam Smith explicitly picks out the *quantitative* point of view, i.e. the curtailment of the labour time needed for the production of a commodity, as the exclusive consideration, in the passage where he is enumerating the advantages of the division of labour:

"*This great increase in the quantity of work which*, in consequence of the division of labour, *the same number of people are capable of performing*, is owing to three different circumstances" ([Garnier,] Book I, Chapter I [p. 18]) [Vol. I, p. 21].

According to him these advantages consist in 1) the *dexterity* the worker attains in his one-sided branch [IV-155] of labour:

"First, the improvement of the dexterity of the workman necessarily increases the *quantity of the work* he can perform; and the division of labour, by *reducing every man's business to some one simple operation*, and by making *this operation the sole employment of his life*, necessarily increases very much the dexterity of the workman." (Hence rapidity of the operations.)

Secondly: saving of the time which gets lost in moving from one task to another. In that connection both "change of place" and "different tools" are required.

"When the two trades can be carried on *in the same workhouse*, the loss of time is no doubt much less. It is even in this case, however, very considerable. A man commonly saunters a little in turning his hand from one sort of employment to another" [Garnier, pp. 20, 21] [Vol. I, p. 23].

Finally Smith mentions

"that the invention of all those machines by which labour is so much facilitated and abridged seems to have been originally owing to the division of labour" [Garnier, p. 22] [Vol. I, p. 24]

(invented by the workers themselves, the whole of whose attention is exclusively directed towards a simple object). And even the influence exerted on the invention of machinery by philosophers or men of speculation is due to the social division of labour, for it is through it that

"philosophy or speculation becomes, like every other employment, the principal or sole trade occupation of a particular class of citizens" [Garnier, p. 24] [Vol. I, p. 25].

Adam Smith remarks that if on the one hand the division of labour is the product, the result, of the natural diversity of human talents, the latter are to a much greater degree the result of the development of the division of labour. In this he follows his teacher Ferguson.

"The difference of natural talents in different men is, in reality, much less than we are aware of; and the very different genius which appears to distinguish men of different professions, when grown up to maturity, is *not so much the cause as the effect of* the division of labour.... All must have had the same duties to perform" (without the division of labour and without exchange, which he makes into the *basis* of the division of labour), "and the same work to do, and there could have been no such difference of employment as could alone give occasion to any great difference of talents". "By nature a philosopher is not in genius and disposition half so different from a street porter, as a mastiff is from a greyhound" [Garnier, pp. 33-35] [Vol. I, pp. 33-35].

Smith explains the very existence of the division of labour by referring to

> "*men's inclination to trade and exchange*", without which "every man must have procured to himself every necessary and conveniency of life" ([Garnier,] Book I, Chapter II, [p. 34]) [Vol. I, p. 34].

Thus he assumes exchange in order to explain the division of labour, and assumes the division of labour IN ORDER THAT THERE BE SOMETHING TO EXCHANGE.

The naturally evolved division of labour precedes exchange, and the exchange of products as commodities first develops *between different communities, not within the same community.* (The division of labour rests in part not only on the naturally evolved differences between human beings themselves, but on natural elements of production found available by these different communities.[195]) Of course, the development of the product into a commodity and the exchange of commodities react back onto the division of labour, so that exchange and division enter into a relation of interaction.

[IV-156] Smith's main merit in dealing with the division of labour is that he stresses it and puts it in the forefront, indeed views it directly as a productive power of labour (i.e. capital). In his conception of it, however, he is dependent on the contemporary level of development of *manufacture*, which was still far removed from the modern factory. Hence also the relative preponderance conceded to the division of labour over machinery, which still appears merely as its appendage.

In the whole section on the division of labour Adam Smith essentially follows his teacher *Adam Ferguson*, often to the extent of copying from him ([A. Ferguson,] *Essai sur l'histoire de la société civile*, translated by M. Bergier, Paris, 1783). Under conditions of barbarism the human being inclines to sloth:

> "He is, perhaps, by the diversity of his wants, discouraged from industry; or, by his divided attention, prevented from acquiring skill in any kind of labour" ([A. Ferguson, l.c.,] Vol. II, p. 128).[a]

Among the different circumstances which gradually lead men "to subdivide their professions without any conscious end in mind", Ferguson similarly indicates "*the prospect of being able to*

---

[a] Here and below Marx quotes Ferguson in French.— *Ed.*

exchange one commodity for another", although he does not imitate Smith's one-sidedness in giving it as the sole reason. He goes on to say:

"The artist finds, that the more he can confine his attention to a particular part of any work, his productions are the more perfect, and *grow under his hands in the greater quantities.* Every undertaker in manufacture finds, that the more he can subdivide the tasks of his workmen, and *the more hands he can employ on separate articles,* the more are his expenses diminished, and his profits increased.... The progress of commerce is but a continued subdivision of the mechanical arts" ([p.] 129).

Adam Smith asserts that originally the workers invented the machine, because, owing to the division of labour,

"when the whole of every man's attention is directed towards some one object", they devised "all those machines by which labour is so much facilitated and abridged" ([Garnier,] Book I, Chapter I [p. 22]) [Vol. I, p. 24].

Adam Ferguson speaks of

"the methods, the means, the devices ... which the artist, attentive to his own affair, has invented, to abridge or to facilitate his separate task" (p. 133).

Adam Smith says:

"In the progress of society, philosophy or speculation becomes, like every employment, the principal or sole occupation of a particular class of citizens" ([Garnier,] Book I, Chapter I [pp. 23-24]) [Vol. I, p. 25].

Adam Ferguson:

"This method, which yields such great advantages in regard of industry, can be applied with equal success to more important things, in the various departments of policy and war ... *in this age of separations,* [thinking] itself may become a peculiar craft" (pp. 131, 136).

Ferguson, like Adam Smith, makes special mention of the application of science to industrial practice (p. 136).

What distinguishes him from Adam Smith is the fact that he brings out more sharply and emphatically the negative aspects of the division of labour (and with Ferguson the *quality* of the commodity still plays a role, while Adam Smith, from the capitalist point of view correctly, leaves it aside as a mere ACCIDENT).

"It may even be doubted, whether the measure of national capacity increases with the advancement of arts. Many mechanical arts require no capacity; they succeed perfectly without recourse to sentiment and reason; and ignorance is the mother of industry as well as of superstition. Reflection and fancy are subject to err; but a habit of moving the hand, or the foot, is independent of either. One might therefore say that perfection, in regard of manufactures, consists in the ability to proceed without consulting the mind" (especially, and this is an important point with regard to the workshop) "*in such a manner that the workshop may* [IV-157], *without any great effort of imagination, be considered as an engine, the parts of which are men*" (pp. 134, 135).

The *concept of manufacture* comes out much more clearly here than in *Adam Smith.* Furthermore, Ferguson emphasises the change in the relationship between manufacturer and worker which occurs as a result of the division of labour.

"Even in manufacture, the genius of the master, perhaps, is cultivated, while that of the inferior workman lies waste.... The general officer may be a great proficient in the knowledge of war, while the soldier is confined to a few motions of the hand and the foot. *The former may have gained, what the latter has lost"* (pp. 135, 136).

What he says of the general in relation to the ordinary soldier is true of the capitalist or his MANAGER in relation to the army of workers. The intelligence and independent development which were applied on a small scale in autonomous work are now applied on a large scale for the whole workshop, and monopolised by the boss; the workers are thereby robbed of these attributes.

"He [the general] may practise on a larger scale all the arts of preservation, of deception and of stratagem, which the savage exerts in leading a small party, or merely in defending himself" (p. 136).

Hence Ferguson also expressly treats of the *"subordination"* consequent on the "separation of arts and professions" (l.c., p. 138). Here the *antagonism of capital,* etc.

With regard to entire nations, Ferguson has this to say:

"Nations of tradesmen come to consist of members who, beyond their own particular trade, are ignorant of all human affairs" (p. 130). "We make a nation of helots, and have no free citizens" (l.c., p. 144).

He contrasts this with classical antiquity, although he points out at the same time that slavery was the foundation for the more complete all-round development of the free citizens. (See the *Frenchman,*[196] who indulges in more speechifying on the whole of this Fergusonian theme, but wittily.)

Thus if one takes Ferguson, who was Smith's teacher directly, and Petty, whose example of watchmaking was replaced by Smith with the one of the pin factory,[197] Smith's originality consists only in his *putting the division of labour in the limelight and his one-sided (hence economically correct) estimation of it as a means for increasing the productive power of labour.*

It says in A. Potter, *Political Economy,* New York, 1841 (Part 2 of which is almost exclusively a REPRINT OF Scrope's *Political Economy,* London, 1833):

* "The first essential towards production is labour. To play its part efficiently in this great business, the labour of individuals must be *combined;* or, in other words, the labour required for producing certain results must be *distributed* among several individuals, and those individuals thus be enabled to cooperate" * (Scrope, p. 76).

Potter remarks on this, in a note on the same page:

* "The principle here referred to is usually called the *division of labour.* The phrase is objectionable, since the fundamental idea is that of *concert* and *cooperation,* not of *division.* The term of division applies only to the *process;* this being *subdivided into several operations,* and these being *distributed* or *parcelled out among a number of operatives.* It is thus a *combination of labourers* effected through a *subdivision of processes.*" * It is: COMBINATION OF LABOUR.

The title of Ferguson's book is: *Essay on the History of Civil Society.*

[IV-158] Dugald Stewart, COLLECTED WORKS, ED. BY Sir W. Hamilton, Edinburgh. I cite from VOL. VIII of the COLLECTED WORKS, WHICH IS VOL. I (published in 1855) of the *Lectures on Political Economy.*

On the way in which the division of labour increases the productivity of labour, he says among other things:

* "The effects of the division of labour, and of the use of machines ... both derive their value from the same circumstance, their tendency, to *enable one man to perform the work of many*" * (p. 317).

* "It produces also an *economy of time,* by separating the work into its different branches, all *of which may be carried into execution at the same moment* ... by *carrying on all the different processes at once,* which an individual must have executed separately, it becomes possible to produce a multitude of pins for instance *completely* finished in the same time as a single pin might have been either cut or pointed" * ([p.] 319).

This goes beyond Adam Smith's second argument above, that the single worker who passes through the whole circuit of the different operations loses time in the transition from one operation to another.[a]

The different operations performed successively by a worker in a patriarchal or craft-based business in order to make his product, which are mutually intertwined as different modes of his activity, and follow each other in chronological sequence; the different phases through which his work passes, and in which it undergoes variation, are separated from each other, isolated, as independent operations or processes. This independence becomes solidified, personified, when each simple and monosyllabic process of this kind becomes the exclusive function of a particular worker or a definite number of workers. They are subsumed under these isolated functions. This work is not divided among them; they are divided among the various processes, each of which becomes the exclusive life-process of one of them — in so far as they function as productive labour capacity. The heightened productivity and complexity of the production process as a whole, its enrichment, is therefore purchased at the cost of the reduction of labour capacity

---

[a] See this volume, p. 273.— *Ed.*

in each of its specific functions to nothing but a dry abstraction—a simple quality, which appears in the eternal uniformity of an identical function, and for which the whole of the worker's productive capacity, the multiplicity of his capabilities, has been confiscated. The processes separated out in this way, and performed as functions of these living automatons, allow combination precisely through their division and autonomy; allow these different processes to be carried out *simultaneously* in the same workshop. Here division and combination condition each other. The overall production process of a single commodity appears now as a combined operation, a complex of many operations, all of which complement each other independently, and can be carried out *simultaneously* alongside each other. The complementarity of the different processes is here transferred from the future to the present, whereby a commodity which is begun at one side is finished at the other. At the same time, since these different operations are performed with virtuosity, because they have been reduced to simple functions, there is added to this *simultaneity,* which is in general characteristic of cooperation, a *reduction in labour time,* which is attained in each of the simultaneous and mutually complementary functions which are combined together into a single whole; so that within a given time not only more *whole commodities,* more commodities *finished and ready for use* are in general delivered, but also *more* finished commodities. Through this combination the workshop becomes a mechanism of which the individual workers form the different elements.

But the combination—cooperation, as it appears in the division of labour, no longer as the parallel existence of the same functions or their temporary subdivision, but as the separation of a totality of functions into their constituent elements, and the unification of these different components—now has a twofold existence: it exists on the one hand, if we look at the production process itself, in the workshop as a whole, which, as a total mechanism of this kind (although in fact it is nothing other than the manifestation of the workers' cooperation, their social mode of action in the production process) confronts the workers as [IV-159] an external power, dominating and enveloping them, in fact as the power of capital itself and a form of its existence, under which they are individually subsumed, and to which their social relation of production belongs. On the other hand, it exists in the finished product, which is in turn a commodity belonging to the capitalist.

For the worker himself no combination of activities takes place. The combination is rather a combination of the one-sided functions under which every worker or number of workers is subsumed, group by group. His function is one-sided, abstract, partial. The totality which is formed from this is based precisely on his *merely partial existence* and isolation in his separate function. It is therefore a combination of which he forms a part, but it depends on the fact that his labour is not combined. *The workers form the building blocks of this combination.* However, the combination is not a relation that belongs to them, nor is it subsumed under them as a united group. This point is also directed against Mr. Potter's pretty phrases about combination and concert as opposed to DIVISION.

Here the capitalist mode of production has already seized upon the substance of labour and transformed it. The subsumption of the worker under capital is no longer merely *formal*: the fact that he works for someone else, under alien command and alien supervision. Nor is the situation any longer merely as it was in the case of simple cooperation, where the worker cooperates with many others, performing *the same* work with them at the same time, while his work as such remains unchanged and a merely temporary connection is created, a contiguity, which by the nature of things may easily be dissolved and which in most cases of simple cooperation takes place only for specific, limited periods, to satisfy exceptional requirements, as with harvesting, road-building, etc. Nor is it like manufacture in its simplest form, where the main thing is the simultaneous exploitation of many workers and a saving on fixed capital, etc., and where the worker only formally becomes a part of a whole, whose head is the capitalist, but in which he is not further affected—as a producer—by the fact that many other workers are doing the same thing alongside him, also making boots, etc. With the transformation of his labour capacity into what is merely a function of part of the complete mechanism, the whole of which forms the workshop, he has altogether ceased to be the producer of a commodity. He is only the producer of a one-sided operation, which in general produces something solely in connection with the whole of the mechanism that forms the workshop. He is thus a living constituent of the workshop, and has himself become an accessory to capital through the manner of his work, since his skill can only be exercised in a workshop, only as a link in a mechanism which confronts him as the presence of capital. Originally he had to sell to the capitalist, instead of the commodity, the labour that produced the commodity, because he was not in possession of the objective conditions for the realisation of his labour capacity. Now he has to sell it because his labour capacity only continues to be labour capacity in so far as it is sold to capital. Thus he is now subsumed under capitalist production, has now fallen under the control of capital, no longer just because he lacks the means of labour, but because of his very labour capacity, the nature and manner of his labour; now capital has in its hands no longer just the objective conditions, but the social conditions of subjective labour, the conditions under which his labour continues to be labour at all.[55]

The increase of productive power which arises from the division of labour, this social mode of existence of labour, is therefore not only capital's, instead of the worker's, productive power. The *social form* of the workers' combined labours is the existence of capital over against the worker; combination confronts him as a paramount destiny to which he has fallen victim through the reduction of his labour capacity to an entirely one-sided function, which is nothing apart from the mechanism as a whole, [IV-160] and therefore depends entirely upon it. He has himself become a mere detail.

Dugald Stewart, l.c., calls the workers subordinated to the division of labour

* "living automatons ... employed in the details of the work",* while the
* "employer will be always on the stretch to economize time and labour" * (p. 318).

Dugald Stewart cites maxims from classical antiquity relating to the division of labour within society.

"*Cuncta nihilque sumus.*" "*In omnibus aliquid, in toto nihil.*"[a] "πολλ' ἠπίστατο ἔργα, κακῶς δ'ἠπίστατο πάντα."[b 198]

(this from the *Margites*, cited in the SECOND ALCIBIADES, ONE OF THE SPURIOUS DIALOGUES OF Plato).[c]

Thus, in the *Odyssey*, XIV, 228:

"ἄλλος γάρ τ'ἄλλοισιν ἀνὴρ ἐπιτέρπεται ἔργοις",[d]

and the statement by Archilochus, quoted in Sextus Empiricus

"αλλος ἄλλῳ ἐπ' ἔργῳ καρδίην ἰαίνεται".[e]

Thucydides makes Pericles contrast the agriculturalists of Sparta, where consumption was not mediated through the

---

[a] "We are everything and nothing". "We can do something of everything, but nothing as a whole".— *Ed.*

[b] "He knew many crafts, but he knew all of them badly".— *Ed.*

[c] Pseudo-Plato, *Alcibiades II 147b.*— *Ed.*

[d] "For different men take joy in different works".— *Ed.*

[e] "Men differ as to what things cheer their hearts" (Sextus Empiricus, *Adversus mathematicos*, XI, 44).— *Ed.*

exchange of commodities, hence no division of labour took place either, with the Athenians, describing the Spartans as "αὐτουργοί"ᵃ (working not for gain but for subsistence).

This is what Pericles says about nautical matters in the same speech (Thucydides, Book I, Chapter 142):

"Seamanship, like any other skill, is a matter of art, and practice in it may not be left to odd times, as a sideline; on the contrary, no other pursuit may be carried on as a subsidiary occupation." 199

We shall come to Plato directly, although he actually belongs before *Xenophon*. The latter, who possesses a considerable amount of bourgeois instinct, and is therefore often reminiscent of both bourgeois morality and bourgeois political economy, looks more closely than Plato at the division of labour, in so far as it takes place in the individual workshop as well as on a broad scale. The following account by Xenophon is interesting, 1) because he shows the dependence of the division of labour upon the *size of the market*; and 2) because in contrast to Plato he does not confine himself to the division of occupations, but rather stresses the reduction of labour to simple labour brought about by the division of labour, and the skill which can more easily be attained under that system. Although as a result he is much closer to the modern conception, he still retains the attitude which is characteristic of the ancients: he is concerned only with *use value*, with the improvement of *quality*. He is not interested in the curtailment of labour time any more than is Plato, even in the one passage where, exceptionally and in passing, the latter indicates that *more* use values are provided. Even here it is only a matter of an increased quantity of *use values*; not of the effect of the division of labour on the product as *commodity*.

Xenophon relates that it is not only an honour to receive food from the table of the King of Persia, but a joy as well (because the food tastes better).

"But the food that is sent from the king's board really is much superior in the pleasure it gives to the palate as well. That this should be so, however, is no marvel. For just as all other arts are developed to superior excellence in large cities, in the same way the food at the king's palace is also elaborately prepared with superior excellence. For in small towns the same workman makes dining couches and doors and ploughs and tables and often this same artisan builds houses, and even so he is thankful if he can only find [IV-161] enough employersᵇ to allow him to make a living. *And it is of course impossible for a man of so many trades to be proficient in all of them.* In large cities, on the other hand, *where every workman finds many customers*, one

---

ᵃ "Working for themselves".— *Ed.*

ᵇ Xenophon uses the word ἐργοδότας. Marx comments in brackets: "ἐργοδότης is an employer who contracts the work out".— *Ed.*

trade alone, and often even less than a whole trade, is enough to support a man: one man, for instance, makes shoes for men, another for women. It happens that one man earns a living by only stitching shoes, another by cutting them out, another by cutting the uppers to shape, while there is another who performs none of these operations but only assembles the parts. *It follows therefore that* HE *who performs the simplest work* MUST NEEDS DO THE THING BEST (he is compelled to provide the best work). Exactly the same thing holds true with the art of cooking. He for whom one and the same man arranges the dining couches, lays the table, bakes the bread, prepares now one sort of dish and now another, he must take things as they come. But where it is all one man can do to stew meats and another to roast them, for one man to boil fish and another to bake them, for another to bake bread, and not every sort at that, but where it suffices if he makes one kind that has a high reputation—everything that is prepared in this manner will, I think, necessarily be worked out with superior excellence. Thus Cyrus by far exceeded everyone when, as a sign of attention, he sent someone food prepared in this way." (With this kind of preparation, the food at Cyrus' table surpassed all others in its excellence.) (Xenophon, *Cyropaedia*, ed. E. Poppo, Lipsiae, 1821, Book VIII, Ch. II.) [199]

Plato's discussion in the *Republic* forms the direct basis and point of departure for a group of English writers who wrote about the division of labour after Petty and before Adam Smith. See e.g. *James Harris* (later Earl of Malmesbury), the 3rd TREATISE of *Three Treatises etc.*, 3rd ed., London, 1772, in which however he presents the DIVISION OF EMPLOYMENTS as the NATURAL foundation of SOCIETY (pp. 148-55). He himself says in a footnote that he drew the WHOLE ARGUMENT from Plato.

In the 2nd book of the *Republic*, which we cite from the *edition by Baiter, Orelli etc., Zurich, 1839*, Plato starts with the origin of the πόλις (city and state coincide here).

"The polis ... comes into existence ... once each of us is *no longer self-sufficient*, but has need of many." [IV-162] "It" [the polis] "is founded by our needs." [199]

Now the most immediate requirements are enumerated: food, a dwelling-place, clothing:

"The first and most important requirement is the procurement of food in order to be able to exist and live.... The second is the construction of a dwelling-place, the third the making of clothes and the like."

How should the πόλις satisfy these different needs? One man becomes a farmer, another a house-builder, others become weavers, cobblers, etc. Should each of them divide his labour time, cultivating the land in one part of it, building in the second, weaving in the third, etc., in order to satisfy his different requirements himself, or should he devote the whole of his labour time exclusively to one single occupation, so that he, e.g., produces corn, weaves, etc., not only for himself but also for the others? The second plan is better. For, in the first place, people differ in their natural aptitudes, which means that their capacity to perform different kinds of work differs. // To the range of different needs there corresponds a range of different aptitudes, enabling the individuals to perform the different kinds of work necessary for the satisfaction of those needs. // Someone practising one single skilled craft will perform his task better than one who exercises many skills. If something is carried on merely as a subsidiary occupation, the appropriate time for production will often be allowed to slip by. The work cannot wait for the leisure of the person who has to perform it; rather must the person doing the work be guided by the conditions of his production, etc. Therefore he should not do it as a sideline. Hence if one person exclusively does one particular kind of work (in accordance with the nature of the thing, and at the right time) and does not concern himself with other work, everything will be produced in greater quantity, better, and more easily.

The main emphasis lies on the *better*: the quality. The word πλείω [a] only occurs in the passage we are about to quote; otherwise it is always κάλλιον.[b]

"How will our polis be able to supply all these demands? Will one man have to be a farmer, another a builder, and a third a weaver?" etc.... "Is each one of them to *bring the product of his work into a common stock*? Should our one farmer, for example, provide food enough for four people and spend the whole of his time and industry in producing corn, so as to share with the rest; or should he take no notice of them and grow just a quarter of this corn, for himself, in a quarter of the time, and divide the other three quarters between building his house, weaving his clothes, and making his shoes, so as to save the trouble of sharing with others and attend himself to all his own concerns?... The first plan is easier, of course.... Firstly, no two people are born exactly alike. They have different aptitudes, which fit them for different occupations.... And will a man do *better* working at many trades, or keeping to one only? Keeping to one.... Also, work may be ruined, if you let the right time go by.... For the workman must wait upon the work; it will not wait upon his leisure and allow itself to be done in a spare moment.—Yes, he must.—So the conclusion is that *more will be produced of every thing and the work will be more easily and better done, when every man is set free from all other occupations to do, at the right time, the one thing for which he is naturally fitted.*"

Plato goes on to show how a further division [IV-163] of labour or the setting up of different branches of business becomes necessary. E.g.

"If the farmer is to have a *good* plough and hoe and other farming tools, he will not make them himself. Nor will the house-builder, or the weaver" etc. "Now how does the individual gain a share in the excess product of the other producers, and how do the others participate in the excess of the first individual's product? Through exchange, through selling and buying." [199]

---

a More.— *Ed.*
b Better.— *Ed.*

Plato then examines different kinds of trade and therefore different kinds of trader. Wage labourers are also mentioned, as a particular kind of human being owing their existence to the division of labour.

"There are also the services of yet another class, who have the physical strength for heavy work, though on intellectual grounds they are hardly worth including in our society—wage labourers, as we call them, because they sell the use of their strength for wages."

After he has indicated a large number of different occupations made necessary by the further refinement of city life, etc., he comes to the separation of the craft of war from other crafts, and therefore to the formation of a special warrior estate.

"We agreed ... that no one man can practise many trades satisfactorily....—Well, how do things stand now? Is not the conduct of war an art?...—But we would not allow our shoemaker to try to be also a farmer or weaver or builder, because we wanted our shoes well made. We gave each man one trade, *for which he was naturally fitted*; he would do good work, if he *confined himself to that all his life*, free from other occupations and never letting the right moment slip by. Now in no form of work is efficiency so important as in war.... So it is our business ... to select those men who are by nature fitted to be guardians of the polis" (l.c., pp. 439-41 passim).

Different activities are required to satisfy the different needs there are in a community; different gifts enable people of different natures to perform one activity better than another. Hence the division of labour and the different social estates corresponding to it. What Plato always emphasises as the main point of the system is that it allows each piece of work to be done *better*. Quality, use value, is for him, as for all other writers of antiquity, the decisive point, and the exclusive way of looking at things. For the rest, the basis of his whole conception is an Athenian idealisation of the Egyptian caste system.

The writers of antiquity in general ascribed the remarkable level of industrial development attained by the Egyptians to their hereditary division of labour and the caste system which was based on it.

"In Egypt ... the arts, too, have ... reached the requisite degree of perfection. For it is the only country where craftsmen may not in any way interfere in the affairs of other classes of citizens, but must follow that calling alone which by law is hereditary in their clan.... Among other peoples it is found that tradesmen divided their attention between too many objects.... At one time they try agriculture, at another they take to commerce, at another again they busy themselves with 2 or 3 occupations at once. In free countries they mostly frequent the popular assemblies.... In Egypt, on the contrary, a craftsman is severely punished if he meddles with affairs of state, or carries on several trades at once. Thus," says Diodorus, "there is nothing to disturb their application to their calling.... In addition to having inherited from their forefathers ... numerous rules of their trade, they are [IV-164] eager to discover still more advantageous ways of practising it" (Diodorus, *Historische Bibliothek*, b. I, ch. 74).

With Plato the division of labour is presented as the economic foundation of a community in which each member is dependent on the others, and does not satisfy the whole range of his needs himself, independently, without any connection with other people. The division of labour within the community develops out of the many-sidedness of needs and the one-sidedness of aptitudes, which differ with different people, who therefore perform more successfully in one occupation than in another. The main point for him is that if one person makes a craft into his exclusive vocation, he does it better, and adapts his activity completely to the requirements, the conditions, of the work he has to perform, whereas if he engages in it as a sideline, the work has to wait for the opportunities left to him by his involvement in other matters. This point of view, that the τέχνη[a] cannot be carried on as a πάρεργον, subsidiary occupation, also appears in the passage from Thucydides, cited earlier.

Xenophon goes further, in that he firstly emphasises the reduction of labour to the simplest possible activity, and secondly makes the degree to which the division of labour can be implemented dependent on the extension of the market.

For comparison.

Blanqui distinguishes, in the passage we referred to earlier,[b] between the "*regulated* and in some degree *forced labour* of workers under the system of large-scale manufacture"[c] and the industries of the countryside, carried on as handicrafts or as subsidiary domestic work.

"The disadvantage of manufacture ... is that it subjugates the worker, placing him ... and his family, at the *discretion* of the work.... Compare, for example, the industry of Rouen or Mulhouse with that of Lyons or Nîmes. Both have as their aim the spinning and weaving of two yarns: one of cotton, the other of silk; and yet they do not resemble each other at all. The former only takes place in giant establishments, with much expenditure of capital ... and with the aid of veritable armies of workers, confined in their hundreds, nay their thousands, in gigantic barrack-like factories, as high as towers, and studded with windows resembling loopholes. The latter, in contrast, is entirely patriarchal; it employs a large number of women and children, but without exhausting or ruining them; it allows them to stay in their beautiful valleys of the Drôme, the Var, the Isère, the Vaucluse, cultivating their silkworms and unwinding their cocoons; it never becomes a true factory industry. However, although it is applied to as high a degree in this

---

[a] Skill.— *Ed.*
[b] See this volume, p. 270.— *Ed.*
[c] Marx quotes in French.— *Ed.*

industry as in the first one, *the principle of the division of labour* takes on a special character here. There do indeed exist winders, throwsters, dyers, sizers, and finally weavers; *but they are not assembled in the same workshop, nor are they dependent on a single master*; they are all *independent*. Their capital, which is made up of their tools, their looms, and their braziers, is not large, but it is sufficient to put them on a certain footing of equality with their employer. Here there are no factory regulations, no conditions to submit to; everyone makes his own stipulations, in complete freedom" (A. Blanqui aîné, *Cours d'économie industrielle*, ed. etc. by A. Blaise, Paris, 1838-39, pp. 44-80 passim).[a]

On the basis of modern industry an OUT OF DOORS factory system is growing up once again which shares all the disadvantages of the original system without enjoying any of its advantages. But this does not belong here, and will be dealt with later.[200]

[IV-165] "Everyone knows from experience that if the hands and the intelligence are always applied to the same kind of work and the same products, these will be produced more easily, in greater abundance, and in higher quality, than if each individual makes for himself all the things he needs.... In this way, men are divided up into various classes and conditions, to their own advantage and to that of the commodity" (Cesare Beccaria, *Elementi di economia pubblica*, Custodi, *Parte Moderna*, Vol. XI, [p.] 28).[b]

"For in so vast a city" (as London) "manufactures will beget one another, and each manufacture will be divided into as many parts as possible, whereby the work of each worker will be simple and easy. As for example in the making of a watch: if one man shall make the wheels, another the spring, another shall engrave the dialplate, and another shall make the cases, then the watch will be better and *cheaper*, than if the whole work be put upon one man" (W. Petty, *An Essay Concerning the Multiplication of Mankind etc.*, 3rd ed., [London,] 1698, [p. 35]).

He then goes on to explain how the division of labour brings it about that specific manufactures are concentrated in specific towns, or streets of great towns.

Here "the commodity peculiar to those places is made better and *cheaper* than elsewhere" (l.c.).

Lastly he goes into the commercial advantages, such as the saving on unnecessary incidental expenses, like carriage charges, etc., whereby in consequence of this distribution of interrelated manufactures in one place the prices of their products are reduced and the profit from foreign trade is increased (l.c., [p.] 36).

What from the outset distinguishes Petty's conception of the division of labour from that of classical antiquity is his grasp of its influence on the exchange value of the product, on the product as commodity—its cheapening.

---

[a] Marx quotes in French.— *Ed.*
[b] Marx quotes in Italian.— *Ed.*

The same point of view is put forward, but expressed more emphatically, as the curtailment of the labour time necessary for the production of a commodity, in *The Advantages of the East-India Trade to England Considered etc.*, London, 1720.[201]

What is important is to make each commodity with "THE LEAST AND EASIEST LABOUR". If a thing is made with "LESS LABOUR", it is made "CONSEQUENTLY WITH LABOUR OF LESS PRICE". Thus the commodity is cheapened, and then competition will make it a universal law to reduce labour time to the minimum necessary for its production.

* "If my neighbour, by doing much with little labour, can sell cheap, I must contrive to sell as cheap as he" * [p. 67].

He lays particular stress on the following aspect of the division of labour:

* "The more variety of artists to every manufacture, the less is left to the skill of single persons" * [p. 68].[a]

Later writers such as Harris (see above[b]) merely develop Plato's arguments. Then *Ferguson*.[c] What distinguishes Adam Smith—who in some respects lags behind his predecessors—is that he employs the phrase *"increase of the productive powers of labour"*. Adam Smith's conceptions still remain located in the epoch of large-scale industry's infancy. How much this is the case is shown by his view of machinery as merely the corollary to the division of labour; with him, the workers still make mechanical inventions in order to ease and shorten their labour.

Division of labour through simplification facilitates learning a trade; therefore lessens the overall production costs of labour capacity.

[IV-166] The workshop, which is based on the division of labour, always involves a certain hierarchy of skills, since some operations are more complex than others, some require more physical strength, some a more delicate touch or greater dexterity. In the workshop, as Ure says,

"a workman is assigned to each operation, his wage corresponding to his skill.,,. It is still *the adaptation of the labours to the different individual capacities* ... the division of labour in manifold gradations ... the division of labour according to different degrees of skill".[d]

a Marx quotes this sentence in English and adds its German translation.— *Ed.*

b See this volume, p. 282.— *Ed.*

c See this volume, pp. 273-76.— *Ed.*

d A. Ure, *Philosophie des manufactures etc.*, Vol. I, Brussels, 1836, pp. 28, 30. Marx used this French translation of Ure. He quotes in a mixture of German and French.— *Ed.*

The dexterity of the individual continues to be important.

It is in fact an analysis of the process into operations which can each be performed by an individual worker; each operation is separated from the one that accompanies it, but the fundamental principle remains that of viewing it as a function of the worker, so that in analysis it is distributed among different workers and groups of workers according to their level of skill, physical development, etc. The process is not yet analysed as such, independently of the worker who performs it, whereas in the automatic factory, the system

"decomposes a process into its basic constituents, and embodies each part in the operation of an automatic machine", whereupon one can "entrust a person of ordinary capacity with any of the said elementary parts after a short probation" [p. 32].

"The master manufacturer, by dividing the work to be executed into different operations, each requiring different degrees of skill or of force, can purchase exactly that precise quantity of both which is necessary for each operation; whereas, if the whole work were executed by one worker, that person must possess sufficient skill to perform the most delicate, and sufficient strength to execute the most laborious, of the operations" (Ch. Babbage, *On the Economy of Machinery etc.*, London, 1832, Ch. XIX).

"When — according to the particular nature of the products of each kind of manufacture — the most advantageous method of dividing the manufacturing process into partial operations and the number of workers to be employed in them have been ascertained by experience, then all factories the number of whose workers is not a direct multiple of that number will produce with less economy" (Babbage, l.c., Ch. XXII).

If e.g. 10 workers are needed for various operations, the number of persons employed must be a multiple of 10.

"If that is not the case, the workers cannot each of them constantly be used to perform the same operation in the manufacturing process.... That is one cause of the colossal size of industrial establishments" (l.c.).

Here, as with simple cooperation, we again have the principle of multiples.[a] But now in proportions that are determined in their proportionality by the division of labour itself. In general, it is clear that the larger the scale on which the work is done, the further the division of labour can be carried. In the first place, the correct multiple can be applied in that way. Secondly, the extent to which the operations are subdivided and to which the whole of an individual worker's time can be absorbed by one operation naturally depends on the magnitude of the scale.

If, therefore, the division of labour requires a greater capital, because more raw material is worked up over the same period of

5

ergaro produce Value7

time, whether it is implemented at all depends on the scale on which the work is done, hence on the number of workers who can be simultaneously employed. A greater capital—i.e. its concentration in one hand—is necessary for the development of the division of labour, which in turn uses the productive power attained thereby [IV-167] to work up a greater amount of material, thus increasing the size of this component of capital.

"He who was reduced to doing a very simple operation in a manufactory entered into dependence upon the man who wished to employ him. He no longer produced a complete piece of work, but only part of one, and to do this he had as much need for the assistance of the labour of others as he did for raw materials, machinery, etc.... He was always in a subordinate position over against the head of the workshop ... he confined his demands to what was strictly necessary to make possible the continuation of the labour he offered, while the head of the workshop alone profited from the whole of the increase of the powers of production which was brought about by the division of labour" (Sismondi, *Nouveaux principes etc.*, Vol. 1, pp. 91-92).[a]

"Division of labour shortens the period required for learning an operation" (F. Wayland, *The Elements of Political Economy*, Boston, 1843, p. 76).

*In establishing a manufactory, it is important so to adjust the number and kind of workmen, that, when the different operations of a process have been assigned to different persons, these persons may be in such proportions *as exactly and fully to employ each other*. The more perfectly this is accomplished, the greater will be the economy and, this having been once ascertained, it is also evident that the establishment cannot be successfully enlarged, unless it employ multiples of this number of workmen* (l.c., p. 83).

At the end of his section on the division of labour Adam Smith once again slips back into the assumption that the various workers among whom the labour is divided are the owners and producers of commodities (we shall see that he abandons this illusion later).

"Every workman has a great quantity of his own work to dispose of beyond what he himself has occasion for; and every other workman being exactly in the same situation, he is enabled to exchange a great quantity of goods of his own production for a great quantity, or, what comes to the same thing, for the price of a great quantity of theirs" [Garnier, pp. 24-25] [Vol. I, p. 26].

The transmission of skill from generation to generation is always important. This aspect is decisive in the case of the caste system, as later with guilds.

"Easy labour is only transmitted skill" (Th. Hodgskin, *Popular Political Economy*, London, [Edinburgh,] 1827, p. 48).

"For dividing labour, and distributing the powers of men and machinery, to the greatest advantage, it is in most cases necessary to operate upon a large scale; in other words, to produce wealth in great masses. It is this advantage which gives

---

[a] Marx quotes Sismondi partly in German and partly in French.— *Ed.*

existence to the great manufactories" (J. Mill, *Élémens d'économie politique*. Traduit par J. T. Parisot, Paris, 1823 [p. 11]).[a]

The division of labour—or rather the workshop based on the division of labour—merely increases the surplus value received by the capitalist (at least this is its only *direct* effect, and the direct effect is the only thing we are concerned with here). Or, in other words, this increase in the productive power of labour only stands the test as a productive force of capital in so far as it is applied to use values which are consumed by the workers, hence curtails the labour time necessary for the reproduction of labour capacity. From precisely this circumstance, that the division of labour on a large scale is chiefly applied just to OBJECT OF COMMON USE, Parson Wayland draws the opposite conclusion, that it is the poor, and not the rich, who benefit from its advantages. The parson is in one sense correct, with regard to the MIDDLING CLASS. But here we are not concerned at all with the non-conceptual relation between poor [IV-168] and rich, but with the relation of wage labour and capital. The passage from the parson runs as follows:

* "The greater the cost of the product, the smaller will be the number of persons who are able to purchase it. Hence, the less will be the demand; and hence, also, the less opportunity will there be for division of labour. And, besides, the greater the cost of the article, the greater amount of capital is required in order to produce it by division of labour.... Hence it is, that division of labour is but sparingly used in the manufacture of rich jewelry, and in articles of expensive luxury; while it is so universally used in the production of all articles of common use. Hence we see, that the benefits of the use of natural agents and of division of labour, are vastly greater and more important to the middling and lower classes than to the rich. These means of increased production, reduce the cost of the necessaries and of the essential conveniences of life to the lowest rate, and, of course, bring them, as far as possible, within the reach of all" * (F. Wayland, *The Elements of Political Economy*, Boston, 1843, [pp.] 86-87).

In addition to an increase in the amount of capital, the division of labour requires for its application, as a basic prerequisite, the cooperation, agglomeration, of workers, which will in any case only occur where the population has reached a certain density. // It is required at the same time that the population should be taken from its scattered dwellings in the countryside and collected together in the centres of production. On this see Steuart.[156] This to be discussed in more detail in the section on accumulation.[150] //

* "There is a certain *density of population* which is convenient, both for social intercourse, and for that combination of powers by which the produce of labour is increased" * (James Mill, *Elements of Political Economy*, London, 1821, [p.] 50).

---

[a] Marx quotes in French.— *Ed.*

The development of the division of labour leads to the disappearance of every individual product of labour—although such a product is still entirely possible when the subsumption of labour under capital is purely formal. The finished commodity is the product of the workshop, which is itself a mode of existence of capital. The fact that the exchange value of labour itself—labour, not its product—becomes the only thing the worker is able to sell, is due not only to the nature of the contract between capital and labour but also to the mode of production itself. Labour becomes in fact the worker's sole commodity, and the commodity altogether becomes the general category under which production is subsumed. Our starting-point was the commodity as the most general category of bourgeois production. It first becomes a general category of this kind through the transformation which the mode of production has itself been subjected to by capital.[60]

* "There is no longer any thing which we can call the natural reward of individual labour. Each labourer produces only some part of a whole, and each part, having no value or utility of itself, there is nothing on which the labourer can seize, and say: it is my product, this I will keep for myself" * ([Th. Hodgskin,] *Labour defended against the claims of Capital etc.*, London, 1825, p. 25).

"The progress of wealth has brought about the division of conditions and that of trades; what is exchanged is no longer each person's *superfluous product* but *subsistence itself.*... In this new situation, the life of each man who works and produces depends not on the completion and success of his labour, but on its *sale*" (Sismondi, *Études*, Vol. 1, p. 82).[a]

* The greater productiveness of human industry, and the diminished price of the necessaries of life, conspire to swell productive capital in modern times * (S. P. Newman, *Elements of Political Economy*, Andover and New York, 1835, [pp. 88-] 89).

In so far as in the division of labour one aspect of the worker's natural individuality, as a natural basis, is further developed, it is put in place of his overall capacity for production and trained up to a specific skill, which can only prove itself useful by being exercised in the context of the workshop as a whole; exercised as a particular function of the workshop.

[IV-169] Storch, like Adam Smith, conflates the two types of division of labour, except that with him one type appears as the most extreme development of the other; one appears as the *point of departure* for the other, which is a step forward.

"The division of labour proceeds from the separation of the most widely different professions to the point where several workers divide between them the preparation of one and the same product, as in manufacture" (This should read not product but commodity. Different people work on the same *product* in the

---

a Marx quotes in French.— *Ed.*

other division of labour too.) (H. Storch, *Cours d'économie politique*, avec des notes etc. par J.-B. Say, Paris, 1823, Vol. 1, p. 173).[a]

"It is not sufficient that the capital required for the subdivision of trades should be in readiness in society; it must also be *accumulated in the hands of the entrepreneurs* in sufficiently large quantities to enable them to work on a large scale.... The more the division of trades increases, the greater an outlay of capital in tools, raw material, etc., is required for the constant employment of a given number of workers. Increase of the number of workers with the division of labour. Increased amount of capital in buildings and means of subsistence" (Storch, 1. c., pp. 250, 251).

*"Labour *is united* ... whenever employments are divided.... The greatest *division of labour* takes place amongst those exceedingly barbarous savages who never help each other, who work separately from each other; and division of employment, with all its great results, depends altogether on *combination* of labour, *cooperation*".* (Wakefield, note to his edition of A. Smith, *Wealth of Nations*, London, 1835, Vol. 1, p. 24).

This distinction between the SEPARATION OF EMPLOYMENTS and the "DIVISION OF LABOUR" is Wakefield's hobbyhorse. What he vaguely feels is precisely the distinction, not emphasised by Adam Smith, between the division of labour within society and that within the workshop. Adam Smith has the employments cooperate with one another by means of EXCHANGE, and not only knows—which is a matter of course—but says expressly that the division of labour within the individual manufactory automatically implies its combination. What is a real step forward in Wakefield—and we shall come to this later—is his feeling that the latter division of labour, based on free bourgeois labour, is a form peculiar to the capitalist mode of production and therefore only occurring under definite social conditions.[67]

Adam Smith makes exchange the foundation of the division of labour, whereas it is (but does not have to be) the opposite, its result. Hodgskin remarks correctly that a division of employments, hence of social labour, takes place in all countries and under all political institutions. It exists originally in the family, where it emerges spontaneously from physiological differences, differences of sex and age. Variations in individual organisation, in physical and mental capacities, form a fresh source for the division of employments. But then, owing to the diversity of natural conditions, differences in the soil, in the distribution of water and land, mountain and plain, climate, situation, the presence of minerals in the earth and peculiarities of its own spontaneous creations, there is added the difference in the naturally available instruments of labour, which divides the employments of different

---

[a] Marx quotes partly in German and partly in French.— *Ed.*

tribes, and it is in the exchange between them that we have, in general, to look for the original transformation of product into commodity [195] (see Th. Hodgskin, *Popular Political Economy etc.*, London, 1827, Chs IV, V and VI).[a] Where the population is stagnant, as in [IV-170] Asia, the division of labour is stagnant too.

* "Improved methods of conveyance, like railroads, steam vessels, canals, all means of facilitating intercourse between distant countries act upon the division of labour in the same way as an actual increase in the number of people; they bring more labourers into communication etc." * [p. 119].

Population and the PROGRESS of the same is the chief basis for the DIVISION OF LABOUR.

* "As the number of labourers increases, the productive power of society augments in the compound ratio of that increase, multiplied by the effects of the division of labour and the increase of knowledge" * (l.c., p. 120).

"It is by means of an additional capital only, that the undertaker of any work can ... make a more proper division of labour among his workmen. When the work to be done consists of a number of parts, to keep every man constantly employed in one way, requires a much greater capital than where every man is occasionally employed in every different part of the work" (A. Smith, [Garnier,] Book II, Ch. III [pp. 338-39]) [Vol. II, pp. 115-16].

"The *productive powers of the same number of labourers cannot be increased*, but in consequence either of some addition and improvement to those machines and instruments which facilitate and abridge labour; or of a more proper division and distribution of labour" (l. c.).

"The owner of capital which employs a great number of labourers, necessarily endeavours, for his own advantage, to make such a proper division and distribution of tasks, that the labourers may be enabled to produce the greatest quantity of work possible. For the same reason, he endeavours to supply them with the best machinery which either he or they can think of. *What takes place among the labourers in a particular workhouse, takes place, for the same reason, among those of a great society.* The greater their number, the more they naturally divide themselves into different classes and subdivisions of employment. More heads are occupied in inventing the most proper machinery for executing the work of each, and it is, therefore, more likely to be invented" (A. Smith, [Garnier,] Book I, Ch. VIII [pp. 177-78]) [Vol. I, pp. 145-46].

In the beginning of the present century *Lemontey* (*Œuvres complètes*, Vol. I, Paris, 1840, pp. 245 sq.) wittily reworked Ferguson's discussion of the subject ("Sur l'influence morale de la division du travail").[202]

"Society as a whole has this in common with the interior of a workshop, that it too has its division of labour. If one took as a model the division of labour in a modern workshop, in order to apply it to a whole society, the society best organised for the production of wealth would undoubtedly be that which had a single chief employer, distributing tasks to the different members of the community according to a previously fixed rule. But this is by no means the case. While inside the

---

[a] See this volume, pp. 163-64.— *Ed.*

modern workshop the division of labour is meticulously regulated by the authority of the employer, modern society has no other rule, no other authority for the distribution of labour than free [IV-171] competition" (*Misère de la philosophie,* Paris, 1847, p. 130).[a]

"Under the patriarchal system, under the caste system, under the feudal and guild system, there was division of labour in the whole of society according to fixed rules.... As for the division of labour in the workshop, it was very little developed in all these forms of society. It can even be laid down as a general rule that the less authority presides over the division of labour inside society, the more the division of labour develops inside the workshop, and the more it is subjected there to the authority of a single person. Thus authority in the workshop and authority in society, in relation to the division of labour, are in *inverse ratio* to each other" (l.c., pp. 130, 131).[b]

"The accumulation and concentration of instruments and workers preceded the development of the division of labour inside the workshop.... The development of the division of labour supposes the assemblage of workers in a workshop.... Once the men and the instruments had been brought together, the division of labour, such as it had existed in the form of the guilds, was reproduced, necessarily reflected inside the workshop" (l.c., [pp.] 132, 133).[c]

"The concentration of the instruments of production and the division of labour are as inseparable one from the other as are, in the political sphere, the concentration of public powers and the division of private interests" (l.c., p. 134).[d]

The prerequisites for adopting the division of labour are therefore:

1) *Conglomeration of workers,* for which a certain density of population is necessary. Means of communication can replace density to a certain degree. *Depopulation of the country* (see the 18th century). In a thinly populated country this conglomeration could only take place at a few points. However, conglomeration is also brought about if agriculture only requires a sparse population, and the mass of the population, separated from the land, can therefore conglomerate around the available means of production, the centres of capital. Relative concentration on the one side can be brought forth by relative rarefaction on the other, even with a *given* population, the existence of which originally remains rooted in the non-capitalist mode of production.

What is needed first, therefore, is not an increase in the population, but an increase in the purely industrial population, or a different distribution of the population. The first condition for this is that the population directly employed in the production of

---

[a] K. Marx, *The Poverty of Philosophy* (present edition, Vol. 6, p. 184). Here and further on, Marx quotes from this work in the language of the original (French).— *Ed.*

[b] Ibid., pp. 184-85.— *Ed.*

[c] Ibid., p. 186.— *Ed*

[d] Ibid., p. 187.— *Ed.*

the means of subsistence, in agriculture, be diminished, that people be separated from the land, from mother earth, and that they be thereby set free (FREE HANDS, as Steuart says [156]), mobilised. The separation from agriculture of the kinds of work bound up with it, and the—progressive—limitation of agriculture to fewer hands, is the main condition for the division of labour and for manufacture in general, if it is to emerge not in individual cases, at isolated points, but playing a predominant role. // All this belongs to *accumulation.* // [150] The same population, distributed differently, does not need a greater supply of the means of life, but only a different apportionment, distribution, of them. The capitalist who applies the division of labour, hence employs a greater number of workers agglomerated at one point, pays larger amounts in wages than the master craftsman, requires more variable capital, which is ultimately reduced to means of subsistence; but for this it is necessary that the same wage that was previously paid to the workers by 100 people [IV-172] should now be paid by one. All we have here, then, is a greater concentration of variable capital in fewer hands, and the same thing goes for the means of subsistence for which these wages are exchanged. What is required here is not an *increase* in this part of capital but only its *concentration*; just as we have, not a bigger population, but a greater agglomeration of the population under the command of one and the same capital.

2) *Concentration of the instruments of labour.*

The division of labour leads to a differentiation and accordingly a simplification of the instruments which serve as means of labour; and therefore to their improvement. But under the division of labour the means of labour remains an implement of labour, an instrument which can only be employed thanks to the personal dexterity of the individual worker. It is the conductor of his own skill; in reality it is an artificial organ added on to his natural organs. The same number of workers requires a greater variety of instruments, not more of them. In so far as the workshop is a conglomeration of workers it also presupposes an agglomeration of instruments. And in any case this part of constant capital grows only in the same proportion as does the variable capital, which is laid out in wages, or the number of workers employed simultaneously by the same capital.

The other conditions of labour, particularly accommodation, factory buildings, can be regarded as a new addition to constant capital, since in the days before manufacture the workshop did not yet exist separately from the private house.

With this exception, a greater concentration takes place of the part of capital which consists of the means of labour; not necessarily a growth in capital and by no means a relative growth in capital as compared with the component laid out in wages.

3) *Increase in raw material.* The part of capital laid out in raw material grows *absolutely* against the part laid out in wages, since the same quantity of raw material absorbs a smaller quantity of labour time, or the same quantity of labour time realises itself in a greater quantity of raw material. Nevertheless, this can also have occurred *originally*, without an absolute increase in the raw material in a country. The same amount of raw material available in a country may absorb less labour, i.e. a smaller number of workers over the whole country may be employed in working it up, in transforming it into new product, although this number of workers is now concentrated in larger groups at various points under the command of individual capitalists, instead of being scattered over a wide area, as previously.

In absolute terms, therefore, nothing is required for *manufacture*, i.e. for the workshop based on the division of labour, but a change in the distribution of the different constituents of capital, concentration instead of dispersal. As long as they are dispersed, these conditions of labour do not yet exist as capital, although they do exist as the material constituents of capital, in the same way as the working part of the population exists, although not yet in the quality of wage labourers or proletarians.

Manufacture (as distinguished from the mechanical workshop or the FACTORY) is the mode of production or form of industry which specifically corresponds to the division of labour. It emerges independently, as the *most developed* form of the capitalist mode of production, before the invention of machinery proper (although machines and particularly fixed capital are already being employed).

[IV-173] With Petty and the apologist for the EAST INDIA TRADE, cited earlier (with the moderns, therefore)[a] it is from the outset a characteristic feature of their discussion of the division of labour that the cheapening of the commodity—the diminution of the labour socially necessary for the production of a particular commodity—is the main aspect considered. With Petty this is mentioned in connection with foreign trade. With the EAST INDIAN it is presented directly as a means of underselling competitors on the

---

[a] See this volume, p. 288.— *Ed.*

world market, just as he presents world trade as itself a means for attaining the same result in less labour time.

In Book I, Chapter I, where he treats the division of labour *ex professo*, Adam Smith discusses at the end of the chapter the extraordinary multiplicity of the kinds of work, either derived from different countries or present in their many-sidedness in a single "civilised country", i.e. a country where the product universally assumes the commodity form, which contribute to provide e.g. the furniture, the clothing, the tools of an ordinary day labourer.

"Observe," begins this conclusion, "the accommodation of the most common artificer or day labourer in a civilised and thriving country, and you will perceive that the number of people of whose industry a part, though but a small part, has been employed in procuring him this accommodation, exceeds all computation. The woolen coat, for example, which covers the day labourer, as coarse and rough as it may appear, is the produce of the joint labour of a great multitude of workmen" and so on [Garnier, p. 25] [Vol. I, p. 26].

And Adam Smith concludes his reflections with these words:

"Perhaps the accommodation of an European prince does not always so much exceed that of an industrious and frugal peasant, as the accommodation of the latter exceeds that of some African king, the absolute master of the lives and liberties of ten thousand naked savages" [Garnier, p. 28] [Vol. I, pp. 28-29].

The whole of this passage as well as this way of viewing the matter is copied from de Mandeville, *The Fable of the Bees*, first published in 1705 as a POEM, with the 2nd part, WHICH CONSISTS OF A SERIES OF SIX DIALOGUES (prose), having been published in 1729. In 1714 HE ADDED THE PROSE NOTES WHICH MAKE THE BULK OF THE FIRST VOLUME OF THE WORK AS WE HAVE IT NOW. It says there, among other things:

* "If we trace the most flourishing nations in their origin, we shall find, that, in the remote beginnings of every society, the richest and most considerable men among them were a great while destitute of a great many comforts of life that are now enjoyed by the meanest and most humble wretches; so that many things which were once looked upon as the inventions of luxury are now allowed even to those that are so miserably poor as to become the objects of public charity.... A man would be laughed at that should discover luxury in the plain dress of a poor creature that walks along in a thick parish gown, and a coarse shirt underneath it; and yet what a number of people, how many different trades, and what a variety of skill and tools must be employed to have the most ordinary Yorkshire cloth?" * etc. (*Remark* P., Vol. I, pp. 181-83 of 1724 ed.).

"What a bustle is there to be made in several parts of the world before a fine scarlet or crimson cloth can be produced; what multiplicity of trades and artificers must be employed! Not only such as are obvious, as woolcombers, spinners, the weaver, the cloth-worker, the scourer, the dyer, the setter, the drawer, and the packer; but others that are more remote, and might seem foreign to it,—as the mill-wright, the pewterer, and the chemist, which yet all are necessary, as well as a great number of handicrafts, to have the [IV-174] tools, utensils, and other implements belonging to the trades already named." * He then goes over the contribution to this of shipping, foreign countries, in a word the world market (*Search into the Nature of Society* (APPENDED TO THE SECOND EDITION), pp. 411-13).

The content of all this enumeration is merely this: Once the *commodity* becomes the general form of the product, or production takes place on the basis of exchange value and therefore of the exchange of commodities, the production of each individual, first of all, becomes one-sided, whereas his needs are many-sided. Innumerable independent branches of labour must therefore contribute to satisfy the needs, even the simplest needs, of the individual. Secondly: The whole range of the objective conditions which are required for the production of a single commodity, such as the raw materials, instruments, *matières instrumentales*, enter into the production of that commodity as *commodities*, are conditioned by the sale and purchase of these elementary constituents of the commodity, which have been produced independently of each other.[a] This takes place to the extent that the individual elements which are required for the production of a commodity exist as commodities outside it, hence originally enter into this individual branch of production as commodities from outside, through the agency of circulation. That is to say, this takes place the more the *commodity* becomes the general elementary form of wealth, i.e. the more production ceases to be for the individual the direct creation of his own means of subsistence, and becomes TRADE, as Steuart says,[203] with the *commodity* therefore ceasing to be the form of the part of the individual's production which goes beyond the individual's needs, i.e. the part which is superfluous and therefore saleable for the individual. Here the product as such is still the basis and production is for subsistence. Here the production of commodities still rests on the foundation of a production the main product of which does not become a commodity. It is not yet a situation where subsistence itself depends on sale; where the producer, unless he produces a *commodity*, produces *nothing at all*; where to be a *commodity* is therefore the general, elementary, necessary form of his product, which alone makes it into an element of bourgeois wealth.[60] This distinction is strikingly demonstrated when one compares large-scale modern agriculture with the agriculture in which production for the individual's own subsistence still forms the basis, and which itself creates most of the conditions for its production; so that these conditions do not

---

[a] See this volume, pp. 80-81.— *Ed.*

enter it as quantities of commodities, through the agency of circulation.

In reality, therefore, the views expressed by de Mandeville and others mean nothing more than that the *commodity* is the general elementary form of bourgeois wealth; that what is decisive for the producer is no longer the use value of the product but its exchange value alone, the use value being only the vehicle of the exchange value for him; that he must in fact produce not merely a particular product, but money. This prerequisite, that the product is universally produced as a commodity, hence is mediated by the conditions of its own production as commodities, by circulation, into which they enter, implies an all-embracing division of social labour, or, in other words, the separation of the various mutually conditioning and complementing labours into independent branches of labour only brought into contact with each other through the circulation of commodities, through sale and purchase. Or, it is identical with this situation, since for products to confront each other generally as commodities presupposes a mutual confronting of the activities producing them [...] [a] This way of viewing things is therefore historically important [...] [a]

[V-179] [204] At this stage of the development of society it is more interesting to examine the contrast with the situation where the individual family itself directly satisfies almost all its needs, as we see in e.g. *Dugald Stewart*, l.c., p. 327[-28]:

* "In some parts of the Highlands of Scotland, not many years ago, every peasant, according to the *Statistical Accounts*, made his own shoes of leather tanned by himself. Many a shepherd and cottar too, with his wife and children, appeared at church in clothes which had been touched by no hands but their own, since they were shorn from their sheep and sown in their flaxfields. In the preparation of these, it is added, scarcely a single article had been purchased, except the awl, needle, thimble, and a very few parts of the iron work employed in the weaving. The dyes, too, were chiefly extracted by the women from trees, shrubs, and herbs" * (*Lectures on Political Economy*, Vol. 1, l.c.). [V-179]

[V-175] In contrast to this, at a more advanced stage of the development of bourgeois society, of the kind that already faced Adam Smith, the simple reproduction of these Mandevillian, Harrisian, etc., reflections does not appear without an admixture of pedantic childishness; and in particular the churning out of such remarks by Smith has the effect that he fails to grasp the division of labour clearly and definitely as a specifically capitalist mode of production; while, on the other hand, the extraordinary importance he attaches to the division of labour in manufacture

---

[a] The manuscript is damaged here.— *Ed.*

shows that in his time the modern factory system was only in its origins. *Ure* remarks on this, correctly [a]:

> "When Adam Smith wrote his immortal work on the elements of political economy, automatic machinery being hardly known, he was properly led to regard the division of labour as the grand principle of manufacturing improvement.... But what was in Dr. Smith's time a topic of useful illustration, cannot now be used without risk of misleading the public as to the real principle of modern industry.... The scholastic dogma of the division of labour into degrees of skill has been exploited [205] by our enlightened manufacturers" (Andrew Ure, *Philosophie des manufactures etc.*, Vol. I, Ch. 1) (first appeared in 1835).

This strikingly demonstrates that the division of labour dealt with here—and, in fact, by Adam Smith too—is not a general category common to most states of society, and the most varied ones, but a particular historical mode of production, corresponding to a particular historical stage of development of capital; indeed a mode of production which belonged, in the all-embracing and predominant form in which one sees it in Adam Smith, to the stage of development of capitalist production reached by his own epoch and since then already overcome and passed.

In the passage we have just cited, Ure says,

> 1) "He" (Adam Smith) "therefore concludes that to *each of these operations* a workman can naturally be appropriated, with a wage corresponding to his skill. This *appropriation* forms the very essence of the division of labour."

So we have firstly the *appropriation* of the worker to a particular operation, his subsumption under it. From now on he belongs to this operation, which becomes the exclusive function of his labour capacity now reduced to an abstraction.

Firstly, then, labour capacity is *appropriated* to this specific operation. Secondly, however, since the basis of the operation itself remains the human frame, it happens that this appropriation is at the same time, as Ure says,

> "a distribution, or rather *adaptation of labour* to the different individual abilities".

That is, the operations themselves are adapted in the course of division to the natural and acquired abilities of the workers. This is not a dissolution of a process into its mechanical components, [V-176] but a dissolution that takes into account the fact that these individual processes have to be performed as functions of human labour capacities.

----

[a] Marx quotes Ure in French.— *Ed.*

In the volume of notes he added to his translation of Adam Smith, *Germain Garnier*, in Note 1 to Smith's chapter on the division of labour, pronounced himself opposed to popular education. Garnier says it is contrary to the division of labour, and with it

"our whole social system would be proscribed" (l.c., Vol. V, p. 2).[a]

Some of his comments are worth noting here.

"The labour which feeds, dresses and houses all the inhabitants of a country is a burden which lies on society as a whole, but which it necessarily *transfers* to one part of its members alone" (l.c., p. 2).

And the greater the industrial progress of society, the more do its material demands grow,

"and consequently the more labour will be employed in producing them, preparing them" (the means of subsistence in general) "and bringing them to the consumers. At the same time, however, and *as a consequence of the same progress*, the *class* of people released from this manual labour increases in size relatively to the other class. The latter, therefore, has at once more people to provide for and more abundant and elaborate provisions to furnish for each of them. Thus, the more society prospers, i.e. the more its industry, its commerce, its population grows, etc. ... *the less time* does the man destined to a mechanical trade *have to spare*. The richer society becomes, the more valuable" (this should rather be "the greater the value of") "*the time of the worker*".... "Thus, the more society advances towards a state of splendour and power, *the less time the working class will have to give to studying and to intellectual and speculative work*" (pp. 2-4).

That is to say, the free time of society is based on the absorption of the worker's time by compulsory labour[154]; thus he loses room for intellectual development, for that is time.[153]

"From another angle, *the less time the working class has to exploit the domain of knowledge, the more time remains for the other class*. If the men of this latter class can devote themselves consistently and assiduously to philosophical observations or literary compositions, it is because they are free from all concern for the production, manufacture or transportation of the objects of their daily subsistence, and because other people have undertaken the burden of these mechanical operations for them. Like all other divisions of labour, that between mechanical and intellectual labour becomes more pronounced and more clear-cut in proportion as society advances towards a wealthier condition. This division, like every other, is an effect of past and a cause of future progress.... Ought the government then to work to counteract this division of [V-177] labour and hinder its natural course? Ought it to expend a part of the public money in the attempt to confound and blend together two classes of labour which are themselves striving towards separation?" (l.c., pp. 4, 5).

The amount of production grows when the EFFICIENCY of LABOUR and at the same time the extent and intensity of labour time is

---

[a] Here and below Marx quotes Garnier in French.— *Ed.*

increased, the number of workers remaining the same. On this presupposition, the further growth of production is conditioned by a growth or increase in the number of wage labourers facing capital. This number is in part directly increased by capital, when previously independent craftsmen, etc., are subjected to the capitalist mode of production and thereby converted into wage labourers; and similarly when the introduction of machinery, etc., effects the conversion of women and children into wage labourers. Thus the number of workers undergoes a relative increase even though the total population remains the same. But capital also produces an absolute increase in the number of people, above all of the working class. The population can only grow absolutely, leaving aside the operations we have just mentioned, if not only more children are born but more children grow up, can be nourished until they are old enough to work. The development of the productive forces under the régime of capital increases the quantity of means of subsistence annually produced and cheapens them to such an extent that the *average wage* can be calculated to allow the reproduction of the workers on a larger scale, even though the wage itself falls in value, represents a smaller quantity of materialised labour time. The wage level may even sink, if only the magnitude of the wage's value does not fall in exactly the same proportion as the productive power of labour rises. On the other hand, the life-situation in which capital places the working class, its conglomeration, its deprivation of all the other pleasures of life, the utter impossibility of attaining a higher social standing and maintaining a certain decorum, the vacuity of their lives, the mixing of the sexes in the workshop, the isolation of the worker himself, all these things impel marriage at an early age. The curtailment and practically the abolition of the necessary period of apprenticeship, the early age at which children can themselves step forward as producers, the shortening therefore of the period during which they must be provided for, increases the stimulus to a more rapid production of human beings. If the average age of working-class generations declines, there is always available on the market a superfluous and constantly increasing mass of short-lived generations, and that is all capitalist production needs.

On the one hand, therefore, it can be said (see *Colins*, etc.) that a country is the richer, the more proletarians it has,[a] and that the growth of wealth is displayed in the increase of poverty. On the other hand, *there is a relative growth* in the number of people not

---

[a] See this volume, p. 206.— *Ed.*

dependent on manual labour, and although the mass of workers grows, the population of the social strata they have to provide for materially through their labour grows in the same proportion. (*Colins, Sismondi,* etc.) The rising productivity of capital is directly expressed in the rising quantity of surplus labour appropriated by capital, or the rising amount of profit, which is an amount of value. Not only is this amount of value growing: the same magnitude of value is represented in an incomparably greater amount of use values. The revenue of society (we disregard wages), the part of the revenue which is not [V-178] re-converted back into capital, therefore grows, and thereby also the substance on which lives the stratum of society not directly involved in material production. This applies, in particular, to the part of society which concerns itself with the sciences; just as to the part concerned with the business of circulation (trade, the money business), and to the idlers, who only consume; as well as to the *serving part* of the population. This section of society amounts e.g. in England to 1 million people, more than all the workers directly employed in weaving and spinning in the FACTORIES.[a] With the separation of bourgeois from feudal society this part of the population is very much reduced. At a more developed stage this VOLUNTARY SERFDOM (see *Quesnay* on servants [206]) undergoes an extraordinary increase along with luxury, wealth and the display of wealth. The working class has to feed, and to work for, this gang—who have become separated from the working class—since they themselves are not directly involved in material production. (The same goes for armies.) [V-178]

[V-179] [207] Although the number of workers grows absolutely, it declines relatively, not only in proportion to the constant capital which absorbs their labour, but also in proportion to the part of society not directly involved in material production or indeed engaged in no kind of production whatsoever.

* "In every stage of society, as increased numbers and better contrivances add to each man's power of production, the number of those who labour is gradually diminished.... Property grows from the improvement of the means of production; its sole business is the encouragement of idleness. When each man's labour is barely sufficient for his own subsistence, as there can be no property" //capital//, "there will be no idle men. When one man's labour can maintain five, there will be four idle men for one employed in production: in no other way can the produce be consumed ... the object of society is to magnify the idle at the expense of the industrious, to create power out of plenty.... The industry which produces is the

---

a *Return to an Address of the Honourable. The House of Commons,* dated 24 April 1861.—Ed.

parent of property; that which aids consumption is its child.... It is the *growth of property, this greater ability to maintain idle men,* and *unproductive industry,* that in political economy is called capital" * (Piercy Ravenstone, M.A., *Thoughts on the Funding System, and Its Effects,* London, 1824, pp. 11-13).

"The less numerous the exploiting population, the less of a burden it is to those it exploits" (Colins, *L'économie politique. Source des révolutions et des utopies prétendues socialistes,* Vol. 1, Paris, 1856, [p.] 69).[a]

"If one understands by social progress, in a harmful direction, the increase of poverty resulting from a rise in the numbers of the exploiting class and a fall in the numbers of the exploited class, then there has been, from the 15th to the 19th century, social progress, in a harmful direction" (l.c., [pp.] 70-71). [V-179]

[V-178] The separation of science from labour, in so far as it concerns labour itself—the separation of science from the industrial and agricultural workers to become, in its application, the industries and agriculture, is a subject which belongs to the section on machinery.[208]

(Otherwise all these reflections belong to the concluding chapter on capital and labour.[30])

The mediaeval master is a craftsman as well, and works himself. He is a master of his craft. With manufacture—based as it is on the division of labour—this comes to an end. Apart from the commercial business he conducts as a buyer and seller of commodities, the activity of the capitalist consists in applying all possible methods of exploiting labour, i.e. making it productive, to the maximum.

* "The class of capitalists are from the first partially, and then become ultimately *completely discharged from the necessity of manual labour.* Their interest is that the *productive powers of the labourers they employ* should be the greatest possible. On *promoting that power* their attention is fixed, and almost exclusively fixed. More thought is brought to bear on the best means of effecting all the purposes of human industry; knowledge extends, multiplies its fields of action, and assists industry" * (Richard Jones, *Text-book of Lectures on the Political Economy of Nations,* Hertford, 1852) (Lecture III).

* "The employer will be always on the stretch to economize time and labour" * (Dugald Stewart, l.c., p. 318).

"These speculators, *who are so economical of the labour of workers they would have to pay*" (J. N. Bidaut, *Du Monopole qui s'établit dans les arts industriels et le commerce,* Paris, 1828, p. 13).[a]

* "The *numerical increase of labourers* has been great, through the growing substitution of female for male, and above all childish for adult labour. Three girls at 13, at wages of 6 to 8 sh. a week, have" * (in a large number of cases) * "replaced the one man of mature age, at wages varying from 18 to 45 sh." * (Thomas [de] Quincey, *The Logic of Political Economy,* Edinburgh, 1844, [p.] 147, footnote).

"Economies in the cost of production can only be economies in the quantity of labour employed in production" (Sismondi, *Études etc.,* Vol. I, p. 22).[a]

---

[a] Marx quotes in French.— *Ed.*

[V-180] Adam Smith remarks as follows on the growth of capital, which is a prerequisite of the division of labour, since the division of labour simultaneously increases *the number of workers employed*:

"The quantity of materials which the same number of people can work up, increases in a great proportion as labour comes to be more and more subdivided; and as the operations of each workman are gradually reduced to a greater degree of simplicity, a variety of new machines come to be invented for facilitating and abridging these operations."

(This is peculiar logic—because labour is reduced to an ever greater degree of simplicity, machines are invented to facilitate and abridge it. Hence because labour is facilitated and abridged by the division of labour! He ought to have said, the tools which when combined later give rise to the machine are simplified and subdivided.)

"As the division of labour advances, therefore, in order to give constant employment to an equal number of workmen, an equal stock of provisions, and a greater stock of materials and tools than what would have been necessary in a ruder state of things, must be accumulated beforehand. *But the number of workmen in every branch of business generally increases with the division of labour in that branch, or rather it is the increase of their number which enables them to class and subdivide themselves in this manner*" (A. Smith, [Garnier,] Vol. II, introduction to Book II, pp. 193-94) [Vol. II, pp. 2-3].

In the same place, Adam Smith presents the capitalist to us as always on the watch for ways of raising the productive power of labour. Here the accumulation of capital is a prerequisite for the division of labour and machinery (since this appears as a capitalist mode of production), and, inversely, accumulation is the result of this raising of the productive forces. We read in the same place:

"As the accumulation of stock is previously necessary for bringing about this great increase in the productive powers of labour, so that accumulation naturally leads to this increase. The person who employs his stock in maintaining labour, necessarily wishes to employ it in such a manner as to produce as great a quantity of work as possible. He endeavours, therefore, both to make among his workmen the most proper distribution of employment, and to furnish them with the best machines which he can either invent or afford to purchase. His abilities, in both these respects, are generally in proportion to the extent of his stock, or to the number of people whom it can employ. *The quantity of industry*, therefore, not only increases in every country with the increase of the *stock which employs it*, but, in consequence of that increase, the same quantity of industry produces a much greater quantity of work" ([Garnier,] pp. 194-95) [Vol. II, p. 3].

[V-181] * "Not beyond a fourth part of our whole population provides everything which is consumed by all" * (Th. Hodgskin, *Popular Political Economy*, London, [Edinburgh,] 1827, [p.] 14).

"The base and petty management, which follows him" (the day-labourer) "with wary eyes, overwhelms him with reproaches when he grants himself the slightest relaxation, and claims he is stealing from it when he allows himself an instant of rest" (S. N. Linguet, *Théorie des loix civiles*, Vol. II, London, 1767, p. 466).

In Book I, Chapter 1, where Adam Smith treats the division of labour *ex professo*, he only touches lightly on its (evil) consequences, but in Book V, in contrast, which deals with the revenue of the state, he follows Ferguson in speaking out directly on this subject. We read there Book V (CH. I, ARTICLE II):

"In the progress of *the division of labour*, the employment of the far greater part of those who live by labour, that is, of the great body of the people, comes to be confined to a few very simple operations, frequently to one or two. But the understandings of the greater part of men are necessarily formed by their ordinary employments. The man whose whole life is spent in performing a few simple operations, of which the effects are perhaps always the same, or very nearly the same, has no occasion to exert his understanding or to exercise his invention in finding out expedients for removing difficulties which never occur. He naturally loses, therefore, the habit of developing or exercising these faculties, and generally becomes as stupid and ignorant as it is possible for a human creature to become. The torpor of his moral faculties ... the uniformity of his stationary life naturally corrupts the courage of his mind.... It corrupts even the activity of his body, and renders him incapable of exerting his strength with vigour and perseverance in any other employment than that to which he has been bred. His dexterity at his own particular trade seems, in this manner, to be acquired at the expense of his intellectual, social, and martial virtues. But in every improved and civilised society this is the state into which the labouring poor, that is, the great body of the people, must necessarily fall.... It is otherwise in the *barbarous* societies as they are commonly called, of hunters, of shepherds, and even of husbandmen in that rude state of husbandry which precedes the improvement of manufactures and the extension of foreign commerce. In such societies the varied occupations of every man oblige every man to exert his capacity by continual efforts, etc.... Though [V-182] in a rude society there is a good deal of variety in the occupations of every individual, there is not a great deal in those of the whole society.... In the civilised state, on the contrary, though there is little variety in the occupations of the greater part of individuals, there is an almost infinite variety in those of the whole society" [Garnier, pp. 181-84] [Vol. III, pp. 295-98].

//DIGRESSION: (ON PRODUCTIVE LABOUR)//

A philosopher produces ideas, a poet poems, a clergyman sermons, a professor compendia and so on. A criminal produces crimes. If we take a closer look at the connection between this latter branch of production and society as a whole, we shall rid ourselves of many prejudices. The criminal produces not only crimes but also criminal law, and with this also the professor who gives lectures on criminal law and in addition to this the inevitable compendium in which this same professor throws his lectures onto the general market as "commodities". This brings with it augmentation of national wealth, quite apart from the personal enjoyment which—as a competent witness, Professor Roscher, [tells] us (see   )[209]—the manuscript of the compendium

Page 182 of Notebook V of the Economic Manuscript of 1861-63

brings to its originator himself. The criminal moreover produces the whole of the police and of criminal justice, constables, judges, hangmen, juries, etc.; and all these different lines of business, which form just as many categories of the social division of labour, develop different capacities of the human mind, create new needs and new ways of satisfying them. Torture alone has given rise to the most ingenious mechanical inventions, and employed many honourable craftsmen in the production of its instruments. The criminal produces an impression, partly moral and partly tragic, as the case may be, and in this way renders a "service" by arousing the moral and aesthetic feelings of the public. He produces not only compendia on Criminal Law, not only penal codes and along with them legislators in this field, but also art, belles-lettres, novels, and even tragedies, as not only Müllner's *Schuld* and Schiller's *Räuber* show, but *Oedipus* and *Richard the Third*. The criminal breaks the monotony and everyday security of bourgeois life. In this way he keeps it from stagnation, and gives rise to that uneasy tension and agility without which even the spur of competition would get blunted. Thus he gives a stimulus to the productive forces. While crime takes a part of the redundant population off the labour market and thus reduces competition among the labourers—up to a certain point preventing wages from falling below the minimum—the struggle against crime absorbs another part of this population. Thus the criminal comes in as one of those natural "counterweights" which bring about a correct balance and open up a whole perspective of "useful" occupations. The effects of the criminal on the development of productive power can be shown in detail. Would locks ever have reached their present degree of excellence had there been no thieves? Would the making of bank-notes have reached its present perfection had there been no [V-183] forgers? Would the microscope have found its way into the sphere of ordinary commerce (see Babbage[a]) but for trading frauds? Does not practical chemistry owe just as much to the adulteration of commodities and the efforts to show it up as to the honest zeal for production? Crime, through its ever new methods of attack on property, constantly calls into being new methods of defence, and so is as productive as STRIKES for the invention of machines. And if one leaves the sphere of private crime: would the world market ever have come into being but for national crime? Indeed, would even the nations have arisen? And

---

[a] Ch. Babbage, *Traité sur l'économie...*, Paris, 1833, p. 279.— *Ed.*

has not the Tree of Sin been at the same time the Tree of Knowledge ever since the time of Adam?

In his *Fable of the Bees* (1705) Mandeville had already shown that every possible kind of occupation is productive, and had given expression to the tendency of this whole line of argument:

> * "That what we call Evil in this World, Moral as well as Natural, is the grand Principle that makes us Sociable Creatures, the solid Basis, the *Life and Support of all Trades and Employments* without exception; there we must look for the true origin of all Arts and Sciences; and the moment Evil ceases, the Society must be spoiled if not totally destroyed." *[a]

Only Mandeville was of course infinitely bolder and more honest than the philistine apologists of bourgeois society.

What strikes us in looking at the division of labour, as with all forms of capitalist production, is the character of the antagonism.

[Firstly.] In the division of labour *within* the workshop, the workers are quantitatively distributed, in strict system, between the individual operations according to certain numerical proportions, as required by production as a whole, by the product of their combined labours. If instead we look at the whole of society—the social division of labour—there are now too many producers to be found in one branch of business and now in another. Competition, through which the price of a commodity is now raised above its value and now lowered beneath it, constantly adjusts these inequalities and disproportions, but just as constantly reproduces them. It is the movement of commodity prices, mediated by competition, that regulates the distribution of the mass of producers among the specific branches of production, bringing about a constant efflux from, or influx into, particular spheres of production—the so-called law of supply and demand, which on the one hand determines prices, and on the other hand is determined by them. Even without going into this point more closely, one's eye is immediately struck by the difference between this anarchic distribution of labour within society and the regulated, fixed distribution within the workshop itself.

Secondly. There are different branches of business within society which themselves merely represent the different phases of production a product must pass through in order to attain its ultimate, its final form, the form in which its use value is a finished product, as for example flax cultivation, the spinning of flax, and weaving of linen cloth. These different branches are brought into contact with each other through the circulation of commodities, so

---

ᵃ B. Mandeville, *The Fable of the Bees*, 3rd ed., London, 1724, p. 428.— *Ed.*

that they ultimately cooperate in the manufacture of a product. The flax confronts the spinner [V-184] as a commodity, the yarn confronts the weaver as a commodity. Here the purchase and sale of commodities mediate the connection which exists internally—as an inner necessity—between these branches of production which operate independently of each other. In contrast to this, the division of labour within manufacture presupposes a *direct* combination of the various operations which provide *a particular* product. This product first becomes a commodity as a result of these combined operations. But the portion of the product created by each of these partial operations is not converted into a commodity. Here cooperation is not mediated through the product of one process entering into the other process as a commodity and thus causing the divided labours to supplement each other. Instead, the *direct* combination of labours is the prerequisite here for the entry of their joint product into the market as a commodity.

Thirdly:

// After relative surplus value, absolute and relative surplus value are to be considered in combination.[210] Then their proportional rise and fall. After this, or rather before it, the alteration the mode of production itself undergoes in becoming capitalist. No longer a merely formal subsumption of the labour process under capital.[75] The different means whereby capital creates relative surplus value, raises the productive forces, and increases the mass of products, are all social forms of labour; but they appear, even within production, rather as social forms of capital—modes of capital's existence. So that one not only sees how capital produces, but how capital is itself produced—its own genesis. It then also emerges that this particular form of the social relation of production, the form through which past labour becomes capital, corresponds to a particular stage of development of the material production process, to particular material conditions of production, which are themselves first created historically, conditions of production whose point of departure naturally belongs to a pre-capitalist stage of social production; their formation and development coincides with the genesis of capital itself, until the movement of production starts to take place on the capitalist basis now obtained, from which point there occurs simply an expansion and reproduction of those conditions of production. Moreover, this genesis of capital appears at the same time as a process of divestiture of labour, of alienation, whereby its own social forms are presented as alien powers. Also, in view of the mass of people required by capitalist production, capital appears as a social form, not as a form of the labour of the independent individual. After this we need to show how far capital is productive, which leads on to questions about productive and unproductive labour.[108] Then wages and surplus value as *revenue*, in general the form of *revenue*, which we need for the transition to the accumulation of capital.[127] //

Within the workshop, the different operations are separated out systematically, according to a plan, and different workers are assigned to them according to a rule which they are faced with as a compelling and alien law imposed on them from outside. The interconnection of the combined labours, their unity, similarly confronts the individual worker as the *will*, personal unity, command and overall supervision of the capitalist; just as their own cooperation itself appears to them not as their deed, their own social existence, but as the presence of the capital that keeps them together, as a form of existence of [V-185] capital in the direct production process, the labour process. Within society, in contrast, the division of labour appears free, i.e. in this case *accidental*, admittedly bound together by an inner connection, which however presents itself as just as much the product of circumstances as of the arbitrary actions of the mutually independent individual commodity producers. Although the division of labour as a specifically capitalist mode of production, the division of labour within the workshop, is essentially different from the division of labour in the whole of society, they condition each other. This means in fact only that large-scale industry and free competition are mutually conditioning forms, creations of capitalist production. Nevertheless, we need to avoid any introduction of competition here, for this is the impact of capitals upon each other, hence already presupposes the development of capital as such.

The commodity, as the most elementary form of wealth, was our point of departure. Commodity and money are both elementary modes of the presence, of the existence, of capital, but they first develop into capital under specific conditions. The formation of capital can only take place on the basis of the production and circulation of commodities, hence at a stage of commerce which is already given, and has already grown to a certain volume, whereas the production and circulation of commodities (which includes the circulation of money) on the contrary by no means require capitalist production for their existence, appearing rather as the necessary, given, historical prerequisite of capitalist production.[20]

On the other hand, it is only on the basis of capitalist production that the commodity first becomes the *general* form of the product, that every product has to assume the form of a commodity, that sale and purchase seize hold of not only surplus production but also subsistence itself, and that the different conditions of production themselves enter extensively into the production process itself as commodities, mediated through sale and purchase. If, therefore, on the one hand the commodity appears as the prerequisite for the formation of capital, on the other hand the *commodity*, as the *general* form of the product, appears just as much as essentially the product and result of capital.[60] Products assume in part the form of the commodity under other modes of production. Capital, in contrast, necessarily produces commodities, produces its product as commodity, or it produces nothing. Therefore the general laws formulated in respect of the commodity, e.g. that the value of the commodity is determined by the socially necessary labour time contained in it, first come to be realised with the development of capitalist production, i.e. of capital.[70] This demonstrates how even categories belonging to earlier epochs of production receive a specifically distinct character—an historical character—on the basis of a different mode of production.[211]

The conversion of money—which is itself only a converted form of the commodity—into capital only takes place once labour capacity (not the worker) has been converted into a commodity, hence the category of the commodity has already from the outset taken possession of a whole sphere which was otherwise excluded from it. Only when the working mass of the population have ceased to enter the market as commodity producers, and begun to sell, instead of the product of labour, labour itself, or RATHER their labour capacity, does production in its entire extent, in its entire breadth and depth become *the* p r o d u c t i o n *of commodities*, with all products being converted into commodities, and the objective conditions of every individual sphere of production entering into it as themselves commodities. Only on the basis of capital, of capitalist production, does the commodity in fact become the general elementary form of wealth. But this already implies [V-186] that the development of the division of labour in society, where it appears in an accidental form, and the capitalist division of labour within the workshop, condition and produce each other. For the producer to produce commodities alone, i.e. for the use value of the product to exist for him exclusively as a means of exchange, it is necessary that his production should be based entirely on the social division of labour, that he therefore should satisfy only an entirely one-sided need through his production. On the other hand, however, this general production of products as commodities only takes place on the basis of capitalist production and in the measure of its spread. If, for example, capital has not yet taken control of agriculture, a great part of the product will still be produced directly as means of subsistence, not as commodity; a great part of the working population will not yet have been turned into wage labourers, and a great part of the conditions of labour will not yet have been converted into capital.[95]

Capitalist production, hence the division of labour within the workshop according to certain rules, directly increases the free division of labour within society (quite apart from the extension of the sphere of exchange, the world market, conditioned by mass production), by making the labour of a particular number of workers more effective, therefore by constantly setting free a part of the labour force for new kinds of employment and thereby simultaneously developing needs which were so far latent or not present at all, and modes of labour to satisfy those needs. This process is also promoted by the increase of the population, by the cheapening of the means of subsistence required for the reproduction and multiplication of labour capacities; also by the fact that the surplus value, which becomes a part of revenue, now seeks to realise itself in the most diverse use values.

Where the *commodity* appears as the dominant form of the product, and the individuals, in order to produce anything at all, must produce not merely products, use values, means of subsistence, where the use value of a commodity is for them, rather, simply a material repository of exchange value, a means of exchange, money *potentia*, where they therefore have to produce *commodities*, their relation to each other—in so far as the material interchange between their activities, their relation within production generally, comes into consideration—is that of *owners of commodities*.[20] But just as the commodity first develops in the exchange of commodities—i.e. the circulation of commodities—so also does the owner of commodities develop in the characters of seller and buyer. Sale and purchase, first the representation of the product as commodity, then the representation of the commodity as money and the metamorphosis of the commodity, in which it presents itself in successive stages as commodity, money, and commodity once again, these are the movements through which the production of the mutually independent individuals is *socially* mediated. The *social* form of their product and their production, i.e. the social relation into which the commodity producers as such enter, is constituted precisely by the representation of their product as *commodity* and *money*, and the acts of sale and purchase, the movements in which their product alternately assumes these different functions.

Therefore, whatever the necessary inner connection arising out of the nature of their needs and the manner of the activities themselves that produce them, which binds together the different use values, hence also the different modes of labour producing them, contained within them, so as to form a whole, a totality, a system of activities and riches—in whatever relation the use value of one commodity as a means of consumption or a means of production is a use value for the other owners of commodities— the *social* relation into which the owners of commodities enter is the representation of their product as commodity and money, and the movement in which they confront each other as vehicles for the metamorphosis [V-187] of the commodities. So that if the existence of the products for each other as commodities and therefore the existence of the individuals as owners of commodities, further developed as sellers and buyers, in and for itself presupposes the social division of labour—for without this the individuals would not produce commodities but rather directly use values, means of subsistence for themselves—this presupposes further a particular division of social labour, namely a division which is *formally* absolutely accidental, and is left to the free will and dealings of the commodity producers.

Where this freedom is restricted, the restriction does not come about through the influence of the state or any other external factor, but through the conditions of existence, the characteristics, that make a commodity a commodity. It must possess a use value for society, i.e. the buyers, hence it must satisfy certain real or imagined needs. Here is a basis on which the individual producer of commodities builds, but it is his affair whether he satisfies existing needs or calls forth new ones with his use value, or whether he has miscalculated and produced something useless. His task is to discover a buyer for whom his commodity has a use value. The second condition he has to fulfil is not to utilise more labour in making his commodity than the labour time socially necessary for its production, and this means that he does not need more labour time to produce it than the average producer who is producing the same commodity. The production of the product as a commodity—if the commodity is the necessary form of the product, the general form of production, and hence the satisfaction of the requirements of life is mediated through sale and purchase—therefore necessitates a social division of labour which admittedly rests on a basis of needs, an interconnection of activities, etc., in its content, but in formal terms this interconnection is only *mediated* through the representation of the product as commodity, the confrontation of the producers with each other as owners of commodities, as sellers and buyers. It therefore appears as on the one hand equally the product of a *concealed* natural necessity, which appears in the individuals only as a need, a requirement, a capacity, etc., and on the other hand the result of their independent wills, conditioned only by the essence of the product—namely that it must be both use value and exchange value.

On the other hand: the product only assumes the form of the commodity generally—the relation of the producers to each other as sellers and buyers only becomes the social connection that rules over them—where labour capacity has itself become a commodity for its owner, where the worker has therefore become a wage labourer and money has become capital. The social connection between the owner of money and the worker is also only a connection between owners of commodities.[20] The relation is modified, brings forth new social relations, through the specific nature of the commodity the worker has to sell and the peculiar manner in which the buyer consumes it, and equally the special purpose for which he buys it. Capitalist production brings with it, among other things, the division of labour within the workshop, and it is this, like the other means of production employed by capital, which further develops mass production, hence the irrelevance of the use value of the product for the producer, production merely for sale, production of the product [V-188] merely as a commodity.

This explains, therefore, how the free, apparently accidental, uncontrolled *division of labour within society*, which is left to the commodity producers to deal with at their discretion, corresponds with the systematic, planned, and regulated division of labour within the workshop, which proceeds under the command of capital, and how both develop in step with each other, and produce each other through mutual interaction.

In contrast to this, in forms of society where social division itself appears as a fixed law, an external norm, and is subject to rules, the division of labour, as forming the basis of manufacture, does not take place, or exists only sporadically and in its initial stages. For example, the guild regulations establish a very low

maximum for the number of journeymen a master can set on.
This is precisely what prevents him from becoming a capitalist.
The division of labour is thereby of itself excluded from the
workshop. (This must be dealt with somewhat more extensively.)
Plato's main argument for the division of labour, that if one
person does several different kinds of work, i.e. if he does one or
the other of them as a subsidiary occupation, the product must
wait until an occasion offers itself to the worker for dealing with it,
whereas the work ought to be determined in the opposite way, by
the requirements of the product,[a] has recently been put forward
by the BLEACHERS and DYERS against their inclusion in the FACTORY
ACTS // the Bleaching and Dyeing Works Act CAME INTO OPERATION ON 1ST
August 1861 //. For according to the FACTORY ACT, whose PROVISIONS
in this connection are reproduced for BLEACHING, etc.,

* "during any meal time which shall form any part of the hour and a half
allowed for meals no child, young person, or female shall be employed or allowed
to remain in any room in which any manufacturing process is then carried on; and
all the young persons and females shall have the time for meals *at the same period of
the day*" * (*Factory Report for the half year ending 31st Oct. 1861*).
* "The bleachers complain of the required uniformity of meal times for them,
on the plea that whilst machinery in factories may be stopped without detriment at
any moment, and if stopped the production is all that is lost, yet in the various
operations of *singeing*, washing, bleaching, mangling, calendering and dyeing, none
of them can be stopped at a given moment without risk of damage ... to enforce
the same dinner hour for all the workpeople might occasionally subject valuable
goods to the risk of danger from incomplete operations" * (l.c., pp. 21, 22).

(*The same* DINNER HOUR was fixed because otherwise it would have
been impossible to check whether the workers had received their
MEALTIMES at all.)

Different Kinds of Division of Labour

"Among peoples which have reached a certain level of civilisation, we meet with
three kinds of division of labour: the *first*, which we shall call *general*, brings about
the division of the producers into agriculturalists, manufacturers, and traders, it
corresponds to the three main branches of the nation's labour; the *second*, which
one [V-189] could call *particular*, is the division of each branch of labour into
species. It is thus, for example, that in *primitive* industry one needs to distinguish
the trade of the ploughman from that of the mineworker, etc. *The third division* of
labour, which one should designate as a *division of tasks*, or of *labour* properly so
called, is that which *grows up in the individual crafts and trades*, and which consists in
the division made by numerous workers between themselves of the tasks which
need to be performed to manufacture a single object of use and commerce, each of

---

[a] See this volume, p. 283.— *Ed.*

23*

them having only one kind of work to perform, not resulting in itself in the production of the whole of the *manufactured object*; the latter result only occurs thanks to *the combination of the labour of all the workers* who are occupied in the manufacture of the product. Such is the division of labour which is established in the *majority of the manufactories* and *workshops*, where one sees a greater or lesser number of workers engaged in producing a single kind of *commodity*, all of them *carrying out different tasks*" (F. Skarbek, *Théorie des richesses sociales*, 2nd ed., Vol. I, Paris, 1839, pp. 84-86).[a]

"The third kind of division of labour is that which occurs *within the workshop itself*.... It arises from the moment when there emerge capitals destined to establish manufactures and *heads of workshops* who make all the *advances necessary to put the workers to work*, and who are able, thanks to their reserves, to wait for the return of the outgoings utilised in the manufacture of the products they provide for exchange" (l.c., pp. [94-]95).

Simple Cooperation

"It should be noted further that this partial division of labour can occur even when the workers are engaged in the same task. Masons, for example, engaged in passing bricks from hand to hand to a higher stage of the building, are all performing the same task, and yet there does exist amongst them a sort of division of labour. This consists in the fact that each of them passes the brick through a given space, and, taken together, they make it arrive much more quickly at the required spot than they would do if each of them carried his brick separately to the upper storey" (Skarbek, l.c., pp. 97-98).

[V-190] γ) MACHINERY.
UTILISATION OF THE FORCES OF NATURE AND OF SCIENCE
(STEAM, ELECTRICITY, MECHANICAL AND CHEMICAL AGENCIES)

John Stuart Mill remarks:

* "It is questionable, if all the mechanical inventions yet made have lightened the day's toil of any human being." *[b]

He should have said, OF ANY TOILING HUMAN BEING. But on the basis of capitalist production the purpose of machinery is by no means TO LIGHTEN OR SHORTEN THE DAY'S TOIL of the worker.

* "Articles are cheap, but they are made of human flesh" * ([J. B. Byles,] *Sophisms of Free-Trade*, 7th edit., London, 1850, p. 202).

The purpose of machinery, speaking quite generally, is to lessen the value, therefore the price, of the commodity, to cheapen it, i.e. to shorten the labour time necessary for the production of a commodity, but by no means to shorten the labour time during which the worker is employed in producing this cheaper

---

[a] Here and below Marx quotes Skarbek in French.— *Ed.*

[b] J. St. Mill, *Principles of Political Economy*, Vol. II, London, 1848, p. 312.— *Ed.*

commodity. In fact it is not a matter of shortening the working day but rather, as in any development of productive power on a capitalist basis, of reducing the labour time the worker needs for the reproduction of his labour capacity, in other words for the production of his wages; it is therefore a matter of shortening the part of the working day during which he works for himself, the *paid* part of his labour time, and thereby lengthening the other part of the day, during which he works for capital for no return, the *unpaid* part of the working day, his *surplus labour time*. Why the mania for devouring alien labour time grows everywhere with the introduction of machinery, and why the working day, instead of being shortened is rather extended beyond its natural limits—until legislation is obliged to take a hand—why therefore not only relative surplus labour time but also total labour time increases, is a *phenomenon* we shall examine in Chapter 3.[212]
[V-190]

[V-196][213] * "Simultaneously, however, with the increase of numbers has been the increase of toil. The labour performed by those engaged in the processes of manufacture, *is three times as great* as in the beginning of such operations. Machinery has executed, no doubt, the work that would demand the sinews of millions of men; but it has also *prodigiously multiplied* the labour of those who are governed by its fearful movements" * (*Ten Hours' Factory Bill. Lord Ashley's Speech*, London, 1844, p. 6).

[V-190] Only in isolated cases does the capitalist intend to secure a *direct reduction of wages* by introducing machinery, although this is always the case when he replaces skilled labour with simple labour, and the labour of grown men with that of women and children. The value of the commodity is determined by the *socially necessary* labour time contained in it. With the introduction of new machinery, and as long as the major part of production continues to be based on the old means of production, the capitalist can sell his commodity *at less than* its social value, even though he sells it at more than its individual value, i.e. for more *labour time* than he requires to manufacture it under the new production process. Here, therefore, the surplus value appears to originate for him from selling—from his taking advantage of the other owners of commodities, from the fact that the commodity's price has risen above its value; not from the reduction in necessary labour time and the lengthening of surplus labour time. Yet, this too is merely the way things appear. Through the exceptional productive power attained here by labour in contrast to average labour in the same branch of industry, it becomes higher labour in relation to the average, so that e.g. an hour of this higher labour would be equal to $^5/_4$ hours of average labour; simple labour raised to a higher power. But the capitalist pays it as average labour. Thus a smaller number of hours of labour becomes equal to a greater number of hours of average labour. He pays for this labour as average labour and sells it as what it is, higher labour, a given quantity of which = a greater quantity of average labour. Here, therefore, the worker needs to work, on our assumption, for a shorter time than the average worker in order to produce [V-191] the same value. He therefore in fact works less labour time—than the average worker—in order to produce an equivalent for his wages, or in other words to produce the means of subsistence necessary for the reproduction of his labour capacity. He therefore gives the capitalist a greater number of hours of labour as surplus labour, and it is only this relative surplus labour which provides the latter, when selling the commodity, with the excess of its price over its value. The capitalist only realises this surplus labour time, or this surplus value, which is the same thing, by selling the commodity; the surplus value therefore originates not in the sale but in the reduction of necessary labour time and the concomitant relative increase of surplus labour time. Even if the capitalist who introduces the new machinery were to pay a higher than average wage, the surplus realised by him over and above the normal surplus value, the surplus value realised by the other capitalists in the same branch of industry, would originate solely from the fact that the wage was not increased *in the same proportion* as this labour rose above the level of average labour, that a relative increase in surplus labour time continued to occur. Therefore this case can also be subsumed under the general law that surplus value = surplus labour.

In its early stages machinery is mostly nothing but a more powerful craftsman's tool; but as soon as it is applied in the capitalist fashion, it presupposes *simple cooperation*, and indeed, as we shall see later,[214] simple cooperation appears as a much more important element in the application of machinery than in the system of manufacture resting on the division of labour, where it only asserts itself in the principle of MULTIPLES, i.e. the principle that the different operations are not only distributed between different workers but according to certain numerical proportions, in which a definite number of workers, organised in groups, is assigned to, subsumed under, each individual operation. In the *mechanical workshop*, the most developed form of the capitalist application of machinery, it is essential that many should do *the same thing*. Indeed, this is its main principle. The application of machinery further presupposes as the original condition of its existence the system of manufacture based on the division of labour, since the *construction of machines*—hence the existence of the machine—is itself based on a workshop in which the principle of the division of labour has been completely implemented. Only at a further stage of development does the construction of machines itself take place on the basis of machinery, by means of the mechanical workshop.

"In the infancy of mechanical engineering, a machine-factory displayed the division of labour in manifold gradations—the file, the drill, the lathe, having each its different workmen in the order of skill; but the dexterous hands of the filer and driller are now superseded by the planing, the key-groove cutting, and the drilling machines; and those of the iron and brass turners, by the self-acting slide-lathe" (*Ure*, l.c., Vol. I, pp. 30-31).

On the one hand, the division of labour developed under the system of manufacture is repeated within the mechanical workshop, although on a greatly reduced scale; on the other hand, as we shall see later on, the mechanical workshop overturns the most essential principles of the system of manufacture based on the division of labour.[215] And finally, the application of machinery increases the division of labour within society, that is to say it multiplies the number of specialised branches of industry and independent spheres of production.

Its fundamental principle is the replacement of skilled labour by *simple* labour; hence also the reduction of the amount of wages to the average wage, or the reduction of the worker's necessary labour to the average minimum and the reduction of the production cost of labour capacity to the production cost of simple labour capacity.

[V-192] The increase in productive power achieved through simple cooperation and the division of labour costs the capitalist nothing. They are natural forces provided free of charge by social labour in the particular forms it takes on under the rule of capital. The application of machinery does not just bring the productive forces of social labour into play, as opposed to the labour of the isolated individual. It transforms simple natural forces, such as water, wind, steam, electricity, etc., into powers of social labour. This apart from the exploitation of the mechanical laws which operate in the actual working part of the machinery (i.e. the part which directly transforms the raw material, mechanically or chemically). However, this form of increasing the productive forces, *hinc*[a] [of reducing] necessary labour time, is distinguished

---

[a] Hence.— *Ed.*

as follows: A part of the pure force of nature which is applied is, in this, its applicable form, a product of labour, as for example the conversion of water into steam. Where the motive power is naturally available, e.g. when water is available as a waterfall and the like //it is highly characteristic, by the way, that in the course of the 18th century the French let their water work horizontally, whereas the Germans always made artificial earthworks for it[216] //, the medium through which its motion is transferred to the actual machinery, e.g. the water-wheel, is the product of labour. But this point is even truer for the machinery itself which directly recasts the raw material. Therefore machinery, unlike simple cooperation or the division of labour in manufacture, is a productive force which has been produced; it costs money; when it enters into the sphere of production in which it functions as machinery, functions as a part of the constant capital, it does so as a commodity (directly as machinery, or indirectly as a commodity which must be consumed in order to give the motive power the required form). Like any portion of constant capital, the machinery adds to the product the value contained in it, i.e. it makes it dearer to the extent of the labour time required for its own production. In this chapter we are exclusively examining the ratio of variable capital to the magnitude of the value in which it is reproduced, in other words the ratio of the necessary labour employed in a sphere of production to the surplus labour; we therefore deliberately refrain from investigating the ratio of surplus value to constant capital, and to the total amount of capital advanced. Nevertheless, the analysis of the application of machinery demands that we also investigate the other parts of capital, besides that laid out in wages. For the principle that the employment of means whereby productive power is increased increases relative surplus time and therewith relative surplus value, rests upon the cheapening of the commodities, hence the curtailment of the labour time necessary for the reproduction of labour capacity, in consequence of these CONTRIVANCES through which productive power is increased, i.e. more use values are produced by the same number of workers in the same period of time. In the case of the employment of machinery, however, this result is only attained by an increase in the outlay of capital, by the consumption of already existing values, therefore by the introduction of an element which increases the magnitude of the product's, the commodity's, value to the amount of its own value.

To begin with, as far as the raw material is concerned, its value naturally remains the same, in whatever manner it is treated—it is, to be precise, the value it has when it enters the process of production. [V-193] Furthermore, the employment of machinery reduces the amount of labour absorbed by a given amount of raw material, or, in other words, increases the amount of raw material transformed into product over a given labour time. Considering both these elements, the commodity produced with the assistance of machinery contains less labour time than the one produced without machinery, it represents a smaller magnitude of value, it is cheaper. But this result is only attained by the industrial consumption of commodities—commodities existing in the machinery—whose value enters into the product.

Therefore, since the value of the raw material remains the same whether machinery is employed or not, and since the amount of labour time which converts a given amount of raw material into product and hence into commodity is reduced by the employment of machinery, it follows that the cheapening of the commodities produced by machines depends on one circumstance alone: the labour time contained in the machinery itself is less than the labour time contained in the labour capacity replaced by it; the value of machinery which enters into the commodity is less than—i.e. = less labour time than—the value of the labour replaced by it. And this value = the value of the number of labour capacities whose employment is made unnecessary by machinery.

As machinery emerges from the stage of infancy, as it diverges in dimensions and character from the craft tool it originally replaced, it becomes more massive and expensive; more labour time is required to produce it, and its absolute value rises, although it becomes cheaper relatively, i.e. although more efficient machinery costs less in proportion to its efficiency than less efficient machinery, i.e. the amount of labour time it costs to produce it grows in a much smaller proportion than the amount of labour time it replaces. But in any case its absolute dearness rises progressively, it therefore adds to the commodity produced by it a value which is greater absolutely, particularly in comparison with the craft tool or even the simple instruments of labour or those based on the division of labour which it replaces in the production process. Why then is the commodity produced by this more expensive instrument of production cheaper than the commodity produced without it? Why is the labour time contained in the machinery itself less than the labour time replaced by it? This is due to the two following circumstances:

1) As the efficiency of the machinery grows, as the productive power of labour is thus raised, the quantity of use values and

therefore of commodities which are produced in the same labour time with the help of machinery grows, in the proportion to which the machinery enables one worker to do the work of many workers. This means an increase in *the number of commodities in which the value of the machinery re-appears.* The total value of the machinery only re-appears in the totality of the commodities in whose production it has assisted as a means of labour; this total value is distributed in aliquot parts among the individual commodities which when added together make up the total amount of the commodities. Therefore, the greater this total amount the smaller the portion of the machinery's value that re-appears in the individual commodity. In spite of the difference in value between the machinery and the tool or simple instrument of labour, a smaller portion of value will enter the commodity from the machinery than from the instrument of labour and from the labour capacity replaced by the machine, in proportion as the value of the machine is spread over a greater total amount of products, of commodities. A spinning machine which absorbs a given labour time in 1,000 pounds of cotton re-appears in the individual pound of yarn as a fraction of value of only $^1/_{1000}$, whereas if it only helped to spin 100 pounds in the same time, $^1/_{100}$ of its value would re-appear in the single pound of yarn, it would therefore contain in this case ten times more labour time, ten times more value, be 10 times dearer, than in the first case. [V-194] Machinery can therefore only be employed (on a capitalist basis) under circumstances in which mass production, production on a large scale, is possible (see p. 201, *quotation from Rossi*).

[V-201][217] "The division of labour and the use of powerful machines are only possible in establishments which offer enough labour to all classes of worker and provide results on a large scale. The more considerable the product the smaller the *proportional expenditure* on tools and machines. If two equally powerful machines produce respectively 100,000 metres and 200,000 metres of the same cloth in the same space of time, you may say that the first machine costs twice as much as the second, that one of these enterprises has employed a capital double that employed in the other" (Rossi, *Cours d'économie politique,* p. 334).[a] [V-201]

[V-194] 2) It is already the case in manufacture resting on the division of labour as in industry on the craft basis, etc., that the instruments of labour (in the same way as other parts of the conditions of labour, like factory buildings) enter into the *labour process* to their *whole extent,* either directly as means of labour or indirectly as conditions (such as buildings) which are necessary for

---

[a] Marx quotes in French.— *Ed.*

the labour process to take place. But they only enter into the *valorisation process* piece by piece, *partially*—i.e. they enter to the extent to which they are used up in the labour process, to the extent to which their exchange value is consumed in the labour process simultaneously with their use value. Their use value as means of labour enters into the labour process wholly, but it is preserved over a period which comprises a number of labour processes, during which these means of labour serve repeatedly for the production of the same kind of commodity, i.e. serve over and over again as means of labour used by new labour for working up new material. Their use value as means of labour of this kind is only used up at the end of a period, which may be shorter or longer, during which the same labour process has been constantly repeated. Their exchange value therefore only re-appears completely in the total amount of commodities they have helped to produce during such a period—the whole period, from their entry into the labour process to their removal from it. Only a certain aliquot part of the value of the instrument of labour therefore enters into each individual commodity. If the instrument served for 90 days, $1/90$ of its value would re-appear in the commodities produced on each day. A notional average calculation necessarily enters the picture here, for the value of the instrument only re-appears as a whole in the whole period of labour processes during which it has been completely used up—therefore in the sum total of the commodities it has helped to produce during this period. The calculation is therefore made in this way: on each day on the average an equal aliquot part of the instrument's use value is used up (this is the fiction), and therefore an equal aliquot part of the value of the instrument re-appears in the product of this one day.

With the introduction of machinery, as a result of which the means of labour assumes a very extensive value and is represented in a massive quantity of use values, there is an increase in this difference between the labour process and the valorisation process, which becomes a significant element in the development of productive power and in the character of production. If a workshop is equipped with mechanical looms, and they perform their function, e.g., over 12 years, the wear and tear of the machinery, etc., during the labour process in the course of one day is insignificant, and therefore the portion of the value of the machinery which re-appears in the individual commodity or even in the product of a whole year is relatively insignificant. Past, objectified labour here enters massively into the labour process, whereas only a relatively insignificant portion of this part of capital, the portion used up in the same labour process, enters into the valorisation process and therefore re-appears in the product as part of the value. Therefore, however considerable the magnitude of the value that is represented by the machinery that enters into the labour process, and the factory buildings, etc., associated with it, the part of this overall value that enters into the daily valorisation [V-195] process, hence into the value of the commodity, is always relatively small; it makes the commodity relatively more expensive, but only insignificantly, to a much smaller extent than the manual labour replaced by the machinery would have done. Therefore, however large the part of the capital laid out in machinery may appear to be in comparison with the part laid out for the living labour which this machinery serves as means of production, this proportion appears to be very small if the part of the value of the machinery which re-appears in the individual commodity is compared with the living labour absorbed in the same commodity, and the part of the value added to the individual product by both of them—machinery and labour— appears to be small in proportion to the value of the raw material itself.

It is with the coming of machinery that social production on a large scale first obtains the power of introducing into the labour process in their entirety, wholly as means of production, products which represent a large amount of past labour, hence large masses of value, whereas only a relatively small aliquot part of those products enters into the valorisation process taking place during the individual labour process. The capital which enters in this form into every individual labour process is large, but the proportion in which its use value is used up, consumed, during this labour process, making necessary the replacement of its value, is relatively small. The machinery functions in its entirety as means of labour, but it only adds value to the product in the proportion to which the labour process diminishes its value, a devaluation which is conditioned by the degree of the reduction of its use value through wear and tear during the labour process.

The conditions enumerated under 1) and 2), on which it depends whether the commodity produced by the dearer instrument is cheaper than the commodity produced by the cheaper one, or whether the value contained in the machinery itself is smaller than the value of the labour capacities it replaces, therefore amount to the following: The first condition is mass production; this depends on the degree to which the amount of commodities 1 worker can produce *in the same labour time* is large in comparison with the amount he would produce without machinery. In other words, it depends on the degree to which *labour is replaced by machinery*; hence the number of labour capacities which is used in regard to the amount of the product *is reduced* as far as possible, as many labour capacities as possible are replaced by the machinery, and the part of the capital which is laid out in labour appears relatively small in comparison with the part of the capital which is laid out in machinery. And secondly: however large the part of the capital which consists in machinery, the part of the value of the machine which re-appears in the individual commodity, the part of the value, therefore, which is added by the machinery to the individual commodity, is small in comparison with the parts of the value of labour and raw material contained in the same commodity, and indeed small because during a given labour time the machinery enters in its entirety into the labour process but only a relatively insignificant portion of it enters into the valorisation process; the whole of the machinery enters into the labour process, but there always enters merely an aliquot part of the total magnitude of the machinery's value [into the valorisation process].

Accordingly, the following criticism of Ricardo needs itself to be corrected:

"Ricardo speaks of * 'a portion of the labour of the engineer in making machines' " * as contained, e.g., in a pair of stockings. * "Yet the *total labour* that produced each single pair of stockings, if it is of a single pair we are speaking, includes the *whole* labour of the engineer, not a portion; for one machine makes many pairs, and none of those pairs could have been done without any part of the machine" * (*Observations on Certain Verbal Disputes in Political Economy*, London, 1821, [p.] 54).

[V-196] The part of the capital laid out in raw material grows disproportionately more rapidly in comparison with the part laid out in wages than where there is a mere division of labour. The new and relatively large amount of capital laid out in means of labour, machinery, etc., comes additionally into consideration. The progress of industry is therefore accompanied by a growth in the AUXILIARY part of capital[218] as against the part laid out in living labour.

[V-197] One of the first effects of the introduction of new machinery, before it has become dominant in its branch of production, is *to prolong* the labour time of those workers who continue to work with the old, imperfect means of production. Although the commodity produced with the machinery is sold at *more than* its individual value, i.e. at more than the quantity of labour time contained in it, it is sold *at less than* the previous social, general value of the same species of product. The labour time socially necessary for the production of this particular commodity has therefore *fallen*, but not the labour time necessary for the worker using the old instruments of production. If, therefore, 10 hours of labour time suffice for the reproduction of his labour capacity, the product of his 10 hours is no longer *10 hours of necessary labour time*, that is to say labour time necessary under the new social conditions of production for the manufacture of this product; it is instead perhaps only 6 hours. Therefore, if he works for 14 hours, those 14 hours of his represent only *10 hours of necessary labour time* and only 10 hours of necessary labour time have been realised in them. Hence the value of the product also does not exceed the value of the product of 10 hours of general, necessary, social labour. If he works independently, he will have to prolong his labour time. If he works as a wage labourer, hence necessarily also works surplus time, then however much the absolute labour time is prolonged, average surplus labour for the capitalist will only emerge through a reduction of his wage below the previous AVERAGE, i.e. he works more hours but less of them are appropriated by him personally, not because his labour has become more productive but because it has become less productive, not because he creates the same quantity of product in less labour time but because the quantity falling to his share is reduced.

The surplus value (= surplus labour, absolute as well as relative) which capital brings into existence through the employment of machinery does not arise from the *labour capacities replaced* by the machinery but from the labour capacities employed by it.

"According to Baines * a first rate cotton-spinning factory cannot be built, filled with machinery, and fitted with the steam engines and gasworks, under £100,000. A steam-engine of 100 horse power will turn 50,000 spindles, which will produce 62,500 miles of fine cotton thread per day. In such a factory 1,000 persons will spin as much thread as 250,000 persons could without machinery" * (S. Laing, *The National Distress*, London, 1844, p. 75).

In this case the surplus value of the capital comes not from the saving made on the labour of 250 persons, but from the 1 person who replaces them; not from the 250,000 persons replaced, but from the 1,000 employed. It is their surplus labour which is realised in the surplus value. The use value of the machine, and its replacement of human labour is its use value, does not determine its value; this is determined by the labour required to produce the machine itself. And this value, which it possesses before being employed, before entering into the production process, is the sole value it adds to the product *qua* machinery. The capitalist paid for this value when he bought the machine.

On the presupposition that the commodities are sold at their value, the *relative surplus value* created by capital by means of the machinery, as in applying all other ARRANGEMENTS which increase the productive power of labour and thereby reduce the price of the individual product, consists simply in this, that the commodities necessary for the reproduction of labour capacity are cheapened, hence that there is a reduction of the labour time necessary for the reproduction of labour capacity, which is only an equivalent of the labour time contained in wages; and therefore that the surplus labour time is prolonged, with the [V-198] overall length of the working day remaining the same. (There are a number of circumstances modifying this, which will be dealt with later.) This curtailment of necessary labour time is a result which redounds to the benefit of capitalist production as a whole and reduces the production costs of labour capacity altogether, because on our assumption the commodity produced by the machinery in fact contributes to the reproduction of labour capacity. However, this is not a motive for the individual capitalist to introduce machinery—it is a general result which is not particularly advantageous to him.

Firstly: Machinery may be introduced, either in replacement of a craft-based industry (as e.g. in the case of spinning), hence in subjecting a branch of industry for the first time to the capitalist mode of production; or in revolutionising a form of manufacture which previously rested merely on the division of labour (as in a factory for making machines); or, lastly, in driving out older by more efficient machinery or in extending the field of application of machinery in a workshop to parts of the operation it had not as yet previously seized hold of. In all these cases, as remarked above, it prolongs *necessary labour time* for the workers still subsumed under the old mode of production, and also prolongs their overall working day. On the other hand, in workshops where it is newly introduced it *curtails* necessary labour time, relatively speaking. If 2 hours of labour by a hand loom weaver are only equivalent to 1 socially necessary hour of labour after the introduction of the POWER LOOM, 1 hour of labour by the POWER LOOM WEAVER is now, before the POWER LOOM has been introduced generally into this form of weaving, of greater magnitude than one hour of necessary labour. Its product has a higher value than the product of one hour of labour. It is the same as if simple labour were realised in it at a higher power, or a higher sort of weaving labour were realised in it. This concerning the extent to which the capitalist who employs the POWER LOOM, while admittedly selling the product of 1 hour below the level of the old hour of labour, below its previous socially necessary value, even so sells it at more than its individual value, i.e. at more than the labour time he himself has to employ to produce it with the help of the POWER LOOM. The worker therefore needs to work fewer hours for the reproduction of his wage, his necessary labour time is curtailed in the same measure as his labour has become higher labour in the same branch, that is to say the product of an hour of his labour is sold at perhaps more than the product of two hours of labour in the workshops where the old mode of production still prevails. If, therefore, the normal day remains the same—equally long— surplus labour time increases here because necessary labour time has been curtailed. This would occur even in the case of an increase in wages, always on the assumption that in the new circumstances the worker does not employ *as large* an aliquot part of the day as previously in replacing his wage or reproducing his labour capacity. This curtailment of necessary labour time is of course temporary, and it disappears once the general introduction of machinery into this branch has reduced the value of the commodity again to the labour time contained in it. Nevertheless, this is at the same time an incentive to the capitalist to raise the labour time he employs above the general level of the necessary labour time in the same sphere of production, by introducing ever new, small improvements. This is true whatever branch of production the machinery is employed in, and it is independent of whether the commodities produced by the machinery enter into the consumption of the worker himself.

Secondly. It is a general experience that as soon as machinery is employed in the capitalist way—i.e. emerges from the infant stage in which it originally appears in many branches, namely as merely a more productive form of the old handicraft tool, which is, however, still employed in the old industrial mode [V-199] by independent workers and their families—once it takes on an independent existence as a form of capital vis-à-vis the worker, the *absolute labour time*, the overall working day, is not curtailed but prolonged. The investigation of this CASE belongs to Chapter III.[212] But the main points should be presented here. In this context we must distinguish between two things. *Firstly* the new conditions in which the worker finds himself and which enable the capitalist forcibly to prolong labour time. *Secondly* the motives which impel capital to undertake this operation.

In looking at 1) we have firstly to consider the converted form of labour, its apparent ease, which transfers all muscular exertion to the machinery, and similarly all skill. For the first reason, prolongation does not initially come up against physical impracticability; the second change breaks the resistance of the worker, who can no longer dig his heels in because his dexterity, still predominant under the system of manufacture, has now been broken; instead of this capital is able to replace skilled workers by unskilled ones, who therefore are more under its control. Then the new class of workers, who enter the situation as a determining element, alter the character of the whole workshop, and by their nature are more obedient to the despotism of capital. The element, namely, of female and child labour. Once the working day has been prolonged forcibly by tradition, generations are required, as in England, before the workers are capable of bringing it back to its normal limits. Thus the prolongation of the day beyond its natural limits, nightwork, is an offshoot of the factory system.

* "It is evident that the long hours of work were brought about by the circumstance of so great a number of destitute children being supplied from the different parts of the country" * (from the WORKHOUSES) * "that the masters were independent of the hands, and that, having once established the custom by means of the miserable materials which they procured in this way, they could impose it upon their neighbours with the greater facility" * (J. Fielden, *The Curse of the Factory System*, London, 1836, [p. 11]).

* "'Mr. E., a manufacturer, informed me that he employs females exclusively at his power looms; it is so universally; gives a decided preference to married females, especially those who have families at home dependent on them for support; they are attentive, docile, more so than unmarried females, and are compelled to use their utmost exertions to procure the necessaries of life.' Thus are the virtues, the peculiar virtues, of the female character to be perverted to her injury,—thus all that is most dutiful and tender in her nature is to be made the means of her bondage and suffering!" * (*Ten Hours Factory Bill. The Speech of Lord Ashley*, London, 1844, p. 20).

Fielden, already cited above, says:

* "As improvements in machinery have gone on, the *avarice* of masters has prompted many to exact more labour from their hands than they were fitted by nature to perform" * (Fielden, l.c., [p.] 34).

A keen appetite for alien labour (surplus labour) is not a feature specific to the person who employs machinery, it is the driving motive of the whole of capitalist production. Since the FACTORY MASTER is now in a better position to indulge this urge, he quite naturally lets go of the reins. A further remark: As long as the motive force proceeds from human beings (and indeed animals too) [V-200] it can only physically function for a certain portion of the day. A steam engine, etc., needs no rest. It can continue operating for any length of time. [V-200]

[V-199] However, there are yet further circumstances which give this urge a very special impetus in the case of the employment of machinery.

[V-200] Machinery, etc., is valorised over a lengthy period, during which the same labour process is constantly repeated in order to produce new commodities. This period is determined by calculating the average time it takes for the whole value of the machinery to be transferred to the product. The extension of labour time beyond the limits of the normal working day shortens the period over which the capital laid out in the machinery is replaced by the total amount of production. Let us assume the period is 10 years if 12 hours are worked every day. If 15 hours are worked every day, hence if the day is lengthened by $^1/_4$, over one week this makes $1^1/_2$ days=18 hours. The whole week comes to 90 hours on our assumption. $^{18}/_{90}=^1/_5$ week. And so $^1/_5$ of the 10 years would be saved; 2 years, therefore. HENCE the capital laid out in machinery would have been replaced in 8 years. Either it has in fact been used up in that time. Then the reproduction process has been hastened. If not—if the machinery is still capable of functioning—the ratio of variable capital to constant capital is raised, because the latter continues to function without however having to enter into the valorisation process any more. This brings about an increase, if not in the surplus value (which has already grown as a result of the prolongation of labour time), at least in the ratio of that surplus value to the total amount of capital laid out—and therefore an increase in profit. And additionally: When new machinery is introduced the improvements come thick and fast. Thus a large part of the old machinery constantly loses part of its value or becomes entirely unusable before it has passed through its circulation period, or its value has re-appeared in the value of the commodities. The more the reproduction period is curtailed, the slighter this danger is, and the more the capitalist is able, the value of the machinery having returned to him in a shorter period, to introduce the new improved machinery and sell cheaply the old machinery, which can again be profitably employed by another capitalist, since it enters into his production as from the outset the representative of a smaller magnitude of value. (We shall deal with this point in more detail under *fixed capital*, bringing in *Babbage*'s examples as well.[a])

What has been said here is valid not only for machinery but for the whole of the fixed capital which the employment of machinery brings in its train and is the condition for.

Yet, the capitalist is by no means concerned merely to get back the amount of value laid out in the fixed capital as soon as possible, so as to protect it from devaluation and to possess it again in disposable form; he is concerned above all with the profitable employment of this capital—of the great quantity of capital fixed in a form in which it both decays as exchange value and is useless as use value, except to the extent that it is brought into contact with the living kind of labour whose fixed capital it constitutes. Since the part of capital laid out in wages has become much smaller in relation to the total capital—particularly in relation to the fixed capital—and since the magnitude of surplus value depends not only on its rate but on the number of working days simultaneously employed, while profit depends on the ratio of this surplus value to the total capital, the consequence is a fall in the rate of profit. The simplest means to prevent this is of course to prolong the absolute surplus labour as far as possible by prolonging the working day, thereby making the fixed capital the means of appropriating the greatest possible quantity of unpaid labour. If the factory is not in operation, the manufacturer regards this as being robbed by the workers; for his capital has obtained a form in fixed capital in which it is directly a draft entitling him to alien labour. This is all expressed very naively by Mr. Senior, who in the year 1837 still was of the opinion [V-201] that the working day—hence absolute labour time—would necessarily have to become longer with the development of machinery.

Senior says, giving, moreover, the honourable Mr. Ashworth as his authority:

"THE DIFFERENCE BETWEEN THE HOURS OF WORK USUAL OVER THE WHOLE WORLD IN COTTON FACTORIES AND OTHER EMPLOYMENTS derives from two sources. 1) THE GREAT PROPORTION OF FIXED TO CIRCULATING CAPITAL, WHICH MAKES LONG HOURS OF WORK DESIRABLE" (Senior, *Letters on the Factory Act etc.*, London, 1837, p. 11) (XI, 4).[219]

---

[a] Ch. Babbage, *Traité sur l'économie...*, pp. 375-78.— *Ed.*

With the constant growth of fixed capital in relation to circulating capital

* "the motives to long hours of work will become greater, as the only means by which a large proportion of fixed capital can be made profitable. 'When a labourer,' said Mr. Ashworth to me, 'lays down his spade, he renders useless, for that period, a capital worth 18d. When one of our people leaves the mill, he renders useless a capital that has cost £100,000 220'" * (l.c., [p.] 14).

HE *RENDERS USELESS*! After all the machinery is there—such a great capital has been invested in it—precisely to squeeze labour out of the worker. In fact he has already committed a great crime against A CAPITAL THAT HAS COST £100,000 BY LEAVING THE MILL AT ALL!

(this was the original reason for nightwork: "later our FACTORIES usually worked 80 hours a WEEK") (XI, 5).

"If a steam engine, or other kind of machine, only works for some hours or some days a week, there is a loss of energy. If it works for the whole day it produces more, and it produces still more if it works night and day" (J. G. Courcelle-Seneuil, *Traité théorique et pratique des entreprises industrielles etc.*, 2nd ed., Paris, 1857, p. 48).[a]

"The first machines for weaving patent net, when first installed, were very expensive, costing from £1,000 to £1,200 [or £1,300]. Though the machines increased the quantity produced, the possessors were nevertheless unable, with the workers' working time being limited to 8 hours, to compete with the old methods in price terms. This disadvantage arose from the large capital the instalment of the machinery cost; but the manufacturers quickly perceived that with the same expense of fixed capital, and a small ADDITION to their circulating capital, they could work the same machines during the whole 24 hours" (Babbage, p. 279).[b]

[V-206] * "It is self-evident, that, amid the ebbings and flowings of the market, and the alternate contractions and expansions of demand, occasions will constantly recur, in which the manufacturer may employ additional floating capital without employing additional fixed capital ... if *additional quantities of raw material can be worked up without incurring an additional expense for buildings and machinery*" * (R. Torrens, *On Wages and Combination*, London, 1834, p. 64).221

This is, in general, an advantage associated with the prolongation of labour time—SAVING OF AN ADDITIONAL EXPENSE FOR BUILDINGS AND MACHINERY. [V-206]

[V-201] *Thirdly*. To the extent that the employment of machinery curtails the labour time during which the same commodity can be produced, it lessens the value of the commodity and makes the labour more productive, because it provides more product in the same time. To that extent the machinery only affects the productive power of normal labour. But a definite quantity of labour time continues to be represented in the same magnitude of value. Therefore as soon as competition has reduced

---

a Marx quotes in French.— *Ed.*
b Ch. Babbage, *Traité sur l'économie...*— *Ed.*

the price of the commodity produced by machinery to its value, the employment of machinery can only increase the *surplus value*, the profit [V-202] of the capitalist, in so far as the cheapening of the commodity leads to a reduction in the value of wages or the value of labour capacity or in the time necessary for the reproduction of labour capacity.

There is, however, an additional circumstance here owing to which the employment of machinery increases absolute labour time, and therefore absolute surplus value, even without any prolongation of the working day. This happens through the, so to speak, *condensation of labour time*, in which every part of the time increases its labour content; the intensity of labour grows; there is growth not only in the productivity (hence the quality) of the labour owing to the employment of machinery, but in the *quantity of labour* performed within a given period. The pores of time are so to speak shrunk through the compression of labour. One hour of labour thereby represents the same quantity of labour as perhaps $^6/_4$ hours of the average labour performed without the employment of machinery or with the employment of less efficient machinery.

Where machinery has already been introduced, the improvements which reduce the number of workers in relation to the amount of commodities produced and the machinery employed are accompanied by the circumstance that the labour of the individual worker who replaces 1 or 2 workers grows with the improvements in the machinery, hence that the machinery only enables him to do what 2 or 3 workers did previously by compelling him to increase his labour and fill each period of time more intensively with labour. Thus labour capacity is more rapidly worn out during the same hour of labour.

Let us look first at the way those who have investigated factory labour at different times have spoken about the growth in labour accompanying improvements in machinery. This follows on the one hand from the greater rapidity of the machine, which the worker has to follow; and on the other hand from the greater quantity of machine labour the individual worker has to overlook, as for example when the number of spindles on the MULE is increased, with double rows of spindles (DOUBLE DECKING) as well, or when 1 weaver has to supervise 2 or 3 POWER LOOMS instead of 1.

* "The labour now undergone in the factories is much greater than it used to be, owing to the greater attention and activity required by the greatly increased speed which is given to the machinery that the children have to attend to, when we

compare it with what it was 30 or 40 years ago"* (J. Fielden, *The Curse of the Factory System*, [London, 1836,] p. 32). This was in the year 1836. John Fielden was himself a manufacturer.

Lord Ashley (now Earl of Shaftesbury) stated in his speech on the Ten Hours Factory Bill on March 15, 1844:

* "The labour performed by those engaged in the processes of manufacture, is 3 times as great as in the beginning of such operations. Machinery has executed, no doubt, the work that would demand the sinews of millions of men; but it has also prodigiously multiplied the labour of those who are governed by its fearful movements"* (l.c., [p.] 6). * "In 1815, the labour of following a pair of mules spinning cotton yarn of Nos. 40—reckoning 12 hours to the working day—involved a necessity for walking 8 miles. In 1832, the distance travelled in following a pair of mules spinning cotton-yarn on the same numbers, was 20 miles, and frequently more. But the amount of labour performed by those following the mules, is not confined merely to the distance walked. There is far more to be done. In 1835,[a] the spinner put up daily on each of these mules 820 stretches; making a total of 1,640 stretches in the course of the day. In 1832, the spinner put upon each mule 2,200 stretches, making a total of 4,400. In 1844, according to a return furnished by a practised operative spinner, the person working puts up in the same period 2,400 stretches on each mule, making a total of 4,800 stretches in the [V-203] course of the day; and in some cases, the amount of labour required is even greater"* (pp. 6, 7).

* "I have a document here, signed by 22 operative spinners of Manchester, in which they state that 20 miles is the very least distance travelled, and they believe it to be still greater. I have another document sent to me in *1842*, stating that the labour is *progressively increasing*—increasing not only because the distance to be travelled is greater, but because the quantity of goods produced is multiplied, while the hands are, in proportion, fewer than before; and, moreover, because an inferior species of cotton is now often spun, which it is more difficult to work"* (l.c., pp. 8, 9).

* "In the carding room there has been also *a great increase of labour*—one person there does the work formerly divided between two. In the weaving room where a vast number of persons are employed, and principally females ... the labour has increased, within the last few years, fully 10 per cent, owing to the increased speed of the machinery. In 1838, the number of hanks spun per week was 18,000; in 1843 it amounted to 21,000. In 1819, the number of picks in power loom weaving per minute was 60—in 1842 it was 140, showing a vast increase of labour, because more nicety and attention are required to the work in hand"* (p. 9).

// As long as machinery enables a manufacturer to sell the commodity for more than its *individual* value, the following passage applies, showing that even in this case the surplus value derives from a curtailment of necessary labour time, is itself a form of relative surplus value:

* "A man's profit does not depend upon his command of the *produce* of other men's labour, but upon his command of *labour itself*. If he can sell"* (by raising the

[a] This should be 1815 or 1825. See the corresponding passage in Volume I of *Capital.—Ed.*

MONEY PRICES of the commodities) * "his goods at a higher price, while his workmen's wages remain unaltered, he is clearly benefited by the rise, whether other goods rise, or not. A smaller proportion of what he produces is sufficient to put that labour into motion, and a larger proportion consequently remains for himself" * (*Outlines of Political Economy* (by a Malthusian), etc., London, 1832, pp. 49-50).[222] //

The FACTORY REPORTS show that in those branches of industry which were covered (until April 1860) by the FACTORY ACT, and in which therefore the working week had been reduced by law to 60 hours, wages did not fall (comparing 1859 with 1839) but RATHER rose, whereas they positively fell during this period in factories where

"THE LABOUR OF CHILDREN, YOUNG PERSONS AND WOMEN" was still "UNRESTRICTED".

The reference here is to

"PRINTING, BLEACHING and DYEING WORKS, in which until 1860 THE HOURS OF WORK REMAIN NOW THE SAME AS THEY WERE 20 YEARS SINCE, IN WHICH THE PROTECTED CLASSES UNDER THE FACTORY ACTS ARE AT TIMES EMPLOYED 14 AND 15 HOURS PER DAY." [a]

[V-204] The following list shows in general that, with the progress of industry in the last 20 years, wages have fallen considerably in a number of branches of industry.

* *Calico printing, dyeing and bleaching, 60 hours per week.*

Fustian dyeing, 61 hours per week.

	1839	1859		1839	1859
Colour mixer	35s.	32	Dressers	18	22
Machine printer	40	38	Bleachers	21	18
Foreman	40	40	Dyers	21	16
Block Cutter	35	25	Finishers	21	22
Block printer	40	28			
Dyer	18	16			
Washer and Labourer	16 and 15	ditto			

(*Factory Reports*. For Half Year ending 30 April 1860, p. 32).* [V-204]

[V-203] In the first kind of factory, production increased more, relatively speaking, than previously, and at the same time the profits of the manufacturers increased, as is demonstrated by the rapid spread of the factories.

---

[a] *Reports of the Inspectors of Factories for the Half Year Ending 30th April 1860*, pp. 31-32.— Ed.

* "The great improvements that have been made in machinery, of all kinds, have vastly improved their productive powers, improvements to which a stimulus was doubtless given, especially as regards *the greater speed of the machines* in a given time, by the restrictions of the hours of work. These improvements, and the *closer application* which the operatives are enabled to give, have had the effect ... of as much work being turned off in the shortened time as used to be in the longer hours" * (*Factory Reports for the Half Year Ending October 31, 1858*, [p.] 10. Cf. *Reports for the Half Year Ending 30th April 1860*, p. 30 sqq.).

[V-204] The phenomenon that the Ten Hours' Bill has not cut down the profits of the English manufacturers, in spite of the shortening of the working day, is explained by two reasons:

1) The English hour of labour stands above the Continental one, it is related to it as more complex labour to simple labour. (Hence the relation of the English to the foreign manufacturer is the same as the relation of a manufacturer who has introduced new machinery to his competitor.)

* "All things being equal, the English manufacturer can turn out a considerably larger amount of work in a given time than a Foreign manufacturer, so much as to counterbalance the difference of the working days, between 60 hours a week here and 72 or 80 elsewhere; and the means of transport in England enable the manufacturer to deliver his goods upon a railway, almost at his factory, whence they may be almost directly shipped for exportation" * (*Reports of Inspectors of Factories. 31 October 1855*, London, 1856, [p.] 65).

2) What is lost through the reduction of absolute labour time is gained in condensation of labour time, so that in fact 1 hour of labour is now equal to $^6/_5$ or more hours of labour. Just as the absolute extension of the working day beyond certain limits (beyond the natural day) is defeated by natural obstacles, so does the condensed working day have its limits. It is questionable whether the amount of labour which is now provided in the factories under the Ten Hours' Law would be possible at all for 12 hours at e.g. an equal level of intensity.

* "In fact one class of manufacturers, the spinners of woollen yarn,"

(since they do not wish to employ TWO SETS OF HALF-TIMERS, children under 13 years who work for 6 hours)

* "now rarely employ children under 13 years of age, i.e. half-timers. They have introduced improved and new machinery of various kinds, which altogether supersedes the necessity of the employment of children, for instance, as an illustration, by the addition of an apparatus, called a *piecing machine*, to existing machines, the work of 6 or 4 half-timers, according to the peculiarity of each machine, can be performed by one young person ... the half-time system had some share in stimulating the invention of the piecing machine" * (*Factory Reports for the Half Year Ending 31 October 1858*, London, 1858, pp. 42-43).

In any case this effect of the shortening of absolute labour time shows us how the manufacturers look for means of curtailing necessary labour time in order to prolong relative surplus labour time. It also shows us how machinery not only enables one individual to perform the labour of many, but increases the amount of labour required of that individual, thus giving the hour of labour a higher value, and thereby lessening the proportion of his time the worker himself needs for the reproduction of his wage.

[V-205] As we have said,[a] this occurs as a result of the increase both in the machine's rapidity of action and in the amount of working machinery the individual worker has to supervise. This result is attained partly through changes in the construction of the machine which supplies the motive power, changes enabling a machine of the same weight to set in motion, and in more rapid motion, with a relative, and often an absolute reduction in cost, a greater quantity of machinery than before.

* "The facts thus brought out by the Return appear to be that the Factory system is increasing rapidly; that *although the same number of hands are employed in proportion to the horsepower as at former periods there are fewer hands employed in proportion to the machinery*; that the steam engine is enabled to drive an increased weight of machinery by economy of force, and other methods, and that an increased quantity of work can be turned off by improvements in machinery, and in methods of manufacture, by increased speed of the machinery, and by a variety of other causes" * (*Factory Reports for the Half Year Ending 31st October 1856*, p. 20).

"In the * Report for October 1852, Mr. Horner quotes ... a letter from Mr. Jas. Nasmyth, the eminent civil engineer, of Paticroft, near Manchester, explaining the nature of recent improvements in the steam engine, whereby the same engine is made to perform more work with a diminished consumption of fuel.... 'It would not be very easy to get an exact return as to the increase of performance or work done by the identical engines to which some or all of these improvements have been applied; I am confident, however, that could we obtain an exact return, the result would show, that from the same weight of steam-engine machinery, we are now at least obtaining *50* per cent more duty or work performed on the average, and that ... in many cases, the identical steam engines which, in the days of the restricted speed of *220* feet per minute, yielded 50 horsepower, are now yielding upwards of 100.'"

* "The return of 1838," * says Horner * (*Reports, 31st October 1856*), "gave the number of steam engines and of water wheels, with the amount of horsepower employed. At that time the figures represented a much more accurate estimate of the actual power employed than do the figures in the returns either of *1850* or *1856*. The figures given in the Returns are all of the *nominal* power of the engines and wheels, not of the power actually employed or capable of being employed. The modern steam engine of 100 horsepowers is capable of being driven at a much greater force than formerly, arising from the improvements in its construction, the capacity and construction of the boilers, etc., and thus the nominal power of a modern manufacturing steam engine cannot be considered more than an index from which its real capabilities are to be calculated" * (l.c., pp. 13-14).

---

a See this volume, pp. 335-36.— *Ed*.

Fourthly: Replacement of simple cooperation by machinery.

Just as machinery removes or revolutionises cooperation in its developed form of division of labour, so also in many cases does it do away with or revolutionise simple cooperation. For example, if operations such as mowing corn, sowing seed, etc., require the simultaneous employment of many hands, they can be replaced by mowing or sowing machines. The same with the production of wine, when the wine-press replaces treading by foot. This is equally true of the application of steam engines to raise building materials to the top of a building or to the height at which they [V-206] are required.

"The TURNOUT of the Lancashire WORKMEN IN THE BUILDING TRADE (1833) HAS INTRODUCED A CURIOUS APPLICATION OF THE STEAM-ENGINE. This machine is now employed in some towns, instead of MANUAL LABOUR, IN HOISTING THE VARIOUS BUILDING MATERIALS TO THE TOP OF THE EDIFICES WHERE THEY ARE INTENDED TO BE USED" ([E. C. Tufnell,] *Character, Object and Effects of Trades' Unions etc.*, London, 1834, [p.] 109).

Fifthly: Invention and employment of machinery against STRIKES, *etc., and against wage demands.*

STRIKES usually originate from attempts either to prevent a cut in wages or enforce an increase in wages, or to settle the limits of the normal working day. What is at stake in a strike is always the limitation of the positive or relative amount of surplus labour time or the appropriation of part of it by the worker himself. The capitalist counters this with the introduction of machinery. Here the machine appears directly as a means of curtailing necessary labour time; it also appears as a form of capital—an instrument of capital—a power of capital—*over* labour—for the suppression of any claim by labour to autonomy. Here machinery *comes into play as a form of capital inimical to labour in intention* as well. SELFACTORS, WOOL-COMBING MACHINES in the spinning industry, the so-called "CONDENSER" which replaces the hand-turned "SLUBBING MACHINE" (in the woollen industry as well), etc., are all machines invented in order to defeat STRIKES.

[V-207] Likewise

the self-acting apparatus for executing the dyeing and rinsing operations was invented "under the high pressure of the same despotic confederacies" (namely the workers' associations)

(what is being referred to here is the printing of calico, where from 4 to 6 colours can now be printed at once with the application of steam-driven engraved cylinders). Ure comments further, with reference to the invention of a new machine in the weaving industry:

"The combined malcontents, who fancied themselves impregnably intrenched behind the old lines of division of labour, found their flanks turned and their defences rendered useless by the new mechanical tactics, and were obliged to surrender at discretion" (l.c., p. 142). [V-207]

[V-206] The result of these new machines is either to make the previous kind of work completely superfluous (as the SELFACTOR makes the spinner superfluous) or to lessen the number of workers required and make the new kind of work simpler in comparison with the previous kind (as the work of the COMBER with COMBING MACHINES).

"The most frequent cause of STRIKES in the COTTON TRADE has been the introduction of improved machinery, and especially the ENLARGEMENT OF MULES, by means of which the number of SPINDLES A SPINNER IS CAPABLE OF SUPERINTENDING HAS BEEN CONTINUALLY INCREASING.... A MASTER, ON THE INTRODUCTION of such improved machinery into his establishment stipulates with his spinners to pay them LESS PER PIECE, but still at such a rate that, OWING TO THE GREATER POWER OF THE MACHINE, their weekly EARNINGS shall rise rather than fall.... But such a BARGAIN is INJURIOUS TO THE MASTERS AND MEN IN THE MANUFACTORIES WHERE THE IMPROVED MACHINE IS NOT INTRODUCED" ([E. C. Tufnell,] *Character, Object and Effects of Trades' Unions etc.*, London, 1834, [pp.] 17-18).

"1829 A SERIOUS TURNOUT. A LITTLE BEFORE THIS TIME, SEVERAL MASTERS HAD ERECTED MULES, CARRYING FROM 4-500 SPINDLES, WHICH ENABLED THE SPINNERS WHO WORKED AT THEM TO RECEIVE A LESS SUM IN THE PROPORTION OF 3 to 4 FOR A GIVEN QUANTITY OF WORK, AND at the same time TO EARN *AT LEAST* AN EQUAL AMOUNT OF WAGES WITH THOSE WHO WERE EMPLOYED ON THE OLD MACHINERY. 21 MILLS AND 10,000 PERSONS WERE THROWN IDLE FOR 6 MONTHS by this STRIKE" (l.c., p. 19).

"The STRIKE of 1833 at Messrs. Hindes and Derham (WEST RIDING OF YORKSHIRE) was the cause of the INVENTION OF A WOOL-COMBING MACHINE, WHICH WHOLLY SUPERSEDED THE LABOUR OF THAT CLASS OF MEN, WHO WERE THE CHIEF RINGLEADERS IN THIS AFFAIR; AND WHICH HAS STRUCK A BLOW AT THEIR COMBINATION, THAT IT CAN NEVER RECOVER" (pp. 61-62).

[V-207] Similarly "THE *INTRODUCTION OF STEAM* AS AN *ANTAGONIST TO* HU-MAN POWER" (P. Gaskell (Surgeon), *Artisans and Machinery etc.*, London, 1836, p. 23).

"THE SURPLUS HANDS would readily enable the MANUFACTURERS TO LESSEN THE RATE OF WAGES; BUT THE CERTAINTY THAT ANY CONSIDERABLE REDUCTION WOULD BE FOLLOWED BY IMMEDIATE IMMENSE LOSSES FROM TURNOUTS, EXTENDED STOPPAGES, AND VARIOUS OTHER IMPEDIMENTS WHICH WOULD BE THROWN IN THEIR WAY, MAKES THEM PREFER THE SLOWER PROCESS OF MECHANICAL IMPROVEMENT, BY WHICH, THOUGH THEY MAY TRIPLE PRODUCTION, THEY REQUIRE NO NEW MEN" (l.c., p. 314).

* "The factory operatives should keep in wholesome remembrance the fact that theirs is really a low species of skilled labour; and that there is none which is more easily acquired or of its quality more amply remunerated, or which, by a short training of the least expert can be more quickly as well as abundantly supplied." "The master's machinery really plays a far more important part in the business of production than the labour and skill of the operative, which 6 months' education can teach, and a common labourer can learn" * (*The Master Spinners and Manufacturers' Defence Fund. Report of the Committee Appointed for the Receipt and Apportionment of This Fund, to the Central Association of Master Spinners and Manufacturers*, Manchester, 1854, pp. 17, 19).

Ure says with regard to the "Iron Man" (SELF-ACTING MULE [223]):

"When capital enlists science in her service, the refractory hand of labour will always be taught docility" (p. 140).

"The necessity of enlarging the spinning-frames, created by the decrees of the workers' associations, has recently given an extraordinary stimulus to mechanical science.... In *doubling the size of his mule,* the owner is enabled to get rid of indifferent or restive workers, and to become once more the master of his mill, which is no small advantage" (Ure, Vol. II, p. 134).

This expedient tends

"to raise, or uphold at least, the *wages of each spinner,* but to diminish the *numbers of workers necessary* for the same quantity of work, so that those employed would prosper, but the combined body of workers would thereby be impoverished" (l.c., [pp.] 133, 134).

"The Iron Man ... a creation destined to *restore order* among the industrous classes" (p. 138).[a]

"The first MANUFACTURERS, WHO HAD TO TRUST ENTIRELY TO HAND LABOUR, WERE SUBJECTED PERIODICALLY TO SEVERE IMMEDIATE LOSSES through the REFRACTORY SPIRIT OF THEIR HANDS, WHO TIMED THEIR OPPORTUNITY, WHEN THE MARKETS WERE PARTICULARLY PRESSING, TO URGE THEIR CLAIMS.... A CRISIS WAS RAPIDLY APPROACHING, which WOULD HAVE CHECKED THE PROGRESS OF MANUFACTURES, WHEN STEAM AND ITS APPLICATION TO MACHINERY AT ONCE TURNED THE CURRENT AGAINST THE MEN" (Gaskell, l.c., [pp.] 34, 35).

[V-208] *Sixthly. Presumption of the workers in wishing to appropriate part of the productivity of their labour brought about by machinery.*

"TRADES UNIONS IN THEIR DESIRE TO MAINTAIN WAGES *ENDEAVOUR TO SHARE IN THE PROFITS OF IMPROVED MACHINERY....* They demand higher wages because LABOUR IS ABBREVIATED ... in other words: they endeavour TO ESTABLISH A *DUTY ON MANUFACTURING IMPROVEMENTS*" (*On Combinations of Trades,* New Edit., London, 1834, p. 42).

"The principle of adjusting WAGES TO THE SUPPOSED PROFITS OF THE EMPLOYER, which is involved in claiming higher remuneration from improved machinery, is wholly INADMISSIBLE. The application of this principle is not, however, confined to one description of profit. The dyers, on August 7th 1824, TURNED OUT ... setting forth in a placard that their masters had obtained AN INCREASE OF PRICE FOR DYEING, MORE THAN ADEQUATE TO THE ADVANCE THEY CLAIM.... WAGES thus change their character completely, and either absorb or become an *ad valorem* tax upon profits" (l.c., pp. 43, 44).

Seventhly. More CONTINUITY OF LABOUR. *Utilisation of waste etc. More work can be done at a* FINISHING *stage if more raw materials are provided with the help of machinery.*

Continuity of labour generally increases with the employment of machinery (of fixed capital altogether).

The machine has the further effect that it provides a more plentiful supply of the material of labour for the branches of

---

[a] Marx quotes Ure in French.— *Ed.*

industry for which its product serves as raw material. For example in the 18th century the HANDLOOM WEAVERS always suffered from the IMPOSSIBILITY OF SUPPLYING THEMSELVES with MATERIALS (yarn) FOR THEIR LABOUR. CONSIDERABLE VACATIONS were FREQUENTLY OCCURRING IN THIS RESPECT, and at these periods they found themselves suffering "PRIVATIONS".

"What was now gained from the improvement in the spinning machine had arisen not so much from any INCREASE IN THE RATE OF PAYMENT FOR LABOUR, as from A MARKET GENERALLY UNDERSTOCKED, AND A CONSTANTLY INCREASING PRODUCTION OF YARN, WHICH ENABLED THEM TO WORK FULL HOURS" (Gaskell, l.c., p. 27).

This is one of the main results of machinery,

"this possibility of continuously WORKING FULL HOURS IN THE SAME DEPARTMENT".

This would be the possibility of WORKING FULL HOURS for the small man who works on his own account. For the capitalist it is the possibility of having other people work FULL HOURS.

What the spinning machine does for weaving, by providing the yarn, was done for the spinner by the invention of the COTTON GIN in 1793, by Eli Whitney, of Connecticut. This machine provides the cotton. The plantation owner had enough black slaves to sow a large amount of COTTON, but not enough to separate the fibres from the seed. This therefore considerably reduced the amount of raw production, and increased what it cost to produce e.g. a pound of cotton.

*"It was an average day's work to separate a pound of cotton fibre perfectly from the seed.... Whitney's invention enabled the owner of his gin to separate the seed completely from [100] pounds of fibres per day per hand, [and] the efficiency of the gin [has] since increased." *[224]

[V-209] The same thing in *India*.

*"The next evil in India is one which one would scarcely expect to find in a country which exports more labour than any other in the world, with the exception perhaps of China and England — *the impossibility of procuring a sufficient number of hands to clean the cotton*. The consequence of this is that large quantities of the crop are left unpicked, while another portion is gathered from the ground, where it has fallen, and of course discoloured and partially rotten, so *that for want of labour at the proper season*, the cultivator is actually forced to submit to the loss of a large part of that crop, for which England is so anxiously looking"* (*Bengal Hurkaru.* Bi-Monthly Overland Summary of News, 22nd July 1861).
*"A common *churka* worked by a man and woman turned out 28 lbs daily. Dr. Forbes' churka worked by 2 men and a boy turns out 250 lbs daily"* (*Bombay Chamber of Commerce Report for 1859-60*, p. 171). *"16 of these (last named machines), driven by bullocks, would clean a ton of cotton per day, which was equal to the ordinary day's work of 750 people"* (*Paper Read before the Society of Arts, on the 17th April 1861*).

Machinery can work with materials which are too inferior to be worked by hand.

* "The demand for cheap goods" * (woollen in the West Riding of Yorkshire) * "has given an immense impulse to this kind of manufacture, the economy of which consists not so much in improved machinery and labour-saving processes, as in the employment of an inferior staple and woollen rags, brought again, by powerful machinery, to the original condition of wool, and then either spun into yarn for inferior cloths, or mixed with new wool, spun into yarn for better kinds of cloths. This manufacture prevails nowhere to so great an extent as in England, although it is considerable in Belgium" * (*Reports of Inspectors of Factories for 31st October 1855*, London, 1856, [p.] 64).

* "There is frequently a great saving of materials, as in the change from making boards with the adze, to that of making them with the saw; and again the labour of natural agents is so much cheaper, that many articles which would otherwise have been worthless, are now deserving of attention, as they may now be profitably endowed with some form of value" * (F. Wayland, *The Elements of Political Economy*, Boston, 1843, '[pp.] 72-73).

In production on a large scale, moreover, the waste products are so considerable that they themselves can in turn more readily become simple articles of commerce, whether for agriculture or for other branches of industry.

[V-210] *Eighthly. Replacement of labour.*

"Perfection of the crafts means nothing other than the discovery of new ways of making a product *with fewer people*, or (which is the same thing) in *less time than previously*" (Galiani, *Della Moneta*, Custodi, *Parte Moderna*, p. 158 [159]).[a]

This is true as much for simple cooperation or the division of labour as it is for machinery—*fewer people* and *less time* for the manufacture of a product are identical. If someone can do in 1 hour what he previously did in 2, one person can do in one working day what previously was done by two; and what therefore previously required two simultaneous working days. Therefore every means of reducing the necessary labour time of an individual worker implies at the same time a reduction in the number of workers required to bring about the same effect. If we look now at the employment of machinery, is there only a difference of degree in this reduction, or is there some specific additional feature?

Sir James Steuart says in his *Principles of Political Economy*, Book I, Ch. XIX:

"Machines therefore I consider as a method of augmenting (*virtually*) the number of the industrious, without the expense of feeding an additional number" [p. 123].

---

a Marx quotes in Italian.— *Ed.*

Indeed, in the same passage he asks:

"Wherein does the effect of a machine differ from that of new inhabitants?" (l. c.).[a]

_____

//Price *of the* commodity and wages.[225] We [shall] SPEAK [in] ANOTHER PLACE of Proudhon's nonsense. BUT WHAT HE IS REPLIED TO BY MR. *Eugène Forcade,* ONE OF THE BEST ECONOMICAL CRITICS IN FRANCE, IS AS FALSE AND RIDICULOUS AS Proudhon's ASSERTIONS. Forcade SAYS:

"If Proudhon's objection ... that 'the worker cannot buy back his own product'" (on account of the interest which is added to it)[b] "were correct, not only would it apply to the profits of capital; it would *eliminate the very possibility of industry.* If the worker is compelled to pay 100 for something for which he has only received 80, *if his wages can buy back only the value he has put into a product,* this amounts to saying that the worker cannot buy back anything"

// hence even if he gets back the WHOLE VALUE he has put into the product, THAT IS TO SAY, IF THERE EXISTS NO PROFIT AND NO OTHER FORM OF SURPLUS VALUE EXPRESSING SURPLUS LABOUR; and holding such notions Forcade claims TO UNDERSTAND ANYTHING WHATEVER OF POLITICAL ECONOMY! Proudhon's nonsense consists in his belief that the worker must buy back with the money he receives (as wages) a higher value in commodities than is contained in the money, or in other words that the commodity is sold *above* its value because profit, etc., is realised in the sale. But now here comes Forcade, declaring that industry becomes *impossible* as soon as the wage is only able to buy back in a product the value that the worker has put into it. The reverse is true. Capitalist industry becomes impossible if the wage is sufficient to buy back in a product the whole of the value the worker has put into it. In that case, there would neither be surplus value, nor profit, nor interest, nor rent, nor capital. IN *FACT*: Forcade's comment has a bearing not only on the "worker" but on the producer in general //,

"that wages cannot pay for anything".

(Thus we have IN FACT the general proposition: if the *producer* can only buy back in a product the value he has put into it, the producer cannot pay for anything. Because the commodity contains constant capital apart from the labour added.)

"In fact *the cost price* always contains something more than the wage"

_____

a Marx quotes in French.— *Ed.*
b P. J. Proudhon, *Qu'est-ce que la propriété?,* p. 201, and *Gratuité du crédit. Discussion entre M. Fr. Bastiat et M. Proudhon,* pp. 207-08.— *Ed.*

(This is already a very crude way of putting it. He means to say that there is always something more than the last piece of labour added to, and realised in, the commodity.)

"e.g. the *price of the raw material, often paid out abroad....*"

(And even if it were not paid out abroad the situation would not be changed in the least. Forcade's objection, which [V-211] is based on a crude misconception, remains the same. The point is this: the amount of the total product which forms the payment of wages CONTAINS NO PARTICLE OF VALUE DUE TO THE VALUE OF THE RAW MATERIAL, etc., ALTHOUGH EVERY SINGLE COMMODITY, CONSIDERED FOR ITSELF, IS COMPOSED OF THE VALUE DUE TO THE LAST LABOUR ADDED AND TO THE VALUE OF THE RAW MATERIALS, etc., INDEPENDENT OF THAT LABOUR. The same applies to the whole of that part of the PRODUCE which constitutes the SURPLUS VALUE. (Profit, etc.) AS TO THE VALUE OF THE CONSTANT CAPITAL, IT IS REPLACED EITHER BY ITSELF, *in natura*, OR BY EXCHANGE WITH OTHER FORMS OF CONSTANT CAPITAL.)

"Proudhon has forgotten the continual growth of the national capital; he has forgotten that this growth takes effect for all workers, both the entrepreneurs and the labourers" (*Revue des Deux Mondes*, Vol. 24, Paris, 1848, *Eugène Forcade*, [pp.] 998, 999).

And with this meaningless phrase Forcade endeavours to evade solving the problem; and yet he is indisputably one of the "most critical" political economists! [a]

Here we want to bring together immediately the whole of Proudhon's rubbish.[226] //

---

[a] The passage on Forcade and Proudhon was written by Marx in a mixture of German, French and English.— *Ed.*

348

[VI-220] 5) THEORIES OF SURPLUS VALUE[228]

All economists share the error of examining surplus value not as such, in its pure form, but in the particular forms of profit and rent. What theoretical errors must necessarily arise from this will be shown more fully in Chapter III, in the analysis of the greatly changed form which surplus value assumes as profit.[229]

a) [*SIR JAMES STEUART*]

Before the Physiocrats, surplus value—that is, profit, in the form of profit—was explained purely from *exchange*, the sale of the commodity above its value. Sir James Steuart on the whole did not get beyond this restricted view; he must rather be regarded as the man who reproduced it in scientific form. I say "in scientific form". For Steuart does not share the illusion that the surplus value which accrues to the individual capitalist from selling the commodity above its value is a creation of new wealth. He distinguishes therefore between *positive* profit and *relative* profit.

* "*Positive profit,* implies no loss to anybody; it results from an *augmentation* of labour, industry, or ingenuity, and has the effect of swelling or augmenting the *public good....* Relative profit, is what implies a loss to somebody; it marks a vibration of the balance of wealth between parties, but implies *no addition to the general stock....* The *compound* is easily understood; it is that species of profit ... which is partly *relative*, and partly *positive* ... both kinds may subsist inseparably in the same transaction" * (*Principles of Political Oeconomy,* Vol. I, *The Works of Sir James Steuart etc.,* ed. by General Sir James Steuart, his son, etc., in 6 vols, London, 1805,[8] pp. 275-76).

Positive profit arises from "*augmentation* of labour, industry and ingenuity". *How* it arises from this Steuart makes no attempt to explain. The further statement that the effect of this profit is to

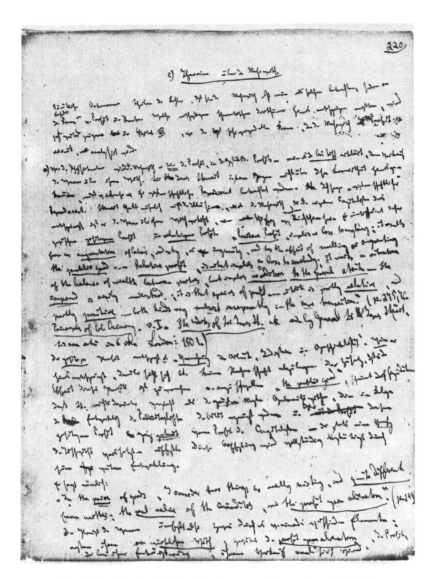

Page 220 of Notebook VI of the Economic Manuscript of 1861-63

augment and swell "*THE PUBLIC GOOD*" seems to indicate that Steuart means by it nothing but the greater mass of use values produced in consequence of the development of the productive powers of labour, and that he thinks of this positive profit as quite distinct from the capitalist's profit—which always presupposes an increase of exchange value. This interpretation is fully confirmed by his further exposition.

He says to wit:

* "In the *price* of goods, I consider two things as really existing, and *quite different from* one another; the *real value* of the commodity, and *the profit upon alienation*" * (p. 244).

The price of goods therefore comprises two elements that are completely different from each other: firstly their *real value*, secondly, the PROFIT UPON ALIENATION, the profit realised through their transfer to another person, their sale.

[VI-221] This PROFIT UPON ALIENATION therefore arises from the price of the goods being greater than their real value, or from the goods being sold *above* their value. Gain on the one side therefore always involves loss on the other. No ADDITION TO THE GENERAL STOCK is created. Profit, i.e., surplus value, is relative and resolves itself INTO "A VIBRATION OF THE BALANCE OF WEALTH BETWEEN PARTIES". Steuart himself rejects the idea that surplus value can be explained in this way. His theory of "VIBRATION OF THE BALANCE OF WEALTH BETWEEN PARTIES", however little it touches the nature and origin of surplus value itself, remains important in considering the distribution of surplus value among different classes and among different categories such as profit, interest and rent.

That Steuart limits all profit of the individual capitalist to this "RELATIVE PROFIT", PROFIT UPON ALIENATION, is shown by the following:

The "REAL VALUE", he says, is determined by the "QUANTITY" of labour, which "UPON AN AVERAGE A WORKMAN OF THE COUNTRY IN GENERAL MAY PERFORM ... IN A DAY, A WEEK, A MONTH etc.". Secondly: "THE VALUE OF THE WORKMAN'S SUBSISTENCE AND NECESSARY EXPENSE, BOTH FOR SUPPLYING HIS PERSONAL WANTS, AND ... THE INSTRUMENTS BELONGING TO HIS PROFESSION, WHICH MUST BE TAKEN UPON AN AVERAGE AS ABOVE." Thirdly: "THE VALUE OF THE MATERIALS" (pp. 244-45). "THESE THREE ARTICLES BEING KNOWN, THE PRICE OF MANUFACTURE IS DETERMINED. IT CANNOT BE LOWER THAN THE AMOUNT OF ALL THE THREE, THAT IS, THAN THE *REAL VALUE*; *WHATEVER IS HIGHER, IS THE MANUFACTURER'S PROFIT*. THIS WILL BE IN PROPORTION TO *DEMAND*, AND THEREFORE WILL FLUCTUATE ACCORDING TO CIRCUMSTANCES" (l. c., p. 245). "HENCE APPEARS THE NECESSITY OF A GREAT DEMAND, IN ORDER TO PROMOTE FLOURISHING MANUFACTURES ... THE INDUSTRIOUS REGULATE THEIR LIVING AND EXPENSE ACCORDING TO THEIR CERTAIN PROFIT" (l. c., [p.] 246).[230]

From this it is clear that: The profit of the "MANUFACTURER", of the individual capitalist, is always RELATIVE PROFIT, always PROFIT UPON

ALIENATION, always derived from the excess of the price of the commodity over its real value, from its sale above its value. If therefore all commodities were sold at their *value*, no profit would exist.

Steuart wrote a special chapter on this; he examines in detail: "HOW PROFITS CONSOLIDATE INTO PRIME COST" (l.c., Vol. III, p. 11 sq.).

Steuart on the one hand rejects the conception of the Monetary and Mercantile systems, according to which the sale of commodities above their value, and the profit resulting therefrom, creates surplus value, a positive increase of wealth.* On the other hand he holds to their view that the profit of the individual capital is nothing but this excess of the price over the [VI-222] value, the PROFIT UPON ALIENATION. This however according to him is only *relative*, the gain on the one side being compensated by the loss on the other, and consequently this movement is nothing more than "A VIBRATION OF THE BALANCE OF WEALTH BETWEEN PARTIES".

In this respect Steuart is therefore the rational expression of the Monetary and Mercantile systems.

His service to the theory of capital is that he shows how the process of separation takes place between the conditions of production, as the property of a definite class, and labour capacity. He gives a great deal of attention to this *genesis* of capital—without as yet seeing it directly as the genesis of capital, although he sees it as a condition for large-scale industry. He examines the process particularly in agriculture; and he rightly considers that manufacturing industry proper only came into being through this process of separation in agriculture. In Adam Smith's writings this process of separation is assumed to be already completed.

(Steuart's book [appeared in] *1767* (London),[8] *Turgot's* [was written in] *1766*,[34] Adam Smith's [in] *1775*.)[231]

b) THE PHYSIOCRATS

The analysis of *capital*, within the bourgeois horizon, is essentially the work of the Physiocrats. It is this service that makes them the true fathers of modern political economy. In the first place, the analysis of the various *objective components* in which

* Even the Monetary system, however, thinks of this profit as arising not within a country, but only in exchange with other countries. In this it remains stuck in the Mercantile system [which assumed] that this value takes the form of money (gold and silver) and the surplus value is therefore expressed in the balance of trade, which is settled with money.

capital exists and into which it resolves itself in the course of the labour process. It is not a reproach to the Physiocrats that, like all their successors, they thought of these objective forms of existence—such as tools, raw materials, etc.—as capital, in isolation from the social conditions in which they appear in capitalist production; in a word, in the form in which they are elements of the labour process in general, independently of its social form—and thereby made of the capitalist form of production an eternal, natural form of production. For them the bourgeois forms of production necessarily appeared as natural forms. It was their great merit that they conceived these forms as physiological forms of society: as forms arising from the natural necessity of production itself, forms that are independent of anyone's will or of politics, etc. They are material laws, the error is only that the material law of a definite historical social stage is conceived as an abstract law governing equally all forms of society.

In addition to this analysis of the objective elements of which capital consists within the labour process, the Physiocrats established the forms which capital assumes in circulation (fixed capital, circulating capital, even though as yet they give them other names), and in general the connection between the process of circulation and the reproduction process of capital. We shall come back to this in the chapter on circulation.[232]

In these two principal points Adam Smith inherited the legacy of the Physiocrats. His service—in this connection—is limited to fixing the abstract categories, to the greater consistency of the baptismal names which he gave to the distinctions made by the Physiocrats in their analysis.

[VI-223] As we have seen,[a] the basis for the development of capitalist production is, *in general*, that *labour capacity*, as the *commodity* belonging to the workers, confronts the conditions of labour as commodities maintained in the form of capital and existing independently of the workers. The determination of the *value* of labour capacity, as a commodity, is of vital importance. This value is equal to the labour time required to produce the means of subsistence necessary for the reproduction of labour capacity, or to the price of the means of subsistence necessary for the existence of the worker as a worker. It is only on this basis that the difference arises between the *value* of labour capacity and the *valorisation* of labour capacity—a difference which exists with no other commodity, since there is no other commodity

---

a See this volume, pp. 111-17.— *Ed.*

whose use value, and therefore also the use of it, can increase its *exchange value* or the exchange values resulting from it.

Therefore the foundation of modern political economy, whose business is the analysis of capitalist production, is the conception of the *value of labour capacity* as something fixed, as a given magnitude—as indeed it is in practice in each particular case. The *minimum of wages* therefore correctly forms the pivotal point of Physiocratic theory. They were able to establish this although they had not yet recognised the nature of value itself, because this *value of labour capacity* is manifested in the price of the necessary means of subsistence, hence in a sum of definite use values. Consequently, without being in any way clear as to the nature of value, they could conceive the value of labour capacity, so far as it was necessary to their inquiry, as a definite magnitude. If moreover they made the mistake of conceiving this *minimum* as an unchangeable magnitude—which in their view is determined entirely by nature and not by the stage of historical development, which is itself a magnitude subject to fluctuations—this in no way affects the abstract correctness of their conclusions, since the difference between the value of labour capacity and its valorisation does not at all depend on whether the value is assumed to be great or small.

The Physiocrats transferred the inquiry into the origin of surplus value from the sphere of circulation into the sphere of direct production, and thereby laid the foundation for the analysis of capitalist production.

Quite correctly they lay down the fundamental principle that only that labour is *productive* which creates a *surplus value,* in whose product therefore a higher value is contained than the sum of the values consumed during the production of this product. Since the value of raw and other materials is given, while the value of the labour capacity is equal to the minimum of wages, this surplus value can clearly only consist in the excess of labour which the labourer returns to the capitalist over and above the quantity of labour that he receives in his wage. But it does not appear in this form with the Physiocrats, because they have not yet reduced [a] value in general to its *simple substance*—the quantity of labour or labour time.

[VI-224] Their method of exposition is, of course, necessarily governed by their general view of the nature of value, which to

---

[a] In the manuscript, the word "reducirt" (reduced) was substituted, presumably by Engels, for "realisirt" (realised).— *Ed.*

them is not a definite social mode of existence of human activity (labour), but consists of material things—land, nature, and the various modifications of these material things.

The difference between the *value* of labour capacity and its *valorisation*—that is, the surplus value which the purchase of labour capacity secures for the user of labour capacity—appears most palpably, most incontrovertibly, of all *branches of production*, in *agriculture*, the primary production. The sum total of the means of subsistence which the labourer consumes from one year to another, or the mass of material substance which he consumes, is smaller than the sum total of the means of subsistence which he produces. In manufacture the workman is not generally seen directly producing either his means of subsistence or the surplus additional to his means of subsistence. The process is mediated through purchase and sale, through the various acts of circulation, and the analysis of value in general is necessary for it to be understood. In agriculture it shows itself directly in the surplus of use values produced over use values consumed by the labourer, and can therefore be grasped without an analysis of value in general, without a clear understanding of the nature of value. Therefore also when value is reduced to use value, and the latter to material substance in general. Hence for the Physiocrats agricultural labour is the only *productive labour*, because it is the only labour that *creates a surplus value*, and *rent* is the *only form of surplus value* which they know. The workman in manufacture does not increase the material substance; he only alters its form. The material—the mass of material substance—is given to him by agriculture. It is true that he adds value to the substance, not through his labour, but through the production costs of his labour: through the total means of subsistence which he consumes during his labour, equivalent to the minimum of wages, which he receives from agriculture. Because agricultural labour is conceived as the only productive labour, the form of surplus value which distinguishes agricultural labour from industrial labour, *rent*, is conceived as the only form of surplus value.

Profit on capital in the true sense, of which rent itself is only an offshoot, therefore does not exist for the Physiocrats. Profit is seen by them as only a kind of higher wages paid by the landowners, which the capitalists consume as revenue (and which therefore enters into their production costs in the same way as the minimum wages of the ordinary workmen); this increases the value of the raw material, because it enters into the consumption costs which the capitalist, [the] industrialist, consumes while he is producing the product, transforming the raw material into a new product.

Surplus value in the form of *interest on money*—another branch of profit—is consequently declared by one section of the Physiocrats, such as Mirabeau the elder, to be usury and contrary to nature. Turgot on the other hand derives his justification of it from the fact that the money capitalist could buy land, that is, rent, and that therefore his money capital must create for him as much surplus value as he would receive if he converted it into landed property. This means therefore that interest on money too is not newly created value, not surplus value; it only explains why a part of the surplus value gained by the landowners finds its way to the money capitalists in the form of interest, just as it is explained on other grounds [VI-225] why a part of this surplus value finds its way to the industrial capitalist in the form of profit. Because *agricultural labour* is the only productive labour, the only labour that creates surplus value, the *form of surplus value* which distinguishes agricultural labour from all other branches of labour, *rent*, is the *general form of surplus value*. Industrial profit and interest on money are merely different categories into which rent is divided and, in certain portions, passes from the hands of the landowners into the hands of other classes. This is the direct opposite to the view held by later economists beginning with Adam Smith, because they rightly consider *industrial profit* to be the *form* in which surplus value is *originally* appropriated by capital, hence as the original general form of surplus value—they present interest and rent as mere offshoots of industrial profit, which is distributed by the industrial capitalists to various classes, who are co-owners of surplus value.

In addition to the reason already stated—that agricultural labour is the labour in which the creation of surplus value appears in material and tangible form, and apart from the process of circulation—there were a number of other considerations which explain the standpoint of the Physiocrats.

First, because in agriculture rent appears as a third element, as a form of surplus value which is not found in industry or merely has a transient existence. It was surplus value over and above surplus value (profit), and so the most palpable and most conspicuous form of surplus value, surplus value raised to the second power.

"By means of agriculture," as *Karl Arnd*, the home-bred economist, says in *Die naturgemässe Volkswirthschaft etc.* (Hanau, 1845, pp. 461-62), "a value is created—in the rent of land—which is not to be met with in industry and trade; a value which remains over when the wages and the rent of the capital employed have been completely replaced."

Secondly: leaving foreign trade out of account—as the Physiocrats rightly did and had to do in an abstract study of bourgeois society—it is clear that the number of workmen engaged in manufacture, etc., and completely detached from agriculture (the "free hands", as Steuart calls them [a] [156])—is determined by the mass of agricultural products which the farm labourers produce in excess of their own consumption.

* "It is obvious that the relative numbers of persons who can be maintained without agricultural labour, must be measured wholly by the productive powers of the cultivators" * (R. Jones, *On the Distribution of Wealth*, London, 1831, pp. 159-60).

As agricultural labour thus forms the natural basis (on this, see an earlier notebook [b]) not only for surplus labour in its own sphere, but also for the independent existence of all other branches of labour, and therefore also for the surplus value created in them, it is clear that it was bound to be considered the creator of surplus value, so long as the substance of value was regarded as definite, concrete labour, and not abstract labour with its measure, labour time.

[VI-226] *Thirdly.* All surplus value, not only relative but absolute, depends on a given productivity of labour. If the productivity of labour had reached only such a stage of development that a man's labour time no more than sufficed to keep him alive, to produce and reproduce his own means of subsistence, then there would be no surplus labour and no surplus value, and there would be no difference at all between the value of labour capacity and [the result of] its valorisation. The possibility of surplus labour and of surplus value therefore arises from a given productive power of labour, a productive power which enables labour capacity to create more than its own value, to produce more than the needs dictated by its life process. And indeed this productivity, this level of productivity which is presupposed as the starting-point, must first—as we saw in the *second* point above—make its appearance in agricultural labour. It appears therefore as *a gift of nature, a productive power of nature.* Here, in agriculture, from the very beginning there is generally

---

[a] J. Steuart, *An Inquiry into the Principles of Political Oeconomy: being an Essay on the Science of Domestic Policy in Free Nations...*, in three volumes, Vol. I, Dublin, 1770, p. 31.— *Ed.*

[b] See this volume, pp. 192-93.— *Ed.*

co-operation of the forces of nature—the increase of human labour power through the use and exploitation of the forces of nature—working automatically. This utilisation of the forces of nature on a large scale appears in manufacture only with the development of large-scale industry. A definite stage in the development of agriculture, whether in the country concerned or in other countries, forms the basis for the development of capital. Up to this point absolute surplus value coincides with relative. (*Buchanan*—a great adversary of the Physiocrats—makes this point even against Adam Smith, when he tries to show that agricultural development preceded the emergence of modern town industry.[a])

Fourthly. Since it is the great and specific contribution of the Physiocrats that they derive value and surplus value not from circulation but from production, they necessarily begin, in contrast to the Monetary and Mercantile systems, with that branch of production which can be thought of in complete separation from and independently of circulation, of exchange; and which presupposes exchange not between man and man but only between man and nature.

Hence the contradictions in the Physiocratic system.

It is in fact the first system which analyses capitalist production, and presents the conditions within which capital is produced, and within which capital produces, as eternal natural laws of production. On the other hand, it has rather the character of a bourgeois reproduction of the feudal system, of the dominion of landed property; and the industrial spheres within which capital first develops independently are presented as "unproductive" branches of labour, mere appendages of agriculture. The first condition for the development of capital is the separation of landed property from labour, the emergence of land, the primary condition of labour, as an independent force, a force in the hands of a separate class, confronting the free labourer. The Physiocrats therefore present the landowner as the true capitalist, that is, the appropriator of surplus labour. Feudalism is thus portrayed and explained *sub specie* of bourgeois production; agriculture is treated as the branch of production in which capitalist production—that is, the production of surplus value—exclusively appears. While feudalism is thus made bourgeois, bourgeois society is given a feudal semblance.

---

[a] See D. Buchanan, *Observations on the Subjects Treated of in Dr. Smith's Inquiry into the Nature and Causes of the Wealth of Nations,* Edinburgh, London, 1814, pp. 137-46.— *Ed.*

This semblance deceived Dr. Quesnay's adherents among the nobility, such as the crotchety and patriarchal Mirabeau the elder. Among the later representatives [VI-227] of the Physiocrats, especially *Turgot*, this illusion disappears completely, and the Physiocratic system is presented as the new capitalist society prevailing within the framework of feudal society. This therefore corresponds to bourgeois society in the epoch when the latter breaks its way out of the feudal order. Consequently, the starting-point is in France, in a predominantly agricultural country, and not in England, a predominantly industrial, commercial and seafaring country. In the latter country attention was naturally concentrated on circulation, on the fact that the product acquires value, becomes a commodity only when it becomes the expression of general social labour, money. In so far, therefore, as the question concerned not the form of value, but the magnitude of value and valorisation, PROFIT UPON EXPROPRIATION[233]—that is, relative profit as Steuart describes it—is what catches the eye. But if the creation of surplus value in the sphere of production itself is what has to be established, it is necessary first of all to go back to that branch of labour in which surplus value is found independently of circulation—that is, agriculture. The initiative was therefore taken in a predominantly agricultural country. Ideas related to those of the Physiocrats are to be found in fragmentary form in older writers who preceded them, partly in France herself, for example, Boisguillebert. But it is only with the Physiocrats that these ideas develop into an epoch-making system.

The agricultural labourer, depending on the minimum of wages, the *strict nécessaire*,[a] reproduces more than this *strict nécessaire*, and this more is rent, *surplus value*, which is appropriated by the owners of the fundamental condition of labour—nature. So what they say is not: the labourer works more than the labour time required for the reproduction of his labour capacity; the value which he creates is therefore greater than the value of his labour capacity; or the labour which he gives in return is greater than the quantity of labour which he receives in the form of wages. But what they say is: the amount of use values which he consumes during the period of production is smaller than the amount of use values which he creates, and so a surplus of use values is left over.—Were he to work only for the time required to reproduce his own labour capacity, there would be nothing over.

---

[a] The most indispensable, the absolutely necessary.— *Ed.*

But the Physiocrats only stuck to the point that the productivity of the earth enables the labourer, in his day's labour, which is assumed to be a fixed quantity, to produce more than he needs to consume in order to continue to exist. The surplus value appears therefore as a *gift of nature*, through whose co-operation a definite quantity of organic matter—plant seeds, a number of animals—enables labour to transform more inorganic matter into organic.

On the other hand, it is taken for granted that the landowner confronts the labourer as a capitalist. He pays for the labour capacity, which the labourer offers to him as a commodity, and he receives in return not only an equivalent, but appropriates for himself the valorisation of this labour capacity. The alienation of the objective condition of labour from labour capacity itself is presupposed in this exchange. The starting-point is the feudal landowner, but he comes on to the stage as a capitalist, as a mere owner of commodities, who valorises the goods exchanged by him for labour, getting back not only their equivalent, but a surplus over this equivalent, because he pays for the labour capacity only as a commodity. He confronts the free labourer as an owner of commodities. In other words, this landowner is in essence a capitalist. In this respect too the Physiocratic system hits the mark, inasmuch as the separation of the labourer from the soil and from the ownership of land is a fundamental condition [VI-228] for capitalist production and the production of capital.

Hence the contradictions in this system: it was the first to explain *surplus value* by the appropriation of the labour of others, and in fact to explain this appropriation on the basis of the exchange of commodities; but it did not see that value in general is a form of social labour and that surplus value is surplus labour. On the contrary, it conceived value merely as use value, merely as material substance, and surplus value as a mere gift of nature, which returns to labour, in place of a given quantity of organic material, a greater quantity. On the one hand, it stripped rent—that is, the true economic form of landed property—of its feudal wrapping, and reduced it to mere surplus value in excess of the labourer's wage. On the other hand, this surplus value is explained again in a feudal way, as derived from nature and not from society; from man's relation to the soil, not from his social relations. Value itself is resolved into mere use value, and therefore into material substance. But again what interests [the Physiocrats] in this material substance is its quantity—the excess of the use values produced over those consumed; that is, the purely quantitative relation of the use values to each other, their mere exchange value, which in the last resort comes down to labour time.

All these are contradictions of capitalist production as it works its way out of feudal society, and interprets feudal society itself only in a bourgeois way, but has not yet discovered its own peculiar form—somewhat as philosophy first builds itself up within the religious form of consciousness, and in so doing on the one hand destroys religion as such, while on the other hand, in its positive content, it still moves only within this religious sphere, idealised and reduced to terms of thought.

Hence also, in the conclusions which the Physiocrats themselves draw, the ostensible veneration of landed property becomes transformed into the economic negation of it and the affirmation of capitalist production. On the one hand, all taxes are put on rent, or in other words, landed property is in part confiscated, which is what the legislation of the French Revolution sought to carry through and which is the final conclusion of the fully developed Ricardian modern political economy.[234] By placing the burden of tax entirely on rent, because it alone is surplus value—and consequently any taxation of other forms of income ultimately falls on landed property, but in a roundabout way, and therefore in an economically harmful way, that hinders production—taxation and along with it all forms of State intervention, are removed from industry itself, and the latter is thus freed from all intervention by the State. This is ostensibly done for the benefit of landed property, not in the interests of industry but in the interests of landed property.

Connected with this is *laissez faire, laissez aller*[235]; unhampered free competition, the removal from industry of all interference by the State, monopolies, etc. Since industry [as the Physiocrats see it] creates nothing, but only transforms values given it by agriculture into another form; since it adds no new value to them, but returns the values supplied to it, though in altered form, as an equivalent; it is naturally desirable that this process of transformation should proceed without interruptions and in the cheapest way; and this is only realised through free competition, by leaving capitalist production to its own devices. The emancipation of bourgeois society from the absolute monarchy set up on the ruins of feudal society thus takes place only in the interests of the feudal landowner transformed into a capitalist [VI-229] and bent solely on enrichment. The capitalists are only capitalists in the interests of the landowner, just as political economy in its later development would have them be capitalists only in the interests of the working class.

It can be seen therefore how little the modern economists, [such as] M. Eugène Daire (who published the works of the Physiocrats together with his prize essay on them), have understood the Physiocrats when they treat their specific theories—of the exclusive productivity of agricultural labour, of rent as the only surplus value, and of the landowners' pre-eminent status in the system of production—as if they had no connection and were only fortuitously associated with their proclamation of free competition, the principle of large-scale industry, of capitalist production. At the same time it is understandable how the feudal semblance of this system, in the same way as the aristocratic tone of the Enlightenment, was bound to win a number of feudal lords as enthusiastic supporters and propagandists of a system which, in its essence, proclaimed the rise of the bourgeois system of production on the ruins of the feudal.

We will now examine a number of passages, partly to elucidate and partly in support of theses advanced above.

With *Quesnay* himself, in the *Analyse du tableau économique*, the nation consists of 3 classes of citizens:

> *"the productive class"* (AGRICULTURAL LABOURERS), *"the class of landowners* and *the sterile class"* ("all the citizens occupied with other services and with other labours than those of agriculture") (*Physiocrates etc.*, éd. Eugène Daire, Paris, 1846, Part 1, p. 58).[a]

Only the agricultural labourers, not the landowners, appear as a productive class, as a class which creates surplus value. The importance of this class of landowners, which is not "sterile", because it is the representative of "surplus value", does not rest on its being the creator of surplus value, but exclusively on the fact that it appropriates surplus value.

[With] *Turgot* [the Physiocratic system is] most fully developed. In some passages in his writings the pure gift of nature is presented as *surplus labour*, and on the other hand the necessity for the labourer to yield up what there is in excess of his necessary wage [is explained] by the separation of the labourer from the conditions of labour, and their confronting him as the property of a class which uses them to trade with.

The first reason why agricultural labour alone is productive is that it is the natural basis and pre-condition for the independent pursuit of all other forms of labour.

---

[a] Here and below Marx quotes Quesnay in French.— *Ed.*

"His" (the husbandman's) "labour, in the sequence of the labours divided among the different members of the society, retains the same primacy ... as the labour which provided his own food had among the different kinds of labour which, when he worked alone, he was obliged to devote to his different kinds of wants. We have here neither a primacy of honour nor of dignity; it is one of *physical necessity*.... What his labour causes the land to produce beyond his personal wants is the only fund for the wages which all the other members of the society receive in exchange for their labour. The latter, in making use of the price of this exchange to buy in their turn the products of the husbandman, only return to him" (as matter) "exactly what they have received from him. We have here a very essential difference [VI-230] between these two kinds of labour" (*Réflexions sur la formation et la distribution des richesses* (1766).[34] Turgot, *Oeuvres*, édit. Daire, Vol. I, Paris, 1844, [pp.] 9-10).

How then does surplus value arise? It does not arise from circulation, but it is realised in circulation. The product is sold at its value, not *above* its value. There is no excess of price over value. But because it is sold at its value, the seller realises a surplus value. This is only possible because he has not himself paid in full for the value which he sells, that is, because the product contains a portion of value which has not been paid for by the seller, which he has not offset by an equivalent. And this is the case with agricultural labour. The seller sells what he has not bought. Turgot at first presents this unbought element as a *pure gift of nature*. We shall see, however, that in his writings this pure gift of nature becomes imperceptibly transformed into the surplus labour of the LABOURERS which the landowner has not bought, but which he sells in the products of agriculture.

"As soon as the labour of the husbandman *produces more than* his wants, he can, with this superfluity *that nature accords him as a pure gift* over and above the wages of his toil, buy the labour of the other members of the society. The latter, in selling it to him, gain only their livelihood; but the husbandman gathers, beyond his subsistence, a wealth which is independent and disposable, *which he has not bought and which he sells.* He is, therefore, the sole source of the riches, which, by their circulation, animate all the labours of the society, *because he is the only one whose labour produces over and above the wages of labour*" (l.c., [p.] 11).

In this first conception we have, to begin with, the essence of surplus value—that it is value realised in sale, without the seller having given an equivalent for it, without his having bought it. *Unpaid value.* But in the second place this is conceived as a pure gift of nature, this excess over the *wage of labour*; because after all it is a gift of nature, it depends on the productivity of nature that the labourer is able to produce in his day's labour more than is necessary for the reproduction of his labour capacity, more than the amount of his wages. In this first conception the total product is still appropriated by the labourer himself. And this total product is divided into 2 parts. The first forms his wages; he is presented as his own wage labourer, who pays himself the part of the product that is necessary for the reproduction of his labour · capacity, for his subsistence. The second part, which is the excess over the first, is *a gift of nature* and forms surplus value. The nature of this surplus value, of this pure gift of nature, will however take clearer shape, when the premiss of the proprietor who cultivates his land is abandoned and the two parts of the product, wages and surplus value, accrue to different classes, the one to the wage labourer, the other to the landowner.

The formation of a class of wage labourers, whether in manufacture or in agriculture itself—at first all MANUFACTURERS appear only as *stipendiés*,[a] wage labourers of the cultivating proprietor—requires the separation of the conditions of labour from labour capacity, and the basis for this separation is that the land itself becomes the private property of one part of society, so that the other part is cut off from this objective condition for valorisation of its labour.

"In the early stages there was no need to distinguish the proprietor from the cultivator.... In this early time, as every industrious man would find as much land as he [VI-231] wished, he could not be tempted *to work for others*.... But in the end all land found its master, and those who could not have properties had at first no other resource than that of *exchanging the labour of their arms*, in the employment of the *stipendiary* class" (i.e., the class of ARTISANS, of all non-agricultural labourers) "for the superfluous portion of the produce of the cultivating proprietor" (p. 12). The cultivating proprietor with the considerable surplus which the land gave to his labour, could "pay men to cultivate his land; and for men who live on wages, it was as good to earn them in this business as in any other. *Thus ownership* [of land] *had to be separated from the labour of cultivation, and soon it was....* The landowners began to shift the labour of cultivating the soil on to the wage labourers" (p. 13).

In this way, therefore, the relation between capital and wage labour arises in agriculture itself. It first arises when a number of people find themselves cut off from ownership of the conditions of labour—above all from the land—and have nothing to sell but their labour itself.

For the wage labourer, however, who can no longer produce commodities, but must sell his labour itself, the *minimum* of wages, the equivalent of the necessary means of subsistence, necessarily becomes the law which governs his exchange with the owner of the condition of labour.

"The mere workman who has only his arms and his industry, has nothing unless he succeeds in selling his labour to others.... In every kind of work it cannot

---

[a] Those who are paid (wages or a salary).— *Ed.*

fail to happen, and as a matter of fact it does happen, that the wages of the workman are limited to what is necessary to procure him his subsistence" (l.c., [p.] 10).

Then as soon as wage labour has arisen,

"the produce of land is divided into two parts: the one includes the subsistence and the profits of the husbandman, which are the reward of his labour and the condition upon which he undertakes to cultivate the field of the proprietor. What remains is that independent and disposable part which the *land gives as pure gifts to him who cultivates it,* over and above his advances and the wages of his labour; and this is the portion of the proprietor, or the revenue with which the latter can live without labour and which he uses as he will" ([p.] 14).

This pure gift of the land, however, is now already defined as a gift which it gives "to him who cultivates it", and thus as a gift which it makes to labour; as the productive power of labour applied to the land, a productive power which labour possesses through using the productive power of nature and which it thus derives from the land—but it derives it from the land only as labour. In the hands of the landowner, therefore, the surplus appears no longer as a "gift of nature", but as the appropriation—without an equivalent—of another's labour, which through the productivity of nature is enabled to produce means of subsistence in excess of its own needs, but which, because it is wage labour, is restricted to appropriating for itself, out of the product of the labour, only "what is necessary to procure him" [the workman] "his subsistence".

"The *cultivator* produces *his own wages,* and, in addition, the revenue which serves to pay the whole class of artisans and other stipendiaries.... *The proprietor has nothing except through the labour of the cultivator*" (therefore not through a pure gift of nature); "he receives from him his [VI-232] subsistence and that wherewith he pays the labours of other stipendiaries ... the cultivator has need of the proprietor only by virtue of conventions and laws" (l.c., [p.] 15).

Thus in this passage surplus value is explicitly stated to be the part of the cultivator's labour which the proprietor appropriates to himself without giving any equivalent, and he sells the product of his labour, therefore, without having bought it. Only what Turgot has in mind is not exchange value as such, the labour time itself, but the surplus of products which the cultivator's labour supplies to the proprietor over and above his own wages; which surplus of products, however, is only the embodiment of the amount of time which he works gratis for the proprietor in addition to the time which he works for the reproduction of his wages.

We see thus how, *within the limits of agricultural labour,* the Physiocrats have a correct grasp of surplus value; they see it as a product of the wage labourer's labour, although they in turn conceive this labour in the concrete form in which it appears in use values.

The capitalist exploitation of agriculture—

"leasing or letting of land"—is, it may be noted in passing, described by Turgot as "the most advantageous method of all, but it presupposes a country that is already rich" (l.c., p. 21).

// In considering surplus value it is necessary to turn from the sphere of circulation to the sphere of production. That is to say, to deduce surplus value not from the exchange of commodity for commodity, but from exchange as it occurs within production, between the owners of the conditions of labour and the labourers themselves. These too confront each other as owners of commodities, and consequently there is no assumption here of production independent of exchange. //

// In the Physiocratic system the proprietors are the salarians,[a] labourers and MANUFACTURERS in all other branches of industry being wage labourers or stipendiaries. Consequently also the governing and the governed. //

Turgot analyses the conditions of labour as follows:

"In every craft, it is necessary that the workman should have tools in advance, that he should have a sufficient quantity of the materials upon which he has to labour; it is necessary that he should subsist while waiting for the sale of his finished goods" ([p.] 34).

All these advances, these conditions in which alone labour can be performed, which are therefore *pre-conditions* of the labour process, are originally provided gratis by the land:

It is the land which "has provided the first fund of advances prior to all cultivation", in fruits, fish, game, etc., in tools such as tree branches, stones, in domestic animals, which multiply through the process of procreation, and moreover each year yield products in milk, fleeces, "hides and other materials, which, with the wood obtained in the forests, have formed the first fund for the works of industry" (p. 34).

Now these conditions of labour, these advances to labour become *capital* as soon as they have to be advanced to the labourer by a third person, and this is the case from the moment when the labourer owns nothing but his labour capacity itself.

"*When* a large part of the society had *only their arms to maintain them*, it was necessary that those who thus lived on wages should begin by having *something in advance*, either to procure the materials upon which to labour or to maintain them while waiting for the payment of their wages" (pp. 37-38).

---

[a] The payers of wages.— *Ed.*

[VI-233] Turgot defines *"capitals"* as

"accumulated movable values" (l.c., p. 38). Originally the proprietor or cultivator pays wages directly each day and supplies the material, for example, to the spinner of flax. As industry develops, larger advances and continuity of the process of production are necessary. This is then undertaken by the possessor of capital. In the price of his products he must recover all his *advances* and a profit equal to "what his money would have been worth to him if he had employed it in the purchase of an estate", besides his wages, "for doubtless, if the profit were the same, he would have preferred to live without any exertion on the revenue of the land he could have acquired with the same capital" ([pp.] 38-39).

The "stipendiary industrial class" is itself subdivided "into capitalist entrepreneurs and simple workers", etc. ([p.] 39).

Agricultural entrepreneurs are in the same position as these entrepreneurs. They must similarly get all their advances replaced, along with the profit as shown above.

"All this must first be deducted from the price of the products of the earth; the *surplus* serves the cultivator for paying the proprietor for the permission he has given him to make use of his field for setting his enterprise on foot. This is the price of the lease, the revenue of the proprietor, the *net produce*; for all the land produces, up to the amount that replaces the advances of every kind and the profits of the person who has made the advances, cannot be regarded as a revenue, but only as *the return of the expenses of cultivation*; when one considers that, if the cultivator did not get them back, he would take care not to employ his resources and his toil in cultivating the field of another" (l.c., p. 40).

Finally:

"Although capitals are partly formed by saving from the profits of the working classes, yet, as these profits always come from the earth—inasmuch as they are all paid either from the revenue, or as part of the expenditure which serves to produce the revenue—it is evident the capitals come from the land just as much as the revenue does; or, rather, that they are nothing but the accumulation of the part of the values produced by the land that the proprietors of the revenue, or those who share it with them, can lay by every year without using it for the satisfaction of their wants" ([p.] 66).

It is quite right that, if rent is the only surplus value, accumulation takes place only from rent. What the capitalists accumulate apart from rent, they pinch from their wages (their revenue, destined for their consumption—since this is how profit is defined).

As profit, like wages, is reckoned in with the costs of cultivation, and only the surplus forms the revenue of the proprietor, the latter—in spite of the honourable status given him—is in fact excluded from the costs of cultivation (and thereby from being an agent of production), just as with the Ricardians.

The emergence of the Physiocrats was connected both with the opposition to Colbertism and, in particular, with the hullabaloo over the John Law system.[236]

[VI-234] The confusion of value with material substance, or rather the equating of value with it, and the connection between this view and the whole outlook of the Physiocrats, comes clearly to light in the following extracts from *Ferdinando Paoletti: I veri mezzi di render felici le società* (in part directed against Verri, who in his *Meditazioni sulla economia politica* (1771),[a] had attacked the Physiocrats).[b] (Paoletti of Toscana, op. cit., Custodi, *Parte Moderna*, Vol. XX.)

"Such a *multiplication of matter*" as are the products of the earth "has certainly never taken place through industry, nor is it possible. This gives matter only form, it only modifies it; consequently nothing is created by industry. But, the objection may be raised, industry gives matter form, and consequently it is productive; even if this is not a production of matter, it is nevertheless one of form. Very well, then, I won't contest this. But *that is not creation of wealth; on the contrary, it is nothing but an expense....* Political economy presupposes, and takes as the object of its investigation, material and real production, which is found only in agriculture, since this alone multiplies the substances and products which form wealth.... Industry buys raw materials from agriculture, in order to work them up; its labour—as we have already said—gives these raw materials only a form, but it adds nothing to them and does not multiply them" ([pp.] 196-97). "Give the cook a measure of peas, with which he is to prepare your dinner; he will put them on the table for you well cooked and well dished up, but in the same quantity as he was given, but on the other hand give the same quantity to the gardener for him to put into the ground; he will return to you, when the right time has come, at least four-fold the quantity that he had been given. This is the true and only production" [p.] 197). "Things receive value through the needs of men. Therefore the value or the increase of value of commodities is not the result of industrial labour, but of the labourers' outlays" ([p.] 198). "Hardly has a new manufacture of any kind made its appearance, but it immediately spreads within and outside the country; and see! very soon competition from other industrialists and merchants brings the price down to its correct level, which ... is determined by the value of the raw material and the costs of the labourers' maintenance" ([pp.] 204-05).[c]

Agriculture is the first of all branches of industry to use the forces of nature for production on a considerable scale. Their use in manufacturing industry becomes apparent only at a higher stage of industrial development. The following quotation shows how, in this connection, Adam Smith still reflects the prehistory of large-scale industry and for this reason upholds the Physiocratic point of view, and how Ricardo answers him from the standpoint of modern industry.

[VI-235] In Book II, Ch. 5 Adam Smith says with reference to the rent of land:

---

[a] In the manuscript Marx presumably by mistake gives the title of another work of Verri, *Pensier sopra l'agricoltura.—Ed.*

[b] See this volume, pp. 375-76.—*Ed.*

[c] Marx quotes in Italian.—*Ed.*

* "It is the work of nature which remains after deducting or compensating everything which can be regarded as the work of man. It is seldom less than a fourth, and frequently more than a third of the whole produce. No equal quantity of productive labour employed in manufactures, can ever occasion so great a reproduction. *In them nature does nothing, man does all*; and the reproduction must always be in proportion to the strength of the agents that occasion it." *[a]

On which Ricardo comments [in his *On the Principles of Political Economy, and Taxation*], 2nd ed., 1819, note to pp. 61, 62:

* "Does nature nothing for man in manufactures? Are the powers of wind and water, which move our machinery, and assist navigation, nothing? The pressure of the atmosphere and the elasticity of steam, which enable us to work the most stupendous engines—are they not the gifts of nature? to say nothing of the effects of the matter of heat in softening and melting metals, of the decomposition of the atmosphere in the process of dyeing and fermentation. There is not a manufacture which can be mentioned, in which nature does not give her assistance to man, and give it too, generously and gratuitously." *

That the Physiocrats regarded profit as only a deduction from rent:

* "The Physiocrats say, for instance, of the price of a piece of lace, one part merely replaces what the labourer consumed, and the other part is only transferred from one man's pocket" //i.e., that of the LANDLORD// "to another's" * (*An Inquiry into those Principles, Respecting the Nature of Demand and the Necessity of Consumption, Lately Advocated by Mr. Malthus etc.*, London, 1821,[b] p. 96).

The view of Adam Smith and his followers that the accumulation of capital is due to personal stinting and saving and self-denial of the capitalists also originates from the view of the Physiocrats that profit (including interest) is merely revenue for the consumption of the capitalist. They could say this because they only regarded land rent as the true economic, so to speak legitimate, source of accumulation.

"He," says Turgot, i.e., the husbandman, "is the only one whose labour produces *over and above the wages of labour*" (Turgot, l.c., p. 11).

Here the entire profit is thus reckoned in with the wages of labour.

[VI-236] "The cultivator creates over and above that restitution" (of his own wages) "the revenue of the proprietor; and the artisan creates no revenue, either for himself or for others" (l.c., p. 16). "All the land produces up to the amount that replaces the advances of every kind and the profits of the person who has made the advances, *cannot be regarded as a revenue*, but only as *the return of the expenses of cultivation*" (l.c., [p.] 40).

---

[a] Adam Smith, *An Inquiry into the Nature and Causes of the Wealth of Nations*, in two volumes, Vol. I, London, 1776, p. 442.— *Ed.*

[b] The manuscript has "1829", the change has been made in somebody else's hand.— *Ed.*

Adolphe Blanqui. *Histoire de l'économie politique*, Brussels, 1839, says on p. 139 [237]:

[The Physiocrats were of the opinion that] "Labour applied to the cultivation of the soil produced not only the wherewithal to maintain the labourer throughout the entire duration of the task, but also an *excess of value*" (surplus value) "which could be added to the mass of already existing wealth. They called this excess the *net product.*" [a]

(Thus they conceive surplus value in the form of the use values in which it appears.)

"The net product had necessarily to belong to the owner of the land and constituted in his hands a revenue fully at his disposal. What then was the net product of the other industries?... Manufacturers, merchants, workmen, all were the employees, the *stipendiaries* of agriculture, sovereign creator and dispenser of all wealth. The products of the labour of these latter represented in the system of the *Economists* [238] only the equivalent of what they had consumed during the task, so that after their work was completed, the sum total of wealth was absolutely the same as before, *unless the workmen or the masters had placed in reserve*, i.e., s a v e d, *what they had the right to consume*. Thus, then, labour applied to the soil was the only labour productive of wealth, and labour in other industries was regarded as s t e r i l e, *because no increase in the general capital resulted from it.*"

(Thus the Physiocrats saw the production of surplus value as the essence of capitalist production. It was this phenomenon that they had to explain. And it remained the problem, after they had eliminated the profit of expropriation of the Mercantile system. [233]

"In order to acquire money," says *Mercier de la Rivière*, "one must buy it, and, after this purchase, one is no richer than one was before; one has simply received in money the same value that one has given in commodities" (Mercier de la Rivière, *L'ordre naturel et essentiel des sociétés politique*, Vol. II, p. 338). [b]

This holds good both for [VI-237] purchase and for sale, as also for the result of the whole metamorphosis of the commodity, or the result of purchase and sale, the exchange of different commodities at their value, hence the exchange of equivalents. Whence, therefore, comes surplus value? That is, whence comes capital? That was the problem for the Physiocrats. Their error was that they confused the *increase of material substance*, which because of the natural processes of vegetation and generation distinguishes agriculture and stockraising from manufacture, with the *increase of exchange value*. Use value was their starting-point. And the use value of all commodities, reduced, as the scholastics say, to a universal, was the material substance of nature as such, whose increase in the same form occurs only in agriculture.)

---

[a] Here and below Marx quotes Blanqui in French.— *Ed.*
[b] Here and below Marx quotes Mercier de la Rivière in French.— *Ed.*

Germain Garnier, the translator of Adam Smith and himself a Physiocrat, correctly expounds their *theory of savings*, etc. First he says that manufacture, as the Mercantilists maintained of all production, can *only* produce surplus value through the PROFIT OF EXPROPRIATION, by selling commodities above their value, so that only A NEW DISTRIBUTION OF VALUES CREATED takes place, BUT NO NEW ADDITION TO THE CREATED VALUES.

"The labour of artisans and manufacturers, opening no new source of wealth, *can only be profitable through advantageous exchanges*, and has only a purely relative value, a value which will not be repeated if there is no longer the opportunity to *gain on the exchanges*" (his translation *Recherches sur la nature et les causes de la richesse des nations*, Vol. V, Paris, 1802, p. 266 [239]).

Or the savings which they make, the VALUES which they secure over and above those which they expend, must be stinted from their own consumption.

"The labour of artisans and manufacturers, though only able to add to the general amount of the wealth of society the savings made by the wage labourers and the capitalists, may well tend by these means to enrich society" (l.c., p. 266).

And in greater detail:

"The labourers in agriculture enrich the State by the very product of their labour; labourers in manufactures and commerce, on the contrary, cannot enrich it otherwise than through *savings on their own consumption.* This assertion of the Economists is a consequence of the distinction which they have established, and appears to be quite incontestable. Indeed, the labour of artisans and manufacturers cannot add anything else to the value of the material than the *value* of their own labour, i.e., the value of the wages and profits which this labour should have earned, at the rates actually current in the country [VI-238] for the one and the other. For these wages, whether they be small or large, are the reward of labour; they are what the labourer has the right to consume and is presumed to consume; because it is only in consuming them that he can enjoy the fruits of his labour, and this enjoyment is all that in reality constitutes his reward. Similarly profits, whether they be high or low, are also regarded as the daily and continuous consumption of the capitalist, who is naturally presumed to proportion his enjoyments to the revenue that his capital gives him. Thus unless the workman curtails a part of the comforts to which he has the right in accordance with the current rate of wages assigned *to his labour*; unless the capitalist resigns himself to saving a part of the revenue which his capital brings him, both the one and the other will consume, in proportion as the piece of work is completed, the whole value resulting from this work. The total quantity of the wealth of society will then be, after their labour is over, the same as it was before, *unless they have saved* a part of what they had the right to consume and what they could consume without being charged with wasting; in which case the total quantity of the wealth of society will have been increased *by the whole value of these savings.* Consequently it is correct to say that the agents of manufacture and commerce can *only add to the total quantity of wealth existing in society by their privations alone*" (l.c., pp. 263-64).

Garnier is also quite correct in noting that Adam Smith's theory of accumulation through savings rests on this Physiocratic foundation (Adam Smith was strongly infected by the Physiocrats, as he nowhere shows more strikingly than in his critique of the Physiocrats).

Garnier says:

"Finally, if the Economists have maintained that manufacturing and commercial industry can only add to the national wealth by privations, Smith has likewise said that industry would be practised in vain, and the capital of a country would never grow larger, unless the economy augmented it by its savings" (Book II, ch. 3 [p. 326]). "Smith is therefore in full agreement with the Economists and so on" (l.c., p. 270).

[VI-239] Among the immediate historical circumstances which facilitated the spread of Physiocratic theory and even its emergence, Adolphe Blanqui, in the work already mentioned, adduces:

"Of all the values which shot up in the feverish atmosphere of the *system*" (Law's), "nothing remained except ruin, desolation and bankruptcy. *Landed property alone* did not go under in the storm."

// For this reason M. Proudhon, in *Philosophie de la misère*, puts landed property only after credit. //

"It even improved its position by changing hands and by being *subdivided on a large scale*, perhaps for *the first time* since feudalism" (l.c., p. 138).

In particular,

"The innumerable changes of ownership which were effected under the influence of the system, began the process of parcelling out property.... Landed property arose for the first time from the condition of torpor in which the feudal system had kept it for so long. This was a real awakening for agriculture.... It" (the land) "passed now from out of a condition of mortmain and came into circulation" (pp. 137-38).

Turgot as well as *Quesnay* and his other adherents also want *capitalist* production in agriculture. Thus Turgot:

"The leasing or letting of land ... this latter method" (large-scale agriculture, based on the modern system of leases) "is the most advantageous of all, but it presupposes a country that is already rich" (see Turgot, l.c., p. 21).

And *Quesnay* in his *Maximes générales du gouvernement économique d'un royaume agricole*:

"The pieces of land which are employed in growing grain should as far as possible be joined together in large-scale farms which can be managed by rich farmers" (i.e., capitalists) "since the expenses for the maintenance and repair of the buildings are smaller and therefore the costs are correspondingly much lower and the net product much greater in the case of large agricultural undertakings than in the case of small" [pp. 96-97].

In the same passage Quesnay admits that the increased productivity of agricultural labour accrues to the "net revenue", and therefore in the first place to the landowner, i.e., the owner of surplus value, and that the relative increase of the latter arises not from the land but from the social and other ARRANGEMENTS for raising the productivity of labour. [VI-240] For he says in the same place:

"Every advantageous" //i.e., advantageous to the net product// "economy in labour which can be accomplished with the aid of animals, machines, water-power and so on, will be of benefit to the population," etc. [pp. 96-97].

At the same time Mercier de la Rivière (l.c., Vol. II, p. 407) has an inkling that surplus value at least in manufacture has something to do with the manufacturing workers themselves. (Turgot extended this to all production, as already mentioned.) In the passage cited he exclaims:

"Moderate your enthusiasm, ye blind admirers of the false products of industry! Before ye extol its miracles, open your eyes and see how many live in poverty or at least, in need, among those producers who understand the art of converting 20 sous into the value of a thousand écus. *Who then benefits by this enormous increase in value? What do you say! Comforts are unknown to those through whose hands it is accomplished. Take warning then by this contrast!*"

Contradictions in the system of the Economists,[238] taken as a whole. Among others, Quesnay was for the absolute monarchy.

"There must be only one supreme power.... The system of opposing forces in a government is ruinous. It merely indicates discord among the great and the suppression of the small people" (in the above-mentioned *Maximes générales etc.*) [p. 81].

Mercier de la Rivière:

"By the very fact that man is intended to live in a community, he is intended to live under a despotism" ([*L'Ordre naturel et essentiel des sociétés politiques*], Vol. I, p. 281).

And to crown all the "Friend of the People",[240] the Marquis de Mirabeau—Mirabeau *le père*! It was precisely this school, with its *laissez faire, laissez aller*, that overthrew Colbertism [236] and all forms of government interference in the activities of civil society. It allowed the State to live on only in the pores of this society, as Epicurus placed his gods in the pores of the world[941]! The glorification of landed property in practice turns into the demand that taxes should be put exclusively on ground rent, [and this implies] the virtual confiscation of landed property by the State, just as with the radical section of the Ricardians.[234] The French Revolution, in spite of the protests of Roederer and others, accepted this taxation theory.

Turgot himself [was] the radical bourgeois minister who prepared the way for the French Revolution. For all their sham feudal pretences the Physiocrats were working hand in hand with the Encyclopaedists[242]!

[VI-241] We shall come back again later to the great service rendered by the Physiocrats RESPECTING THE ANALYSIS OF CAPITAL.[232]

Meanwhile just this point: surplus value (according to them) is due to the productivity of a special kind of labour, agricultural labour. And on the whole this special productivity is due to nature itself.

———

In the Mercantile system, surplus value is only relative—what one wins, the other loses: PROFIT UPON ALIENATION or OSCILLATION OF WEALTH BETWEEN DIFFERENT PARTIES.[a] So that within a country, if we consider the total capital, no creation of surplus value in fact takes place. It can only arise in the relations between one nation and other nations. And the surplus realised by one nation as against the other takes the form of money (the balance of trade), because it is precisely money that is the direct and independent form of exchange value. In opposition to this—for the Mercantile system in fact denies the creation of absolute surplus value—the Physiocrats seek to explain absolute surplus value: the *net product.* And since the net product is fixed in their minds as use value, agriculture [is for them] the sole creator of it.

———

Turgot sought to anticipate the measures of the French Revolution. By the edict of *February 1776* he abolished the guilds. (This edict was revoked three months after it was promulgated.) Similarly he annulled the road-making *corvée des paysans.*[b] He tried to introduce the *impôt unique*[c] on rent of land.

———

One of the most naïve representatives of Physiocratic theory— how far removed he is from Turgot!—is the old smeller-out of demagogues[243] and royal Prussian Privy Councillor Schmalz. For instance:

———

a See this volume, p. 348 et seq.— *Ed.*
b Compulsory labour exacted of the peasants.— *Ed.*
c Single tax.— *Ed.*

"If nature pays him" (the lessor of the land,[a] the landowner) "*even double the legal interests*, on what plausible ground could anyone dare to deprive him of it?" (*Économie politique*, traduit par Henri Jouffroy, etc., Vol. I. Paris, 1826, p. 90 [244]).[b]

The minimum of wages is so formulated by the Physiocrats that the consumption (or expenditure) of the labourers is equal to the wage *that they receive*.[c] Or as Mr. Schmalz puts it in a general way:

"The average wage in a trade is equal to the average of what a man in this trade consumes during the time of his labour" (l.c., p. 120).

"*Rent of land* is the one and only element of the national revenue; [VI-242] and interest on capitals employed and the wages of all kinds of labours only make the product of this rent pass and circulate through everyone's hands" (Schmalz, l.c., Vol. I, [pp.] 309-10).

"The utilisation of the land, its faculty, its capacity for the annual reproduction of rent, is all that constitutes the national wealth" (l.c., p. 310).

"If we go back to the foundations, to the first elements of the *value* of all objects, whatsoever they may be, we are forced to recognise that this value is nothing other than that of the simple products of nature; that is to say, although labour may have given a new value to these objects and raised their price, this new value, or this price, is only made up nevertheless of the total values put together of all the natural products which, because of the new form that labour has given them, have been destroyed, consumed, or used by the labourer in one way or another" (l.c., p. 313).

"This kind of labour" (agriculture proper) "being the only labour that contributes to the production of *new bodies*, it is therefore the only labour that can, up to a certain point, be considered productive. As for labours in working up material or in industry ... they simply give a new form to bodies which nature has produced" (Schmalz, l.c., pp. 15-16).

Against the superstition of the Physiocrats.

Verri (Pietro): *Meditazioni sulla economia politica.* (First printed 1771), Custodi, *Parte Moderna*, Vol. XV, p. [21,]22:

"All the phenomena of the universe, whether produced by the hand of man or through the universal laws of physics, are not actual *new creations*, but merely a *modification* of matter. *Joining together* and *separating* are the only elements which the human mind always finds on analysing the concept of *reproduction*; and it is just the same with the *reproduction of value* and of *wealth*, when earth, air and water in the fields are transformed into corn, or when the hand of man transforms the

---

[a] The words "the lessor of the land" were written in French in the manuscript.— *Ed.*

[b] Here and below Marx quotes Schmalz in French.— *Ed.*

[c] In the manuscript part of this sentence was written by Marx in French.— *Ed.*

secretions of an insect into silk, or some pieces of metal are arranged to make the mechanism of a watch."

Further:

The Physiocrats call "the class of manufacturing labourers *sterile*, because in their view *the value of manufactured products is equal to the raw material* plus *the means of subsistence which the labourers consume during the time of manufacture*" (l.c., p. 25).

[VI-243] On the other hand, Verri calls attention to the constant poverty of the *contadini*[a] in contrast to the progressive enrichment of the *artigiani*,[b] and then goes on to say:

"This proves that the artisan, in the price which he receives, gets not only the *replacement of his outlay on consumption, but a certain sum over and above that; and this sum is a new quantity of value created* in the annual production" (l.c., p. 26).

"The value reproduced is that part of the price of an agricultural or industrial product which *exceeds the original value* of the material and the outlay on consumption incurred while it is being produced. In agriculture the seed and the consumption of the peasant must be deducted: equally in manufacture one must deduct the raw material and the worker's consumption; and so every year a *reproduced value* is created, *to the amount of the part that remains*" (l.c., pp. 26-27).

c) *ADAM SMITH*

Adam Smith, like all economists WORTH SPEAKING OF, takes over from the Physiocrats the conception of the AVERAGE wage, which he calls the *prix naturel du salaire*.

"A man must always live by his work, and his wages must at least be sufficient to maintain him. They must even upon most occasions be somewhat more, otherwise it would be impossible for him to bring up a family, and the race of such workmen could not last beyond the first generation" ([Garnier,] t. I, l. I, ch. VIII, p. 136) [Vol. I, pp. 113-14].[194]

Adam Smith expressly states that the development of the productive powers of labour does not benefit the labourer himself. He says (l. I, ch. VIII [*An Inquiry into the Nature and Causes of the Wealth of Nations*] edit. McCulloch, London, 1828):

* "The produce of labour constitutes the natural recompense or wages of labour. In that original state of things, which precedes both the *appropriation of land* and the *accumulation of stock*, the whole produce of labour belongs to the labourer. He has neither landlord nor master to share with him. Had this state continued, the wages of labour *would have augmented with all those improvements in its productive powers*, to which the *division of labour* gives occasion. All things would gradually have become cheaper." *[245]

---

[a] Agricultural population.— *Ed.*
[b] Artisans.— *Ed.*

//At any rate *all those things requiring a smaller quantity of labour for their reproduction, but they "would" not only have become cheaper; they have, in point of fact, become cheaper.*//

* "They would have been produced by a smaller quantity of labour; and as the commodities produced by equal quantities of labour would naturally in this state of things be exchanged for one another, they would have been purchased likewise with [VI-244] the produce of a smaller quantity. But this original state of things, in which the labourer enjoyed the whole produce of his own labour, could *not last beyond the first introduction of the appropriation of land and the accumulation of stock.* It was at an end, therefore, long before the most considerable improvements were made in the productive powers of labour, and it would be to no purpose to trace further what might have been its effects upon the recompense or wages of labour" * (Vol. I, pp. 107-09).

Here Adam Smith very acutely notes that the really great development of the productive power of labour starts only from the moment when it is transformed into wage labour, and the conditions of labour confront it on the one hand as landed property and on the other as capital. The development of the productive power of labour thus begins only under conditions in which the labourer himself can no longer appropriate its results. It is therefore quite useless to investigate how this growth of productive powers might have influenced or would influence "WAGES", taken here as equal to the product of labour, on the premiss that the product of labour (or the value of this product) belonged to the labourer himself.

Adam Smith is very copiously infected with the conceptions of the Physiocrats, and often whole strata run through his work which belong to the Physiocrats and are in complete contradiction with the views specifically advanced by him. This is so, for example, in the theory of rent, etc. For our present purpose we can completely disregard these passages in his writings, which are not characteristic of himself, but in which he is a mere Physiocrat.[246]

In the first part of this work, when dealing with the analysis of the commodity, I have already pointed out[a] Adam Smith's inconsistency in his treatment of how exchange value is determined. In particular, [I have shown] how he sometimes confuses, and at other times replaces, the determination of the value of *commodities* by the quantity of labour required for their production, with its determination by the quantity of living labour with which commodities can be bought, or, what is the same thing, the

---

[a] K. Marx, *A Contribution to the Critique of Political Economy*. Part One (present edition, Vol. 29, pp. 299-300).— *Ed.*

quantity of commodities with which a definite quantity of living labour can be bought. Here he makes the *exchange value* of labour the measure for the value of commodities. In fact, he makes *wages* the measure; for wages are equal to the quantity of commodities bought with a definite quantity of living labour, or to the quantity of labour that can be bought by a definite quantity of commodities. The value of labour, or rather of labour capacity, changes, like that of any other commodity, and is in no way specifically different from the value of other commodities. Here value is made the measuring rod and the basis for the explanation of value—so we have a *cercle vicieux*[a].

From the exposition that follows, however, it will be seen that this vacillation and this jumbling up of completely heterogeneous determinations do not affect Smith's investigations into the nature and origin of surplus value, because in fact, without even being aware of it, everywhere in his analysis, he keeps firmly to the correct determination of the exchange value of commodities—that is, its determination by the quantity of labour or the labour time expended on them.

[VI-245] Secondly, however, this contradiction in Adam Smith and his passing from one kind of explanation to another is based upon something deeper, which Ricardo, in exposing this contradiction, overlooked or did not rightly appreciate, and therefore also did not solve.[247] Let us assume that all labourers are producers of commodities, and not only produce their commodities but also sell them. The value of these commodities is determined by the necessary labour time contained in them. If therefore the commodities are sold at their value, the labourer buys with one commodity, which is the product of 12 hours' labour time, another 12 hours' labour time in the form of another commodity, i. e., 12 hours' labour time which is embodied in another use value. The value of his labour is therefore equal to the value of his commodity, i. e., it is equal to the product of 12 hours' labour time. The selling and buying again, in a word, the whole process of exchange, the metamorphosis of the commodity, alters nothing in this. It alters only the form of the use value in which this 12 hours' labour time appears. The value of labour is therefore equal to the value of the product of labour. In the first place, equal quantities of objectified labour are exchanged in the commodities—in so far as they are exchanged at their value. Secondly, however, a certain quantity of living labour is exchanged

---

[a] Vicious circle.— *Ed.*

for an equal quantity of objectified labour, because, firstly, the
living labour is objectified in a product, a commodity, which
belongs to the labourer, and secondly, this commodity is in turn
exchanged for another commodity which contains an equally large
quantity of labour. In fact, therefore, a certain quantity of living
labour is exchanged for an equal amount of objectified labour.
Thus it is not only commodity exchanging for commodity in the
proportion in which they represent an equal quantity of objectified labour time, but a quantity of living labour exchanging for a
commodity which represents the same quantity of labour objectified.

On this assumption the value of labour (the quantity of
commodities which can be bought with a given quantity of labour,
or the quantity of labour which can be bought with a given
quantity of commodities) could serve as the measure of the value
of a commodity just as well as the quantity of labour contained in
it, since the value of labour always represents the same quantity of
objectified labour as the living labour requires for the production
of this commodity; in other words, a definite quantity of living
labour time would always command a quantity of commodities
which represents an equal amount of objectified labour time. But
in all modes of production—and particularly in the capitalist
mode of production—in which the objectified conditions of labour
belong to one or several classes, while on the other hand nothing
but labour capacity belongs to another class, the working class,
what takes place is the opposite of this. The product or the value
of the product of labour does not belong to the labourer. A
definite quantity of living labour does not command the same
quantity of objectified labour, or a definite quantity of labour
objectified in a commodity commands a greater quantity of living
labour than is contained in the commodity itself.

But as Adam Smith quite correctly takes as his starting-point the
commodity and the exchange of commodities, and thus the
producers initially confront each other only as possessors of
commodities, sellers of commodities and buyers of commodities,
he therefore discovers (so it seems to him) that in the exchange
between capital and wage labour, [VI-246] objectified labour and
living labour, the general law at once ceases to apply, and
commodities (for labour too is a commodity in so far as it is
bought and sold) do not exchange in proportion to the quantities
of labour which they represent. *Hence* he concludes that labour
time is no longer the immanent measure which regulates the
exchange value of commodities, from the moment when the

conditions of labour confront the wage labourer in the form of landed property and capital. He should on the contrary, as Ricardo rightly points out,[248] have drawn the opposite conclusion, that the expressions "quantity of labour" and "value of labour" are now no longer identical, and that therefore the relative value of commodities, although determined by the labour time contained in them, is not determined by the value of labour, since that was only correct so long as the latter expression remained identical with the former. Later on, when we deal with Malthus,[249] we can show how wrong and absurd it would be, even when the labourer appropriated his own product, i. e., the value of his own product, to make this value or the value of labour the measure of value, in the same sense in which labour time or labour itself is the measure of value and the value-creating element. For even in that case the labour which can be bought with a commodity cannot serve as a measure in the same sense as the labour contained in it. One would be merely an index to the other.

In any case Adam Smith feels the difficulty of deducing the exchange between capital and labour from the law that determines the exchange of commodities, since the former apparently rests on quite opposite and contradictory principles. And indeed the contradiction could not be solved so long as capital was set directly against labour instead of against labour capacity. Adam Smith was well aware that the labour time expended on the reproduction and maintenance of labour capacity is very different from the labour which it [labour capacity] itself can perform. Thus he himself quotes from Cantillon's *Essai sur la nature du commerce...*:

"The labour of an able-bodied slave, the same author adds, is computed to be worth double his maintenance; and that of the meanest labourer, he thinks, cannot be worth less than that of an able-bodied slave" (Garnier, t. I, l. I, ch. VIII, p. 137) [Vol. I, p. 114].

On the other hand it is strange that Adam Smith did not grasp how little the objection he raises has to do with the law that determines the exchange of commodities for each other. That commodities A and B exchange in proportion to the labour time contained in them is in no way upset by the proportions in which the producers A or B divide the products A and B, or rather their value, between themselves. If a part of A goes to the landowner, another to the capitalist, and a third part to the labourer, no matter what the share of each may be, this does not alter the fact that A itself exchanges with B according to its value. The relation between the labour time contained in commodities A and B is in no way affected by how the labour time contained in A and B is appropriated by various persons.

"When the exchange of broadcloth for linen has been accomplished, the producers of broadcloth will share in the linen in a proportion equal to that in which they previously shared in the broadcloth" (*Misère de la philosophie*, p. 29).[a]

It is this, too, that later the Ricardians rightly maintained against [VI-247] Adam Smith. Thus the Malthusian John Cazenove says:

*"Interchange of commodities and distribution must be kept distinct from each other ... the circumstances which affect the one do not always affect the other. For instance, a reduction in the cost of producing any particular commodity will alter its relation to all others: but it will not necessarily alter its own distribution, nor will it in any way affect theirs. Again, a general reduction in the value of commodities affecting them *all alike* will not alter their relation to each other. It might or might not affect their distribution etc."* (John Cazenove: Preface to his edition of Malthus's *Definitions in Political Economy*, London, 1853 [p. VI]).

But since the "distribution" of the value of the product between capitalist and worker is itself based on an EXCHANGE between commodities—commodities and labour capacity—Adam Smith is justifiably STARTLED. The fact that he had also made the value of labour, or the extent to which a commodity (or money) can purchase labour, the measure of value, has a disturbing effect on Smith's argument when he comes to the theory of prices, shows the influence of competition on the rate of profit, etc.; it deprives his work of all unity, and even excludes a number of essential questions from his inquiry. As we shall soon see, however, it did not affect his exposition of *surplus value in general*, because here he keeps consistently to the correct determination of value by the labour time expended in different commodities.

So now to his treatment of the question.

But first we must mention one other circumstance. Adam Smith mixes up different things. First he states in Book I, Ch. V:

"Every man is rich or poor according to the degree in which he can afford to enjoy the necessaries, conveniences and amusements of human life. But after the division of labour has once thoroughly taken place, it is but a very small part of these with which a man's own labour can supply him. The far greater part of them he must derive from the *labour of other people*, and he must be rich or poor *according to the quantity of that labour which he can command, or which he can afford to purchase. The value of any commodity*, therefore, to the person who possesses it, and who means not to use or consume it himself, but to *exchange it for other commodities, is equal to the quantity of labour* which it enables him to purchase or command. Labour, therefore, is the *real* measure of the *exchangeable value* of all commodities" ([Garnier,] t. I, pp. 59, 60) [Vol. I, pp. 53-54].

---

[a] Marx quotes his book *Misère de la philosophie...*, Paris, Brussels, 1847 (present edition, Vol. 6, p. 126).— *Ed.*

Further:

"They" (the goods) *"contain the value of a certain quantity of labour, which we exchange* [VI-248] *for what is supposed at the time to contain the value of an equal quantity of labour....* It was not by gold or by silver, but by labour, that all the wealth of the world was originally purchased; and its value, to those who possess it, and who want to exchange it for some new productions, is precisely equal to the quantity of labour which it can enable them to purchase or command" ([Garnier,] [l.] 1, [ch.] V, pp. 60-61) [Vol. I, p. 54].

Finally:

"*Wealth*, as Mr. Hobbes says, is *power*. But the person who either acquires, or succeeds to a great fortune, does not necessarily acquire or succeed to any political power, either civil or military... The power which that possession immediately and directly conveys to him, is the power of purchasing, the right to command *all the labour of other people* o r *all the produce of this labour which is then in the market"* ([Garnier,] l.c., p. 61) [Vol. I, pp. 54-55].

It can be seen that in all these passages Adam Smith confuses *the labour of other people* with the *produce of this labour.* The exchange value of the commodity which anyone possesses consists—after the division of labour—in the commodities belonging to someone else which he can buy, i.e., in the quantity of someone else's labour which is contained in them, the quantity of someone else's materialised labour. And this quantity of the labour of others is equal to the quantity of labour that is contained in his own commodity. As he expressly says:

"The goods contain the value of a certain quantity of labour, which we exchange for what is supposed at the time to contain *the value of an equal quantity of labour.*"

The emphasis here is on the CHANGE brought about by the *division of labour*: that is to say, that wealth no longer consists in the product of one's own labour, but in the quantity of the labour of others which this product commands, the social labour which it can buy, the quantity of which is determined by the quantity of labour it itself contains. In fact, only the concept of exchange value is here involved—that my labour now counts only as social labour, and consequently its product determines my wealth by its command over an equal quantity of social labour. My commodity, which contains a definite quantity of necessary labour time, gives me command over all other commodities of equal value, and therefore over an equal quantity of the labour of others realised in other use values. The emphasis here lies on the equalisation, brought about through the division of labour and exchange value, of *my* labour with the labour of *others*, in other words, with social labour (the fact that *my* labour too, or the labour contained in my commodities, is already *socially* determined, and has fundamentally changed its character, escapes Adam), and not at all on the difference between *objectified* labour and *living* labour, and the specific laws of their exchange. In fact, Adam Smith is here saying nothing more than that the value of commodities is determined by the labour time contained in them, and that the wealth of the owner of commodities consists in the quantity of social labour at his disposal.

However, the equating here of *labour* and *product of labour* [VI-249] in fact provides the first occasion for the confusion between the determination of the value of commodities by the quantity of labour contained in them, and the determination of their value by the quantity of living labour that they can buy, in other words, their determination by the value of labour. When Adam Smith says:

> "His fortune is greater or less precisely in proportion to the extent of this power, or to the quantity of either of other men's labour, or, *what is the same thing*" (here is the false identification) "*of the produce of other men's labour*, which it enables him to purchase or command" ([Garnier,] l.c., p. 61) [Vol. I, p. 55],

he might just as well have said: it is in proportion to the quantity of social labour contained in his own commodity or FORTUNE; as indeed he also says:

> "They" (the goods) "contain the value of a certain quantity of labour, which we exchange for what is supposed at the time to contain the value *of an equal quantity of labour.*"

(The word *value* is here superfluous and meaningless.) The false conclusion emerges already in this Chapter V, when for example he says:

> "Labour, therefore, never varying in its *own value*, is alone the ultimate and real standard by which the value of all commodities can at all times and places be estimated and compared" ([Garnier,] p. 66) [Vol. I, p. 58].

What is true of labour itself and consequently of its measure, labour time—that the value of commodities is always proportionate to the labour time realised in them, no matter how the *value of labour* may change—is here claimed for this changing value of labour itself.

Here Adam Smith is examining only commodity exchange in general: the nature of exchange value, of the division of labour and of money. The parties to the exchange still confront each other only as owners of commodities. They buy the labour of others in the form of a commodity, just as their own labour appears in the form of a commodity. The quantity of social labour which they command is therefore equal to the quantity of labour contained in the commodity with which they themselves make the purchase. But when in the following chapters he comes to the exchange between objectified labour and living labour, between capitalist and worker, and then *stresses* that the value of the commodity is now no longer determined by the quantity of labour it itself contains, but by the quantity—which is different from this—of living labour of others which it can command, i.e., buy, he is not in fact saying by this that commodities themselves no longer exchange in proportion to the labour time they contain; but that the *increase of wealth,* the increase of the value contained in the commodity, and the extent of this increase, depends upon the greater or less quantity of living labour which the objectified labour sets in motion. And put in this way it is correct. Smith, however, remains unclear on this point.

[VI-250] In Chapter VI of Book I Adam Smith passes on from those relations in which it is assumed that the producers confront one another only as sellers and possessors of commodities to the relations of exchange between those who possess the conditions of labour and those who possess labour capacity alone.

"In that early and rude state of society which *precedes both the accumulation of stock and the appropriation of land, the proportion between the quantities of labour necessary for acquiring different objects of exchange,* seems to be the only circumstance which can afford any rule for exchanging them for one another.... It is natural that what is usually the produce of two days' or two hours' labour, should be worth double of what is usually the produce of one day's or one hour's labour" (Garnier, t. I, l. 1, ch. VI, pp. 94-95) [Vol. I, p. 81].

That is to say, the labour time necessary to produce different commodities determines the proportion in which they exchange for one another, or their *exchange value.*

"In this state of things, the whole produce of labour belongs to the labourer; and the quantity of labour commonly employed in acquiring or producing any commodity, is the only circumstance which can regulate the quantity of labour which it ought commonly to purchase, command, or exchange for" ([Garnier,] l.c., [p.] 96) [Vol. I, p. 82].

Consequently, on this assumption the labourer is a mere seller of commodities, and one commands the labour of another only in so far as he buys the other's commodity with his commodity. He thus commands with his commodity only so much of the other's labour as is contained in his own commodity, since both exchange only commodities against each other, and the exchange value of the commodities is determined by the labour time or quantity of labour they contain.

But, Adam continues:

"As soon as *stock has accumulated in the hands of particular persons,* some of them will naturally employ it in setting to work industrious people, whom they will supply with materials and subsistence, *in order to make a profit by the sale of their work,* o r *by what their labour adds to the value of the materials*" ([Garnier,] l.c., p. 96) [Vol. I, pp. 82-83].

STOP, BEFORE we follow the passage further. *D'abord,*[a] whence come the industrious people who possess neither means of subsistence nor materials of labour—people who are hanging in mid air? If we strip Smith's statement of its naïve phrasing, it means nothing more than: capitalist production begins from the moment when the conditions of labour belong to one class, and another class has at its disposal only labour capacity. This separation of labour from the conditions of labour is the pre-condition of capitalist production.

Secondly, however, what does Adam Smith mean when he says that the EMPLOYERS OF LABOUR set labourers to work "in order *to make a profit by the sale of their work,* o r by what their labour [VI-251] adds to the value of the materials"? Does he mean by this that the profit comes from the *sale,* that the commodity is sold *above* its value—that is, what Steuart calls PROFIT UPON ALIENATION, which is nothing but A VIBRATION OF WEALTH BETWEEN PARTIES? Let him answer for himself.

"In exchanging *the complete manufacture* either for money, *for labour*" (here again is a source of new error) "or for other goods, over and above what may be sufficient to pay the price of the materials, and the wages of the workmen, *something must be given* for the profits of the undertaker of the work, who hazards his stock in this adventure" ([Garnier,] l.c.) [Vol. I, p. 83].

(We shall return to this "hazarding" later, see Notebook VII, p. 173,[250] in the chapter on the apologetic accounts of profit.) This something given for the *profits* of the undertaker, when the complete manufacture is exchanged, does it come from the sale of the commodity above its value, is it Steuart's PROFIT UPON ALIENATION?

"The *value,*" Adam continues immediately, "*which the workmen add to the materials,* therefore, resolves itself *in this case*" (when capitalist production has begun) "*into two parts, of which the one pays their wages, the other the profits of their employer upon the whole stock of materials and wages which he advanced*" ([Garnier,] l.c., pp. 96-97) [Vol. I, p. 83].

Here therefore Adam Smith explicitly states: the profit which is made on the sale of the complete manufacture originates not from *the sale* itself, not from the sale of the commodity *above* its value, is not PROFIT UPON ALIENATION. The value, that is, the quantity of labour

---

[a] In the first place.— *Ed.*

which the workmen add to the material, falls rather into 2 parts. One pays their wages or is paid for through their wages. By this transaction the workmen give in return only as much labour as they have received in the form of wages. The other part forms the profit of the capitalist, i.e., it is a quantity of labour which he sells without having paid for it. If therefore he sells the commodity at its value, i.e., for the labour time contained in it, in other words if he exchanges it for other commodities in accordance with the law of value, then his profit originates from the fact that he has not *paid for* a part of the labour contained in the commodity, but has nevertheless *sold* it. Adam Smith has thereby himself refuted the idea that the circumstance that the whole product of his labour no longer belongs to the labourer, that he is obliged to share it or its value with the owner of capital, invalidates the law that the proportion in which commodities exchange for each other, or their exchange value, is determined by the quantity of labour time materialised in them. Indeed, on the contrary, he traces the profit of the capitalist precisely to the fact that he has not paid for a part of the labour added to the commodity, and it is from this that his profit on the sale of the commodity arises. We shall see how further on Adam Smith even more explicitly derives profit from the labour performed by the workman over and above the quantity of labour with which he *pays for* his wages, that is to say, replaces it by an equivalent.[a] Thereby he has recognised the true origin of surplus value. At the same time he has expressly stated that it does not arise from the [VI-252] advanced funds, whose value—however useful they may be in the real labour process—merely reappears in the product; but that it arises exclusively from the new labour which the workmen *add to the materials* in the new process of production, in which those funds figure as means of labour or instruments of labour.

On the other hand, the phrase "in exchanging the complete manufacture either for money, *for labour,* or for other goods" is wrong (and arises from the confusion mentioned earlier).

If he exchanges the commodity for money or for a commodity, his profit arises from his selling more labour than he has paid for, from the fact that he does not exchange an equal quantity of objectified labour for an equal quantity of living labour. Adam Smith therefore must not put the exchange either for money or for other goods on the same footing as the exchange of the complete manufacture for labour. For in the first exchange the

---

[a] See this volume, pp. 394-98.— *Ed.*

surplus value originates from the fact that the commodities are exchanged at their value, for the labour time contained in them, which however is in part *unpaid for*. Here it is assumed that the capitalist does not exchange an equal quantity of past labour for an equal quantity of living labour; that the quantity of living labour appropriated by him is greater than the quantity of living labour he has paid for. Otherwise the workman's wage would be equal to the value of his product. The profit on the exchange of the complete manufacture for money or commodities, if they are exchanged at their value, arises therefore from the fact that the exchange between the complete manufacture and the living labour is subject to other laws; that no equivalents are exchanged here. These CASES, therefore, must not be lumped together.

Profit is consequently nothing but a deduction from the value which the workmen have added to the material of labour. They add to the material, however, nothing but a new quantity of labour. The workman's labour time therefore resolves itself into two parts: one for which he has received an equivalent, his wages, from the capitalist; the other which he gives to him gratis and which constitutes the *profit*. Adam Smith rightly points out that only the part of the labour (value) which the workman newly adds to the material resolves itself into wages and profit, that is to say, the newly-created surplus value in itself has nothing to do with the part of the capital which has been advanced (as materials and instruments).

Adam Smith, who has thus reduced profit to the appropriation of the unpaid labour of others, at once goes on to say:

"The profits of stock, it may perhaps be thought, are only a different name for the wages of a particular sort of labour, the labour of inspection and direction" ([Garnier,] p. 97) [Vol. I, p. 83].

And he refutes this false view of the LABOUR OF SUPERINTENDENCE. We shall return to this later, in another chapter.[76] Here it is only important to stress that Adam Smith very clearly recognises, brings out and expressly emphasises the contradistinction between his view of the origin of profit and this apologetic view. After pointing out this contradistinction he proceeds:

[VI-253] "In this state of things the whole produce of labour does not always belong to the labourer. He must in most cases share it with the *owner of the stock* which employs him. Neither is the quantity of labour commonly employed in acquiring or producing any commodity, the only circumstance which can regulate the quantity which it ought commonly to purchase, command or exchange for. An *additional quantity*, it is evident, must be due for the profits of the stock which advanced the wages and furnished the materials of that labour" ([Garnier,] l. c., p. 99) [Vol. I, p. 85].

This is quite correct. Given capitalist production, objectified labour—in the form of money or commodity—always purchases, besides the quantity of labour which it itself contains, an "additional quantity" of living labour "for the profits of the stock"; which however in other words means nothing but that it appropriates for nothing, appropriates without paying for it, a part of the living labour. Adam Smith is superior to Ricardo in that he so strongly emphasises how this CHANGE begins with capitalist production. On the other hand, he is inferior to Ricardo in that he is never able to free himself from the viewpoint—though it is one he himself refuted by his own analysis—that through this CHANGED RELATION BETWEEN MATERIALISED LABOUR AND LIVING LABOUR a CHANGE takes place IN THE DETERMINATION OF THE RELATIVE VALUE OF COMMODITIES, which in relation to each other represent nothing but MATERIALISED LABOUR, GIVEN QUANTITIES OF REALISED LABOUR.

After thus presenting surplus value in the one form, the form of profit, as part of the labour which the worker performs over and above the part of the labour WHICH PAYS HIS WAGES, he does the same with the other form of surplus value, *rent of land.* One of the objective conditions of labour alienated from labour and therefore confronting it as other men's property, is *capital*; the other is the *land* itself, the land as *landed property.* Therefore after dealing with the *owner of capital,* Adam Smith continues:

"As soon as the land of any country has all become private property, the landlords, like *all other men,* love to reap where they never sowed, and demand a *rent* even for its natural produce... He" (the labourer) "must *give up* to the landlord *a portion of what his labour either collects or produces.* This portion, or, what comes to the same thing, the price, of this portion, constitutes the *rent of land*" ([Garnier,] l. c., pp. 99-100) [Vol. I, pp. 85-86].

Like industrial profit proper, rent of land is only a part of the labour which is added by the labourer to the materials and *which he gives up,* hands over to the owner of the land without being paid for it; hence, only a part of the surplus labour performed by him over and above the part of the labour time which he works TO PAY HIS WAGES or to return an equivalent for the labour time contained in his wages.

Thus Adam Smith conceives *surplus value*—that is, surplus labour, the excess of labour performed and realised in the commodity *over and above* the paid labour, the labour which has received its equivalent in the wages—as the *general category,* [VI-254] of which profit proper and rent of land are merely branches. Nevertheless, he does not distinguish surplus value as such as a category on its own, distinct from the specific forms it

assumes in profit and rent. This is the source of much error and
inadequacy in his inquiry, and of even more in the work of
Ricardo.

Another form in which surplus value appears is *intérêt du
capital*,[a] interest on money. But this

> *"interest on money is always"* (Adam Smith says in the same chapter) *"a derivative
> revenue,* which, if it is not paid from the *profit* which is made by the use of the
> money, must be paid from some other source of revenue"

(therefore either rent or wages. In the latter case, assuming the
average wage, it does not originate from surplus value but is a
deduction from the wage itself or—and in this form, as we shall
later have occasion to see, it appears in undeveloped capitalist
production—it is only another form of profit[251])

> "unless perhaps the borrower is a spendthrift, who contracts a second debt in
> order to pay the interest of the first" ([Garnier,] l. c., pp. 105-06) [Vol. I, p. 90].

Interest is therefore either a part of the *profit* made with the
capital lent; in this case it is only a secondary form of profit itself,
a branch of profit, and thus only a further division between
different persons of the surplus value appropriated in the form of
profit. Or it is paid out of rent. In which case the same holds
good. Or the borrower pays the interest out of his own or
someone else's capital. In which case it in no way constitutes
surplus value, but is merely a different distribution of existing
wealth, VIBRATION OF THE BALANCE OF WEALTH BETWEEN PARTIES, as in PROFIT
UPON ALIENATION.[b] Excluding the latter case, when interest is not in
any way a form of surplus value and excluding the case where it is
a deduction from the wage or itself a form of profit; Adam does not
mention this latter case, interest is therefore only a secondary form
of surplus value, a mere part of profit or of rent (affecting merely
their distribution), and therefore also is nothing but a part of unpaid
surplus labour.

> * "The stock which is lent at interest is always *considered* as a capital by the
> lender. He expects that in due time it is to be restored to him, and that in the
> meantime the borrower is to pay him a certain annual rent for the use of it. The
> borrower may use it either as a *capital*, or as a *stock reserved for immediate
> consumption*. If he uses it as a capital, he employs it in the maintenance of
> productive labourers, *who reproduce the value with a profit*. He can, in this case, both
> restore the capital and pay the interest, without alienating or encroaching upon any
> other source of revenue. If he uses it as a stock reserved for immediate
> consumption, he acts the part of a prodigal, and dissipates in the maintenance of
> the idle, what was destined for the support of the industrious. He can, in this case,

---

neither restore the capital nor pay the interest, without either alienating or encroaching upon some other source of revenue, such as the property or rent of land" * (McCulloch edit., Vol. II, b. II, ch. IV, [p.] 127).

[VI-255] Thus whoever borrows money, which here means capital, either uses it himself as capital, and makes a profit with it. In this case the interest which he pays to the lender is nothing but a part of the profit under a *special name*. Or he consumes the borrowed money. Then he increases the wealth of the lender by reducing his own. What takes place is only a different distribution of the wealth that passes from the hand of the spendthrift into that of the lender, but there is no generation of surplus value. In so far therefore as interest in any way represents surplus value, it is nothing but a part of profit, which itself is nothing but a definite form of surplus value, that is, unpaid labour.

Finally, Adam Smith observes that in the same way all incomes of persons who live on the proceeds of taxes are paid either from wages, and are therefore a deduction from wages themselves; or have their source in profit and rent, thus representing only claims whereby various social strata share in the consumption of profit and rent, which themselves are nothing but different forms of surplus value.

"All taxes, and all the revenue which is founded upon them, all salaries, pensions, and annuities of every kind, are ultimately derived from some one or other of those three original sources of revenue, and are paid either immediately or mediately from the wages of labour, the profits of stock, or the rent of land" ([Garnier,] l. c., l. I, ch. VI, p. 106) [Vol. I, p. 90].

Thus interest on money, along with taxes or revenues derived from taxes—in so far as they are not deductions from wages themselves—are merely shares in profit and rent, which are themselves in turn reducible to surplus value, that is, unpaid labour time.

This is Adam Smith's general theory of surplus value.

In yet another passage Adam Smith sums up his views on the whole question, making it all the more clear how far he is from even attempting in any way to prove that the value added by the labourer to the product (after deducting the *frais de production*,[a] the value of raw material and of the instruments of labour) is no longer determined by the labour time contained in the product, because the labourer does not himself appropriate this value in full, but has to share it—the value or the product—with the capitalist and the landowner. The way in which the value of a

---

[a] Costs of production.— *Ed.*

commodity is distributed among the producers of this commodity naturally alters nothing in the nature of this value or in the relative value of commodities to one another.

* "As soon as land becomes private property, the landlord demands a share of almost all the produce which the labourer can either raise, or collect from it. *His rent makes the first deduction from the produce of the labour which is employed upon land.* It seldom happens that the person who tills the ground has wherewithal to maintain himself till he reaps the harvest. His maintenance is generally advanced to him from the stock of a master, the farmer who employs him, and who would have no interest to employ him, unless he was to share in the produce of his labour, or unless his stock was to be replaced to him with a profit. *This profit makes a second deduction* [VI-256] *from* [*the produce of*] *the labour which is employed upon land.* The produce of almost all other labour is liable to *the like deduction of profit.* In all arts and manufactures the greater part of the workmen stand in need of a master to advance them the materials of their work, and their wages and maintenance till it be completed. *He shares in the produce of their labour, or in the value which it adds to the materials upon which it is bestowed; and in this share consists his profit"* * ([McCulloch edit.,] l.c., Vol. I, b. I, ch. VIII, pp. 109-10).

Here therefore Adam Smith in plain terms describes rent and profit on capital as mere *deductions* from the workman's product or the value of his product, which is equal to the quantity of labour added by him to the material. This deduction however, as Adam Smith has himself previously explained, can only consist of that part of the labour which the workman adds to the materials, over and above the quantity of labour which only pays his wages, or which only provides an equivalent for his wages; that is, the surplus labour, the unpaid part of his labour. (Therefore, incidentally, profit and rent or capital and landed property can never be a *source of value.*)

We see the great advance made by Adam Smith beyond the Physiocrats in the analysis of surplus value and hence of capital. In their view, it is only one definite kind of concrete labour— agricultural labour—that creates surplus value. Therefore what they examine is the use value of labour, not labour time, general social labour, which is the sole source of value. In this special kind of labour, however, it is *nature*, the land, which in fact creates the surplus value, consisting in an increase of (organic) matter—the excess of the matter produced over the matter consumed. They see it, however, still in quite a restricted form and therefore distorted by fantastic ideas. But to Adam Smith, it is general social labour—no matter in what use values it manifests itself—the mere quantity of necessary labour, which creates value. Surplus value, whether it takes the form of profit, rent, or the secondary form of interest, is nothing but a part of this labour, appropriated by the owners of the objective conditions of labour in the exchange with living labour. For the Physiocrats, therefore, surplus value appears only in the form of rent of land. For Adam Smith, rent, profit and interest are only different forms of surplus value.

When I speak of surplus value, in relation to the total sum of capital advanced, as *profit on capital*, this is because the capitalist directly engaged in production *directly* appropriates the surplus labour, no matter under what categories he has subsequently to share this surplus value with the landowner or with the lender of capital. Thus the farmer pays the landowner directly. And the manufacturer, out of the surplus value he has appropriated, pays rent to the owner of the land on which the factory stands, and interest to the capitalist who has advanced capital to him.

[VI-257] // There are now still to be examined: 1) Adam Smith's confusion of surplus value with profit; 2) his views on productive labour; 3) how he makes rent and profit *sources of value*, and his false analysis of the natural price of commodities, in which the value of raw materials and instruments is not supposed to have a separate existence, and therefore not to be considered, apart from the price of the 3 SOURCES OF REVENUE. //

Wages or the equivalent with which the capitalist buys the temporary disposal of labour capacity are not a commodity in its immediate form, but the commodity metamorphosed, money, the commodity in its independent form as exchange value, as the direct materialisation of social labour, of general labour time. With this money the labourer naturally buys commodities at the same price as any other possessor of money // disregarding here such details as, for example, that he buys on less favourable conditions and in worse circumstances, etc. //. He faces the seller of commodities as does every other possessor of money—as a buyer. He enters commodity circulation itself not as a labourer, but as pole Money facing pole Commodity, as possessor of a commodity in its general, always exchangeable form. His money is once more transformed into commodities, which are to serve him as use values, and in this process he buys commodities at the current market price—generally speaking, at their value. In this transaction he carries through only the act $M—C$, which indicates a change of form, but, as a general rule, by no means a change in magnitude of value. Since however, by his labour materialised in the product, he has added not only as much labour time as was contained in the money he received, he has paid not only an equivalent but has given surplus labour gratis—which is precisely the source of the profit—he has thus *in fact* (the mediating process, the sale of his labour capacity, is not relevant when we are dealing with the result) given a higher value than the value of the sum of money which forms his wages. IN RETURN, he has bought with more labour time the quantity of labour realised in the money which comes to him as wages. It can therefore be said that in the same way he has indirectly bought all the commodities into which the money (which is only the independent expression of a definite quantity of social labour time) he received is converted with more labour time than they contain, although he buys them at the same price as any other buyer or possessor of a commodity in its first transformation. Conversely, the money with which the capitalist buys labour contains a smaller quantity of labour, less labour time, than the quantity of labour or labour time of the workman contained in the commodity produced by him. Besides the quantity of labour contained in this sum of money which forms the wage, the capitalist buys an additional quantity of labour for which he does not pay, an excess over the quantity of labour contained in the money he pays out. And it is precisely this additional quantity of labour which constitutes the surplus value created by capital.

But as the money [VI-258] with which the capitalist buys labour (in the actual result, even though mediated through EXCHANGE not with labour directly, but with labour capacity) is nothing other than the converted form of *all other commodities*, their independent existence as exchange value, it can equally well be said that all commodities in exchange with living labour buy more labour than they contain. It is precisely this more that constitutes surplus value. It is Adam Smith's great merit that it is just in the chapters of Book I (chapters VI, VII, VIII) where he passes from simple commodity exchange and its law of value to exchange between objectified and living labour, to exchange between capital and wage labour, to the consideration of profit and rent in general— in short, to the origin of surplus value—that he feels some flaw has emerged. He senses that somehow—whatever the cause may be, and he does not grasp what it is—in the actual result the law is suspended: more labour is exchanged for less labour (from the labourer's standpoint), less labour is exchanged for more labour (from the capitalist's standpoint). His merit is that he emphasises— and it obviously perplexes him—that with the *accumulation of capital* and the *appearance of property in land*—that is, when the conditions of labour assume an independent existence over against labour itself—something new occurs, apparently (and actually, in the result) the law of value changes into its opposite. It is his theoretical strength that he feels and stresses this contradiction, just as it is his theoretical weakness that the contradiction shakes his confidence in the general law, even for simple commodity exchange; that he does not perceive how this contradiction arises, through labour capacity itself becoming a commodity, and that in the case of this specific commodity its use value—which therefore has nothing to do with its exchange value—is precisely the energy which creates exchange value. Ricardo is ahead of Adam Smith in that these apparent contradictions—in their result real contradictions—do not confuse him. But he is behind Adam Smith in that he does not even suspect that this presents a problem, and therefore the *specific* development which the law of value undergoes with the formation of capital does not for a moment puzzle him or even attract his attention. We shall see later how what was a stroke of genius with Adam Smith becomes reactionary with Malthus as against Ricardo's standpoint.[249]

Naturally, however, it is at the same time this deep insight of Adam Smith's that makes him irresolute and uncertain, cuts the firm ground from under his feet, and prevents him—in contrast to Ricardo—from reaching a consistent and comprehensive theoretical view of the abstract general foundations of the bourgeois system.

[VI-259] The above-quoted statement by Adam Smith that the commodity buys more labour than it contains, or that labour pays a higher value for the commodity than the latter contains, is thus formulated by Hodgskin in his *Popular Political Economy*:

* "The *natural price* (or *necessary* price) means the whole *quantity of labour* nature requires from man, that he may produce any commodity.... Labour was the original, is now and ever will be the only purchase money in dealing with nature. Whatever quantity of labour may be requisite to produce any commodity, the labourer must always, in the present state of society, give a great deal more labour to acquire and possess it than is requisite to buy it from nature. Natural Price so increased to the labourer is *Social Price,** we must always attend to the difference between natural and social price" (Thomas Hodgskin, *Popular Political Economy etc.*, London, 1827, [pp.] 219-20).

In this presentation Hodgskin reproduces both what is correct and what is confused and confusing in Adam Smith's view.

We have seen how Adam Smith explains *surplus value* in general, of which the rent of land and profit are only different forms and component parts. As he presents it, the part of capital which consists of raw material and means of production has nothing directly to do with the creation of surplus value. The latter arises exclusively from the ADDITIONAL QUANTITY OF LABOUR which the labourer gives *over and above* the part of his labour which forms only the equivalent for his wages. Therefore it is only that part of the capital advanced which consists in wages from which surplus value directly arises, since it is the only part of capital which not only reproduces itself but produces an OVERPLUS. In profit, on the other hand, the surplus value is calculated on the total amount of capital advanced, and besides this modification yet further ones are added through the equalisation of profits in the various spheres of production of capital.

Because Adam makes what is in substance an analysis of surplus value, but does not present it explicitly in the form of a definite category, distinct from its special forms, he subsequently mixes it up directly with the further developed form of profit. This error persists with Ricardo and all his disciples. Hence arise (particularly with Ricardo, all the more strikingly because he works out the fundamental law of value in more systematic unity and consistency, so that the inconsistencies and contradictions stand out more strikingly) a series of inconsistencies, unresolved contradictions and fatuities, which the Ricardians (as we shall see later in the section on profit) attempt to solve with phrases in a scholastic way.[252] Crass empiricism turns into false metaphysics, scholasticism, which toils painfully to deduce undeniable empirical phenomena by simple formal abstraction directly from the general law, or to show by cunning argument that they are in accordance with that law.

At this point where we discuss Adam Smith we will give an example, because the confusion creeps in immediately not when he is dealing *ex professo*[a] with profit or rent—those particular forms of surplus value—but where he is thinking of them only as forms of surplus value in general, as DEDUCTIONS FROM THE LABOUR BESTOWED BY THE LABOURERS UPON THE MATERIALS.[b]

[VI-260] After Adam Smith has said, in Book I, Chapter VI:

"The value which the workmen *add* to the materials, therefore, resolves itself in this case into two parts, of which the one pays their wages, the other the profits of their employer upon the whole stock of materials and wages which he advanced",

he continues:

"He" (the entrepreneur) "could have no interest to employ them, unless he expected from the sale of their work something more than what was sufficient to replace his stock to him; and he could have no interest to employ a great stock rather than a small one, unless his profits were to bear some proportion to the extent of his stock" [Garnier, pp. 96-97] [Vol. I, p. 83].

Remarquons d'abord[c]: surplus value, the OVERPLUS which the

---

a Specifically.— *Ed.*

b See this volume, p. 391.— *Ed.*

c We note first.— *Ed.*

entrepreneur makes over and above the amount of value required to replace his stock, is reduced by Adam Smith to that part of the labour which the workmen add to the materials over and above the quantity that pays their wages—thus making this OVERPLUS arise purely from the part of the capital which is laid out in wages. Then, however, he immediately conceives this OVERPLUS in the form of profit—i.e., he thinks of it not in relation to the part of the capital from which it arises, but as an overplus over the total value of the capital advanced, "upon the whole stock of materials *and* wages which he advanced". (It is oversight that the means of production are here left out of account.) [253] He therefore conceives surplus value directly in the form of profit. Hence the difficulties that soon appear.

The capitalist, Adam Smith says,

"could have no interest to employ them, unless he expected from the sale of their work *something more* than what was sufficient to replace his stock to him".

Once capitalist relations are assumed, this is quite correct. The capitalist does not produce in order to satisfy his needs with the product; he produces with absolutely no direct regard for consumption. He produces in order to produce surplus value. But this premiss—which amounts to no more than that, capitalist production being assumed, the capitalist produces for the sake of surplus value—is not made use of by Adam Smith to *explain surplus value*, as some of his silly disciples subsequently did; i.e., he does not explain the existence of surplus value by the interests of the capitalist, by his desire for surplus value. On the contrary, he has already derived surplus value from the value which the workmen add to the materials over and above the value which they add in exchange for the wages they have received. But then he goes on at once: the capitalist would have no interest to employ a great stock rather than a small one, unless his profits were to bear some proportion to the extent of the stock advanced. Here profit is no longer explained by the nature of surplus value, but by the "interest" of the capitalist. Which is downright silly.

Adam Smith does not sense that, by thus directly confusing surplus value with profit and profit with surplus value, he is upsetting the law of the origin of surplus value which he has just established. [VI-261] If surplus value is only the part of the value (or of the quantity of labour) a d d e d by the workman *in excess* of the part that he adds to the materials to replace the wages, why should that 2nd part grow as the direct result of the value of the capital advanced being in one case greater than in the other? The contradiction becomes even clearer in the example which Adam Smith himself gives immediately following on this, in order to refute the view that profit is WAGES for the "SO-CALLED LABOUR OF SUPERINTENDENCE".

For he says:

"They" (the profits of stock) "are, however, altogether different from wages, are regulated by quite different principles, and bear no proportion to the quantity, or the ingenuity of this supposed labour of inspection and direction. *They are regulated altogether by the value of the stock employed,* and are greater or smaller in proportion to the extent of this stock. Let us suppose, for example, that in some particular place, where the *common annual profits of* manufacturing *stock are ten per cent* there are two different manufactures, in each of which twenty workmen are employed, at the rate of 15 pounds a year each, or at the expense of 300 a year in each manufactory. Let us suppose, too, that the coarse materials annually wrought up in the one cost only 700 pounds, while the finer materials in the other cost 7,000. The capital annually employed in the one will, in this case, amount only to 1,000 pounds; whereas that employed in the other will amount to 7,300 pounds. At the rate of ten per cent, therefore, the undertaker of the one will expect a yearly profit of about 100 pounds only; while that of the other will expect about 730 pounds. But though their profits are so very different, their labour of inspection and direction may be either altogether or very nearly the same" [Garnier, pp. 97-98] [Vol. I, pp. 83-84].

From surplus value in its general form we come straight to a general rate of profit, which has nothing directly to do with it. *Mais passon outre!*[a] In both manufactories 20 workmen are employed; in both their wages are the same, £300. Proof therefore that it is not perhaps a case of a higher kind of labour being employed in one as compared with the other, so that one hour's labour and therefore also one hour's surplus labour would in one be equal to several hours' surplus labour in the other. On the contrary, the same average labour is assumed in both, as the equality of their wages shows. How then can the surplus labour which the workers add, beyond the price of their wages, be worth seven times as much in one factory as in the other? Or why should the workers in one factory, because the materials they work up in it are 7 times as costly as in the other, provide 7 times as much surplus labour as in the other, although in both factories they receive the same wages, and therefore work the same time to reproduce [VI-262] their wages?

The seven times greater profit in the one manufactory as compared with the other—or in general the law of profit, that it is in proportion to the magnitude of the capital advanced—thus *prima facie* contradicts the law of surplus value or of profit (since

---

[a] But let us pass on!—*Ed.*

Adam Smith treats the two as identical) that it consists purely of the unpaid surplus labour of the workmen. Adam Smith puts this down with quite naïve thoughtlessness, without the faintest suspicion of the contradiction it presents. All his disciples—since none of them considers surplus value in general, as distinct from its determinate forms—followed him faithfully in this. With Ricardo, as already noted, it merely comes out even more strikingly.

As Adam Smith resolves surplus value not only into profit but also into the rent of land—two particular kinds of surplus value, whose movement is determined by quite different laws—he should certainly have seen from this that he ought not to treat general abstract form as directly identical with any of its particular forms. With all later bourgeois economists, as with Adam Smith, lack of theoretical understanding needed to distinguish the different forms of the economic relations remains the rule in their coarse grabbing at and interest in the empirically available material. Hence also their inability to form a correct conception of money, in which what is in question is only various changes in the form of exchange value, while the magnitude of value remains unchanged.

Lauderdale, in *Recherches sur la nature et l'origine de la richesse publique (traduit par Lagentie de Lavaïsse, Paris, 1808)*, raises the objection to Adam Smith's exposition of surplus value—which he says corresponds with the views already advanced by Locke—that according to it capital is not an original source of wealth, as Smith makes out, but only a derivative source. The relevant passages run:

"Above a century ago, Mr. Locke stated pretty nearly the same opinion" (as Adam Smith).... "'Money,' he said, 'is a barren thing and produces nothing; the only service it renders is that it by compact transfers that profit that was the reward of one man's labour into another man's pocket'" (Lauderdale, p. 116).[a]

"If this, however, was a just and accurate idea of the profit of capital, it would follow that the profit of stock must be a derivative, and not an original source of wealth; and capital could not therefore be considered as a source of wealth, its profit being only a transfer from the pocket of the labourer into that of the proprietor of stock" (l.c., pp. 116-17) [James Maitland Lauderdale, *An Inquiry into the Nature and Origin of Public Wealth...*, Edinburgh and London, 1804, pp. 157-58].[a]

In so far as the value of the capital reappears in the product, it cannot be called a "source of wealth". Here it is only as ACCUMULATED LABOUR, as a definite quantity of materialised labour, that it adds its own value to the product.

---

[a] Marx quotes Lauderdale partly in French and partly in German.— *Ed.*

Capital is productive of value only as a *relation*, in so far as it is a coercive force on wage labour, compelling it to perform surplus labour, or spurring on the productive power of labour to produce relative surplus value. In both cases it only produces value as [VI-263] the power of labour's own objectified conditions over labour when these are alienated from labour; only as one of the forms of wage labour itself, as a condition of wage labour. But in the sense commonly used by economists, as stored up labour existing in money or commodities, capital—like all conditions of labour, even the unpaid natural forces—functions productively in the labour process, in the production of use values, but it is never a source of value. It creates no new value, and only adds exchange value to the product at all in so far as it has exchange value, i.e., only in so far as it itself consists in objectified labour time, so that labour is the source of its value.

Lauderdale is right in this respect—that Adam Smith, after explaining the nature of surplus value and of value, wrongly presents capital and land as independent sources of exchange value. They are sources of revenue for their owners in so far as they are titles to a certain quantity of surplus labour, which the labourer must perform over and above the labour time required to replace his wages. Thus Adam Smith says for example:

"*Wages, profit, and rent,* are the *three original sources* of all revenue, *as well as of all exchangeable value*" ([Garnier,] l. I, ch. VI [p. 105]) [Vol. I, p. 89].

Just as it is true that they are the three original sources of all revenue, so it is false that they also are the three original sources *of all exchangeable value*, since the value of a commodity is exclusively determined by the labour time contained in it. After just presenting rent and profit as mere DEDUCTIONS from the value or from the labour added by the workman to the raw material, how can Adam Smith call them original sources of exchangeable value? (They can only be that in the sense that they set in motion the original source, that is to say, that they compel the workman to perform surplus labour.) In so far as they are titles (conditions) for the appropriation of a part of the value, that is, of the labour objectified in the commodity, they are sources of income for their owners. But the distribution or appropriation of value is certainly not the source of the value that is appropriated. If this appropriation did not take place, and the workman received the whole product of his labour as his wage, the value of the commodities produced would be just the same as before, although it would not be shared with the landowner and the capitalist.

The fact that landed property and capital are sources of income for their owners, i.e., give them the power to appropriate a part of the values created by labour, does not make them sources of the value which they appropriate. But it is equally wrong to say that wages are an original source of exchangeable value, although wages, or rather the continuous sale of labour capacity, is a source of income for the labourer. It is the labour and not the wages of the labourer that creates value. Wages are only already existing value, or if we consider the whole of production, the part of the value created by the labourer which he himself appropriates; but this appropriation does not create value. His wages can therefore rise or fall without this affecting the value of the commodity produced by him.

Here we will leave entirely out of account how far Adam Smith regards rent as a constituent element of the price of commodities. For our present inquiry this question is all the more unimportant because he treats rent just as he treats profit, as a mere part of surplus value, a DEDUCTION FROM THE LABOUR ADDED BY THE LABOURER TO THE RAW MATERIAL,[a] and consequently [VI-264] in fact also as a DEDUCTION FROM PROFIT, inasmuch as the total unpaid surplus labour is *directly* appropriated by the capitalist in his relations with labour; it does not matter under what categories he may later have to share this surplus value with owners of the conditions of production—the landowner or the lender of capital. For the sake of simplicity we shall therefore speak only of wages and profit as the two categories into which newly-created value is divided.

Let us assume that 12 hours of labour time are materialised in a commodity (*leaving out of account* the value of the raw material and instruments of labour consumed in it). We can express its value as such only in *money*. Let us therefore assume that 12 hours of labour time are likewise materialised in 5s. Thus the value of the commodity=5s. By the natural price of commodities Adam Smith understands nothing but their value expressed in money. (The market price of the commodity, of course, stands either above or below its value. Indeed, as I shall show later, even the average price of commodities is *always different* from their value.[254] Adam Smith, however, does not deal with this in his discussion of natural price. Moreover, neither the market price nor still less the fluctuations in the average price of commodities can be comprehended except on the basis of an understanding of the nature of value.)

See this volume, p. 391.—*Ed.*

If the surplus value contained in the commodity is 20 per cent of its total value, or what amounts to the same thing, 25 per cent of the necessary labour contained in it, then this value of 5s., the natural price of the commodity, can be resolved into 4s. wages and 1s. surplus value (which here we will call profit, following Adam Smith). It would be correct to say that the magnitude of value of the commodity determined independently of wages and profit, or its natural price, can be resolved into 4s. wages (the price of the labour) and 1s. profit (the price of the profit). But it would be wrong to say that the value of the commodity arises from adding together or combining the price of the wages, which is regulated independently of the value of the commodity, and the price of the profit. If this were the case there would be absolutely no reason why the total value of the commodity should not be 8s., 10s., etc., according to whether one assumes the wages=5s. and the profit 3s., and so on.

When Adam Smith is examining the "natural rate" of wages or the "natural price" of wages, what guides his investigation? The natural price of the means of subsistence required for the reproduction of labour capacity. But by what does he determine the natural price of these means of subsistence? In so far as he determines it at all, he comes back to the correct determination of value, namely, the labour time required for the production of these means of subsistence. But when he abandons this correct course, he falls into *cercle vicieux.* By what is the natural price of the means of subsistence determined, which determine the natural price of wages? By the natural price of "wages", of "profit", of "rent", which constitute the natural price of those means of subsistence as of all commodities. And so *in infinitum.* The twaddle about the law of demand and supply of course does not help us out of this *cercle vicieux.* For the "natural price" or the price corresponding to the value of the commodity is supposed to exist just when demand meets supply, i.e., when the price of the commodity does not stand above or below its value as a result of fluctuations in demand and supply; when, in other words, the cost price [255] of the commodity (or the value of the commodity supplied by the seller) is also the price which the demand pays.

[VI-265] But as we have said: In investigating the natural price of wages Adam Smith in fact falls back—at least in certain passages—on the correct determination of the value of the commodity. On the other hand, in the chapter dealing with the natural rate or the natural price of profit he gets bogged down, so far as the real problem is concerned, in meaningless commonplaces and tautologies. In fact, at first it was the value of the commodity which he saw as regulating wages and profit and rent. Then however he sets to work the other way round (which was closer to what empirical observation showed and to everyday ideas), and now the natural price of commodities is supposed to be calculated and discovered [a] by adding together the natural prices of wages, profit and rent. It is one of Ricardo's chief merits that he put an end to this confusion. We shall return to this point briefly when we are dealing with him.[256]

Here there is only this further point to be noted: the *given magnitude* of value of the commodity, serving as a fund for the payment of wages and profit, appears empirically to the industrialist in the form that a definite market price of the commodity holds good for a shorter or longer time, in spite of all fluctuations in wages.

It is necessary therefore to call attention to this peculiar train of thought in Adam Smith's book: first the value of the commodity is examined, and in some passages correctly determined—so correctly determined that he traces out in general form the origin of surplus value and of its specific forms, hence deriving wages and profit from this value. But then he takes the opposite course, and seeks on the contrary to deduce the value of commodities (from which he has deduced wages and profit) by adding together the natural prices of wages, profit and rent. It is this latter circumstance that is responsible for the fact that he nowhere correctly explains the influence of oscillations of wages, profit, etc., on the prices of commodities—since he lacks the basis [for such an explanation].

We come to another point, which is linked with the analysis of the price or value of the commodity (since the two are here still assumed to be identical). Let us assume that Adam Smith has calculated correctly—i.e., the value of the commodity being given, he has correctly resolved it into the constituent parts in which this value is distributed among the various agents of production—but has not on the contrary tried to deduce value from the price of these constituent parts. Thus we shall leave this aside and also the one-sided way in which wages and profit are presented only as forms of distribution, and hence both as revenues in the same sense that their owners can consume. Apart from all this, Adam Smith himself raises a question, and this again shows his

---

[a] Marx wrote the word "ausgerechnet" (calculated) above the word "aufgefunden" (discovered) without indicating its place in the line.— *Ed.*

superiority over Ricardo—not that he finds the right solution to the question he raises, but that he raises it at all.

// The following quotation should be added to what has been said above in regard to Adam Smith making the categories in which the value of the commodity is appropriated into sources of this value: After he has refuted the view that profit is only another name for the wages of the capitalist, or WAGES OF LABOUR OF SUPERINTENDENCE, he concludes:

"In the *price* of commodities, therefore, the *profits* of stock constitute a *source of value* altogether *different* from the wages [of labour], and regulated by quite different principles" ([Garnier,] l. I, ch. VI, [p. 99]) [Vol. I, p. 85].

Adam Smith has just shown that the value added by the workmen to the materials is divided between them and the capitalists in the form of wages and profit; labour is therefore the only *source of value,* and the price of wages and the price of profits arise out of this source of value. But these prices themselves, whether wages or profit, are not a *source of value.* //

[VI-266] What Adam Smith says is:

"These three parts" (wages, profit and rent of the landowner) "seem either immediately or ultimately to make up the *whole* price of corn."

(Of all commodities. Adam Smith here takes corn, because in some commodities rent does not enter into the price as a constituent part.)

"A *fourth part,* it may be thought, is necessary for replacing the stock of the farmer, or for compensating the wear and tear of his labouring cattle, and other instruments of husbandry. But it must be considered, that the price of an instrument of husbandry, such as a labouring horse, is itself made up of the same three parts: the rent of the land upon which he is reared, the labour of tending and rearing him, and the profits of the farmer, who advances both the rent of this land, and the wages of this labour."

// Here profit appears as the primary form, which also includes rent. //

"Though the price of the corn, therefore, may pay the price as well as the maintenance of the horse, the *whole* price still resolves itself, either immediately or ultimately, into the same three parts of rent, labour and profit" ([Garnier,] l. I, ch. VI, [p. 101]) [Vol. I, pp. 86-87].

(Here it is perfectly preposterous that all of a sudden he says labour instead of wages, while he does not put landed property or capital for rent and profit.)

But was it not equally obviously necessary to consider that just as the farmer included the price of the horse and the plough in the price of the corn, the horse breeder or the plough maker from whom the farmer bought the horse and the plough, would include in the price of the horse and the plough the price of the instruments of production (in the case of the former, perhaps another horse) and of raw materials such as feeding stuffs and iron, whereas the fund from which the horse breeder and plough maker *paid* wages and profit (and rent) consisted only in the new labour which they *added* in their sphere of production to the amount of value present in their constant capital? Since therefore Adam Smith admits, in relation to the farmer, that the price of his *blé*[a] includes, besides the wages, profit and rent paid by him to himself and others, also a *4th constituent part* which is different from these—the value of the constant capital he has used up, such as horses, agricultural implements, etc.—this must also hold good for the horse breeder and the manufacturer of agricultural implements; and it is of no avail for Adam Smith to send us from pillar to post. Incidentally, the example of the farmer is peculiarly unhappily chosen for sending us from pillar to post, for in this case the ITEMS of constant capital include one that does not at all need to be bought from SOMEBODY ELSE, namely the seed; and does this constituent part of the value resolve itself into wages, profit or rent for ANYBODY?

But for the present let us proceed, and see whether Smith sticks to his view that the value of every commodity is resolvable into one or all of the sources of revenue: wages, profit, rent; and can therefore, being destined for consumption, be devoured or at any rate used up in one way or another for personal use (not industrial consumption). *D'abord* [VI-267] another preliminary point. In the case for example of gathering berries and such like it can be assumed that their value consists entirely of wages, although here also as a rule some appliances, such as baskets and so on, are required as means of labour. But examples of this kind are quite irrelevant here, where we are dealing with capitalist production.

To start with, once more the repetition of the view expressed in Book I, Chapter VI;

B. II, Ch. II, (Garnier, Vol. II, p. 212) states:

"It has been shown ... that the price of the greater part of commodities resolves itself into three parts, of which one pays the wages of the labour, another the profits of the stock, and a third the rent of the land" [Vol. II, pp. 17-18].

According to this, the whole value of any commodity resolves itself into revenue, and therefore falls to the share of one or

---

[a] Corn.— *Ed.*

another of the classes which live on this revenue, as a fund for consumption. Now since the total production of a country, each year for example, consists solely of the total of the values of the commodities produced, and since the value of each single one of these commodities is resolved into revenues, so also must their sum, the annual product of labour, the gross revenue, be consumable annually in this form.[257] And so immediately after this passage Smith himself raises the point:

"Since this is the case, it has been observed, with regard to every particular commodity, taken separately, it must be so with regard to *all* the commodities which compose the whole annual produce of the land and labour of every country, taken complexly. The *whole price* or *exchangeable value* of the annual produce, must resolve itself into the same three parts, and be parcelled out among the different inhabitants of the country, either as the wages of their labour, the profits of their stock, or the rent of their land" ([Garnier,] l.c., p. 213) [Vol. II, p. 18].

This is IN FACT the necessary consequence. What is true of the individual commodity is necessarily true of the total sum of commodities. But *quod non*,[a] says Adam. He goes on:

"But though the whole value of the annual produce of the land and labour of every country is thus divided among, and constitutes a revenue to, its different inhabitants; yet, as in the rent of a private estate, we distinguish between the *gross rent* and the *neat rent*, so may we likewise in the revenue of *all the inhabitants* of a great country" [Garnier, l. c., p. 213] [Vol. II, p. 18].

(*Halt la!*[b] Above he told us the direct opposite: in the case of the individual farmer we can distinguish a 4th part into which the value of his wheat for example resolves itself, namely the part which merely replaces the constant capital used up. This is *directly* true for the individual farmer. But when we go further into it, what is constant capital for him resolves itself at an earlier point, in another person's hand before it became capital in his, into wages, profit, etc., in a word into revenue. Therefore if it is true that commodities, considered in the hands of an individual producer, contain one part of the value which does not form revenue, then it is untrue for "all the inhabitants of a great country", because what in one person's hand is constant capital derives its value from the fact that it came from another person's hand as the aggregate price of wages, profit and rent. Now he says the direct opposite.)

Adam Smith continues:

[VI-268] "The *gross* rent of a private estate comprehends whatever is paid by the farmer; the *neat rent*, what remains free *to the landlord*, after deducting the

a Not so.— *Ed.*
b But stop.— *Ed.*

expense of management, of repairs, and all other necessary charges; or what, without hurting his estate, he can afford to place in his stock reserved for immediate consumption, or to spend upon his table", etc. "His real wealth is in proportion, not to his *gross,* but to his *neat* rent" [Garnier, pp. 213-14] [Vol. II, pp. 18-19].

(In the first place, Smith brings in here something improper. What the farmer pays as rent to the landowner, just as what he pays as wages to the labourers, is like his own profit, part of the value or price of the commodity, which resolves itself into revenue. The question is however whether the commodity contains yet another constituent part of its value. He admits this here, as he should admit it in the case of the farmer, but that should not prevent the latter's corn (i.e., the price *or* exchange value of his corn) from being resolvable merely into revenue. Secondly, a note in passing. The real wealth of which an individual farmer, considered *as a farmer,* can dispose, depends on his profit. But on the other hand, as owner of commodities he can sell the whole farm, or if the land does not belong to him, he can sell all constant capital there is on it such as draught cattle, agricultural implements, etc. The value which he can realise in this way, therefore the wealth at his disposal, is conditioned by the value, that is the size of the constant capital belonging to him. However, he can only sell this again to another farmer, in whose hands it is not disposable wealth but constant capital.) //So we are still just where we were.//

"The *gross* revenue of all the inhabitants of a great country comprehends the *whole* annual produce of their land and labour"

(previously we were told that this total (its value) resolves itself into wages, profits and rents, nothing but different forms of net revenue);

"the *neat* revenue, what remains free to them, after deducting the expense of maintaining, first, their *fixed,* and, secondly, their *circulating capital*";

(so he now deducts instruments of labour and raw materials);

"or what, without encroaching upon their capital, they can place in their *stock reserved for consumption*".

(So now we learn that the price or exchangeable value of the total stock of commodities, just as in the case of the individual capitalist, so also for the whole country, is resolvable into a fourth part which does not form a revenue for anyone and cannot be resolved into wages, profit or rent.)

"The whole expense of maintaining the *fixed capital* must evidently be excluded from the *neat* revenue of the society. Neither *the materials necessary* for supporting their useful machines and instruments of trade, their profitable buildings, etc., nor the *produce of the labour necessary* for fashioning those materials into the proper form, can ever make any part of it. The *price of that labour* may indeed make a part of it; as the workmen so employed may place *the whole value* [VI-269] *of their wages* in their *stock reserved for consumption.* But in other sorts of labour, both the price and the produce go to this or that stock; the price to that of the workmen, the produce to that of other people, whose subsistence, conveniences, and amusements, are augmented by the labour of those workmen" ([Garnier,] l.c., pp. 214-15) [Vol. II, pp. 19-20]. All the same, nearer the right view than the others.[a]

Here Adam Smith once more shies away from the question which he has to answer—the question concerning the fourth part of the total price of the commodity, which is not resolved into either wages, profit or rent. First something that is quite wrong: with makers of machinery, as with all other industrial capitalists, the labour which fashions the raw materials of the machine, etc., into the proper form in fact consists of necessary and surplus labour, and therefore resolves itself not only into the wages of the workmen, but also into the profit of the capitalist. But the value of the materials and the value of the instruments with which they are fashioned by the workmen into the proper form, is resolvable into neither the one nor the other. That products which are destined by their nature not for individual consumption but for industrial consumption do not enter into the stock reserved for immediate consumption, has nothing at all to do with it. Seed, for example (that portion of the corn which serves for sowing), by its nature could also enter into the stock for consumption; but by its economic function it must enter into the stock for production. But furthermore it is quite wrong to say with regard to the products destined for individual consumption that both the full price and the product enter into the *stock for consumption.* Linen, for example, when not used for sail-cloth or other productive purposes, all goes as a product into consumption. But not its price, for one part of this price replaces the linen yarn, another part looms and so on, and only a part of the price of the linen is converted into revenue of any kind.

Just now Adam told us that the materials necessary for machines, profitable buildings, etc. "can never make any part of this *neat* revenue", any more than the machines and so on fashioned from them can; presumably, therefore, they form a part of the gross revenue. Shortly afterwards, l.c., Book II, Chapter II, p. 220, he says on the contrary:

---

[a] This sentence was added by Marx in pencil.—*Ed.*

"The machines and instruments of trade, etc., which compose the *fixed capital* either of an individual or of a society, make no part *either of the gross or of the neat revenue* of either; so money etc...." [Garnier] [Vol. II, p. 23].

Adam's twistings and turnings, his contradictions and wanderings from the point, prove that, once he had made wages, profit and rent the constituent component parts of exchangeable value or of the total price of the product, he had got himself stuck in the mud and had to get stuck.[a]

Say, who tries to hide his dull superficiality by repeating in absolute general phrases Smith's inconsistencies and blunders, says:

"If we consider a nation as a whole, it has no net product; for since the *products* have only a value equal to the *costs* of their production, when these *costs* are deducted, the whole *value* of the *products* is deducted.... The *annual revenue* is the *gross revenue*" (*Traité d'économie politique*..., 3rd ed., Vol. II, Paris, 1817, p. 469).

The value of the total annual products is equal to the quantity of labour time materialised in them. [VI-270] If this aggregate value is deducted from the annual product, then in fact, so far as value is concerned, there remains no value, and by this deduction both the net revenue and the gross revenue have come to a final end. But Say thinks that the annually produced[b] values are annually consumed. Hence for the whole nation there is no net product, but only a gross product. In the first place, it is not true that the annually produced[b] values are annually consumed. This is not the case for a large part of the fixed capital. A large part of the annually produced values enters into the labour process without entering into the valorisation process, i.e., without their total value being annually consumed. But in the second place: a part of the annual consumption of values consists of values that are used not as the stock for consumption, but as MEANS OF PRODUCTION, and which are returned to production (either in the same form or in the form of an equivalent), just as they originated in production. The second part consists of the values which can enter into individual consumption over and above the first part. These form the net product.[258]

Storch says of this trash of Say's:

"It is evident that the value of the annual product is divided partly into capital and partly into profits, and that each *of these parts of the value of the annual product goes regularly to purchase the product needed by the nation*, as much for the purpose of preserving its capital as for renewing its consumable stock" (Storch, *Cours*

---

[a] See this volume, p. 405.— *Ed.*

[b] In the manuscript the word "producirten" (produced) was substituted in pencil, presumably by Engels, for the original "consumirten" (consumed).— *Ed.*

d'économie politique, Vol. V: *Considérations sur la nature du revenu national,* Paris, 1824,[259] pp. 134-35).[a] "Let us then imagine a family which through its own labour is self-sufficing in all its needs, such as there are so many examples of in Russia ... is the *revenue* of such a family equal to the gross product coming from its land, its capital and its industry? Can it live in its barns or its stables, eat its seed and forage, clothe itself with its labouring cattle, amuse itself with its agricultural implements? According to Mr. Say's thesis, all these questions would have to be answered in the affirmative" (l.c., pp. 135-36).[b] "Say regards the gross product as the revenue of society; and from this he concludes that society can consume a value equal to this product" (l.c., p. 145).[b] "The (net) revenue of a nation is not the excess of values produced over *the totality of values consumed,* as Say imagines it to be, but only over the *values consumed in order to produce.* Therefore, if a nation consumes all this excess in the year it is produced, it consumes all its (net) revenue" (l.c., p. 146).[b] "If it is admitted that the revenue of a nation is equal to its gross product, so that no *capital* is to be deducted, then it must also be admitted that this nation may consume unproductively the entire value of its annual product, without in the least reducing its future revenue" (l.c., [p.] 147).[a] " *The products which represent the capital of a nation are not consumable" (l.c., p. 150)* (constant capital).[c]

Ramsay (George)—An Essay on the Distribution of Wealth (Edinburgh, 1836)—remarks on the same subject, namely, Adam Smith's fourth part of the total price, or what I call constant capital as distinct from the capital laid out in wages:

[VI-271] "Ricardo," he says, "overlooks the fact that the whole product is not only divided up between WAGES and PROFIT, but that a part of it is also NECESSARY FOR REPLACING FIXED CAPITAL" (p. 174, note).[260]

By "FIXED CAPITAL" Ramsay in fact means not only instruments of production, etc., but also the raw material—in short, what I call constant capital within each sphere of production. When Ricardo speaks of the division of the product into profit and wages, he always assumes that the capital advanced to production itself and consumed in it has been deducted. Nevertheless, on the main issue Ramsay is right. Because Ricardo does not make any further examination at all of the constant part of capital, and pays no attention to it, he makes gross errors and in particular confuses profit with surplus value, besides errors in investigating oscillations in the rate of profit etc.

Let us hear now what Ramsay himself says:

"In what manner is a comparison to be instituted between the product and the *stock expended upon it?... In regard to a whole nation ... it is evident that all the various elements of the stock expended must be reproduced in some employment or another, otherwise the industry of the country could not go on as formerly. The

[a] Marx quotes in French.— *Ed.*

[b] Marx quotes partly in German and partly in French.— *Ed.*

[c] Marx added the words "constant capital", in pencil, thus correcting Storch's inaccuracy. Marx quoted Storch in French.— *Ed.*

raw material of manufactures, the implements used in them, as also in agriculture, the extensive machinery engaged in the former, the buildings necessary for fabricating or storing the produce, must all be parts of the total return of a country, as well as of the advances of all its master-capitalists. Therefore, the quantity of the former may be compared with that of the latter, each article being supposed placed as it were beside that of a similar kind"* (Ramsay, l.c., pp. 137-39). "Now as regards the individual capitalist, since he does not *replace* his outgoings IN KIND, by far the GREATER NUMBER must be obtained by EXCHANGE, A CERTAIN PORTION OF THE PRODUCT BEING NECESSARY FOR THIS PURPOSE. Hence each INDIVIDUAL MASTER-CAPITALIST COMES TO LOOK MUCH MORE TO THE EXCHANGEABLE VALUE OF THE PRODUCT THAN TO ITS QUANTITY" (l.c., [pp.] 145-46).a * "The more the *value* of *the product* exceeds the *value of the capital* advanced, the greater will be the profit. Thus, then, will he estimate it, by comparing value with value, not quantity with quantity.... Profit must rise or fall exactly as the proportion of the gross produce, or of its *value*, required to *replace necessary advances*, falls or rises.* The RATE OF PROFIT therefore depends UPON TWO CIRCUMSTANCES; 1) *the proportion of the whole produce which goes to the labourers; secondly, the proportion which must be set apart for replacing, either in kind or by exchange, the fixed capital"* (l.c. [pp.] 146-48, passim).a

(What Ramsay here says on the rate of profit has to be considered in Chapter III, on profit.[261] It is important that he rightly lays stress on this element. On the one hand what Ricardo says is correct—that the cheapening of commodities which form constant capital (which Ramsay calls fixed capital) always depreciates a part of the existing capital. This is especially true of fixed capital proper—machinery, etc. It is of no advantage to the individual capitalist that the surplus value rises in relation to the total capital, if the rise in this rate has been due to a fall in the total value of his constant capital (which he already had before the depreciation). But this is true only to a very small extent for that part of the capital which consists of raw materials or finished commodities (which do not form part of the fixed capital). The existing amount of these that can be depreciated in this way is always only an insignificant magnitude compared with the total production. It holds good for each capitalist only to a slight extent for the part of his capital expended as circulating capital. On the other hand—since the profit=the proportion of the surplus value to the total advanced capital, and since the quantity of labour that can be absorbed depends not on the value but on the quantity of raw materials and on the EFFICIENCY of the means of production—not on their exchange value but on their use value—it is clear that the greater the productivity of industry in the branches whose [VI-272] product enters into the formation of constant capital, the smaller the outlay of constant capital required

---

a Marx quotes Ramsay with slight changes and additions.— *Ed.*

to produce a given quantity of surplus value; consequently the greater the proportion of this surplus value to the whole advanced capital, and therefore the higher the rate of profit for a given amount of surplus value.)

(What Ramsay considers doubly—replacement of product by product in the process of reproduction for the whole country, and replacement of value by value for the individual capitalist—are two aspects, both of which, in relation to the individual capital, must be taken into account in the *circulation process of capital, which is at the same time its reproduction process.*) [262]

Ramsay did not solve the real difficulty which occupied Adam Smith's attention and entangled him in all kinds of contradictions. Put plainly, it is this: The whole capital (as value) resolves itself into labour, is nothing but a certain quantity of objectified labour. The paid labour, however, is equal to the wages of the labourers, the unpaid labour is equal to the capitalists' profit. So the whole capital must be resolvable, directly or indirectly, into wages and profit. Or is labour somewhere performed which consists neither of wages nor profit, and merely has the purpose of replacing the values used up in production which are, however, the conditions of reproduction? But who performs this labour, since all labour performed by the labourer is resolved into two quantities, one which maintains his own capacity to produce, and the other which forms the profit of capital?

[INQUIRY INTO HOW IT IS POSSIBLE FOR THE ANNUAL PROFIT AND WAGES TO BUY THE ANNUAL COMMODITIES, WHICH BESIDES PROFIT AND WAGES ALSO CONTAIN CONSTANT CAPITAL]

To rid the problem of any spurious admixture, there is one more point to mention at the outset. When the capitalist transforms a part of his profit, of his revenue, into capital—into means of labour and materials of labour—both are paid for by that part of the labour which the labourer has performed gratis for the capitalist. Here we have a new quantity of labour forming the equivalent for a new quantity of commodities, commodities which as use values consist of means of labour and materials of labour. This therefore enters into the accumulation of capital and presents no difficulty; we have here the growth of the constant capital beyond its previous limits, or the formation of new constant capital in excess of the amount of constant capital that already exists and must be replaced. The difficulty is the reproduction of the *existing* constant capital, not the formation of new constant capital in excess of what has to be reproduced. The new constant capital obviously originates in profit, and has existed for a moment in the form of revenue which is later transformed into capital. This part of the profit consists of the surplus labour time, which, even without the existence of capital, must constantly be performed by society, in order to have at its disposal, so to speak, a fund for development, which the very increase of population makes necessary.

(There is a good explanation of constant capital, but only in so far as concerns its use value, in Ramsay, l.c., p. 166, which runs:

* "Be the amount of the gross return" * (of the FARMER, for example) * "small or great, the quantity of it required for replacing what has been consumed in these different forms, can undergo no alteration whatever. This quantity must be considered as *constant*, so long as production is carried on the same scale." *)

So we must first start from the FACT: new formation of constant capital—as distinct from the reproduction of the existing constant capital—flows from profit as its source; that is, assuming on the one hand that the wages only suffice for the reproduction of labour capacity, and on the other that the whole surplus value is embraced under the category "profit",. since it is the industrial capitalist who *directly appropriates* the whole surplus value, [irrespective of] to whom and where he has to surrender some of it later.

("THE MASTER-CAPITALIST IS THE GENERAL DISTRIBUTOR OF WEALTH who undertakes to pay to the LABOURERS, the WAGES—to the (MONEYED) CAPITALIST, the interest—to the proprietor, the rent of his land" (Ramsay, [l.c.], p. 218-[19]).[263]

[In calling the whole] surplus value profit, we regard the capitalist: 1) * as the person who immediately appropriates the whole surplus value created; 2) as the distributor of that surplus value between himself, the moneyed capitalist, and the proprietor of the soil.*)

[VII-273] That this new constant capital arises from profit however means nothing but that it is due to a part of the surplus labour of the labourers. Just as the savage, in addition to the time he needs for hunting, must necessarily use some time for making his bow; or just as in patriarchal agriculture, the peasant, in addition to the time spent in tilling the soil, must use a certain quantity of labour time in producing most of his implements.

But the question here is: Who is it that labours in order to replace the equivalent of the constant capital already expended in production? The part of the labour which the labourer performs for himself replaces his wages, or, considered in relation to the whole of production, creates his wages. On the other hand, his surplus labour which forms the profit is in part a consumption fund for the capitalist, and in part is transformed into additional capital. But the capitalist does not replace the capital already used up in his own production out of this surplus labour or profit. But the necessary labour which forms the wages and the surplus labour which forms the profit make up the whole working day, and no other labour is performed in addition to these. (The contingency of the capitalist's LABOUR OF SUPERINTENDENCE is included in wages. In this aspect he is the wage worker, even though not of another capitalist, yet of his own capital.) What then is the source, the labour, that replaces the constant capital?

The part of the capital expended in wages is replaced (leaving surplus labour out of account) by new production. The labourer consumes the wages, but he adds as much new labour as he has destroyed of old labour; and if we consider the whole working class, without allowing the division of labour to confuse us, he reproduces not only the same value but the same use values, so that, according to the productivity of his labour, the same value, the same quantity of labour, is reproduced in a greater or smaller quantity of these same use values.

If we take society at any one moment, there exists simultaneously in all spheres of production, even though in very different proportions, a definite constant capital—presupposed as a condition of production—that once for all belongs to production and must be given back to it, as seed must be given back to the land. It is true that the *value* of this constant part can fall or rise, depending on whether the commodities of which it is composed have to be reproduced at less or greater cost. This *change in value*, however, never alters the fact that in the process of production, into which it enters as a condition of production, it is a postulated value which must reappear in the value of the product. Therefore this change of value of the constant capital can here be ignored. In all circumstances it is a definite quantity of *past, objectified* labour, which passes into the value of the product as a determining factor. In order to bring out more clearly the nature of the problem, let us therefore assume that the production costs[264] or the value of the constant part of the capital similarly remain unchanged, remain constant. It also makes no difference that for example the whole value of the constant capital may not pass into the products in a single year, but, as is the case with fixed capital, only passes into the aggregate products of a series of years. For the question here centres on that part of the constant capital which is actually consumed within the year, and therefore also must be replaced within the year.

The question of the reproduction of the constant capital clearly belongs to the section on the reproduction process or circulation process of capital [265] — which however is no reason why the kernel of the matter should not be examined here.

[VII-274] Let us first take the labourer's wages. He receives, then, a certain sum of money in which say 10 hours' labour are materialised, if he works 12 hours for the capitalist. These wages are converted into means of subsistence. These means of subsistence are all commodities. Assume that the price of these commodities is equal to their value. But in the value of these commodities there is one component part which covers the value of the raw materials they contain and the means of production used up in them. All the component parts of the value of these commodities taken together, contain, however, like the wages spent by the labourer, only 10 hours' labour. Let us assume that $2/3$ of the value of these commodities consists of the value of the constant capital they contain, and $1/3$, on the other hand, of the labour which has finally made the product into a finished article for consumption. Thus the labourer, with his 10 hours of living labour, replaces $2/3$ of constant capital and $1/3$ of living labour (added to the article in the course of the year). If there were no constant capital in the means of subsistence, the commodities, which he buys, the raw material in them would have cost nothing, and no instrument of labour would have been required to make them. In that case there are two possibilities. Either the commodities, as before, would contain 10 hours' labour; then the labourer replaces 10 hours' living labour by 10 hours' living labour. Or the same quantity of use values into which his wages are converted and which he needed for the reproduction of his labour capacity would have cost only $3\frac{1}{3}$ hours' labour (with NO instrument of labour and no raw material which is itself a product of labour). In this case the labourer has only to perform $3\frac{1}{3}$ hours' necessary labour, and his wages would in fact fall to $3\frac{1}{3}$ [hours'] objectified labour time.

Let us assume that the commodity is linen: 12 yards (the actual price does not matter here)=36s. or £1 16s. Of this, let $1/3$ be labour added, $2/3$ for raw material (yarn) and wear and tear of machinery. Let the necessary labour time=10 hours; the surplus labour therefore=2. Let one hour's labour, expressed in money=1s. In this case the 12 hours' labour=12s., wages=10s., profit=2s. Let us assume that labourer and capitalist spent the whole of their wages and profit, that is 12 s. (the total value that has been added to the raw material and machinery, the whole quantity of new labour time materialised in the transformation of yarn into linen), on linen itself as a consumption article. (And it is possible that subsequently more than one labour day will be spent on their own product.) A yard of linen costs 3s. With the 12s. labourer and capitalist together—adding wages and profit together—can only buy 4 yards of linen. These 4 yards of linen contain 12 hours' labour, of which however only 4 are newly-added labour, 8 representing the labour realised in the constant capital. With the 12 hours' labour wages and profit together buy only $^1/_3$ of their total product, because $^2/_3$ of this total product consist of constant capital. The 12 hours' labour are divisible into 4+8, of which 4 replace themselves, while 8—independently of the labour added in the weaving process—replace such labour as entered into the weaving process in already materialised form, as yarn and machinery.

In regard to that part of the product, of the commodity, which exchanges against or is bought by wages and profit as an article of consumption (or for any other purpose, even reproduction, for the purpose for which the commodity is bought makes no difference to the transaction), it is therefore clear that the part of the value of the product which is formed by the constant capital is paid for from the fund of newly-added labour, which is resolved into wages and profit. How much or how little of constant capital and how much or how little of the labour added in the last production process is bought by wages and profit combined, in what proportions the labour most recently added and in what proportions the labour realised in constant capital is paid for, depends on the original proportion in which they entered as component parts of value into the finished commodity. To simplify matters we assume the proportion of $^2/_3$ labour realised in constant capital to $^1/_3$ newly-added labour.

[VII-275] Now two things are clear:

First. The proportion we have assumed in the case of the linen—i.e., in the case where labourer and capitalist realise wages and profit in the commodities they have themselves produced, when they buy back a part of their product—this proportion remains the same when they expend the same quantity of value on other products. On the assumption that every commodity contains $^2/_3$ of constant capital and $^1/_3$ most recently added labour, wages and profit together could always only purchase $^1/_3$ of the product. The 12 hours' labour time=4 yards of linen. If these 4 yards of linen are transformed into money, then they exist as 12s. If these 12s. are retransformed into some commodity other than linen, they buy a commodity of the value of 12 hours' labour, of which 4 are most recently added labour, 8 labour realised in constant capital. Consequently, this proportion holds good generally provided the other commodities contain the same original proportion of labour most recently added and of labour realised in constant capital as linen.

Secondly. If the daily most recently added labour = 12 hours, of these 12 hours only 4 replace themselves—i.e., the living, most recently added labour; while 8 pay for the labour realised in the constant capital. But who pays for the 8 hours of living labour which are not replaced by living labour? It is precisely the 8 hours of realised labour contained in the constant capital that are exchanged for the 8 hours of living labour.

There is not the slightest doubt, therefore, that the part of the finished commodity which is bought by wages and profit combined—which together however are nothing but the total quantity of labour most recently added to the constant capital—is replaced in all its elements: the most recently added labour contained in this part as well as the quantity of labour contained in the constant capital. Further, there is not the slightest doubt that the labour contained in the constant capital has here received its equivalent from the fund of living labour most recently added to it.

But now comes the difficulty. The *total product* of the 12 hours of weaving labour, and this product is absolutely different from what this weaving labour has itself produced, = 12 yards of linen, of the value of 36 hours' labour or 36s. But wages and profit together, or the total labour time of 12 hours can buy back *only* 12 of these 36 hours' labour, or of the total product only 4 yards, not a piece more. What happens to the other 8 yards? (Forcade, Proudhon.[a])

First we note than the 8 yards represent nothing but the constant capital advanced. It has however been given a changed form of use value. It exists as a new product, no longer as yarn, loom, etc., but as linen. These 8 yards of linen, just like the 4 others which have been bought by wages and profit, contain— considered as value—$1/3$ labour added in the weaving process, and $2/3$ pre-existing labour materialised in the constant capital. In the

---

a The names of Forcade and Proudhon were added by Marx in pencil in the manuscript. The reference is to Notebook V of the 1861-1863 manuscript (see this volume, pp. 345-46).— *Ed.*

case of the 4 yards previously discussed $^1/_3$ of the newly-added labour covered the weaving labour contained in these 4 yards, i.e. covered itself; $^2/_3$ of the weaving labour on the other hand covered the constant capital the 4 yards contained. But now we have it the other way round: in the 8 yards of linen, $^2/_3$ of the constant capital covers the constant capital they contain, and $^1/_3$ of the constant capital covers the newly-added labour.

What then happens to the 8 yards of linen, which have absorbed the value of the whole constant capital which has been maintained during the 12 hours' weaving labour, or which went into the production process, but is now in the form of a product destined for direct, individual (not industrial) consumption?

The 8 yards belong to the capitalist. Were he to consume them himself, besides the $^2/_3$ of a yard representing his profit, [VII-276] then he could not reproduce the constant capital contained in the 12 hours' weaving process; in general—with regard to the capital contained in this 12 hours' process—he is no longer able to function as a capitalist. He therefore sells the 8 yards of linen, transforming them into money to the amount of 24s. or 24 hours' labour. But here we come to the difficulty. To whom does he sell them? Into whose money does he transform them? But we shall return to this in a moment. Let us first have a look at the further process.

When he has transformed into money, sold, converted into the form of exchange value, the 8 yards of linen—i.e., the part of the value of his product which=the constant capital he advanced— he buys again with it commodities of the same kind (with regard to their use value) as those which originally composed his constant capital. He buys yarn and looms and so on. He divides the 24s. between raw materials and means of production, in the proportions in which these are required for the manufacture of new linen.

His constant capital is therefore replaced, in terms of use value, by new products of the same labour as that of which it originally consisted. The capitalist has reproduced the constant capital. This new yarn, looms, etc., however (on the assumption with which we began) likewise consist of $^2/_3$ of constant capital and $^1/_3$ of most recently added labour. While the first 4 yards of linen (most recently added labour and constant capital) have thus been paid for exclusively by newly-added labour, these 8 yards of linen are replaced by their own newly-produced elements of production, which consist partly of newly-added labour and partly of constant capital. Hence it seems that at least a part of the constant capital exchanges for constant capital in another form. The replacement of the products is real, because at the same time as the yarn is being worked up into linen, flax is being worked up into yarn and flax seed into flax; in the same way, while the loom is wearing out, a new loom is being made; and similarly, while the latter is being manufactured, new wood and iron is being produced. The elements are produced in one sphere of production at the same time as they are being worked up in the others. But in all these *simultaneous* processes of production, although each of them represents a higher stage of the product, constant capital is simultaneously being used up in varying proportions.

The value of the finished product, the linen, therefore resolves itself into two parts, of which one repurchases the simultaneously produced elements of constant capital, while the other is expended on articles of consumption. For the sake of simplification no account is here taken of the retransformation of part of the profit into capital; i.e., as throughout this inquiry, it is assumed that wages+profit, or the total of the labour added to the constant capital, are consumed as revenue.

The only question left is: Who buys the part of the total product with whose value the elements of constant capital that have meanwhile been newly produced are again bought? Who buys the 8 yards of linen? We assume, in order to leave no *faux-fuyants*[a] that it is a type of linen specially intended for individual consumption, and is not, like perhaps sail-cloth, for industrial consumption. Here also the purely intermediary operations of commerce—so far as they are only mediatory—must be left completely out of account. For example, if the 8 yards of linen were sold to a merchant, and even if they pass through the hands of not 1 but 20 merchants and are 20 times bought and resold, then at the 20th time they must at last be sold by the merchant to the actual consumer, who therefore actually pays the producer or the *last*, the 20th merchant, who as far as the consumer is concerned represents the *first merchant*, i.e., the actual producer. These intermediary transactions postpone or, if you like, mediate the final transaction, but they do not explain it. The question remains exactly the same whether it is: who buys the 8 yards of linen from the linen manufacturer, or: [VII-277] who buys them from the 20th merchant into whose hand they have come through a series of exchanges?

The 8 yards of linen, just as the first 4 yards, must pass into the

---

[a] Loopholes.— *Ed.*

fund for consumption. That is to say, they can only be paid for out of wages and profit, for these are the only sources of revenue for the producers, who figure here as the only consumers. The 8 yards of linen contain 24 hours' labour. Let us now assume (taking 12 hours as the generally valid normal working day) that labourer and capitalist in two other branches spend their whole wages and profit on linen, as labourer and capitalist in the weaving industry have done with their whole day's labour (the labourer his 10 hours, the capitalist the 2 hours' surplus value made on his labourer, that is, on 10 hours). Then the linen weaver would have sold the 8 yards, the *value* of his constant capital for 12 yards would be replaced, and this value could again be spent on the particular commodities of which the constant capital consists, *because* these commodities, yarn, loom, etc., available on the market, have been produced at the same time as yarn and loom were being worked up into linen. *The simultaneous production* of yarn and loom as products alongside the production process into which they enter as products but from which they do not emerge as products, explains how it is that the part of the *value* of the linen=the value of the material, loom, etc., worked up into it can be again transformed into yarn, loom, etc. If this production of the elements of linen did not proceed simultaneously with the production of the linen itself, the 8 yards of linen, even when they have been sold and transformed into money, could not be retransformed once more from money into the constant elements of linen. As for example is now the case with the YARN or CLOTH of the cotton manufacturers, as a result of the American Civil War. The mere sale of their product is no guarantee for them that it will be retransformed, since there is no COTTON on the market.

On the other hand, however, although there may be new yarn, new looms, etc., on the market, and therefore production of new yarn and looms had taken place while finished yarn and finished loom were being transformed into linen—in spite of the simultaneous production of yarn and loom alongside the production of the linen—the 8 yards of linen cannot be retransformed into these material elements of constant capital for the weaving industry before they are sold, before they are converted into money. The continuous real production of the elements of linen, running side by side with the production of linen itself, therefore does not yet explain to us the reproduction of the constant capital, before we know whence comes the fund to buy the 8 yards of linen, to give them back the form of money, of independent exchange value.

In order to solve this last difficulty we have assumed that B and C—which can stand for shoemaker and butcher—have spent their total wages and profit, that is, the 24 hours' labour time which they have at their disposal, entirely on linen. And this gets us over our difficulty with A, the linen weaver. His whole product, the 12 yards of linen in which 36 hours' labour is realised, has been replaced by wages and profit alone—i.e. by the whole of the labour time newly added to the constant capital in the spheres of production A, B and C. All the labour time contained in the linen, both that already existing in its constant capital and that newly added in the weaving process, has been exchanged against labour time which did not previously exist as constant capital in any sphere of production, but which was added simultaneously to the constant capital in the 3 production spheres A, B and C, *in the last stage* [*of production*].

Though therefore it is still wrong to say that the original value of the linen was composed of wages and profit alone—since however it was made up of the value=the total of wages and profit=12 hours' weaving, and the 24 hours' labour which, independently of the weaving process, was contained in the yarn, loom, in a word, the constant capital—it would on the other hand be correct to say that the equivalent of the 12 yards of linen, the 36s. for which they have been sold, is composed of wages and profit alone; that is, not only the weaving labour but also the labour contained in yarn and loom are replaced entirely by newly-added labour, namely 12 hours' labour in A, 12 hours in B and 12 hours in C.

The value of the commodity sold is itself divided [VII-278] into newly-added labour (wages and profit) and pre-existing labour (value of the constant capital); that is the value for the seller (IN FACT [the value] of the commodity). On the other hand, the purchasing value, the equivalent given by the buyer to the seller,[a] is made up entirely of newly-added labour, wages and profit. But as every commodity, before it is sold, is a commodity for sale and becomes money through a mere change of form, so every commodity, after it has been sold, would be made up of other component parts of value than it is composed of as a buying commodity (as money), which is absurd. Further: the labour performed by society for example in one year would not only cover itself—so that if the total quantity of commodities is divided

---

[a] In the manuscript the words "the buyer to the seller" were substituted in pencil, presumably by Engels, for "the seller to the buyer".— *Ed.*

into two equal parts, one half of the year's labour would form an equivalent for the other half—but $^1/_3$ of the labour, which forms the current year's labour in the total labour contained in the annual product, would cover $^3/_3$ of the labour, would be equal to a magnitude 3 times greater than itself. This is still more absurd.

In the above example we have SHIFTED the difficulty, pushed it on from A to B and C. But this has only increased the difficulty, not made it simpler. *In the first place*, in dealing with A we had the way out that 4 yards, containing as much labour time as had been added to the yarn, that is, the total wages and profit in A, were consumed in linen itself, in the product of A's own labour. With B and C this is not the case, since they consume the total labour time added by them, their total wages and profit, in the product of sphere A, in linen, and so not in the product of B or C. They have therefore to sell not only the part of their product representing the 24 hours' labour of constant capital, but also the part of their product which represents the 12 hours' labour newly added to the constant capital. B must sell 36 hours' labour, not only 24 like A. C is in same position as B. *Secondly*, in order to sell A's constant capital, to get it off his hands and transform it into money, we need the whole most recently added labour not only of B but also of C. *Thirdly*, B and C cannot sell any part of their product to A, since the whole part of A which constitutes revenue has already been expended in A itself by the producers of A. Nor can they replace the constant part of A by any part of their own product, since on the assumption we have made their products are not production elements for A but commodities which enter into individual consumption. The difficulty increases at each further step.

In order to exchange the 36 hours contained in A's product (that is, $^2/_3$ or 24 hours in constant capital, $^1/_3$ or 12 hours in newly-added labour) entirely for labour added to constant capital, A's wages and profit—the 12 hours' labour added in A—had to consume $^1/_3$ of the product of A itself. The other $^2/_3$ of the total product=24 hours represented the value contained in the constant capital. This value was exchanged for the total quantity of wages and profit or newly-added labour in B and C. But in order that B and C should be able, with the 24 hours in their products that make up their wages [and profit], to buy linen, they must sell these 24 hours in the form of their own products—and in addition to replace the constant capital they must sell 48 hours of their own products. They have therefore to sell products of B and C to the amount of 72 hours, in exchange for the total quantity of profit and wages in the other spheres D, E, etc.; and this means (with a normal 12 hours' day) that 12×6 hours (=72) or the labour added in 6 other spheres of production must be realised in the products B and C; [VII-279] that is, the profit and wages or the total labour added to their respective constant capital in D, E, F, G, H, I.

In these circumstances the value of the total product of B+C would be paid for entirely in newly-added labour, that is, the aggregate wages and profit, in production spheres D, E, F, G, H, I. But in these 6 spheres the total produce would then have to be sold (since no part of these products would be consumed by their producers themselves, as they have already put their whole revenue into products B and C), and no part of it could be accounted for within their own spheres; that is, the product of 6×36 hours' labour=216, of which 144 represent constant capital and 72 (6×12) newly-added labour. Now in order in turn to transform the products of D, etc., similarly into wages and profit, i.e., into newly-added labour, all the newly-added labour in the 18 spheres $K^1 - K^{18}$, i.e., the total sum of wages and profit in these 18 spheres, must be entirely expended on the products of spheres D, E, F, G, H, I. These 18 spheres $K^1 - K^{18}$ would have to sell — since they consumed none of their products themselves, but had already spent their entire revenue in the 6 spheres D — I — 18×36 hours' labour or 648 hours' labour, of which 18×12 or 216 are in most recently added labour, and 432 in labour contained in the constant capital. In order therefore to transform this total product of $K^1 - K^{18}$ into the labour added or total wages and profit in other spheres, the labour added in the spheres $L^1 - L^{54}$ would be required; that is to say, 12×54=648 hours' labour. Spheres $L^1 - L^{54}$, in order to exchange their total product=1,944 hours (of which 648=12×54=newly-added labour and 1,296 hours' labour=the labour contained in the constant capital) for newly-added labour, would have to absorb the newly-added labour of spheres $M^1 - M^{162}$, for 162×12=1,944; these in their turn must absorb the newly-added labour of spheres $N^1 - N^{486}$ and so on.

This is the beautiful progression *in infinitum* which we arrive at if all products are resolved into wages and profit, newly-added labour—if not only the labour added in the commodity but also its constant capital have to be paid for by newly-added labour in another sphere of production.

In order to convert the labour time contained in product A, 36 hours ($^1/_3$ newly-added labour, $^2/_3$ constant capital), into newly-added labour, i.e., to have it paid for by wages and profit, we at first assumed that $^1/_3$ of the product (whose value=the total of wages+profit) was consumed or bought—which is the same thing—by the producers of A themselves. This was the progress[266]:

1) *Production sphere A.* Product=*36* hours' labour. 24 hours' labour, constant capital. 12 hours' labour, newly added. $^1/_3$ of the product consumed by the SHAREHOLDERS of the 12 hours, wages and profit, labourer and capitalist. There remain to be sold $^2/_3$ of the product of A, equivalent to the 24 hours' labour contained in the constant capital.

2) *Production spheres B^1—B^2.* Product=*72* hours' labour; of which 24 labour added, 48 constant capital. They buy with it the $^2/_3$ of A's product, replacing the value of A's constant capital. But they have now to sell the 72 hours' labour, of which the value of their total product consists.

3) *Production spheres C^1—C^6.* Product=*216* hours' labour; of which 72 added labour (wages and profit). They buy with it the entire product of B^1—B^2. But they have now to sell 216, of which 144 are constant capital.

[VII-280] 4) *Production spheres D^1—D^{18}.* Product=648 hours' labour, 216 labour added, and 432 constant capital. With the labour added they buy the total product of production spheres C^1—C^6=216. But they have to sell 648.

5) *Production spheres E^1—E^{54}.* *Product*=1,944 hours' labour; 648 labour added and 1,296 constant capital. They buy the total product of production spheres D$^{1-18}$. But they have to sell 1,944.

6) *Production spheres F^1—F^{162}.* *Product*=5,832 of which 1,944 added labour and 3,888 constant capital. With the 1,944 they buy the product of E^1—E^{54}. They have to sell 5,832.

7) *Production spheres G^1—G^{486}.*

In order to simplify the problem, only one working day of 12 hours is assumed throughout, in every production sphere, divided between capitalist and labourer. It does not solve the problem to increase the number of working days, but complicates it needlessly.

So, to get a clearer picture of the law of this series[267]:

1) *A. Product*=36 hrs. Constant capital=24 hrs. *Total of wages and profit* or *newly-added labour*=12 hrs. The latter is consumed by capital and labour in the form of the product of A itself.

A's product to be sold, equal to its constant capital, =24 hrs.

2) *B^1—B^2.* We need here 2 days' labour, that is, 2 production spheres, to pay for A's 24 hrs.

Product=2×36, or 72 hrs, of which 24 hrs labour and 48 constant capital.

Product of B^1 and B^2 to be sold=72 hours' labour, no part of it consumed in their own spheres.

6) $C^1 - C^6$. We need here 6 days' labour, because 72=12×6, and the total product of $B^1 - B^2$ has to be consumed by the labour added in $C^1 - C^6$. Product=6×36=216 hours' labour, of which 72 newly added, 144 constant capital.

18) $D^1 - D^{18}$. We need here 18 days' labour, because 216=12×18; so, since there is $^2/_3$ constant capital per day's labour, 18×36 is the total product=648 (432 constant capital).

And so on.

The figures 1, 2, [etc.] placed at the beginning of paragraphs signify the working days or the different kinds of labour in different production spheres, as we assumed 1 working day in each sphere.

Therefore: 1) *A. Product=36* hrs. Added labour *12* hrs. *Product to be sold* (constant capital)=24 hrs.

Or:

1) *A. Product to be sold* or *constant capital*=24 hrs. Total product 36 hrs. *Labour* added *12 hrs. Consumed in A itself.*

2) $B^1 - B^2$. Buys with added labour=24 hrs A. *Constant capital* 48 hrs. *Total product* 72 hrs.

6) $C^1 - C^6$. Buys with added labour *72* hrs $B^1 - B^2(=12×6)$. *Constant capital* 144, total product=216, etc.

[VII-281] Therefore:

1) *A.* Product=3 working days (36 hrs). 12 hrs added labour. *24 hrs* constant capital.

2) B^{1-2}. Product=2×3=6 working days (*72 hrs*). Added labour=12×2=*24 hrs. Constant capital*=48=2×24 hrs.

6) C^{1-6}. *Product*=3×6 working days=3×72 hrs=216 hours' labour. *Added labour*=6×*12*=72 hours' labour. *Constant capital*=2×72=144.

18) D^{1-18}. *Product*=3×3×6 working days=3×18 working days =54 working days=648 hours' labour. Added labour= 12×18=*216. Constant capital*=432 hours' labour.

54) E^{1-54}. *Product*=3×54 working days=162 working days= 1,944 hours' labour. Added labour=54 working days=648 hours' labour; 1,296 constant capital.

162) $F^1 - F^{162}$. *Product*=3×162 [=] 486 working days=5,832 hours' labour, of which 162 working days or 1,944 hours' labour are added labour, and 3,888 constant capital.

486) G^{1-486}. *Product = 3 × 486 working days*, of which 486 working

days or 5,832 hours' labour are labour added, and 11,664 constant capital etc.

Here we would already have the goodly total of $1+2+6+18+54+162+486$ different working days in different production spheres=729 different production spheres, which already implies a considerably ramified society.

In order to sell the total product of A (where only 12 hours' labour=1 working day is added to the constant capital of 2 working days, and wages and profit consume their own product), that is, only the 24 hours' constant capital—and moreover to sell it again entirely for newly-added labour, for wages and profit—we need 2 working days in B^1 and B^2; which however require a constant capital of 4 working days, so that the total product of $B^{1\text{-}2}$=6 working days. These must be *all* sold, because *from here on* it is assumed that each subsequent sphere does not consume any of its own product, but spends its profit and wages only on the product of the preceding sphere. In order to replace these 6 working days of the product of $B^{1\text{-}2}$, 6 working days are necessary, which however presuppose a constant capital of 12 working days. The total product of $C^{1\text{-}6}$ therefore=18 working days. In order to replace these by labour, 18 working days $D^{1\text{-}18}$ are necessary, which however presuppose a constant capital of 36 working days; so that the product=54 working days. To replace these, 54 working days are needed, $E^{1\text{-}54}$, which presuppose a constant capital of 108. Product=162 working days. Finally, to replace these, 162 working days are needed, which however presuppose a constant capital of 324 working days; that is, total product 486 working days, etc. This is F^1—F^{162}. Finally, to replace this product of $F^{1\text{-}162}$, we need 486 working days ($G^{1\text{-}486}$), which however presuppose a constant capital of 972 working days. So the total product of $G^{1\text{-}486}$=972+486=1,458 working days.

But now let us assume that with sphere G we reach an end to the SHIFTING; and [VII-282] our progression would soon bring us to an end in any society. How would the matter stand then? We have a product comprising 1,458 working days of which 486 newly-added labour and 972 labour realised in constant capital. The 486 working days can then be spent in the previous sphere $F^{1\text{-}162}$. But what is to buy the 972 working days contained in the constant capital? Beyond G^{486} there is no new sphere of production and therefore no new sphere of exchange. In the spheres that lie behind it, except for $F^{1\text{-}162}$, there is nothing to be exchanged. Moreover, $G^{1\text{-}486}$ has expended all its wages and profit up to the last centime in $F^{1\text{-}162}$. Therefore the 972 working days realised in the total product of $G^{1\text{-}486}$, which are the equivalent of the constant capital it contains, remain unsaleable. It has thus not helped us at all to shift through nearly 800 branches of production the difficulty of the 8 yards of linen of sphere A, or the 24 hours' labour, the 2 working days, representing in its product the value of the constant capital.

It is no use imagining that the reckoning would have a different result if perhaps A did not spend its whole wages and profits in linen, but spent a part of it on the product of B and C. The limit of the outlays, the hours of labour added which are contained in A, B, C, can always only command a labour time equal to themselves. If they buy more of one product, then they buy less of the other. It would only confuse the reckoning, but in no way alter result.

Que faire donc?[a]

In the above calculation we find [268]:

	Working days	Labour added	Constant capital
A Product =	3	1	2
B " =	6	2	4
C) " =	18	6	12
D) " =	54	18	36
E) " =	162	54	108
F) " =	486	162	324
Total:	729	243	486

($1/3$ of A's product consumed by A itself)

If the last 324 working days of constant capital in this account=the constant capital which the farmer replaces for himself, subtracts from his product and returns to the land—and so has not to be paid for by new labour—then the account would balance. The riddle, however, would only be solved because a part of the constant capital replaces itself.

In fact therefore we have had consumed 243 working days, corresponding to the newly-added labour. The value of the final product, 486 working days=the value of the total constant capital contained in A—F, which also =486 working days. In order to account for this, we assume 486 days of new labour in G, from which however the only satisfaction we get is that instead of

---

[a] What then is to be done?— *Ed.*

having to account for a constant capital of 486 days, [VII-283] we have to account for a constant capital of 972 working days in G's product, which is equal to 1,458 working days (972 constant capital+486 labour). If now we want to get out of our difficulty by supposing that G works without constant capital, so that the product only =486 days of newly-added labour, the account would of course be cleared; but we would have solved the problem of who pays for the part of the value contained in the product which forms the constant capital, by assuming a case in which the constant capital equals nil and hence forms no part of the value of the product.

In order to sell A's total product entirely for newly-added labour, in order to resolve it into profit and wages, *the whole of the labour added in A, B and C*[269] must be spent on the labour realised in product A. Likewise to sell the total product of $B+C$, all labour newly added in D^1-D^{18} [is needed].[270] Similarly, to buy the total product of D^1-D^{18}, all labour added in E^{1-54}. To buy the total product of E^{1-54}, all labour added in F^{1-162}. And finally, to buy the total product of F^{1-162}, the total labour time added in G^{1-486}. At the end, in these 486 production spheres represented by G^{1-486}, the total labour time added=the total product of the 162 spheres F, and this total product which is replaced by labour is as large as the constant capital in A, B^{1-2}, C^{1-6}, D^{1-18}, E^{1-54}, F^{1-162}. But the constant capital of sphere G, twice the size of the constant capital used in $A-F^{162}$, is not replaced and cannot be replaced.

IN FACT we have found, on our assumption that in all production spheres the proportion of the newly-added to the pre-existing labour=1:2, that always twice as many new production spheres must use all their new labour to buy the product of the preceding spheres—the labour added of A, B^{1-2} and C^{1-6}, to buy A's total product; the labour added of 18 D or $D^{1-18(2\times9)}$, to buy the product of A, B, C, and so on.[271] In short, that twice as much newly-added labour as the product itself contains is always needed, so that there must be twice as much newly-added labour in the last production sphere G as there actually is, in order to buy the total product. In a word, we find in the result of G what was already there in our starting-point A, that the newly-added labour cannot buy any greater quantity of its own product than it itself amounts to and that it can *not* buy the labour pre-existing in the constant capital.

It is therefore impossible for the value of the revenue to cover the value of the total product. But since, apart from the revenue, no fund exists from which this product sold by producers to (individual) consumers can be paid for, it is impossible for the value of the total product, minus the value of the revenue, ever to be sold, paid for or (individually) consumed. On the other hand it is necessary for every product to be sold and paid for at its price (on the assumption that price here=value).

For that matter, it might have been foreseen from the outset that introducing the acts of exchange, sales and purchases between different commodities or the products of different production spheres, would not bring us a step forward. In A, the first commodity, the linen, we had $^1/_3$ or [VII-283a] 12 hours of newly-added labour and 2×12 or 24 hours of pre-existing labour in the capital. Wages and profit could only repurchase that part of the product of commodity A—and therefore also of any equivalent of commodity A in any other product—which is equal to 12 hours' labour. They could not buy back their own constant capital of 24 hours, hence they could not repurchase the equivalent of this constant capital in any other commodity either.

It is possible for the relation of added labour to constant capital to be different in commodity B. But however different the proportion may be of constant capital to newly-added labour in the various spheres of production, we can calculate the average, and so say that in the product of the whole society or of the whole capitalist class, in the total product of capital, the newly-added labour=a, the labour pre-existing as constant capital=b. In other words, the proportion of 1:2 which we assumed in A, the linen, is only a symbolical expression of $a:b$ and is not intended to imply anything more than that definite and definable relation of some kind or other exists between these two elements—the living labour added in the current year or in any other period selected, and the past labour pre-existing as constant capital. If the 12 hours added to the yarn buy not only linen, but for example linen only to the amount of 4 hours, then they could buy some other product to the amount of 8 hours, but they could never buy more than 12 hours altogether; and if they buy another product to the value of 8 hours, then 32 hours' linen in all must be sold by A. The example A therefore holds good for the total capital of the entire society, and though the problem can be complicated by introducing the exchange of different commodities, the problem itself remains unchanged.

Let us assume that A is the total product of society: then $^1/_3$ of this total product can be bought by the producers for their own consumption, bought and paid for with the total of their wages and their profits,=the total newly-added labour, the amount of their aggregate revenue. They have no fund with which to pay for, to buy and consume, the other $^2/_3$. Just as the newly-added labour, the $^1/_3$ which consists of profit and wages, is itself covered by its own product, or withdraws only that part of the value of the product which contains $^1/_3$ of the total labour, newly-added labour or its equivalent, so must the $^2/_3$ of pre-existing labour be covered by its own product. That is to say, the constant capital remains equal to itself and replaces itself out of that part of the value which represents the constant capital in the total product. The exchange between various commodities, the series of purchases and sales between different spheres of production, brings about a change in form only in the sense that the constant capitals in the various production spheres mutually replace each other in the proportion in which they were originally contained in them.

We must now examine this more closely.

// Many examples can be given to show how often in the course of his work, when he is explaining actual facts, Adam Smith treats the quantity of labour contained in the product as value and determining value. Some of these are quoted by Ricardo.[a] His whole doctrine of the influence of the division of labour and improved machinery on the price of commodities is based on it. Here one passage will be enough to cite. In Book I, Chapter XI, Adam Smith speaks of the cheapening of many manufactured goods in his time, as compared with earlier centuries, and he concludes with the words:

"It cost a greater quantity of labour [VII-283b] to bring the goods to market. When they were brought thither, therefore, they must have purchased, or exchanged for the price, of a greater quantity" ([Garnier,] t. II, p. 156) [Vol. I, p. 404]. //

This view—that the annual product of the country is divided into wages and profits (rents, interest, etc., included in the latter)—is expressed by Adam Smith, Book II, Chapter II, in examining the circulation of money and the credit system (on this, compare later *Tooke*), where he says:

"The circulation of every country may be considered as divided into two different branches; the circulation of the DEALERS[b] with one another, and the circulation between the dealers and the consumers" (Garnier explains that by DEALERS Adam Smith here means "all traders, manufacturers, artisans, and so on; in a word, the agents of the trade and industry of a country"). "Though the same pieces of money, whether paper or metal, may be employed sometimes in the one circulation and sometimes in the other; yet as both are constantly going on at the same time, each requires a certain stock of money, of one kind or another, to carry it on. *The value of the goods circulated between the different dealers never can exceed the*

---

a D. Ricardo, *On the Principles...*, London, 1821, Ch. I, Section I.— *Ed.*

b Marx gives the English term in brackets after its French equivalent.— *Ed.*

value of those circulated between the dealers and the consumers; whatever is bought by the dealers being ultimately destined to be sold to the consumers" ([Garnier,] t. II, l. II, ch. II, pp. 292-93) [Vol. II, pp. 79-80].

To this, as well as Tooke, we must come back later.[272]

Let us return to our example. The day's product of A, a linen weaving factory,=12 yards=36s.=36 hours' labour, of which 12 are newly-added labour divisible into wages and profit, and 24 hours or 2 days=the value of the constant capital, which now however, instead of the old form of yarn and loom, exists in the form of linen, but in a quantity of linen=24 hours=24 s. In this there is the same quantity of labour as in the yarn and loom which it replaces, and with it therefore the same quantity of yarn and loom can be bought again (on the assumption that the value of yarn and loom has remained the same, that the productivity of labour in these branches of industry has not altered). The spinner and the loom maker must sell the whole of their year's or their day's product (which for our purpose here is the same thing) to the weaver, for he is the only person for whom their commodity has use value. He is their only consumer.

But if the weaver's constant capital=2 working days (his daily consumed constant capital), then for one working day of the weaver there are two working days of spinner and machine maker—2 working days which may themselves be divided in very different proportions into labour added and constant capital. But the total daily product of spinner and machine maker together (assuming that the machine maker makes only looms)—constant capital and added labour together—cannot amount to more than 2 days' labour while that of the weaver, because of the 12 hours' labour newly added by him, amounts to 3 working days. It is possible that spinner and machine maker consume as much living labour time as the weaver. Then the labour time contained in their constant capital must be smaller. However that may be, they can in no case use the same quantity of labour (*summa summarum*[a]) objectified and living, as the weaver. It would be possible for the weaver to use proportionately less living labour time than the spinner (the latter for example would certainly use less than the flax-grower); in that case the excess of his constant capital over the variable part of his capital must be so much greater.

[VII-284] The weaver's constant capital thus replaces the entire capital of the spinner and the loom maker, not only their own constant capital but the labour newly added in the spinning

---

[a] Grand total.— *Ed.*

process and in the manufacture of machines. The new constant capital therefore here replaces other constant capitals completely and, besides that, the total amount of the labour newly added to them. By the sale of their commodities to the weaver, spinner and loom maker have not only replaced their constant capital but have received payment for their newly-added labour. His constant capital replaces for them their own constant capital and realises their revenue (wages and profit together). In so far as the weaver's constant capital replaces for them only their own constant capital, which they have handed over to him in the forms of yarn and loom, constant capital in one form has only been exchanged for constant capital in another form. There has in fact been no change of value in the constant capital.

Let us now go further back. The spinner's produce is divided into two parts, flax, spindles, coal, etc., in a word his constant capital, and the newly-added labour; similarly for the machine maker's total product. When the spinner replaces his constant capital, he pays not only for the total capital of the spindle manufacturer, etc., but also for that of the flax-grower. His constant capital pays for the one part of their constant capital + the labour added. Then as for the flax-grower, his constant capital— after deducting agricultural implements, etc.—consists of seed, manure, etc. We will assume—as in agriculture must always be the case, *plus ou moins*[a] directly—that this part of the farmer's constant capital is an annual deduction from his own product, which he must return each year, out of his own product, to the land—that is, to production itself. Here we find a part of the constant capital which replaces itself and is never sold, and therefore also is never paid for, and is never consumed, never enters into individual consumption. Seed, etc., are the equivalent of so much labour time. The value of the seed, etc., enters into the value of the total product; but the same value, because it is the same amount of products (on the assumption that the productivity of labour has remained the same), is also deducted again from the total product and returned to production, not entering into circulation.

Here we have at least one part of the constant capital—that which can be regarded as the raw material of agriculture—which replaces itself. Here therefore is an important branch—the most important branch in size and in the amount of capital it contains—of the annual production in which an important part of

---

[a] More or less.— Ed.

the constant capital, the part which consists of raw materials (apart from artificial fertilisers, etc.), replaces itself and does not enter into circulation, and is therefore not replaced by any form of revenue. Therefore the spinner is not obliged to repay to the flax-grower this part of the constant capital (the part of the constant capital the flax-grower himself replaces and pays for); nor has the weaver to pay this part to the spinner, nor the buyer of the linen to the weaver.

Let us assume that all those who directly or indirectly participated in the production of the 12 yards of linen (=36 s.=3 working days or 36 hours' labour) were paid in linen itself. It is clear in the first place that the producers of the elements of the linen, of the constant capital of the linen, *could not consume* their *own product*, since these products are produced for production and do not enter into immediate [VII-285] consumption. They must therefore spend their wages and profits on linen—on the product which finally enters into individual consumption. What they do not consume in linen, they must consume in some other consumable product exchanged for linen. As much (in value) linen is therefore consumed by others as they consume in other consumable products instead of linen. It is the same as if they had themselves consumed it in linen, since as much as they consume in another product is consumed in linen by the producers of other products. The whole problem must therefore be cleared up, without any reference to exchange, by considering how the 12 yards of linen are divided up between all the producers who have taken part in its production or in the production of its elements.[273]

$5\,^1/_3$ yards or 16 hours' labour represent the constant capital of the spinner and of the loom maker. Let us assume that of the spinner's constant capital $^2/_3$ is raw material and is spent on flax; then the flax-grower can consume these $^2/_3$ entirely in linen, since his constant capital //but here we take the wear and tear of his implements of labour, etc.=0// is not put into circulation at all; he has already deducted it and reserved it for reproduction. He can therefore buy $^2/_3$ of the $5\,^1/_3$ yards of linen[274] or 16 hours' labour,=$3\,^5/_9$ yards, or $10\,^2/_3$ hours' labour. So there remains to be accounted for only $5\,^1/_3-3\,^5/_9$ yards, or $16-10\,^2/_3$ hours' labour, i.e., $1\,^7/_9$ yards or $5\,^1/_3$ hours' labour. These $1\,^7/_9$ yards or $5\,^1/_3$ hours' labour resolve themselves into the constant capital of the loom maker and the total product of the spinning machinery maker, who are assumed to be one person.

[VII-286] Therefore once again: 1 hr.=1 s. 12 yards=36 s. 1 yard=3 s.

Weaver	Total product	Constant capital	Weaving la- bour added	Consumption
	12 yards linen (36 s.) (36 hours' labour)	8 yards (24 hours) (24 s.)	12 hours	12 hours =12s. =4 yards

Of the weaver's *constant capital* let $3/4$=yarn and $1/4$=loom (means of production in general). The weaver thus pays 6 yards or 18 hours to the spinner and 2 yards or 6 hours to the machine maker, etc.

	Spinner				Machine maker		
Total product	Constant capital	Spinning labour added	Consump- tion	Total product	Constant capital	Labour added	Consump- tion
6 yards (18s.) (18 hours)	4 yards (12s.) (12 hours)	2 yards 6s. 6 hours	2 yards =6s.	2 yards 6s. 6 hours	$4/3$ yards	$2/3$ yard	$2/3$ yard

Of the 8 yards which replace the weaver's constant capital, therefore, 2 yards (=6 s.=6 hours) are consumed by the spinner, and $2/3$ of a yard (2 s.=2 hours' labour) by the maker of looms, etc.

What remains for us to account for is thus $8-2\,2/3$ yards=$5\,1/3$ yards (=16 s.=16 hours' labour). These remaining $5\,1/3$ yards (=16 s.=16 hours' labour) are resolved as follows: We assume that in the 4 yards which represent the spinner's constant capital, that is, the elements of his yarn, $3/4$ is the equivalent of the flax, and $1/4$ of the spinning machine. The elements of the [VII-287] spinning machine will be reckoned in further on with the constant capital of the loom maker. The two are assumed to be the same person.

Of the 4 yards which replace the spinner's constant capital, $3/4$=3 yards are therefore resolved into *flax*. A considerable part of the constant capital in the flax, used in its production, has not however to be replaced; for the flax-grower has already returned it to the land in the form of seed, manure, fodder, cattle, etc. Therefore in the part of his product that he sells, only the wear and tear of his instruments of labour, etc., has to be included as constant capital. Here we must rate the labour added at $2/3$ at least and the constant capital to be replaced at $1/3$ at the most.

Thus:

	Total product	Constant capital	Farm labour	Consumable
Flax	3 yards 9s. 9 hours' labour	1 yard 3s. 3 hours' labour	2 yards 6s. 6 hours' labour	2 yards 6s. 6 hours' labour

Thus what we have still to account for is:
1 yard (3 s., 3 hours' labour), equal to the flax-grower's constant capital:
1 $^1/_3$ yards (4 s., 4 hours' labour), equal to the constant capital for the loom;
finally
1 yard (3 s., 3 hours' labour) for the *total product* contained in the spinning machine.
First what the machine maker can consume for the spinning machine has to be deducted:

	Total product	Constant capital	Engineering labour added	Consumable
Spinning machine	1 yard 3s. 3 hours' labour	$^2/_3$ yard 2s. 2 hours' labour	$^1/_3$ yard 1s. 1 hour's labour	$^1/_3$ yard 1s. 1 hour's labour

Moreover, the agricultural machinery, the flax-grower's constant capital, has to be divided into its consumable and other parts:

	Total product	Constant capital	Engineering labour	Consumable
Agri- cultural machine	1 yard 3s. 3 hours' labour	$^2/_3$ yard 2s. 2 hours' labour	$^1/_3$ yard 1s. 1 hour's labour	$^1/_3$ yard 1s. 1 hour's labour

If therefore we put together that·part of the total product which represents machinery, it amounts to 2 yards for the loom, 1 yard for the spinning machine, 1 yard for the agricultural machine, 4 yards in all (12 s., 12 hours' labour or $^1/_3$ of the total product, 12 yards of linen). Of these 4 yards, the machine maker can consume $^2/_3$ of a yard for the loom, $^1/_3$ for the spinning machine, ditto $^1/_3$ for the agricultural machinery, in all 1 $^1/_3$ yards. 2 $^2/_3$ yards are left, that is, $^4/_3$ constant capital for the loom, $^2/_3$ for the spinning machine, and $^2/_3$ for the agricultural machine=$^8/_3$=2 $^2/_3$ yards

($=8$ s.$=8$ hours' labour). This therefore forms the machine builder's constant capital which has to be replaced. Of what now does this constant capital consist? On the one hand, of its raw material, iron, wood, leather belting; and so on. But on the other hand, of that part of the machine he works with (which he may have built himself) which he uses in building machines and which gets worn out. Let us assume that the raw material amounts to $^2/_3$ of the constant capital, and the machine-building machine to $^1/_3$. This latter $^1/_3$ is to be examined later. The $^2/_3$ for wood and iron [VII-288] amount to $^2/_3$ of the $2\,^2/_3$ yards$=^8/_3$ yards$=^{24}/_9$ yards. $^1/_3$ of this$=^8/_9$, therefore $^2/_3=^{16}/_9$ yards.

Let us then assume that here in machinery is $^1/_3$ and added labour $^2/_3$ (since there is nothing for raw material); then $^2/_3$ of the $^{16}/_9$ yards replace labour added, and $^1/_3$ machinery. Thus what is left again for machinery is $^{16}/_{27}$ yard. The constant capital of the producers of iron and wood, in short, of the extractive industry, consists only of instruments of production—which we here call machinery in general—and not of raw material.

Therefore $^8/_9$ yard for the machine-building machine, $^{16}/_{27}$ yard for the machinery used by the producers of iron and wood. So $^{24}/_{27}+^{16}/_{27}=^{40}/_{27}=1\,^{13}/_{27}$ yards. This, therefore, has in turn to be put down to the machine builder's account.

Machinery. $^{24}/_{27}$ of a yard forms the replacement for the machine-building machine. But this in turn is divided into raw material (iron, wood, etc.), the part of the machinery used up in building the machine-building machine, and labour added. So, if each of the elements is $^1/_3$ of the total, $^8/_{27}$ of a yard would go for the labour added, and $^{16}/_{27}$ of a yard would be left for the *constant capital* to be replaced in the machine-building machine, that is, $^8/_{27}$ of a yard for raw material and $^8/_{27}$ of a yard to replace the part of the value representing the machinery used up in working up this raw material (together $^{16}/_{27}$ of a yard).

On the other hand the $^{16}/_{27}$ of a yard, which replace the iron and wood producers' machinery, likewise consist of raw material, machinery and labour added. This last$=^i/_3$, that is$=\dfrac{16}{27\times 3}=\dfrac{16}{81}$ of a yard, and the constant capital in this part of the machinery consists of $^{32}/_{81}$ of a yard, of which $^{16}/_{81}$ is for the raw material, $^{16}/_{81}$ to make good the wear and tear of the machinery.

Thus there remains in the machine builder's hands, as constant capital to make good the wear and tear of his machinery, $^8/_{27}$ of a yard, with which he replaces the wear and tear of his machine-building machine, and $^{16}/_{81}$ of a yard for the wear and tear of the iron and wood producers' machinery that has to be replaced. Apart from this he had, for the replacement of his constant capital, $^8/_{27}$ of a yard for the raw material (contained in the machine-building machine) and $^{16}/_{81}$ for the raw material contained in the iron and wood producers' machines. Of this, however, another $^2/_3$ consist of labour added and $^1/_3$ of machinery used up. Therefore $^2/_3$ of the $^{24}/_{81} + ^{16}/_{81} = ^{40}/_{81}$ is paid for labour, that is, $\dfrac{26\,^2/_3}{81}$. Of this raw material, [VII-289] $\dfrac{13\,^1/_3}{81}$ is again left to replace machinery. This $\dfrac{13\,^1/_3}{81}$ of a yard therefore comes back to the machinery manufacturer.

Now there would again be in the hands of the latter: $^8/_{27}$ of a yard for the replacement of the wear and tear of the machine-building machine, $^{16}/_{81}$ to replace the wear and tear of the iron, etc., producers' machinery, and $\dfrac{13\,^1/_3}{81}$ for the part of the value to replace the machinery in the raw material, iron, etc.

And so we might go on calculating to infinity, with ever smaller fractions, but never able to divide the 12 yards of linen without a remainder.

Let us briefly resume the course of our inquiry up to this point.

We said at the start that in the different spheres of production there are different proportions as between the newly-added labour (which partly replaces the variable capital laid out in wages, and partly forms the profit, the unpaid surplus labour) and the constant capital to which this labour is added. We could however assume an average proportion, for example, a—labour added, b—constant capital; or we could assume that the proportion of the latter to the former is $2:1=^2/_3 : ^1/_3$. If this holds good in each production sphere of capital, we went on, then the labour added (wages and profit together) in one particular sphere of production can always only buy $^1/_3$ of its own product, since wages and profit together form only $^1/_3$ of the total labour time realised in the product. But the other $^2/_3$ of the product, which replace his constant capital, also belong to the capitalist. If he wishes to continue production, however, he must replace his constant capital, that is, retransform $^2/_3$ of his product into constant capital. To do this, he must sell the $^2/_3$.

But to whom? We have already deducted $^1/_3$ of the product that can be bought with the total of wages and profit. If this total represents 1 day's labour or 12 hours, then the part of the product whose value is equal to the constant capital represents 2 days' labour or 24 hours. So we assume that [the second] $^1/_3$ of the product is bought by profit and wages in another branch of production, and the last $^1/_3$ is bought in turn by profit and wages in a third branch of production. But then we have exchanged the constant capital of Product I for wages and profit exclusively, i.e., for newly-added labour, by making the whole labour added to Products II and III be consumed in the form of Product I. Of 6 working days contained in Products II and III, in both newly-added and pre-existing labour, none has been replaced or bought by the labour contained in either Product I or in Products II and III. So we had in turn to make the producers of other products spend all their labour added on Products II and III, and so on. Finally we had to come to a halt at a Product X, in which the labour added was as much as the constant capital of all the earlier products; but its own constant capital $^2/_3$ larger, would be unsaleable. Thus we have not come one step forward with the problem. In the case of Product X, as in the case of Product I, the question remains: to whom is the part of the product sold which replaces the constant capital? Or is $^1/_3$ new labour added to the product to replace the $^1/_3$ new labour+$^2/_3$ pre-existing labour contained in the product? Is $^1/_3=^3/_3$?

So from this it became clear that the SHIFTING of the difficulty from Product I to Product II, etc., in a word, bringing in an intermediate link merely amounting to the exchange of commodities, was of no avail.

[VII-290] So we had to pose the question in a different way.

We assumed that the 12 yards of linen=36 s.=36 hours' labour were a product containing 12 hours' labour or 1 working day of the weaver (necessary labour and surplus labour together, that is, the equivalent of the total of profit and wages), while $^2/_3$ represented the value of the constant capital, yarn and machinery, etc., contained in the linen. We further assumed, in order to eliminate any recourse to quibbles and intermediate transactions, that the linen was of a kind destined only for individual consumption, and therefore could not serve in turn as raw material for some new product. By this we assumed that it was a product that had to be paid for from wages and profit, that it must be exchanged for revenue. And finally to simplify things we assume that no part of the profit is reconverted into capital, but that the whole profit is spent as revenue.

As for the first 4 yards, the first $^1/_3$ of the product, equal to the 12 hours' labour added by the weaver, we soon settled that. They are resolved into wages and profit; their value is the same as the value of the weaver's total profit and wages. They are therefore consumed by him and his workmen themselves. This solution for the 4 yards is unconditionally valid. For if profit and wages are consumed not in linen but in some other product, this can only happen because the producers of some other product consume the part of it which is consumable by them in linen and not in their own product. If of the 4 yards of linen, for example, only 1 is consumed by the linen weaver himself, and 3 yards in meat, bread, and cloth, then just the same as before, the value of the 4 yards of linen is consumed by the linen weavers themselves; only they have consumed $^3/_4$ of this value in the form of other commodities, while the producers of these other commodities have consumed in the form of linen the meat, bread and cloth consumable by them as wages and profit. // Here, as throughout this inquiry, it is of course always assumed that the commodity is sold and sold at its value. //

But now comes the real problem. The weaver's constant capital exists now in the form of 8 yards of linen (=24 hours' labour=24 s.); if he wants to continue production, he must transform these 8 yards of linen into money, £1 4s., and with this £1 4s. he must buy newly-produced commodities, to be found on the market, of which his constant capital consists. To simplify the problem, let it be assumed that he does not replace his machinery within a period of years, but that every day, out of the proceeds of his product, he has to replace *in natura* the part of the machinery that is equal to the part of the value of the machinery worn out each day. He must replace the part of the product=the value of the constant capital consumed by him with the elements of this constant capital, or the objective conditions of production for his labour. On the other hand, his product, the linen, does not enter any other sphere of production as a condition of production, but passes into individual consumption. He can therefore replace the part of his product which represents his constant capital only by exchanging it for revenue or for the part of the value of the product of other producers which consists of wages and profit, *hinc*[a] of newly-added labour. The problem is thus posed in its correct form. The question is only: in what conditions can it be solved?

A difficulty that arose in our first presentation of it has now been partly overcome. Although in each sphere of production the

---

[a] Hence.— *Ed.*

labour added=$^1/_3$, the constant capital, on the assumption made, =$^2/_3$, this $^1/_3$ labour added—or the total value of the revenue (of wages and profit; as already noted earlier, no account is here taken of the part of the profit which is again transformed into capital)—is only consumable in the products of the branches of industry which work directly for individual consumption. The products of all other branches of industry can only be consumed as capital, can only enter into industrial consumption.

[VII-291] The constant capital represented by the 8 yards (=24 hours=24s.) consists of yarn (raw material) and machinery. Let us say $^3/_4$ raw material and $^1/_4$ machinery. (Under raw material we can here also reckon all *matériaux instrumentaux* such as oil, coal, etc. But for the sake of simplicity it is better to disregard these.) The yarn would cost 18s. or 18 hours' labour=6 yards; the machinery 6s.=6 hours' labour=2 yards.

If therefore the weaver uses his 8 yards to buy yarn for 6 yards and machinery for 2 yards, with his constant capital of 8 yards he has covered not only the constant capital of the spinner and the loom manufacturer, but also the labour newly added by them. A part of what appears as the weaver's constant capital therefore represents newly-added labour on the part of the spinner and the machinery manufacturer, and consequently is for them not CAPITAL but revenue.

Of the 6 yards of linen, the spinner can himself consume $^1/_3$=2 yards (=the labour newly added, profit and wages). But 4 yards replace for him only flax and machinery. Say 3 yards for flax, 1 yard for machinery. He must pass on the payment for these. Of the 2 yards the machinery manufacturer can himself consume $^2/_3$ of a yard; but $^4/_3$ only replace for him iron and wood, in a word, raw material, and the machinery used for building the machine. Say, of the $^4/_3$ yards, 1 yard for raw material and $^1/_3$ of a yard for machinery.

Of the 12 yards of linen, we have consumed up to this point: 1) 4 for the weaver, 2) [2] for the spinner, and 3) $^2/_3$ for the machine builder; together $6\,^2/_3$. So $5\,^1/_3$ remain to be accounted for. And these $5\,^1/_3$ are distributed as follows:

The spinner has to replace, out of the value of 4 yards, 3 for flax, 1 for machinery.

The machinery manufacturer has to replace, out of the value of $^4/_3$ yards, 1 for iron, etc., $^1/_3$ for machinery (what he has himself used up in building the machines).

The 3 yards for flax are therefore paid by the spinner to the flax-grower. In the case of the latter, however, there is the special feature that a part of his constant capital (namely, seed, manure, etc., in short all products of the land which he returns to the land) does not enter at all into circulation, and consequently does not need to be deducted from the product that he sells; this product on the contrary expresses only added labour, and consequently consists entirely of wages and profit (except for the part which replaces machinery, artificial fertilisers, etc.). So let us assume as before that $^1/_3$ of the total product is labour added; then 1 yard of the 3 would come under this category. Taking as before for the 2 other yards that $^1/_4$ is for machinery, that would be $^2/_4$ yard. The other $^6/_4$, on the other hand, would also be for labour added, since in this part of the flax-grower's product there is no constant capital, which he has already deducted earlier. So $2\,^2/_4$ yards would go for the flax-grower's wages and profit. What remains is $^2/_4$ yard for replacement of machinery. Thus of the $5\,^1/_3$ yards which we had to consume, $2\,^2/_4$ have gone $(5\,^4/_{12}-2\,^6/_{12}=2\,^{10}/_{12}=2\,^5/_6$ yards$)$. This last $^2/_4$ of a yard would therefore be used by the flax-grower to buy machinery.

The machinery manufacturer's account would now stand like this: of the constant capital for the loom he had laid out 1 yard for iron, etc.; $^1/_3$ of a yard for the wear and tear of the machine-building machine in producing the loom.

In addition, however, the spinner buys from the machinery manufacturer spinning machinery for 1 yard, and the flax-grower buys from him agricultural implements for $^2/_4$ of a yard. Of these $^6/_4$ yards, the machinery manufacturer has to consume $^1/_3$ for labour added, and to expend $^2/_3$ for the constant capital laid out in the spinning machine and the agricultural implements. $^6/_4$ however$=^{18}/_{12}$. So the machine builder would have $^6/_{12}$ of a yard [VII-292] again for consumption, $^{12}/_{12}$ or 1 yard to convert into constant capital. (Of the $2\,^5/_6$ yards not yet consumed, $^1/_2$ yard therefore has gone. $^{14}/_6$ yards are left, or $2\,^2/_6$, or $2\,^1/_3$ yards.)

Of this yard the machinery manufacturer would have to expend $^3/_4$ on raw material, iron and wood, etc., $^1/_4$ to pay to himself for the replacement of the machine-building machine.

So the total account would now stand like this:

Machinery manufacturer's constant capital	For the loom: *1 yard* for raw material, $^1/_3$ *of a yard* for wear and tear of his own machinery. For spinning machine and agricultural implements: $^3/_4$ *of a yard* for raw material, $^1/_4$ of a yard for wear and tear of his own machinery.

HENCE: $1\,^3/_4$ yards for raw material, $^1/_3+^1/_4$ for wear and tear of his own machinery.

The $1^3/_4$ yards or $^7/_4$ yards therefore buy from the iron and wood manufacturers iron and wood to this value. $^7/_4=^{21}/_{12}$. But here a new question arises. In the case of the flax-grower, the raw material which is part of the constant capital did not enter into the product he sold, because it had already been deducted. In this case we must resolve the total product into labour added and machinery. If we even assumed that here the added labour=$^2/_3$ of the product, the machinery=$^1/_3$, $^{14}/_{12}$ would be consumable. And $^7/_{12}$ would remain as constant capital for machinery. This $^7/_{12}$ would come back to the machinery manufacturer.

What was left of the 12 yards would then amount to $^1/_3+^1/_4$ yard, which the machinery manufacturer would have to pay to himself for the wear and tear of his own machinery, and $^7/_{12}$ of a yard, which the iron and wood manufacturers return to him for machinery. Hence $^1/_3+^1/_4=^4/_{12}+^3/_{12}=^7/_{12}$. In addition, the $^7/_{12}$ returned by the iron and wood manufacturers. (Together $^{14}/_{12}=1\,^2/_{12}=1\,^1/_6$.)

The iron and wood manufacturers' machinery and instruments of labour must be bought from the machinery manufacturer, just as those of the weaver, the spinner and the flax-grower. Thus of the $^7/_{12}$ of a yard, let $^1/_3=^2/_{12}$, be labour added. This $^2/_{12}$ of a yard can therefore also be consumed. The remaining $^5/_{12}$ (actually $^4/_{12}$ and $\dfrac{^2/_3}{12}$, but there's no need to be so exact) represents the constant capital contained in the wood-cutter's axe and the iron manufacturer's machinery, $^3/_4$ pig-iron, wood, etc., and $^1/_4$ machinery used up. (Of the $^{14}/_{12}$ yards $^{12}/_{12}$ is left, or 1 yard=3 hours' labour=3s.) Therefore of the 1 yard, $^1/_4$ of a yard for replacement of the machine-building machine and $^3/_4$ of a yard for wood, iron, etc.

Hence for the wear and tear of the machine-building machine $^7/_{12}$ of a yard+$^1/_4$ of a yard=$^7/_{12}+^3/_{12}=^{10}/_{12}$ of a yard. On the other hand it would now be quite pointless again to resolve the $^3/_4$ of a yard for wood and iron into their component parts and to return a part of it once more to the machinery manufacturer, who would return a part of it again to the iron [VII-293] and wood manufacturers. Something would always be left over and a *progressus in infinitum.*

Let us then take the problem as it now stands.

$^{10}/_{12}$ or $^5/_6$ of a yard in value has to be replaced by the machinery manufacturer himself in the worn-out machine.

$^3/_4$ or $^9/_{12}$ of a yard represents an equal amount of value in wood and iron. The machinery manufacturer has given it to the iron and wood manufacturers, in order to replace his raw material. We have in hand the residuum of $^{19}/_{12}$ or $1\,^7/_{12}$ yards.

The balance of $^5/_6$ of a yard which the machinery manufacturer keeps for making good his wear and tear$=^{15}/_6$s.$=^{15}/_6$ hours' labour, that is, $2\,^3/_6$, or $2\,^1/_2$s., or $2\,^1/_2$ hours' labour. The machinery manufacturer cannot accept any linen for this value; he would himself have to sell it again, in order with the $2\,^1/_2$s. to make good the wear and tear of his machinery, in a word, to make new machine-building machines. But to whom is he to sell it? To producers of other products (other than iron and wood)? But these producers have consumed in linen all that they were able to consume in this form. Only the 4 yards which constitute the weaver's wages and profit are exchangeable for other products (apart from those contained in the constant capital or the labour of which this capital consists). And we have already accounted for these 4 yards. Or is he to pay workers with it? But we have already deducted from his products all that labour has added to them, and we have taken it as all consumed in linen.

To put the matter in another way:

The *weaver* has to replace for *machinery*	=2 yards	=6s.		=6	hours' labour
The *spinner*	ditto	ditto	=1	"	=3	"	=3	"	"
The *flax-grower*	ditto	ditto	= $^2/_4$	"	=$1\,^1/_2$	"	=$1\,^1/_2$	"	"
The *iron and wood producers*	ditto	ditto	= $^7/_{12}$	"	=$1\,^3/_4$	"	=$1\,^3/_4$	"	"

Total yards expended on machinery or the part of the value of the linen which consists of machinery	ditto	=$4^1/_{12}$ yards	=$12^1/_4$s.	=$12^1/_4$ hours' labour

To simplify the calculation, say 4 yards=12s.=12 hours' labour. Of this, for labour (profit and wages) $^1/_3=^4/_3$ yards=$1\,^1/_3$ yards.

$2\,^2/_3$ remain for constant capital. Of this, $^3/_4$ for raw material, $^1/_4$ for wear and tear of machinery. $2\,^2/_3=^8/_3=^{32}/_{12}$. Of this $^1/_4=^8/_{12}$.

This $^8/_{12}$ of a yard for wear and tear of machinery is all that the machinery manufacturer is still burdened with. For he pays $^{24}/_{12}$ or 2 yards to the iron and wood manufacturers for raw material.

[VII-294] It is wrong, then, to charge the iron and wood manufacturers again for machinery, since all that they have to replace in machinery, namely $^7/_{12}$ of a yard, has already been brought into the machinery manufacturer's account. In the latter's

ITEM, the whole of the machinery that they need for the production of iron and wood has already been included, and it therefore cannot come a second time into the reckoning. The last 2 yards for iron and wood (the residuum of $2\,^8/_{12}$) consist therefore entirely of labour, since there is no raw material used, and can therefore be consumed in linen.

Thus the whole residuum is $^8/_{12}$ of a yard or $^2/_3$ of a yard for wear and tear of the machinery used by the machinery manufacturer.

The whole problem was partly solved by the fact that the part of the farmer's *constant capital*, which does not itself consist of labour newly added or in machinery, does not circulate at all, but is already deducted, replaces itself in its own production, and therefore also—apart from the machinery—his whole *circulating* product consists of wages and profit and consequently can be consumed in linen. This was one part of the solution.

The other part was that what appears in one sphere of production as constant capital, in other spheres of production appears as new labour added during the same year. What in the weaver's hand appears as constant capital consists in large part of the revenue of the spinner, machinery manufacturer, flax-grower and iron and wood producers (also of the collier, etc.; but for the sake of simplification this is not brought into it). (This is so clear that, for example, when the same manufacturer both spins and weaves, his constant capital seems to be smaller than that of the weaver and the labour added by him greater, i. e., the part of his product which consists of labour added, revenue, profit and wages. Thus in the case of the weaver revenue=4 yards=12s., constant capital=8 yards=24s. If he both spins and weaves, his revenue=6 yards. His constant capital=6 yards ditto; that is, 2 yards=loom, 3 yards flax, and 1 yard spinning machinery.)

Thirdly, however, the solution so far found is that all production processes which supply only raw material or means of production for the product which finally enters into individual consumption, cannot consume their revenue—profit and wages, the [labour] newly added—in their own product, but they can consume the part of the value of this product which represents revenue only in the consumable product, or, what is the same thing, [they have to exchange it] for a consumable product of other producers containing the same amount of value. Their newly-added labour enters into the final product as a component part of the value, but is only consumed in the form of the final product, while as a use value it is contained in the final product as raw material or machinery used up.

Hence the part of the problem which now remains to be solved is reduced to this: What happens to the $^2/_3$ of a yard for the wear and tear—not of the machines used in production, for these represent new labour, that is, new labour which gives the raw material (which has itself no raw material that costs anything) the form of new machinery but—[what happens] to the depreciation of the machinery manufacturer's machine-building machine? Or to put it another way: Under what conditions can the machinery manufacturer consume the $^2/_3$ of a yard=2s.=2 hours' labour in linen, and at the same time replace his machinery? That is the real question. This takes place in fact. It necessarily takes place. Hence the problem: how is this phenomenon to be explained?

[VII-295] Here we leave entirely out of account the part of the profit which is transformed into new capital (both circulating and fixed, variable and constant capital). It has nothing to do with our problem, for here new variable capital as well as the new constant capital are created and replaced by *new* labour (a part of the surplus labour).

So putting this CASE on one side, the total of labour newly added, in a year e. g.,=the total of profit and wages, i. e.,=the total of the annual *revenue* spent on products which enter into individual consumption, such as food, clothing, heating, dwelling-house, furniture, etc.

The total of these products going into consumption is=in value to the total labour added annually (to the total value of the revenue). This quantity of labour must=total labour contained in these products, both the added and the pre-existing labour. In these products not only the labour newly added, but also the constant capital they contain, must be paid for. Their value therefore=the total of profit and wages. If we take linen as the example, then the linen represents for us the aggregate of the products entering into individual consumption annually. This linen must not only be equal to the value of all its elements of value, but its whole use value must be consumable by the various producers who take their share of it. Its whole value must be resolvable into profit and wages, i. e., labour newly added each year, although it consists of labour added and constant capital.

This is partly explained, as we have said, by:

First. A part of the constant capital required for the production of the linen does not enter into it, either as use value or as exchange value. This is the part of the flax which consists of seed, etc.; the part of the constant capital of the agricultural product which does not enter into circulation, but is directly or indirectly returned to production, to the land. This part replaces itself, so it does not need to be repaid out of the linen. // A peasant may sell his whole harvest, say 120 qrs. But then he must buy from another peasant for example 12 qrs of seed, and the latter has then to use as seed, out of his 120 qrs, 24 qrs instead of 12 qrs, $^1/_5$ instead of $^1/_{10}$ of his product. As before 24 qrs of the 240 qrs are given back to the land as seed. Of course, this makes a difference in the circulation. In the first case, where each deducts $^1/_{10}$, 216 qrs enter circulation. In the second case 120 qrs of the first and 108 qrs of the second enter circulation, that is, 228 qrs. As in the previous case, 216 qrs reach the actual consumers. Here therefore we have an example of the fact that the total of values as between DEALERS and DEALERS is greater than the total of values as between DEALERS and CONSUMERS.[a] // (Moreover there is the same difference in all cases in which a part of the profit is transformed into new capital; moreover, transactions between DEALERS and DEALERS extend over many years, etc.)

This part [required] for the production of the linen, i. e. the consumable products, therefore does not have to replace a considerable part of the constant capital required for its production.

Secondly. A large part of the constant capital required for the linen, that is, for the annual consumable product, appears at one level as constant capital, at another level as labour newly added, and consequently in fact consists of profit and wages, revenue, for one, while the same sum of value appears as capital for another. Thus a part of [the weaver's] constant capital is reducible to the labour of the spinner, etc.

[VII-296] *Thirdly.* In all the intermediate processes that are necessary to produce the consumable product, a large part of the products, apart from the raw material and certain *matériaux instrumentaux*, never passes into the use value, but only enters into the consumable product as a component part of its value—such as machinery, coal, oil, tallow, leather belting, etc. In each of these processes which in fact always only produce the constant capital for the next stage—in so far as, through the division of social labour, they take the form of separate branches of business—the product of each stage is divided into one part representing the newly-added labour (consisting of profit and wages, and, with the

---

a See this volume, pp. 429-30.— *Ed.*

proviso made above,[a] forms revenue), and another part which represents the value of the constant capital consumed. It is therefore clear that in each of these spheres of production only that part of the product can be consumed by its own producers which represents wages and profit—only that part which remains over after deducting the quantity of products equal to the value of the constant capital they contain. But none of these producers consumes any part whatever of the products of the previous stage, or of the products of all the stages, which in fact produce nothing but constant capital for a further stage.

Thus although the final product—the linen, which represents all consumable products—consists of newly-added labour and constant capital, and so the final producers of this consumable product can only consume that part of it which consists of the labour most recently added, of their total wages and profits, their revenue—nevertheless all the producers of constant capital consume or realise their newly-added labour only in the consumable product. Thus although this consists of labour added and constant capital, its purchase price consists—in addition to that part of the product which=the quantity of labour most recently added—of the total quantity of all the labour added in the production of its constant capital. They realise all added labour in the consumable product instead of in their own product—so that in this respect it is the same as if the consumable product consisted entirely of wages and profit, of labour added.

From the consumable product, the linen (the exchange of consumable products for each other and the previous transformation of the commodities into money makes no difference), the producers from whose sphere of production it emerges as a FINISHED product themselves deduct the part of the product equal to their revenue=the labour most recently added by them=the total wages and profit. With the other part of the consumable product they pay the component part of the value due to the producers who have directly supplied them with their constant capital. All of this part of their consumable product therefore covers the value of the revenue and constant capital of the producers of this constant capital in its nearest stage. The latter however keep only the part of the consumable product whose value=their revenue. With the other part they pay in turn the producers of their constant capital=revenue+constant capital. *The account, however, can only be settled* if it is only revenue, newly-added labour, not constant capital, that has to be replaced by the last part of the linen, the consumable product. For on the assumption we have made the linen enters only into consumption and does not in turn form the constant capital of another phase of production.

This has already been shown to be the case for a part of the product of agriculture.

In general, it is only products that enter as raw materials into the final product of which it can be said that they are consumed as products. Other products enter into the consumable product only as component parts of value. The consumable product is bought by revenue, that is, by wages and profit. Its total value must therefore be resolvable into wages and profit, that is, into the labour added in all its stages. The question now arises: in addition to the part of the product of agriculture which is returned to [VII-297] production by its producers themselves—seed, cattle, manure, etc.—is there yet another part of the constant capital which does not enter into the consumable product as a component part of value, but is replaced *in natura* in the process of production itself?

Fixed capital in all its forms can of course only be considered here to the extent that its value enters into production and is consumed.

Apart from agriculture (including cattle-raising and fish farming, and forestry, in which reproduction is artificially organised, etc.)—and so apart from all raw materials for clothing, actual means of sustenance and a large part of the products entering into fixed capital in industry, such as sails, rope, belting, etc.—in mining there is the partial replacement of constant capital *in natura* out of the product, so that the part which enters into circulation does not have to replace this part of the constant capital. For example, in coal production some of the coal is used to work the steam-engine which pumps out water or raises coal.

The value of the annual product therefore partly=the part of the labour pre-existing in coal and consumed in producing the coal, and partly=the quantity of labour added (leaving out of account wear and tear of machinery, etc.). Of the total product, however, the part of the constant capital which consists in coal itself is directly deducted and returned to production. No one has to replace this part for the producer, because he replaces it himself. If the productivity of labour has neither fallen nor risen, then too the part of the value which this part of the product represents remains unchanged,=a definite aliquot part of the quantity of labour existing in the product—partly pre-existing [labour], partly the quantity of labour added during the year. In the other mining industries too there is a partial replacement of the constant capital *in natura.*

Waste products—as for example cotton waste and so on—are fed to the fields as fertiliser or become raw material for other branches of industry, as for example linen rags [in the production] of paper. In such cases, as in the former case, part of an industry's constant capital may be directly exchanged for the constant capital of another industry. For example, cotton for cotton waste used as fertiliser.

In general, however, there is a cardinal difference between the production of machines and primary production (of raw materials: iron, wood, coal) and the other phases of production: in the latter, there is no interaction between them. Linen cannot be a part of the spinner's constant capital, nor can yarn (as such) be part of the constant capital of the flax-grower or machinery manufacturer. But the raw material of machinery—apart from such agricultural products as leather belting, rope, etc.—is wood, iron and coal, while on the other hand machinery in its turn enters as a means of production into the constant capital of the producers of wood, iron, coal, etc. In fact, therefore, both replace each other a part of their constant capital *in natura.* Here there is exchange of constant capital for constant capital.

Here it is not merely a question of accounting. The producer of iron debits the machinery manufacturer for the wear and tear of the machinery used up in producing the iron and the machinery manufacturer debits for the wear and tear of his machinery in constructing the machines. Let the producers of iron and coal be the same person. First, he himself replaces the coal, as we have seen. Secondly, the value of his total product of iron and coal=the value of the labour added+the labour pre-existing in the worn-out machinery. After deducting from this total product the quantity of iron that replaces the value of the machinery, the quantity of iron which is left represents the labour added. The latter part forms the raw material of manufacturers of machinery, instruments, etc. The machinery manufacturer pays the iron manufacturer for this latter part in linen. In exchange for the first part, he supplies him with machinery to replace the old.

On the other hand, the part of the machinery manufacturer's constant capital which represents the wear and tear of his machine-building machines, instruments, etc.—and therefore consists neither of raw material (leaving out of account here the machinery used [VII-298] and the part of the coal which replaces itself) nor of labour added, and so neither of wages nor profit—this wear and tear is in fact made good by the machinery manufacturer appropriating for himself one or two of his own machines to serve as machine-building machines. This part of his product merely comes to an excess consumption of raw material. For it does not represent labour newly added, since in the total product of the labour so many machines=the value of the labour added, so many machines=the value of the raw material, and so many machines=the part of the value that was contained in machine-building machines. It is true that this last part does contain labour added. But in terms of value this=zero, since the labour contained in the raw material and in the machinery used up is not reckoned in the group of machines that represents labour added; and the part which replaces the new labour and machinery is not reckoned in the 2nd group, which replaces the raw material; and consequently in the 3rd part—considered in terms of value— neither labour added nor raw material is contained, but this group of machines represents only the wear and tear of the machinery.

The machinery of the machinery manufacturer himself is not sold. It is replaced *in natura*, deducted from the total product. Consequently the machines which he sells represent only raw material (which consists only of labour, if he has already been charged for the wear and tear of the raw material producer's machinery) and labour added, and therefore are resolvable into linen for himself and for the raw material producer. As for what specially concerns the relations between the machinery manufacturer and the producer of raw materials, the latter has deducted, in respect of the part of his machinery that has been WASTED, a quantity of iron equal to its value. He exchanges this with the machinery manufacturer, so that each of them pays the other *in natura*, and this process has nothing to do with the division of revenue between them.

So much for this question, to which we shall return in connection with the circulation of capital.[265]

In reality, the constant capital is replaced by being constantly produced anew and in part by reproducing itself. The part of the constant capital which enters into the consumable product is however paid for out of the living labour which enters into the non-consumable products. Because the latter labour is not paid for in its own products, it can resolve the whole consumable product into revenue. A part of the constant capital is, seen in terms of the year, only seemingly constant capital. Another part, although it enters into the total product, does not enter into the consumable product either as a component part of its value or as a use value, but is replaced *in natura*, remaining always incorporated in production.

Here we have considered how the total consumable product is divided up and resolved into all the component parts of value and conditions of production that have entered into it.

But always there are, simultaneously and side by side, the consumable product (which, in so far as it consists of wages=the variable part of capital), the production of the consumable product, and the production of all parts of the constant capital required for its production, whether it enters into it or not. In the same way, each capital is always simultaneously divided into constant and variable capital, and although the constant capital, like the variable, is continuously replaced by new products, it always continues to exist in the same manner, as long as the same kind of production continues.

[VII-299] The relation between the machinery manufacturer and the primary producers—of iron, wood, etc.—is that they in fact exchange with each other a part of their constant capital (which has nothing in common with the transformation of a part of the constant capital of one into revenue for the other[275]), because their products—although one is a previous stage for the other—on both sides enter as means of production into the constant capital of the other. In return for the machinery which the producer of iron, wood, etc., needs, he gives the machine builder iron, wood, etc., to the value of the machine to be replaced. This part of the machine builder's constant capital is for him just the same as seed is for the peasant. It is part of his annual product which he replaces *in natura* for himself and which is not resolved into revenue for him. On the other hand, what is thus replaced for the machine builder in the form of raw material is not only the raw material contained in the iron producer's machine, but also the part of the value of this machine which consists of labour added and wear and tear of his own machinery. Thus it replaces for him not only the wear and tear of his own machinery, but can be regarded as accounting for (replacing) a part of the wear and tear contained in the other machines.

It is true that this [machine sold] to the producer of iron also contains component parts of value=the raw material and the labour added. But on the other hand there is correspondingly less wear and tear to be accounted for in the other machines. This part of their [the iron producers', etc.] constant capital—that is, of the product of their annual labour which replaces only the part of value of the constant capital representing wear and tear—therefore does not enter into the machines which the machine builder sells to other industrialists. But as regards the wear and tear in these other machines, it is in fact [replaced] for the machine builder by the above-mentioned $^2/_3$ of a yard of linen, the equivalent of 2 hours' labour. With that, he buys pig-iron, wood, etc., to the same value, and replaces the wear and tear in another form of his constant capital—[in the form] of iron. Thus a part of his raw material replaces for him the value of his wear and tear, in addition to the value of the raw material. This raw material, however, as far as the producer of iron, etc., is concerned, consists only of the labour time added, as the machinery of these producers of raw materials (iron, wood, coal, etc.) has already been accounted for.

Thus all the elements of the linen are resolved into a sum of quantities of labour=the amount of labour newly added, but not equal to the amount of the total labour contained in the constant capital and perpetuated by reproduction.

That the quantity of labour consisting partly of living labour, partly of pre-existing labour, which forms the total of commodities which enter each year into individual consumption, and thus are consumed as revenue, cannot be greater than the labour added annually, is for that matter a tautology. For the revenue=the total of profit and wages=the total labour newly added=the total of the commodities which contain an equal quantity of labour.

The case of iron producer and machine builder is only one EXAMPLE. Between different spheres of production, where the products of each enter into the other as means of production, an exchange *in natura* takes place too (even though concealed by a series of money transactions) between the constant capital of the one and that of the other. In so far as this is the case, the consumers of the final product which enters into consumption have not got to replace this constant capital, since it has already been replaced.

Adam Smith's contradictions are of significance because they contain problems which it is true he does not solve, but which he reveals by contradicting himself. His correct instinct in this connection is best shown by the fact that his successors take opposing stands based on one aspect of his teaching or the other.

NOTES
AND
INDEXES

NOTES

[1] After completing the economic manuscript of 1857-58 (see present edition, vols 28 and 29), Marx started work to realise his idea of a substantial economic work to encompass all aspects of life in capitalist society. The first step was the publication, in 1859, of *A Contribution to the Critique of Political Economy*. Part One. In the Preface to this work, Marx sets out the plan of his ambitious project: "I examine the system of bourgeois economy in the following order: *capital, landed property, wage-labour; the State, foreign trade, world market...* The first part of the first book, dealing with Capital, comprises the following chapters: 1. The commodity; 2. Money or simple circulation; 3. Capital in general. The present part consists of the first two chapters" (see present edition, Vol. 29, p. 261).

From extant correspondence (see present edition, Vol. 40) it is clear that after publishing Part One Marx intended to start immediately on the second part, which was to consist of a chapter on capital in general. However, certain other circumstances, his preoccupation with *Herr Vogt* among them, prevented him from carrying through this intention. Preparatory work continued up to the summer of 1861 (drafting plans, reviewing the 1857-58 manuscript and excerpts dealing with capital, making new excerpts, etc.), and in August 1861 Marx began writing. Viewed as the second part of *A Contribution to the Critique of Political Economy*, the manuscript of 1861-63 originally bore the same title. But soon its size grew considerably and reached 23 notebooks, 1,472 large pages in all. In addition to the main title, the covers of the first two notebooks were given the subtitle "Third Chapter. Capital in General".— 5

[2] This note was made on the inside cover of Notebook I (which Marx marked "A"), presumably once it was complete. Other notes on the cover have been inserted in the relevant passages of the manuscript by the compilers.—6

[3] This note was originally made on the inside cover of Notebook II, which Marx also marked "A".— 6

[4] In the economic manuscript of 1857-58, Marx had pointed out that "exchange value expresses the *social form* of value" (see present edition, Vol. 29, p. 244), but he still used these concepts interchangeably. Only starting with the

second edition of Volume I of *Capital* in 1872 did he begin to differentiate clearly between them.— 11

5 Marx summarised the following passage from MacLeod: "When currency is employed in this method, that is when it is employed in producing articles which are themselves intended to be subservient to the production of other articles, it is usually called CAPITAL, and the use of the word Capital is also extended to apply to the article itself so produced to act as an agent in the production of others" (H. D. MacLeod, *The Theory and Practice of Banking*, Vol. I, London, 1855, p. 55).— 13

6 Part of the text from pages 16 and 17 of the manuscript has been transferred here in accordance with Marx's note: "Addition to I 1) a, p. 4, line 2."— 13

7 Commenting on Malthus' views on pp. XIII—758-759 of the manuscript of 1861-63, Marx quotes Malthus' *Definitions in Political Economy* and Torrens' *Essay on the Production of Wealth* (see present edition, Vol. 32). On pp. XIV— 777-778 of the manuscript Marx deals once more with Ricardo's followers' critique of Malthus' concept of "the mere consumers" (Vol. 32).— 14

8 This work by James Steuart was first published in 1767. In his Excerpt Notebook VII, Marx copied out passages from the six-volume edition of this work published in London in 1805. When writing his synopsis, Marx mistakenly put 1801 as the year of publication. This error occurred again in the manuscript of 1861-63 and in all four editions of Volume I of *Capital.*— 16, 348, 352

9 As part of his economic studies in the summer of 1858, Marx wrote a synopsis of Aristotle's *Republic,* noting, among other things, that the latter drew a distinction between economics and chrematistics. Both the extant part of the original version of *A Contribution to the Critique of Political Economy* and the published version emphasise that Aristotle counterposed the two forms of circulation: $C—M—C$ and $M—C—M$ (see present edition, Vol. 29, pp. 370 and 488). In Part II, Ch. IV of Volume I of *Capital* Marx dealt in more detail with Aristotle's views on the subject (see present edition, Vol. 35).— 19

10 Marx described the nature of the general connection between the productivity of labour and value—the inverse ratio between the labour time contained in the commodity and the productivity of labour—in Part One of *A Contribution to the Critique of Political Economy* (see present edition, Vol. 29, p. 279).— 20, 167, 235, 242

11 Part of the text from page 14 of the manuscript has been transferred here in conformity with Marx's note: "Addition to a."— 20

12 This and the following paragraph reproduce, in places verbatim, a passage from the economic manuscript of 1857-58 (see present edition, Vol. 28, pp. 190-92).— 20

13 Later, in notebooks XIII and XIV of the manuscript of 1861-63, Marx returns to his analysis of Malthus' views and the critique of his theory of "the mere consumers" (see present edition, Vol. 32).— 28

14 This quotation is followed by Marx's German translation.— 28

15 In the economic manuscript of 1857-58 Marx already described merchant's capital and usurer's capital as, on the one hand, the historically earliest forms of capital and, on the other, as derived, secondary forms of it in developed bourgeois production (see present edition, Vol. 28, pp. 184-85 and 430-36;

Vol. 29, pp. 231-32). In notebooks XI and XV of the manuscript of 1861-63 Marx again takes up his analysis of these forms of capital as the historical prerequisites for the emergence of industrial capital (see present edition, vols 31 and 33).—29, 103

[16] Initially, the Greek word κεφάλαιον meant "the principal", "the basic", and later, "a sum of money", "capital". Marx borrowed the etymological entry from Ducange's *Glossarium mediae et infimae latinitatis,* Vol. II, Paris, 1842, pp. 139-41. Cf. also Marx's notes in the Economic Manuscripts of 1857-58 (see present edition, Vol. 28, p. 437).—31

[17] A detailed analysis of interest-bearing capital is contained in Notebook XV of this manuscript (see present edition, Vol. 32).—31

[18] Marx takes up this issue in Notebook XXI of the manuscript, in the fragment entitled "Transitional Forms" (see present edition, Vol. 34).—32

[19] In his analysis of capital in the manuscript of 1861-63 Marx followed the plan he had evolved when working on the economic manuscript of 1857-58. On April 2, 1858, he wrote to Engels about the structure of the book: "*Capital* falls into 4 sections. a) Capital *en général..* b) *Competition,* or the interaction of many capitals. c) *Credit,* where capital, as against individual capitals, is shown to be a universal element. d) *Share capital* as the most perfected form (turning into communism) together with all its contradictions" (see present edition, Vol. 40, p. 298).

During his work on the manuscript of Volume III of *Capital,* Marx decided to discuss some questions on credit in the section devoted to capital (Ch. XXV) (see present edition, Vol. 37).—33

[20] While working on the manuscript of 1861-63, Marx repeatedly described the prerequisites for analysing capital proper. He thus pointed out a characteristic feature of the dialectical approach to the subject, the transition from the abstract to the concrete, and continued, as it were, his criticism of the vulgar economists, which he had begun in the manuscript of 1857-58 (see present edition, Vol. 28, pp. 180-81, 195-96, 248), for their attempts to reduce the fundamental production relation between the wage labourer and the capitalist to a simple relation between commodity owners, as it appears on the surface of capitalist production in the process of simple commodity circulation.—33, 35, 37, 39, 69, 105, 134, 312, 314, 316

[21] Cf. Marx's description of the historical conditions of the existence of the worker as a *free* worker in the original version of the beginning of Chapter Three of *A Contribution to the Critique of Political Economy* (present edition, Vol. 29, pp. 504-05).—35, 37, 38, 87, 109, 111, 131

[22] Marx returned to his analysis of the historical conditions that gave rise to the free worker, i.e. to a discussion of primitive accumulation, in notebooks XXII and XXIII of the manuscript (see present edition, Vol. 34). The most logical and complete form of his analysis of how the relation between the wage labourer and the capitalist emerged is to be found in Volume I of *Capital,* Part VIII, "The So-Called Primitive Accumulation" (see present edition, Vol. 35).— 38

[23] In Part One of *A Contribution to the Critique of Political Economy* Marx returns several times to the prerequisites for money circulation (see present edition, Vol. 29, pp. 338-39, 357).— 39

²⁴ Marx presents the correlation between the development of money as a hoard and the historical stages in the development of the social process of production in Part One of *A Contribution to the Critique of Political Economy* (see present edition, Vol. 29, pp. 361-65).— 39

²⁵ *Being-for-itself* ("Fürsichsein", "Fürsichseiendes") is a Hegelian term denoting the condition of an attribute regarded in its fixity or relative self-containment.— 39, 114

²⁶ Cf. Marx's description of production as given in the Introduction to the economic manuscript of 1857-58 (present edition, Vol. 28, p. 25).— 40

²⁷ Marx analysed bourgeois economists' views on the genesis of surplus value in the economic manuscript of 1857-58 (see present edition, Vol. 28, pp. 251-56).— 41

²⁸ Cf. the beginning of Chapter Three in the original version of *A Contribution to the Critique of Political Economy* (present edition, Vol. 29, p. 502).— 41

²⁹ Marx described the relation between master and journeyman on p. XXI—1303 of the manuscript of 1861-63, in the section dealing with the formal and the real subsumption of labour under capital (see present edition, Vol. 34).— 42, 94

³⁰ After the publication of Part One of *A Contribution to the Critique of Political Economy*, Marx drafted a plan for Chapter Three ("Chapter on Capital"). In this, item 5 is "Wage Labour and Capital" (see present edition, Vol. 29, p. 514). While working on the manuscript of 1861-63, Marx became convinced that the material on this issue should be transferred to the end of Section III, "Capital and Profit", as can be seen from the draft plan of this section on p. XVIII—1139 of the manuscript (see present edition, Vol. 33).— 42, 304

³¹ Cf. a similar definition of value as the law of market prices in the economic manuscript of 1857-58 (present edition, Vol. 28, pp. 74-75).— 44

³² According to the plan given in the Preface to Part One of *A Contribution to the Critique of Political Economy*, Marx intended to consider these issues in a separate book entitled *Wage Labour*, a comprehensive research he was planning to undertake into bourgeois economy (see present edition, Vol. 29, p. 261).— 44, 82

³³ On pp. XX—1284-1296 of the manuscript of 1861-63, Marx repeatedly turned to the analysis of wages (see present edition, Vol. 34). See also this volume, p. 224.— 45, 195, 232

³⁴ Turgot wrote his chief economic work in 1766. It was first published by Dupond de Nemours in 1769-70.— 46, 352, 363

³⁵ Part of the text from page 26 of the manuscript has been transferred here in conformity with Marx's note: "Addition to p. 23."— 46

³⁶ Marx again touches upon this issue as being a consequence of the factory system on pp. XX—1243-1244 of the manuscript of 1861-63 (see present edition, Vol. 33).— 46

³⁷ The passage in question is quoted by Marx in the Additions to the chapter "Absolute Surplus Value" (see this volume, p. 217). Later, he used this quotation in *Capital*, Vol. I, Ch. X (see present edition, Vol. 35).— 47

[38] In the manuscript of 1861-63 Marx comments repeatedly on Bailey's attacks on Ricardo's labour theory of value (see this volume, p. 101). This quotation, coming from *A Critical Dissertation*, occurs again on p. XIV—827, where Marx gives a detailed analysis of Bailey's views on value (see present edition, Vol. 32).—48, 101

[39] Cf. the description of use value in Part One of *A Contribution to the Critique of Political Economy* (present edition, Vol. 29, pp. 269-70). On use value entering into the process of production of capital as the "economic determination of form", see the economic manuscript of 1857-58 and the original text of the beginning of Chapter Three of *A Contribution to the Critique of Political Economy* (present edition, Vol. 28, p. 237 and Vol. 29, pp. 252, 504).—53, 55, 103, 105

[40] Marx gave a detailed analysis of the development of money from the difference between use value and exchange value in the economic manuscript of 1857-58 (see present edition, Vol. 28, pp. 78-85, 88). Cf. also Part One of *A Contribution to the Critique of Political Economy* (present edition, Vol. 29, pp. 287-90).—54

[41] On the inside cover of Notebook I marked "A" (see Note 2), Marx copied out a fragment from the manuscript of 1857-58 containing a short résumé of the problem of the exchange between labour and capital and the transition to the question of the actual consumption of the commodity labour capacity, i.e. to an analysis of the labour process and of the process of valorisation (see present edition, Vol. 28, pp. 204-05). This fragment has, therefore, been placed at the beginning of the section "The Labour Process".—54

[42] In the economic manuscript of 1857-58, Marx criticised Frédéric Bastiat, one of the preachers of economic harmony between the classes in capitalist society, for reducing all economic relations to a simple relation of circulation (see present edition, Vol. 28, pp. 244-45).—54

[43] In the section "The Labour Process" Marx turns repeatedly to his description of real labour as the source of use value, which he gave in Part One of *A Contribution to the Critique of Political Economy* (see present edition, Vol. 29, p. 278). Here he examines the subject in greater detail.—55, 63

[44] Following Hegel, Marx uses the notion "ideal" in the sense of action mediated by consciousness. Thus, Marx interprets the "idealisation" of the materials of nature, as is clear from the text that follows, as giving a product, through labour, that is, through *man's conscious activity*, a "higher use value".—55

[45] Marx gives a description of the interdependence of the division of labour, exchange and exchange value in the original text of Chapter Two of *A Contribution to the Critique of Political Economy* (see present edition, Vol. 29, pp. 464-68).—55

[46] Cf. Marx's description of the worker's indifference to the specificity of his labour in the economic manuscript of 1857-58 (present edition, Vol. 28, pp. 222-23).—55

[47] Cf. this passage with Marx's statement concerning the analysis of the use values of commodities as such in Part One of *A Contribution to the Critique of Political Economy* (present edition, Vol. 29, p. 270).—55

[48] Cf. Marx's definition of the simple moments of the labour process in the economic manuscript of 1857-58 (present edition, Vol. 28, pp. 224-25).—56

[49] Cf. the description of productive consumption in the economic manuscript of 1857-58 (present edition, Vol. 28, p. 227).—58

⁵⁰ Cf. the description of the means and instruments of labour as "objectification of living labour" in the economic manuscript of 1857-58 (present edition, Vol. 28, p. 285).—58

⁵¹ Cf. Marx's definition of a "higher use value" in the economic manuscript of 1857-58 (present edition, Vol. 28, p. 237).—58, 63

⁵² The rest of this paragraph and the beginning of the next one contain passages with minor changes taken from the economic manuscript of 1857-58 (see present edition, Vol. 28, pp. 226-27).—59

⁵³ In the economic manuscript of 1857-58 Marx stressed that "for use value, only the *quality* of the labour already objectified is relevant" (present edition, Vol. 28, p. 288).—62

⁵⁴ Cf. Part One of *A Contribution to the Critique of Political Economy* (present edition, Vol. 29, p. 270), in which Marx gives a similar description of use value as a result of the labour process as such.—64

⁵⁵ Marx had already pointed out the changes in the character of the labour process resulting from its subsumption under capital in the economic manuscript of 1857-58 (see present edition, Vol. 29, pp. 81-84). In the manuscript of 1861-63, Marx repeatedly noted the varying impact of the capitalist relation on the character of the labour process and the creation by capital of a mode of production corresponding to it.—64, 92, 137, 262, 271, 280

⁵⁶ In the economic manuscript of 1857-58, Marx had already criticised economists who, as apologists of bourgeois society, confused capital with the material elements of the labour process (see present edition, Vol. 28, pp. 188-89, 235-36). In the manuscript of 1861-63, Marx took up the issue once more in the section "Unity of the Labour Process and the Valorisation Process" (see this volume, pp. 95 and 98-99) and when considering Thomas Hodgskin's views on p. XV—864 (see present edition, Vol. 32).—65, 95, 98, 140, 143, 150, 154

⁵⁷ The remark in parenthesis probably means that Marx wanted to give another definition of productive labour as a moment of the labour process as such. Later, in Ch. VII of Volume I of *Capital*, having left this passage virtually unchanged, he supplied a footnote pointing out the specifics of the application of this concept to the capitalist production process (see present edition, Vol. 35).—65

⁵⁸ In the section "Forms Preceding Capitalist Production" of the economic manuscript of 1857-58, Marx dealt at length with the conditions of human labour already present in nature (see present edition, Vol. 28, pp. 412, 416).—65, 134

⁵⁹ At the end of the section "Forms Preceding Capitalist Production" of the economic manuscript of 1857-58, Marx already stated that, just as wealth existing in the form of money constituted an historical prerequisite for the emergence of industrial capital, an analysis of the role of money was a theoretical prerequisite for an analysis of capital (see present edition, Vol. 28, pp. 427-36).—69

⁶⁰ In the manuscript of 1861-63, in the course of his further analysis, Marx repeatedly pointed to one of the specific features of his method for analysing capitalist production relations: the transformation of the prerequisite for the analysis into its result (of the commodity as the most elementary form of wealth

into a product of capital) (see this volume, pp. 96-97 and 291 and also Vol. 32, p. XV—899). Marx returns to this issue in the manuscript of Volume I of *Capital*, Chapter Six, "The Results of the Direct Process of Production" (see present edition, Vol. 34).—69, 97, 291, 298, 313

[61] In the Introduction to the economic manuscript of 1857-58 Marx exhaustively criticised the way bourgeois economists broke down the subject of research into production, distribution, exchange and consumption (see present edition, Vol. 28, pp. 17-37). Cf. also Marx's note on p. XIV—793 of the manuscript of 1861-63 on James Mill's "unsatisfactory divisions" (present edition, Vol. 32).— 69, 159

[62] Marx discusses the question of the relations of distribution being determined by the relations of production in the manuscript of Volume III of *Capital*, Ch. LI (see present edition, Vol. 37). Cf. also the presentation of this problem in the economic manuscript of 1857-58 (present edition, Vol. 29, p. 142).— 70, 145, 159

[63] Marx returned to this question in Notebook V of the manuscript of 1861-63 (see this volume, p. 325 et seq.). Cf. also Marx's letter to Engels of August 20, 1862, in which he inquires about the method of calculating the wear and tear of machinery (present edition, Vol. 41, pp. 411-12).— 70

[64] For more detail, see the section on the Physiocrats in Notebook VI of the manuscript of 1861-63 (this volume, pp. 352-76). Cf. also the pertinent passage in the economic manuscript of 1857-58 (present edition, Vol. 28, pp. 253-55).— 70, 167

[65] At the bottom of page 36 of Notebook I of the manuscript of 1861-63, Marx copied out two paragraphs from the economic manuscript of 1857-58 with slight changes (see present edition, Vol. 28, pp. 236-37).— 71

[66] Cf. Marx's description of labour as a source of use value and exchange value presented in Part One of *A Contribution to the Critique of Political Economy* (present edition, Vol. 29, p. 277).— 71

[67] Marx is referring to Wakefield's theory of colonisation. He already touched on the views of this English economist in the economic manuscript of 1857-58 (see present edition, Vol. 28, pp. 208, 484-85). Later, Marx devoted a whole chapter (Ch. XXIII) to this theory in Volume I of *Capital* (see present edition, Vol. 35).— 75, 116, 257, 292

[68] When analysing the boundaries of capitalist production in the economic manuscript of 1857-58, Marx cited J. R. McCulloch's views to illustrate how the vulgar economists denied the existence of overproduction. McCulloch reduced production based on capital to production for immediate use value, to all intents and purposes identifying production with consumption under capitalism and reducing the goal of the capitalist production process to the consumption of its products by the producers themselves (see present edition, Vol. 28, pp. 338-39). On pp. XIII—707, 717 of the manuscript of 1861-63, Marx returns to this question when describing the specifics of the capitalist production process (present edition, Vol. 32).—81, 133

[69] In the economic manuscript of 1857-58, when evolving the concept of value, Marx proceeded from ordinary (simple) average labour, on which he based the determination of exchange value by labour time (see present edition, Vol. 28, pp. 249, 531). The problem of the definition of simple labour, and the need for further research into the law of the reduction of complex labour to

simple labour was formulated for the first time in the economic manuscript of 1857-58 and then, in more detail, in Part One of *A Contribution to the Critique of Political Economy* (see present edition, Vol. 29, pp. 222, 272-73).—81, 90, 231

[70] Cf. the definition of necessary labour time as it is formulated in Part One of *A Contribution to the Critique of Political Economy* (present edition, Vol. 29, p. 274).—82, 242, 313

[71] Cf. the economic manuscript of 1857-58, where Marx says that "Californian gold is the product of simple labour" (present edition, Vol. 29, p. 222).—82

[72] Cf. the definition of the use value of the commodity labour capacity in the original version of *A Contribution to the Critique of Political Economy* (present edition, Vol. 29, p. 506).—87

[73] Marx discussed the socialists' inability to explain surplus value theoretically in his economic manuscript of 1857-58 (see present edition, Vol. 28, p. 340) and in Part One of *A Contribution to the Critique of Political Economy* (Vol. 29, p. 301).—89

[74] Cf. Marx's similar statement concerning the consumption of material by labour and capital's consumption of labour by means of the material in the economic manuscript of 1857-58 (present edition, Vol. 28, p. 237).—93

[75] The formal subsumption of the labour process under capital and the formation by capital of a corresponding mode of production, i.e. the real subsumption of the labour process under capital, are examined in detail in Notebook XXI of the manuscript of 1861-63 (see present edition, Vol. 34).—93, 188, 262, 311

[76] Marx repeatedly discussed the various aspects of "labour of superintendence" in the manuscript of 1861-63 (see this volume, pp. 262, 387 and 413, and also vols 32 and 33, pp. XIV—782, XV—919, 924, XVIII—1100). A special analysis of this issue is to be found in *Capital*, Vol. III, Ch. XXIII (see present edition, Vol. 37).—94, 262, 387

[77] Marx re-examines the way Ricardo confused capital with the objective conditions of the labour process on p. XII—653 of the manuscript of 1861-63 (see present edition, Vol. 32). Cf. also Marx's criticism of Ricardo's views in the economic manuscript of 1857-58 (present edition, Vol. 28, pp. 188, 235-36).—95

[78] The English bourgeois economists' phrase, "capital employs labour", was also used by Ricardo: "capital, or ... the means of employing labour". Marx returned several times to this problem in the manuscript of 1861-63 (see present edition, vols 32 and 34, pp. XII—663, XIV—808, XV—864, XXI—1317).—95

[79] Marx later reproduced this description of John Wade's work in Volume I of *Capital* in a note to the chapter "The Working-Day" (see present edition, Vol. 35).—96

[80] In the economic manuscript of 1857-58 (see present edition, Vol. 28, pp. 94-95, 171; Vol. 29, pp. 40, 77-78, 431-32, 487) and Part One of *A Contribution to the Critique of Political Economy* (Vol. 29, pp. 275-76, 289), Marx repeatedly noted the fusion of production relations with their objective being, which is manifested in the fact that social relationships of persons appear in money and capital as social relationships of things.—96, 135

81 Marx takes this quotation from: J. Colins, *L'économie politique. Source des révolutions et des utopies prétendues socialistes,* Vol. 3, Paris, 1857, p. 358.—97

82 The section which is to be found at the end of Notebook XVII and the beginning of Notebook XVIII of the manuscript of 1861-63, deals again with this question (see present edition, Vol. 33). Marx considered this problem in detail in Volume II of *Capital* (see present edition, Vol. 36).—97, 99

83 Here, Marx develops an earlier idea of the interdependence of the natural conditions of production at the first stage of the development of human society and the product of the labour process as a result of man's social activities (see present edition, Vol. 28, pp. 188-89, 511). See also Note 58.— 97

84 A reference to A. Turgot, *Réflexions sur la formation et la distribution des richesses,* pp. 34-35. Marx again stresses this idea on p. XIX—1163 of this manuscript (see present edition, Vol. 33).—97

85 Marx quotes B. Franklin's definition of man from: [Thomas Bentley,] *Letters on the Utility and Policy of Employing Machines to Shorten Labour; Occasioned by the Late Disturbances in Lancashire...,* London, 1780, pp. 2-3. In his Notebook VII of excerpts covering 1859-63, Marx copied out the following passage from that work: "Man has been defined many ways ... a *tool-making animal,* or *engineer* (Franklin), has by some been adopted as the best and most characteristic definition of men."—98

86 Marx refers to pp. 153-54 of his Notebook VII of excerpts, covering 1859-62, where he wrote down passages from Volumes One and Three of Colins' three-volume work *L'économie politique...* (Paris, 1856-57).—98

87 Cf. Marx's description of the individual as a member of a community, given in the economic manuscript of 1857-58 (present edition, Vol. 28, pp. 409-10).— 98

88 The assertions made by James Mill and J. B. Say on the impossibility of overproduction, under capitalism were critically analysed by Marx in the economic manuscript of 1857-58 (present edition, Vol. 28, pp. 338-39, 352).—99

89 In the economic manuscript of 1857-58, Marx had proved the bourgeois economists' views on capital as an original source of value existing apart from labour to be unsound (see present edition, Vol. 28, pp. 470, 473). Marx repeatedly took up this question in the manuscript of 1861-63 (the section "Capital and Profit"), and when analysing the views of Malthus, Torrens and Ramsay (see present edition, vols 32 and 33).—103

90 The passages that follow have been transferred here from the inside cover of Notebook II, marked "A". Marx copied them out, with minor changes, from the economic manuscript of 1857-58 (see present edition, Vol. 28, pp. 212, 219-20).— 103

91 In the chapter "Piece-Wages" of Volume I of *Capital* (see present edition, Vol. 35), Marx quotes a pertinent passage from A. Ure's *The Philosophy of Manufactures,* London, 1835.—104

92 Cf. in Marx's economic manuscript of 1857-58: "Such belletristic phrases, which by means of some sort of analogy relate everything to everything else, may even appear profound when are said for the first time, and the more so the more they identify the most disparate things. If repeated, and especially if repeated

complacently, as statements of scientific value, they are *tout bonnement* foolish. Suitable only for belletristic story-tellers and empty chatterboxes who besmear all sciences with their liquorice-sweet rubbish" (see present edition, Vol. 28, pp. 219-20).— 104, 159

93 The relation of superordination and subordination under capitalism viewed as a purely economic relation, as distinct from its forms in pre-bourgeois societies, had previously been discussed, in general terms, in the economic manuscript of 1857-58 (see present edition, Vol. 28, pp. 96, 100-01, 176, 424-25).— 106, 132

94 In the manuscript of Volume III of *Capital*, Ch. XXXVI (see present edition, Vol. 37), Marx, defining interest-bearing capital, in which valorisation appears in its pure form and the production of surplus value is concealed, wrote that "this accounts for the fact that even some political economists, particularly in countries where industrial capital is not yet fully developed, as in France, cling to interest-bearing capital as the fundamental form of capital".— 109

95 Marx had written about the formation of bourgeois landed property by capital as a necessary prerequisite for the existence of wage labour in the economic manuscript of 1857-58 (see present edition, Vol. 28, pp. 206-09).— 112, 314

96 In the economic manuscript of 1857-58, Marx repeatedly discussed the inverse relation between object and subject, and the nature of the objective conditions of labour under capitalism that confront labour capacity as an alien, independent power (see present edition, Vol. 28, pp. 233-34, 381-83, 389-90).— 113

97 Similar criticism of Bastiat's attempts to represent the form of wage labour as inessential, merely superficial and having nothing to do with the economic relation of labour and capital, is contained in the economic manuscript of 1857-58 (see present edition, Vol. 28, p. 248).— 114, 148

98 In examining the views of James Mill on pp. XIV—795-796 of the manuscript of 1861-63, Marx resumes his critique of the views on "the price of labour's being advanced" by capital expounded by a number of bourgeois economists (see present edition, Vol. 32).— 115

99 This quotation from F. Wayland's work has been transferred here from pp. II—61-62 of the manuscript. Marx set it off from the main text by a line; it is marked by two crosses and supplied with the note: "To p. 60". On p. 61 of the main text, the same note was made after the word "Wakefield" (see this volume, p. 116). The quotation and Marx's note make it clear, however, that he probably intended to illustrate the passage marked in the main text by another quotation, one from Wakefield's work on the development of capitalist relations in the colonies. That is why the quotation from Wayland is given as a footnote here.— 115

100 Marx makes a brief remark about this only on p. XXIII—1461 of the manuscript of 1861-63. He dealt with this question in more detail in Chapter Six of the manuscript of Volume I of *Capital*, "The Results of the Direct Process of Production" (see present edition, Vol. 34).— 115, 142

101 Cf. the presentation of this problem in the economic manuscript of 1857-58 (present edition, Vol. 28, pp. 511-14). See also this volume, pp. 138-50.— 117, 134

102 In the economic manuscript of 1857-58, Marx had already drawn an analogy between coal, oil and means of subsistence, as being instrumental materials in the labour process (see present edition, Vol. 29, p. 82).—117, 133, 143, 144, 157

103 These figures differ from the earlier ones. While making the calculations, Marx changed the figures from which he proceeded initially. At first, the value of the product (£5) was composed of the following elements: raw material, £2 10s.; wear and tear of the machinery, £1; the value added by fresh labour, £1 10s. Later, he estimated the raw material at £1 10s., wear and tear of the machinery, at £1, and the value added by fresh labour, at £2 10s. A confusion arose later from the fact that, having switched to new figures in his calculations, in one instance Marx referred to the initial value of raw material, i.e. £2 10s.—120

104 As Marx himself wrote about the value magnitudes in the given example, "the figures are here a matter of indifference" (see this volume, p. 120). In this case, as in the above, he does not stick to the natural indices initially adopted. At first he assumed the amount of cotton spun daily to be 80 lbs (6 2/3 lbs per hour), whereas later he cites different figures: the amount of cotton spun per hour is 6 lbs, or 72 lbs for 12 hours.—125, 127

105 Marx critically analysed Rossi's views in the economic manuscript of 1857-58 (see present edition, Vol. 28, pp. 511-14).—135, 141

106 Cf. Marx's description of pre-bourgeois property in the economic manuscript of 1857-58 (present edition, Vol. 28, pp. 428-32). Marx took up this issue once more on pp. XXI—1328-1329 of the manuscript of 1861-63 (see present edition, Vol. 34).—135

107 Marx considered the distinction between services and productive wage labour in the economic manuscript of 1857-58 (see present edition, Vol. 28, pp. 202-03, 393-99). In notebooks VII, IX and XXI of the manuscript of 1861-63, he examined in detail the economic specificity of services in capitalist society (see present edition, vols 31 and 34).—136, 137

108 When discussing the views of bourgeois economists in the manuscript of 1861-63, Marx returned more than once to the nature of productive and non-productive labour under the conditions of bourgeois production (see present edition, vols 31 and 34, pp. VII—300, IX—419, XXI—1317-1331).—136, 312

109 Marx discussed the role of trade in establishing the capitalist mode of production in the economic manuscript of 1857-58 (see present edition, Vol. 29, pp. 227-36) and reproduced the fragment from it in Notebook XV of the manuscript of 1861-63 (see present edition, Vol. 33).—136

110 Marx had already pointed out in the economic manuscript of 1857-58 that Say's definition of capital as a sum of values was unsound (see present edition, Vol. 28, p. 182).—138

111 In Ramsay this passage reads as follows: "The sources of national wealth would unquestionably be as great in the former case as in the latter. Nothing can prove more strongly that circulating capital...."—139

112 Marx returned to the analysis of Ramsay's views in Notebook XVIII of the manuscript of 1861-63 (see present edition, Vol. 33).—140

113 The problem of the functioning of fixed capital in the process of reproduction and partial valorisation of the product had been exhaustively examined by Marx

32*

in the economic manuscript of 1857-58 (see present edition, Vol. 29, pp. 8-128).
In the manuscript of 1861-63 he made no special study of this question, although
he took it up again when analysing the views of certain bourgeois economists in notebooks IX and XVII (see present edition, vols 31 and
33).— 140

114 On pp. XXII—1403-1404 of the manuscript of 1861-63, summing up the
material contained in the works of bourgeois economists dealing with the
primitive accumulation of capital, Marx noted that the concentration of small
farms in few hands and the competition between big farmers had helped turn
independent peasants into wage labourers stripped of all property (see present
edition, Vol. 34).— 142

115 Marx borrowed this quotation, which he had translated himself, from the
economic manuscript of 1857-58 (see present edition, Vol. 28, p. 511).— 146

116 Marx probably borrowed the quotations from Say and Sismondi, as well as the
phrase immediately preceding them, from the economic manuscript of 1857-58
(see present edition, Vol. 28, p. 235). The figure LX denotes a page in one of
Marx's Brussels notebooks of excerpts for 1845, where a synopsis of Sismondi's
quoted work is to be found.— 150

117 Cf. the relevant passage in the economic manuscript of 1857-58 (present
edition, Vol. 28, p. 230). Further on Marx copied out some passages from it (see
this volume, pp. 159-61).— 151

118 Cf. the relevant passage in the economic manuscript of 1857-58 (present
edition, Vol. 28, p. 229).— 151

119 R. Torrens says: "In that early period of society which precedes the separation
of the community into a class of capitalists and a class of labourers, and in
which the individual who undertakes any branch of industry, performs his own
work, the total quantity of labour, accumulated and immediate, expended on
production, is that on which comparison and competition turn, and which, in
the transactions of barter or sale, ultimately determines the quantity of one
commodity which shall be received for a given quantity of another"
(pp. 33-34).— 151

120 Pages 23-30 of the London Notebook XVI of excerpts contain a synopsis of the
work Gratuité du crédit, from which Marx copied this quotation.— 153

121 Cf. the relevant passage in the economic manuscript of 1857-58 (present
edition, Vol. 28, pp. 195-96).— 154

122 Marx quotes J. B. Say from: J. Colins, L'économie politique..., Vol. 3, Paris, 1857,
p. 376.— 155

123 Marx renders Say's idea. See J. B. Say, Traité d'économie politique, Vol. II, Paris,
1817, pp. 484, 464, 480. Cf. also Marx's critique of Say's determination of the
price of land in Ch. XIX of Volume I of Capital (present edition, Vol. 35).—
155

124 Marx quotes the same passage from P. Verri at the end of the section dealing with
the Physiocrats (see this volume, p. 376).— 156

125 Marx made a detailed analysis of this problem in Chapter Six, "The Results of the
Direct Process of Production", of the manuscript of Volume I of Capital (see
present edition, Vol. 34). See also Note 100.— 158

126 Marx is referring to item 4 of Section I in the Draft Plan of the Chapter on Capital for *A Contribution to the Critique of Political Economy*, which he drew up after Part One had been published (see present edition, Vol. 29, pp. 513-14). Marx examined questions relating to the primitive accumulation of capital in Notebook XXII of the manuscript of 1861-63 (see present edition, Vol. 34); he made extensive use of the corresponding section of the economic manuscript of 1857-58 (see present edition, Vol. 28, pp. 387-99).—159, 192

127 Marx described surplus value as income in notebooks XV and XXII of the manuscript of 1861-63 (see present edition, vols 32 and 34).—159, 312

128 Marx examined all these questions in notebooks II and III of the economic manuscript of 1857-58, in the section "Exchange between Capital and Labour" (see present edition, Vol. 28, pp. 213-21, 231-36).—159

129 This refers to Notebook III of the economic manuscript of 1857-58 (see present edition, Vol. 28, pp. 231-34).—159

130 Marx reproduced these data on p. 186 of the first edition of Volume I of *Capital*. As his letter to Engels of May 7, 1868 indicates (see present edition, Vol. 43), these data refer to the factory of which Engels was co-owner. According to Marx (see his letter to Engels of May 16), Engels himself put them down in his notebook.—161

131 In a letter to Engels of September 28, 1861, Marx thanked him for the "*Manchester Guardians* most useful to me" (see present edition, Vol. 41, p. 321).—162

132 Marx deals with this question in notebooks XVI and XVII of the manuscript of 1861-63 (see present edition, Vol. 33).—163

133 Originally Marx left the end of Notebook II (pp. 89-94 of the manuscript) blank and, starting most probably in late 1861, filled it in with additional material as he worked on the subsequent part of this manuscript.—163

134 Marx refers to the analysis of the impact made on profit and the rate of profit by changes in the value of constant capital. This analysis is to be found in Notebook XVI of the manuscript of 1861-63 (see present edition, Vol. 33).—165

135 Marx borrowed the facts pertaining to the economic development of Hungary from a work by Richard Jones, *An Essay on the Distribution of Wealth...*, London, 1831, a synopsis of which is to be found in Marx's London Notebook IX of excerpts for 1851.—167

136 Marx borrowed the statistics from "Coal mine accidents. Abstract of return to an address of the Honourable the House of Commons, dated 3 May 1861. Ordered, by the House of Commons, to be printed, 6 February 1862".
   Marx later used this material in *Capital*, Vol. III, Ch. V (see present edition, Vol. 37).—168

137 Marx touched briefly on this issue on pp. XVI—985-986 of the manuscript of 1861-63 (see present edition, Vol. 33). A detailed analysis of the concentration of workers and the economy in the employment of constant capital as factors increasing the rate of profit can be found in *Capital*, Vol. III, Ch. V (see present edition, Vol. 37).—169

138 Marx reproduces this quotation in the Additions to the chapter "Absolute Surplus Value" (see this volume, p. 224).—170

[139] The passages on pp. 170-71 of this volume were borrowed by Marx from the economic manuscript of 1857-58 (see present edition, Vol. 28, pp. 221-22, 231-32).—170

[140] This paragraph, containing a mathematical interpretation of the production of surplus value, was probably inserted by Marx later, between the heading and the text. Marx deals in more detail with the mathematical interpretation of capitalist production as production of surplus value in Chapter Six, "The Results of the Direct Process of Production", of the manuscript of Volume I of *Capital* (see present edition, Vol. 34).—172

[141] Marx made these calculations on the inside cover of Notebook I, without referring specifically to the text. The calculations have been inserted here by the compilers of the volume.—178

[142] According to the original plan, Marx considered this problem in the section on capital and profit in Notebook XVI of the manuscript of 1861-63 (see present edition, Vol. 33).—178

[143] In the given instance, apart from the "primary" converted forms of surplus value—profit, interest and rent—Marx operates with its "secondary" form— taxes. Here as earlier in the manuscript (see this volume, p. 158), he breaks down surplus value into different kinds of income as industrial capitalists did in everyday practice.—179, 206

[144] Cf. this volume, pp. 199-204. See also Marx's criticism of Senior's "last hour" theory in *Capital*, Vol. I, Ch. IX (present edition, Vol. 35).—179, 199

[145] These points, which Marx had planned to consider in the section dealing with surplus value, were touched upon in the economic manuscript of 1857-58, e.g. the civilising influence of capital (see present edition, Vol. 28, pp. 336-38, 466); the relation of labour time to free time (Vol. 29, p. 97); and the relation of population and capital (Vol. 28, pp. 325-26). Marx gave a detailed analysis of Proudhon's erroneous thesis in Notebook IV of the manuscript of 1857-58 (Vol. 28, pp. 352-62).—180

[146] Marx wrote briefly on the extremely hard work done by the English bakers in the Additions to this chapter (see this volume, p. 228). In notebooks XVIII and XIX of the manuscript of 1861-63 Marx three times cited facts illustrating the merciless exploitation of dressmakers in London which was an additional source of surplus value for the employers (see present edition, vols 33 and 34).—181

[147] *Killing No Murder* was the title of a pamphlet that appeared in England in 1657. Its author, Edward Sexby, stated that it was a patriotic duty that Lord Protector Oliver Cromwell, a hated and cruel tyrant, be assassinated.—185

[148] A reference to a quotation from Wakefield's work *England and America. A Comparison of the Social and Political State of Both Nations.* In two vols. Vol. I, London, 1833, p. 55. Marx uses it on p. XXIII—1448 of the manuscript of 1861-63 (see present edition, Vol. 34).—185

[149] The dependence of the amount of surplus value on the surplus labour of an individual worker and the number of simultaneously employed workers was defined by Marx as a law of surplus value (see this volume, p. 206).—185

[150] Marx had touched on some aspects of the interdependence of the growth of capital and that of the population in the economic manuscript of 1857-58 (see present edition, Vol. 29, pp. 147-48). Later, in the manuscript of 1861-63, he

noted repeatedly that this question should be examined specially when
analysing accumulation (e.g. see this volume, p. 190). Marx realised his idea in
Part VII of Volume I of *Capital* (see present edition, Vol. 35).—189, 190, 290,
295

151 Marx analysed this problem thoroughly in *Capital,* Vol. I, Ch. XXV (see
present edition, Vol. 35).—189

152 Marx again took up the question of the drop in the value of labour capacity as
a result of women and children being drawn into capitalist exploitation on
pp. XX—1243, 1257 of the manuscript of 1861-63 (see present edition, vols 33
and 34).—189

153 Quite early, in his economic manuscript of 1857-58, Marx gave a description
of time as scope for the development of human capacities (see present edition,
Vol. 29, p. 93). On p. XX—1244 of the manuscript of 1861-63 he repeats this
definition (see present edition, Vol. 33).—191, 301

154 Marx's first detailed description of the antagonistic form of free time as free
time only for the few in societies based on the appropriating of the surplus
labour of the toiling majority is to be found in the economic manuscript of
1857-58 (see present edition, Vol. 28, pp. 324-25).—191, 192, 196, 301

155 This definition of wealth as disposable time was inserted later and is a
translation of a quotation from the work *The Source and Remedy of the National
Difficulties,* London, 1821, p. 6: "Wealth is disposable time and nothing more."
Marx quoted it in the original language in the Additions to the chapter "Absolute
Surplus Value" (see this volume, p. 204), most probably after looking through the
economic manuscript of 1857-58, where he first used this quotation (see present
edition, Vol. 28, p. 324). He analysed this definition once again in Notebook XIV
of the manuscript of 1861-63 (see present edition, Vol. 32).—192

156 In the economic manuscript of 1857-58 Marx gave a description of Steuart's
economic views in general and his ideas concerning the historical appearance of
"free hands", i.e. the separation of labour capacity from the conditions of
production, in particular (see present edition, Vol. 28, p. 395 and Vol. 29,
p. 164). When examining Steuart's views in Notebook VI of the manuscript of
1861-63, Marx stressed in particular his contribution to the scientific solution of
this problem (see this volume, p. 352).—193, 290, 295, 357

157 Marx uses this quotation from Richard Jones on two other occasions: on
p. VI—225 of the manuscript of 1861-63 (see this volume, p. 357), and when
analysing the views of the English economist on p. XVIII—1122 of this
manuscript (see present edition, Vol. 33).—193

158 A similar description is to be found in the economic manuscript of 1857-58
(see present edition, Vol. 28, pp. 183, 395, 397, 426) and in the original
version of Part One of *A Contribution to the Critique of Political Economy* (see
present edition, Vol. 29, p. 481).—197

159 Marx reproduces these two quotations on p. XIV—852 of the manuscript of
1861-63, when examining the views of the author of *The Source and Remedy of
the National Difficulties.* By the "value of capital" the author of the pamphlet
implies the ratio of the quantity of surplus labour appropriated by the capitalist
to the size of the capital he uses (see present edition, Vol. 32).—204

160 Marx erroneously named W. Jacob's *Consideration on the Protection Required by
British Agriculture etc.,* London, 1814 as the source of the quotation. The

correction has been made in conformity with the London Notebook IV of excerpts, which contains this quotation from J. G. Büsch among excerpts copied out from Jacob's book.—204

161 Cf. Marx's remarks concerning Joseph Townsend and Giammaria Ortes in *Capital*, Vol. I, Ch. XXV (see present edition, Vol. 35). He reproduces there the quoted passage from Townsend's work and the excerpt from H. Fr. Storch quoted further in the text.—205

162 Cf. excerpts from the work by Symons at the end of the Chapter on Capital in the economic manuscript of 1857-58 (present edition, Vol. 29, pp. 206-07).—212

163 Marx goes back to examining Richard Jones' views on rent in Notebook XXII of this manuscript (see present edition, Vol. 33).—212

164 Marx borrowed the data on Wallachian and Moldavian peasants cited below from: É. Regnault, *Histoire politique et sociale des principautés danubiennes*, Paris, 1855, pp. 304-11.—214

165 The *Règlement organique*, the first constitution of the Danubian Principalities (Moldavia and Wallachia), was introduced in 1831 by P. D. Kiselev, head of the Russian administration there. The principalities had been occupied by the Russian troops after the Russo-Turkish War of 1828-29. Under the *Règlement*, the legislative power in each of the principalities was granted to the assembly, elected by big landowners, and executive power to the *hospodars*, representatives of the landed gentry, the clergy and the towns, elected for life. The *Règlement* consolidated the dominant position of the top stratum of the boyars and the clergy by perpetuating the feudal order, including the *corvée*.—214

166 A reference to the *Factory Acts* of 1850, which introduced the 10-hour working day. In the chapter "The Working-Day" (Volume I of *Capital*) Marx went into the history of this act (see present edition, Vol. 35).—216

167 Newmarch, "Address". In: *Report of the Thirty-First Meeting of the British Association for the Advancement of Science; held at Manchester in September 1861*, London, 1862, pp. 201-03. Between late August and mid-September 1861, Marx was staying with Engels in Manchester; while there, he attended sittings of the Economic Science and Statistics Section held as part of the Association's 31st annual meeting which took place on September 4-11, 1861.—216

168 Marx first gave a German translation from *The Daily Telegraph* and then quoted the original, preceding it with the words: "The original runs".—217

169 When recounting facts from the history of factory legislation, including the quotation from Blanqui given below, Marx used A. Redgrave's material from the *Reports of the Inspectors of Factories ... for the Half Year ending 31st October 1855*, London, 1856, pp. 77-81, 87.—220

170 L. Horner wrote on page 9 of his report of April 30, 1859 (which Marx quotes) that it would probably be his last one. He managed, however, to continue his work as Inspector of Factories and published one more report, covering the half year ending October 31, 1859. See Marx's letter to Engels of January 11, 1860 (present edition, Vol. 41, p. 5).—223

171 Marx inserted pages 124a-124h into Notebook III later. He wrote on page 124a: "To p. 124."—224

172 Page 196 of Notebook V of the manuscript of 1861-63 has been inserted here in conformity with Marx's note: "This quotation belongs to Notebook III, p. 'e' after p. 124."—228

173 Marx considered this problem in Notebook XVI of the manuscript of 1861-63 (see present edition, Vol. 33).—229

174 Marx quotes, in his own translation into German, the French edition of Babbage's work *Traité sur l'économie des machines et des manufactures.* Translated from the English by Éd. Biot. Paris, 1833, p. 5.—229

175 Marx is referring to a story about Leibniz which Hegel recounts in his *Science of Logic*: "The tenet that there are no two identical things is difficult to comprehend, and, according to an anecdote, was found puzzling at a certain court, where Leibniz voiced it, thereby prompting the ladies to search among leaves on the trees in the hope of finding two identical ones" (G.W.F. Hegel, "Wissenschaft der Logik", *Werke*, Bd. 4, Berlin, 1834, S. 45).—232

176 *Fluxions* and *fluents* are concepts of the calculus of fluxions, the earliest form of differential and integral calculus, developed by Newton. He used the term fluents to denote the values of a system which (the values) change simultaneously and constantly, depending on time, and the term fluxions to denote the velocities with which the fluents change. Thus, fluxions are time derivatives of fluents.—233

177 Marx returns to this question while analysing Ramsay's views on p. XVIII—1096 of the manuscript of 1861-63 (see present edition, Vol. 33).—236

178 Marx is probably referring to John Stuart Mill who, when considering the ratio of the rate of profit to wages in his *Essays on Some Unsettled Questions of Political Economy* (London, 1844), proceeds from the assumption that the "labourer is paid in the very article he produces". Marx cites this tenet when analysing Mill's views on p. VII—322 of the manuscript of 1861-63 (see present edition, Vol. 31).—238

179 The following discussion concerning the influence of the increase in labour productivity on the ratio of necessary to surplus labour time largely corresponds to the respective passage in the economic manuscript of 1857-58 (see present edition, Vol. 28, pp. 259-66).—245

180 Marx began, by mistake, to number the pages of Notebook IV of the manuscript of 1861-63 from 138 (instead of 132).—245

181 In this instance Marx is in error, for the decrease in necessary labour time from $^5/_6$ to $^3/_6$ of the working day means that the value of labour capacity has decreased by 40% and made up 60% of the initial magnitude. Marx pointed out this mistake several pages later.—246, 247

182 Summing up his analysis of the effect increases in the productivity of labour have on the magnitude of surplus value, Marx notes, in the economic manuscript of 1857-58, that all this "*really belongs in the doctrine of profit*" (see present edition, Vol. 28, p. 266). He takes up this problem again in the manuscript of 1861-63, in the section on capital and profit, Notebook XVI (see present edition, Vol. 33).—247

183 Marx returns to this problem on pp. XX—1284-1294 of the manuscript of 1861-63 (see present edition, Vol. 34).—250

184 *The Standard,* London, No. 11610, October 26, 1861 and *The Evening Standard,* London, No. 11610, October 26, 1861 do not mention the fact cited by Marx.—250

185 The text that follows was written on the inside cover of Notebook IV (which Marx marked 138a). It is a summary of the corresponding passage from the economic manuscript of 1857-58 dealing with the ratio of the increase in the productivity of labour to the magnitude of relative surplus value (see present edition, Vol. 28, pp. 264-66).—251

186 Cf. the pertinent passage on pp. XIV—808-809 of the manuscript of 1861-63, where Marx returns to his examination of Ricardo's views on this issue and the critique levelled at him by an anonymous author (see present edition, Vol. 32). Cf. also Note 78.—254

187 The remark about production under slavery and the mention of Cairnes were made later: Cairnes' book *The Slave Power* (London) did not appear before May 1862, when Notebook IV of the manuscript of 1861-63 was already complete. Marx refers to p. 47 of the book, a copy of which he had in his own library. This page contains Marx's markings.—255, 262

188 Marx bases this remark on the work by S. N. H. Linguet, *Théorie des loix civiles, ou principes fondamentaux de la société,* Vol. I, London, 1767.—256

189 Marx takes up this question again on pp. XVI—985-986 and XXI—1318-1320 of the manuscript of 1861-63 (see present edition, vols 33 and 34). He studied the question most thoroughly in Volume III of *Capital,* in the chapter "Economy in the Employment of Constant Capital" (see present edition, Vol. 37).—258, 270

190 On pp. XIX—1180 and XX—1250 of the manuscript of 1861-63, in the section dealing with machines, Marx merely points to the continuity of labour as a consequence of the introduction of machinery (see present edition, Vol. 33). He dealt with this question at greater length in *Capital,* Vol. II, Ch. XV (see present edition, Vol. 36).—259

191 Part of the text from the inside cover of Notebook IV, marked "138a", has been transferred here in conformity with Marx's note: "To p. 148."—263

192 When writing this section, notably the first part, Marx based himself on the work by D. Stewart, *Lectures on Political Economy,* Vol. 1, Edinburgh, 1855.—264

193 Marx is referring to the terminology D. Stewart used in his work *Lectures on Political Economy,* p. 310 et seq.—266

194 Marx quotes Garnier's translation of the work by Adam Smith: *Recherches sur la nature et les causes de la richesse des nations,* Paris, 1802. Marx made excerpts from this book in the spring of 1844, while living in Paris. In the present volume, all quotations from *Recherches...* are given according to the English original (A. Smith, *An Inquiry into the Nature and Causes of the Wealth of Nations.* By J. R. McCulloch. In four volumes. Edinburgh, London, 1828). The page numbers from the latter edition are given in square brackets. The French translation of Smith's work does not always coincide with the English original, which is disregarded here. Marx made extensive use of the 1828 English edition when working on the manuscript of 1861-63.—268, 376

[195] Marx repeatedly stressed this idea, both in the economic manuscript of 1857-58 (see present edition, Vol. 28, pp. 40, 96, 107, 187) and in Part One of *A Contribution to the Critique of Political Economy* (Vol. 29, pp. 290-91).—274, 293

[196] Marx is probably referring to C. F. Bergier, who translated Adam Ferguson's book into French and wrote an introduction to it.—276

[197] Cf. *A Contribution to the Critique of Political Economy.* Part One (see present edition, Vol. 29, p. 293).—276

[198] These two Latin proverbs and the quotation from Alcibiades II occur in the note supplied by editor W. Hamilton to p. 311 of Stewart's book.—280

[199] Marx provides the German translation of this quotation in ancient Greek.—281, 282, 283

[200] Marx returns to this question in connection with a critical analysis of Ure's *The Philosophy of Manufactures,* on pp. XX—1246-1247 of the manuscript of 1861-63 (see present edition, Vol. 33).—286

[201] Below, Marx quotes passages from pages 67-68 of Henry Martyn's work *The Advantages of the East-India Trade to England...* from MacCulloch, *The Literature of Political Economy...,* London, 1845, p. 101.—287

[202] Cf. Marx's assessment of P. E. Lemontey's views on the consequences of the division of labour in *The Poverty of Philosophy* (see present edition, Vol. 6, p. 180).—293

[203] In the economic manuscript of 1857-58, Marx twice uses the pertinent quotation from page 166 of Steuart's work *An Inquiry into the Principles of Political Oeconomy,* Vol. I, Dublin, 1770 (see present edition, Vol. 29, pp. 163, 234). He uses it again on p. XV—949 of the manuscript of 1861-63 (see present edition, Vol. 33).—298

[204] Part of the text from p. 179 has been transferred here in conformity with Marx's note: "To the beginning of p. 175."—299

[205] On p. XX—1249 of the manuscript of 1861-63, Marx pointed out the discrepancy between the English original and the French translation of Ure's book (see present edition, Vol. 33); the French text has "*exploité*" and the English original, "exploded".—300

[206] This reference to Quesnay was inserted by Marx later, probably on the basis of an excerpt from Quesnay's *Fermiers* (published by Daire in 1846) which he made in Additional Notebook C (May 1863).—303

[207] Part of the text from p. 179 has been transferred here in conformity with Marx's note: "To p. 178."—303

[208] Marx wrote about this on pp. XX—1262-1263, 1278-1279 of the manuscript of 1861-63 (see present edition, Vol. 34).—304

[209] Marx left a blank space here for the source. In the summer of 1862, Marx borrowed from Lassalle Wilhelm Roscher's book, *Die Grundlagen der Nationalökonomie,* Stuttgart, Augsburg, 1858 (Roscher: *System der Volkswirtschaft,* Bd. 1). See Marx's letter to Lassalle of June 16, 1862 (present edition, Vol. 41, pp. 377-78). On p. 47 of his book Roscher says about production: "As a rule, the more it [production] is perfected, the greater is—as effect and cause of efficient operation—the producer's satisfaction in his production." The reference is probably made to this particular passage.—306

²¹⁰ Marx partially realised this plan in Notebook XX of this manuscript (see present edition, Vol. 34).—311

²¹¹ Marx wrote about the specifically historical character of economic categories within the framework of the capitalist mode of production in the Introduction to the manuscript of 1857-58 (see present edition, Vol. 28, pp. 41-42).—313

²¹² By Chapter 3 Marx might have meant either the section on relative surplus value (the third chapter of the first part of his investigation of capital), or the third part of the Chapter on Capital, "Capital and Profit" (see present edition, Vol. 29, p. 516). The first draft of Chapter 3 is to be found in the manuscript of 1857-58 (Vol. 29, pp. 129-251), where it is marked as Section Three of the Chapter on Capital. In the later sections of the manuscript of 1861-63, Marx refers to Section Three, or Part Three instead of Chapter 3 (see present edition, vols 31 and 33).

The question of a longer working day as a consequence of the introduction of machinery by capitalists was later considered by Marx in Chapter XV of Volume I and in Chapter V of Volume III of *Capital* (see present edition, vols 35 and 37).—319, 331

²¹³ Part of the text from p. 196 has been transferred here in accordance with Marx's note: "To p. 190."—319

²¹⁴ Marx takes up this issue once more on pp. XIX—1237-1238 of the manuscript of 1861-63 (see present edition, Vol. 33).—320

²¹⁵ See Notebook XIX of the manuscript of 1861-63 (present edition, Vol. 33).—321

²¹⁶ Marx cites this fact, drawing on data provided by the German scientist Johann Heinrich Moritz von Poppe. Marx copied relevant passages from the latter's work on p. XIX—1166 of the manuscript of 1861-63 (see present edition, Vol. 33).—322

²¹⁷ The quotation from Rossi's work has been transferred here from p. 201 in accordance with Marx's note: "To the beginning of p. 194."—324

²¹⁸ To designate constant capital Marx here uses Richard Jones' term "auxiliary capital". Cf. Marx's note concerning Richard Jones' use of the term on p. XVIII—1128 of the manuscript of 1861-63 (present edition, Vol. 33).—327

²¹⁹ Here and below the figure XI stands for Marx's London Notebook XI of excerpts where the synopsis of Senior's work is to be found (pp. 4-5).—333

²²⁰ Senior operates not with the total sum of the capital advanced, equalling £100,000, but with the sum of £100 falling to each individual worker. This correction was made by Marx when making a synopsis of Senior's work in the London Notebook XI of excerpts.—334

²²¹ The quotation from Torrens has been transferred here from p. 206 in conformity with Marx's note: "To p. 201."—334

²²² A detailed analysis of this work, published anonymously (its author was John Cazenove, a follower of Malthus) was made by Marx in Notebook XIV of this manuscript (see present edition, Vol. 32).—337

²²³ A reference to the self-acting mule invented by the British engineer Richard Roberts in 1825. The workers nicknamed this loom the "Iron Man", because it automatically performed many of the operations in the spinning industry which had hitherto been performed manually.—342

[224] The source of this English quotation has not been established. The figure "100" before the word "pounds" has been added on the strength of a similar passage in Chapter XV of Volume I of *Capital*, where Marx describes, in his own words, Eli Whitney's cotton gin (see present edition, Vol. 35).—343

[225] In the economic manuscript of 1857-58, Marx had discussed Proudhon's thesis concerning the worker's inability to buy back his product (see present edition, Vol. 28, pp. 352-62). He does the same, in a more concise form, in *Capital*, Vol. III, Ch. XLIX (see present edition, Vol. 37).—345

[226] This intention was not realised. In March 1862 Marx abandoned a systematic exposition of the problems pertaining to relative surplus value, and took up a detailed analysis of bourgeois theories of surplus value. Only in late 1862-early 1863 did he return to the problem of the capitalist use of machinery, as his letters to Engels of January 24 and 28, 1863 indicate (see present edition, Vol. 41, pp. 446, 449), filling in the empty pages of Notebook V, as well as notebooks XIX and XX. Accordingly, this part of Notebook V is included in Volume 33.—346

[227] These notes were made on the inside covers of notebooks VI and VII respectively.—347

[228] *Theories of Surplus Value*, on which Marx embarked in March 1862, is the fifth, concluding section of the first chapter of research into capital, "The Production Process of Capital". Originally, the fourth section was to consider the connection of relative and absolute surplus value. *Theories of Surplus Value* was to be an historical introduction to the chapter on surplus value, similar to the historical notes introducing the chapters on commodity and on money in *A Contribution to the Critique of Political Economy*.

In the course of Marx's work on the manuscript, *Theories of Surplus Value* underwent considerable changes. In both length and content it far surpassed the original plan. As well as considering the views of bourgeois economists, Marx put forward a number of major theoretical propositions in it.

Theories of Surplus Value appeared in English for the first time in an abridged form in 1951: K. Marx, *Theories of Surplus Value*. A selection from the volumes published between 1905 and 1910 as *Theorien über den Mehrwert*, edited by Karl Kautsky, taken from Karl Marx's preliminary manuscript for the projected fourth volume of *Capital*. Transl. from the German by G. A. Bonner and Emile Burns, London, Lawrence & Wishart, 1951.

The work was first published in full between 1963 and 1971: K. Marx, *Theories of Surplus-Value* (Vol. IV of *Capital*), Part I, Moscow, Foreign Languages Publishing House, 1963; Part II, Moscow, Progress Publishers, 1968; Part III, Moscow, Progress Publishers, 1971.—348

[229] Marx is referring to part three of his work, "Third Chapter. Capital in General". In the Draft Plan of the Chapter on Capital drawn up in 1860, this part is entitled "III. Capital and Profit" (see present edition, Vol. 29, p. 516). The beginning of this work is to be found on pp. XVI—973-1021 and XVII—1022-1028 of the manuscript (see present edition, Vol. 33).—348

[230] Marx is paraphrasing Steuart's ideas. Steuart says: "I. The first thing to be known of any manufacture when it comes to be sold, is, how much of it a person can perform in a day, a week, a month, according to the nature of the work, which may require more or less time to bring it to perfection. In making such estimates, regard is to be had only to what, upon an average only, a workman of the country in general may perform,... II. The second thing to be known, is the value of the

workman's subsistence and necessary expense, both for supplying his personal
wants, and providing the instruments belonging to his profession, which must be
taken upon an average as above;... III. The third and last thing to be known, is the
value of the materials..." (James Steuart, *An Inquiry into the Principles of Political
Oeconomy.* In: Steuart, *The Works, Political, Metaphysical, and Chronological...*,
Vol. I, London, 1805, p. 246).—351

231 Marx is referring to the work by Adam Smith *An Inquiry into the Nature and
Causes of the Wealth of Nations.* In two volumes, London, 1776. Garnier's French
translation, which Marx owned and used (A. Smith, *Recherches...*, Vol. I, Paris,
1802) indicated, on page 1, that the first edition appeared in late 1775-early 1776.
That was probably why a mistake was made over the year of publication of Adam
Smith's work.—352

232 Marx is referring to the second part of his work. In the plan for the Chapter on Capital drafted in 1860, this part is entitled "II. Circulation Process of
Capital". Some of the notes pertaining to this chapter (concerning Quesnay's
economic table) are to be found on pp. X—422-437 of the manuscript of
1861-63 (see present edition, Vol. 31). Marx wrote more on the subject on
pp. XXIII—1433-1434 of the manuscript (see present edition, Vol. 34). The
questions of circulation were not developed further in this manuscript. Marx
returned to them only in the manuscript of 1863-65. They are studied in
Part III of Volume II of *Capital* (see present edition, Vol. 36).—353, 374

233 In the manuscript of 1861-63, Marx uses the terms "profit upon alienation"
and "profit upon expropriation" interchangeably. Steuart does not use the
latter term.—359, 370

234 Marx repeatedly pointed to this "conclusion" of Ricardian political economy, as
well as to the practical conclusions drawn from it by the radical Ricardians, in
the manuscript of 1861-63. See pp. X—458, XI—496-497, 516-517 (present
edition, Vol. 31); pp. XIV—791, XV—902-903 (Vol. 32); pp. XVIII—1120,
1139 (Vol. 33). See also K. Marx, *The Poverty of Philosophy* (present edition,
Vol. 6, p. 203).—361, 373

235 "*Laissez-faire, laissez-aller*" (also "*laissez-faire, laissez-passer*"), the formula of
economists who advocated Free Trade and non-intervention by the state in
economic affairs.—361

236 Colbert, a champion of Mercantilism, was Controller-General of Finances under
Louis XIV. The economic policy he pursued objectively promoted the primitive
accumulation of capital, even though it served the interests of the absolutist
state. Further development of capitalism required fulfilment of the new
economic and political tasks, as defined by the Physiocrats in the struggle
against Mercantilism.
    At the same time, the advance of the Physiocratic doctrine was facilitated by
the fiasco of John Law's system. The latter tried to enhance the country's
wealth through a series of finance and credit projects and greater state
intervention. The issue of paper money not backed by gold and speculation in
bonds produced the first paper currency inflation and the bankruptcy of the
bank and joint-stock company he had set up. Under those conditions land
became the most stable property, which accounted for the Physiocrats' emphasis on agriculture. The nascent French bourgeoisie's rejection of Colbertism
and of Law's system, as well as the objective changes under way in material
production itself, contributed to the establishment of the Physiocratic doctrine.—
367, 373

237 In 1839 and 1843, the Société typographique Belge, Adolfe Wahlen et compagnie published two collections of economic works under the general title *Cours d'économie politique.* Both collections opened with J. A. Blanqui's *Histoire de l'économie politique en Europe.* Marx used the 1843 edition, which he had in his library and from which he quoted Rossi. It is probable that the 1843 edition reproduced the title page of the 1839 collection, which presumably explains Marx's reference to this source.—370

238 The *Economists* was the name given to the French Physiocrats in the second half of the 18th and the first half of the 19th century. By the 1850s the name acquired a more general meaning and ceased to denote exponents of a particular economic doctrine.—370, 373

239 Volume V of Adam Smith's *Recherches sur la nature...* (1802 edition) contains translator's (Germain Garnier's) notes, which Marx quotes here and below.—371

240 In his lifetime *Mirabeau le père* was nicknamed "L'Ami des hommes" (the "Friend of the People"), after the title of one of his works.—373

241 Epicurus believed that gods existed in the space between the worlds and were unconcerned with either the development of the Universe or human affairs.—373

242 The *Encyclopaedists* were the authors of the French *Encyclopédie ou Dictionnaire raisonné des sciences, des arts et des métiers,* which appeared in 1751-72 and consisted of 28 volumes. Among them were the most prominent people of the Enlightenment. Most of the credit for the publication must go to Diderot, who supervised the work, as well as to D'Alembert, who wrote the famous Introduction to the *Encyclopédie.* Quesnay and Turgot, prominent Physiocrats, wrote a number of entries expounding the basic propositions of their doctrine. This work, reflecting as it did a diversity of views, made a substantial contribution to the ideological preparation for the French Revolution.

The collaboration between the Physiocrats and the Encyclopaedists can be explained by the fact that both trends helped spread bourgeois ideas, thus paving the way for bourgeois society.—374

243 The *demagogues* were members of an opposition movement among German intellectuals. The word gained currency in this sense after the Carlsbad Conference of Ministers of German States in August 1819, which adopted a special resolution against the "intrigues of demagogues".—374

244 Schmalz's book appeared in Berlin in 1818, under the title *Staatswirthschaftslehre in Briefen an einen teutschen Erbprinzen,* Parts One and Two.—375

245 Taken from Notebook VII of excerpts (1859-62), p. 210. On p. 188 this quotation from Adam Smith is in French. On p. 210 Marx wrote: "To p. 188. Here and further, Smith is quoted in English; edit. *McCulloch. London. 1828.*"—376

246 Marx critically examines the Physiocratic part of Smith's doctrine in Notebook VI of the manuscript (see this volume, pp. 368-72), as well as on pp. XII—626-632 of the manuscript (see present edition, Vol. 31).—377

247 See pp. XII—650-651 of the manuscript of 1861-63 (present edition, Vol. 32), as well as D. Ricardo, *On the Principles...,* London, 1819, Chapter I, Section I.—378

248 See Note 247 and also pp. XII—652-654 of the manuscript of 1861-63 (present edition, Vol. 32).—380

249 A detailed analysis of Malthus' theory of value and surplus value is given in Marx's manuscript of 1861-63 on pp. XIII—753-767 (see present edition, Vol. 32).—380, 394

250 Marx is referring to Notebook VII of excerpts (1859-62), p. 173. In connection with the passage from Adam Smith quoted earlier, he ridicules the latter's attempts to derive profit from "the undertaker's hazard".

Marx planned to put the chapter on the apologetic accounts of profit in the third section of his work (see present edition, Vol. 33, p. XVIII—1139), but this chapter was never written. Some of the problems that were to constitute its subject-matter were considered in the manuscript of 1861-63. See, for instance, pp. X—425-427 (present edition, Vol. 31).—385

251 Marx examined the question of the "antediluvian forms" of capital on pp. XV—899-901 of the manuscript of 1861-63 (see present edition, Vol. 32). See also *Capital*, Vol. III, Part V, Ch. XXXVI (present edition, Vol. 37).—389

252 See Note 229, and pp. XIV—791-805 of the manuscript of 1861-63 (present edition, Vol. 32).—395

253 Later Marx specified the concept of the means of production. In Section 1, Chapter VII of Volume I of *Capital*, by the means of production he implies "both the instruments and the subject of labour" (see present edition, Vol. 35).—396

254 Here, Marx uses the term "average price" to denote the same concept as "price of production", i.e. the cost of production plus average profit. The correlation between the market price of commodities and their average price is examined in Notebook XII of this manuscript.

The very term "average price" indicates that Marx has in mind "the average market price over a long period, or the central point towards which the market price gravitates" (see p. XII—605 of the manuscript of 1861-63, present edition, Vol. 31).—400

255 Marx uses the term "cost price" ("Kostenpreiss" or "Kostpreiss") in three different meanings: 1) in the sense of the cost of production for the capitalist ($c+v$); 2) in the sense of the "immanent cost of production" of the commodities ($c+v+s$), which is identical to the value of the commodity, and 3) in the sense of the price of production ($c+v$+average profit). In the given passage, the term is used in its second sense. In notebooks X-XIII of the manuscript (see present edition, vols 31 and 32), it is used as the price of production, or the average price. There Marx identifies the two terms. Thus on p. XI—529 he writes about "average prices or, as we shall call them, *cost prices* which are different from the values themselves and are not directly determined by the values of the commodities but by the capital advanced for their production+the average profit" (see present edition, Vol. 31). On p. XII—624 Marx observes: "...The price which is required for the supply of the commodity, the price which is required for it to come into existence at all, to appear as a commodity on the market, is of course its *price of production* or *cost price*" (ibid.).

In notebooks XIV-XV of the manuscript (see present edition, vols 32 and 33), the term "Kostenpreiss" is used now in the sense of the price of production, and now in that of production costs for the capitalist.

The treble usage of the term "Kostenpreiss" is explained by the fact that, in political economy, the word "Kosten" was used in three senses, as Marx noted in particular on pp. XIV—788-790 and XV—928 of the manuscript of 1861-63 (see present edition, Vol. 32). Apart from these usages in the classical works of bourgeois political economy, a fourth one exists: the vulgar meaning of the term "production costs" as used by J. B. Say, who interpreted production costs as something paid for the "productive services" performed by labour, capital or land. Marx opposed this vulgar interpretation (see p. XI—506 of the manuscript of 1861-63, present edition, Vol. 31; pp. XIII—693-694 of the manuscript, present edition, Vol. 32).—401

256 Marx critically analysed Smith's theory of cost prices and its refutation by Ricardo on pp. XI—549-560 of the manuscript (see present edition, Vol. 31).—402

257 Here and up to the end of p. 267 of the manuscript there follows a passage that breaks up the previous narrative, so Marx precedes p. 268 of the manuscript with the words: "Adam Smith continues."—405

258 A critique of Say's views on this issue is also to be found on p. VII—300 of the manuscript of 1861-63 (see present edition, Vol. 31).—408

259 Storch's *Considérations*, put out in 1824 as a separate edition, was in 1852 published as Part V of *Cours d'économie politique*. Marx uses the 1824 edition.—409

260 Here Marx sets forth Ramsay's views. The exact quotation runs as follows: "Mr. Ricardo saw very well, that the question of profit was entirely one of proportion; but unfortunately, one seems always to consider the whole produce as divided between wages and profits, forgetting the part necessary for replacing fixed capital" (George Ramsay, *An Essay on the Distribution of Wealth,* Edinburgh, London, 1836, p. 174, note).—409

261 See pp. XVIII—1091-1098 of the manuscript of 1861-63 (present edition, Vol. 33) and also Note 229.—410

262 Marx repeatedly returned to these two aspects of simple reproduction in this manuscript (e.g. see this volume, pp. 411-51; pp. VIII—350-356 and IX—379 of the manuscript, present edition, Vol. 31). In the later notebooks of this manuscript Marx also discussed simple reproduction, and in Notebook XXII (Vol. 34) outlined the preliminary conclusions of his own theory of reproduction.—411

263 The paragraph that follows was probably added by Marx later, while working on Notebook VII, which is borne out by the use of inner margins.—412

264 The term "*production costs*" ("Produktionskosten") is used here in the sense of the "immanent costs of production", i.e. $c+v+s$. Cf. Note 255.—413

265 Marx is here referring to "II. Circulation Process of Capital" in the Draft Plan of the Chapter on Capital written in 1860 (see present edition, Vol. 29, pp. 514-16). In Volume II of *Capital* the reproduction of constant capital is considered in Part III, "The Reproduction and Circulation of the Aggregate Social Capital" (present edition, Vol. 36).—414, 449

266 Below, while preserving the numerical values cited here, Marx changed the letters designating the production spheres (with the exception of A). In place of

B and C, he uses B^1-B^2 (or B^{1-2}); in place of D, E, F, G, H, and I, he uses C^1-C^6 (or C^{1-6}); in place of K^1-K^{18}, D^1-D^{18} (or D^{1-18}); in place of L^1-L^{54}, E^1-E^{54} (or E^{1-54}); in place of M^1-M^{162}, F^1-F^{162} (or F^{1-162}); in place of N^1-N^{486}, G^1-G^{486} (or G^{1-486}).—423

[267] The points from 1) to 486) on pp. 423-24 of this volume designate the number of necessary working days in these production spheres.—423

[268] The table that follows is based on the relevant calculations written down on the back cover of Notebook I of this manuscript.—426

[269] Letters B and C designate the same production spheres as prior to p. 423 of this volume (see Note 266). Marx refers to two production spheres, in each of which newly-added labour makes up one working day. The sum total of the newly-added labour in spheres A, B and C amounts to three working days, i.e. to the labour objectified in the product of sphere A.—427

[270] Here, B and C no longer signify the two production spheres; otherwise their product would have amounted to only 6 working days, whereas Marx refers to 18 working days. Marx does not use them, however, in the sense of B^1-B^2 and C^1-C^6 either (B^1-B^2 means a group of two production spheres; C^1-C^6 designates a group of six production spheres; the total product of these eight spheres makes up 24 working days). Here, Marx is referring to a group consisting of six production spheres. Their total product is 18 working days and, consequently, may be exchanged for the newly-added labour in D^1-D^{18}, also equalling 18 working days.—427

[271] According to Marx's calculation, each subsequent group includes twice as many production spheres as all the preceding ones put together. Thus, group D^{1-18}, which covers 18 production spheres, consists of twice as many spheres as all preceding groups taken together (A—one sphere, B^{1-2}—two spheres, C^{1-6}—six spheres; nine spheres in all). That is why Marx wrote: D^{1-18} (2×9).—427

[272] Marx goes back to this question on p. IX—390 of the manuscript of 1861-63 (see present edition, Vol. 31).—430

[273] Further on, the manuscript originally contained the following passage, which Marx crossed out: "Spinner and loom maker, who we assume also makes spinning machinery, have added $1/3$ in labour, their constant capital amounting to $2/3$ of yarn and loom. Of the 8 yards of linen (or 24 hours) or 24s., which replace their total product, they can consequently consume $8/3$ [yards]$=2^2/3$ [yards] of linen or 8 hours' labour or 8s. Therefore $5^1/3$ yards or 16 hours' labour remain to be accounted for. Spinner's constant capital consists of flax and the spinning machinery (coal, etc., are not taken into account in this example), $1/3$ in the form of raw material$=$flax$=16/3$ hours' labour$=5^1/3$ hours' labour or $\dfrac{1\,7/3}{3}$: $17/9$ yards$=18/9$ yards. All of them can be purchased by the flax-grower because he compensates his constant capital himself, at least when it comes to the seeds (setting aside, for the time being, the wear and tear of fixed capital, the instruments of labour), by deducting the necessary amount from his product. Thus we have to account only for $5^2/3-18/9$ yards (or $16-5^1/3$

hours' labour)$-5^2/_3$ yards$=1^7/_3=5^1/_9$. Thus, $5^1/_9-1^7/_9=3^7/_9$ (or $10^1/_3$ hours' labour)."—432

274 By earlier calculations, $5^1/_3$ yards of linen represent the total constant capital of the spinner and of the loom maker. Therefore, to determine the flax-grower's share, one should proceed not from $5^1/_3$ yards of linen, but from a smaller figure. Marx eventually corrected this error and assumed that the spinner's constant capital was represented by only 4 yards of linen.—432

275 The untenability of the bourgeois doctrine stating that a part of the constant capital of one is transformed into revenue for the other, is demonstrated in *Capital*, Vol. II, chapters XIX-XX and Vol. III, Ch. XLIX (see present edition, vols 36 and 37).—450

482

NAME INDEX

A

Archilochus (7th cent. B.C.)—Greek elegiac poet.—280

Aristotle (384-322 B.C.)—Greek philosopher.—19

Arkwright, Sir Richard (1732-1792)—English industrialist; invented the cotton spinning machine named after him.—229

Arnd, Karl (1788-1878)—German economist.—356

Ashley, Anthony Cooper, Earl of Shaftesbury (1801-1885)—English politician, Tory, philanthropist.—169, 227, 319, 331, 336

Ashworth, Edmund (1801-1881)—English manufacturer, liberal.—228, 333

B

Babbage, Charles (1792-1871)—English mathematician and economist.—229, 288, 309, 333, 334

Bailey, Samuel (1791-1870)—English economist and philosopher; criticised Ricardo's labour theory of value.—23, 48, 100, 101

Baines, Sir Edward (1800-1890)—English economist, liberal.—328

Baiter, Johann Georg (1861-1877)—one of the publishers of Plato's *Republic.*—282

Baker, Robert—British official, inspector of factories in the 1850s and 1860s.—170, 228

Bastiat, Frédéric (1801-1850)—French economist, preached harmony of class interests in bourgeois society.—114, 148

Beccaria, Cesare Bonesana (1738-1794)—Italian lawyer, publicist and economist of the Enlightenment.—286

Bentham, Jeremy (1748-1832)—English utilitarian philosopher, sociologist.—230

Bergier, Claude François—translated into French, and wrote the Introduction to, Ferguson's *An Essay on the History of Civil Society.*—274, 276

Bidaut (first half of the 19th cent.)—French journalist, civil servant.—304

Blaise, Adolphe Gustave (1811-1886)—French economist, published works by Jérôme Adolphe Blanqui.—286

Blanqui, Jérôme Adolphe (1798-1854)—French vulgar political economist.—221, 270, 285, 286, 370, 372

Boisguillebert, Pierre le Pesant, sieur de (1646-1714)—French economist, father of French classical political economy, predecessor of the Physiocrats.—359

Bright, John (1811-1889)—English manufacturer and politician, a Free Trade leader and founder of the Anti-Corn Law League.—250

Brotherton, Joseph (1783-1857)—English manufacturer, M.P.—203

Broughton—a county magistrate.—217

Buchanan, David (1779-1848)—English journalist and economist, disciple of Adam Smith and commentator of his works.—358

Büsch, Johann Georg (1728-1800)—German economist, Mercantilist.—204

Byles, John Barnard (1801-1884)—English lawyer, member of the Privy Council, Tory; wrote on law, economics and other subjects.—226, 318

C

Cairnes, John Elliot (1823-1875)—British economist and journalist, opposed slavery in the US South.—255, 262

Cantillon, Richard (1680-1734)—English economist, predecessor of the Physiocrats.—380

Carey, Henry Charles (1793-1879)—American economist, advocated harmony of class interests in capitalist society.—151

Carli, Gian Rinaldo (1720-1795)—Italian scholar; wrote on money and the corn trade; opposed Mercantilism.—258

Carlyle, Thomas (1795-1881)—British essayist, historian and idealist philosopher, Tory; criticised the English bourgeoisie from the position of Romanticism; relentless opponent of the working-class movement from 1848 onwards.—226

Cato, Marcus Parcius the Elder (324-149 B.C.)—Roman statesman and

philosopher, leader of the aristocratic republican party.—222

Cazenove, John (19th cent.)—English vulgar economist, disciple of Malthus whose works he published.—91, 138, 152, 336, 381

Chalmers, Thomas (1780-1847)—English Protestant theologian and economist, disciple of Malthus.—100, 152

Cherbuliez, Antoine Élisée (1797-1869)—Swiss economist; tried to combine Sismondi's theory with elements of Ricardo's.—152, 157-58

Child, Sir Josiah (1630-1699)—English economist and banker, merchant; Mercantilist; President of the Court of Directors of the East India Company (1681-83 and 1686-88).—222

Colins, Jean Guillaume César Alexandre Hippolyte (1783-1859)—French economist.—98, 206, 302, 304

Courcelle-Seneuil, Jean Gustave (1813-1892)—French economist, author of works on the practical economics of industrial enterprises, on credit and banking.—211, 334

Culpeper, Sir Thomas (1578-1662)—English economist, advocate of Mercantilism.—222

Custodi, Pietro (1771-1842)—Italian economist, published works by Italian economists of the late 16th-early 19th centuries.—23, 286, 368, 375

D

Daire, Louis François Eugène (1798-1847)—French economist; published works on political economy.—29, 46, 362

Dale, David (1739-1806)—founded a cotton mill in New Lanark, of which Robert Owen was later appointed manager.—230

De Quincey, Thomas (1785-1859)—English writer and economist; commented on Ricardo's works; his own

484 Name Index

works reflect the disintegration of the Ricardian school.—304

Destutt de Tracy, Antoine Louis Claude, comte de (1754-1836)—French economist, philosopher, advocate of constitutional monarchy.—22, 263

Diodorus Siculus (c. 90-21 B.C.)—Greek historian.—253, 284

E

Eden, Sir Frederick Morton (1766-1809)—English economist and historian, disciple of Adam Smith.—46, 96, 205

Edward III (1312-1377)—King of England (1327-77).—45, 226

Epicurus (341-270 B.C.)—Greek materialist philosopher.—373

F

Ferguson, Adam (1723-1816)—Scottish historian, philosopher and sociologist.—273, 274, 275, 276, 277, 287, 293, 306

Fielden, John (1784-1849)—English manufacturer, philanthropist, proponent of factory legislation.—228, 331, 336

Forbes, Charles—Scottish landowner.—343

Forcade, Eugène (1820-1869)—French publicist, vulgar economist.—345, 346, 416

Franklin, Benjamin (1706-1790)—American physicist, economist and politician; took part in the American War of Independence.—28, 30, 98

G

Galiani, Ferdinando (1728-1787)—Italian economist, criticised the Physiocrats; maintained that the value of a commodity is determined by its usefulness; at the same time he made correct conjectures about the nature of the commodity and money.—23, 205, 344

Garnier, Germain, marquis (1754-1821)—French economist and politician, monarchist; follower of the Physiocrats, translator and critic of Adam Smith.—268, 272, 273, 275, 289, 293, 297, 301, 305, 306, 371, 372, 380, 384, 404, 429

Gaskell, Peter—English physician and liberal journalist.—341, 342, 343

Goethe, Johann Wolfgang von (1749-1832)—German poet.—112, 168

H

Hamilton, Sir William (1788-1856)—Scottish idealist philosopher; published the works of Dugald Stewart.—214, 277, 299, 304

Harris, James (1709-1780)—English philologist and philosopher, M.P., Lord Chancellor (1763-65).—282, 287, 299

Hobbes, Thomas (1588-1679)—English philosopher.—382

Hodgskin, Thomas (1787-1869)—English economist and journalist, utopian socialist; drew socialist conclusions from the Ricardian theory.—163, 203, 289, 291, 293, 305, 394

Horace (65-8 B.C.)—Roman poet.—47, 271

Horner, Leonard (1785-1864)—English geologist and public figure, inspector of factories (1833-56), member of the Factories Inquiry Commission in 1833 and of the Children's Employment Commission in 1841; upheld the workers' interests.—200, 218, 219, 220, 222, 223, 228, 339

Howell—inspector of factories in England.—220

J

Jacob, William (c. 1762-1851)—English businessman, author of several works on economics.—206, 248

R

Ramsay, George Sir (1800-1871)—English economist, follower of classical political economy.—27, 117, 139, 140, 150, 161, 165, 203, 236, 252, 408, 409, 410, 411, 412

Ravenstone, Piercy (d. 1830)—English Ricardian economist; opposed Malthus; upheld the workers' interests.—252, 304

Redgrave, Alexander—English inspector of factories.—219, 221, 222

Regnault, Elias Georges Soulange Oliva (1801-1868)—French historian and publicist, civil servant.—216

Ricardo, David (1772-1823)—English economist.—45, 47, 95, 100, 101, 151, 253, 254, 327, 368, 369, 378, 380, 388, 389, 394, 395, 398, 402, 403, 409, 410, 429

Roederer, Pierre Louis, comte de (1754-1835)—French politician.—373

Roscher, Wilhelm George (1817-1894)—German economist, professor at Leipzig University; founder of the historical school of political economy.—306

Rossi, Pellegrino Luigi Edoardo, count (1787-1848)—Italian economist, lawyer, politician; in 1848, head of the government in the Papal States.—117, 135, 141, 142, 144, 145, 146, 147, 148, 149, 150, 324

Rumford—see Thompson, Benjamin, Count of Rumford

S

Sadler, Michael Thomas (1780-1835)—English economist and politician, philanthropist, sympathised with the Tory party.—260

Saint Germain Leduc, Pierre Etienne Denis—see Leduc, Pierre Etienne Denis, dit Saint Germain

Saunders, Robert John—English inspector of factories in the 1840s.—228

Say, Jean Baptiste (1767-1832)—French economist, representative of vulgar political economy.—13, 25, 69, 97, 98, 135, 137, 138, 150, 151, 154, 161, 205, 292, 408, 409

Schiller, Johann Christoph Friedrich von (1759-1805)—German poet, dramatist and philosopher.—309

Schmalz, Theodor Anton Heinrich (1760-1831)—German lawyer and economist, Physiocrat.—374, 375

Schouw, Joakim Frederick (1789-1852)—Danish scholar, botanist.—230

Scrope, George Julius Poulett (1797-1876)—English geologist and economist; opposed Malthus; M.P.—276

Senior, Nassau William (1790-1864)—English economist; vulgarised Ricardo's theory.—179, 199, 200, 201, 202, 203, 333

Sextus Empiricus (A.D. late 2nd-early 3rd cent.)—Greek sceptic philosopher.—280

Shaftesbury, Anthony Ashley Cooper—see Ashley, Anthony Cooper, Earl of Shaftesbury

Sismondi, Jean Charles Léonard Simonde de (1773-1842)—Swiss economist, exponent of economic romanticism.—12, 13, 98, 149, 150, 152, 157, 158, 210, 289, 291, 303, 304

Skarbek, Frédérick Florian (1792-1866)—Polish economist and writer, follower of Adam Smith.—318

Smith, Adam (1723-1790)—Scottish economist.—69, 93, 152, 266, 268, 269, 271, 272, 273, 274, 275, 276, 277, 282, 287, 289, 291, 292, 293, 297, 299, 301, 305, 306, 347, 352, 353, 356, 358, 368, 369, 371, 372, 376, 377, 378, 379, 380, 381, 382, 384, 385, 386, 387, 388, 389, 390, 391, 392, 393, 394, 395, 396, 397, 398, 399, 400, 401, 402, 403, 404, 406, 407, 408, 409, 411, 429, 451

Sparks, Jared—(1789-1866)—American historian and publisher; founded the

INDEX OF LITERARY AND MYTHOLOGICAL NAMES

INDEX OF QUOTED
AND MENTIONED LITERATURE

WORKS BY KARL MARX AND FREDERICK ENGELS

Marx, Karl

A Contribution to the Critique of Political Economy. Part One (present edition, Vol. 29)
— Zur Kritik der politischen Oekonomie, Erstes Heft. Berlin, 1859.—9, 10, 15, 18, 25, 29, 33, 34, 38, 40, 50, 62, 101, 265, 266, 377

Economic Manuscripts of 1857-58 (present edition, vols 28-29)
—Grundrisse der Kritik der politischen Ökonomie 1857-58.—20, 54, 59, 71, 103, 150, 159, 170, 281

The Poverty of Philosophy. Answer to the "Philosophy of Poverty" by M. Proudhon (present edition, Vol. 6)
—Misère de la philosophie. Réponse à la philosophie de la misère de M. Proudhon. Paris, Bruxelles, 1847.—297, 321

Engels, Frederick

The Condition of the Working-Class in England. From Personal Observations and Authentic Sources (present edition, Vol. 4)
—Die Lage der arbeitenden Klasse in England. Nach eigner Anschauung und authentischen Quellen. Leipzig, 1845.—216

Outlines of a Critique of Political Economy (present edition, Vol. 3)
—Umrisse zu einer Kritik der Nationalökonomie. In: *Deutsch-Französische Jahrbücher*, 1-2 Lfg. Paris, 1844.—30

WORKS BY DIFFERENT AUTHORS

Aristoteles. *De republica* Libri VIII. In: *Aristotelis opera* ex recensione I. Bekkeri. Accedunt Indices Sylburgiani. Tomus X. Oxonii, 1837.—19

Arnd, K. *Die naturgemässe Volkswirthschaft, gegenüber dem Monopoliengeiste und dem Communismus, mit einem Rückblicke auf die einschlagende Literatur.* Hanau, 1845.—356-57

Ashley, [A.] *Ten Hours' Factory Bill. The Speech of Lord Ashley, M. P., in the House of Commons, on Friday, March 15th, 1844.* London, 1844.—227, 319, 331, 336

Babbage, Ch. *On the Economy of Machinery and Manufactures.* London, 1832.—229, 288
— *Traité sur l'économie des machines et des manufactures.* Traduit de l'anglais sur la troisième édition, par Éd. Biot. Paris, 1833.—333, 334

[Bailey, S.] *A Critical Dissertation on the Nature, Measures, and Causes of Value; Chiefly in Reference to the Writings of Mr. Ricardo and His Followers.* By the Author of Essays on the Formation and Publication of Opinions. London, 1825.—23, 47, 100-01

Baines, Ed. *History of the Cotton Manufacture in Great Britain: with a Notice of the Early History in the East, and in All the Quarters of the Globe; a Description of the Great Mechanical Inventions, Which Have Caused Its Unexampled Extension in Britain; and a View of the Present State of the Manufacture, and the Condition of the Classes Engaged in Its Several Departments.* Embellished and Illustrated with Portraits of Inventors, Drawings of Machinery, etc. In: Laing, S., *National Distress; its Causes and Remedies.* London, 1844.—328

Bastiat, Fr. *Gratuité du Crédit. Discussion entre M. Fr. Bastiat et M. Proudhon.* Paris, 1850.—153, 345

Beccaria, C. *Elementi di economia pubblica.* In: *Scrittori Classici Italiani di Economia Politica. Parte Moderna.* T. XI. Milano, 1804.—286

[Bentley, Th.] *Letters on the Utility and Policy of Employing Machines to Shorten Labour; Occasioned by the Late Disturbances in Lancashire...* London, 1780.—98

Bible

The Old Testament 1 Moses.—160, 205

Bidaut, J. N. *Du monopole qui s'établit dans les arts industriels et le commerce, au moyen des grands appareils de fabrication.* Deuxième livraison. *Du monopole de la fabrication et de la vente.* Paris, 1828.—304

Blanqui, [J. A.] *Des classes ouvrières en France, pendant l'année 1848.* Première partie. Paris, 1849.—221
— *Cours d'économie industrielle.* Recueilli et ann. par Ad. Blaise. Paris, 1838-39.—270, 285-86
— *Histoire de l'économie politique en Europe depuis les anciens jusqu'à nos jours.* In: *Cours d'économie politique.* Bruxelles, 1843.—370, 372

Buchanan, D. *Observations on the Subjects Treated of in Dr. Smith's Inquiry into the Nature and Causes of the Wealth of Nations.* Edinburgh, London, 1814.—358

Büsch, J. G. *Abhandlung von dem Geldumlauf in anhaltender Rücksicht auf die Staatswirthschaft und Handlung.* Erster Teil. Zweite vermehrte und verbesserte Auflage. Hamburg und Kiel, 1800.—204

[Byles, J. B.] *Sophisms of Free-Trade and Popular Political Economy Examined.* By a Barrister. Seventh edition: with Corrections and Additions. London, 1850.—226, 318

Cairnes, [J.] E. *The Slave Power: its Character, Career and Probable Designs: Being an Attempt to Explain the Real Issues Involved in the American Contest.* London, 1862.—255, 262

[Cantillon, R.] *Essai sur la nature du commerce en général.* Traduit de l'anglais. Londres, 1755.—380

Carey, H. C[h]. *Principles of Political Economy. Part the First: of the Laws of the Production and Distribution of Wealth.* Philadelphia, 1837.—151

[Cazenove, J.] *Outlines of Political Economy: Being a Plan and Short View of the Laws Relating to the Production, Distribution, and Consumption of Wealth;...* London, 1832.—91, 337, 381

Chalmers, Th. *On Political Economy in Connexion with the Moral State and Moral Prospects of Society.* Second edition. Glasgow, 1832.—100, 152

Cherbuliez, A. *Richesse ou pauvreté.* Paris, 1841.—152, 157

Colins, [J.G.C.A.H.] *L'économie politique. Source des révolutions et des utopies prétendues socialistes.*
—Tome premier. Paris, 1856.—304
—Tome troisième. Paris, 1857.—97, 98, 206, 302-03

Courcelle-Seneuil, J. G. *Traité théorique et pratique des entreprises industrielles, commerciales et agricoles ou manuel des affaires.* Deuxième edition, revue et augm. Paris, 1857.—211, 334

Crawfurd, J. *On the Cotton Supply.* In: *The Journal of the Society of Arts, and of the Institutions in Union.* London, April 19, 1861.—344

Daire, E. *Mémoire sur la doctrine des physiocrates.* Paris, 1847.—362

De Quincey, Th. *The Logic of Political Economy.* Edinburgh and London, 1844.—304

Destutt de Tracy, [A. L. C.] *Élémens d'idéologie. IV e et V e parties. Traité de la volonté et de ses effets.* Paris, 1826.—22, 263

Diodor von Sicilien. *Historische Bibliothek.* Übers. von Julius Friedrich Wurm. (Abth. 1) Bd. 1. Stuttgart, 1827.—253, 285

Ducange, Ch. D. *Glossarium mediae et infimae latinitatis conditum a Carolo Dufresne Domino Du Cange.* Cum supplementis integris monachorum Ordinis S. Benedicti D. P. Carpenterii Adelungii, aliorum, suisque digessit G. A. L. Henschel. Tomus Secundus. Parisiis, 1842.—31

Eden, F. M. *The State of the Poor: or, an History of the Labouring Classes in England, from the Conquest to the Present Period; in which are particularly considered their Domestic Economy, with Respect to Diet, Dress, Fuel and Habitation; and the Various Plans which, from Time to Time, have been proposed, and adopted, for the Relief of the Poor; together with Parochial Reports Relative to the Administration of Work-houses, and Houses of Industry; the State of Friendly Societies; and other Public Institutions; in several Agricultural, Commercial, and Manufacturing Districts.* With a Large Appendix;... In three volumes. Vol. I. London, 1797.—46, 96, 205-06

Ferguson, A. *Essai sur l'histoire de la société civile.* Ouvrage traduit de l'anglais par Bergier. Tome second. Paris, 1783.—274, 275, 276, 306
—*An Essay on the History of Civil Society.* Edinburgh, 1767.—276, 277

Fielden, J. *The Curse of the Factory System; or, a short Account of the origin of Factory Cruelties; of the attempts to protect the Children by Law; of their present Sufferings; our duty towards them; Injustice of Mr. Thomson's Bill; the Folly of the Political Economists; a Warning against sending the Children of the South into the Factories of the North.* Halifax. [London,] 1836.—228, 331, 336

Forcade, E. *La guerre du socialisme.* Deuxième partie. *L'économie politique révolutionnaire et sociale.* In: *Revue des Deux Mondes,* 1848. Tome quatrième. Bruxelles, 1848.—345, 346, 416

Franklin, B. *A Modest Inquiry into the Nature and Necessity of a Paper Currency.* In: Franklin, B. *The Works; Containing Several Political and Historical Tracts not Included in Any Former Edition, and Many Letters Official and Private Not Hitherto Published;* with Notes and a Life of the Author. By Jared Sparks. Volume II. Boston, 1836.—28

Galiani, F. *Della moneta.* In: *Scrittori classici Italiani di Economia Politica. Parte Moderna.* Tomo III, IV. Milano, 1803.—23, 205, 344

[Garnier, G.] See Smith, A., *Recherches sur la nature et les causes de la richesse des nations.* Traduction nouvelle, avec des notes et observations; par Germain Garnier. Tome cinquième. Paris, 1802.—301, 371-72

Gaskell, P. *Artisans and Machinery: the Moral and Physical Condition of the Manufacturing Population Considered with Reference to Mechanical Substitutes for Human Labour.* London, 1836.—341, 342-43

Goethe, J. W. von. *An Suleika.*—168
— *Faust.* Der Tragödie erster Teil.—112

Harris, J. *Dialogue Concerning Happiness.* In: Harris, *Three Treatises...* 3 ed. rev. and corr. London, 1772.—282

Hegel, G. W. F. *Wissenschaft der Logik.* Hrsg. von Leopold von Henning. Th. 1: *Die objektive Logik.* Abth. 2: Die Lehre vom Wesen. Berlin, 1834.—232

Hind, J. *The Elements of Algebra.* Designed for the Use of Students in the University. 4th ed. Cambridge, 1839.—178

[Hodgskin, Th.] *Labour Defended Against the Claims of Capital; or, the Unproductiveness of Capital Proved.* With Reference to the Present Combinations amongst Journeymen. By a Labourer. London, 1825.—291
— *Popular Political Economy. Four Lectures Delivered at the London Mechanics' Institution.* London, Edinburgh, 1827.—203, 289, 293, 305, 394

Homer. *Odyssey.*—280

Horace (Quintus Horatius Flaccus). *Ars Poetica.*—47
— *Satires.*—271

Horner, L. *Letter to Senior.* May 23, 1837. In: Senior, N. W., *Letters on the Factory Act..* London, 1837.—200

An Inquiry into those Principles, Respecting the Nature of Demand and the Necessity of Consumption, Lately Advocated by Mr. Malthus, from which it is Concluded, that Taxation and the Maintenance of Unproductive Consumers can be Conducive to the Progress of Wealth. London, 1821.—15, 137, 156, 204, 210, 369

Jacob, W. *Considerations on the Protection Required by British Agriculture, and on the Influence of the Price of Corn on Exportable Productions.* London, 1814.—204
— *An Historical Inquiry into the Production and Consumption of the Precious Metals.* In two volumes. Vol. II. London, 1831.—248
— *A Letter to Samuel Whitbread, being a Sequel to Considerations on the Protection Required by British Agriculture; to which are added Remarks on the Publications of a*

Fellow of University College, Oxford; of Mr. Ricardo, and Mr. Torrens. London, 1815.—206

Jones, R. *An Essay on the Distribution of Wealth, and on the Sources of Taxation.* London, 1831.—193, 212, 357
— *Text-book of Lectures on the Political Economy of Nations, delivered at the East India College, Haileybury.* Hertford, 1852.—259, 304

Laing, S. *National Distress; its Causes and Remedies.* London, 1844.—328

Lauderdale, [J. M.] *Recherches sur la nature et l'origine de la richesse publique, et sur les moyens et les causes qui concourent à son accroissement.* Traduit de l'anglais, par E. Lagentie de Lavaïsse. Paris, 1808.—398

Leduc, [P. E. D.]S.-G. *Sir Richard Arkwright ou naissance de l'industrie cotonnière dans la Grande-Bretagne. (1760 à 1792).* Paris, 1842.—229

Lemontey, P. E. *Influence morale de la division du travail considérée sous le rapport de la conservation du gouvernement et de la stabilité des institutions sociales.* In: Oeuvres complètes. Édition revue et préparée par l'auteur. Tome premier. Paris, 1840.—293

[Linguet, S. N. H.] *Théorie des loix civiles, ou principes fondamentaux de la société.* Tome second. Londres, 1767.—305

Macaulay, Th. B. *The History of England from the Accession of James the Second.* Tenth edition. Volume I. London, 1854.—47, 222

MacCulloch, J. R. *The Literature of Political Economy: a Classified Catalogue of Select Publications in the Different Departments of That Science, with Historical, Critical, and Biographical Notices.* London, 1845.—271, 287
— *The Principles of Political Economy: with a Sketch of the Rise and Progress of the Science.* Edinburgh, London, 1825.—210

Macleod, H. D. *The Theory and Practice of Banking: with the Elementary Principles of Currency; Prices; Credit; and Exchanges.* Volume I. London, 1855.—13

Macnab, H. G. *Examen impartial des nouvelles vues de M. Robert Owen, et de ses établissemens à New-Lanark en Écosse, pour le Soulagement et l'Emploi le plus utile des classes ouvrières et des Pauvres, et pour l'Éducation de leurs Enfans, etc., etc., avec des observations sur l'Application de ce système à l'Économie politique de tous les Gouvernemens, etc.* Traduit de l'anglais par Laffon de Ladébat. Paris, 1821.—230

Malthus, T[h.] R. *Definitions in Political Economy, Preceded by an Inquiry into the Rules which Ought to Guide Political Economists in the Definition and Use of their Terms; with Remarks on the Deviation from these Rules in their Writings.* A New edition with a Preface, Notes and Supplementary Remarks by John Cazenove. London, 1853.—138, 152, 381
— *Principles of Political Economy Considered with a View to their Practical Application.* Second edition, with Considerable Additions from the Author's Own Manuscript and an Original Memoir. London, 1836.—45

[Mandeville, B. de.] *The Fable of the Bees: or, Private Vices, Publick Benefits.* London, 1714.—297
— *The Fable of the Bees: or, Private Vices, Publick Benefits.* 2 ed., enl. with many add. London, 1723.—297

— *The Fable of the Bees: or, Private Vices, Publick Benefits.* 3 ed. London, 1724.—297, 310
— *The Fable of the Bees.* Part II. London, 1729.—297
— *The Grumbling Hive; or, Knaves Turn'd Honest.* London, 1705.—297, 310

[Martyn, H.] *The Advantages of the East-India Trade to England Considered, wherein all the Objections, and c. to that Trade are fully Answered.* 8 vo. London, 1720. In: MacCulloch, J. R. *The Literature of Political Economy: a Classified Catalogue of Select Publications in the Different Departments of That Science, with Historical, Critical, and Biographical Notices.* London, 1845.—271, 287

The Master Spinners and Manufacturers' Defence Fund. Report of the Committee Appointed for the Receipt and Apportionment of this Fund, to the Central Association of Master Spinners and Manufacturers. Manchester, 1854.—342

[Mercier de la Rivière, P. P.] *L'ordre naturel et essentiel des sociétés politiques.* T. 1-2. Londres, 1767.—370, 373

Mill, J. *Élémens d'économie politique.* Traduit de l'anglais par J. T. Parisot. Paris, 1823.—290
— *Elements of Political Economy.* London, 1821.—13, 98-99, 151, 210, 290

Mill, J. St. *Essays on Some Unsettled Questions of Political Economy.* London, 1844.—150, 211, 238
— *Principles of Political Economy with Some of their Applications to Social Philosophy.* In two volumes, Vol. II. London, 1848.—318

Mülner, A. *Die Schuld.*—309

Newman, F. W. *Lectures on Political Economy.* London, 1851.—209

Newman, S. P[h.] *Elements of Political Economy.* Andover, New York, 1835.—156, 291

Newmarch, W. *Address.* In: *Report of the Thirty-First Meeting of the British Association for the Advancement of Science; Held at Manchester in September 1861.* London, 1862.—216

Observations on Certain Verbal Disputes in Political Economy, Particularly Relating to Value, and to Demand and Supply. London, 1821.—157, 254, 327

On Combination of Trades. New ed. London, 1834.—342

Opdyke, G. *A Treatise on Political Economy.* New York, 1851.—30

Ortes, G. *Della economia nazionale.* Venezia, 1774.—205
— *Della economia nazionale.* Libri sei. In: *Scrittori classici Italiani di Economia Politica. Parte Moderna.* Tomo XXI. Milano, 1804.—205

Paoletti, F. *I veri mezzi di render felici le società.* In: *Scrittori classici Italiani di Economia Politica. Parte Moderna.* Tomo XX. Milano, 1804.—368

Petty, W. *An Essay Concerning the Multiplication of Mankind: Together with another Essay in Political Arithmetick, Concerning the Growth of the City of London: with the Measures, Periods, Causes, and Consequences thereof. 1682. London, 1698.* In: Petty, W. *Several Essays in Political Arithmetick*: the Titles of which Follow in the Ensuing Pages. London, 1699.—286

Plato. *De republica.* In: Plato, *Opera quae feruntur omnia.* Recogn. Georgius Baiterus, Caspar Orellius, Augustus Guilielmus Winckelmannus. Vol. 13. Turici, 1840.— 282-84

[Pseudo-Plato.] *Alcibiades secundus.*—280

Potter, A. *Political Economy: its Objects, Uses, and Principles: considered with Reference to the Condition of the American People.* New York, 1841.—276

Proudhon, [P. J.] *Gratuité du crédit. Discussion entre M. Fr. Bastiat et M. Proudhon.* Paris, 1850.—153, 345
— *Qu'est-ce que la propriété? Ou recherches sur le principe du droit et du gouvernement.* Premier mémoir. Paris, 1841.—345, 416
— *Système des contradictions économiques, ou philosophie de la misère.* Tome II. Paris, 1846.—372

Quesnay, [F.] *Analyse du tableau économique.* In: *Physiocrates. Quesnay, Dupont de Nemours, Mercier de la Rivière, L'Abbé Baudeau, Le Trosne, avec une introduction sur la doctrine des Physiocrates, des commentaires et des notices historiques, par M. Eugène Daire.* Première Partie. Paris, 1846.—70, 362
— *Fermiers.* In: *Physiocrates...* Première Partie. Paris, 1846.—303
— *Maximes générales du gouvernement économique d'un royaume agricole, et notes sur ces maximes.* In: *Physiocrates...* Première Partie. Paris, 1846.—70, 372, 373

Ramsay, G. *An Essay on the Distribution of Wealth.* Edinburgh, London, 1836.—27, 139, 165, 203, 236, 252, 409, 410, 412

Ravenstone, P. *Thoughts on the Funding System, and its Effects.* London, 1824.—252, 303-04

Regnault, É. *Histoire politique et sociale des principautés danubiennes.* Paris, 1855.—216

Ricardo, D. *On the Principles of Political Economy, and Taxation.* Second edition. London, 1819.—369
— *On the Principles of Political Economy, and Taxation.* Third edition. London, 1821.—45, 95, 101, 151, 429

Roscher, W. *Die Grundlagen der Nationalökonomie.* Dritte, vermehrte und verbesserte Auflage. Stuttgart und Augsburg, 1858.—306

Rossi, P. [L. E.] *Cours d'économie politique. Année 1836-1837* (contenant les deux volumes de l'édition de Paris). In: *Cours d'économie politique.* Bruxelles, 1843.—142, 145, 146, 148, 149, 151, 324
— *De la méthode en économie politique. De la nature et définition du travail.* In: *Économie politique. Recueil de monographies; examen des questions sociales, agricoles, manufacturières et commerciales. Année 1844.* T. I. Bruxelles, 1844.—145

Sadler, M. Th. *The Law of Population: A Treatise, in six books, in Disproof of the Superfecundity of Human Beings, and Developing the Real Principle of their Increase.* Volume the First. London, 1830.—260

Say, J.-B. *Cours complet d'économie politique pratique; ouvrage destiné à mettre sous les yeux des hommes d'état, des propriétaires fonciers, et des capitalistes, des savants, des agriculteurs, des manufacturiers, des négociants, et en général de tous les citoyens, l'économie des sociétés.* Seconde édition, Tome I. Paris, 1840.—97
— *Lettres à M. Malthus, sur différens sujets d'économie politique, notamment sur les causes de la stagnation générale du commerce.* Paris, 1820.—137
— *Traité d'économie politique, ou simple exposition de la manière dont se forment, se*

distribuent et se consomment les richesses. Troisième édition, à laquelle se trouve joint un épitome des principes fondamentaux de l'économie politique. Tome second. Paris, 1817.—13, 25, 69, 150, 154-55, 408

Schiller, J. C. F. *The Robbers.*—309

Schmalz, [Th. A. H.] *Économie politique, ouvrage traduit de l'allemand par Henri Jouffroy.* Revu et annoté sur la traduction, par M. Fritot. Tome premier. Paris, 1826.—374, 375

Schouw, J. F. *Die Erde, die Pflanzen und der Mensch.* Naturschilderungen. Aus dem Dänischen unter Mitwirkung des Verfassers von H. Zeise. Zweite Auflage. Leipzig, 1854.—230

Scrope, G. P. *Principles of Political Economy, Deduced from the Natural Laws of Social Welfare, and Applied to the Present State of Britain.* London, 1833.—276

Senior, N. W. *Letters on the Factory Act, as It Affects the Cotton Manufacture, addressed to the Right Honourable the President of the Board of Trade, to which are Appended, a Letter to Mr. Senior from Leonard Horner, Esq. and Minutes of a Conversation between Mr. Edmund Ashworth, Mr. Thomson and Mr. Senior.* London, 1837.—199-200, 333

[Sexby, E.] *Killing no Murder.* 1657.—185

Sextus Empiricus. *Adversus mathematicos.*—280

Shakespeare, W. *Richard III.*—309

Sismondi, J. C. L. Simonde de. *Études sur l'économie politique.* Tome premier. Bruxelles, 1837.—291, 304
—Tome deuxième. Bruxelles, 1838.—98, 150, 152
—*Nouveaux principes d'économie politique, ou de la richesse dans ses rapports avec la population.* Seconde édition. Tome premier. Paris, 1827.—12, 13, 149, 150, 157, 158, 210, 289

Skarbek, F. *Théorie des richesses sociales. Suivie d'une bibliographie de l'économie politique.* Seconde édition. Tome premier. Paris, 1839.—317, 318

Smith, A. *An Inquiry into the Nature and Causes of the Wealth of Nations.* In two volumes. Vol. I. London, 1776.—368, 369
—*An Inquiry into the Nature and Causes of the Wealth of Nations.* With a Commentary, by the Author of "England and America" [E. G. Wakefield], vols 1-4. Vol. 1. London, 1835.—152, 292
—*An Inquiry into the Nature and Causes of the Wealth of Nations.* With a Life of the Author, an Introductory Discourse, Notes, and Supplemental Dissertations. By J. R. McCulloch. In four volumes. Vol. I. Edinburgh, London, 1828.—376, 377, 391;
—Vol. II. Edinburgh, London, 1828.—389
—*Recherches sur la nature et les causes de la richesse des nations.* Traduction nouvelle, avec des notes et observations; par Germain Garnier. Tome premier. Paris, 1802.—93, 268, 272, 273, 275, 289, 293, 297, 376, 380-90, 393-97, 399, 403
—Tome second. Paris, 1802.—293, 305, 404-08
—Tome quatrième. Paris, 1802.—306
—Tome cinquième. Paris, 1802.—371

— *On Wages and Combination.* London, 1834.—334

Townsend, J. *A Dissertation on the Poor Laws.* By a Well-wisher to Mankind. 1786. Republished, London, 1817.—205

[Tufnell, E. C.] *Character, Object and Effects of Trades' Unions; with Some Remarks on the Law Concerning Them.* London, 1834.—340, 341

Turgot, [A. R. J.] *Réflexions sur la formation et la distribution des richesses.* Paris, 1769-1770.—352, 363
— *Réflexions sur la formation et la distribution des richesses.* In: Turgot, [A. R. J.] *Oeuvres.* Nouvelle édition. Classée par ordre de matières avec les notes de Dupont de Nemours augmentée de lettres inédites, des questions sur le commerce, et d'observations et de notes nouvelles par MM. E. Daire et H. Dussard et précédée d'une notice sur la vie et les ouvrages de Turgot par M. E. Daire. Tome premier. Paris, 1844.—29, 46, 97, 363-67, 369, 372-73

Ure, A. *Philosophie des manufactures, ou économie industrielle de la fabrication du coton, de la laine, du lin et de la soie, avec la description des diverses machines employées dans les ateliers anglais.* Traduit sous les yeux de l'auteur, et augmenté d'un chapitre inédit sur l'industrie cotonnière française. Tome I. Bruxelles, 1836.—287, 288, 300, 321
—Tome II. Bruxelles, 1836.—341, 342
— *The Philosophy of Manufactures: or, an Exposition of the Scientific, Moral, and Commercial Economy of the Factory System of Great Britain.* London, 1835.—104

Virgil (Publius Virgilius Maro). *Aeneid.*—210

Verri, P. *Meditazioni sulla economia politica ... con annotazioni di Gian-Rinaldo Carli.* In: *Scrittori classici Italiani di Economia Politica. Parte Moderna.* Tomo XV. Milano, 1804.—155, 156, 161, 258, 368, 375, 376

Wade, J. *History of the Middle and Working Classes; with a Popular Exposition of the Economical and Political Principles which Have Influenced the Past and Present Condition of the Industrious Orders. Also an Appendix...* Third edition. London, 1835.—96, 156, 224, 226

[Wakefield, E. G. *A Commentary to Smith's "Wealth of Nations".*] See Smith, A. *An Inquiry into the Nature and Causes of the Wealth of Nations...* Vol. 1. London, 1835.—152
— *England and America. A Comparison of the Social and Political State of Both Nations.* In two volumes. Vol. I. London, 1833.—185

Wakefield, E. G. *A View of the Art of Colonization, with Present Reference to the British Empire; in Letters between a Statesman and a Colonist.* London, 1849.—75, 116, 256-67

Wayland, F. *The Elements of Political Economy.* Boston, 1843.—26, 98, 115, 154, 289-90, 344

Xenophon. *Cyropaedia.*—281, 282

DOCUMENTS

Bombay Chamber of Commerce. Report for 1859-1860.—343

Coal Mine Accidents. Abstract of Return to an Address of the Honourable the House of Commons, dated 3 May 1861. Ordered, by the House of Commons, to be Printed, 6 February 1862.—168

Factories Regulation Acts. Ordered, by the House of Commons, to be Printed, 9 August 1859.—218

Reports of the Inspectors of Factories to Her Majesty's Principal Secretary of State for the Home Department,
— *For the Quarter ending 30th June 1843, March 15th 1844.* London, 1844.—28, 331, 336
— *For the Half Year Ending 31st October 1855.* London, 1856.—220, 221, 222, 238
— *For the Half Year Ending 30th April 1856.* London, 1856.—222
— *For the Half Year Ending 31st October 1856.* London, 1857.—47, 218, 219, 220, 338, 339
— *For the Half Year Ending 31st October 1857.* London, 1857.—219
— *For the Half Year Ending 30th April 1858.* London, 1858.—219, 220
— *For the Half Year Ending 31st October 1858.* London, 1858.—223, 338
— *For the Half Year Ending 30th April 1859.* London, 1859.—222, 223
— *For the Half Year Ending 31st October 1859.* London, 1860.—224
— *For the Half Year Ending 30th April 1860.* London, 1860.—223, 337, 338
— *For the Half Year Ending 31st October 1860.* London, 1860.—224, 225
— *For the Half Year Ending 31st October 1861.* London, 1862.—227, 317

Return to an Address of the Honourable. The House of Commons, dated 24 April 1861. Ordered, by the House of Commons, to be Printed, 11 February 1862.—303

Twenty-Second Annual Report of the Registrar-General of Births, Deaths, and Marriages in England. Presented to Both Houses of Parliament by Command of Her Majesty. London, 1861.—169

ANONYMOUS ARTICLES
PUBLISHED IN PERIODIC EDITIONS

The Bengal Hurkaru. July 22, 1861: *We are afraid..*.—343

The Daily Telegraph, January 17, 1860: *On His Last Circuit..*.—217

The Journal of the Society of Arts, and of the Institutions in Union, on the 17 April 1860. Volume VIII.—344

The Manchester Guardian, September 18, 1861: *As the Manufacturers...*—162

The Standard, No. 11610, October 26, 1861.—250

The Times, No. 24082, November 5, 1861: *Every Government has its Traditions.*—250

INDEX OF PERIODICALS